Emergency Substitutions

Using the ingredients recommended in a recipe is best. But if you have to substitute, try the following:

Instead Of	Amount	Use
Baking powder	1 teaspoon	1/4 teaspoon baking soda plus 1/2 teaspoon cream of tartar
Balsamic vinegar	1 tablespoon	1 tablespoon sherry or cider vinegar
Beer	1 cup	1 cup nonalcoholic beer, apple cider or beef broth
Bread crumbs, dry	1/4 cup	1/4 cup finely crushed cracker crumbs, corn flakes or quick-cooking or old-fashioned oats
Broth, chicken, beef or vegetable	1 cup	1 teaspoon chicken, beef or vegetable bouillon granules (or 1 cube) dissolved in 1 cup boiling water
Brown sugar, packed	1 cup	1 cup granulated sugar plus 2 tablespoons molasses or dark corn syrup
Bulgur, cooked	1 cup	1 cup cooked couscous or brown rice
Buttermilk or sour milk	1 cup	1 tablespoon lemon juice or white vinegar plus enough milk to make 1 cup; let stand a few minutes. Or 1 cup plain yogurt.
Chocolate		
Semisweet baking	1 ounce	1 ounce unsweetened baking chocolate plus 1 tablespoon sugar
Semisweet chips	1 cup	6 ounces semisweet baking chocolate, chopped
Unsweetened baking	1 ounce	3 tablespoons baking cocoa plus 1 tablespoon shortening or margarine
Corn syrup		
Light	1 cup	1 cup sugar plus 1/4 cup water
Dark	1 cup	1 cup light corn syrup; 3/4 cup light corn syrup plus 1/4 cup molasses; or 1 cup maple-flavored syrup
Cornstarch	1 tablespoon	2 tablespoons all-purpose flour or 4 teaspoons quick-cooking tapioca
Cream of mushroom soup	1 can (10 3/4 ounces)	Thick White Sauce (page 441)—except stir in 1 can (2 1/2 ounces) sliced mushrooms, drained and chopped, with the milk
Eggs	1 large	2 egg whites; 1/4 cup fat-free cholesterol-free egg product; 2 egg yolks (for custards or puddings); or 2 egg yolks plus 1 tablespoon water (for cookies or bars)
Fats, solid	Any amount	Butter, margarine, lard, shortening, vegetable oil or spread with at least 65 percent fat. Also see Fats (page 16).
Flour		
All-purpose	1 cup	1 cup plus 2 tablespoons cake flour
Cake	1 cup	1 cup minus 2 tablespoons all-purpose flour
Self-rising	1 cup	1 cup all-purpose flour plus 1 1/2 teaspoons baking powder and 1/2 teaspoon salt
Garlic, finely chopped	1 medium clove	1/8 teaspoon garlic powder or 1/4 teaspoon instant minced garlic
Gingerroot, grated or finely chopped	1 teaspoon	3/4 teaspoon ground ginger
Herbs, chopped fresh	1 tablespoon	3/4 to 1 teaspoon dried herbs
Honey	1 cup	1 1/4 cups sugar plus 1/4 cup water or apple juice
Jicama, chopped	1/2 cup	1/2 cup chopped water chestnuts
Leeks, sliced	1/2 cup	1/2 cup sliced shallots or green onions
Lemon juice, fresh	1 tablespoon	1 tablespoon bottled lemon juice or white vinegar
Lemon peel, grated	1 teaspoon	1 teaspoon dried lemon peel
Milk, regular or low-fat	1 cup	1/2 cup evaporated milk plus 1/2 cup water; or nonfat dry milk prepared as directed on package
Mushrooms, fresh	1 cup cooked sliced	1 can (4 ounces) mushroom pieces and stems, drained
Mustard, yellow	1 tablespoon	1 teaspoon ground mustard
Poultry seasoning	1 teaspoon	1/4 teaspoon ground thyme plus 3/4 teaspoon ground sage
Pumpkin or apple pie spice	1 teaspoon	Mix 1/2 teaspoon ground cinnamon, 1/4 teaspoon ground ginger, 1/8 teaspoon ground allspice and 1/8 teaspoon ground nutmeg.
Raisins	1/2 cup	1/2 cup currants, dried cherries, dried cranberries, chopped dates or chopped prunes
Red pepper sauce	3 or 4 drops	1/8 teaspoon ground red pepper (cayenne)
Sesame seed	1 tablespoon	1 tablespoon finely chopped blanched almonds
Tomato juice	1 cup	1/2 cup tomato sauce plus 1/2 cup water
Tomato paste	1/2 cup	1 cup tomato sauce cooked uncovered until reduced to 1/2 cup
Tomato sauce	2 cups	3/4 cup tomato paste plus 1 cup water
Tomatoes, canned	1 cup	About 1 1/3 cups cut-up fresh tomatoes, simmered 10 minutes
Wine		
Red	1 cup	1 cup nonalcoholic wine, apple cider, beef broth, tomato juice or water
White	1 cup	1 cup nonalcoholic wine, white grape juice, apple juice, chicken broth or water
Yeast, regular or quick active dry	1 package (1/4 ounce)	2 1/4 teaspoons regular or quick active dry; or 1 package (0.6 ounce) compressed cake yeast
Yogurt, plain	1 cup	1 cup sour cream

Betty Crocker's COOKBOOK

EVERYTHING YOU NEED TO KNOW TO COOK TODAY

IDG Books Worldwide, Inc.
An International Data Group Company

Foster City, CA • Chicago, IL • Indianapolis, IN • New York, NY

IDG BOOKS WORLDWIDE, INC.
An International Data Group Company
919 E. Hillsdale Boulevard
Suite 400
Foster City, CA 94404

For general information on IDG Books Worldwide's books in the U.S.,
please call our Consumer Customer Service department at 800-762-2974.
For reseller information, including discounts and premium sales,
please call our Reseller Customer Service department at 800-434-3422.

Contact the Library of Congress for complete Cataloging-in-Publication Data
ISBN: 0-7645-6079-4
UPC: 785555027145   EAN: 9780764560798

GENERAL MILLS, INC.

Betty Crocker Kitchens
Manager, Publishing: Lois L. Tlusty
Editor: Lori Fox
Associate Editor: Joyce Gauck
Recipe Development: Grace Wells
Food Stylists: Nancy J. Johnson, Carol Grones and Sue Finley
Nutritionists: Nancy Holmes, R.D. and Mary Dahlberg Johnson, DTR
Photographic Services
Photographer: Steven B. Olson

Cover Design: Edwin Kuo and Michele Laseau
Book Design: Michele Laseau
Photography Art Director: Emily Oberg

For consistent baking results, the Betty Crocker Kitchens recommend
Gold Medal Flour.

Manufactured in China
10 9 8 7 6 5 4 3 2
Ninth Edition

Cover photo: Zesty Italian Chicken (page 287)

Contents

Introduction

Dear Friends,

Here it is—my newest edition of *Betty Crocker's Cookbook*, also fondly known as "Big Red." This indispensable kitchen resource brings 50 years of cooking and baking success from my kitchen to yours.

This updated edition of America's most trusted cookbook includes the latest information on cooking and baking, over 950 great-tasting recipes and all-new color photography. It's loaded with charts for cooking meats, poultry, grains, legumes and vegetables. We added a Grilling chapter because it's a favorite way to cook—for family and casual entertaining. The new Vegetarian chapter satisfies the ever-growing popularity of meatless eating. Learn about the types of vegetarians, nutrition guidelines for vegetarian eating and vegetarian ingredients. Check out Tofu and Tempeh Know-How on pages 369 to 371.

Look for "Learn with Betty" throughout my book—it's a series of mini cooking lessons with photographs. Ever wonder "What do perfect scrambled eggs look like?" or "Why do my chocolate chip cookies always come out flat?" Find out on pages 147 and 202. We've also flagged recipes that are low-fat or fast and added slow cooker and bread machine directions for convenience and versatility.

The tried-and-true classics all are here too, from Macaroni and Cheese (page 308) to Meat Loaf (page 240), Old-Fashioned Baked Beans (page 361) and Chocolate Chip Cookies (page 146). We don't stop there—lots of new and exciting tastes are added to this edition! Check out Brie with Caramelized Onions, Pistachio and Cranberry (page 27), Chai Tea (page 39) and artisan-style breads such as Asiago Bread (page 72) and Sun-Dried Tomato and Olive Bread (page 71). Travel the globe without leaving your kitchen by trying Tandoori Chicken and Chutney (page 294) and Greek Lamb Chops (page 267).

Bigger and better describes how our chapters have expanded to match the way you're cooking today. For starters, each chapter begins with current, comprehensive information in an easy-to-read format describing the basics about the recipes within that chapter. You'll also find specifics about methods, techniques and equipment, helpful tips, solutions to common problems, ingredient glossaries, ingredient selection and storage, cooking charts and much more. More illustrations, how-to photos and food identification photos are sprinkled throughout the pages.

We hope you will enjoy this cookbook, as have thousands of other families, for years to come!

Betty Crocker

p.s. Enjoy homemade goodness in your kitchen.

Cooking Basics & Ingredients

Low-Fat = 3g or less, except main dishes with 6g or less   **Fast** = Ready in 30 minutes or less   ■ = Bread Machine directions   ● = Slow Cooker directions

Lighter = 1/3 fewer calories or 50% less fat

Measuring Ingredients

Graduated Nesting Measuring Cups

Cups usually range in size from 1/4 cup to 1 cup. Some sets also include 1/8 (2 tablespoons), 2/3, 3/4 and 2 cups. Use them to measure dry ingredients, such as flour, sugar and oats, and solid fats, such as shortening. Do not use them to measure liquids.

For flour, baking mix and sugar, spoon the ingredient lightly into the cup, then level it off with the straight edge of a spatula or knife. You don't need to sift powdered sugar unless it's lumpy.

Glass Measuring Cups

You can buy glass cups for measuring liquids in 1-, 2-, 4- and 8-cup sizes. To get an accurate reading, place the measuring cup on a flat surface and read the measurement at eye level. Before measuring sticky liquids, such as honey, molasses and corn syrup, wipe the cup lightly with oil or lightly spray with cooking spray so it's easier to remove the liquid. Do not use to measure dry ingredients.

Graduated Measuring Spoons

Spoons range in size from 1/4 teaspoon to 1 tablespoon. Some sets contain a 1/8 teaspoon and a 3/4 teaspoon. Use spoons to measure liquids and dry ingredients.

For thin liquids, pour them into the spoon until full.

For thick liquids and dry ingredients, pour or scoop them into the spoon until full, then level them off with the straight edge of a spatula or knife.

For cereal and dry bread crumbs, pour them into the cup. Level them off with the straight edge of a spatula or knife.

For shredded cheese, chopped nuts, coconut and soft bread crumbs, spoon them into the cup and pat down very lightly.

For solid fats and brown sugar, spoon them into the cup and pack down firmly with a spatula or spoon.

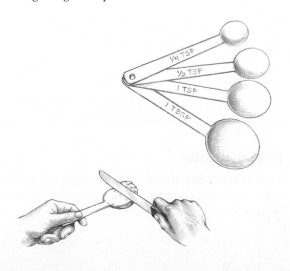

Mixing Ingredients

If you've ever been confused by cooking terms and tools, this guide will help clear things up and help make your time in the kitchen easier, too.

Mixing Terms

Beat: Combine ingredients vigorously with a spoon, fork, wire whisk, hand beater or electric mixer until smooth.

Blend: Combine ingredients with a spoon, wire whisk or rubber scraper until very smooth, or to combine ingredients in a blender or food processor.

Cut in: Thoroughly combine butter, margarine or shortening with dry ingredients. As you cut in the fat, it will begin to clump with the dry ingredients. Use a pastry blender with an up-and-down rocking motion until the particles are the desired size, such as the size of a pea. Or cut in by crisscrossing two knives or using the side of a table fork.

Fold: Lightly combine ingredients without removing air. With a rubber spatula, cut down vertically through the mixture. Next, slide the spatula across the bottom of the bowl and up the side, turning the mixture over. Continue this down-across-up-over motion while rotating the bowl 1/4 turn with each series of strokes.

Mix: Combine ingredients in any way that distributes them evenly.

Process: Use a food processor or mini-chopper to liquefy, blend, chop, grind or knead food.

Stir: Combine ingredients with a circular or figure-eight motion until thoroughly blended.

Whip: Beat ingredients to add air and increase volume until light and fluffy (cream, egg whites).

Mixing Tools

Fork or Hand Beater: Use a fork or hand beater to lightly beat eggs, sauces and salad dressings as well as some batters.

Hands: Use your hands for mixing doughs, streusel toppings and very thick mixtures, such as meat loaf. Wash your hands thoroughly before and after handling the food, or if you prefer, wear plastic or rubber gloves.

Pastry Blender: Use a pastry blender for cutting solid fat into flour for pie crusts and biscuit doughs. Lift it up and down with a rocking motion.

Rubber Spatula: Use a rubber spatula for folding, mixing and stirring batters or sauces. Use a heatproof rubber spatula for mixing hot foods in saucepans and skillets.

Spoon: Use a spoon for general all-purpose mixing and stirring. Most people prefer sturdy wooden or plastic cooking spoons.

Wire Whisk: Use a wire whisk for beating eggs, egg whites and thin batters as well as for stirring puddings, sauces and gravies to remove lumps.

Electric Mixing Appliances

Blender: For liquefying or blending mixtures or chopping small amounts of nuts, herbs or bread crumbs. Most batters or doughs are too thick for a blender.

Food Processor: For blending, pureeing, chopping, slicing, dicing, grinding, pulverizing and shredding many foods. Some food processors mix and knead dough.

Hand Blender: For liquefying or blending mixtures. This smaller, less-powerful blender may not perform as well as a regular one for some mixtures.

Handheld Mixer: For all but the thickest batters. Use for recipes in this book that specify "electric mixer." We used a handheld mixer for testing recipes.

Mini-Chopper: For mixing small amounts of sauces and dips or chopping small amounts of vegetables, nuts and herbs.

Stand Mixer: Has a more powerful motor than a hand-held mixer, and it frees up your hands. It may have added attachments, including a dough hook.

Stocking the Pantry

You can prepare quick meals or make an easy snack or dessert without planning ahead if you keep the essential ingredients on hand in your kitchen. Check the following lists for the foods you like to serve, and add them to your cupboard, refrigerator or freezer. Then keep a running shopping list, and add items as your supply runs low.

Cupboard

- Breads (buns, loaves, pitas, tortillas)
- Canned
    Beans (black, kidney, navy)
    Broth (beef, chicken, vegetable)
    Meats (chicken, salmon, tuna)
    Tomatoes (diced or peeled whole)
- Cereals
- Coffee and tea
- Cookies and crackers
- Herbs and spices
- Jams and jellies
- Ketchup
- Main-dish mixes
- Mayonnaise
- Mustard
- Olives
- Pasta (fettuccine, macaroni, spaghetti)
- Pasta sauces (Alfredo, pesto, spaghetti)
- Peanut butter
- Pickles
- Rice and rice mixtures
- Salsa
- Salt and pepper
- Soft drinks
- Soups (canned or dried)
- Soy sauce and marinating sauces
- Syrups (butterscotch, chocolate, maple)
- Tomato sauce and tomato paste
- Vegetable oil
- Vinegar

Refrigerator

- Cheeses (Cheddar, cottage, Parmesan)
- Eggs
- Fruit juice
- Margarine or butter
- Milk
- Packaged salad greens
- Sour cream
- Yogurt

Freezer

- Chicken (skinless, boneless breasts)
- Fruit juice concentrate
- Ground beef or turkey
- Ice cream or frozen yogurt
- Vegetables (packaged)

Baking

- Baking cocoa
- Bisquick®
- Baking powder and baking soda
- Brownie mix
- Cake mix and canned frosting
- Flour
- Sugars (brown, granulated, powdered)
- Vanilla and almond extracts

Nonfood Supplies

- All-purpose spray cleanser
- Aluminum foil
- Dishwater detergent and liquid detergent
- Food-storage bags
- Napkins and paper towels
- Nonabrasive scrubbing pads
- Plastic wrap
- Sponges
- Storage containers
- Toothpicks
- Waxed paper

HELPFUL HOW-TO'S

Peel: *Cut off outer covering with a knife or vegetable peeler, or strip off outer covering with fingers.*

Slice: *Cut into flat pieces of the same size.*

Julienne: *Cut into long, thin slices. Stack the slices, and cut into matchlike sticks.*

Cube or Dice: *To cube, cut into 1/2-inch or wider strips; cut across strips into cubes. To dice, cut into 1/2-inch or narrower strips; cut across strips to dice.*

Chop: *Cut into pieces of irregular sizes.*

Snip: *Cut into very small pieces with a kitchen scissors.*

Cut Up: *Cut into small irregular pieces with a kitchen scissors or knife.*

Shred: *Cut into long, thin pieces by rubbing food across the large holes of a shredder or by using a knife to slice very thinly.*

Grate: *Cut into tiny particles by rubbing food across the small rough holes of a grater.*

HELPFUL HOW-TO'S

Crush: *Press with side of knife, mallet or rolling pin to break into small pieces. For garlic, chop into small pieces after crushing.*

Simmer: *Cook in liquid on the stove top just below the boiling point while bubbles rise slowly and break just below the surface. Simmering usually is done after reducing heat from a boil.*

Boil: *Heat liquid on the stove top until bubbles rise continuously and break on the surface and steam is given off. Pasta is usually cooked in boiling water.*

Cutting an Orange into Sections: *Cut along the membrane of both sides of one orange section. Remove that section, and continue with the rest of the orange.*

Peeling and Cutting Up Pineapple: *Cut pineapple lengthwise into fourths. Cut off the rind and the core. Cut pineapple into chunks, removing any "eyes" or spots left from the rind.*

Removing the Hull from a Strawberry: *Cut out the hull, or "cap," with the point of a paring knife.*

Seeding a Jalapeño Chili: *Cut stem off jalapeño chili. Cut chili lengthwise in half; scrape out the seeds. The flesh, ribs and seeds contain irritating, burning oils so be especially careful not to rub your face or eyes. Be sure to wear protective gloves and be sure to wash the oils from your hands.*

Seeding a Tomato: *Cut tomato crosswise in half. Gently squeeze each half to force out the seeds.*

Separating Eggs: *Eggs are easiest to separate when cold. Use an inexpensive egg separator placed over a small bowl. Crack egg, allowing yolk to fall into center of separator, and white will slip through the slots. Do not pass the yolk back and forth from shell half to shell half. Bacteria may be present on the outside of the shell, which could contaminate the yolk or white.*

Pots and Pans

There are many useful and attractive pots and pans to choose from. These are some of the basic types and sizes that are particularly good to have in your kitchen.

For Cooking

Dutch Oven, Stockpot: These are bigger pots, usually 4-quart size or more, and are perfect for cooking soup, stew and pasta.

Saucepans: These come in a range of sizes from 1 to 3 quarts; some have a nonstick finish. They're used for cooking or reheating food on a stove top and should have tight-fitting lids.

Skillet, Frying Pan, Sauté Pan: Used for frying almost any kind of food. They are normally identified by size such as 10- or 12-inch, or capacity such as 3-, 4- or 5-quart, and have a long handle. Although they often can be used interchangeably, some have sloping sides and some have straight sides, and they may vary in depth and capacity. In this book, we use the word *skillet*.

Specialty Pans: There are any number of additional stove-top pans that often have a special purpose. Some of these are crepe pans, omelet pans, chicken fryers and pans for stir-frying and grilling.

For Baking

Angel Food Cake Pan (Tube Pan): A round metal pan with a tube or cylinder in the middle. The bottom of this pan is often removable to make it easier to get the cake out of the pan. Used for angel food, chiffon and sponge cakes.

Baking Dishes: These are made of heat-resistant glass and are usually round, square or rectangular. Although they can be used to bake cakes and other desserts, they are perfect for lasagna and other main dishes.

Baking Pans: These metal pans come in a variety of shapes and sizes and are often used for cakes and other desserts.

Bundt Cake Pan: A round, fluted pan with a center tube.

Casserole: A covered or uncovered piece of cookware for baking and serving food.

Cookie/Baking Sheet: This is flat and rectangular and may be open on one or more sides. The open sides allow for good air circulation in the oven when baking cookies, biscuits, scones and shortcakes. For more about cookie sheets, see Cookie and Bar Basics page 137.

Custard Cups: Small, deep, individual bowl-shaped dishes with a flat bottom. These glass, heatproof bowls can be used to bake popovers and individual custards.

Jelly Roll Pan: A rectangular metal baking pan measuring 15 1/2 × 10 1/2 × 1 inch for sheet cakes or sponge cakes for jelly rolls.

Muffin Pan: A pan with individual cups for baking muffins or cupcakes. The cups range in size from small (or miniature) to jumbo.

Pie Plate or Pie Pan: A round glass or metal, heat-resistant plate or pan with a flared side, especially designed for baking pies.

Pizza Pan: A round metal pan with low or no sides for baking pizza. Some are perforated to help crisp the pizza crust.

Popover Pan: A dark pan with deep cups especially designed for baking popovers.

Soufflé Dish: A round, open dish with high, straight sides and smooth interior especially designed for baking soufflés.

Springform Pan: A round, deep pan with a removable side. Especially designed for cheesecakes and desserts that should not be inverted to remove them from the pan.

Cooking Terms Glossary

Just like any other activity, cooking has its own vocabulary. This glossary isn't a complete list, but it will help you learn some of the most common terms. For other food or cooking definitions, see Ingredients Glossary (page 14), Microwave Basics (page 543) and Grilling (page 331).

Al Dente: Description for the doneness of pasta cooked until tender but firm to the bite.

Bake: To cook food in an oven with dry heat. Bake food uncovered for a dry, crisp top (breads, cakes, cookies, chicken) or covered to retain moistness (vegetables, casseroles, stews).

Baste: Spoon liquid over food (pan juices over turkey) during cooking to keep it moist.

Batter: An uncooked mixture of flour, eggs, liquid and other ingredients. Batter is thin enough to be spooned or poured (muffins, pancakes).

Blanch: Plunge food into boiling water for a brief time to preserve color, texture and nutritional value or to remove the skin (vegetables, fruits, nuts).

Boil: Heat liquid until bubbles rise continuously and break on the surface and steam is given off. In a rolling boil, the bubbles form rapidly and the surface "rolls."

Bread: Coat a food (fish, meat, vegetables) by dipping into a liquid (beaten egg or milk), then into bread crumbs, cracker crumbs or cornmeal before frying or baking. See also Coat.

Broil: Cook directly under a red-hot heating unit.

Brown: Cook quickly over high heat, causing the surface of the food to turn brown.

Caramelize: Melt sugar slowly over low heat until it becomes a golden brown, caramel-flavored syrup. Or sprinkle granulated, powdered or brown sugar on top of a food, then place it under a broiler until the sugar is melted and caramelized.

Chill: Place food in the refrigerator until it's thoroughly cold.

Chop: Cut food into coarse or fine irregular-shaped pieces, using a knife, food chopper, blender or food processor.

Coat: Cover food evenly with crumbs or sauce. See also Bread.

Cool: Allow hot food to stand at room temperature until it reaches a desired temperature. Placing hot food on a wire rack will help it cool more quickly. Occasional stirring will help a mixture cool more quickly and evenly.

Core: Remove the center of a fruit (apple, pear, pineapple). Cores contain small seeds (apple, pear) or are woody (pineapple).

Cover: Place a cover, lid, plastic wrap or aluminum foil over a container of food.

Crisp-tender: Description of doneness for vegetables cooked so they retain some of their crisp texture.

Crush: Press into very fine particles; for example, crushing a clove of garlic with a chef's knife or garlic press.

Cube: Cut food into squares 1/2 inch or larger, using a knife.

Cut up: Cut food into small irregular pieces, using a kitchen scissors or knife. Or cut a large food into smaller pieces (broiler-fryer chicken).

Dash: Less than 1/8 teaspoon of an ingredient.

Deep-fry or French-fry: Cook in hot fat that's deep enough to float the food. See also Fry, Panbroil, Panfry, Sauté.

Deglaze: After panfrying a food, remove excess fat from the skillet, then add a small amount of liquid (broth, water, wine) and stir to loosen browned bits of food in the skillet. This mixture is used as a base for sauce.

Dice: Cut food into squares smaller than 1/2 inch, using a knife.

Dip: Moisten or coat a food by submerging it, covering all sides.

Dissolve: Stir a dry ingredient (flavored gelatin, yeast, sugar) into a liquid ingredient (boiling water, hot water, tea) until the dry ingredient dissolves.

Dough: A stiff but pliable mixture of flour, liquid and other ingredients (often including a leavening). Dough can be dropped from a spoon (cookies), rolled (pie crust) or kneaded (bread).

Drain: Pour off liquid by putting the food into a strainer or colander that has been set in the sink. If draining fat from meat, place the strainer in a disposable container. If you're saving the liquid, place the strainer in a bowl or other container.

Drizzle: Pour topping in thin lines from a spoon or liquid measuring cup in an uneven pattern over food (glaze over cake or cookies).

Dust: Sprinkle lightly with flour, granulated sugar, powdered sugar or baking cocoa (dusting coffee cake with powdered sugar).

Flake: Break lightly into small pieces, using a fork (cooked fish).

Flute: Pinching pastry with your fingers to make a finished, decorative edge. (See Pastry Edges, page 120.)

Fry: Cook in hot fat over moderate or high heat. See also Deep-fry, Panbroil, Panfry, Sauté.

Garnish: Decorate food with small amounts of other foods that have a distinctive color or texture (parsley, fresh berries, chocolate curls).

Glaze: Brush, spread or drizzle an ingredient (meat stock, jam, melted chocolate) on hot or cold food to give it a glossy appearance or hard finish.

Grate: Rub a hard-textured food (chocolate, citrus peel, Parmesan cheese) against the small, rough, sharp-edged holes of a grater to reduce it to tiny particles. When grating citrus peel, be sure to grate only the outer skin, not the bitter white inner membrane.

Grease: Rub the bottom and sides of a pan with shortening, using pastry brush, waxed paper or paper towel. Or spray with cooking spray. Grease pans to prevent food from sticking during baking (muffins, some casseroles). Don't use butter or margarine for greasing, unless specified in a recipe, because they usually contain salt that may cause hot foods to stick.

Grease and flour: After greasing a pan with shortening, sprinkle it with small amount of flour and shake the pan to distribute it evenly. Then, turn the pan upside down and tap the bottom to remove excess flour. Grease and flour pans to prevent sticking during baking.

Grill: See page 331.

Heat oven: Turn the oven control(s) to the desired temperature, allowing the oven to heat thoroughly before adding food. Heating, also called preheating, takes about 10 minutes for most ovens.

Hull: Remove the stem and leaves with a knife or huller (strawberries).

Husk: Remove the leaves and outer shell (corn on the cob).

Julienne: Cut into thin, matchlike strips with a knife or food processor (fruits, vegetables, meats).

Knead: Work dough on a floured surface into a smooth, elastic mass, using your hands or an electric mixer with dough hooks. Kneading develops the gluten in flour and gives an even texture and a smooth, rounded top. See How to Make Yeast Dough, page 65.

Marinate: Let food stand in a marinade—a savory, acidic liquid—in a glass or plastic container for several hours to add flavor or to tenderize. Always refrigerate marinating foods.

Melt: Turn a solid (chocolate, butter) into liquid by heating.

Microwave: Cook, reheat or thaw food in a microwave oven. See Microwave Basics, page 543.

Mince: Cut food into very fine pieces—smaller than chopped, but bigger than crushed—with a knife.

Mix: Combine ingredients evenly, using any method.

Panbroil: Cook meat or other food quickly in an ungreased or lightly greased skillet.

Panfry: Fry meat or other food in a skillet, using varying amounts of fat and usually pouring off the fat from the meat during cooking. See also Deep-fry, Fry, Panbroil, Sauté.

Peel: Cut off the outer covering with a knife or vegetable peeler (apples, potatoes). Also, strip off the outer covering with your fingers (bananas, oranges).

Poach: Cook in simmering liquid just below the boiling point (eggs, fish).

Pound: Flatten boneless cuts of chicken and meat, using a meat mallet or the flat side of a meat pounder, until they're a uniform thickness.

Puree: Blend food until it's smooth, using a blender or food processor.

Reduce: Boil liquid, uncovered, to evaporate some of the liquid and intensify the flavor of the remaining liquid.

Reduce heat: Lower the heat on the stove top so that a mixture continues to cook slowly and evenly without scorching.

Refrigerate: Place food in the refrigerator to chill or store it.

Roast: Cook meat, uncovered, on rack in a shallow pan in the oven without adding liquid.

Roll: Flatten dough into a thin, even layer, using a rolling pin (cookies, pie crust).

Roll up: Roll a flat food spread with a filling—or with the filling placed at one end—beginning at one end until it is tube-shaped (jelly roll, enchilada).

Sauté: Cook over medium-high heat in a small amount of fat, using a frequent tossing or turning motion. See also Deep-fry, Fry, Panbroil, Panfry.

Scald: Heat liquid to just below the boiling point and tiny bubbles form at the edge. A thin skin will form on the top of scalded milk.

Score: Lightly cutting the surface of a food about 1/4 inch deep, using a knife. Scoring helps cooking and flavoring or it may be used for appearance (meat, yeast bread).

Sear: Brown meat quickly over high heat.

Season: Add flavor with salt, pepper, herbs, spices and seasoning mixes.

Shred: Cut into long, thin pieces using the round, smooth holes of shredder, a knife or food processor.

Simmer: Cook in liquid on the stove top just below the boiling point while bubbles rise slowly and break just below the surface. Simmering usually is done after reducing heat from a boil.

Skim: Remove the top layer of fat or foam that floats on top from a soup or broth, using a spoon, ladle or skimmer (a flat utensil with holes in it).

Slice: Cut into flat pieces about the same size (bread, meat).

Snip: Cut into very small pieces with a kitchen scissors.

Soft Peaks: Egg whites or whipping cream beaten until the moist, glossy peaks are rounded or curl when you lift the beaters from the bowl. See also Stiff Peaks.

Soften: Let cold food stand at room temperature, or microwave at low power setting, until no longer hard (butter, margarine, cream cheese).

Steam: Cook food by placing it on a rack or in a special steamer basket over a small amount of boiling water in a covered pan. See also Vegetables and Fruit (page 491).

Stew: Cook slowly in a small amount of liquid for a long time (stewed fruit, beef stew).

Stiff Peaks: Egg whites or whipping cream beaten until moist, glossy peaks stand up straight when you lift the beaters from the bowl. See also Soft Peaks.

Stir-fry: A Chinese method of quickly cooking similar-size pieces of food in a small amount of hot oil over high heat, lifting and stirring constantly with a turner or large spoon.

Strain: Pour a mixture or liquid through a fine sieve or strainer to remove larger particles.

Tear: Break into pieces with your fingers.

Toast: Brown lightly in a toaster, oven, broiler or skillet (bread, coconut, nuts).

Toss: Mix ingredients lightly with a lifting motion (salads, pasta with sauce).

Whip: Beat ingredients to add air and increase volume until the ingredients are light and fluffy (cream, egg whites).

Zest: The outside colored layer of citrus fruit (oranges, lemons) that contains aromatic oils and flavor. It also means to remove the outside layer of citrus fruit in fine strips, using a knife, citrus zester or vegetable peeler.

Ingredients Glossary

Using the right ingredients will help you be successful when you cook. In this list, you'll find ingredients used in this cookbook as well as other common ingredients.

Baking Powder: Leavening mixture which includes baking soda, an acid plus a moisture absorber. Double-acting baking powder forms carbon dioxide, the gas which makes doughs rise, twice: once when mixed with moist ingredients and once during baking. It's not interchangeable with baking soda because baking soda needs something acidic to be mixed with it in order for it to work while baking powder already contains the acid it needs to work.

Baking Soda: Leavening also called bicarbonate of soda. Must be mixed with an acid ingredient (such as lemon juice, buttermilk or molasses) to release its carbon dioxide gas bubbles, which makes baked goods rise.

Balsamic Vinegar: Italian vinegar made from white Trebbiano grape juice, then aged in barrels, producing a vinegar darker in color and sweeter than other vinegars. To keep the flavor intact, many balsamic vinegars contain sulfites, which can cause an allergic reaction.

Bisquick: A convenience baking mix made from flour, shortening, baking powder and salt. Use for biscuits, muffins, other quick breads, cakes, cookies and some main dishes.

Bouillon/Broth/Stock: The liquid made from cooking vegetables, meat, poultry or fish. It's used for making soups and sauces. Beef, chicken and vegetable canned broths and dehydrated bouillon cubes, granules and pastes are available in the soup section of the supermarket.

Capers: Unopened flower buds of a Mediterranean plant. Capers look like tiny wrinkled peas, and they're usually pickled in vinegar brine. Sharp and tangy, they're used to flavor salad dressings, sauces and condiments.

Cheese: See pages 208 to 212.

Chilies: A family of more than two hundred varieties, chilies are used in cooking around the world. Available fresh and dried in red, green, yellow and purple. Chilies range in length from 1/4 inch to 12 inches. Beware of the ribs and seeds—they're actually hotter than the outside flesh because they contain concentrated amounts of an oil, *capsaicin*, which gives chilies their kick but can irritate and burn the eyes, nose and skin. Wear rubber gloves while handling chilies and wash your hands thoroughly with soap (to break down the oils) afterward. Don't cut chilies under running water because the irritating oils can become airborne.

- **Anaheim chilies:** Slim chilies in various shades of green, between 5 and 8 inches long, mildly hot. Available in cans labeled whole or diced mild green chilies, they get their name from the California city that opened a chili pepper cannery.
- **Ancho chilies:** Dried, ripened poblano chilies.
- **Cascabel chilies:** Medium hot, with a distinctive nutty flavor. Dark, blood-red in color, they're plum shaped and about 1 1/2 inches in diameter. In Spanish, *cascabel* means "little round bell" or "rattle," referring to the sound they make when shaken. These chilies are also known as *chili bola*.
- **Chipotle chilies:** Smoked, dried jalapeño chilies. Buy them loose in the dried form, pickled or canned in adobo sauce. Chipotle chilies are often used in sauces.
- **Fresno chilies:** Tapered chili that's light green when young, red when mature. Shaped like an Anaheim chili, but with the all the heat of a jalapeño. Fresno chilies are often used in guacamole.
- **Habanero chilies:** Orange when ripe, it's the fire engine of the chili family. Considered the hottest of all chilies, it looks like a little lantern. Handle with care so the oils don't burn you.
- **Hungarian Wax chilies:** Large—up to five inches long—yellow chili, mild to medium hot. Also known as banana peppers or yellow wax chilies. They're often pickled.
- **Jalapeño chilies:** A jade green or red chili, two to three inches long, that packs a heat wallop. The smallest ones are the hottest. Called *escabeche* when pickled, *chipotle* when dried and smoked. Jalapeños are a favorite for nachos, salsas and other sauces.

CHILIES

Pasilla

Poblano

Ancho

Chipotle

Jalapeño

Anaheim

Banana

Casabel

Thai

Serrano

Habanero

- **Poblano chilies:** Dark green and slightly flat with a pointed tip, mild to hot. Best known for their use in *chiles rellenos*. When dried, they're called *ancho chilies*.

- **Serrano chilies:** Range in color from bright green to scarlet, among the hottest chilies. Look for them fresh, canned, dried or pickled.

Chocolate: Cocoa beans are shelled, roasted and ground to make a thick paste called chocolate liquor, the base for all chocolate. Cocoa butter is the fat or oil from the cocoa bean. Chocolate liquor is processed to make the many varieties of chocolate below. Not all chocolate is the same and quality varies, so follow package directions when melting.

- **Baking cocoa:** Dried chocolate liquor, with the cocoa butter removed, is ground into unsweetened cocoa. Baking cocoa isn't a direct substitute for cocoa drink mixes that contain added powdered milk and sugar.

- **Semisweet, bittersweet, sweet and milk chocolate:** Contains from 10 to 35 percent chocolate liquor, varying amounts of cocoa butter, sugar and, for some, milk and flavorings. Available in bars and chips for baking or eating.

- **Unsweetened chocolate:** Contains 50 to 58 percent cocoa butter. Bitter in flavor, it's used primarily in baking.

- **White chocolate (white baking bar):** It is not true chocolate because it doesn't contain cocoa or chocolate liquor. Made from cocoa butter, sugar, milk solids and vanilla. Often called white baking chips or vanilla baking bar.

Coconut: The firm, creamy white meat of the coconut, the fruit of the coconut palm. It's available shredded or flaked in cans or plastic bags and usually comes sweetened. Unsweetened coconut may be found in specialty or gourmet food stores or in Asian and Indian grocery stores.

Coffee: Use brewed coffee or instant coffee granules as an ingredient. For more about coffee, see pages 35 to 37.

Corn Syrup: Clear, thick liquid made from corn sugar mixed with acid. It doesn't crystallize and is especially good for pecan pie, frostings, fruit sauces and jams. Dark and light corn syrup are interchangeable.

Cornstarch: A thickener for soups, sauces and desserts that comes from a portion of the corn kernel. It makes clear sauces, not opaque like those thickened with flour. To substitute all-purpose flour in a sauce, use half as much cornstarch.

Cream: Cream is the smooth, rich dairy product that naturally separates from whole milk (typically milk is homogenized to prevent this natural separation from occurring). Cream is churned to make butter and buttermilk; it's also pasteurized and processed into several forms:

- **Half-and-half:** A blend of milk and cream, contains 10 to 12 percent butterfat. It won't whip, but you can use it in place of whipping or heavy cream in many recipes.

- **Sour cream:** Commercially cultured with lactic acid to give it a tangy flavor. Regular sour cream is 18 to 20 percent butterfat. Reduced-fat sour cream is made from half-and-half and can be substituted for regular sour cream in most recipes. Fat-free sour cream has all the fat removed and

may not be successful in all recipes that call for regular sour cream.

- **Whipping or heavy cream:** The richest cream available in the United States, it has 36 to 40 percent butterfat. It doubles in volume when whipped.

Cream of tartar: After wine is made, the acid left in the wine barrels is processed into cream of tartar. Add cream of tartar to egg whites in the beginning stages of beating for more stability and volume.

Eggs: See page 199.

Fats: Solid fats and oils add richness and flavor to food. In cooking, they improve browning, help bind ingredients together, tenderize baked goods and are used for frying. But not all fats are created equal in texture and flavor. In our recipes, we call for different fats because of their cooking and baking characteristics.

- **Butter:** A saturated fat made from cream that must be at least 80 percent butterfat by USDA standards. It's high in flavor and has a

BUTTER, MARGARINE AND VEGETABLE OIL SPREAD FAT COMPARISON

Margarine 80% Fat
(11g fat per tablespoon)

Vegetable Oil Spread 53% Fat
(7g fat per tablespoon)

Butter 80% Fat
(11g fat per tablespoon)

Vegetable Oil Spread
70% Fat
(10g fat per tablespoon)

Vegetable Oil Spread 40% Fat
(6g fat per tablespoon)

melt-in-your-mouth texture. Butter is sold in solid sticks or whipped in tubs. Only use sticks for baking; whipped butter will give a different texture because of the air beaten into it.

- **Butter-margarine blends:** Available in sticks and tubs, blends usually are a combination of 60 percent margarine and 40 percent butter and are interchangeable with butter or margarine. Only use sticks for baking.

- **Lard:** A saturated fat made from rendered and refined pork fat, lard is not used as much now as in the past. Lard makes very tender, flaky biscuits and pastry.

- **Margarine:** An unsaturated butter substitute made with at least 80 percent fat by weight and flavoring from dairy products. Most margarine uses vegetable oils made from soybeans, cottonseed and corn. Use it as a table spread and for cooking and baking. Sold in sticks and as soft spreads in tubs. Only use sticks for baking.

- **Oils for cooking:** Low in saturated fats and containing no cholesterol, these liquid fats are delicate to bland in flavor and are treated to withstand high-temperature cooking and long storage. Look for these cooking oils in our recipes:

  Cooking spray: Used to spray cooking and baking pans to prevent food from sticking. You also can spray it directly on food for low-fat cooking.

  Olive oil: This oil has become incredibly popular in the United States, not only for its flavor but also for its potential health benefits. Olive oil naturally contains no cholesterol, but it does contain fat—the highest amount of monounsaturated fat of any vegetable oil, which may contribute to heart health. It is classified in several ways, including extra virgin, virgin, olive oil and light olive oil.

  Vegetable oil: An economical blend of oils from various vegetables, such as corn, cottonseed, peanut, safflower, canola and soybean. Use for all cooking and baking.

- **Reduced-calorie or low-fat butter or margarine:** Water and air have been worked into these products, and they contain at least 20 percent less fat than regular butter or margarine. Do not use for baking or cooking.

- **Shortening:** Vegetable oils that are hydrogenated so they'll be solid at room temperature. Shortening is used especially for flaky, tender pastry and to grease baking pans. Use butter-flavored and regular shortening interchangeably. Sold in cans and in sticks.

- **Vegetable-oil spreads:** Margarine products with less than 80 percent fat (vegetable oil) by weight usually are labeled as vegetable-oil spreads. They're sold in sticks for all-purpose use, including some baking if they contain more than 65 percent fat, so check the label. Vegetable-oil spreads sold in tubs shouldn't be used for baking. They're also sold as a liquid in squeeze bottles. Use the squeezable spread for topping veggies, popcorn or basting, but not for baking.

Flour: The primary ingredient in breads, cakes, cookies and quick breads. The main difference between the different varieties of flour is the amount of gluten-forming protein they contain and you'll want more or less protein depending on what you are baking. The main job of gluten is to give structure to baked goods.

- **All-purpose flour:** Selected wheats blended for all kinds of baking. Available both bleached and unbleached.

- **Bread flour:** Made from hard wheat, which is higher in gluten-forming protein and gives more structure and volume to bread than all-purpose flour. It's the best choice for making bread machine breads and other yeast breads. It can also be used for quick breads and cookies, but it doesn't make tender cakes or pastries.

- **Cake flour:** Milled from soft wheat, which has less gluten, cake flour results in tender, fine-textured cakes.

- **Quick-mixing flour:** Enriched, all-purpose flour that's granular and processed to blend easily with liquid to make gravies or sauces or thicken main dishes.

- **Rye flour:** Milled from rye grain and low in gluten-forming protein, it is usually combined with wheat flour to increase a dough's gluten-forming capabilities.

- **Self-rising flour:** A convenience flour made from a blend of hard and soft wheats that includes leavening and salt. For best results, don't substitute self-rising flour for other kinds, unless directed in a recipe, because it will throw off the leavening and salt proportions.

- **Whole wheat flour:** Ground from the complete wheat kernel, whole wheat flour gives breads and other baked goods a nutty flavor and dense texture. Stone-ground whole wheat flour has a coarser texture than roller-milled whole wheat flour. Graham flour is a slightly different grind of whole wheat flour but can be used interchangeably with whole wheat flour. It is best to store whole wheat flour in the freezer or refrigerator to keep the fat in the wheat germ from becoming rancid. Be sure to allow the amount of flour measured for your recipe to come to room temperature before adding it to other ingredients.

Garlic: Plump, pungent, egg-size bulbs encased in papery skin and made up of individual cloves, garlic belongs to the same family as chives, onions and shallots. Available in numerous forms: fresh, peeled and in jars, as a paste, as juice, dried, powdered, flaked. Used to season a broad range of dishes from many cultures. Also may be roasted whole until the cloves become buttery soft, then spread on crackers or bread or used as an ingredient.

Gelatin: An odorless and colorless powder, its thickening power is released when it's mixed with hot liquid. Gelatin is pure protein, processed from beef and veal bones and cartilage or pig skin. Available flavored and sweetened.

Gingerroot: Plump tubers with knobby branches. Side branches have a milder tangy ginger flavor than the main root, which can have a hot "bite." Grate unpeeled gingerroot, or peel and chop or slice, to season foods such as stir-fries, sauces and baked goods. Wrap tightly in plastic and store in the refrigerator.

Herbs: See pages 445 to 447.

Honey: A natural sweetener produced by bees. The buzz about honey is that it adds distinctive flavor to salads, salad dressings, dips, sauces, beverages and baked goods. Because honey can contain spores of *clostridium*

botulinum, which has been a source of infection for infants, do not feed honey to children less than 1 year old. Honey is safe for persons one year of age and older. Store honey at room temperature; it can be refrigerated but will crystallize more easily and quickly. To make crystallized honey liquid again, heat a saucepan of water to boiling, remove from the heat and place the container of honey in the hot water until the crystals disappear. Or it can be liquefied in the microwave (page 545).

Leavening: Ingredients that cause baked goods to rise and develop lighter textures. See also see Baking Powder, Baking Soda, Yeast.

Legumes: See page 357.

Maple Syrup: Golden brown sweetener made by boiling down the sap of sugar maple trees. Used as a topping and as an ingredient, maple syrup has a slight caramel flavor. Refrigerate after opening. Maple-flavored syrup usually is corn syrup combined with a little pure maple syrup. Pancake syrups usually are corn syrup with added maple flavoring.

Mayonnaise/Salad Dressing: Smooth, rich mixture made from egg yolks, vinegar and seasonings, which is beaten to make a permanent emulsion that retains its creamy texture during storage. Available in jars in reduced-fat and fat-free versions. Salad dressing is a similar product, but it's lower in fat because it's made with a starch thickener, vinegar, eggs and sweetener. Salad dressing can be substituted for mayonnaise in salads or spreads, but use only mayonnaise in hot or cooked dishes, unless a recipe was developed for salad dressing, because salad dressing may separate when heated.

Milk: Refers to cow's milk throughout this cookbook.

- **Buttermilk:** Thick, smooth liquid made by culturing skim or part-skim milk with lactic acid bacteria. Adds a tangy flavor to baked goods. It is called buttermilk because originally it was the liquid left after churning butter.

- **Evaporated milk:** Whole milk with more than half of the water removed before the mixture is homogenized. Evaporated milk is a little thicker than whole milk and has a slightly "cooked" taste. Use it in recipes calling for evaporated milk, or mix with an equal amount of water to replace whole milk. Do not use it as a substitute for sweetened condensed milk in recipes.

- **Fat-free (skim) milk:** Contains virtually no fat.
- **1% low-fat milk:** Has 99 percent of milk fat removed.
- **2% reduced-fat milk:** Has 98 percent of milk fat removed.
- **Sweetened condensed milk:** Made when about half of the water is removed from whole milk and sweetener is added. Recipes using sweetened condensed milk include bars, candies and pies. Do not substitute it in recipes calling for evaporated milk.
- **Whole or regular milk:** Has at least 4 percent milk fat.

Mushrooms: An exciting crop of fresh, dried and canned mushrooms has sprung up in recent years. A great flavor trick is to combine white mushrooms with a more flavorful variety, such as portabella or crimini. Cooked together, the whites will pick up the stronger flavor of their counterpart. It saves money because whites are the least expensive, but you get the full taste of the more expensive variety. To prep fresh mushrooms, cut a thin slice from the bottom of the stem. Gently wipe with a cloth or soft brush or rinse quickly with cold water (do not soak in water); pat dry with paper towels. See page 491 for more information on mushrooms.

Mustard: From plants grown for their sharp-tasting seeds and calcium-rich leaves (mustard greens). Gives pungent flavor to foods.

- **Ground mustard:** Finely ground dried mustard seed.
- **Mustard:** Yellow mustard (also called American mustard) is made with mild white mustard seed and mixed with sugar, vinegar and seasonings. Dijon mustard, from Dijon, France, is made from brown mustard seed mixed with wine, unfermented grape juice and seasonings. You'll find a wealth of other mustard varieties at your supermarket or local gourmet or cooking shop.
- **Mustard seed:** Whole seeds used for pickling and to season savory dishes.

Pasta: See page 385.

Pesto: A pasta sauce traditionally made from fresh basil, pine nuts, Parmesan cheese, garlic and olive oil, which is ground or blended until smooth. Make it fresh (page 438), or look for it in the refrigerator case or in tubes and jars in the tomato product section of your supermarket.

Phyllo (Filo): Paper-thin pastry sheets whose name comes from the Greek word for leaf. It's the pastry favored for many Greek and Middle Eastern main dishes and sweets. Available frozen and refrigerated. Sheets dry out quickly; so when working with phyllo, cover the unused sheets with waxed paper and a damp kitchen towel.

Pine Nuts: Small white nuts from several varieties of pine trees. Also known as *pinon* and *pignoli*. Often used in Mediterranean and Mexican dishes. With their high fat content, these nuts turn rancid quickly, so store them in the refrigerator to preserve their flavor.

Puff Pastry: This dough got its name because it puffs when it is baked. Dozens of layers of chilled butter rolled between sheets of pastry dough result in an extremely flaky dough. This dough is the basis of croissants, puff pastry shells and desserts such as Napoleons.

Red Pepper Sauce: Condiment made from hot chili peppers and cured in either salt or vinegar brine. Many varieties and levels of hotness are available.

Rice: See page 345.

Roasted Bell Peppers: Sweet red or other color bell peppers that have been roasted and packed in jars. Popular for appetizers, soups and main dishes.

Salad Dressing: See Mayonnaise.

Salsa: A Mexican sauce of tomatoes, onions, green chilies and cilantro. Make it at home (see Tomato Salsa, page 456), or buy it fresh, canned or bottled. Green salsa, or *salsa verde*, is made with tomatillos. Also, any sauce of fresh chopped fruits and/or vegetables.

Scallion: With their long, straight green tops and thin white bottoms, scallions are often referred to as green onions. The terms are used interchangeably in recipes.

Shallot: An onion with multiple cloves that resemble garlic. The papery skin that covers the bulbs ranges in color from beige to purple and should be removed. Shallots and onions can be used interchangeably.

Soy Sauce: A brown sauce made from soybeans, wheat, yeast and salt used in cooking and as a condiment especially in Chinese and Japanese cooking.

Sugar: Sweetener produced from sugar beets or cane sugar. Available in several forms:

- **Artificial sweeteners:** A variety of products is available. It's not recommended for baking because it isn't really sugar and the flavor may break down.

- **Brown (packed):** Brown sugar today is made by mixing white sugar with molasses. Available in light and dark varieties; dark brown sugar has the more intense flavor. If brown sugar hardens, store in a closed container with a slice of apple or a slice of fresh bread for 1 to 2 days.

- **Granulated:** Standard white sugar available in quantities ranging from 1-pound boxes to 100-pound bags, as well as in cubes and 1-teaspoon packets.

- **Molasses:** A dark, thick syrup from the sugar refining process.

- **Powdered:** Granulated sugar that has been processed into a fine powder and used for frostings and for dusting pastries and cakes.

Tomatillo: Easily mistaken for a small green tomato, tomatillos grow in a paper husk that's removed before use. Citrusy in flavor, tomatillos are commonly used in salsas and Mexican sauces.

Tortilla: The everyday bread of Mexico, tortillas look like a very thin pancake. Made from ground wheat or corn, tortillas can be eaten plain or as a "wrap" around both hot and cold fillings. Both fresh and fried (hard shell) tortillas are available in varieties such as blue corn, spinach and tomato.

Truffle: This European fungus is one of the world's most expensive foods. It grows wild near the roots of trees; truffle hunters sometimes employ trained pigs and dogs to sniff out the treasured morsels. Roundish with thick, wrinkled skin and pungent flavor, truffles are used in sauces and omelets and as a garnish. Available fresh, canned and as a paste in a tube.

Worcestershire sauce: Common condiment made from exotic blend of ingredients: garlic, soy sauce, tamarind, onions, molasses, lime, anchovies, vinegar and other seasonings. Although named for Worcester, England, where it was first bottled, Worcestershire sauce was developed in India by the British.

Yeast: Leavening whose fermentation causes yeast bread to rise. The combination of warmth, food (sugar) and liquid causes yeast to release carbon dioxide bubbles that, in turn, cause dough to rise. Yeast is very sensitive; too much heat will kill it, and cold will stunt its growth. Always use yeast before its expiration date.

- **Bread machine yeast:** A strain of yeast that's finely granulated and works exceptionally well in bread machines.

- **Brewer's yeast:** Special nonleavening yeasts used in making beer. Due to its rich vitamin B content, it is also sold as a food supplement. Do not use brewer's yeast for making bread; the bread will not rise.

- **Compressed cake or fresh active yeast:** This yeast is sold in moist cakes in two sizes, 0.6 ounce and 2 ounces. Because it has not undergone the drying process, it doesn't need to be dissolved before using. Simply crumble the cake into dry ingredients or soften in warm water first. This yeast is especially good for breads starting with a sponge or those with a long rising time. One 0.6 ounce cake of yeast is equal to 1 package of dry yeast—they are interchangeable.

- **Quick active dry yeast:** Dehydrated yeast that allows bread to rise in less time than regular yeast. Quick active dry yeast can be used interchangeably with bread machine yeast.

- **Regular active dry yeast:** Dehydrated yeast that can be used in most yeast bread recipes. For use in bread machines, you may need to increase the amount to 1 teaspoon for each 3/4 teaspoon of bread machine yeast.

Appetizers & Beverages

Low-Fat = 3g or less, except main dishes with 6g or less   **Fast** = Ready in 30 minutes or less   ■ = Bread Machine directions   ● = Slow Cooker directions

Brie with Caramelized Onion, Pistachio and Cranberry (page 27)

Lighter = 1/3 fewer calories or 50% less fat

Appetizer Basics

Americans have a love affair with appetizers! Whether they're veggies and dip, elegant canapés, or a handful of popcorn, we love to eat them at parties, at restaurants (ever ordered just appetizers instead of a full meal?) and when sitting in front of the TV. Appetizers answer to a lot of different names and can be light and nibbly or can serve as the beginning to a meal. Here are a few different types of appetizers and several different ways they can be served:

Canapé: Small pieces of toast, bread, crackers or baked pastry topped with various cheeses, an anchovy or some type of spread. They can be hot or cold, easy or elaborate.

Crudité: Raw veggies cut into slices, sticks or pieces, usually served with a dip.

Dips and dunks: These tasty mixtures are the perfect consistency, not too thin or too thick, for dipping chips, crudités and fruit.

Finger Food: Any portion of food that can be eaten with fingers (no utensils required)! Think Crostini (page 31) or Original Chex® Party Mix (page 33).

First Course: One or two appetizers served at the beginning of a sit-down meal. Usually a knife and fork is needed to eat these appetizers.

Hors d'oeuvre: In French, *hors d'oeuvre* means "outside the work" of the main meal, or bite-size foods, served hot or cold, and eaten apart from the regular meal, often with cocktails. Hors d'oeuvres can range from canapés and crudité to olives and nuts.

Spreads: Spreads are thicker than dips, so you'll need a knife to spread them on bread or hearty crackers.

Entertaining with Appetizers

You'll find an assortment of sweet and savory, elegant and casual appetizer recipes in this book. If you're hosting a party, you can make all your appetizers from scratch or you can head to the deli or supermarket to pick up crackers and cheese, prepared dips and spreads, chicken wings, meatballs, even the cut-up veggies.

Think about serving an appetizer buffet instead of a sit-down dinner. Plan it just like you would a regular meal with a blend of hot and cold, mild and spicy, colors and textures. See Menu Planning Basics, page 529.

Host a bring-your-favorite-appetizer party. Provide one or two appetizers yourself, along with beverages. Ask guests to bring the recipes to exchange, too!

Creamy Pesto Dip *Fast*

Prep: 5 min ✳ 1 cup

Avoid the time-consuming preparation of cut-up vegetables by purchasing a package of baby cut carrots and cut-up broccoli, cauliflower and celery available in the produce section of the grocery store.

1 container (8 ounces) sour cream
1/4 cup basil pesto
Assorted fresh vegetables, if desired

1. Mix sour cream and pesto until well blended.

2. Serve with vegetables.

2 Tablespoons: Calories 80 (Calories from Fat 70); Fat 8g (Saturated 3g); Cholesterol 15mg; Sodium 60mg; Carbohydrate 1g (Dietary Fiber 0g); Protein 1g **% Daily Value:** Vitamin A 4%; Vitamin C 0%; Calcium 4%; Iron 0% **Diet Exchanges:** 2 Fat

Creamy Yogurt Fruit Dip

Caesar Vegetable Dip *Fast*

Prep: 10 min ✱ About 1 1/4 cups

Dress up this dip by serving it in a hollowed-out red, yellow or green bell pepper half. Baby carrots, halved radishes, bell pepper slices and cucumber spears are tasty vegetables for dipping.

1/2 cup sour cream
1/4 cup mayonnaise or salad dressing
1/4 cup creamy Caesar dressing
2 tablespoons shredded Parmesan cheese
2 tablespoons chopped red bell pepper
1 hard-cooked egg, chopped
Assorted raw vegetables, if desired

1. Mix sour cream, mayonnaise and Caesar dressing until smooth. Stir in cheese. Serve immediately, or cover and refrigerate 30 minutes to blend flavors if desired.

2. Spoon into serving bowl. Sprinkle with bell pepper and egg. Serve with vegetables.

1 Tablespoon: Calories 55 (Calories from Fat 45); Fat 5g (Saturated 1g); Cholesterol 15mg; Sodium 65mg; Carbohydrate 1g (Dietary Fiber 0g); Protein 1g **% Daily Value:** Vitamin A 2%; Vitamin C 2%; Calcium 0%; Iron 0% **Diet Exchanges:** 1 Fat

Creamy Yogurt Fruit Dip

Fast & Low-Fat

Prep: 10 min ✱ About 2 cups

Select a variety of fruits for dippers, such as sliced apples and pears, sliced cantaloupe and honeydew melon, strawberries and pineapple chunks.

1 package (8 ounces) light cream cheese (Neufchâtel), softened
1 container (6 ounces) orange yogurt
1/2 cup orange marmalade
1/8 teaspoon ground nutmeg
2 tablespoons coarsely chopped pecans
Shredded orange peel
Cut-up fruit, if desired

1. Beat cream cheese in medium bowl with electric mixer on medium speed until creamy. Beat in yogurt, marmalade and nutmeg until smooth. Serve immediately, or cover and refrigerate for 30 minutes to blend flavors if desired.

2. Spoon into serving bowl. Top with pecans, orange peel and, if desired, additional nutmeg. Serve with fruit.

1 Tablespoon: Calories 40 (Calories from Fat 20); Fat 2g (Saturated 1g); Cholesterol 5mg; Sodium 35mg; Carbohydrate 5g (Dietary Fiber 0g); Protein 1g **% Daily Value:** Vitamin A 2%; Vitamin C 0%; Calcium 0%; Iron 0% **Diet Exchanges:** 1/2 Fruit

Guacamole *Low-Fat*

Prep: 20 min; Chill: 1 hr ✱ About 2 3/4 cups

Look for ripe avocados that yield to gentle pressure but are still just slightly firm. If you can only find firm avocados, just let them stand at room temperature for a day or two until they ripen.

2 jalapeño chilies*
2 ripe large avocados
2 tablespoons lime or lemon juice
2 tablespoons finely chopped cilantro
1/2 teaspoon salt
Dash of pepper
1 clove garlic, finely chopped
2 medium tomatoes, finely chopped (1 1/2 cups)
1 medium onion, chopped (1/2 cup)
Tortilla chips, if desired

1. Remove stems, seeds and membranes from chilies; chop chilies (page 9). Cut avocados lengthwise in half; remove pit and peel. Mash avocados.

To remove an avocado pit, firmly and carefully strike the exposed pit with the sharp edge of a knife. While grasping the avocado, twist the knife to loosen and remove the pit.

2. Mix chilies, avocados and remaining ingredients except tortilla chips in glass or plastic bowl.

3. Cover and refrigerate 1 hour to blend flavors. Serve with tortilla chips.

*2 tablespoons canned chopped green chilies can be substituted for the jalapeño chilies.

1 Tablespoon: Calories 10 (Calories from Fat 10); Fat 1g (Saturated 0g); Cholesterol 0mg; Sodium 30mg; Carbohydrate 1g (Dietary Fiber 1g); Protein 0g **% Daily Value:** Vitamin A 0%; Vitamin C 4%; Calcium 0%; Iron 0% **Diet Exchanges:** One serving is free

Lighter "Guacamole": For 0 grams of fat and 5 calories per serving, substitute 1 can (15 ounces) asparagus cuts, drained then blended or processed in food processor until smooth, for avocados. Stir in 1/4 cup fat-free mayonnaise.

INTERESTING DIPPERS

When deciding what to serve with dips, dunks and spreads, you'll find lots of dippers to choose from. Check out the variety of crackers now available. Look for different sizes, shapes, colors and flavors. Scan the snack aisle, too. Big pretzel sticks, flavored chips and snacks in unusual shapes will also work well. And fresh vegetables are always a crisp and colorful addition. Try zucchini slices, jicama sticks (resembling a turnip, jicama is a crunchy vegetable with a flavor similar to water chestnuts), radishes cut into rose shapes or baby corn on the cob (found in jars near the canned vegetables). Whatever you choose, keep in mind that dippers should be sturdy enough to stand up to the dip without breaking.

Spinach Dip

Prep: 15 min; Chill: 4 hr ✱ *About 3 1/2 cups*

1 package (10 ounces) frozen chopped spinach, thawed
1 cup mayonnaise or salad dressing
1 cup sour cream
1 package (1.4 ounces) vegetable soup and recipe mix
1 can (8 ounces) water chestnuts, drained and chopped
1 medium green onion, chopped (1 tablespoon)
1 round uncut loaf bread (about 1 pound), if desired

1. Squeeze spinach to drain; spread on paper towels and pat dry. Mix spinach, mayonnaise, sour cream, soup mix, water chestnuts and onion. Cover and refrigerate at least 4 hours to blend flavors and soften soup mix.

2. Cut 1- to 2-inch slice off top of bread loaf; hollow out loaf, leaving 1/2- to 1-inch shell of bread on side and bottom. Reserve scooped-out bread and top of loaf; cut or tear into pieces to use for dipping. Spoon spinach dip into hollowed-out loaf. Arrange bread pieces around loaf.

3. Or serve dip in bowl with raw vegetable sticks or assorted chips and crackers for dipping.

1 Tablespoon: Calories 40 (Calories from Fat 35); Fat 4g (Saturated 1g); Cholesterol 5mg; Sodium 80mg; Carbohydrate 1g (Dietary Fiber 0g); Protein 0g **% Daily Value:** Vitamin A 4%; Vitamin C 2%; Calcium 0%; Iron 0% **Diet Exchanges:** 1 Fat

Lighter Spinach Dip: For 2 grams of fat and 30 calories per serving, use reduced-fat mayonnaise and sour cream.

Hot Crab Dip

Prep: 15 min; Bake: 20 min ✱ *About 2 1/2 cups*

1 package (8 ounces) cream cheese, softened
1/4 cup grated Parmesan cheese
1/4 cup mayonnaise or salad dressing
1/4 cup dry white wine or apple juice
2 teaspoons sugar
1 teaspoon ground mustard
4 medium green onions, thinly sliced (1/4 cup)
1 clove garlic, finely chopped
1 can (6 ounces) crabmeat, drained, cartilage removed and flaked*
1/3 cup sliced almonds, toasted (page 177)
Assorted crackers or sliced raw vegetables, if desired

1. Heat oven to 375°.

2. Mix all ingredients except crabmeat, almonds and crackers in medium bowl until well blended. Stir in crabmeat.

3. Spread crabmeat mixture in ungreased pie plate, 9 × 1 1/4 inches, or shallow 1-quart casserole. Sprinkle with almonds.

4. Bake uncovered 15 to 20 minutes or until hot and bubbly. Serve with crackers.

*6 ounces imitation crabmeat, coarsely chopped, can be substituted for the canned crabmeat.

1 Tablespoon: Calories 50 (Calories from Fat 35); Fat 4g (Saturated 2g); Cholesterol 10mg; Sodium 50mg; Carbohydrate 1g (Dietary Fiber 0g); Protein 2g **% Daily Value:** Vitamin A 2%; Vitamin C 0%; Calcium 2%; Iron 0% **Diet Exchanges:** 1 Fat

Hot Artichoke Dip

Prep: 10 min; Bake: 25 min ✱ *About 1 1/2 cups*

To save time, mix ingredients in a microwavable casserole. Cover with plastic wrap, folding one edge or corner back 1/4 inch to vent steam. Microwave on Medium-High (70%) 4 to 5 minutes, stirring after 2 minutes, until hot.

1/2 cup mayonnaise or salad dressing
1/2 cup grated Parmesan cheese
4 medium green onions, chopped (1/4 cup)
1 can (14 ounces) artichoke hearts, drained and coarsely chopped
Crackers or cocktail rye bread, if desired

1. Heat oven to 350°.

2. Mix mayonnaise and cheese in small bowl. Stir in onions and artichoke hearts. Spoon into 1-quart casserole.

3. Cover and bake 20 to 25 minutes or until hot. Serve warm with crackers.

1 Tablespoon: Calories 50 (Calories from Fat 35); Fat 4g (Saturated 1g); Cholesterol 4mg; Sodium 105mg; Carbohydrate 2g (Dietary Fiber 1g); Protein 1g **% Daily Value:** Vitamin A 0%; Vitamin C 0%; Calcium 4%; Iron 2% **Diet Exchanges:** 1 Fat

Lighter Hot Artichoke Dip: For 1 gram of fat and 20 calories per serving, use 1/3 cup plain fat-free yogurt and 3 tablespoons reduced-fat mayonnaise for the 1/2 cup mayonnaise.

HOT ARTICHOKE-SPINACH DIP: Increase mayonnaise and Parmesan cheese to 1 cup each. Stir in 1 package (10 ounces) frozen chopped spinach, thawed and squeezed to drain. Spoon into 1-quart casserole. Bake as directed.

Hummus *Fast & Low-Fat*

Prep: 10 min ✴ *About 2 cups*

Serve this Middle Eastern favorite as a dip, a spread, a sandwich filling or as a salad.

1 can (15 to 16 ounces) garbanzo beans, drained and
   liquid reserved
1/2 cup sesame seed
1 clove garlic, cut in half
3 tablespoons lemon juice
1 teaspoon salt
Chopped fresh parsley
Pita bread wedges, crackers or raw vegetables, if
   desired

1. Place reserved bean liquid, the sesame seed and garlic in blender or food processor. Cover and blend on high speed until mixed.

2. Add beans, lemon juice and salt. Cover and blend on high speed, stopping blender occasionally to scrape sides if necessary, until uniform consistency.

3. Spoon into serving dish. Garnish with parsley. Serve with pita bread wedges.

1 Tablespoon: Calories 40 (Calories from Fat 20); Fat 2g (Saturated 0g); Cholesterol 0mg; Sodium 95mg; Carbohydrate 4g (Dietary Fiber 1g); Protein 2g **% Daily Value:** Vitamin A 0%; Vitamin C 0%; Calcium 0%; Iron 2% **Diet Exchanges:** 1 Vegetable

Easy Fiesta Salsa Spread *Fast*

Prep: 10 min ✴ *8 servings*

1 package (8 ounces) cream cheese
1/4 cup salsa
1/4 cup apricot preserves or orange marmalade
1 tablespoon chopped avocado, if desired
1 tablespoon finely shredded Cheddar or Monterey Jack
   cheese
1 tablespoon chopped fresh cilantro
1 tablespoon chopped ripe olives
Assorted crackers or sliced raw vegetables, if desired

1. Place block of cream cheese on serving plate with shallow rim.

2. Mix salsa and preserves; spread over cream cheese. Sprinkle with remaining ingredients except crackers. Serve with crackers.

1 Serving: Calories 135 (Calories from Fat 90); Fat 10g (Saturated 6g); Cholesterol 30mg; Sodium 125mg; Carbohydrate 8g (Dietary Fiber 0g); Protein 3g **% Daily Value:** Vitamin A 10%; Vitamin C 4%; Calcium 2%; Iron 2% **Diet Exchanges:** 1/2 Starch, 2 Fat

EASY CURRY SPREAD: Omit all ingredients except cream cheese and assorted crackers. Spread 1/3 cup chopped chutney over cream cheese. Sprinkle with 1 to 2 teaspoons curry powder, 1 tablespoon chopped peanuts, 1 tablespoon chopped green onion, 1 tablespoon currants or chopped raisins and 1 tablespoon chopped cooked egg yolk.

EASY SHRIMP SPREAD: Omit all ingredients except cream cheese and assorted crackers. Spread 1/3 cup cocktail sauce over cream cheese. Sprinkle with 1/2 cup cooked tiny shrimp, 1 tablespoon chopped green onion and 1 tablespoon chopped ripe olives.

Layered Mexican Snack Platter

Layered Mexican Snack Platter *Fast*

Prep: 20 min ✱ *16 servings*

1 can (15 ounces) refried beans
2 tablespoons salsa, chili sauce or ketchup
1 1/2 cups sour cream
1 cup Guacamole (page 23) or prepared guacamole
1 cup shredded Cheddar cheese (4 ounces)
2 medium green onions, chopped (2 tablespoons)
Tortilla chips, if desired

1. Mix refried beans and salsa. Spread in thin layer on 12- or 13-inch serving plate or pizza pan.

2. Spread sour cream over beans, leaving about 1-inch border of beans around edge. Spread guacamole over sour cream, leaving border of sour cream showing.

3. Sprinkle cheese over guacamole. Sprinkle onions over cheese. Serve immediately, or cover with plastic wrap and refrigerate until ready to serve. Serve with tortilla chips.

1 Serving: Calories 75 (Calories from Fat 45); Fat 5g (Saturated 2g); Cholesterol 10mg; Sodium 210mg; Carbohydrate 6g (Dietary Fiber 2g); Protein 4g **% Daily Value:** Vitamin A 4%; Vitamin C 14%; Calcium 4%; Iron 4% **Diet Exchanges:** 1 Vegetable, 1 Fat

Gouda and Sun-Dried Tomato Cheese Ball

Prep: 20 min; Chill: 2 hr ✱ *About 3 cups*

1 tub (8 ounces) soft cream cheese
2 cups shredded Gouda or Colby cheese (8 ounces)
1/4 cup chopped fresh chives
1/4 cup sliced oil-packed sun-dried tomatoes, drained
1/4 teaspoon garlic powder
3/4 cup chopped pecans
Assorted crackers, if desired

1. Mix cream cheese and Gouda cheese in medium bowl until blended. Stir in chives, tomatoes and garlic powder.

2. Shape mixture into 1 large or 2 small balls or logs; roll in pecans. Wrap in plastic wrap. Refrigerate until firm, at least 2 hours but no longer than 2 weeks. Serve with crackers.

1 Tablespoon: Calories 50 (Calories from Fat 35); Fat 4g (Saturated 2g); Cholesterol 10mg; Sodium 60mg; Carbohydrate 1g (Dietary Fiber 0g); Protein 2g **% Daily Value:** Vitamin A 2%; Vitamin C 0%; Calcium 4%; Iron 0% **Diet Exchanges:** 1 Fat

Brie with Caramelized Onions, Pistachio and Cranberry

Prep: 15 min; Cook: 15 min; Bake: 10 min
✱ *8 to 10 servings*

Delicious anytime, this makes an especially nice holiday appetizer because of the reds and greens. You can make the onion topping up to 24 hours ahead of time, refrigerate and reheat before spooning over the Brie.

2 tablespoons butter or stick margarine*
1 medium onion, cut into fourths and thinly sliced
1/2 cup dried cranberries
1 tablespoon packed brown sugar
1 tablespoon balsamic vinegar
Vegetable oil
1 round (15 ounces) Brie cheese
1/4 cup coarsely chopped pistachio nuts, slivered
    almonds or walnuts
Crackers, if desired

1. Heat oven to 350°.

2. Melt butter in 10-inch skillet over medium heat. Cook onion in butter 10 minutes, stirring frequently. Stir in cranberries, brown sugar and vinegar. Cook about 5 minutes, stirring frequently, until mixture is thickened and caramelized.

3. Lightly brush ovenproof plate with oil. Place cheese on center of plate. Bake uncovered 8 to 10 minutes or until cheese is soft and partially melted.

4. Spoon onion topping over cheese. Sprinkle with nuts. Serve with crackers.

Spreads with at least 65% vegetable oil can be used

1 Serving: Calories 245 (Calories from Fat 160); Fat 18g (Saturated 10g); Cholesterol 45mg; Sodium 470mg; Carbohydrate 12g (Dietary Fiber 3g); Protein 12g **% Daily Value:** Vitamin A 16%; Vitamin C 8%; Calcium 22%; Iron 4% **Diet Exchanges:** 1 Medium-Fat Meat, 1 Fruit, 1 Fat

Roasted Garlic

Prep: 10 min; Bake: 50 min ✱ *2 to 8 servings*

Garlic bulbs, sometimes called heads of garlic, are made up of as many as fifteen sections called cloves.

1 to 4 bulbs garlic
2 teaspoons olive or vegetable oil for each garlic bulb
Salt and pepper to taste
Sliced French bread, if desired

1. Heat oven to 350°.

2. Carefully peel paperlike skin from around each bulb of garlic, leaving just enough to hold garlic cloves together. Cut 1/4- to 1/2-inch slice from top of each bulb to expose cloves. Place cut side up on 12-inch square of aluminum foil.

3. Drizzle each bulb with 2 teaspoons oil. Sprinkle with salt and pepper. Wrap securely in foil. Place in pie plate or shallow baking pan.

4. Bake 45 to 50 minutes or until garlic is tender when pierced with toothpick or fork. Let stand until cool enough to handle. To serve, gently squeeze soft garlic out of cloves. Spread garlic on bread.

1 Serving: Calories 50 (Calories from Fat 45); Fat 5g (Saturated 1g); Cholesterol 0mg; Sodium 150mg; Carbohydrate 0g (Dietary Fiber 0g); Protein 0g **% Daily Value:** Vitamin A 0%; Vitamin C 0%; Calcium 0%; Iron 0% **Diet Exchanges:** 1 Fat

To prepare garlic for roasting, carefully peel paperlike skin from around each bulb of garlic, leaving just enough to hold garlic cloves together. Cut 1/4- to 1/2-inch slice from top of each bulb to expose cloves. Place cut side up on 12-inch square of aluminum foil.

Buffalo Chicken Wings

Buffalo Chicken Wings

Prep: 20 min; Bake: 32 min ✱ 2 dozen

12 chicken wings (about 2 pounds)
2 tablespoons butter or stick margarine, melted*
1/2 cup all-purpose flour
1/2 teaspoon salt
1/4 teaspoon pepper
1 cup barbecue sauce
1 tablespoon red pepper sauce
1/2 teaspoon Cajun seasoning
1/4 teaspoon ground cumin
1 bottle (8 ounces) blue cheese dressing, if desired
Celery, carrot and zucchini sticks, if desired

1. Heat oven to 425°. Cut each chicken wing at joints to make 3 pieces; discard tip. Cut off excess skin; discard.

2. Melt butter in rectangular pan, 13 × 9 × 2 inches, in oven. Mix flour, salt and pepper in large heavy-duty resealable plastic bag. Add chicken; seal bag tightly. Shake until chicken is completely coated with flour mixture. Place chicken in pan.

3. Bake uncovered 20 minutes. Mix barbecue sauce, pepper sauce, Cajun seasoning and cumin. Turn chicken. Pour sauce mixture over chicken; toss until evenly coated with sauce.

4. Bake uncovered 10 to 12 minutes longer or until light golden brown on outside and juice of chicken is no longer pink when centers of thickest pieces are cut. Serve with dressing and celery sticks.

Spreads with at least 65% vegetable oil can be used (page 45).

1 Appetizer: Calories 70 (Calories from Fat 35); Fat 3g (Saturated 2g); Cholesterol 15mg; Sodium 170mg; Carbohydrate 3g (Dietary Fiber 0g); Protein 5g **% Daily Value:** Vitamin A 2%; Vitamin C 2%; Calcium 0%; Iron 2% **Diet Exchanges:** 1 Medium-Fat Meat

Mahogany Chicken Wings

Prep: 15 min; Chill: 1 hr; Bake: 50 min ✱ *2 1/2 dozen*

15 chicken wings (about 2 1/2 pounds)
1/2 cup soy sauce
1/2 cup honey
1/4 cup molasses
2 tablespoons chili sauce
1 teaspoon ground ginger
2 cloves garlic, finely chopped

1. Cut each chicken wing at joints to make 3 pieces; discard tip. Cut off excess skin; discard. (See illustration, right.) Place chicken in shallow glass or plastic bowl. Mix remaining ingredients; pour over chicken. Cover and refrigerate 1 hour, turning occasionally.

2. Heat oven to 375°. Line broiler pan with aluminum foil.

3. Remove chicken from marinade; reserve marinade. Place chicken in single layer on rack in foil-lined broiler pan; brush with marinade.

4. Bake 30 minutes; turn. Bake about 20 minutes longer, brushing occasionally with marinade, until deep brown and juice of chicken is no longer pink when centers of thickest pieces are cut. Discard any remaining marinade.

1 Appetizer: Calories 70 (Calories from Fat 25); Fat 3g (Saturated 1g); Cholesterol 10mg; Sodium 270mg; Carbohydrate 7g (Dietary Fiber 0g); Protein 4g **% Daily Value:** Vitamin A 0%; Vitamin C 0%; Calcium 0%; Iron 2% **Diet Exchanges:** 1/2 Lean Meat, 1/2 Fruit

Cut each chicken wing at joints to make 3 pieces; discard tip. Cut off excess skin; discard.

WELCOMING AROMA

Create a welcoming aroma in your home when entertaining during the chilly fall and winter seasons. Heat 1 quart water, 1 teaspoon vanilla, 4 cinnamon sticks and 4 whole cloves to boiling. Reduce the heat, and simmer uncovered. Check it often, and be sure to add water as it cooks away.

Baked Coconut Shrimp

Baked Coconut Shrimp   *Low-Fat*

Prep: 30 min; Bake: 8 min ✱ About 40 shrimp

Apricot Sauce (below)
1/4 cup all-purpose flour
2 tablespoons packed brown sugar
1/4 teaspoon salt
Dash of ground red pepper (cayenne)
1 large egg
1 tablespoon lime juice
1 cup shredded coconut
1 pound uncooked peeled deveined medium shrimp,
    thawed if frozen (about 40)
2 tablespoons butter or stick margarine, melted*

1. Make Apricot Sauce.

2. Heat oven to 425°. Spray rack in broiler pan with cooking spray.

3. Mix flour, brown sugar, salt and red pepper in shallow bowl. Beat egg and lime juice in another shallow bowl. Place coconut in third shallow bowl.

4. Coat each shrimp with flour mixture. Dip each side into egg mixture. Coat well with coconut. Place on rack in broiler pan. Drizzle with butter.

5. Bake 7 to 8 minutes or until shrimp are pink and firm and coating is beginning to brown. Serve with sauce.

Apricot Sauce

3/4 cup apricot preserves
1 tablespoon lime juice
1/2 teaspoon ground mustard

Mix all ingredients in 1-quart saucepan. Cook over low heat, stirring occasionally, just until preserves are melted. Refrigerate while making shrimp.

*Spreads with at least 65% vegetable oil can be used (page 45).

1 Shrimp: Calories 40 (Calories from Fat 10); Fat 1g (Saturated 1g); Cholesterol 15mg; Sodium 35mg; Carbohydrate 6g (Dietary Fiber 0g); Protein 2g **% Daily Value:** Vitamin A 0%; Vitamin C 0%; Calcium 0%; Iron 2% **Diet Exchanges:** 1/2 Starch

Cheesy Potato Skins

Prep: 15 min; Bake: 1 hr 15 min; Broil: 11 min ✱ *8 servings*

4 large potatoes (about 2 pounds)
2 tablespoons butter or stick margarine, melted*
1 cup shredded Colby–Monterey Jack cheese (4 ounces)
1/2 cup sour cream
8 medium green onions, sliced (1/2 cup)

1. Heat oven to 375°. Prick potatoes. Bake potatoes 60 to 1 hour 15 minutes or until tender. Let stand until cool enough to handle.

2. Cut potatoes lengthwise into fourths; carefully scoop out pulp, leaving 1/4-inch shells. Save potato pulp for another use.

3. Set oven control to broil. Place potato shells, skin sides down, on rack in broiler pan. Brush with butter.

4. Broil with tops 4 to 5 inches from heat 8 to 10 minutes or until crisp and brown. Sprinkle cheese over potato shells. Broil about 30 seconds or until cheese is melted. Serve hot with sour cream and green onions.

**Spreads with at least 65% vegetable oil can be used (page 45).*

1 Serving: Calories 180 (Calories from Fat 90); Fat 10g (Saturated 7g); Cholesterol 30mg; Sodium 120mg; Carbohydrate 19g (Dietary Fiber 2g); Protein 6g **% Daily Value:** Vitamin A 8%; Vitamin C 8%; Calcium 10%; Iron 6% **Diet Exchanges:** 1 Starch, 2 Fat

Lighter Cheesy Potato Skins: For 5 grams of fat and 135 calories per serving, decrease cheese to 1/2 cup; use fat-free sour cream.

Quesadillas ***Fast***

Prep: 10 min; Bake: 5 min ✱ *18 appetizers*

If all the quesadillas won't fit on your cookie sheet, bake them in batches. You can bake more as needed.

2 cups shredded Colby or Cheddar cheese (8 ounces)
6 flour tortillas (8 to 10 inches in diameter)
1 small tomato, chopped (1/2 cup)
4 medium green onions, chopped (1/4 cup)
2 tablespoons canned chopped green chilies
Chopped fresh cilantro or parsley

1. Heat oven to 350°.

2. Sprinkle 1/3 cup of the cheese evenly over half of each tortilla. Top cheese with remaining ingredients. Fold tortilla over filling. Place on ungreased cookie sheet.

3. Bake about 5 minutes or until hot and cheese is melted. Cut each into 3 or 4 wedges, beginning cuts from center of folded side.

1 Appetizer: Calories 95 (Calories from Fat 45); Fat 5g (Saturated 3g); Cholesterol 15mg; Sodium 150mg; Carbohydrate 9g (Dietary Fiber 1g); Protein 4g **% Daily Value:** Vitamin A 2%; Vitamin C 0%; Calcium 8%; Iron 2% **Diet Exchanges:** 1/2 Starch, 1 Fat

Lighter Quesadillas: For 1 gram of fat and 45 calories per serving, use reduced-fat cheese and tortillas.

Crostini ***Fast***

Prep: 15 min; Bake: 8 min ✱ *12 appetizers*

Crostini is Italian for "little toasts." These crunchy bites can be topped with a variety of savory foods for delicious appetizers. We've used fresh tomatoes, basil and mozzarella, but feel free to experiment with different spreads and toppings.

12 slices Italian bread, 1/2 inch thick
1/4 cup olive or vegetable oil
1 large tomato, chopped (1 cup)
3 tablespoons chopped fresh basil leaves
1 tablespoon large capers or chopped ripe olives
1/2 teaspoon salt
1/2 teaspoon pepper
12 slices (1 ounce each) mozzarella cheese

1. Heat oven to 375°.

2. Place bread slices on ungreased cookie sheets. Drizzle 1 teaspoon oil over each slice bread.

3. Mix tomato, basil, capers, salt and pepper. Spread half of the tomato mixture over bread slices; top each with cheese slice. Spread remaining tomato mixture over cheese.

4. Bake about 8 minutes or until bread is hot and cheese is melted. Serve hot.

1 Appetizer: Calories 175 (Calories from Fat 90); Fat 10g (Saturated 4g); Cholesterol 15mg; Sodium 380mg; Carbohydrate 12g (Dietary Fiber 1g); Protein 10g **% Daily Value:** Vitamin A 5%; Vitamin C 2%; Calcium 22%; Iron 4% **Diet Exchanges:** 1 Starch, 1 High-Fat Meat

Oven Caramel Corn

Popcorn *Fast*

Prep: 5 min; Cook: 5 min ✱ About 12 cups

1/2 cup unpopped popcorn (not microwave popcorn)
1/4 cup vegetable oil
Salt, if desired

1. Pour popcorn and oil into 4-quart Dutch oven. Tilt Dutch oven to spread popcorn evenly. Cover and cook over medium-high heat until 1 kernel pops; remove from heat. Let stand 1 minute, then return to heat.

2. Cook, shaking pan occasionally, until popcorn stops popping. Immediately pour into serving bowl. Sprinkle with salt; toss until evenly coated. Serve warm.

1 Cup: Calories 70 (Calories from Fat 45); Fat 5g (Saturated 1g); Cholesterol 0mg; Sodium 0mg; Carbohydrate 6g (Dietary Fiber 1g); Protein 1g **% Daily Value:** Vitamin A 0%; Vitamin C 0%; Calcium 0%; Iron 0% **Diet Exchanges:** 1/2 Starch, 1/2 Fat

Oven Caramel Corn

Prep: 20 min; Bake: 1 hr; Cool: 30 min ✱ About 15 cups

15 cups popped popcorn
1 cup packed brown sugar
1/2 cup butter or stick margarine*
1/4 cup light corn syrup
1/2 teaspoon salt
1/2 teaspoon baking soda

1. Heat oven to 200°.

2. Place popcorn in very large roasting pan, very large bowl, or divide popcorn between 2 ungreased rectangular pans, 13 × 9 × 2 inches.

3. Heat brown sugar, butter, corn syrup and salt in 2-quart saucepan over medium heat, stirring occasionally, until bubbly around edges. Continue cooking 5 minutes without stirring; remove from heat. Stir in baking soda until foamy.

4. Pour sugar mixture over popcorn; toss until evenly coated. If using bowl, transfer mixture to 2 ungreased rectangular pans, 13 × 9 × 2 inches.

5. Bake 1 hour, stirring every 15 minutes. Spread on aluminum foil or cooking parchment paper. Cool completely, about 30 minutes. Store tightly covered.

Do not use vegetable oil spreads (page 17).

1 Cup: Calories 200 (Calories from Fat 100); Fat 11g (Saturated 5g); Cholesterol 15mg; Sodium 170mg; Carbohydrate 25g (Dietary Fiber 1g); Protein 1g **% Daily Value:** Vitamin A 4%; Vitamin C 0%; Calcium 2%; Iron 2% **Diet Exchanges:** 1 Starch, 1 Fruit, 1 Fat.

NUTTY OVEN CARAMEL CORN: Decrease popcorn to 12 cups. Add 3 cups walnut halves, pecan halves or unblanched whole almonds

Original Chex® Party Mix

Prep: 20 min; Bake: 1 hr ✱ About 12 cups

6 tablespoons butter or stick margarine*
2 tablespoons Worcestershire sauce
1 1/2 teaspoons seasoned salt
3/4 teaspoon garlic powder
1/2 teaspoon onion powder
3 cups Corn Chex® cereal
3 cups Rice Chex cereal
3 cups Wheat Chex cereal
1 cup mixed nuts
1 cup pretzels
1 cup garlic-flavor bite-size bagel chips or regular-size bagel chips, broken into 1-inch pieces

1. Heat oven to 250°.

2. Melt butter in large roasting pan in oven. Stir in Worcestershire sauce, seasoned salt, garlic powder and onion powder. Gradually stir in remaining ingredients until evenly coated.

3. Bake 1 hour, stirring every 15 minutes. Spread on paper towels to cool. Store in airtight container.

Do not use vegetable oil spreads (page 17).

1/2 Cup: Calories 140 (Calories from Fat 65); Fat 7g (Saturated 1g); Cholesterol 0mg; Sodium 340mg; Carbohydrate 18g (Dietary Fiber 2g); Protein 3g **% Daily Value:** Vitamin A 4%; Vitamin C 2%; Calcium 0%; Iron 26% **Diet Exchanges:** 1 Starch, 1 Fat

Lighter Chex Party Mix: For 2 grams of fat and 90 calories per serving, decrease butter to 3 tablespoons. Omit mixed nuts; use fat-free bagel chips.

Baked Tortilla Chips

Fast & Low-Fat

Prep: 10 min; Bake: 8 min ✱ 4 dozen

4 corn or flour tortillas (8 inches in diameter)
2 tablespoons butter or stick margarine, melted*
Chili powder, if desired

1. Heat oven to 375°.

2. Brush tortillas lightly with butter. Sprinkle with chili powder. Cut each tortilla into 12 wedges or pieces with kitchen scissors. Place in single layer in 2 ungreased jelly roll pans, 15 1/2 × 10 1/2 × 1 inch, or on 2 cookie sheets.

3. Bake uncovered 6 to 8 minutes or until light brown and crisp. Cool slightly (chips will continue to crisp as they cool). Serve warm or cool. Store in tightly covered container up to 3 weeks at room temperature.

Do not use vegetable oil spreads (page 17).

1 Chip: Calories 15 (Calories from Fat 10); Fat 1g (Saturated 0g); Cholesterol 2mg; Sodium 5mg; Carbohydrate 1g (Dietary Fiber 0g); Protein 0g **% Daily Value:** Vitamin A 0%; Vitamin C 0%; Calcium 0%; Iron 0% **Diet Exchanges:** 1 Serving is free

BAKED PITA CHIPS: Split 6 pita breads (6 inches in diameter) around edge with knife to make 12 rounds. Brush with melted butter. Sprinkle with dried basil leaves and grated Parmesan cheese if desired. Cut each round into 8 wedges. Bake as directed.

Nachos *Fast*

*Prep: 5 min; Bake: 4 min * 4 servings*

28 tortilla chips
1 cup shredded Monterey Jack or Cheddar cheese
    (4 ounces)
1/4 cup canned chopped mild green chilies, if desired
1/4 cup salsa

1. Heat oven to 400°. Line cookie sheet with aluminum foil.

2. Place tortilla chips on cookie sheet. Sprinkle with cheese and chilies.

3. Bake about 4 minutes or until cheese is melted. Top with salsa. Serve hot.

1 Serving: Calories 165 (Calories from Fat 100); Fat 11g (Saturated 6g); Cholesterol 25mg; Sodium 320mg; Carbohydrate 9g (Dietary Fiber 1g); Protein 8g **% Daily Value:** Vitamin A 10%; Vitamin C 4%; Calcium 20%; Iron 4% **Diet Exchanges:** 1/2 Starch, 1 High-Fat Meat, 1/2 Fat

Cinnamon-Sugared Nuts

*Prep: 10 min; Bake: 30 min * 2 cups*

1 tablespoon slightly beaten large egg white
2 cups pecan halves, unblanched whole almonds or
    walnut halves
1/4 cup sugar
2 teaspoons ground cinnamon
1/4 teaspoon ground nutmeg
1/4 teaspoon ground cloves

1. Heat oven to 300°.

2. Mix egg white and pecan halves in medium bowl until pecans are coated and sticky.

3. Mix remaining ingredients; sprinkle over pecans. Stir until pecans are completely coated. Spread pecans in single layer in ungreased jelly roll pan, 15 1/2 × 10 1/2 × 1 inch.

4. Bake uncovered about 30 minutes or until toasted. Cool completely, or serve slightly warm. Store in airtight container at room temperature up to 3 weeks.

1/4 Cup: Calories 210 (Calories from Fat 160); Fat 18g (Saturated 1g); Cholesterol 2mg; Sodium 5mg; Carbohydrate 12g (Dietary Fiber 2g); Protein 2g **% Daily Value:** Vitamin A 0%; Vitamin C 0%; Calcium 2%; Iron 4% **Diet Exchanges:** 1 Starch, 3 Fat

Savory Pecans *Fast*

*Prep: 5 min; Bake: 10 min * 2 cups*

2 cups pecan halves, walnut halves or peanuts
2 medium green onions, chopped (2 tablespoons)
2 tablespoons butter or stick margarine, melted*
1 tablespoon soy sauce
1/4 teaspoon ground red pepper (cayenne)

1. Heat oven to 300°.

2. Mix all ingredients. Spread pecans in single layer in ungreased jelly roll pan, 15 1/2 × 10 1/2 × 1 inch.

3. Bake uncovered about 10 minutes or until pecans are toasted. Serve warm, or cool completely. Store in airtight container at room temperature up to 3 weeks

Do not use vegetable oil spreads (page 17).

1/4 Cup: Calories 210 (Calories from Fat 190); Fat 21g (Saturated 3g); Cholesterol 10mg; Sodium 135mg; Carbohydrate 5g (Dietary Fiber 2g); Protein 2g **% Daily Value:** Vitamin A 2%; Vitamin C 0%; Calcium 0%; Iron 4% **Diet Exchanges:** 1/2 Starch, 4 Fat

---

MICROWAVING NACHOS

Nachos can be microwaved in serving-size amounts: Arrange 7 tortilla chips in a circle on a microwavable paper plate. Sprinkle 1/4 cup of the cheese over chips. Sprinkle with 1 tablespoon green chilies. Microwave uncovered on High 20 to 30 seconds or until cheese is melted. Top with 1 tablespoon salsa.

Beverage Basics

Aah. What can beat a glass of cool lemonade on a sultry summer day or a cup of steaming coffee on a frosty morning? Beverages do more than quench our thirst, they also add sparkle to a party, warmth to a cozy get-together, color and flavor to any meal.

We have the recipes if you want to stir up a beverage from scratch, but you'll also find an incredible selection of ready-to-drink beverages at your supermarket—from punches and fruit juices to soda pop, bottled sparkling water, and nonalcoholic beer and wine, plus flavored coffees and teas.

Coffee

The perfect cup of coffee—for a coffee drinker, it's a never-ending quest. What makes a perfect cup? Four things: the type of coffee beans, the style of roast, the equipment used, and most important, your own taste preferences. Let's start with the beans:

- Coffee beans are actually the seeds of a cherry-red fruit produced by the coffee plant, which grows in the tropics. These seeds are picked green, and it is not until they are cleaned, dried, roasted and sometimes blended with other beans, that they become the product we are most familiar with.

- The commercial varieties of beans belong to two main species: arabica and robusta. The **arabica** coffee plant produces the most desirable beans because it grows at higher elevations and its beans have a rich flavor and aroma. **Robusta** beans thrive at lower altitudes and have a less complex flavor. Most coffee in the supermarket is made from robusta beans, which are often blended with a small amount of arabica beans to give a fuller body blend.

- Each coffee-growing region of the world produces beans with its own distinctive characteristics: Colombian coffee is rich, Kenyan coffee has a slightly sweet-tart flavor, and Sumatran coffee is full-bodied with little acidity. Ask around at your local coffee shop or grocery store to see what type of bean or blend of beans you may be interested in trying.

Roasting brings out the flavor in the bean and determines the richness, mellowness and smoothness of the coffee. The longer the bean is roasted, the darker and stronger-flavored the coffee. Beans may be roasted with or without added flavorings such as vanilla or hazelnut. Most gourmet coffee companies have their own specialty roasts. Sample them all until you find your favorite!

The main commercial roasts you'll find are:

- **American Roast:** Chestnut brown in color with a caramel-like flavor. There will be no traces of a dark roast flavor.

- **Cinnamon Roast:** Light cinnamon in color with a strong nutlike flavor. This roast is the highest in acidity.

- **French Roast:** Very dark brown in color with a large amount of oil on the bean surface and a bitter taste dominated by pungent aromatic flavors. This roast may also be called New Orleans Roast.

- **Full City Roast:** Dark brown in color with no traces of oil on the bean surface. Flavor is fully developed and can range from caramel to chocolate-like with some hints of a dark roast flavor. This roasting method results in the coffee losing some acidity.

- **Italian Roast:** Black in color with large amounts of oil on the bean surface and a strong burnt flavor that is bitter and pungent.

- **Vienna Roast:** Dark brown in color with a small amount of oil on the bean surface and a noticeable dark roast flavor.

And finally, depending on what type of equipment you use to brew coffee, there is a specific type of grind to use for a great cup of coffee. Most coffee in the supermarket is labeled "for all coffeemakers."

- **Automatic drip coffeemaker:** Medium grind.

- **Espresso maker:** Fine grind.

- **Percolator:** Coarse grind.

- **Plunger or French press coffeemaker:** Coarse grind.

As far as personal taste, that is up to you. Do you like a deep, rich, full flavor or something lighter? The best way to figure out what you like is by asking around at your favorite coffee shop or sampling the daily varieties of brews.

Storing Coffee

Air and moisture are coffee's worst enemies since they dry up the precious oils that give coffee its wonderful flavor. To preserve flavor, store whole beans and ground coffee in an airtight container in the cupboard. It will keep at room temperature for about a month. Or place the airtight container in the freezer for up to three months. Some manufacturers of vacuum-packed ground coffee suggest storing it tightly covered in the refrigerator after opening the can. Opinions vary on the best way to store coffee, so be sure to check the labels on brands of coffee, too.

Decaffeinated Coffee

Some people want to avoid caffeine, a stimulant that is present in regular coffee. Any bean can be decaffeinated; however, it loses some aroma and flavor in the decaffeinating process.

Caffeine is removed by either the water process or solvent (chemical) process. The solvent process is faster, less expensive and disturbs fewer of the flavor components. But if you're concerned about solvent residues, you may want to choose water-processed decaf.

Instant Coffee

Quickly dissolved in either hot or cold water, instant coffee powders are made by brewing pure ground coffee and evaporating the water. Freeze-dried coffee crystals are made from brewed coffee frozen into a slush before the water has evaporated. Because of this process, freeze-dried coffee is slightly more expensive than other instant coffees. For the best cup of instant coffee, pour boiling water over the coffee in the cup, rather than stirring the coffee into the water.

How to Make Coffee

Remember that perfect cup of coffee? Here's how to make it:

- Start with a clean pot. Wash the pot and filter basket after each use with hot, soapy water—but not abrasive scouring pads—to get rid of any bitter oils that may cling to the inside. Rinse well with hot water. Check manufacturer's directions for periodic cleaning of the entire coffeemaker.

- Choose the correct grind for your coffeemaker. Check the manufacturer's recommendations if you're not sure.

- Use freshly ground beans and fresh cold water. For the best flavor, grind coffee beans just before using. The "magic formula" preferred by many coffee lovers is 2 level tablespoons of ground coffee per 3/4 cup (or 6 ounces) of water—this makes a stronger cup of coffee (see below for other formulas).

- Serve hot coffee as soon as it's done brewing. Just as air is the beans worst enemy, heat destroys the flavor of coffee if left on the burner too long. If you aren't going to drink it right away, remove the grounds and keep the heat very low, or pour the coffee into an insulated container.

- Never reheat coffee, it becomes very bitter. However, leftover coffee can be covered and refrigerated until cold and used for iced coffee.

COFFEE BREWING STRENGTH (PER SERVING)*

Strength of Brew	Ground Coffee (level tablespoon)	Water
Regular	1	3/4 cup (6 ounces)
Strong	2	3/4 cup (6 ounces)

*Best general recommendation

Specialty Coffees

Although specialty coffee drinks may seem like a new phenomenon, European, Middle Eastern and African cultures have been savoring them for centuries. Once available only in coffeehouses and cafes, inexpensive, scaled-down equipment now lets you make these coffee drinks at home, too. Dress any of them up with sprinkles of cinnamon, nutmeg, cardamom or cocoa—or even a dash of your favorite liqueur.

- **Café au lait:** Equal parts of hot coffee and hot milk, originally popular in France as a breakfast beverage.

- **Café latte:** One-third espresso plus two-thirds hot steamed milk, usually without a foamy cap.

- **Café mocha:** One-third espresso plus chocolate syrup (usually 1 to 2 tablespoons per serving) and two-thirds steamed milk. It's usually topped with whipped cream and a sprinkle of sweetened cocoa.

- **Cappuccino:** Espresso plus hot steamed milk topped with a cap of foamed milk. In the U.S., it's often sprinkled with cinnamon and served with a biscotti cookie for dipping. In Italy, cappuccino is a breakfast beverage; Americans drink it any time of day.

- **Espresso:** Made using a special coffeemaker with a pressurized brewing chamber that uses steaming-hot water for brewing and a steam valve for steaming and foaming or frothing milk.

- **Flavored instant coffee mixes:** Available in a delightful variety of flavors, from chocolate mint to raspberry cream. Mix according to package directions.

- **Iced coffee:** Starts with very strong brewed coffee. It's chilled in the refrigerator, then served over ice.

- **Iced coffee frappé:** Made in a blender with cold coffee, ice, sugar, and cream or milk. This coffee slush is served with a drizzle of chocolate syrup.

- **Irish coffee:** A blend of strong coffee, a tablespoon or two of Irish or other whiskey and a small amount of sugar. It's usually topped with whipped cream. It's often served after dinner, with or in place of dessert.

- **Turkish coffee:** A combination of equal parts of sugar and coffee and 1/2 cup water. It's boiled twice, then served in espresso cups without removing the grounds.

Tea

When you cozy up with a cup of tea, you're joining people around the world in enjoying a beverage that's steeped in tradition, from the afternoon high tea of the English to the tea ceremony of the Japanese. Next to water, tea is the most commonly consumed beverage in the world.

Tea, an evergreen shrub related to the magnolia, was first cultivated in China several thousand years ago and was originally considered a medicine.

There are three main types of tea:

- **Black tea:** Made from dried and fermented leaves. It contains the most caffeine, about 50 to 65 percent of the amount in coffee. Some familiar varieties are Darjeeling, Assam and Ceylon orange pekoe.

- **Green tea:** Unfermented and pale green in color with a light, fresh flavor. Gunpowder, so named because it's rolled in little balls that "explode" when they come in contact with water, and Lung Ching are two popular green teas.

- **Oolong tea:** Partially fermented and a cross between green and black teas. You'll also recognize it as "Chinese restaurant tea." Imperial oolong is prized for its honey flavor, while Formosa oolong tastes a little like peaches.

Black, green and oolong teas are just the processing methods—there are literally thousands of varieties of teas, including:

- **Blended tea:** A combination of teas. Some of the best known are English breakfast, Earl Grey, Russian-style and spiced blends.

- **Chai:** A newcomer to the American tea scene, but it has long been a staple in India. It's made from black tea brewed with water, milk, sugar and spices, such as cinnamon, cardamom, cloves and black peppercorns. Chai is served in some coffeehouses and can also be made at home or bought packaged, often as a concentrate.

- **Decaffeinated tea:** Fits well with today's emphasis on healthful living because almost all the caffeine is removed during processing. Brew and enjoy decaffeinated tea just as you would regular tea.

- **Herb tea:** Really not a tea at all because it doesn't contain tea leaves. Also called a *tisane*, herb tea is made by steeping blends of dried herbs, flowers and spices in boiling water. Some of the most popular herbal teas are chamomile, peppermint, lemon balm and rose hip.

- **Instant tea:** Quickly dissolves in either hot or cold water and is made by brewing tea and evaporating the water. Buy it unsweetened or sweetened with sugar or sweetener. Or try flavors such as lemon, peach and raspberry. Make instant tea according to the directions on the container.

- **Specialty tea:** Flavored with spices or flowers, such as jasmine, chrysanthemum blossoms and orange or lemon peel.

Tea Equipment

Making tea is very simple, and so is the equipment you'll need:

- **Infuser:** An infuser holds loose tea leaves. They come in all shapes and sizes.

- **Tea strainer:** A strainer comes in handy when you brew with loose tea leaves and you don't have an infuser. Hold it over the cup as you pour to catch the leaves.

- **Teapot:** Choose one made of glass, china or earthenware. Look for an opening wide enough to transfer tea bags or leaves into, a stay-cool handle, and a lid that stays on while pouring.

How to Make Tea

Brewing tea is as easy as 1, 2, 3! Choose your tea, then:

1. Start with a spotlessly clean teapot. Warm or "hot the pot" by filling it with hot water. Empty it before adding the tea.

2. Bring fresh, cold water to a full boil in a teakettle.

3. Add tea to the warm pot, about 1 teaspoon of loose tea or 1 tea bag for each 3/4 cup of water. Pour the boiling water* over the tea. Let it steep for 3 to 5 minutes to bring out the full flavor (tea is not ready once the color has changed). Stir the tea once to ensure an even brew. Remove the tea bags or infuser, or strain the tea as you pour. If you prefer weaker tea, add hot water after brewing the tea. Serve with milk or cream, lemon and sugar, and enjoy!

Some experts suggest that green tea is the exception; make it with very hot water—about 170° to 190°—not boiling water.

Iced Tea

Iced tea is an America tradition. We drink it to cool down on a hot summer day, sip it with meals year-round and refresh ourselves with it after exercise. To make clear, crisp iced tea:

- Brew a pot of tea, using double the amount of tea.

- Remove the tea bags or strain the tea while pouring it into ice-filled glasses or a pitcher. Put a metal knife or spoon into the glasses or pitcher to keep the glass from cracking from the heat of the tea.

- If you're making tea in advance, let it cool to room temperature before putting it in the refrigerator so it won't become cloudy.

- Keep iced tea in the refrigerator for only 8 hours, then throw it out. Because bacteria can multiply during brewing, we don't recommend sun tea.

Punches

There's something welcoming about a big bowl of punch—guests gather round it, chat and get acquainted. Punch is a snap to pour together, and there are almost as many kinds of punch as there are kinds of parties. Following are a few tips for festive punches:

- Chill all ingredients for cold punches before mixing. You can mix fruit juices and spices ahead and refrigerate, but add soda pop, sparkling water and alcohol just before serving.

- Instead of using ice cubes, try an ice ring. Check to be sure the ring mold will fit your punch bowl, then fill it with the same juices as in the punch and freeze. Perk it up with pieces of fresh fruit—strawberries, cherries, kiwifruit, grapes and star fruit.

For hot punches, start with a heat-resistant punch bowl, then warm it by rinsing with hot water before pouring in the punch. Or serve hot punches in an attractive saucepan right from the stove or in a fondue pot, chafing dish or slow cooker.

Hot Spiced Cider

Chai Tea *Fast & Low-Fat*

Prep: 6 min: Cook: 4 min ✱ *4 servings*

If you have a sweet tooth, stir in a little more honey to suit your taste.

2 cups water
4 bags black tea
2 cups milk
2 tablespoons honey
1/2 teaspoon ground ginger
1/2 teaspoon ground nutmeg
1/4 teaspoon ground cinnamon

1. Heat water to boiling in 2-quart saucepan. Add tea bags; reduce heat. Simmer uncovered 2 minutes. Remove tea bags.

2. Stir remaining ingredients into tea. Heat to boiling. Stir with wire whisk to foam milk.

1 Serving (about 1 cup): Calories 95 (Calories from Fat 20); Fat 2g (Saturated 2g); Cholesterol 10mg; Sodium 65mg; Carbohydrate 15g (Dietary Fiber 0g); Protein 4g **% Daily Value:** Vitamin A 6%; Vitamin C 0%; Calcium 14%; Iron 0% **Diet Exchanges:** 1 Skim Milk

Hot Spiced Cider *Fast & Low-Fat*

Prep: 5 min: Cook: 20 min ✱ *6 servings*

6 cups apple cider
1/2 teaspoon whole cloves
1/4 teaspoon ground nutmeg
3 sticks cinnamon

1. Heat all ingredients to boiling in 3-quart saucepan over medium-high heat; reduce heat. Simmer uncovered 10 minutes.

2. Strain cider mixture to remove cloves and cinnamon if desired. Serve hot.

1 Serving (about 1 cup): Calories 115 (Calories from Fat 0); Fat 0g (Saturated 0g); Cholesterol 0mg; Sodium 10mg; Carbohydrate 29g (Dietary Fiber 0g); Protein 0g **% Daily Value:** Vitamin A 0%; Vitamin C 2%; Calcium 2%; Iron 4% **Diet Exchanges:** 2 Fruit

HOT BUTTERED RUM SPICED CIDER: Make as directed. For each serving, place 1 tablespoon butter (do not use margarine or vegetable oil spreads), 1 tablespoon packed brown sugar and 2 tablespoons rum in mug. Fill with hot cider.

Strawberry and Orange Smoothies

Hot Chocolate *Fast*

Prep: 5 min; Cook: 15 min ✱ 6 servings

3 ounces unsweetened baking chocolate
1 1/2 cups water
1/3 cup sugar
Dash of salt
4 1/2 cups milk

1. Heat chocolate and water in 1 1/2-quart saucepan over medium heat, stirring constantly, until chocolate is melted and mixture is smooth.

2. Stir in sugar and salt. Heat to boiling; reduce heat. Simmer uncovered 4 minutes, stirring constantly. Stir in milk. Heat just until hot (do not boil because skin will form on top).

3. Beat with hand beater until foamy, or stir until smooth. Serve immediately.

1 Serving (about 1 cup): Calories 220 (Calories from Fat 100); Fat 11g (Saturated 7g); Cholesterol 15mg; Sodium 150mg; Carbohydrate 24g (Dietary Fiber 2g); Protein 8g **% Daily Value:** Vitamin A 10%; Vitamin C 0%; Calcium 22%; Iron 6% **Diet Exchanges:** 1 Fruit, 1 Skim Milk, 1 1/2 Fat

Lighter Hot Chocolate: For 1 gram of fat and 120 calories per serving, substitute 1/3 cup baking cocoa for the chocolate; use fat-free (skim) milk. Mix cocoa, sugar and salt in saucepan; stir in water. Continue as directed in step 2.

Strawberry Smoothie

Fast & Low-Fat

Prep: 5 min ✱ 4 servings

Keep the green leaves on the strawberries that will be used to garnish the Strawberry Smoothie.

1 pint (2 cups) strawberries
1 cup milk
2 containers (6 ounces each) strawberry yogurt
    (1 1/3 cups)

1. Reserve 4 strawberries for garnish. Cut out the hull or "cap," from remaining strawberries.

2. Place remaining strawberries, the milk and yogurt in blender. Cover and blend on high speed about 30 seconds or until smooth.

3. Pour mixture into 4 glasses. Garnish each with reserved strawberry.

1 Serving (about 1 cup): Calories 130 (Calories from Fat 20); Fat 2g (Saturated 1g); Cholesterol 10mg; Sodium 80mg; Carbohydrate 24g (Dietary Fiber 2g); Protein 6g **% Daily Value:** Vitamin A 4%; Vitamin C 70%; Calcium 20%; Iron 2% **Diet Exchanges:** 1 Fruit, 1 Skim Milk

STRAWBERRY-BANANA SMOOTHIE: Substitute 1 medium banana, cut into chunks, for 1 cup of the strawberries.

Orange Smoothie *Fast & Low-Fat*

Prep: 5 min ✳ *4 servings*

1 quart (4 cups) vanilla frozen yogurt or ice cream, slightly softened
1/2 cup frozen (thawed) orange juice concentrate
1/4 cup milk
Orange slices, if desired

1. Place yogurt, orange juice concentrate and milk in blender. Cover and blend on medium speed about 45 seconds, stopping blender occasionally to scrape sides, until thick and smooth.

2. Pour mixture into glasses. Garnish with orange slices.

1 Serving (about 1 cup): Calories 260 (Calories from Fat 20); Fat 2g (Saturated 2g); Cholesterol 10mg; Sodium 120mg; Carbohydrate 51g (Dietary Fiber 0g); Protein 10g **% Daily Value:** Vitamin A 4%; Vitamin C 84%; Calcium 32%; Iron 0% **Diet Exchanges:** 2 1/2 Fruit, 1 Skim Milk

Chocolate Milk Shakes *Fast*

Prep: 10 min ✳ *2 servings*

Turn these shakes into malts by adding about 1 tablespoon natural-flavor or flavored malted milk powder before blending.

3/4 cup milk
1/4 cup chocolate-flavored syrup
3 scoops (1/2 cup each) vanilla ice cream

1. Place milk and syrup in blender. Cover and blend on high speed 2 seconds.

2. Add ice cream. Cover and blend on low speed about 5 seconds or until smooth. Pour into glasses. Serve immediately.

1 Serving (about 1 cup): Calories 340 (Calories from Fat 115); Fat 13g (Saturated 8g); Cholesterol 50mg; Sodium 160mg; Carbohydrate 50g (Dietary Fiber 1g); Protein 7g **% Daily Value:** Vitamin A 14%; Vitamin C 2%; Calcium 24%; Iron 4% **Diet Exchanges:** 2 Starch, 1 Fruit, 3 Fat

> **Lighter Chocolate Milk Shakes:** For 1 gram of fat and 275 calories per serving, use fat-free (skim) milk; substitute fat-free frozen yogurt for the ice cream.

BERRY MILK SHAKES: Substitute strawberry or cherry topping or frozen strawberries or raspberries in syrup, thawed and undrained, for the chocolate-flavored syrup.

CHILLING BOTTLED AND CANNED DRINKS

If you just purchased bottled or canned drinks and want to serve them right away, here's how to chill them quickly. Completely submerge them in a bucket or large pot filled with half ice and half water for about 20 minutes. This also works well for carbonated beverages that will be added at the last minute to a punch or used to mix with other ingredients.

Eggnog

Prep: 35 min; Chill: 2 hr ✱ *10 servings*

A cooked egg custard rather than uncooked eggs is used to make this eggnog to avoid any food-safety problems associated with uncooked eggs. Leftover 'nog? Try blending equal parts fresh fruits and eggnog for a creamy brunchtime smoothie. Or, substitute eggnog for the milk in your favorite quick bread or cake recipe. Delicious! Leftover eggnog will keep, covered, for two days.

Soft Custard (below)
1 cup whipping (heavy) cream
2 tablespoons powdered sugar
1/2 teaspoon vanilla
1/2 cup light rum*
1 or 2 drops yellow food color, if desired
Ground nutmeg

1. Make Soft Custard.

2. Just before serving, beat whipping cream, powdered sugar and vanilla in chilled medium bowl with electric mixer on high speed until stiff. Gently stir 1 cup of the whipped cream, the rum and food color into custard.

3. Pour custard mixture into small punch bowl. Drop remaining whipped cream in mounds onto custard mixture. Sprinkle with nutmeg. Serve immediately. Store covered in refrigerator for up to 2 days.

Soft Custard

3 large eggs, slightly beaten
1/3 cup sugar
Dash of salt
2 1/2 cups milk
1 teaspoon vanilla

Mix eggs, sugar and salt in heavy 2-quart saucepan. Gradually stir in milk. Cook over medium heat 10 to 15 minutes, stirring constantly, until mixture just coats a metal spoon; remove from heat. Stir in vanilla. Place saucepan in cold water until custard is cool. (If custard curdles, beat vigorously with hand beater until smooth.) Cover and refrigerate at least 2 hours but no longer than 24 hours.

*2 tablespoons rum extract and 1/3 cup milk can be substituted for the rum.

1 Serving (about 1/2 cup): Calories 155 (Calories from Fat 90); Fat 10g (Saturated 6g); Cholesterol 95mg; Sodium 55mg; Carbohydrate 12g (Dietary Fiber 0g); Protein 4g **% Daily Value:** Vitamin A 10%; Vitamin C 0%; Calcium 10%; Iron 0% **Diet Exchanges:** 1 Skim Milk, 1 1/2 Fat

Lighter Eggnog: For 4 grams of fat and 100 calories per serving, substitute 2 eggs plus 2 egg whites for the 3 eggs and 2 1/4 cups fat-free (skim) milk for the milk in the Soft Custard. Substitute 2 cups frozen (thawed) reduced-fat whipped topping for the beaten whipping cream, powdered sugar and vanilla.

Lemonade *Fast & Low-Fat*

Prep: 10 min ✱ 6 servings

3 cups water
1 cup lemon juice (about 4 lemons)
1/2 cup sugar
Lemon or orange slices, if desired
Fresh mint leaves, if desired

1. Mix water, lemon juice and sugar until sugar is dissolved.

2. Serve over ice. Garnish with lemon slices and mint.

1 Serving: Calories 75 (Calories from Fat 0); Fat 0g (Saturated 0g); Cholesterol 0mg; Sodium 10mg; Carbohydrate 19g (Dietary Fiber 0g); Protein 0g **% Daily Value:** Vitamin A 0%; Vitamin C 16%; Calcium 0%; Iron 0% **Diet Exchanges:** 1 Fruit

LIMEADE: Substitute lime juice (about 10 limes) for the lemon juice and increase sugar to 3/4 cup. Garnish with lime slices and strawberries if desired.

Tangy Citrus Punch

Fast & Low-Fat

Prep: 10 min ✱ 24 servings

Make this punch ahead of time by combining the juice concentrates and water in a half-gallon pitcher or large mixing bowl and refrigerating. Just before serving, pour into a punch bowl and add the soda pop.

1 can (12 ounces) frozen pineapple-orange juice concentrate, thawed
1 can (12 ounces) frozen limeade concentrate, thawed
1 can (12 ounces) frozen lemonade concentrate, thawed
3 cups cold water
1 liter (4 1/4 cups) lemon-lime soda pop, chilled
Lime, lemon and orange slices, if desired

1. Mix juice concentrates and water in punch bowl.

2. Just before serving, stir in soda pop. Float fruit slices in punch.

1 Serving (about 1/2 cup): Calories 125 (Calories from Fat 0); Fat 0g (Saturated 0g); Cholesterol 0mg; Sodium 5mg; Carbohydrate 31g (Dietary Fiber 0g); Protein 0g **% Daily Value:** Vitamin A 0%; Vitamin C 24%; Calcium 0%; Iron 2% **Diet Exchanges:** 2 Fruit

MAKING AN ICE RING

Here's an easy way to make an ice ring for chilling a bowl of punch, using a ring mold or bundt cake pan. Make sure the mold you choose is smaller than your punch bowl. Arrange 1/4-inch slices of lemons, limes and oranges or other sliced fruit or berries in ring mold. Slowly add just enough water or fruit juice to partially cover fruit (too much water will make the fruit float); freeze. When frozen, add enough water or juice to fill mold three-fourths full; freeze overnight to make sure ice ring is solid. When you're ready to serve the punch, run hot water over bottom of the mold to loosen the ice ring. Remove the ice ring from the mold, and float it, fruit side up, in the punch. Or use the same method to make floating ice disks from muffin cups, which take less time to freeze.

Sangria *Fast & Low-Fat*

Prep: 10 min ✳ *8 servings*

2/3 cup lemon juice
1/3 cup orange juice
1/4 cup sugar
1 bottle (750 milliliters) dry red wine or nonalcoholic
    red wine
Lemon and orange slices, if desired

1. Strain juices into half-gallon glass pitcher. Stir sugar into juices until sugar is dissolved.

2. Stir wine into juice mixture. Add ice if desired. Garnish with lemon and orange slices.

1 Serving (about 1/2 cup): Calories 95 (Calories from Fat 0); Fat 0g (Saturated 0g); Cholesterol 0mg; Sodium 10mg; Carbohydrate 10g (Dietary Fiber 0g); Protein 0g **% Daily Value:** Vitamin A 0%; Vitamin C 14%; Calcium 0%; Iron 2% **Diet Exchanges:** 1 Fruit, 1 Fat

Sparkling Raspberry Tea

Fast & Low-Fat

Prep: 5 min ✳ *6 servings*

2 cups brewed tea (page 38), chilled
2 cups raspberry or cranberry-raspberry juice, chilled
2 cups sparkling water, chilled
Raspberries, lime slices or lemon slices, if desired
Fresh mint leaves, if desired

1. Mix tea, juice and water. Serve over ice.

2. Garnish with raspberries and mint.

1 Cup: Calories 40 (Calories from Fat 0); Fat 0g (Saturated 0g); Cholesterol 0mg; Sodium 20mg; Carbohydrate 10g (Dietary Fiber 0g); Protein 0g **% Daily Value:** Vitamin A 0%; Vitamin C 6%; Calcium 0%; Iron 2% **Diet Exchanges:** 1/2 Fruit

Quick Cranberry Punch

Fast & Low-Fat

Prep: 10 min ✳ *12 servings*

For festive ice cubes, cut lemon, lime or orange peel into star shapes, and freeze with cranberries in cranberry juice or water in ice-cube trays.

1 can (6 ounces) frozen pink lemonade concentrate,
    thawed
4 cups cranberry juice cocktail, chilled
2 cans (12 ounces each) ginger ale, chilled

1. Make lemonade in large pitcher as directed on can.

2. Stir in cranberry juice cocktail and enough ice to chill. Just before serving, stir in ginger ale.

3/4 Cup: Calories 110 (Calories from Fat 0); Fat 0g (Saturated 0g); Cholesterol 0mg; Sodium 10mg; Carbohydrate 27g (Dietary Fiber 0g); Protein 0g **% Daily Value:** Vitamin A 0%; Vitamin C 54%; Calcium 0%; Iron 2% **Diet Exchanges:** 2 Fruit

Breads

Low-Fat = *3g or less, except main dishes with 6g or less*   **Fast** = *Ready in 30 minutes or less*   ■ = *Bread Machine directions*   ● = *Slow Cooker directions*

Caramel Sticky Rolls (page 82)

Lighter = 1/3 fewer calories or 50% less fat

Quick Bread Basics

Quick breads are just that—quick and easy to make. Because they don't rely on yeast to rise, they really live up to their name! It takes just minutes to stir up a batch of pancakes or waffles, muffins, nut bread, biscuits or scones.

What makes quick breads so quick? It's the baking soda and double-acting baking powder that gets them going. When leavening meets liquid in a batter or dough, carbon dioxide (a harmless gas) is given off, forming tiny bubbles that create a framework for the bread. This reaction happens not once but twice: once during mixing and again during baking. To make sure your baking soda and baking powder are fresh, check the container for an expiration date. Buy only a small container so you'll use it up quickly.

Pans and Pan Preparation

To make golden and tender crusts, use shiny pans and cookie sheets.

Dark pans or pans with dark nonstick coating absorb heat easier than shiny pans; watch breads so they don't get too brown. Follow the manufacturer's instructions for both baking and greasing. Many pan makers suggest reducing the oven temperature by 25°, and some recommend not greasing or using any cooking spray.

If you're using insulated pans, you may need to increase the baking time slightly.

When making muffins and quick bread loaves, usually only the bottoms of the pans are greased so that the batter doesn't form a lip (overhanging or hard, dry edges) around the edge during baking.

Mixing Quick Breads

Mix according to each recipe's instruction; some batters are mixed until smooth, others until the ingredients are just moistened. But one thing's the same: If you mix quick breads too much, they become tough.

For butter or margarine, we recommend using the stick form. You also can use the stick form of vegetable oil spreads that have *at least* 65 percent fat, although the batter consistency may be slightly softer.

For quick breads, we don't recommend using vegetable oil spreads with less than 65 percent fat, reduced-fat butter or any tub or whipped product, whether it's spread, butter or margarine. Because they contain more water and less fat, you'll end up with a bread that's tough and wet or gummy.

Baking Quick Breads

Bake quick breads on the oven rack placed in the center of the oven, unless noted otherwise in the recipe, for best heat circulation.

Ovens vary, so check for doneness at the minimum baking time; if the bread isn't done, bake for another 1 to 2 minutes before checking again.

Remove quick breads from the pan to a wire rack for cooling shortly after they finish baking; this gives them a dry, crisp surface. If left in the pan, the surface will end up steamed and soft.

To reheat quick breads in the microwave, see Microwave Cooking and Heating Chart, page 544.

Tips for Muffins

- Grease only the bottoms of the muffin cups with shortening for nicely shaped muffins with rounded tops and no overhanging edges. For some recipes, you may have to grease the whole cup so the muffins won't stick. Better yet, use paper baking cups for easy baking, easy cleanup.

- Stir the dry ingredients into the wet ingredients just until the flour is moistened. Muffin batter *should be* lumpy. If you mix the batter too much, the muffins will turn out tough with pointed tops instead of nice rounded ones.

- Take the guesswork out of filling muffin cups: Use a spring-handled ice-cream scoop! The different scoop sizes are identified by a number; we recommend a No. 20 or 24. After filling the cups, be sure to wipe up any batter spills on the pan so they don't burn.

- When muffins are done, take them out of the muffin pan immediately so they don't get soggy. Muffins baked in paper cups should lift right out. Otherwise, loosen the muffins with a knife or metal spatula, then lift them out. Sometimes a recipe will specify that muffins be left in the pan for a few minutes before removing. This lets fragile muffins set up on the sides to steam a bit so the muffins are easier to remove.

Specialty Muffins

Convert your favorite twelve-muffin recipe to mini or jumbo muffins or to regular or jumbo muffin tops using the guidelines below. After you've figured out the bake times for your muffin recipe, note it on the recipe for future use.

- The bake times for the specialty muffins have quite a range—sometimes up to 10 minutes from the suggested minimum time to the maximum. Always check at the minimum time to see if the muffins are done, then check every minute or two until done.
- Muffin batters with large pieces of nuts, fruit or chocolate work better as medium or jumbo muffins because the pieces are too big for mini muffins. For mini muffins, use miniature chips and small pieces of fruit and nuts.
- Muffin batters that are very rich work better as mini muffins because a larger muffin may be too much of a good thing for one serving.
- Pans for baking muffin tops often have a dark nonstick surface. Be sure to check the manufacturer's instructions to see if reducing the oven temperature by 25° is recommended.

MUFFIN CURES

Great Muffins Are
Golden brown
Slightly rounded with
  bumpy tops
Tender and light
Even-textured with medium,
  round holes
Moist inside
Easy to remove from the pan

Problem	Possible Cause
Pale muffins	• oven too cool
Peaked and smooth tops	• too much mixing
Tough and heavy	• too much flour
	• too much mixing
Uneven texture with long holes or tunnels	• too much mixing
Dry	• too much flour
	• oven too hot
	• baked too long
Stick to pan	• pan not properly greased
Dark crust but center not done	• oven too hot

SPECIALTY MUFFIN BAKING CHART

Muffin Size	Muffin Cup Size	Oven Temperature	Bake Time	Yield
Muffins				
Mini	1 3/4 x 1 inch (small)	400°	10 to 17 minutes	24
Jumbo	3 1/2 x 1 3/4 inches (large)	375°	25 to 35 minutes	4
Muffin Tops				
Regular	2 3/4 x 3/8 inch	400°	8 to 10 minutes	18
Jumbo	4 x 1/2 inch	400°	15 to 20 minutes	6

Bran Muffins

Prep: 10 min: Bake 25 min ✱ *12 muffins*

These hearty muffins can be frozen for as long as three months and reheated as you need them. Be sure to place them in resealable plastic freezer bags or freezer containers.

1 1/4 cups Fiber One® cereal, crushed, or 2 cups bran
    cereal flakes, crushed*
1 1/3 cups milk
1/2 cup raisins, if desired
1/2 teaspoon vanilla
1/4 cup vegetable oil
1 large egg
1 1/4 cups all-purpose flour**
1/2 cup packed brown sugar
3 teaspoons baking powder
1/4 teaspoon salt
1/4 teaspoon ground cinnamon, if desired

1. Heat oven to 400°. Grease bottoms only of 12 medium muffin cups, 2 1/2 × 1 1/4 inches, with shortening, or line with paper baking cups.

2. Mix cereal, milk, raisins and vanilla in medium bowl. Let stand about 5 minutes or until cereal has softened.

3. Beat in oil and egg with fork. Mix remaining ingredients; stir into cereal mixture just until moistened. Divide batter evenly among muffin cups.

4. Bake 20 to 25 minutes or until toothpick inserted in center comes out clean. If baked in greased pan, let stand about 5 minutes in pan, then remove from pan to wire rack; if baked in paper baking cups, immediately remove from pan to wire rack. Serve warm if desired.

*To crush cereal, place in plastic bag or between sheets of waxed paper or plastic wrap and crush with rolling pin. Or crush in blender or food processor.
**If using self-rising flour, decrease baking powder to 1 teaspoon and omit salt.

1 Muffin: Calories 160 (Calories from Fat 55); Fat 6g (Saturated 1g); Cholesterol 20mg; Sodium 250mg; Carbohydrate 25g (Dietary Fiber 2g); Protein 4g **% Daily Value:** Vitamin A 6%; Vitamin C 2%; Calcium 12%; Iron 10% **Diet Exchanges:** 1 1/2 Starch, 1 Fat

Chocolate Chip Muffins *Fast*

Prep: 10 min: Bake: 20 min ✱ *12 muffins*

3/4 cup milk
1/4 cup butter or stick margarine, melted*
1 large egg
1 3/4 cups all-purpose flour**
1/2 cup miniature semisweet chocolate chips
1/2 cup chopped walnuts or pecans
1/3 cup packed brown sugar
2 1/2 teaspoons baking powder
1 teaspoon salt

1. Heat oven to 400°. Grease bottoms only of 12 medium muffin cups, 2 1/2 × 1 1/4 inches, or line with paper baking cups.

2. Beat milk, butter and egg in large bowl with fork or wire whisk. Stir in remaining ingredients just until flour is moistened. Divide batter evenly among muffin cups (about 2/3 full).

3. Bake 18 to 20 minutes or until golden brown. If baked in greased pan, let stand about 5 minutes in pan, then remove from pan to wire rack; if baked in paper baking cups, immediately remove from pan to wire rack. Serve warm if desired.

*Spreads with at least 65% vegetable oil can be used (page 45).
**If using self-rising flour, omit baking powder and salt.

1 Muffin: Calories 205 (Calories from Fat 90); Fat 10g (Saturated 4g); Cholesterol 30mg; Sodium 340mg; Carbohydrate 26g (Dietary Fiber 1g); Protein 4g **% Daily Value:** Vitamin A 4%; Vitamin C 0%; Calcium 8%; Iron 8% **Diet Exchanges:** 1 Starch, 1 Fruit, 1 1/2 Fat

Blueberry Muffins

Blueberry Muffins

Prep: 10 min; Bake: 25 min ✳ *12 muffins*

Streusel Topping (right), if desired
3/4 cup milk
1/4 cup vegetable oil
1 large egg
2 cups all-purpose flour*
1/2 cup sugar
2 teaspoons baking powder
1/2 teaspoon salt
1 cup fresh, canned (drained) or frozen blueberries

1. Heat oven to 400°. Grease bottoms only of 12 medium muffin cups, 2 1/2 x 1 1/4 inches, with shortening, or line with paper baking cups.

2. Make Streusel Topping; set aside.

3. Beat milk, oil and egg in large bowl with fork or wire whisk. Stir in flour, sugar, baking powder and salt all at once just until flour is moistened (batter will be lumpy). Fold in blueberries. Divide batter evenly among muffin cups. Sprinkle each with about 1 tablespoon topping.

4. Bake 20 to 25 minutes or until golden brown. If baked in greased pan, let stand about 5 minutes in pan, then remove from pan to wire rack; if baked in paper baking cups, immediately remove from pan to wire rack. Serve warm if desired.

Streusel Topping
1/4 cup all-purpose flour
1/4 cup packed brown sugar
1/4 teaspoon ground cinnamon
2 tablespoons firm butter or stick margarine**

Mix flour, brown sugar and cinnamon in medium bowl. Cut in butter, using pastry blender or crisscrossing 2 knives, until crumbly.

*If using self-rising flour, omit baking powder and salt.
**Spreads with at least 65% vegetable oil can be used (page 45).

1 Muffin: Calories 170 (Calories from Fat 55); Fat 6g (Saturated 1g); Cholesterol 20mg; Sodium 190mg; Carbohydrate 27g (Dietary Fiber 1g); Protein 3g **% Daily Value:** Vitamin A 2%; Vitamin C 0%; Calcium 6%; Iron 6% **Diet Exchanges:** 1 Starch, 1 Fruit, 1 Fat

APPLE-CINNAMON MUFFINS: Omit blueberries. Beat in 1 cup chopped peeled apple (about 1 medium) with the milk. Stir in 1/2 teaspoon ground cinnamon with the flour. Bake 25 to 30 minutes.

BANANA MUFFINS: Omit blueberries. Decrease milk to 1/3 cup. Beat in 1 cup mashed very ripe bananas (2 medium) with the milk. Use packed brown sugar for the sugar.

CRANBERRY-ORANGE MUFFINS: Omit blueberries. Beat in 1 tablespoon grated orange peel with the milk. Fold 1 cup cranberry halves into batter.

Tips for Nut Breads

- For fruit or nut breads, grease only the bottoms of the loaf pans to give the loaves a gently rounded top and avoid ridges at the edges of the loaf.
- Chop or shred fruits, vegetables or nuts *before* you start making the batter. If you start the batter and then stop to chop, the batter may get too stiff.
- Mix quick breads by hand, because it's easy to mix the batter too much with an electric mixer.
- It's okay if the top of the loaf gets a large, lengthwise crack.
- Cool nut breads completely before slicing so they don't crumble. Even better, store them tightly covered for 24 hours before cutting. Cut with a sharp, thin-bladed knife, using a light sawing motion.
- After cooling, wrap loaves tightly and store them in the refrigerator for up to a week or freeze up to three months.

Mini Nut Bread Loaves

For tasteful gifts or bite-size treats, make mini loaves using miniature loaf pans, muffin pans or small cake molds in special shapes.

NUT BREAD CURES

Great Nut Bread Has

Golden brown, rounded top
Crack (or split) lengthwise along the top
Thin, tender crust
Moist texture with small even holes
Fruits and/or nuts evenly distributed

Problem	Possible Cause
Didn't rise	• too much mixing
	• check expiration date on leavening
Tough	• too much mixing
	• not enough fat
Tunnels	• too much mixing
Rims around the edges	• sides of pan were greased
Compact	• too much flour
	• too little leavening
Crumbly	• not cooled completely; cut too soon after baking

- To determine how much batter a pan will hold, fill it to the top with water, then pour the water into a measuring cup. Consult the chart below to see how much batter you should use for the size pan you have.
- Let the baked breads cool for a few minutes, then loosen the edges with a table knife or metal spatula and carefully remove them from the pans. Cool completely on a wire rack.

MINI NUT BREAD LOAVES BAKING CHART

Approximate Pan Size	Amount of Batter	Approximate Bake Time at 350°
1/3 cup	1/4 cup	15 to 20 minutes
1/2 cup	1/3 cup	15 to 20 minutes
2/3 to 3/4 cup	1/2 cup	25 to 35 minutes
1 cup	3/4 cup	35 to 40 minutes

Zucchini Bread

Prep: 15 min; Bake: 1 hr; Cool: 2 hr 10 min
✻ *2 loaves, 24 slices each*

3 cups shredded zucchini (2 to 3 medium)
1 2/3 cups sugar
2/3 cup vegetable oil
2 teaspoons vanilla
4 large eggs
3 cups all-purpose* or whole wheat flour
2 teaspoons baking soda
1 teaspoon salt
1 teaspoon ground cinnamon
1/2 teaspoon ground cloves
1/2 teaspoon baking powder
1/2 cup coarsely chopped nuts
1/2 cup raisins, if desired

1. Move oven rack to low position so that tops of pans will be in center of oven. Heat oven to 350°. Grease bottoms only of 2 loaf pans, 8 1/2 × 4 1/2 × 2 1/2 inches, or 1 loaf pan, 9 × 5 × 3 inches, with shortening.

2. Mix zucchini, sugar, oil, vanilla and eggs in large bowl. Stir in remaining ingredients except nuts and raisins. Stir in nuts and raisins. Divide batter evenly between pans.

3. Bake 8-inch loaves 50 to 60 minutes, 9-inch loaf 1 hour 10 minutes to 1 hour 20 minutes, or until toothpick inserted in center comes out clean. Cool 10 minutes in pans on wire rack.

4. Loosen sides of loaves from pans; remove from pans and place top side up on wire rack. Cool completely, about 2 hours, before slicing. Wrap tightly and store at room temperature up to 4 days, or refrigerate up to 10 days.

*If using self-rising flour, omit baking soda, salt and baking powder.

1 Slice: Calories 95 (Calories from Fat 35); Fat 4g (Saturated 1g); Cholesterol 15mg; Sodium 110mg; Carbohydrate 13g (Dietary Fiber 0g); Protein 2g **% Daily Value:** Vitamin A 0%; Vitamin C 0%; Calcium 0%; Iron 2% **Diet Exchanges:** 1/2 Starch, 1 Vegetable, 1/2 Fat

CRANBERRY BREAD: Omit zucchini, cinnamon, cloves and raisins. Stir in 1/2 cup milk and 2 teaspoons grated orange peel with the oil. Stir 3 cups fresh or frozen (thawed and drained) cranberries into batter. Bake 1 hour to 1 hour 10 minutes.

PUMPKIN BREAD: Substitute 1 can (15 ounces) pumpkin (not pumpkin pie mix) for the zucchini.

Banana Bread   *Low-Fat*

Prep: 15 min; Bake: 1 hr; Cool: 2 hr 10 min
✻ *2 loaves, 24 slices each*

Don't throw away those bananas that are turning brown and soft. They're just right for banana bread.

1 1/4 cups sugar
1/2 cup butter or stick margarine, softened*
2 large eggs
1 1/2 cups mashed very ripe bananas (3 medium)
1/2 cup buttermilk
1 teaspoon vanilla
2 1/2 cups all-purpose flour**
1 teaspoon baking soda
1 teaspoon salt
1 cup chopped nuts, if desired

1. Move oven rack to low position so that tops of pans will be in center of oven. Heat oven to 350°. Grease bottoms only of 2 loaf pans, 8 1/2 × 4 1/2 × 2 1/2 inches, or 1 loaf pan, 9 × 5 × 3 inches, with shortening.

2. Mix sugar and butter in large bowl. Stir in eggs until well blended. Stir in bananas, buttermilk and vanilla; beat until smooth. Stir in flour, baking soda and salt just until moistened. Stir in nuts. Divide batter evenly between pans.

3. Bake 8-inch loaves about 1 hour, 9-inch loaf about 1 hour 15 minutes, or until toothpick inserted in center comes out clean. Cool 10 minutes in pans on wire rack.

4. Loosen sides of loaves from pans; remove from pans and place top side up on wire rack. Cool completely, about 2 hours, before slicing. Wrap tightly and store at room temperature up to 4 days, or refrigerate up to 10 days.

*Spreads with at least 65% vegetable oil can be used (page 45).
**If using self-rising flour, omit baking soda and salt.

1 Slice: Calories 70 (Calories from Fat 20); Fat 2g (Saturated 1g); Cholesterol 15mg; Sodium 95mg; Carbohydrate 12g (Dietary Fiber 0g); Protein 1g **% Daily Value:** Vitamin A 2%; Vitamin C 0%; Calcium 0%; Iron 2% **Diet Exchanges:** 1/2 Starch, 1/2 Fruit

BLUEBERRY-BANANA BREAD: Omit nuts. Stir 1 cup fresh or frozen blueberries into batter.

Sour Cream Coffee Cake

Prep: 30 min; Bake: 1 hr; Cool: 30 min ✱ *16 servings*

Brown Sugar Filling (right)
3 cups all-purpose* or whole wheat flour
1 1/2 teaspoons baking powder
1 1/2 teaspoons baking soda
3/4 teaspoon salt
1 1/2 cups sugar
3/4 cup butter or stick margarine, softened**
1 1/2 teaspoons vanilla
3 large eggs
1 1/2 cups sour cream
Vanilla Glaze (right)

1. Heat oven to 350°. Grease bottom and side of angel food cake pan (tube pan), 10 × 4 inches, 12-cup bundt cake pan or 2 loaf pans, 9 × 5 × 3 inches, with shortening.

2. Make Brown Sugar Filling; set aside. Mix flour, baking powder, baking soda and salt; set aside.

3. Beat sugar, butter, vanilla and eggs in large bowl with electric mixer on medium speed 2 minutes, scraping bowl occasionally. Beat about one-fourth of the flour mixture and sour cream at a time alternately into sugar mixture on low speed until blended.

4. For angel food or bundt cake pan, spread one-third of the batter (about 2 cups) in pan, then sprinkle with one-third of the filling; repeat twice. For loaf pans, spread one-fourth of the batter (about 1 1/2 cups) in each pan, then sprinkle each with one-fourth of the filling; repeat once.

5. Bake angel food or bundt cake pan about 1 hour, loaf pans about 45 minutes, or until toothpick inserted near center comes out clean. Cool 10 minutes in pan(s) on wire rack. Remove from pan(s) to wire rack. Cool 20 minutes. Drizzle with Vanilla Glaze. Serve warm or cool.

Brown Sugar Filling

1/2 cup packed brown sugar
1/2 cup finely chopped nuts
1 1/2 teaspoons ground cinnamon

Mix all ingredients.

Vanilla Glaze

1/2 cup powdered sugar
1/4 teaspoon vanilla
2 to 3 teaspoons milk

Mix all ingredients until smooth and thin enough to drizzle.

*If using self-rising flour, omit baking powder, baking soda and salt.
**Spreads with at least 65% vegetable oil can be used (page 45).

1 Slice: Calories 355 (Calories from Fat 145); Fat 16g (Saturated 9g); Cholesterol 75mg; Sodium 360mg; Carbohydrate 49g (Dietary Fiber 1g); Protein 5g **% Daily Value:** Vitamin A 12%; Vitamin C 0%; Calcium 6%; Iron 8% **Diet Exchanges:** Not Recommended

Apple Coffee Cake

Apple Coffee Cake

Prep: 15 min; Bake: 25 min; Cool: 20 min ✱ *9 servings*

Some common cooking apples are Cortland, Northern Spy, Rome Beauty, Winesap, Golden Delicious and Granny Smith. You might even want to poke around your farmers' markets to see if there are local varieties that are tasty for baking.

Streusel Topping (right)
2 cups Original Bisquick®
2/3 cup milk
3 tablespoons sugar
1 large egg
2 medium cooking apples, peeled and thinly
    sliced (2 cups)
2 tablespoons chopped nuts
Glaze (right)

1. Heat oven to 400°. Grease bottom and sides of square pan, 9 × 9 × 2 inches, with shortening.

2. Make Streusel Topping; set aside.

3. Stir Bisquick milk, sugar and egg until blended; beat vigorously 30 seconds. Spread half of the batter in pan. Arrange apple slices on batter; sprinkle with half of the topping. Spread remaining batter over apple slices; sprinkle with remaining topping. Sprinkle with nuts.

4. Bake 20 to 25 minutes or until toothpick inserted in center comes out clean. Cool 20 minutes in pan on wire rack. Drizzle with Glaze. Serve warm or cool.

Streusel Topping

2/3 cup Original Bisquick
2/3 cup packed brown sugar
1 teaspoon ground cinnamon
1/2 teaspoon ground nutmeg
1/4 cup firm butter or stick margarine*

Mix Bisquick, brown sugar, cinnamon and nutmeg. Cut in butter, using pastry blender or crisscrossing 2 knives, until mixture is crumbly.

Glaze

1/2 cup powdered sugar
2 to 3 teaspoons milk

Mix ingredients until smooth and thin enough to drizzle.

Spreads with at least 65% vegetable oil can be used (page 45).

1 Serving: Calories 335 (Calories from Fat 110); Fat 12g (Saturated 5g); Cholesterol 40mg; Sodium 560mg; Carbohydrate 54g (Dietary Fiber 1g); Protein 4g **% Daily Value:** Vitamin A 6%; Vitamin C 0%; Calcium 10%; Iron 10% **Diet Exchanges:** Not Recommended

Lighter Apple Coffee Cake: For 6 grams fat and 285 calories per serving, use Reduced Fat Bisquick and fat-free (skim) milk. Substitute 1/4 cup fat-free, cholesterol-free egg product for the egg. Decrease butter to 2 tablespoons in Streusel Topping.

Danish Puff

Prep: 30 min; Bake: 1 hr; Cool: 30 min ✱ *10 to 12 servings*

1 cup all-purpose flour*
1/2 cup butter or stick margarine, softened**
2 tablespoons water
1/2 cup butter or stick margarine**
1 cup water
1 cup all-purpose flour*
1 teaspoon almond extract
3 large eggs
Powdered Sugar Glaze (right)
1/4 cup sliced almonds

1. Heat oven to 350°.

2. Place 1 cup of the flour in small bowl. Cut in 1/2 cup butter, using pastry blender or crisscrossing 2 knives, until mixture looks like small peas. Sprinkle 2 tablespoons water over mixture; mix in with fork. Round dough into a ball; divide in half. Pat each half into 12 × 3-inch strip about 3 inches apart on ungreased cookie sheet.

3. Heat 1/2 cup butter and 1 cup water to a rolling boil in 2 1/2-quart saucepan. Stir in 1 cup flour and the almond extract. Stir vigorously over low heat about 1 minute or until mixture forms a ball; remove from heat.

4. Beat in eggs, all at once; continue beating until smooth. Divide in half; spread each half evenly over strips.

5. Bake about 1 hour or until topping is crisp and golden brown. Cool 30 minutes. Frost with Powdered Sugar Glaze. Sprinkle with almonds.

Powdered Sugar Glaze

1 1/2 cups powdered sugar
2 tablespoons butter or stick margarine, softened**
1 1/2 teaspoons vanilla
1 to 2 tablespoons warm water

Mix all ingredients until smooth and spreadable.

Self-rising flour can be used.
**Spreads with at least 65% vegetable oil can be used (page 45).*

1 Serving: Calories 385 (Calories from Fat 215); Fat 24g (Saturated 14g); Cholesterol 120mg; Sodium 160mg; Carbohydrate 38g (Dietary Fiber 1g); Protein 5g **% Daily Value:** Vitamin A 18%; Vitamin C 0%; Calcium 2%; Iron 8% **Diet Exchanges:** Not Recommended

BISCUIT CURES

Great Baking Powder Biscuits Are

Light golden brown
  outside
High with fairly smooth,
  level tops
Tender and light
Flaky and slightly moist
  inside

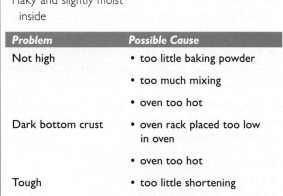

Problem	Possible Cause
Not high	• too little baking powder
	• too much mixing
	• oven too hot
Dark bottom crust	• oven rack placed too low in oven
	• oven too hot
Tough	• too little shortening
	• too much mixing or handling
	• too much flour
Not flaky	• too little shortening
	• too much mixing
	• not kneaded enough

Tips for Biscuits

- One secret to making flaky biscuits is thoroughly blending or "cutting in" the shortening and dry ingredients. A pastry blender, which breaks the shortening into little lumps, works great for cutting in. If you don't have one, you can crisscross two table knives through the flour and shortening or use a wire whisk.

- For nice-looking biscuits and even baking, roll or pat the dough to an even thickness. Here's a clever trick for rolling dough to the right thickness every time: Use two sticks, 1/2 inch thick and 14 inches long, as a guide. Place the ball of dough between the sticks, and roll or pat the dough to the thickness of the sticks. Anyone who works with wood can make a pair of these guides. See photo in How to Make Biscuits, below.

- Use a biscuit cutter dipped in flour to cut the dough, pushing the cutter straight down through the dough. If you twist as you cut, the biscuits will be uneven. Cut the biscuits as close together as possible.

- If you don't have a biscuit cutter, use the end of an opened 6-ounce juice can or other narrow can or glass, or use cookie cutters for fun shapes. Dip in flour before cutting.

- After cutting as many biscuits as possible, lightly press—don't knead—the scraps of dough together. Roll or pat the remaining dough to 1/2-inch thickness and cut. These biscuits will look slightly uneven.

HOW TO MAKE BISCUITS

1. Cut shortening into flour mixture until the mixture looks like fine crumbs.

2. Stir in milk until dough leaves side of bowl (dough will be soft and sticky).

3. Roll or pat the dough 1/2 inch thick. Cut dough with a cutter that has been dipped in flour.

Baking Powder Biscuits *Fast*

Prep: 10 min; Bake: 12 min ✱ *12 biscuits*

Try the Sausage Biscuits (right) as a great twist and an easy meal. Split the biscuits, add a slice of cheese and you have a delicious handheld breakfast sandwich.

2 cups all-purpose flour*
1 tablespoon sugar
3 teaspoons baking powder
1 teaspoon salt
1/2 cup shortening
3/4 cup milk

1. Heat oven to 450°.

2. Mix flour, sugar, baking powder and salt in medium bowl. Cut in shortening using pastry blender or criss-crossing 2 knives, until mixture looks like fine crumbs. Stir in milk until dough leaves side of bowl (dough will be soft and sticky).

3. Place dough on lightly floured surface. Knead lightly 10 times. Roll or pat 1/2 inch thick. Cut with floured 2 to 2 1/4-inch round cutter. Place on ungreased cookie sheet about 1 inch apart for crusty sides, touching for soft sides.

4. Bake 10 to 12 minutes or until golden brown. Immediately remove from cookie sheet. Serve warm.

If using self-rising flour, omit baking powder and salt.

1 Biscuit: Calories 160 (Calories from Fat 80); Fat 9g (Saturated 2g); Cholesterol 0mg; Sodium 330mg; Carbohydrate 18g (Dietary Fiber 1g); Protein 3g **% Daily Value:** Vitamin A 0%; Vitamin C 0%; Calcium 8%; Iron 6% **Diet Exchanges:** 1 Starch, 2 Fat

BUTTERMILK BISCUITS: Decrease baking powder to 2 teaspoons; add 1/4 teaspoon baking soda with the sugar. Substitute buttermilk for the milk. (If buttermilk is thick, using slightly more than 3/4 cup may be necessary.)

DROP BISCUITS: Grease cookie sheet with shortening. Increase milk to 1 cup. Drop dough by 12 spoonfuls onto cookie sheet.

PESTO BISCUITS: Decrease shortening to 1/3 cup, salt to 1/2 teaspoon and milk to 1/2 cup. Cut 1/4 cup pesto into flour mixture with the shortening. Sprinkle with grated Parmesan cheese before baking if desired.

SAUSAGE BISCUITS: Decrease shortening to 1/3 cup and salt to 1/4 teaspoon. Cook 1/2 pound bulk pork sausage in 10-inch skillet over medium heat, stirring occasionally, until no longer pink; drain, cool slightly and crumble. Stir sausage into flour-shortening mixture before adding milk.

Praline Pan Biscuits *Fast*

Prep: 15 min; Bake: 15 min ✱ *12 biscuits*

1/3 cup butter or stick margarine*
1/3 cup packed brown sugar
1/3 cup chopped pecans
2 cups Original Bisquick®
1/2 cup milk

1. Heat oven to 425°.

2. Heat butter and brown sugar in 1-quart saucepan over low heat, stirring constantly, until melted. Pour into round pan, 9 × 1 1/2 inches, or square pan, 8 × 8 × 2 inches. Sprinkle with pecans.

3. Mix Bisquick and milk until dough forms; beat 30 seconds. If dough is too sticky, gradually mix in enough baking mix (up to 1/4 cup) to make dough easy to handle.

4. Place dough on surface dusted with Bisquick; gently roll in Bisquick to coat. Knead 10 times. Divide dough into 12 equal pieces; gently shape each piece into a ball. Place balls on brown sugar mixture in pan.

5. Bake 12 to 15 minutes or until golden brown. Turn pan upside down onto heatproof serving plate. Leave pan over biscuits a few minutes to allow brown sugar mixture to drizzle over biscuits. Cool slightly before serving.

Spreads with at least 65% vegetable oil can be used (page 45).

1 Biscuit: Calories 170 (Calories from Fat 90); Fat 10g (Saturated 4g); Cholesterol 15mg; Sodium 330mg; Carbohydrate 19g (Dietary Fiber 1g); Protein 2g **% Daily Value:** Vitamin A 4%; Vitamin C 0%; Calcium 4%; Iron 4% **Diet Exchanges:** 1 Starch, 2 Fat

Easy Garlic-Cheese Biscuits *Fast*

Prep: 10 min; Bake: 10 min ✻ 10 to 12 biscuits

These biscuits are so yummy, they've found themselves on restaurant menus. This recipe is frequently requested by our consumers.

2 cups Original Bisquick
2/3 cup milk
1/2 cup shredded Cheddar cheese (2 ounces)
1/4 cup butter or stick margarine, melted*
1/4 teaspoon garlic powder

1. Heat oven to 450°.

2. Mix Bisquick, milk and cheese until soft dough forms; beat vigorously 30 seconds. Drop dough by 10 to 12 spoonfuls about 2 inches apart onto ungreased cookie sheet.

3. Bake 8 to 10 minutes or until golden brown. Mix butter and garlic powder; brush on warm biscuits before removing from cookie sheet. Serve warm.

Spreads with at least 65% vegetable oil can be used (page 45).

1 Biscuit: Calories 165 (Calories from Fat 90); Fat 10g (Saturated 5g); Cholesterol 20mg; Sodium 410mg; Carbohydrate 15g (Dietary Fiber 0g); Protein 4g **% Daily Value:** Vitamin A 6%; Vitamin C 0%; Calcium 8%; Iron 4% **Diet Exchanges:** 1 Starch, 2 Fat

> **Lighter Easy Garlic-Cheese Biscuits:** For 2 grams of fat and 105 calories per serving, use Reduced Fat Bisquick, fat-free (skim) milk and reduced-fat Cheddar cheese. Omit butter. Increase garlic powder to 1/2 teaspoon; stir in with the Bisquick. Spray warm biscuits with butter-flavored cooking spray if desired.

EASY HERBED-CHEESE BISCUITS: Stir in 3/4 teaspoon dried dill weed, dried rosemary leaves, crumbled, or Italian seasoning with the baking mix.

Scones

Prep: 15 min; Bake: 16 min ✻ 8 scones

In a hurry? Just drop dough from a large spoon into 8 equal mounds on ungreased cookie sheet. Flatten to about 1/2 inch with floured fingers. Bake as directed.

1 3/4 cups all-purpose flour*
3 tablespoons sugar
2 1/2 teaspoons baking powder
1/2 teaspoon salt
1/3 cup firm butter or stick margarine**
1 large egg, beaten
1/2 cup currants or raisins
4 to 6 tablespoons half-and-half
Additional half-and-half
White coarse sugar crystals (decorating sugar) or
    granulated sugar

1. Heat oven to 400°.

2. Mix flour, 3 tablespoons sugar, baking powder and salt in large bowl. Cut in butter, using pastry blender or crisscrossing 2 knives, until mixture looks like fine crumbs. Stir in egg, currants and just enough of the 4 to 6 tablespoons half-and-half so dough leaves side of bowl.

3. Place dough on lightly floured surface; gently roll in flour to coat. Knead lightly 10 times. Roll or pat into 8-inch circle on ungreased cookie sheet. Cut into 8 wedges with sharp knife that has been dipped in flour, but do not separate wedges. Brush with additional half-and-half; sprinkle with sugar crystals.

4. Bake 14 to 16 minutes or until golden. Immediately remove from cookie sheet; carefully separate wedges. Serve warm.

If using self-rising flour, omit baking powder and salt.
**Spreads with at least 65% vegetable oil can be used (page 45).*

1 Scone: Calories 250 (Calories from Fat 90); Fat 10g (Saturated 6g); Cholesterol 50mg; Sodium 360mg; Carbohydrate 37g (Dietary Fiber 1g); Protein 4g **% Daily Value:** Vitamin A 8%; Vitamin C 0%; Calcium 10%; Iron 10% **Diet Exchanges:** 1 1/2 Starch, 1 Fruit, 1 1/2 Fat

LEMON–POPPY SEED SCONES: Omit currants. Stir in 1 tablespoon grated lemon peel and 1 tablespoon poppy seed with the egg.

SPICY FRUIT SCONES: Add 3/4 teaspoon ground cinnamon and 1/8 teaspoon ground cloves with the flour. Substitute finely chopped dried apricots, figs or dates for the currants if desired.

Scones (page 56)

Dumplings *Fast*

Prep: 10 min; Cook: 20 min ✱ 10 dumplings

These dumplings are similar to biscuits except they are cooked on top of simmering stew. They are a great addition to Beef Stew (page 465), Burgundy Beef Stew (page 465) and Rabbit Italiano (page 269).

1 1/2 cups all-purpose flour*
1 tablespoon parsley flakes, if desired
2 teaspoons baking powder
1/2 teaspoon salt
3 tablespoons shortening
3/4 cup milk

1. Mix flour, parsley, baking powder and salt in medium bowl. Cut in shortening using pastry blender or crisscrossing 2 knives, until mixture looks like fine crumbs. Stir in milk.

2. Drop dough by 10 spoonfuls onto hot meat or vegetables in boiling stew (do not drop directly into liquid or dumplings may become soggy). Cook uncovered 10 minutes. Cover and cook 10 minutes longer.

If using self-rising flour, omit baking powder and salt.

1 Dumpling: Calories 105 (Calories from Fat 35); Fat 4g (Saturated 1g); Cholesterol 0mg; Sodium 220mg; Carbohydrate 15g (Dietary Fiber 1g); Protein 3g **% Daily Value:** Vitamin A 0%; Vitamin C 0%; Calcium 8%; Iron 4% **Diet Exchanges:** 1 Starch, 1/2 Fat

HERB DUMPLINGS: Substitute 2 teaspoons chopped fresh or 1 teaspoon dried herbs (such as basil, sage or thyme leaves or celery seed) for the parsley.

Popovers *Low-Fat*

Prep: 10 min; Bake: 40 min ✳ 6 popovers

Popovers can be baked ahead and reheated. When just out of the oven, pierce each popover with the point of a knife to let the steam out, and cool completely on a wire rack. When it's time to eat, just reheat on an ungreased cookie sheet at 350° for 5 minutes.

2 large eggs
1 cup all-purpose flour*
1 cup milk
1/2 teaspoon salt

1. Heat oven to 450°. Generously grease 6-cup popover pan or six 6-ounce custard cups with shortening. Place custard cups on cookie sheet.

2. Beat eggs slightly in medium bowl with fork or wire whisk. Beat in remaining ingredients just until smooth (do not overbeat or popovers may not puff as high). Fill cups about half full.

3. Bake 20 minutes.

4. Reduce oven temperature to 325° for popover pan or 350° for custard cups. Bake about 20 minutes longer or until deep golden brown. Immediately remove from cups. Serve hot.

Do not use self-rising flour.

1 Popover: Calories 120 (Calories from Fat 25); Fat 3g (Saturated 1g); Cholesterol 75mg; Sodium 240mg; Carbohydrate 18g (Dietary Fiber 1g); Protein 6g **% Daily Value:** Vitamin A 4%; Vitamin C 0%; Calcium 6%; Iron 6% **Diet Exchanges:** 1 Starch, 1 Fat

Tips for Pancakes and French Toast

- For even browning, heat the griddle or skillet on medium heat or set at 375° about 10 minutes before cooking pancakes or French toast. Depending on the pan, griddle or your stove, you may have to adjust the temperature.

- Mix pancake batter right in a 4- or 8-cup glass measuring cup with a handle and spout, which makes for easy pouring onto the griddle.

- Get that spatula ready! Turn pancakes as soon as they puff and the bubbles just begin to break. The second side never browns as evenly as the first.

- Serve pancakes and French toast immediately, or keep them warm in a *single* layer on a wire rack or paper towel–lined cookie sheet in a 200° oven. If you stack warm pancakes, they'll become soggy.

Pancakes *Fast*

Prep: 5 min; Cook: 10 min ✳ Nine 4-inch pancakes

Consider mixing the batter in a 4- or 8-cup glass measuring cup with a handle and spout. Then pouring the batter onto the griddle will be easy.

1 large egg
1 cup all-purpose* or whole wheat flour
3/4 cup milk
1 tablespoon granulated or packed brown sugar
2 tablespoons vegetable oil
3 teaspoons baking powder
1/4 teaspoon salt
Butter, stick margarine or shortening

1. Beat egg in medium bowl with hand beater until fluffy. Beat in remaining ingredients except butter just until smooth. For thinner pancakes, stir in additional 1 to 2 tablespoons milk.

2. Heat griddle or skillet over medium heat or to 375°. (To test griddle, sprinkle with a few drops of water. If bubbles jump around, heat is just right.) Grease griddle with butter if necessary.

3. For each pancake, pour slightly less than 1/4 cup batter from cup or pitcher onto hot griddle. Cook pancake until bubbly on top, puffed and dry around edges. Turn and cook other side until golden brown.

Pancakes are ready to turn when they are bubbly on top, puffed and dry around edges.

If using self-rising flour, omit baking powder and salt.

1 Pancake: Calories 110 (Calories from Fat 45); Fat 5g (Saturated 1g); Cholesterol 25mg; Sodium 250mg; Carbohydrate 13g (Dietary Fiber 0g); Protein 3g **% Daily Value:** Vitamin A 2%; Vitamin C 0%; Calcium 12%; Iron 4% **Diet Exchanges:** 1 Starch, 1/2 Fat

BERRY PANCAKES: Stir 1/2 cup fresh or frozen (thawed and well drained) blackberries, blueberries or raspberries into batter.

BUTTERMILK PANCAKES: Substitute 1 cup buttermilk for the 3/4 cup milk. Decrease baking powder to 1 teaspoon. Add 1/2 teaspoon baking soda.

Puffy Oven Pancake

Prep: 10 min; Bake: 30 min ✳ *2 to 4 servings*

More like a popover than a pancake, this oven pancake puffs up high around the edges and should be served quickly, before it sinks.

2 tablespoons butter or stick margarine*
2 large eggs
1/2 cup all-purpose flour**
1/2 cup milk
1/4 teaspoon salt
Lemon juice and powdered sugar or cut-up fruit, if desired

1. Heat oven to 400°. Melt butter in pie plate, 9 × 1 1/4 inches, in oven; brush butter over bottom and side of pie plate.

2. Beat eggs slightly in medium bowl with wire whisk or hand beater. Beat in flour, milk and salt just until mixed (do not overbeat or pancake may not puff). Pour into pie plate.

3. Bake 25 to 30 minutes or until puffy and deep golden brown. Serve immediately sprinkled with lemon juice and powdered sugar or topped with fruit.

*Spreads with at least 65% vegetable oil can be used (page 45).
**Do not use self-rising flour.

1 Serving: Calories 315 (Calories from Fat 160); Fat 18g (Saturated 10g); Cholesterol 245mg; Sodium 460mg; Carbohydrate 27g (Dietary Fiber 1g); Protein 12g **% Daily Value:** Vitamin A 18%; Vitamin C 0%; Calcium 10%; Iron 12% **Diet Exchanges:** 2 Starch, 1 Lean Meat, 2 Fat

APPLE OVEN PANCAKE: Make Puffy Oven Pancake as directed—except sprinkle 2 tablespoons packed brown sugar and 1/4 teaspoon ground cinnamon evenly over melted butter in pie plate. Arrange 1 cup thinly sliced peeled baking apple (1 medium) over sugar. Pour batter over apple. Bake 30 to 35 minutes. Immediately loosen edge of pancake and turn upside down onto heatproof serving plate.

DOUBLE OVEN PANCAKE: Melt 1/3 cup butter in rectangular pan, 13 × 9 × 2 inches. Use 4 large eggs, 1 cup all-purpose flour, 1 cup milk and 1/4 teaspoon salt.

Banana-Pecan Pancakes *Low-Fat*

Prep: 10 min; Cook: 30 min
✳ *Twenty-seven 4-inch pancakes*

2 large eggs
2 cups all-purpose flour*
2 cups buttermilk
2 cups mashed ripe bananas (4 medium)
1/4 cup granulated or packed brown sugar
1/4 cup vegetable oil
2 teaspoons baking powder
1 teaspoon baking soda
1/2 teaspoon salt
1 cup chopped pecans, toasted (page 177), if desired

1. Beat eggs in medium bowl with hand beater until fluffy. Beat in remaining ingredients except pecans just until smooth. Stir in pecans. For thinner pancakes, stir in additional 1 to 2 tablespoons buttermilk.

2. Heat griddle to 375° or heat skillet over medium heat. Grease griddle with butter if necessary. (To test griddle, sprinkle with a few drops of water. If bubbles jump around, heat is just right.)

3. For each pancake, pour slightly less than 1/4 cup batter from cup or pitcher onto hot griddle. Cook pancakes until puffed and dry around edges. Turn and cook other sides until golden brown.

*If using self-rising flour, omit baking powder, baking soda and salt.

1 Pancake: Calories 90 (Calories from Fat 25); Fat 3g (Saturated 1g); Cholesterol 15mg; Sodium 150mg; Carbohydrate 14g (Dietary Fiber 1g); Protein 2g **% Daily Value:** Vitamin A 0%; Vitamin C 10%; Calcium 4%; Iron 4% **Diet Exchanges:** 1 Starch

Crepes

Prep: 10 min; Cook: 25 min ✷ 12 crepes

Crepe is French for "pancake." Crepes are much thinner than regular pancakes and can be filled with jam or cut-up fruit, then folded or rolled.

1 1/2 cups all-purpose flour*
1 tablespoon sugar
1/2 teaspoon baking powder
1/2 teaspoon salt
2 cups milk
2 tablespoons butter or stick margarine, melted**
1/2 teaspoon vanilla
2 large eggs
Butter, stick margarine or shortening
Applesauce, sweetened strawberries, currant jelly or
    raspberry jam, if desired
Powdered sugar, if desired

1. Mix flour, sugar, baking powder and salt in medium bowl. Stir in remaining ingredients. Beat with hand beater until smooth.

2. Lightly butter 6- to 8-inch skillet. Heat over medium heat until bubbly.

3. For each crepe, pour scant 1/4 cup batter into skillet. Immediately rotate skillet until thin layer of batter covers bottom. Cook until light brown. Run wide spatula around edge to loosen; turn and cook other side until light brown. Repeat with remaining batter, buttering skillet as needed.

4. Stack crepes, placing waxed paper between each; keep covered. If desired, spread applesauce, sweetened strawberries, currant jelly or raspberry jam thinly over each warm crepe; roll up. (Be sure to fill crepes so when rolled the more attractive side is on the outside.) Sprinkle with powdered sugar if desired. Unfilled crepes can be wrapped airtight and frozen up to 2 months.

If using self-rising flour, omit baking powder and salt.
**Spreads with at least 65% vegetable oil can be used (page 45).*

1 Crepe: Calories 110 (Calories from Fat 35); Fat 4g (Saturated 2g); Cholesterol 45mg; Sodium 160mg; Carbohydrate 15g (Dietary Fiber 0g); Protein 4g **% Daily Value:** Vitamin A 4%; Vitamin C 0%; Calcium 6%; Iron 4% **Diet Exchanges:** 1 Starch, 1/2 Fat

French Toast   *Fast & Low-Fat*

Prep: 5 min; Cook: 16 min ✷ 8 slices

3 eggs
3/4 cup milk
1 tablespoon sugar
1/4 teaspoon vanilla
1/8 teaspoon salt
Butter, stick margarine or shortening
8 slices sandwich bread or 1-inch-thick slices French
    bread

1. Beat eggs, milk, sugar, vanilla and salt with wire whisk or hand beater until smooth.

2. Heat griddle or skillet over medium heat or to 375°. (To test griddle, sprinkle with a few drops water. If bubbles jump around, heat is just right.) Grease griddle with butter if necessary.

3. Dip bread into egg mixture. Place on griddle. Cook about 4 minutes on each side or until golden brown.

1 Slice: Calories 165 (Calories from Fat 25); Fat 3g (Saturated 1g); Cholesterol 80mg; Sodium 190mg; Carbohydrate 31g (Dietary Fiber 1g); Protein 4g **% Daily Value:** Vitamin A 2%; Vitamin C 0%; Calcium 4%; Iron 6% **Diet Exchanges:** 2 Starch

OVEN FRENCH TOAST: Heat oven to 500°. Generously butter jelly roll pan, 15 1/2 × 10 1/2 × 1 inch. Heat pan in oven 1 minute; remove from oven. Arrange dipped bread in hot pan. Drizzle any remaining egg mixture over bread. Bake 5 to 8 minutes or until bottoms are golden brown; turn bread. Bake 2 to 4 minutes longer or until golden brown.

Waffles with Raspberry Sauce (page 197)

Waffles *Fast*

Prep: 5 min: Bake: 5 min per waffle
✱ *Six 7-inch round waffles*

Waffle irons, also called waffle bakers or waffle makers, are available in a variety of shapes and sizes. Each waffle iron uses a different amount of batter, so you may end up with more or fewer waffles.

2 large eggs
2 cups all-purpose* or whole wheat flour
1 3/4 cups milk
1/2 cup vegetable oil**
1 tablespoon granulated or packed brown sugar
4 teaspoons baking powder
1/4 teaspoon salt
Fresh berries if desired

1. Heat waffle iron.

2. Beat eggs in large bowl with hand beater or wire whisk until fluffy. Beat in remaining ingredients just until smooth.

3. Pour a scant 2/3 cup batter from cup or pitcher onto center of hot waffle iron. (Check manufacturer's directions for recommended amount of batter.) Close lid of waffle iron.

4. Bake about 5 minutes or until steaming stops. Carefully remove waffle. Serve immediately. Top with fresh berries. Repeat with remaining batter.

*If using self-rising flour, omit baking powder and salt.
**1/2 cup butter or stick margarine, melted, can be substituted for the oil.

1 Waffle: Calories 380 (Calories from Fat 200); Fat 22g (Saturated 4g); Cholesterol 75mg; Sodium 480mg; Carbohydrate 38g (Dietary Fiber 1g); Protein 9g **% Daily Value:** Vitamin A 6%; Vitamin C 0%; Calcium 28%; Iron 14% **Diet Exchanges:** 2 1/2 Starch, 4 Fat

Corn Bread

Prep: 10 min; Bake: 25 min ✱ 12 servings

There are many versions of corn bread. This one, sometimes called Yankee Corn Bread, is sweeter than the Southern Buttermilk Corn Bread recipe (right).

1 cup milk
1/4 cup butter or stick margarine, melted*
1 large egg
1 1/4 cups yellow, white or blue cornmeal
1 cup all-purpose flour**
1/2 cup sugar
1 tablespoon baking powder
1/2 teaspoon salt

1. Heat oven to 400°. Grease bottom and side of round pan, 9 × 1 1/2 inches, or square pan, 8 × 8 × 2 inches, with shortening.

2. Beat milk, butter and egg in large bowl with hand beater or wire whisk. Stir in remaining ingredients all at once just until flour is moistened (batter will be lumpy). Pour into pan.

3. Bake 20 to 25 minutes or until golden brown and toothpick inserted in center comes out clean. Serve warm if desired.

Spreads with at least 65% vegetable oil can be used (page 45).
**If using self-rising flour, omit baking powder and salt.*

1 Serving: Calories 175 (Calories from Fat 45); Fat 5g (Saturated 3g); Cholesterol 30mg; Sodium 260mg; Carbohydrate 29g (Dietary Fiber 1g); Protein 4g **% Daily Value:** Vitamin A 4%; Vitamin C 0%; Calcium 10%; Iron 6% **Diet Exchanges:** 2 Starch, 1/2 Fat

CORN MUFFINS: Grease bottoms only of 12 medium muffin cups, 2 1/2 × 1 1/4 inches, with shortening, or line with paper baking cups. Fill cups about 3/4 full.

Southern Buttermilk Corn Bread

Prep: 10 min; Bake: 30 min ✱ 12 servings

1 1/2 cups yellow, white or blue cornmeal
1/2 cup all-purpose flour*
1 1/2 cups buttermilk
1/4 cup vegetable oil or shortening
2 teaspoons baking powder
1 teaspoon sugar
1 teaspoon salt
1/2 teaspoon baking soda
2 large eggs

1. Heat oven to 450°. Grease bottom and side of round pan, 9 × 1 1/2 inches, square pan, 8 × 8 × 2 inches, or 10-inch ovenproof skillet with shortening.

2. Mix all ingredients. Beat vigorously 30 seconds. Pour into pan.

3. Bake round or square pan 25 to 30 minutes, skillet about 20 minutes, or until golden brown. Serve warm.

If using self-rising flour, decrease baking powder to 1 teaspoon and omit salt.

1 Serving: Calories 140 (Calories from Fat 55); Fat 6g (Saturated 1g); Cholesterol 35mg; Sodium 370mg; Carbohydrate 19g (Dietary Fiber 1g); Protein 4g **% Daily Value:** Vitamin A 2%; Vitamin C 0%; Calcium 8%; Iron 6% **Diet Exchanges:** 1 Starch, 1 Fat

CHEESY MEXICAN CORN BREAD: Decrease buttermilk to 1 cup. Stir in 1 can (about 8 ounces) cream-style corn, 1 can (4 ounces) chopped green chilies, well drained, 1/2 cup shredded Monterey Jack or Cheddar cheese (2 ounces) and 1 teaspoon chili powder.

CORN STICKS: Grease 18 corn stick pans with shortening. Fill about 7/8 full. Bake 12 to 15 minutes. Makes 18 corn sticks.

Yeast Bread Basics

Don't you just love the aroma of fresh-baked bread? It's a smell that says "home." And it's one that you can easily bring to your home, even if you're new to baking. Making yeast breads isn't hard; they just take time for rising, and the results are well worth the wait. From Focaccia (page 78), to Caramel Sticky Rolls (page 82), in this chapter you'll find—and learn to make—breads that rise to any ocassion.

Pans and Pan Preparation

For well-browned crusts, use uninsulated pans and cookie sheets. Cookie sheets without a rim or sides also will allow better heat circulation and the bread will brown better. If you're using pans with dark nonstick coating, watch carefully so bread doesn't get too brown. Check the manufacturer's directions for oven temperature; sometimes reducing it by 25° is recommended.

For tender, golden brown crusts on rolls and sweet rolls, use shiny cookie sheets and muffin cups, which reflect heat.

Ingredients

What does it take to make bread? Basically, just a few simple ingredients. Of course, for the best bread, start with fresh, high-quality ingredients.

All-purpose Flour: All-purpose flour is the most widely used flour. The amount of protein in flour varies with the wheat crop; the moisture content can vary, too. That's why most recipes for kneaded dough give a range of amount of flour. Also see Flour, page 17.

Bread Flour: Bread flour is made from a special blend of wheats higher in protein than the wheat used in all-purpose flour. Protein produces gluten, which gives structure and volume to yeast breads. Bread flour is ideal to use in bread machines as well as for all yeast breads. Also see Flour, page 17.

Yeast: Yeast is a living organism that converts its food to alcohol and carbon dioxide. It's the carbon dioxide bubbles that make dough rise. Yeast is very sensitive— too much heat will kill it, and cold will stunt its growth. Always check the expiration date on the yeast package before using.

Most of the recipes in this chapter follow the "quick-mix" method: mixing the yeast with part of the flour, then beating in very warm liquid (120° to 130°). Some recipes, however, still use the traditional method of dissolving the yeast in warm water (105° to 115°).

If you're using quick active dry yeast, rising times may be shorter. Check the manufacturer's directions for the best results.

For best results, be sure to use the temperatures for liquids given in each recipe. Also see Yeast, page 20.

Liquids: Water and milk are the most commonly used liquids. Water gives bread a crisper crust; milk provides a velvety texture and added nutrients.

Sweeteners: Sugar, honey and molasses provide "food" for the yeast to help it grow, enhance the flavor of the bread and help brown the crust. Don't use artificial sweeteners because they don't properly "feed" the yeast.

Salt: Salt is a flavoring needed to control the growth of the yeast and prevent the dough from rising too much, which can cause the bread to collapse. If you reduce the salt in a recipe, you'll need to decrease both rising times, too.

Fat: Butter, margarine, shortening and vegetable oil make bread tender. In addition to tenderness, butter and margarine add flavor.

Eggs: Eggs are sometimes added for flavor, richness and color.

Baking Yeast Breads

Just before baking, give your bread one of these professional finishing touches:

For a shiny crust, brush the top of the bread with an egg or egg white beaten with a little water. If desired, sprinkle with poppy, caraway or sesame seed or rolled oats.

For a softer, deep golden brown crust, brush with softened butter or margarine.

For a crisp crust, brush or spray lightly with water.

For a soft, tender crust, brush with milk.

After glazing (brushing with one of these ingredients), slash the top of the loaf with a sharp ser-rated knife, cutting about 1/4 inch deep, once down the center of the loaf or across the loaf a few times.

Here are some tips for successful bread:

- Always preheat the oven.
- On a lower oven rack, stagger the loaf pans so they don't touch the sides of the oven or each other. The top of each pan should be level with, or slightly above, the middle of the oven.
- If baking round loaves on a cookie sheet, place the sheet on a rack in the center of the oven.
- To tell if bread is done, tap the crust. If the loaf sounds hollow, it's done.
- Remove loaves from the pans immediately so the sides remain crusty, and place them on wire racks away from drafts to cool.

Cutting Bread

Place loaf on a cutting board or other surface suitable for cutting. Slice with a serrated bread knife or an electric knife.

If bread is very fresh or still warm, turn it on its side to avoid squashing the top.

Go beyond slices: cut round loaves into wedges, or cut slices into fingers or fun shapes with cookie cutters. Homemade Croutons (page 430) or Bread Pudding with Whiskey Sauce (page 182) from the leftover pieces.

Storing Bread

Store breads and rolls in airtight containers in a cool, dry place for up to five days. Breads get stale faster if you store them in the refrigerator, so refrigerate them only if they contain meat, cheese or other perishable ingredients or if the weather is hot and humid.

To freeze bread, wrap it tightly in moistureproof and vaporproof wrap and freeze for up to three months. To thaw, let stand, wrapped, at room temperature for 2 to 3 hours. Or microwave it on Defrost (30% power) for 6 to 8 minutes.

To warm thawed baked bread or rolls, wrap in aluminum foil and reheat in the oven at 350° for 15 to 30 minutes. For a crisp crust, unwrap bread for the last 5 minutes of heating.

Types of Yeast Doughs

There are two kinds of yeast doughs: batter and kneaded. Batter breads are shortcut, no-knead yeast breads. Kneaded breads require more time—as well as energy—for kneading. Both kinds need to rise before baking to let the yeast activate.

Batter dough: Because it contains less flour than kneaded dough, batter dough is stickier and is not shaped. Batter bread has a coarser texture than bread that's kneaded and has a pebbled surface.

Kneaded dough: Kneading develops gluten from the protein in flour and produces an even texture and a smooth, rounded top. If dough isn't kneaded enough, the bread will turn out coarse, heavy, crumbly and dry. To knead, follow the directions in How to Make Yeast Dough, page 65.

You also can use a standard countertop electric mixer with a dough-hook attachment. It mixes dough enough for satisfactory loaves of bread, although they may have slightly less volume than those kneaded by hand. A heavy-duty mixer produces loaves with higher volumes; follow the manufacturer's instructions for the size of recipe the mixer can handle, as well as mixing times. And some recipes prepare dough in a food processor. Check the manufacturer's directions.

For rising kneaded doughs, put the dough in a large bowl greased with shortening, turning the dough to grease all sides. Cover loosely with plastic wrap and set in a warm, draft-free place. Or place the covered bowl on a wire rack over a bowl of warm water. You also can let dough rise in the microwave: Fill a measuring cup with water and microwave until the water boils. Set the bowl of dough in the microwave with the steaming water.

HOW TO MAKE YEAST DOUGH

1. *After the first addition of flour has been beaten in, the dough will be very soft and fall in "sheets" off a rubber spatula.*

2. *The second addition of flour makes the dough stiff enough to knead. Mix in only enough flour so dough leaves the side of the bowl and is easy to handle.*

3. *To knead, fold dough toward you. With the heels of your hands, push the dough away from you with a short rocking motion. Move the dough a quarter turn, and repeat the motion.*

4. *When the dough has been kneaded long enough, it will feel springy and be smooth with some blisters on the surface.*

5. *Place dough in a large bowl greased with shortening, turning dough to grease all sides.*

6. *Dough should rise until it has doubled in size. Test by pressing fingertips about 1/2 inch into dough. If the indentations remain, the dough has risen enough.*

7. *Gently push fist into dough to deflate. Fold dough over and form into a ball. This releases large air bubbles to produce a finer texture in traditional loaves.*

Shaping Dough

There's more than one way to shape the perfect loaf of bread. We think one of the best is shown in How to Shape Traditional Yeast Bread Loaves, below. Use it for shaping Traditional White Bread (page 68), Cinnamon Swirl Bread (page 76), and Honey–Whole Wheat Bread (page 74).

Here is a second method for shaping, although we don't recommend it for Cinnamon Swirl Bread (page 76) because when it's cut, the bread won't have an even, spiral appearance.

1. With your hands or a rolling pin, flatten each half of the dough into a 18 × 9-inch rectangle.

2. Fold the rectangle crosswise into thirds, overlapping the two sides. Flatten or roll the dough into a 9-inch square.

3. Roll up the dough square tightly, beginning at one of the open (unfolded) ends and pressing with your thumbs to seal after each turn, to form a loaf.

4. Firmly pinch the edge of the dough into the roll to seal it.

5. Press each end of the roll with the side of your hand to seal; fold the ends under the loaf.

HOW TO SHAPE TRADITIONAL YEAST BREAD LOAVES

1. *Flatten dough with hands or rolling pin into 18 × 9-inch rectangle.*

2. *Tightly roll dough up toward you, beginning at a 9-inch side.*

3. *Pinch edge of dough into roll to seal.*

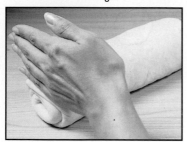

4. *Press each end of roll with side of hand to seal. Fold ends under loaf. Place seam side down in greased pan.*

YEAST BREAD CURES

Great Traditional Yeast Bread and Rolls Are

High and evenly shaped

Uniformly golden or dark brown

Even in texture with no large air holes

Problem	Possible Cause
Not high	• water too hot for yeast
	• too little flour
	• not kneaded enough
	• rising time too short
	• pan too large
Coarse texture	• rising time too long
	• too little flour
	• not kneaded enough
	• oven too cool
Dry and crumbly	• too much flour
	• not kneaded enough
Large air pockets	• dough not rolled tightly when loaf was shaped
Yeasty flavor	• rising time too long
	• temperature too high during rising time

BAKING STONES AND TILES

Breads baked in professional ovens are often placed directly on heavy stones to create a crisp, brown crust. You can do the same in your oven by using a bread stone, pizza stone or unglazed baking tiles available in cookware shops. Let the stone heat in the oven for at least 20 to 30 minutes. (Don't place a cold stone in a hot oven because it may crack; new stones may need to be seasoned by heating at a low temperature once or twice before using it at high temperatures—check the directions that came with your stone.) Sprinkle cornmeal over the stone. Carefully slide the unbaked loaf—just the dough, not dough in a bread pan—directly onto the hot stone by sliding it from a cookie sheet or using a baker's wooden paddle called a *pelle*. After baking, the stone will be very hot; let it cool in the oven before moving it.

Country Loaf (page 69)

Traditional White Bread *Low-Fat*

Prep: 35 min; Rise: 1 hr 50 min; Bake: 30 min
✱ *2 loaves,16 slices each*

6 to 7 cups all-purpose* or bread flour

3 tablespoons sugar

1 tablespoon salt

2 tablespoons shortening

2 packages regular or quick active dry yeast
    (4 1/2 teaspoons)

2 1/4 cups very warm water (120° to 130°)

2 tablespoons butter or stick margarine, melted, if
    desired

1. Mix 3 1/2 cups of the flour, the sugar, salt, shortening and yeast in large bowl. Add warm water. Beat with electric mixer on low speed 1 minute, scraping bowl frequently. Beat on medium speed 1 minute, scraping bowl frequently. Stir in enough remaining flour, 1 cup at a time, to make dough easy to handle.

2. Place dough on lightly floured surface. Knead about 10 minutes or until dough is smooth and springy. Place dough in large bowl greased with shortening, turning dough to grease all sides. Cover bowl loosely with plastic wrap and let rise in warm place 40 to 60 minutes or until double. Dough is ready if indentation remains when touched.

3. Grease bottoms and sides of 2 loaf pans, 8 1/2 × 4 1/2 × 2 1/2 or 9 × 5 × 3 inches, with shortening.

4. Gently push fist into dough to deflate. Divide dough in half. Flatten each half with hands or rolling pin into 18 × 9-inch rectangle on lightly floured surface. Roll dough up tightly, beginning at 9-inch side. Press with thumbs to seal after each turn. Pinch edge of dough into roll to seal. Press each end with side of hand to seal. Fold ends under loaf. (See How to Shape Traditional Yeast Bread Loaves, page 66.) Place seam side down in pan. Brush loaves lightly with butter. Cover loosely with plastic wrap and let rise in warm place 35 to 50 minutes or until double.

5. Move oven rack to low position so that tops of pans will be in center of oven. Heat oven to 425°.

6. Bake 25 to 30 minutes or until loaves are deep golden brown and sound hollow when tapped. Remove from pans to wire rack. Brush loaves with butter; cool.

If using self-rising flour, omit salt.

1 Slice: Calories 95 (Calories from Fat 10); Fat 1g (Saturated 0g); Cholesterol 0mg; Sodium 220mg; Carbohydrate 19g (Dietary Fiber 1g); Protein 3g **% Daily Value:** Vitamin A 0%; Vitamin C 0%; Calcium 0%; Iron 6% **Diet Exchanges:** 1 Starch

Country Loaf *Low-Fat*

Prep: 25 min; Rise: 3 hr; Bake: 40 min
✱ *1 large loaf, 32 slices*

This large, crusty loaf gains a country quality when dusted with flour before baking. Copy the trend in restaurants by serving this bread with a little plate pooled with olive oil and sprinkled with shredded Parmesan cheese and some olives. Be sure to use bread flour because it contains a higher amount of gluten than all-purpose flour.

5 to 5 1/2 cups bread flour
1 teaspoon sugar
1 package regular or quick active dry yeast
    (2 1/4 teaspoons)
2 cups very warm water (120° to 130°)
2 tablespoons olive or vegetable oil
2 teaspoons salt

1. Mix 2 cups of the flour, the sugar and yeast in large bowl. Add warm water. Beat with wire whisk or electric mixer on low speed 1 minute, scraping bowl frequently. Cover tightly with plastic wrap and let stand about 1 hour until bubbly.

2. Stir in oil and salt. Stir in enough remaining flour, 1/2 cup at a time, until a soft, smooth dough forms. Place dough on lightly floured surface. Knead about 10 minutes, adding flour as necessary to keep dough from sticking, until dough is smooth and springy.

3. Place dough in large bowl greased with shortening, turning dough to grease all sides. Cover bowl loosely with plastic wrap and let rise in warm place about 1 hour or until double. Dough is ready if indentation remains when touched.

4. Grease uninsulated cookie sheet with shortening. Place dough on lightly floured surface. Gently shape into an even, round ball, without releasing all of the bubbles in the dough. Stretch sides of dough downward to make a smooth top. Place loaf with smooth side up on cookie sheet. Spray loaf with cool water. Cover loosely with plastic wrap and let rise in warm place 45 to 60 minutes or until almost double.

5. Place square pan, 8 × 8 × 2 or 9 × 9 × 2 inches, on bottom rack of oven; add hot water to pan until about 1/2 inch from the top. Heat oven to 425°.

6. Spray loaf with cool water; sprinkle lightly with flour. Carefully cut three 1/4-inch-deep slashes on top of loaf with sharp serrated knife.

7. Bake 35 to 40 minutes or until loaf is deep golden brown with crisp crust and sounds hollow when tapped. Remove from cookie sheet to wire rack; cool.

1 Slice: Calories 80 (Calories from Fat 10); Fat 1g (Saturated 0g); Cholesterol 0mg; Sodium 150mg; Carbohydrate 17g (Dietary Fiber 1g); Protein 2g **% Daily Value:** Vitamin A 0%; Vitamin C 0%; Calcium 0%; Iron 6% **Diet Exchanges:** 1 Starch

WHOLE WHEAT COUNTRY LOAF: Substitute 2 cups whole wheat flour for 2 cups of the bread flour.

MISTING AND CREATING STEAM

Creating moisture in the oven or on a loaf of bread helps to give the finished loaf a crisp crust. Using a spray bottle with a fine spray, mist the loaf with water a few times during the first 10 minutes of baking. This slows down the formation of the top crust, so the loaf will rise higher as it bakes and form a crisp crust. Or add moisture by placing a metal pan with hot water in the oven with the bread. As the water evaporates in the hot oven, it will dry the surface of the bread so a hard crust is formed.

French Bread *Low-Fat*

Prep: 25 min; Rise: 3 hr 30 min; Chill: 24 hr; Bake: 20 min
✱ *2 loaves, 16 slices each*

The flavor and texture of French bread is developed by making a sponge, which is a bread-dough mixture made with the yeast and some of the flour and water, in the first step and by refrigerating the shaped loaves before baking. Spraying the loaves with water and adding a water pan to the oven help to make a crunchy crust. French Bread is best served the same day it is baked.

1 1/2 cups all-purpose flour*
1 package regular active dry yeast (2 1/4 teaspoons)
1 cup very warm water (120° to 130°)
1 teaspoon salt
1 1/3 to 1 2/3 cups bread flour

1. Mix all-purpose flour and yeast in large bowl. Add warm water. Beat with wire whisk or electric mixer on low speed 1 minute, scraping bowl frequently, until batter is very smooth. Cover tightly with plastic wrap and let stand about 1 hour or until bubbly.

2. Stir in salt and enough bread flour, 1/2 cup at a time, until a soft dough forms. Place dough on lightly floured surface. Knead 5 to 10 minutes or until dough is smooth and springy (dough will be soft). Place dough in large bowl greased with shortening, turning dough to grease all sides. Cover bowl loosely with plastic wrap and let rise in warm place 1 hour to 1 hour 15 minutes or until double. Dough is ready if indentation remains when touched.

3. Grease uninsulated cookie sheet with shortening. Turn dough out of bowl onto lightly floured surface, keeping it in an oval-shaped mound. Sprinkle top of dough with flour. Press straight down with a straight-edged knife lengthwise on dough to divide it into 2 equal parts (the parts will be elongated in shape). Gently shape each part into a narrow loaf, about 16 inches long, stretching the top of the loaf slightly to make it smooth. Place loaves, smooth sides up, about 4 inches apart on cookie sheet.

4. Cover loaves loosely, but airtight, with plastic wrap. (Loaves will expand slightly in the refrigerator.) Refrigerate at least 4 hours but no longer than 24 hours. (This step can be omitted, but refrigerating develops the flavor and texture of the bread. If omitted, continue with next step.)

5. Uncover loaves and spray with cool water; let loaves rise in a warm place about 1 hour or until refrigerated loaves have come to room temperature.

6. Place square pan, 8 × 8 × 2 or 9 × 9 × 2 inches, on bottom rack of oven; add hot water to pan until about 1/2 inch from the top. Heat oven to 475°.

7. Carefully cut 1/4-inch-deep slashes diagonally across loaves at 2-inch intervals with sharp serrated knife. Spray loaves with cool water. Place loaves in oven and spray again.

8. Reduce oven temperature to 450°. Bake 18 to 20 minutes or until loaves are deep golden with crisp crust and sound hollow when tapped. Remove from cookie sheet to wire rack; cool.

*Do not use self-rising flour.

1 Slice: Calories 40 (Calories from Fat 0); Fat 0g (Saturated 0g); Cholesterol 0mg; Sodium 75mg; Carbohydrate 9g (Dietary Fiber 0g); Protein 1g **% Daily Value:** Vitamin A 0%; Vitamin C 0%; Calcium 0%; Iron 2% **Diet Exchanges:** 1/2 Starch

Carefully cut 1/4-inch-deep slashes on top of loaf with sharp serrated knife.

Sun-Dried Tomato and Olive Bread *Low-Fat*

Prep: 25 min; Rise: 3 hr; Bake: 20 min
✻ *2 loaves, 16 slices each*

The tart flavor of sun-dried tomatoes combined with the salty flavor of Greek Kalamata olives distinguish this bread. Shape the dough either into baguettes or rounds.

3 1/2 to 4 cups bread flour
1 tablespoon sugar
1 package regular or quick active dry yeast
   (2 1/4 teaspoons)
1 1/4 cups very warm water (120° to 130°)
1/4 cup chopped sun-dried tomatoes (not oil-packed)
1/4 cup boiling water
1 teaspoon dried basil leaves
2 tablespoons olive or vegetable oil
1 teaspoon salt
1/2 cup Kalamata olives, pitted, cut into fourths and
   very well drained

1. Mix 1 1/2 cups of the flour, the sugar and yeast in large bowl. Add warm water. Beat with wire whisk or electric mixer on low speed 1 minute, scraping bowl frequently. Cover tightly with plastic wrap and let stand about 1 hour until bubbly.

2. Mix sun-dried tomatoes and boiling water in small bowl. Let stand until mixture is completely cooled and tomatoes are rehydrated.

3. Pour tomatoes with the liquid over batter in bowl. Stir in basil, oil and salt. Stir in enough remaining flour, 1/2 cup at a time, until a soft dough forms. Let stand 15 minutes.

4. Place dough on lightly floured surface. Knead 5 to 10 minutes, adding flour as necessary to keep dough from sticking, until dough is smooth and springy. Place dough in large bowl greased with shortening, turning dough to grease all sides. Blot chopped olives with paper towel to dry; sprinkle over dough. Cover bowl loosely with plastic wrap and let rise in warm place about 1 hour or until double. Dough is ready if indentation remains when touched.

5. Grease uninsulated cookie sheet with shortening. Place dough on lightly floured surface. Knead until olives are worked into dough. Divide dough in half. Sprinkle top of dough with flour. Shape each half into a round or 12-inch baguette-shaped loaf. Place dough with smooth side up on cookie sheet. Cover loosely with plastic wrap lightly sprayed with cooking spray and let rise in warm place 45 to 60 minutes or until almost double.

6. Place square pan, 8 × 8 × 2 or 9 × 9 × 2 inches, on bottom rack of oven; add hot water to pan until about 1/2 inch from the top. Heat oven to 475°.

7. Carefully cut three or four 1/4-inch-deep slashes on tops of loaves with sharp serrated knife. Spray loaves with cool water. Place loaves in oven and spray again.

8. Bake 10 minutes. Reduce oven temperature to 400°. Bake about 10 minutes longer or until loaves are deep golden brown with crisp crust and sound hollow when tapped. Remove from cookie sheet to wire rack; cool.

1 Slice: Calories 60 (Calories from Fat 10); Fat 1g (Saturated 0g); Cholesterol 0mg; Sodium 100mg; Carbohydrate 12g (Dietary Fiber 1g); Protein 2g **% Daily Value:** Vitamin A 0%; Vitamin C 0%; Calcium 0%; Iron 4% **Diet Exchanges:** 1 Starch

Asiago Bread

Asiago Bread *Low-Fat*

Prep: 25 min; Rise: 3 hr; Bake: 35 min
✳ *1 large loaf, 24 slices*

When sliced, this large, flour-dusted loaf reveals cheese-lined pockets. Any full-flavored, firm, aged cheese works well. It's a perfect bread for a country-style dinner as well as toasted for breakfast.

3 1/2 to 3 3/4 cups bread flour
1 teaspoon sugar
1 package regular or quick active dry yeast
    (2 1/4 teaspoons)
1 1/4 cups very warm water (120° to 130°)
2 tablespoons olive or vegetable oil
2 teaspoons dried rosemary or thyme leaves, if desired
1 teaspoon salt
1 cup diced Asiago, Swiss or other firm cheese
1/4 cup diced Asiago, Swiss cheese or other firm
    cheese

1. Mix 1 1/2 cups of the flour, the sugar and yeast in large bowl. Add warm water. Beat with wire whisk or electric mixer on low speed 1 minute, scraping bowl frequently. Cover tightly with plastic wrap and let stand about 1 hour or until bubbly.

2. Stir in oil, rosemary and salt. Stir in enough remaining flour, 1/2 cup at a time, until a soft, smooth dough forms. Let stand 15 minutes.

3. Place dough on lightly floured surface. Knead 5 to 10 minutes or until dough is smooth and springy. Knead in 1 cup cheese. Place dough in large bowl greased with shortening, turning dough to grease all sides. Cover bowl tightly with plastic wrap and let rise in warm place 45 to 60 minutes or until double. Dough is ready if indentation remains when touched.

4. Lightly grease uninsulated cookie sheet with shortening. Place dough on lightly floured surface. Gently shape into football-shaped loaf, about 12 inches long, by stretching sides of dough downward to make a smooth top. Place loaf with smooth side up on cookie sheet. Coat loaf generously with flour. Cover loosely with plastic wrap and let rise in warm place 45 to 60 minutes or until almost double.

5. Place square pan, 8 × 8 × 2 or 9 × 9 × 2 inches, on bottom rack of oven; add hot water to pan until about 1/2 inch from the top. Heat oven to 450°.

6. Spray loaf with cool water; sprinkle with flour. Carefully cut 1/2-inch-deep slash lengthwise down center of loaf with sharp serrated knife. Sprinkle 1/4 cup cheese into slash.

7. Bake 10 minutes. Reduce oven temperature to 400°. Bake 20 to 25 minutes longer or until loaf is deep golden and sounds hollow when tapped. Remove from cookie sheet to wire rack; cool.

1 Slice: Calories 105 (Calories from Fat 25); Fat 3g (Saturated 1g); Cholesterol 5mg; Sodium 115mg; Carbohydrate 16g (Dietary Fiber 1g); Protein 4g **% Daily Value:** Vitamin A 0%; Vitamin C 0%; Calcium 6%; Iron 4% **Diet Exchanges:** 1 Starch, 1/2 Fat

Cinnamon-Raisin-Walnut Wheat Bread

Prep: 25 min; Rise: 2 hr; Bake: 40 min
✳ *1 large loaf, 24 slices*

Cinnamon enhances the whole wheat flavor in this country-style loaf, and raisins and walnuts add sweetness and crunch. It makes wonderful bread to use for grilled cheese sandwiches and is a perfect accompaniment to fruit salad or potato soup.

2 cups whole wheat flour
1 package regular or quick active dry yeast
   (2 1/4 teaspoons)
2 cups very warm water (120° to 130°)
2 tablespoons packed brown sugar
2 tablespoons olive or vegetable oil
2 teaspoons ground cinnamon
2 teaspoons salt
2 to 2 1/2 cups bread flour
1 cup coarsely chopped walnuts
1 cup raisins
Cornmeal

1. Mix whole wheat flour and yeast in large bowl. Add warm water. Beat with wire whisk or electric mixer on low speed 1 minute, scraping bowl frequently. Cover tightly with plastic wrap and let stand 15 minutes.

2. Stir in brown sugar, oil, cinnamon, salt and 1 cup of the bread flour; beat until smooth. Stir in enough remaining bread flour, 1/2 cup at a time, until a soft, smooth dough forms.

3. Place dough on lightly floured surface. Knead 5 to 10 minutes or until dough is smooth and springy. Knead in walnuts and raisins. Place dough in large bowl greased with shortening, turning dough to grease all sides. Cover bowl loosely with plastic wrap and let rise in warm place about 1 hour or until double. Dough is ready if indentation remains when touched.

4. Grease uninsulated cookie sheet with shortening; sprinkle with cornmeal. Place dough on lightly floured surface. Gently shape into an even, round ball, without releasing all of the bubbles in the dough. Stretch sides of dough downward to make a smooth top. Place loaf with smooth side up on cookie sheet. Spray loaf with cool water. Cover loosely with plastic wrap and let rise in warm place 45 to 60 minutes or until almost double.

5. Heat oven to 375°. Spray loaf with cool water. Carefully cut 1/4-inch-deep slashes in tic-tac-toe pattern on top of loaf with sharp serrated knife.

6. Place in oven; spray with cool water. Bake 35 to 40 minutes or until loaf is dark brown and sounds hollow when tapped. Remove from cookie sheet to wire rack; cool.

1 Slice: Calories 150 (Calories from Fat 45); Fat 5g (Saturated 1g); Cholesterol 0mg; Sodium 200mg; Carbohydrate 24g (Dietary Fiber 2g); Protein 4g **% Daily Value:** Vitamin A 0%; Vitamin C 0%; Calcium 2%; Iron 6% **Diet Exchanges:** 1 Starch, 1/2 Fruit, 1/2 Fat

APPLE-PECAN BREAD: Substitute chopped dried apples for the raisins and chopped pecans for the walnuts.

FRUIT AND ALMOND BREAD: Omit cinnamon. Substitute diced dried fruit and raisin mixture for the raisins and chopped almonds for the walnuts.

Gently shape by stretching sides of dough downward to make a smooth top.

Honey–Whole Wheat Bread *Low-Fat*

Prep: 35 min; Rise: 1 hr 50 min; Bake: 45 min

✱ *2 loaves, 16 slices each*

3 cups whole wheat flour
1/3 cup honey
1/4 cup shortening
1 tablespoon salt
2 packages regular or quick active dry yeast
   (4 1/2 teaspoons)
2 1/4 cups very warm water (120° to 130°)
3 to 4 cups all-purpose* or bread flour
Butter or stick margarine, melted, if desired

1. Mix whole wheat flour, honey, shortening, salt and yeast in large bowl. Add warm water. Beat with electric mixer on low speed 1 minute, scraping bowl frequently. Beat on medium speed 1 minute, scraping bowl frequently. Stir in enough all-purpose flour, 1 cup at a time, to make dough easy to handle.

2. Place dough on lightly floured surface. Knead about 10 minutes or until dough is smooth and springy. Place dough in large bowl greased with shortening, turning dough to grease all sides. Cover bowl loosely with plastic wrap and let rise in warm place 40 to 60 minutes or until double. Dough is ready if indentation remains when touched.

3. Grease bottoms and sides of 2 loaf pans, 8 1/2 × 4 1/2 × 2 1/2 or 9 × 5 × 3 inches, with shortening.

4. Gently push fist into dough to deflate. Divide dough in half. Flatten each half with hands or rolling pin into 18 × 9-inch rectangle on lightly floured surface. Roll dough up tightly, beginning at 9-inch side. Press with thumbs to seal after each turn. Pinch edge of dough into roll to seal. Press each end with side of hand to seal. Fold ends under loaf. (See How to Shape Traditional Yeast Bread Loaves, page 66.) Place seam side down in pan. Brush loaves lightly with butter. Cover loosely with plastic wrap and let rise in warm place 35 to 50 minutes or until double.

5. Move oven rack to low position so that tops of pans will be in center of oven. Heat oven to 375°.

6. Bake 40 to 45 minutes or until loaves are deep golden brown and sound hollow when tapped. Remove from pans to wire rack. Brush loaves with butter; cool.

*If using self-rising flour, decrease salt to 1 teaspoon.

1 Slice: Calories 100 (Calories from Fat 20); Fat 2g (Saturated 0g); Cholesterol 0mg; Sodium 220mg; Carbohydrate 20g (Dietary Fiber 2g); Protein 3g **% Daily Value:** Vitamin A 0%; Vitamin C 0%; Calcium 0%; Iron 6% **Diet Exchanges:** 1 1/2 Starch

SUNFLOWER-HERB WHOLE WHEAT BREAD: Add 1 tablespoon dried basil leaves and 2 teaspoons dried thyme leaves with the salt. Stir in 1 cup unsalted sunflower nuts with the all-purpose flour.

Dark Pumpernickel Bread *Low-Fat*

Prep: 30 min; Rise: 2 hr; Bake: 30 min ✼ *1 loaf, 14 slices*

The instant coffee gives this bread a darker color but does not add a coffee flavor.

2 packages regular or quick active dry yeast
   (4 1/2 teaspoons)
1 cup warm water (105° to 115°)
1 teaspoon instant coffee (dry)
1 teaspoon salt
1 tablespoon butter or stick margarine, softened*
3 tablespoons dark molasses
2 1/2 to 3 cups bread flour or all-purpose flour**
2 tablespoons baking cocoa
1 tablespoon caraway seed, if desired
3/4 cup rye flour
Cornmeal
Butter or stick margarine, melted, if desired

1. Dissolve yeast in warm water in large bowl. Stir in coffee, salt, 1 tablespoon butter and the molasses. Stir in 1 1/2 cups of the bread flour. Beat with electric mixer on low speed 1 minute, scraping bowl frequently. Beat on medium speed 1 minute, scraping bowl frequently. Stir in cocoa, caraway seed, rye flour and enough remaining bread flour to make dough easy to handle.

2. Place dough on lightly floured surface. Cover loosely with plastic wrap and let rest 15 minutes. Knead 5 to 10 minutes or until smooth. Place dough in large bowl greased with shortening, turning dough to grease all sides. Cover bowl loosely with plastic wrap and let rise in warm place about 1 hour or until double. Dough is ready if indentation remains when touched.

3. Grease cookie sheet with shortening; sprinkle with cornmeal. Gently push fist into dough to deflate. Shape dough into a round, slightly flat loaf. Place on cookie sheet. Cover loosely with plastic wrap lightly sprayed with cooking spray and let rise in warm place 1 hour.

4. Heat oven to 375°.

5. Bake 25 to 30 minutes or until loaf sounds hollow when tapped. Remove from cookie sheet to wire rack. Brush with butter; cool.

*Spreads with at least 65% vegetable oil can be used (page 45).
**If using self-rising flour, omit salt.

1 Slice: Calories 115 (Calories from Fat 10); Fat 1g (Saturated 1g); Cholesterol 5mg; Sodium 180mg; Carbohydrate 26g (Dietary Fiber 2g); Protein 3g **% Daily Value:** Vitamin A 0%; Vitamin C 0%; Calcium 2%; Iron 8% **Diet Exchanges:** 1 1/2 Starch

Bread Machine Directions: Use ingredients listed above—except use 2 1/2 cups bread flour and 1 cup plus 2 tablespoons room-temperature water. Measure carefully, placing all ingredients except cornmeal and melted butter in bread machine pan in the order recommended by the manufacturer. Select Dough/Manual cycle. Remove dough from pan. Continue with step 3 for shaping, rising and baking. Rising time may be shorter because dough will be warm when removed from bread machine.

SWEDISH RYE BREAD: Omit instant coffee, baking cocoa and caraway seed. Add 2 teaspoons anise seed or fennel seed and 2 teaspoons grated orange peel with the rye flour.

Rich Egg Bread *Low-Fat*

Prep: 30 min; Rise: 2 hr; Bake: 35 min ✱ *1 loaf, 16 slices*

3 to 3 1/4 cups all-purpose* or bread flour

1/4 cup sugar

1 1/2 teaspoons salt

1 package regular or quick active dry yeast
    (2 1/4 teaspoons)

1 cup very warm water (120° to 130°)

2 tablespoons vegetable oil

1 large egg

Butter or stick margarine, melted, if desired

1. Mix 1 1/2 cups of the flour, the sugar, salt and yeast in large bowl. Add warm water and oil. Beat with electric mixer on low speed 1 minute, scraping bowl frequently. Beat on medium speed 1 minute, scraping bowl frequently. Add egg; beat until smooth. Mix in enough remaining flour to make dough easy to handle.

2. Place dough on lightly floured surface. Knead about 10 minutes or until dough is smooth and springy. Place dough in large bowl greased with shortening, turning dough to grease all sides. (At this point, dough can be refrigerated up to 24 hours.) Cover bowl loosely with plastic wrap and let rise in warm place about 1 hour or until double. Dough is ready if indentation remains when touched.

3. Grease bottom and sides of loaf pan, 9 × 5 × 3 or 8 1/2 × 4 1/2 × 2 1/2 inches. Gently push fist into dough to deflate. Flatten dough with hands or rolling pin into 18 × 9-inch rectangle. Roll up tightly, beginning at 9-inch side. Pinch edge of dough into roll to seal. Press each end with side of hand to seal; fold ends under loaf. (See How to Shape Traditional Yeast Bread Loaves, page 66.) Place loaf, seam side down, in pan. Cover loosely with plastic wrap lightly sprayed with cooking spray and let rise in warm place about 1 hour or until double.

4. Move oven rack to low position so that top of pan will be in center of oven. Heat oven to 375°. Bake 30 to 35 minutes or until loaf is deep golden brown and sounds hollow when tapped. Remove from pan to wire rack. Brush loaf with butter; cool.

If using self-rising flour, omit salt.

1 Slice: Calories 110 (Calories from Fat 20); Fat 2g (Saturated 0g); Cholesterol 15mg; Sodium 230mg; Carbohydrate 21g (Dietary Fiber 1g); Protein 3g **% Daily Value:** Vitamin A 0%; Vitamin C 0%; Calcium 0%; Iron 6% **Diet Exchanges:** 1 1/2 Starch

Bread Machine Directions: Use ingredients listed above—except use 3 1/4 cups bread flour and room-temperature water. Measure carefully, placing all ingredients except butter in bread machine pan in the order recommended by the manufacturer. Select Dough/Manual cycle; do not use delay cycle. Remove dough from pan. Continue with step 3 for shaping, rising and baking. Rising time may be shorter because dough will be warm when removed from bread machine.

CHALLAH BRAID: Make dough as directed. Lightly grease cookie sheet with shortening. After pushing fist into dough, divide into 3 equal parts. Roll each part into 14-inch rope. Place ropes close together on cookie sheet. Braid ropes gently and loosely; do not stretch. Fasten ends; tuck ends under braid securely. Brush with vegetable oil. Cover loosely with plastic wrap and let rise in warm place 40 to 50 minutes or until double. Heat oven to 375°. Mix 1 egg yolk and 2 tablespoons water; brush over braid. Sprinkle with poppy seed. Bake 25 to 30 minutes or until golden brown.

CINNAMON SWIRL BREAD: Make dough as directed, except stir in 1/2 cup raisins with the second addition of flour if desired. After rolling dough into rectangle, brush with vegetable oil. Mix 1/4 cup sugar and 1 1/2 teaspoons ground cinnamon. Sprinkle evenly over dough. Roll up, let rise and bake as directed.

Sourdough Bread *Low-Fat*

Prep: 4 days; Rise: 1 hr 45 min; Bake: 40 min
✱ *2 loaves, 12 slices each*

1 1/2 cups Sourdough Starter (right)
4 1/4 to 5 1/4 cups bread flour
1 package regular or quick active dry yeast
    (2 1/4 teaspoons)
1 teaspoon salt
1 cup very warm water (120° to 130°)
Cornmeal

1. Make Sourdough Starter 2 to 4 days before making bread. Starter should be the consistency of thin pancake batter; if necessary, stir in enough water to achieve this consistency before measuring. For accuracy, stir starter before measuring. Measure out 1 1/2 cups cold starter, and bring to room temperature (the starter will expand as it warms up).

2. Mix 2 cups of the flour, the yeast (dry) and salt in large bowl. Gradually beat in starter and warm water with electric mixer on low speed. Beat on medium speed 2 minutes, scraping bowl occasionally. Beat on high speed 2 minutes, scraping bowl occasionally. Stir in enough remaining flour to make a soft dough.

3. Place dough on lightly floured surface. Knead about 8 minutes or until smooth. Place dough in large bowl greased with shortening, turning dough to grease all sides. Cover bowl loosely with plastic wrap and let rise in warm place 30 to 60 minutes or until double. Dough is ready if indentation remains when touched.

4. Grease large cookie sheet with shortening; sprinkle with cornmeal. Gently push fist into dough to deflate. Divide dough in half.* Roll each half into 12 × 9-inch rectangle on lightly floured surface. Roll up tightly, beginning at 12-inch side. Pinch seams and ends to seal. Taper ends by gently rolling back and forth. Place loaves, seam sides down, on cookie sheet. Cover loosely with plastic wrap lightly sprayed with cooking spray and let rise in warm place 30 to 45 minutes or until double.

5. Heat oven to 400°. Carefully cut 1/4-inch-deep slashes diagonally across top of each loaf at 2-inch intervals with sharp serrated knife. (For crispy crust, spray loaves with water just before baking and every 5 minutes during the first 10 minutes of baking.) Bake 35 to 40 minutes or until golden brown. Remove from cookie sheet to wire rack; cool.

*To make round loaves, shape each half of dough into 5-inch ball. Continue as directed, except cut 4 slashes, 1/4 inch deep, in crisscross pattern on top of each loaf. Bake as directed, spraying with water for crispy crust if desired.

Sourdough Starter

3 1/2 cups bread flour or all-purpose flour**
1 package regular or quick active dry yeast
    (2 1/4 teaspoons)
2 cups warm water (105° to 115°)

Mix flour and yeast (dry) in 4-quart or larger container. Gradually beat in water until smooth. Cover loosely with plastic wrap and let stand in warm place 2 to 4 days or until bubbly and sour smelling. Transfer to 2-quart or larger plastic container with tight-fitting lid. Refrigerate until ready to use.

TO KEEP STARTER ACTIVE: Once a week, beat in 1 tablespoon bread flour or all-purpose flour and 1 tablespoon warm water until smooth. Cover loosely and let stand in warm place 12 to 14 hours or until bubbly. Cover tightly; refrigerate until ready to use.

TO REPLENISH STARTER: For each 1 1/2 cups of starter used, beat in 1 1/3 cups bread flour or all-purpose flour and 1 1/3 cups warm water until smooth. Cover loosely and let stand in warm place 12 to 24 hours or until bubbly. Cover tightly; refrigerate until ready to use.

**Do not use self-rising flour.

1 Slice: Calories 100 (Calories from Fat 0); Fat 0g (Saturated 0g); Cholesterol 0mg; Sodium 100mg; Carbohydrate 23g (Dietary Fiber 1g); Protein 3g **% Daily Value:** Vitamin A 0%; Vitamin C 0%; Calcium 0%; Iron 8% **Diet Exchanges:** 1 1/2 Starch

Focaccia

Focaccia *Low-Fat*

Prep: 30 min; Rise: 1 hr; Bake: 20 min
✱ *2 breads, 12 slices each*

This bread is sometimes referred to as Italian flat-bread. The dough is versatile and makes wonderful breadsticks (far right) as well as loaves. Serve with a bit of olive oil and shredded Parmesan for dipping.

2 1/2 to 3 cups all-purpose* or bread flour
2 tablespoons chopped fresh or 1 tablespoon dried
    rosemary leaves, crumbled
1 tablespoon sugar
1 teaspoon salt
1 package regular or quick active dry yeast
    (2 1/4 teaspoons)
3 tablespoons olive or vegetable oil
1 cup very warm water (120° to 130°)
2 tablespoons olive or vegetable oil
1/4 cup grated Parmesan cheese

1. Mix 1 cup of the flour, the rosemary, sugar, salt and yeast in large bowl. Add 3 tablespoons oil and the warm water. Beat with electric mixer on medium speed 3 minutes, scraping bowl frequently. Stir in enough remaining flour until dough is soft and leaves sides of bowl.

2. Place dough on lightly floured surface. Knead 5 to 8 minutes or until dough is smooth and springy. Place dough in large bowl greased with shortening, turning dough to grease all sides. Cover bowl loosely with plastic wrap and let rise in warm place about 30 minutes or until almost double. Dough is ready if indentation remains when touched.

3. Grease 2 cookie sheets or 12-inch pizza pans with small amount of oil.

4. Gently push fist into dough to deflate. Divide dough in half. Shape each half into a flattened 10-inch round on cookie sheet. Cover loosely with plastic wrap lightly sprayed with cooking spray and let rise in warm place about 30 minutes or until double.

5. Heat oven to 400°. Gently make depressions about 2 inches apart in dough with fingers. Carefully brush with 2 tablespoons oil; sprinkle with cheese. Bake 15 to 20 minutes or until golden brown. Serve warm or cool.

Do not use self-rising flour.

Gently make depressions about 2 inches apart in dough with fingers.

1 Slice: Calories 80 (Calories from Fat 25); Fat 3g (Saturated 1g); Cholesterol 0mg; Sodium 115mg; Carbohydrate 11g (Dietary Fiber 0g); Protein 2g **% Daily Value:** Vitamin A 0%; Vitamin C 0%; Calcium 0%; Iron 4% **Diet Exchanges:** 1 Starch

Bread Machine Directions: Use ingredients listed above, except use 3 cups bread flour and room-temperature water. Measure carefully, placing all ingredients except 2 tablespoons olive oil and the Parmesan cheese in bread machine pan in the order recommended by the manufacturer. Select Dough/Manual cycle. Remove dough from pan. Continue with step 3. as directed for shaping, rising and baking. Rising time may be shorter because dough will be warm when removed from bread machine.

CARAMELIZED ONION FOCACCIA: Make dough as directed above, except omit rosemary, 2 tablespoons oil and Parmesan cheese. Make onion topping: Heat 1/3 cup olive or vegetable oil in nonstick 10-inch skillet over medium heat. Stir in 4 cups thinly sliced onions (4 medium onions) and 4 cloves garlic, finely chopped, to coat with oil. Cook uncovered 10 minutes, stirring every 3 to 4 minutes. Reduce heat to medium-low. Cook 30 to 40 minutes longer, stirring well every 5 minutes, until onions are light golden brown (onions will shrink during cooking). Continue as directed above, except do not brush dough with oil; after second rising, carefully spread onion mixture over breads. Bake as directed.

BREADSTICKS: Make dough as directed above, except omit 2 tablespoons oil. After kneading, cover loosely with plastic wrap and let rest 30 minutes. Grease 2 cookie sheets with shortening; sprinkle with cornmeal if desired. Divide dough into 12 equal pieces. (To divide, cut dough in half, then continue cutting pieces in half until there are 12 pieces.) Roll and shape each piece into 12-inch rope, sprinkling with flour if dough is too sticky. Place 1/2 inch apart on cookie sheets. Sprinkle with grated Parmesan cheese or coarse salt if desired. Cover loosely with plastic wrap and let rise in warm place about 20 minutes or until almost double. Heat oven to 425°. Bake 10 to 12 minutes or until golden brown.

Dinner Rolls

Prep: 30 min; Rise: 1 hr 30 min; Bake: 15 min ✳ 15 rolls

3 1/2 to 3 3/4 cups all-purpose flour* or bread flour
1/4 cup sugar
1/4 cup butter or stick margarine, softened**
1 teaspoon salt
1 package regular or quick active dry yeast
    (2 1/4 teaspoons)
1/2 cup very warm water (120° to 130°)
1/2 cup very warm milk (120° to 130°)
1 large egg
Butter or stick margarine, melted, if desired

1. Mix 2 cups of the flour, the sugar, 1/4 cup butter, salt and yeast in large bowl. Add warm water, warm milk and egg. Beat with electric mixer on low speed 1 minute, scraping bowl frequently. Beat on medium speed 1 minute, scraping bowl frequently. Stir in enough remaining flour to make dough easy to handle.

2. Place dough on lightly floured surface. Knead about 5 minutes or until dough is smooth and springy. Place dough in large bowl greased with shortening, turning dough to grease all sides. Cover bowl loosely with plastic wrap and let rise in warm place about 1 hour or until double. Dough is ready if indentation remains when touched.

3. Grease rectangular pan, 13 × 9 × 2 inches, with shortening.

4. Gently push fist into dough to deflate. Divide dough into 15 equal pieces. Shape each piece into a ball; place in pan. Brush with butter. Cover loosely with plastic wrap and let rise in warm place about 30 minutes or until double.

5. Heat oven to 375°.

6. Bake 12 to 15 minutes or until golden brown. Serve warm or cool.

*If using self-rising flour, omit salt.
**Spreads with at least 65% vegetable oil can be used (page 45).

1 Roll: Calories 150 (Calories from Fat 35); Fat 4g (Saturated 2g); Cholesterol 25mg; Sodium 190mg; Carbohydrate 26g (Dietary Fiber 1g); Protein 4g **% Daily Value:** Vitamin A 2%; Vitamin C 0%; Calcium 2%; Iron 8% **Diet Exchanges:** 2 Starch

Shape each piece of dough into a ball; place in pan.

Bread Machine Directions: Use ingredients listed above, except use 3 1/4 cups bread flour, 2 tablespoons softened butter, 3 teaspoons yeast and 1 cup room-temperature water for the warm water; omit milk. Measure carefully, placing all ingredients except melted butter in bread machine pan in the order recommended by the manufacturer. Select Dough/Manual cycle; do not use delay cycle. Remove dough from pan. Continue as directed for shaping, rising and baking. Rising time may be shorter because dough will be warm when removed from bread machine.

DO-AHEAD DINNER ROLLS: After placing rolls in pan, cover tightly with aluminum foil and refrigerate 4 to 24 hours. Before baking, remove from refrigerator; remove foil and cover loosely with plastic wrap. Let rise in warm place about 2 hours or until double. If some rising has occurred in the refrigerator, rising time may be less than 2 hours. Bake as directed.

CLOVERLEAF ROLLS: Grease bottoms and sides of 24 medium muffin cups, 2 1/2 × 1 1/4 inches, with shortening. Make dough as directed, except after pushing fist into dough, divide dough into 72 equal pieces. (To divide, cut dough in half, then continue cutting pieces in half until there are 72 pieces.) Shape each piece into a ball. Place 3 balls in each muffin cup. Brush with butter. Cover loosely with plastic wrap and let rise in warm place about 30 minutes or until double. Bake as directed. 24 rolls.

Shape each piece of dough into a ball. Place 3 balls in each muffin cup.

CRESCENT ROLLS: Grease cookie sheet with shortening. Make dough as directed, except after pushing fist into dough, cut dough in half. Roll each half into 12-inch circle on floured surface. Spread with softened butter. Cut each circle into 16 wedges. Roll up each wedge, beginning at rounded edge. Place rolls, with points underneath, on cookie sheet and curve slightly. Brush with butter. Cover loosely with plastic wrap and let rise in warm place about 30 minutes or until double. Bake as directed. 32 rolls.

Cut each circle into 16 wedges. Roll up each wedge, beginning at rounded edge. Place rolls, with points underneath, on cookie sheet and curve slightly.

Herb Buns *Low-Fat*

Prep: 30 min; Rise: 1 hr; Bake: 15 min ✱ 12 buns

1 package regular or quick active dry yeast
   (2 1/4 teaspoons)
1 cup warm water (105° to 115°)
1 teaspoon caraway seed
1/2 teaspoon dried sage leaves
1/4 teaspoon ground nutmeg
2 tablespoons sugar
1/2 teaspoon salt
1 large egg
2 tablespoons shortening
2 1/4 cups all-purpose flour*

1. Grease bottoms and sides of 12 medium muffin cups, 2 1/2 × 1 1/4 inches. Dissolve yeast in warm water in large bowl. Stir in caraway seed, sage, nutmeg, sugar, salt, egg, shortening and 1 cup of the flour. Beat with electric mixer on low speed 1 minute, scraping bowl frequently.

2. Stir in remaining 1 1/4 cups flour until smooth. Scrape batter from side of bowl. Cover loosely with plastic wrap and let rise in warm place about 30 minutes or until double.

3. Stir down batter by beating about 25 strokes. Spoon into muffin cups, filling each about half full. Cover loosely with plastic wrap and let rise 20 to 30 minutes or until batter almost reaches tops of cups.

4. Heat oven to 400°.

5. Bake about 15 minutes or until golden brown. Serve warm or cool.

*If using self-rising flour, omit salt.

1 Bun: Calories 115 (Calories from Fat 25); Fat 3g (Saturated 1g); Cholesterol 15mg; Sodium 105mg; Carbohydrate 20g (Dietary Fiber 1g); Protein 3g **% Daily Value:** Vitamin A 0%; Vitamin C 0%; Calcium 0%; Iron 6% **Diet Exchanges:** 1 Starch, 1/2 Fat

Caramel Sticky Rolls

Prep: 40 min; Rise: 2 hr; Bake: 35 min ✻ 15 rolls

3 1/2 to 4 cups all-purpose* or bread flour
1/3 cup sugar
1 teaspoon salt
2 packages regular or quick active dry yeast
 (4 1/2 teaspoons)
1 cup very warm milk (120° to 130°)
1/4 cup butter or stick margarine, softened**
1 large egg
Caramel Topping (right)
1 cup pecan halves (4 ounces), if desired
Filling (right)
2 tablespoons butter or stick margarine, softened**

1. Mix 2 cups of the flour, the sugar, salt and yeast in large bowl. Add warm milk, 1/4 cup butter and the egg. Beat with electric mixer on low speed 1 minute, scraping bowl frequently. Beat on medium speed 1 minute, scraping bowl frequently. Stir in enough remaining flour to make dough easy to handle.

2. Place dough on lightly floured surface. Knead about 5 minutes or until dough is smooth and springy. Place dough in large bowl greased with shortening, turning dough to grease all sides. Cover bowl loosely with plastic wrap and let rise in warm place about 1 hour 30 minutes or until double. Dough is ready if indentation remains when touched.

3. Make Caramel Topping. Pour into ungreased rectangular pan, 13 × 9 × 2 inches. Sprinkle with pecan halves. Make Filling.

4. Gently push fist into dough to deflate. Flatten dough with hands or rolling pin into 15 × 10-inch rectangle on lightly floured surface. Spread with 2 tablespoons butter; sprinkle with Filling. Roll rectangle up tightly, beginning at 15-inch side. Pinch edge of dough into roll to seal. Stretch and shape until even. Cut roll into fifteen 1-inch slices with dental floss or a sharp serrated knife. Place slightly apart in pan. Cover loosely with plastic wrap and let rise in warm place about 30 minutes or until double.

5. Heat oven to 350°.

6. Bake 30 to 35 minutes or until golden brown. Let stand 2 to 3 minutes; immediately turn upside down onto heatproof tray or serving plate. Let stand 1 minute so caramel can drizzle over rolls; remove pan. Serve warm.

Caramel Topping

1 cup packed brown sugar
1/2 cup butter or stick margarine, softened**
1/4 cup corn syrup

Heat brown sugar and butter to boiling in 2-quart saucepan, stirring constantly; remove from heat. Stir in corn syrup.

Filling

1/2 cup chopped pecans or raisins, if desired
1/4 cup granulated or packed brown sugar
1 teaspoon ground cinnamon

Mix all ingredients.

If using self-rising flour, omit salt.
**Spreads with at least 65% vegetable oil can be used (page 45).*

1 Roll: Calories 335 (Calories from Fat 115); Fat 13g (Saturated 6g); Cholesterol 40mg; Sodium 240mg; Carbohydrate 51g (Dietary Fiber 1g); Protein 5g **% Daily Value:** Vitamin A 8%; Vitamin C 0%; Calcium 4%; Iron 10% **Diet Exchanges:** 2 Starch, 1 Fruit, 2 1/2 Fat

Lighter Caramel Sticky Rolls: For 4 grams of fat and 220 calories per serving, make as directed, except omit Caramel Topping and pecan halves. Line pan with aluminum foil; spray with cooking spray. Drizzle 1 cup caramel ice-cream topping over foil (heat topping slightly if it is stiff). Continue as directed in steps 4, 5 and 6, except omit chopped pecans from Filling.

Bread Machine Directions: Use ingredients listed above, except use 3 1/2 cups bread flour, 1 1/2 teaspoons yeast and 1 cup room-temperature water for the warm milk. Measure carefully, placing all ingredients except Caramel Topping, pecan halves, Filling and 2 tablespoons softened butter in bread machine pan in the order recommended by the manufacturer. Select Dough/Manual cycle; do not use delay cycle. Remove dough from pan. Continue as directed in step 3 for shaping, rising and baking. Rising time may be shorter because dough will be warm when removed from bread machine.

DO-AHEAD CARAMEL STICKY ROLLS: After placing slices in pan, cover tightly with plastic wrap or aluminum foil and refrigerate 4 to 24 hours. Before baking, remove from refrigerator; remove plastic wrap or foil and cover loosely with plastic wrap. Let rise in warm place about 2 hours or until double. If some rising has occurred in the refrigerator, rising time may be less than 2 hours. Bake as directed.

CINNAMON ROLLS: Omit Caramel Topping and pecan halves. Grease bottom and sides of rectangular pan, 13 × 9 × 2 inches, with shortening. Place dough slices in pan. Let rise and bake as directed in steps 4, 5 and 6, except do not turn pan upside down. Remove rolls from pan to wire rack. Cool 10 minutes. Drizzle rolls with Vanilla Glaze (page 13) if desired.

To cut even slices, place a piece of dental floss or heavy thread under the roll, bring ends of floss up and crisscross at top of roll, then pull ends in opposite directions. Or cut with a sharp serrated knife.

Four-Grain Batter Bread *Low-Fat*

Prep: 15 min; Rise: 30 min; Bake: 25 min
✳ *2 loaves, 16 slices each*

This is called a batter bread because the dough is soft and does not require kneading. Just mix it, put it in the pan to rise and bake. Homemade bread doesn't get much easier than that!

Cornmeal
4 1/2 to 4 3/4 cups all-purpose* or bread flour
2 tablespoons sugar
1 teaspoon salt
1/4 teaspoon baking soda
2 packages regular or quick active dry yeast
    (4 1/2 teaspoons)
2 cups milk
1/2 cup water
1/2 cup whole wheat flour
1/2 cup wheat germ
1/2 cup quick-cooking oats

1. Grease bottoms and sides of 2 loaf pans, 8 1/2 × 4 1/2 × 2 1/2 inches, with shortening; sprinkle with cornmeal.

2. Mix 3 1/2 cups of the all-purpose flour, the sugar, salt, baking soda and yeast in large bowl. Heat milk and water in 1-quart saucepan over medium heat, stirring occasionally, until very warm (120° to 130°). Add milk mixture to flour mixture. Beat with electric mixer on low speed until moistened. Beat on medium speed 3 minutes, scraping bowl occasionally.

3. Stir in whole wheat flour, wheat germ, oats and enough remaining all-purpose flour to make a stiff batter. Divide batter evenly between pans. Round tops of loaves by patting with floured hands. Sprinkle with cornmeal. Cover loosely with plastic wrap and let rise in warm place about 30 minutes or until batter is about 1 inch below tops of pans.

4. Heat oven to 400°.

5. Bake about 25 minutes or until tops of loaves are light brown. Remove from pans to wire rack; cool.

*If using self-rising flour, omit salt and baking soda.

1 Slice: Calories 95 (Calories from Fat 10); Fat 1g (Saturated 0g); Cholesterol 0mg; Sodium 90mg; Carbohydrate 19g (Dietary Fiber 1g); Protein 4g **% Daily Value:** Vitamin A 0%; Vitamin C 0%; Calcium 2%; Iron 6% **Diet Exchanges:** 1 Starch

WHOLE WHEAT BATTER BREAD: Increase whole wheat flour to 2 cups. Omit wheat germ and oats. Stir in 1 cup raisins with the second addition of all-purpose flour.

Fresh Herb Batter Bread

Low-Fat

Prep: 10 min; Rise: 40 min; Bake: 45 min
✳ *1 loaf, 20 slices*

3 cups all-purpose flour*
1 tablespoon sugar
1 teaspoon salt
1 package regular or quick active dry yeast
    (2 1/4 teaspoons)
1 1/4 cups very warm water (120° to 130°)
2 tablespoons chopped fresh parsley
2 tablespoons shortening
1 1/2 teaspoons chopped fresh or 1/2 teaspoon dried
    rosemary leaves
1/2 teaspoon chopped fresh or 1/4 teaspoon dried
    thyme leaves
Butter or stick margarine, softened, if desired

1. Grease bottom and sides of loaf pan, 8 1/2 × 4 1/2 × 2 1/2 or 9 × 5 × 3 inches, with shortening.

2. Mix 2 cups of the flour, the sugar, salt and yeast in large bowl. Add water, parsley, shortening, rosemary and thyme. Beat with electric mixer on low speed 1 minute, scraping bowl frequently. Beat on medium speed 1 minute, scraping bowl frequently. Stir in remaining 1 cup flour until smooth.

3. Spread batter evenly in pan and pat into shape with floured hands. Cover loosely with plastic wrap lightly sprayed with cooking spray and let rise in warm place about 40 minutes or until double.

4. Heat oven to 375°.

5. Bake 40 to 45 minutes or until loaf sounds hollow when tapped. Immediately remove from pan to wire rack. Brush top of loaf with butter; sprinkle with additional chopped fresh herbs if desired. Cool.

*If using self-rising flour, omit salt.

1 Slice: Calories 75 (Calories from Fat 10); Fat 1g (Saturated 2g); Cholesterol 0mg; Sodium 120mg; Carbohydrate 15g (Dietary Fiber 1g); Protein 2g **% Daily Value:** Vitamin A 0%; Vitamin C 0%; Calcium 0%; Iron 4% **Diet Exchanges:** 1 Starch

Oatmeal-Molasses Bread

Low-Fat

Prep: 10 min; Rise: 1 hr 30 min; Bake: 55 min
✱ 1 loaf, 16 slices

3/4 cup boiling water
1/2 cup old-fashioned or quick-cooking oats
3 tablespoons shortening
1/4 cup mild-flavor molasses
2 teaspoons salt
1 package regular or quick active dry yeast
(2 1/4 teaspoons)
1/4 cup warm water (105° to 115°)
1 large egg
2 3/4 cups all-purpose flour*
Butter or stick margarine, softened, if desired

1. Grease bottom and side of loaf pan, 9 × 5 × 3 or 8 1/2 × 4 1/2 × 2 1/2 inches, with shortening. Mix boiling water, oats, shortening, molasses and salt in large bowl; cool to lukewarm.

2. Dissolve yeast in warm water. Add yeast mixture, egg and 1 1/2 cups of the flour to the oat mixture. Beat 2 minutes with electric mixer on medium speed, scraping bowl frequently. Stir in remaining 1 1/4 cups flour until completely mixed.

3. Spread batter evenly in pan and pat into shape with floured hands. Cover loosely with plastic wrap and let rise in warm place about 1 hour 30 minutes or until batter is 1 inch from top of 9-inch pan or reaches top of 8 1/2-inch pan.

4. Heat oven to 375°.

5. Bake 50 to 55 minutes or until loaf is brown and sounds hollow when tapped. (If loaf browns too quickly, cover loosely with aluminum foil during last 15 minutes of baking.) Remove from pan to wire rack. Brush top of loaf with butter if desired; cool.

*If using self-rising flour, omit salt.

1 Slice: Calories 125 (Calories from Fat 25); Fat 3g (Saturated 1g); Cholesterol 15mg; Sodium 300mg; Carbohydrate 22g (Dietary Fiber 1g); Protein 3g **% Daily Value:** Vitamin A 0%; Vitamin C 0%; Calcium 2%; Iron 8% **Diet Exchanges:** 1 Starch, 1/2 Fruit, 1/2 Fat

Garlic Bread *Fast*

Prep: 10 min; Bake: 20 min ✳ 18 slices

1 clove garlic, finely chopped, or 1/4 teaspoon garlic
    powder
1/3 cup butter or stick margarine, softened*
1 loaf (1 pound) French bread, cut into 1-inch slices

1. Heat oven to 400°.

2. Mix garlic and butter.

3. Spread butter mixture over 1 side of each bread slice. Reassemble loaf; wrap securely in heavy-duty aluminum foil.

4. Bake 15 to 20 minutes or until hot.

*Spreads with at least 65% vegetable oil can be used (page 45).

1 Slice: Calories 90 (Calories from Fat 35); Fat 4g (Saturated 2g); Cholesterol 10mg; Sodium 170mg; Carbohydrate 13g (Dietary Fiber 1g); Protein 2g **% Daily Value:** Vitamin A 2%; Vitamin C 0%; Calcium 2%; Iron 4% **Diet Exchanges:** 1 Starch

HERB-CHEESE BREAD: Omit garlic. Mix 2 teaspoons chopped fresh parsley, 1/2 teaspoon dried oregano leaves, 2 tablespoons grated Parmesan cheese and 1/8 teaspoon garlic salt with the butter.

ONION BREAD: Omit garlic if desired. Mix 2 tablespoons finely chopped onion or chives with the butter.

SEEDED BREAD: Omit garlic if desired. Mix 1 teaspoon celery seed, poppy seed, dill seed or sesame seed with the butter.

Texas Toast *Fast*

Prep: 5 min; Broil: 4 min ✳ 8 servings

1/4 cup butter or stick margarine, softened*
4 slices thick-cut white bread, about 1 inch thick
1/2 teaspoon seasoned salt

1. Set oven control to broil.

2. Spread butter on both sides of bread slices. Sprinkle with seasoned salt. Place on rack in broiler pan.

3. Broil with tops 4 to 6 inches from heat 2 to 4 minutes, turning once, until lightly toasted. Cut each slice diagonally in half. Serve warm or cool.

*Spreads with at least 65% vegetable oil can be used (page 45).

1 Slice: Calories 85 (Calories from Fat 55); Fat 6g (Saturated 4g); Cholesterol 15mg; Sodium 200mg; Carbohydrate 7g (Dietary Fiber 0g); Protein 1g **% Daily Value:** Vitamin A 4%; Vitamin C 0%; Calcium2 %; Iron 2% **Diet Exchanges:** 1 1/2 Starch, 1 Fat

---

MICROWAVING GARLIC BREAD

Save time by heating the buttered loaf in the microwave. Don't wrap in foil. Instead, divide the loaf in half, and put the halves side by side in a napkin-lined microwavable basket or dinner plate. Cover with a napkin and microwave on Medium (50%) 1 1/2 to 3 minutes, rotating basket 1/2 turn after 1 minute, until bread is warm.

Tips for Bread Machine Breads

Enjoy the old-fashioned aroma and goodness of home-baked bread the fun and easy new-fashioned way: using an electric bread machine! Here are some tips to help you make the best bread machine bread ever.

- Read your bread machine manual carefully, especially the tips and hints. Make sure the machine is assembled correctly.

- Add ingredients in the order specified by the manufacturer.

- *Carefully* measure ingredients with standard measuring cups and spoons. Even little variations can dramatically affect the finished loaf.

- Ingredients should be at room temperature, except for those normally stored in the refrigerator such as milk, sour cream and eggs.

- For best results, use bread machine yeast. Its finer granulation helps the yeast disperse more thoroughly during mixing and kneading. Remember that when the weather is hot and humid, yeast action speeds up; when it's cold out, yeast action slows down.

- For high-volume loaves, use bread flour. For more about flour, also see Flour, page 17.

- Be careful when you peek! Checking the progress of your bread is tempting, but peek only during mixing and kneading. If you open the machine during rising or baking, the loaf can collapse.

- When using the delay cycle, be sure the yeast doesn't come in contact with liquid or wet ingredients. Don't use the delay cycle with recipes that contain eggs, fresh dairy products (butter and margarine can be used), honey, meats or fresh fruits and vegetables because bacteria can grow while these ingredients stand in the bread machine for several hours.

- If you get the urge to experiment by changing the ingredients, make just one change at a time so you can clearly see the result.

- For consistent results, keep your bread machine in the same place, away from drafts and areas of your house where heat and humidity fluctuate widely. Keep the area around your bread machine open for good ventilation.

Classic White Bread   *Low-Fat*

Prep: 5 min; Bake: About 3 hr 30 min
✻ *1 1/2-pound loaf, 12 slices*

1 cup plus 2 tablespoons water
2 tablespoons butter or stick margarine, softened*
3 cups bread flour
3 tablespoons nonfat dry milk
2 tablespoons sugar
1 1/2 teaspoons salt
2 teaspoons bread machine yeast

1. Measure carefully, placing all ingredients in bread machine pan in the order recommended by the manufacturer.

2. Select Basic/White cycle. Use Medium or Light crust color. Remove baked bread from pan to wire rack; cool.

*Spreads with at least 65% vegetable oil can be used (page 45).

1 Slice: Calories 145 (Calories from Fat 20); Fat 2g (Saturated 1g); Cholesterol 5mg; Sodium 310mg; Carbohydrate 29g (Dietary Fiber 1g); Protein 4g **% Daily Value:** Vitamin A 2%; Vitamin C 0%; Calcium 2%; Iron 10% **Diet Exchanges:** 2 Starch

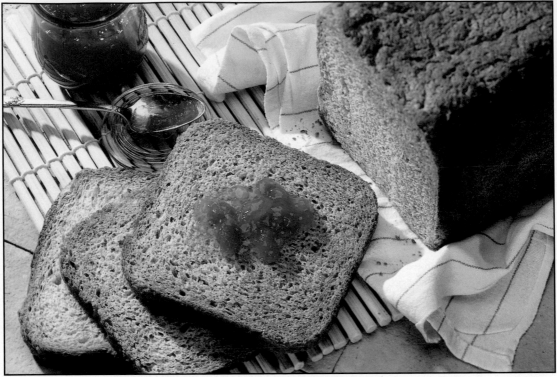

Multigrain Loaf

Whole Wheat Bread *Low-Fat*

Prep: 15 min; Bake: About 4 hr 30 min
✱ *1 1/2-pound loaf, 12 slices*

1 cup plus 2 tablespoons water
3 tablespoons honey
2 tablespoons butter or stick margarine*
1 1/2 cups bread flour
1 1/2 cups whole wheat flour
1/4 cup chopped walnuts, toasted (page 177), if desired
1 teaspoon salt
1 1/2 teaspoons bread machine yeast

1. Measure carefully, placing all ingredients in bread machine pan in the order recommended by the manufacturer.

2. Select Whole Wheat or Basic/White cycle. Use Medium or Light crust color. Do not use delay cycle. Remove baked bread from pan to wire rack; cool.

*Spreads with at least 65% vegetable oil can be used (page 45).

1 Slice: Calories 140 (Calories from Fat 20); Fat 2g (Saturated 0g); Cholesterol 0mg; Sodium 220mg; Carbohydrate 29g (Dietary Fiber 2g); Protein 4g **% Daily Value:** Vitamin A 2%; Vitamin C 0%; Calcium 0%; Iron 8% **Diet Exchanges:** 2 Starch

Multigrain Loaf *Low-Fat*

Prep: 10 min; Bake: About 3 hr 30 min
✱ *1 1/2-pound loaf, 12 slices*

Look for 7-grain cereal in the health food aisle or hot cereal section of your supermarket.

1 1/4 cups water
2 tablespoons butter or stick margarine, softened*
1 1/3 cups bread flour
1 1/3 cups whole wheat flour
1 cup 7-grain or multigrain hot cereal (uncooked)
3 tablespoons packed brown sugar
1 1/4 teaspoons salt
2 1/2 teaspoons bread machine yeast

1. Measure carefully, placing all ingredients in bread machine pan in the order recommended by the manufacturer.

2. Select Whole Wheat or Basic/White cycle. Use Medium or Light crust color. Remove baked bread from pan to wire rack; cool.

Spreads with at least 65% vegetable oil can be used (page 45).

1 Slice: Calories 165 (Calories from Fat 25); Fat 3g (Saturated 1g); Cholesterol 5mg; Sodium 410mg; Carbohydrate 33g (Dietary Fiber 3g); Protein 5g **% Daily Value:** Vitamin A 2%; Vitamin C 0%; Calcium 2%; Iron 10% **Diet Exchanges:** 2 Starch

Jalapeño Corn Bread *Low-Fat*

Prep: 10 min; Bake: About 3 hr 30 min
✳ *1 1/2-pound loaf, 12 slices*

3/4 cup plus 2 tablespoons water
2/3 cup frozen whole kernel corn, thawed
2 tablespoons butter or stick margarine, softened*
1 tablespoon chopped seeded jalapeño chili
3 1/4 cups bread flour
1/3 cup cornmeal
2 tablespoons sugar
1 1/2 teaspoons salt
2 1/2 teaspoons bread machine yeast

1. Measure carefully, placing all ingredients in bread machine pan in the order recommended by the manufacturer.

2. Select Basic/White cycle. Use Medium or Light crust color. Do not use delay cycle. Remove baked bread from pan to wire rack; cool.

Spreads with at least 65% vegetable oil can be used (page 45).

1 Slice: Calories 170 (Calories from Fat 20); Fat 2g (Saturated 1g); Cholesterol 5mg; Sodium 310mg; Carbohydrate 35g (Dietary Fiber 2g); Protein 5g **% Daily Value:** Vitamin A 2%; Vitamin C 0%; Calcium 0%; Iron 10% **Diet Exchanges:** 2 Starch, 1 Vegetable

Cheese-Onion Bread *Low-Fat*

Prep: 5 min; Bake: About 3 hr 30 min
✳ *1 1/2-pound loaf, 12 slices*

We don't recommend this recipe for bread machines that have cast-aluminum pans in a horizontal-loaf shape because our results after several tests were unsatisfactory.

3/4 cup plus 2 tablespoons water
3 cups bread flour
3/4 cup shredded Cheddar cheese (3 ounces)
2 tablespoons sugar
1 tablespoon nonfat dry milk
2 teaspoons instant minced onion
1 teaspoon salt
1 1/4 teaspoons bread machine yeast

1. Measure carefully, placing all ingredients in bread machine pan in the order recommended by the manufacturer.

2. Select Basic/White cycle. Use Medium or Light crust color. Do not use delay cycle. Remove baked bread from pan to wire rack; cool.

1 Slice: Calories 165 (Calories from Fat 25); Fat 3g (Saturated 2g); Cholesterol 10mg; Sodium 240mg; Carbohydrate 29g (Dietary Fiber 1g); Protein 6g % **Daily Value:** Vitamin A 2%; Vitamin C 0%; Calcium 4%; Iron 10% **Diet Exchanges:** 2 Starch

Mediterranean Herbed Bread

Low-Fat

Prep: 10 min; Bake: About 3 hr 30 min
✱ *1 1/2-pound loaf, 12 slices*

1 cup water
1 tablespoon butter or stick margarine, softened*
3 cups bread flour
2 tablespoons sugar
1 tablespoon nonfat dry milk
1 1/2 teaspoons salt
1 teaspoon chopped fresh or 1/2 teaspoon dried
    basil leaves
1 teaspoon chopped fresh or 1/2 teaspoon dried
    oregano leaves
1 teaspoon chopped fresh or 1/2 teaspoon dried
    thyme leaves
2 1/4 teaspoons bread machine yeast

1. Measure carefully, placing all ingredients in bread machine pan in the order recommended by the manufacturer.

2. Select Basic/White cycle. Use Medium or Light crust color. Remove baked bread from pan to wire rack; cool.

*Spreads with at least 65% vegetable oil can be used (page 45).

1 Slice: Calories 145 (Calories from Fat 20); Fat 2g (Saturated 1g); Cholesterol 5mg; Sodium 300mg; Carbohydrate 29g (Dietary Fiber 1g); Protein 4g **% Daily Value:** Vitamin A 0%; Vitamin C 0%; Calcium 0%; Iron 10% **Diet Exchanges:** 2 Starch

Raisin-Cinnamon Bread

Low-Fat

Prep: 5 min; Bake: About 3 hr 30 min
✱ *1 1/2-pound loaf, 12 slices*

If your bread machine doesn't have a Raisin/Nut signal, add the raisins 5 to 10 minutes before the last kneading cycle ends. Check your bread machine's use-and-care book to find out how long the last cycle runs.

1 cup plus 2 tablespoons water
2 tablespoons butter or stick margarine, softened*
3 cups bread flour
3 tablespoons sugar
1 1/2 teaspoons salt
1 teaspoon ground cinnamon
2 1/2 teaspoons bread machine yeast
3/4 cup raisins

1. Measure carefully, placing all ingredients except raisins in bread machine pan in the order recommended by the manufacturer. Add raisins at the Raisin/Nut signal.

2. Select Sweet or Basic/White cycle. Use Medium or Light crust color. Remove baked bread from pan to wire rack; cool.

*Spreads with at least 65% vegetable oil can be used (page 45).

1 Slice: Calories 175 (Calories from Fat 20); Fat 2g (Saturated 1g); Cholesterol 5mg; Sodium 310mg; Carbohydrate 37g (Dietary Fiber 2g); Protein 4g **% Daily Value:** Vitamin A 2%; Vitamin C 0%; Calcium 0%; Iron 10% **Diet Exchanges:** 1 1/2 Starch, 1 Fruit

Cakes & Pies

Cakes & Pies

Low-Fat = 3g or less, except main dishes with 6g or less   **Fast** = Ready in 30 minutes or less   ■ = Bread Machine directions   ● = Slow Cooker directions

Chocolate Cake (page 94)

Lighter = 1/3 fewer calories or 50% less fat

Cake Basics

Special occasions call for cake—and only cake will do—from birthdays and weddings to social events and personal milestones. Cake is a sweet confection that rises to any occasion whether it's a kid's birthday party, a church picnic, lunch at your desk or a fiftieth wedding anniversary. There are almost as many versions of cakes as occasions to enjoy them. There are two main types of cakes; shortening and foam. Both types have some baking tips in common.

Pans and Pan Preparation

Use the size of pan called for in a recipe. How do you determine pan size? Measure the length and width from *inside* edge to *inside* edge. If the pan's too big, your cake will be flat and dry; too small and it'll bulge or overflow the pan.

Shiny metal pans are the first choice for baking cakes. They reflect heat away from the cake for a tender, light brown crust.

If you use dark nonstick or glass baking pans, follow the manufacturer's directions, which may call for reducing the baking temperature by 25° because these pans absorb heat and cakes will cook and brown faster.

Fill cake pans half full. To determine how much batter a specialty pan (such as a heart, star or bell shape) can hold, fill it with water, then measure the water; use half that amount of batter. Extra batter? Make cupcakes!

Mixing Cakes

We tested the cake recipes in this cookbook with electric handheld mixers. Because mixers vary in power, you may need to adjust the speed, especially during the first step of combining ingredients. If using a powerful stand mixer, be careful not mix the batter too much, which causes tunnels (large air holes) or a sunken center.

You can also mix cakes by hand. Stir the ingredients until they're well combined, then beat 150 strokes for each minute of beating time (3 minutes equals 450 strokes). If a cake isn't beaten enough, the volume will be lower.

If a recipe calls for butter or margarine, we recommend using the stick form. You also can use the stick form of vegetable oil spreads that have *at least* 65 percent fat, although the batter consistency might be slightly thinner.

For cakes, we don't recommend using vegetable oil spreads with less than 65 percent fat, reduced-fat butter or any tub or whipped product, whether it's spread, butter, or margarine. Because they contain more water and less fat, you'll end up with a cake that's tough and wet or gummy. (See Fats, page 16.)

Baking Cakes

Bake cakes on the oven rack placed in the center of the oven, unless noted otherwise in the recipe.

Cakes are done when a toothpick poked in the center comes out clean.

Cool cakes on a wire rack away from drafts.

Storing Cakes

Cool unfrosted cakes completely before covering and storing to keep the top from becoming sticky.

Store cakes with a creamy frosting loosely covered with aluminum foil, plastic wrap or waxed paper or under a cake safe or a large inverted bowl.

Serve a cake with fluffy frosting the same day you make it. If there are leftovers, use a cake safe or inverted bowl with a knife slipped under the edge so air can get in.

Store cakes with whipped cream toppings, cream fillings or cream cheese frostings in the refrigerator.

Put cakes containing very moist ingredients such as chopped apples, applesauce, shredded carrots or zucchini, mashed bananas or pumpkin in the refrigerator during humid weather or in humid climates. If stored at room temperature, these cakes tend to mold quickly.

How to Split Cake Layers

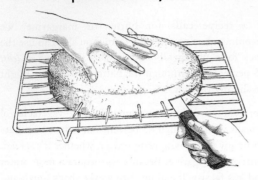

Mark middle points around side of layer with toothpicks. Using picks as a guide, cut through the layer with a long, thin sharp knife.

Split the layer by pulling a piece of dental floss or heavy thread horizontally through the middle of the layer, moving floss in a back-and-forth motion.

Cutting Cakes

For layer cakes, use a sharp, long, thin knife.

For angel food, chiffon and pound cakes, use a long serrated knife and cut with a sawing motion or use an electric knife.

If the frosting sticks to the knife, dip the knife in hot water and wipe with a damp paper towel after cutting each slice.

For fruitcake, use a thin nonserrated or electric knife. Fruitcakes are easy to cut if you make them three to four weeks ahead of time, wrap and store in the refrigerator. Brush occasionally with rum, brandy or bourbon for a rich, mellow flavor.

Baking Cupcakes

Fun, totable cupcakes are perfect for parties and picnics. Make a batch from any of the cake batters; you'll get about twenty-four to thirty-six cupcakes.

- Line medium muffin cups, 2 1/2 × 1 1/4 inches, with paper baking cups. Look for festive cups in colors and special designs at your supermarket, party store or paper warehouse.

- Fill each cup about half full. Bake 20 to 25 minutes or until a toothpick inserted in center comes out clean.

- If you have only one 12-cup muffin pan, cover and refrigerate the rest of the batter while the first batch is baking. Then bake the rest of the batter, adding 1 or 2 minutes to the bake time.

CAKE YIELDS	
Size and Kind	**Number of Servings**
8- or 9-inch one-layer round cake	8
8- or 9-inch two-layer round cake	12 to 16
8- or 9-inch square cake	9
13 × 9 × 2-inch rectangular cake	12 to 16
10 × 4-inch angel food or chiffon cake	12 to 16
12-cup bundt cake or pound cake	16 to 24

Shortening Cakes

At heart, shortening cakes are all the same. They're all made with shortening, butter or margarine, flour, eggs, a liquid and a leavening agent such as baking powder or baking soda. Only the flavorings are different, but what a difference they make! Flavorings determine whether it's a German Chocolate Cake or Pineapple Upside-Down Cake, Easy Butter Cake or Silver White Cake.

Pans and Pan Preparation

Place oven rack in the middle of the oven; place pans in the center of the rack. When baking a layer cake, arrange 8- or 9-inch round pans so they don't touch and there's at least one inch of space between the pans and the sides of the oven. When baking three round pans, refrigerate batter in third pan if all pans will not fit in oven at one time; bake third pan separately.

CAKE CURES

Great Shortening Cakes Are

High, golden brown
Slightly rounded, with a
  smooth top
Fine-grained, even textured,
  not crumbly
Soft, velvety, slightly moist,
  light, tender

Problem	Possible Cause
Pale	• too little sugar
	• baking time too short
Does not rise properly	• too much liquid
	• too much fat
	• pan too large
	• oven too cool
Peaked or cracked on top	• too much flour
	• oven too hot
Rim around edge	• pan sprayed with cooking spray
Coarse grained	• too much shortening
	• underbeaten
Crumbly	• too much shortening
	• too much sugar
	• underbeaten
	• too little egg (use large eggs)
Dry	• too much baking powder
	• baking time too long
Heavy, too moist	• too much liquid
	• too much shortening
	• too little flour
Batter overflows	• too much batter in pan
	• pan too small
	• too much leavening
Sticks to pan	• pan not greased enough
	• pan greased with oil (okay if not removing cake from pan)
	• cake left in pan too long before being removed

To keep cakes from sticking to the pans, generously grease the bottoms and sides with shortening (about 1 tablespoon for each round pan). Sprinkle each greased pan with flour—use baking cocoa for a chocolate cake—then shake the pan until the bottom and sides are well coated; shake out excess flour. For nonstick pans, follow the manufacturer's directions; greasing is usually recommended. Cooking spray can be used, but the cake may be less attractive with high sides and a lip. If used, spray it only on the bottom of the pan; do not sprinkle with flour.

Lightly flour greased pan by adding a small amount of flour, then tilting the pan and tapping it so flour covers all the greased surfaces. Discard any excess flour.

For fruitcakes, line pans with aluminum foil, then grease with shortening. Or line with cooking parchment paper. Leave short "ears" (overhang) of foil on two opposite sides so you can easily lift the baked cake out of the pan. Extend the foil beyond the pan if you plan to store the cake before serving. When the cake is cooled, fold the foil over the top of the cake and seal.

Vegetable oil is not a suitable substitute for shortening, butter or margarine, even when those ingredients are to be melted. Recipes formulated with shortening need the solids for proper structure and texture.

Cool round cakes in their pans on wire racks for 5 to 10 minutes. To remove a cake from the pan, insert a knife between the cake and the pan and slide it around the side to loosen the edge. Put a wire rack on top of the cake. Holding both the rack and the pan firmly, flip them over and lift the pan off the cake. Flip again onto another rack so the cake can cool top side up. Cool completely on wire racks.

Chocolate Cake

Prep: 20 min; Bake: 45 min; Cool: 1 hr 10 min
✱ *12 servings*

This cake could also be called Devil's Food because it's dark, dense and very chocolaty, just the opposite of the white and feathery Angel Food Cake (page 104).

2 1/4 cups all-purpose* or 2 1/2 cups cake flour
1 2/3 cups sugar
3/4 cup butter or stick margarine, softened**
2/3 cup baking cocoa
1 1/4 cups water
1 1/4 teaspoons baking soda
1 teaspoon salt
1 teaspoon vanilla
1/4 teaspoon baking powder
2 large eggs
Fudge Frosting (page 110) or White Mountain Frosting
    (page 112), if desired

1. Heat oven to 350°. Grease bottom and sides of rectangular pan, 13 × 9 × 2 inches, 2 round pans, 9 × 1 1/2 inches, or 3 round pans, 8 × 1 1/2 inches, with shortening; lightly flour.

2. Beat all ingredients except Fudge Frosting with electric mixer on low speed 30 seconds, scraping bowl constantly. Beat on high speed 3 minutes, scraping bowl occasionally. Pour into pan(s).

3. Bake rectangle 40 to 45 minutes, rounds 30 to 35 minutes, or until toothpick inserted in center comes out clean. Cool rectangle in pan on wire rack. Cool rounds 10 minutes; remove from pans to wire rack. Cool completely, about 1 hour.

4. Frost rectangle or fill round layers and frost with Fudge Frosting.

Do not use self-rising flour.
**Spreads with at least 65% vegetable oil can be used (page 91).*

1 Serving: Calories 320 (Calories from Fat 115); Fat 13g (Saturated 8g); Cholesterol 65mg; Sodium 430mg; Carbohydrate 48g (Dietary Fiber 2g); Protein 5g **% Daily Value:** Vitamin A 10%; Vitamin C 0%; Calcium 2%; Iron 10% **Diet Exchanges:** Not Recommended

German Chocolate Cake

Prep: 30 min; Bake: 40 min; Cool: 1 hr 10 min
✱ *12 to 16 servings*

This cake is named after Samuel German, who invented the sweet chocolate bar that is used to make it. It's a classic recipe that has been a favorite for almost fifty years. It is important that your beaters are clean and dry so nothing interferes with your egg whites whipping up nice and high.

4 ounces sweet baking chocolate
1/2 cup water
2 cups sugar
1 cup butter or stick margarine, softened*
4 large eggs
1 teaspoon vanilla
2 1/4 cups all-purpose** or 2 1/2 cups cake flour
1 teaspoon baking soda
1 teaspoon salt
1 cup buttermilk
Coconut-Pecan Filling and Topping (page 113), if desired

1. Heat oven to 350°. Grease bottom and side of 3 round pans, 8 × 1 1/2 or 9 × 1 1/2 inches, with shortening. Line bottoms of pans with waxed paper or cooking parchment paper.

2. Heat chocolate and water in 1-quart saucepan over low heat, stirring frequently, until chocolate is completely melted; cool.

3. Beat sugar and butter in medium bowl with electric mixer on high speed until light and fluffy. Separate eggs; reserve egg whites. Beat egg yolks, one at a time, into sugar mixture. Beat in chocolate and vanilla on low speed. Mix flour, baking soda and salt. Beat flour mixture into sugar mixture alternately with buttermilk on low speed, beating just until smooth after each addition.

4. Using clean beaters, beat eggs whites on high speed until stiff; fold into batter. Pour into pans. Refrigerate batter in third pan if not all pans will fit in oven at one time; bake third pan separately.

5. Bake 8-inch rounds 35 to 40 minutes, 9-inch rounds 30 to 35 minutes, or until toothpick inserted in center comes out clean. Cool 10 minutes; remove from pans to wire rack. Remove waxed paper. Cool completely, about 1 hour.

6. Fill layers and frost top of cake with Coconut-Pecan Filling and Topping, leaving side of cake unfrosted. Store covered in refrigerator.

*Spreads with at least 65% vegetable oil can be used (page 91).
**Do not use self-rising flour.

1 Serving: Calories 445 (Calories from Fat 205); Fat 23g (Saturated 13g); Cholesterol 115mg; Sodium 440mg; Carbohydrate 55g (Dietary Fiber 2g); Protein 6g **% Daily Value:** Vitamin A 14%; Vitamin C 0%; Calcium 4%; Iron 10% **Diet Exchanges:** Not Recommended

Chocolate Snack Cake

Prep: 10 min; Bake: 35 min; Cool: 15 min ✱ *9 servings*

You can leave your mixer in the cupboard when making this easy one-layer cake. Just mix up the batter with a spoon, bake it and enjoy it warm.

1 1/2 cups all-purpose flour*
1 cup sugar
1/4 cup baking cocoa
1 teaspoon baking soda
1/2 teaspoon salt
1/3 cup vegetable oil
1 teaspoon white vinegar
1/2 teaspoon vanilla
1 cup cold water
Ice cream or whipped cream, if desired

1. Heat oven to 350°. Grease bottom and side of round pan, 9 × 1 1/2 inches, or square pan, 8 × 8 × 2 inches, with shortening; lightly flour.

2. Mix flour, sugar, cocoa, baking soda and salt in medium bowl. Mix oil, vinegar and vanilla. Vigorously stir oil mixture and water into flour mixture about 1 minute or until well blended. Immediately pour into pan.

3. Bake 30 to 35 minutes or until toothpick inserted in center comes out clean. Cool 15 minutes. Serve warm or cool with ice cream.

*Do not use self-rising flour.

1 Serving: Calories 230 (Calories from Fat 70); Fat 8g (Saturated 1g); Cholesterol 0mg; Sodium 270mg; Carbohydrate 38g (Dietary Fiber 1g); Protein 2g **% Daily Value:** Vitamin A 0%; Vitamin C 0%; Calcium 0%; Iron 4% **Diet Exchanges:** 1 Starch, 1 1/2 Fruit, 1 Fat

Silver White Cake

Prep: 10 min; Bake: 45 min; Cool: 1 hr 10 min
✻ *12 servings*

2 1/4 cups all-purpose* or 2 1/2 cups cake flour
1 2/3 cups sugar
2/3 cup shortening
1 1/4 cups milk
3 1/2 teaspoons baking powder
1 teaspoon salt
1 teaspoon vanilla or almond extract
5 large egg whites
White Mountain Frosting (page 112) or Chocolate
    Buttercream Frosting (page 110), if desired

1. Heat oven to 350°. Grease bottom and sides of rectangular pan, 13 × 9 × 2 inches, 2 round pans, 9 × 1 1/2 inches, or 3 round pans, 8 × 1 1/2 inches, with shortening; lightly flour.

2. Beat all ingredients except egg whites and White Mountain Frosting in large bowl with electric mixer on low speed 30 seconds, scraping bowl constantly. Beat on high speed 2 minutes, scraping bowl occasionally.

3. Beat in egg whites on high speed 2 minutes, scraping bowl occasionally. Pour into pan(s).

4. Bake rectangle 40 to 45 minutes, 9-inch rounds 30 to 35 minutes, 8-inch rounds 23 to 28 minutes, or until toothpick inserted in center comes out clean or until cake springs back when touched lightly in center. Cool rectangle in pan on wire rack. Cool rounds 10 minutes; remove from pans to wire rack. Cool completely, about 1 hour.

5. Frost rectangle or fill round layers and frost with White Mountain Frosting.

*Do not use self-rising flour.

1 Serving: Calories 310 (Calories from Fat 110); Fat 12g (Saturated 3g); Cholesterol 0mg; Sodium 370mg; Carbohydrate 47g (Dietary Fiber 1g); Protein 5g **% Daily Value:** Vitamin A 0%; Vitamin C 0%; Calcium 10%; Iron 0% **Diet Exchanges:** Not Recommended

CHOCOLATE CHIP CAKE: Fold 1/2 cup miniature or finely chopped regular semisweet chocolate chips into batter.

COCONUT-LEMON CAKE: Spread rectangle or fill layers with Lemon Filling (page 114). Frost with White Mountain Frosting (page 112). Sprinkle cake with about 1 cup flaked or shredded coconut.

MARBLE CAKE: Before pouring batter into pan(s), remove 1 3/4 cups of the batter; reserve. Pour remaining batter into pan(s). Stir 3 tablespoons baking cocoa and 1/8 teaspoon baking soda into reserved batter. Drop chocolate batter by tablespoonfuls randomly onto white batter. Cut through batters with knife for marbled design. Bake and cool as directed in step 4.

CHOOSING PANS

Many types and sizes of pans are available for baking cakes. Check the recipe to see what size is recommended, then measure your pan across the top from inside edges. If your pan is bigger than the recipe suggests, the cake may end up being flat or thin. If your pan is smaller, the cake could be too rounded or possibly cracked on the top. Even if the size is right, the material used to make the pan may cause baking differences. Dark pans with a nonstick finish tend to cause cakes to bake faster and form a darker crust. Some manufacturers recommend lowering the oven temperature by 25° when baking cakes in these pans. Glass dishes often have rounded corners that change the cake shape. If your cake doesn't look perfect, just choose a yummy frosting to cover any imperfections.

Starlight Yellow Cake

Prep: 10 min; Bake: 40 min; Cool: 1 hr 10 min
✻ *12 servings*

2 1/4 cups all-purpose flour*
1 1/2 cups sugar
1/2 cup butter or stick margarine, softened**
1 1/4 cups milk
3 1/2 teaspoons baking powder
1 teaspoon salt
1 teaspoon vanilla
3 large eggs
Chocolate Buttercream Frosting (page 110) or Peanut
   Butter Buttercream Frosting (page 111), if desired

1. Heat oven to 350°. Grease bottom and sides of rectangular pan, 13 × 9 × 2 inches, 2 round pans, 9 × 1 1/2 inches, or 3 round pans, 8 × 1 1/2 inches, with shortening; lightly flour.

2. Beat all ingredients except Chocolate Buttercream Frosting with electric mixer on low speed 30 seconds, scraping bowl constantly. Beat on high speed 3 minutes, scraping bowl occasionally. Pour into pan(s).

3. Bake rectangle 35 to 40 minutes, 9-inch rounds 25 to 30 minutes, 8-inch rounds 30 to 35 minutes, or until toothpick inserted in center comes out clean or until cake springs back when touched lightly in center. Cool rectangle in pan on wire rack. Cool rounds 10 minutes; remove from pans to wire rack. Cool completely, about 1 hour.

4. Frost rectangle or fill round layers and frost with Chocolate Buttercream Frosting.

*If using self-rising flour, omit baking powder and salt.
**Spreads with at least 65% vegetable oil can be used.

1 Serving: Calories 285 (Calories from Fat 90); Fat 10g (Saturated 6g); Cholesterol 75mg; Sodium 420mg; Carbohydrate 44g (Dietary Fiber 1g); Protein 5g **% Daily Value:** Vitamin A 8%; Vitamin C 0%; Calcium 12%; Iron 8% **Diet Exchanges:** 2 Starch, 1 Fruit, 1 1/2 Fat

PEANUT BUTTER CAKE: Substitute peanut butter for the butter. Frost with Fudge Frosting (page 110) if desired.

CHOCOLATE CURLS AND SHAVINGS

To make chocolate curls for garnishing desserts, pull a swivel-bladed vegetable peeler or thin, sharp knife across a block of milk chocolate, using long, thin strokes. The curls will be easier to make if the chocolate is slightly warm, so you can let it stand in a warm place for about 15 minutes before cutting if you like. Semisweet chocolate will make smaller curls. Use a toothpick to lift the curls from the chocolate and to place them on a frosted cake, pie or dessert. Make chocolate shavings the same way by using shorter strokes.

Buttery Snack Cake with Broiled Topping

Buttery Snack Cake with Broiled Topping

Prep: 10 min; Bake: 40 min; Cool: 15 min ✱ *9 servings*

1 1/4 cups all-purpose* or 1 1/2 cups cake flour
1 cup sugar
1/3 cup butter or stick margarine, softened**
3/4 cup milk
1 1/2 teaspoons baking powder
1 teaspoon vanilla
1/2 teaspoon salt
1 large egg
Broiled Coconut Frosting (right)

1. Heat oven to 350°. Grease bottom and sides of square pan, 8 × 8 × 2 or 9 × 9 × 2 inches, or round pan, 9 × 1 1/2 inches, with shortening; lightly flour.

2. Beat all ingredients except Broiled Coconut Frosting with electric mixer on low speed 30 seconds, scraping bowl constantly. Beat on high speed 3 minutes, scraping bowl occasionally. Pour into pan.

3. Bake 35 minutes or until toothpick inserted in center comes out clean. Make Broiled Coconut Frosting.

4. Set oven control to broil. Carefully spread frosting over hot cake. Broil with top of cake about 4 inches from heat about 2 minutes or until frosting is light brown. Watch carefully so frosting does not burn. Cool 15 minutes. Serve warm or cool.

Broiled Coconut Frosting

1 cup flaked coconut
1/3 cup packed brown sugar
1/4 cup butter or stick margarine, softened**
2 tablespoons half-and-half or milk

Mix all ingredients.

*If using self-rising flour, omit baking powder and salt.
**Spreads with at least 65% vegetable oil can be used (page 91).

1 Serving: Calories 350 (Calories from Fat 145); Fat 16g (Saturated 11g); Cholesterol 60mg; Sodium 340mg; Carbohydrate 49g (Dietary Fiber 1g); Protein 4g **% Daily Value:** Vitamin A 12%; Vitamin C 0%; Calcium 8%; Iron 6% **Diet Exchanges:** Not Recommended

Lemon-Poppy Seed Pound Cake (variation of Pound Cake)

Pound Cake

Prep: 20 min; Bake: 1 hr 20 min; Cool: 2 hr 20 min
✳ *24 servings*

2 1/2 cups sugar
1 cup butter or stick margarine, softened*
1 teaspoon vanilla or almond extract
5 large eggs
3 cups all-purpose flour**
1 teaspoon baking powder
1/4 teaspoon salt
1 cup milk or evaporated milk
Powdered sugar, if desired

1. Heat oven to 350°. Grease bottom and side of angel food cake pan (tube pan), 10 × 4 inches, 12-cup bundt cake pan or 2 loaf pans, 9 × 5 × 3 inches, with shortening; lightly flour.

2. Beat sugar, butter, vanilla and eggs in large bowl with electric mixer on low speed 30 seconds, scraping bowl constantly. Beat on high speed 5 minutes, scraping bowl occasionally. Mix flour, baking powder and salt.

Beat flour mixture into sugar mixture alternately with milk on low speed, beating just until smooth after each addition. Pour into pan(s).

3. Bake angel food or bundt cake pan 1 hour 10 minutes to 1 hour 20 minutes, loaf pans 55 to 60 minutes, or until toothpick inserted in center comes out clean. Cool 20 minutes; remove from pan(s) to wire rack. Cool completely, about 2 hours. Sprinkle with powdered sugar.

*Spreads with at least 65% vegetable oil can be used (page 91).
**Do not use self-rising flour.

1 Serving: Calories 225 (Calories from Fat 80); Fat 9g (Saturated 5g); Cholesterol 65mg; Sodium 115mg; Carbohydrate 33g (Dietary Fiber 0g); Protein 3g **% Daily Value:** Vitamin A 8%; Vitamin C 0%; Calcium 2%; Iron 4% **Diet Exchanges:** 1 Starch, 1 Fruit, 2 Fat

LEMON-POPPY SEED POUND CAKE: Substitute 1 teaspoon lemon extract for the vanilla. Fold 1 tablespoon grated lemon peel and 1/4 cup poppy seed into batter.

Carrot Cake with Cream Cheese Frosting (page 111)

Carrot Cake

Prep: 20 min; Bake: 45 min; Cool: 1 hr 10 min

✱ *12 to 16 servings*

1 1/2 cups sugar

1 cup vegetable oil

3 large eggs

2 cups all-purpose flour*

2 teaspoons ground cinnamon

1 teaspoon baking soda

1 teaspoon vanilla

1/2 teaspoon salt

3 cups shredded carrots (5 medium)

1 cup coarsely chopped nuts

Cream Cheese Frosting (page 111), if desired

1. Heat oven to 350°. Grease bottom and sides of rectangular pan, 13 × 9 × 2 inches, or 2 round pans, 8 × 1 1/2 or 9 × 1 1/2 inches, with shortening; lightly flour.

2. Beat sugar, oil and eggs in large bowl with electric mixer on low speed about 30 seconds or until blended.

Add remaining ingredients except carrots, nuts and Cream Cheese Frosting; beat on low speed 1 minute. Stir in carrots and nuts. Pour into pan(s).

3. Bake rectangle 40 to 45 minutes, rounds 30 to 35 minutes, or until toothpick inserted in center comes out clean. Cool rectangle in pan on wire rack. Cool rounds 10 minutes; remove from pans to wire rack. Cool completely, about 1 hour.

4. Frost rectangle or fill round layers and frost with Cream Cheese Frosting. Store covered in refrigerator.

*If using self-rising flour, omit baking soda and salt.

1 Serving: Calories 430 (Calories from Fat 235); Fat 26g (Saturated 4g); Cholesterol 55mg; Sodium 230mg; Carbohydrate 46g (Dietary Fiber 2g); Protein 5g **% Daily Value:** Vitamin A 44%; Vitamin C 2%; Calcium 2%; Iron 8% **Diet Exchanges:** Not Recommended

Lighter Carrot Cake: For 10 grams of fat and 280 calories per serving, substitute 1/2 cup unsweetened applesauce for 1/2 cup of the oil and 1 egg plus 4 egg whites for the eggs. Omit nuts.

APPLE CAKE: Substitute 3 cups chopped tart apples (3 medium) for the carrots.

PINEAPPLE-CARROT CAKE: Add 1 can (8 ounces) crushed pineapple, drained, and 1/2 cup flaked or shredded coconut with the carrots.

ZUCCHINI CAKE: Substitute 3 cups shredded zucchini for the carrots.

Applesauce Cake

Prep: 15 min; Bake: 50 min; Cool: 1 hr 10 min
✱ *12 to 16 servings*

Puzzled by pumpkin pie spice? If you don't have it handy, then just combine 1/2 teaspoon ground cinnamon, 1/4 teaspoon ground ginger, 1/8 teaspoon ground allspice and 1/8 teaspoon ground nutmeg to equal 1 teaspoon pumpkin pie spice.

2 1/2 cups all-purpose flour*
1 1/2 cups unsweetened applesauce
1 1/4 cups sugar
1/2 cup butter or stick margarine, softened**
1/2 cup water
1 1/2 teaspoons baking soda
1 1/2 teaspoons pumpkin pie spice
1 teaspoon salt
3/4 teaspoon baking powder
2 large eggs
1 cup raisins
2/3 cup chopped nuts
Maple-Nut Buttercream Frosting (page 111) or Cream
    Cheese Frosting (page 111), if desired

1. Heat oven to 350°. Grease bottom and sides of rectangular pan, 13 × 9 × 2 inches, or 2 round pans, 8 × 1 1/2 or 9 × 1 1/2 inches, with shortening; lightly flour.

2. Beat all ingredients except raisins, nuts and Maple-Nut Buttercream Frosting in large bowl with electric mixer on low speed 30 seconds, scraping bowl constantly. Beat on high speed 3 minutes, scraping bowl occasionally. Stir in raisins and nuts. Pour into pan(s).

3. Bake rectangle 45 to 50 minutes, rounds 40 to 45 minutes, or until toothpick inserted in center comes out clean. Cool rectangle in pan on wire rack. Cool rounds 10 minutes; remove from pans to wire rack. Cool completely, about 1 hour.

4. Frost rectangle or fill round layers and frost with Maple-Nut Buttercream Frosting.

*Do not use self-rising flour.
**Spreads with at least 65% vegetable oil can be used (page 91).

1 Serving: Calories 355 (Calories from Fat 115); Fat 13g (Saturated 5g); Cholesterol 55mg; Sodium 450mg; Carbohydrate 56g (Dietary Fiber 2g); Protein 5g **% Daily Value:** Vitamin A 6%; Vitamin C 0%; Calcium 4%; Iron 10% **Diet Exchanges:** Not Recommended

BANANA CAKE: Substitute 1 1/2 cups mashed ripe bananas (3 medium) for the applesauce and buttermilk for the water. Omit pumpkin pie spice and raisins. Increase baking powder to 1 teaspoon. Frost with Browned Butter Buttercream Frosting (page 111) or Chocolate Buttercream Frosting (page 110) if desired.

Jeweled Fruitcake

Prep: 15 min; Bake: 1 hr 45 min; Cool: 24 hr ✱ *32 servings*

This fruitcake can be kept in the refrigerator for as long as 2 months. It actually develops flavor and is easier to cut after long storage, so make it ahead of the holidays. If you like, brush occasionally with brandy, rum or bourbon during storage to add a rich mellow flavor.

2 cups dried apricots (11 ounces)
2 cups pitted dates (12 ounces)
1 1/2 cups nuts (8 ounces)
1 cup red and green candied pineapple (7 ounces), chopped
1 cup red and green maraschino cherries (12 ounces), drained
3/4 cup all-purpose flour*
3/4 cup sugar
1/2 teaspoon baking powder
1/2 teaspoon salt
1 1/2 teaspoons vanilla
3 large eggs
Light corn syrup, if desired

1. Heat oven to 300°. Line loaf pan, 9 × 5 × 3 or 8 1/2 × 4 1/2 × 2 1/2 inches, with aluminum foil; grease foil with shortening.

2. Mix all ingredients except corn syrup. Spread in pan.

3. Bake about 1 hour 45 minutes or until toothpick inserted in center comes out clean. If necessary, cover with aluminum foil during last 30 minutes of baking to prevent excessive browning.

4. Remove fruitcake from pan (with foil) to wire rack. For a glossy top, immediately brush with light corn syrup. Allow loaves to cool completely and become firm before cutting, about 24 hours. Wrap tightly and store in refrigerator no longer than 2 months.

If using self-rising flour, omit baking powder and salt.

1 Serving: Calories 155 (Calories from Fat 45); Fat 5g (Saturated 1g); Cholesterol 20mg; Sodium 125mg; Carbohydrate 27g (Dietary Fiber 2g); Protein 2g **% Daily Value:** Vitamin A 6%; Vitamin C 0%; Calcium 2%; Iron 6% **Diet Exchanges:** 1 Starch, 1 Fruit, 1/2 Fat

MINI JEWELED FRUITCAKE LOAVES: Generously grease bottoms and sides of 7 or 8 miniature loaf pans, 4 1/2 × 2 3/4 × 1 1/4 inches, with shortening, or line with aluminum foil and grease with shortening. Divide batter evenly among pans (about 1 cup each). Bake about 1 hour or until toothpick inserted in center comes out clean. Remove from pans to wire rack. Allow loaves to cool completely and become firm before cutting, about 24 hours. 7 or 8 mini loaves.

PETITE JEWELED FRUITCAKE CUPS: Line 24 medium muffin cups, 2 1/2 × 1 1/4 inches, with foil liners. Divide batter evenly among cups (about 1/3 cup each). Bake 35 to 40 minutes or until toothpick inserted in center comes out clean. Remove from pans to wire rack. Cool completely before serving. 24 servings.

Foam Cakes

Angel food, sponge, and chiffon are the lighter-than-air, melt-in-your-mouth members of the foam cake family. They're related because they depend on beaten egg whites for their lightness. But each kind is also a little different:

- Angel food cakes have no added leavening (such as baking powder), shortening or egg yolks, and they have a high proportion of beaten egg whites to flour. No egg yolks and no shortening make angel food cakes a fabulous no-fat sweet. Don't miss the wonderful Angel Food Cake recipe on page 104.
- Sponge cakes use both egg whites and yolks and sometimes a little leavening, but like angel food cakes, they don't contain shortening. See Jelly Roll, page 107.
- Chiffon cakes are a cross between foam and shortening cakes because they're made with leavening, vegetable oil or shortening and egg yolks, as well as beaten whites. See Lemon Chiffon Cake, page 106.

Pans and Pan Preparation

Don't grease and flour the pans unless the recipe calls for it. When baking, the batter must be able to cling to and climb up the side and tube of the pan.

If you're using an angel food cake pan, also called a tube pan, move the oven rack to the lowest position so the cake will bake completely without getting too brown on top.

Mixing Foam Cakes

Start with a clean, dry bowl and beaters so the egg whites will beat properly. Even a speck of grease will keep them from whipping up. Beat the egg whites until they form stiff, straight peaks. Not beating the whites enough or not folding them completely into the batter can cause coarse, low-volume cakes. Beating or folding too much will break down the egg white foam, and you'll end up with a compact cake.

Always fold the batter or the sugar-flour mixture into the beaten egg whites rather than stirring it in. To fold, cut down through the mixture with your spatula, then slide the spatula across the bottom and up the side of the bowl. Rotate the bowl a quarter turn and continue folding just until no white streaks remain. See page 104 for illustration.

Baking Foam Cakes

To test if a foam cake baked in rectangular, round or jelly roll pan is done, poke a toothpick in the center. If it comes out clean, the cake is done.

To test if an angel food cake is done, touch it. If the cracks feel dry and the top springs back when you touch it lightly with your fingertip, the cake is done. If the cake pulls away from the side of the pan or falls out of the pan when turned upside down to cool, it wasn't baked long enough.

After baking, immediately invert a foam cake baked in an angel food cake pan onto a heatproof funnel or bottle and let it hang upside down until it is completely cool.

To remove a foam cake from an angel food cake pan after it is completely cool, slide a stiff knife or metal spatula firmly between the cake and the pan. Move it up and down along the side to loosen the cake, being careful not to damage it. Turn the pan upside down, tap one side against the counter, and the cake will slip out.

To keep a foam cake fresh overnight, leave it in the baking pan and cover it loosely with plastic wrap. When you're ready to serve it, remove it from the pan and frost if desired.

Angel Food Cake *Low-Fat*

Prep: 20 min; Bake: 35 min; Cool: 2 hr ✳ *12 servings*

Stiffly beaten egg whites are the secret to a successful angel food cake, so separate eggs carefully. Even a tiny amount of egg yolk will keep the egg whites from beating up. See page 189 for more information on beating egg whites. Looking for something to do with the leftover egg yolks? Try making Crème Brûlée (page 187), Chocolate Mousse (page 186) or Rice Pudding (page 187).

1 1/2 cups powdered sugar
1 cup cake flour
1 1/2 cups large egg whites (about 12)
1 1/2 teaspoons cream of tartar
1 cup granulated sugar
1 1/2 teaspoons vanilla
1/2 teaspoon almond extract
1/4 teaspoon salt
Vanilla Glaze (page 113) or Chocolate Glaze (page 112),
    if desired

1. Move oven rack to lowest position. Heat oven to 375°.

2. Mix powdered sugar and flour; set aside. Beat egg whites and cream of tartar in large bowl with electric mixer on medium speed until foamy. Beat in granulated sugar, 2 tablespoons at a time, on high speed, adding vanilla, almond extract and salt with the last addition of sugar. Continue beating until stiff and glossy. Do not underbeat.

3. Sprinkle powdered sugar–flour mixture, 1/4 cup at a time, over egg white mixture, folding in with rubber spatula just until sugar–flour mixture disappears. Push batter into ungreased angel food cake pan (tube pan), 10 × 4 inches. Cut gently through batter with metal spatula or knife to break air pockets.

4. Bake 30 to 35 minutes or until cracks feel dry and top springs back when touched lightly. Immediately turn pan upside down onto heatproof funnel or bottle. Let hang about 2 hours or until cake is completely cool. Loosen side of cake with knife or long metal spatula; remove from pan.

5. Spread or drizzle Vanilla Glaze over top of cake.

1 Serving: Calories 180 (Calories from Fat 0); Fat 0g (Saturated 0g); Cholesterol 0mg; Sodium 100mg; Carbohydrate 41g (Dietary Fiber 0g); Protein 4g **% Daily Value:** Vitamin A 0%; Vitamin C 0%; Calcium 0%; Iron 4% **Diet Exchanges:** 1 1/2 Starch, 1 Fruit

HOW TO MAKE ANGEL FOOD CAKES

Beat egg whites and sugar until stiff and glossy.

To fold sugar-flour mixture into beaten egg white mixture, use a rubber spatula to cut down vertically through center of egg whites, across the bottom of the bowl and up the side, turning the egg whites over. Rotate bowl one-fourth turn and repeat. Continue folding in this way just until ingredients are blended.

Use a metal spatula to cut through batter, pushing batter gently against side of pan and tube, to break large air pockets.

Coffee and Cream Chiffon Cake

Prep: 20 min; Bake: 1 hr; Cool: 2 hr ✳ *16 servings*

Chocolate-covered coffee beans are a perfect garnish. If your grocer doesn't have them, try a coffee shop.

1 cup large egg whites (about 8)
1/2 teaspoon cream of tartar
2 cups all-purpose* or 2 1/4 cups cake flour
1 1/2 cups sugar
3 teaspoons baking powder
1 teaspoon salt
3/4 cup cold coffee
1/2 cup vegetable oil
1 teaspoon vanilla
5 egg yolks
Coffee Cream Filling (right)
Sweetened Whipped Cream (page 198), if desired

1. Move oven rack to lowest position. Heat oven to 325°.

2. Beat egg whites and cream of tartar in large bowl with electric mixer on high speed until stiff peaks form; set aside.

3. Mix flour, sugar, baking powder and salt in medium bowl. Beat in coffee, oil, vanilla and egg yolks on low speed 1 minute. Gradually pour coffee mixture over beaten egg whites, folding with rubber spatula just until blended. Push batter into ungreased angel food cake pan (tube pan), 10 × 4 inches. Cut gently through batter with metal spatula or knife to break air pockets.

4. Bake 50 to 60 minutes or until top springs back when touched lightly. Immediately turn pan upside down onto heatproof funnel or bottle. Let hang about 2 hours or until cake is completely cool. Loosen side of cake with knife or long metal spatula; remove from pan.

5. Make Coffee Cream Filling. Cut cake horizontally to make 3 layers. (Mark side of cake with toothpicks and cut with long, thin serrated knife.) Fill layers with Coffee Cream Filling. Top with whipped topping. Store covered in refrigerator.

Coffee Cream Filling

1/3 cup sugar
2 tablespoons cornstarch
Dash of salt
1 1/4 cups whipping (heavy) cream
2 egg yolks
2 tablespoons coffee liqueur or cold strong coffee

Mix sugar, cornstarch, salt, whipping cream and egg yolks in 1-quart saucepan until blended. Heat over medium heat, stirring constantly, until thickened; remove from heat. Stir in liqueur. Refrigerate at least 1 hour until chilled.

*If using self-rising flour, omit baking powder and salt.

1 Serving: Calories 220 (Calories from Fat 80); Fat 9g (Saturated 2g); Cholesterol 65mg; Sodium 270mg; Carbohydrate 31g (Dietary Fiber 0g); Protein 4g **% Daily Value:** Vitamin A 2%; Vitamin C 0%; Calcium 6%; Iron 6% **Diet Exchanges:** 1 Starch, 1 Fruit, 2 Fat

---

FOAM CAKE CURES

Great Foam Cakes Are

High, golden brown with rounded top and cracks in surface
Soft, moist and delicate
Angel Food—feathery and fine-textured
Chiffon—springy and medium-textured
Sponge—springy and fine-textured

Problem	Possible Cause
Low and compact	• underbeaten or extremely overbeaten egg whites (use medium speeds on powerful stand mixers)
	• overfolded batter
	• incorrect cooling (not cooled upside down)
Coarse	• underfolded batter
Tough	• underbeaten egg whites
	• overfolded batter

Lemon Chiffon Cake with Lemon Glaze (variation of Vanilla Glaze, page 113)

Lemon Chiffon Cake

Prep: 20 min; Bake: 1 hr 15 min; Cool: 2 hr ✱ *12 servings*

Chiffon cake combines the lightness of angel food with the richness of a layer cake.

2 cups all-purpose* or 2 1/4 cups cake flour
1 1/2 cups sugar
3 teaspoons baking powder
1 teaspoon salt
3/4 cup cold water
1/2 cup vegetable oil
2 teaspoons vanilla
1 tablespoon grated lemon peel
7 large egg yolks (with all-purpose flour) or 5 large egg
    yolks (with cake flour)
1 cup large egg whites (about 8)
1/2 teaspoon cream of tartar
Lemon Glaze (page 113), if desired

1. Move oven rack to lowest position. Heat oven to 325°.

2. Mix flour, sugar, baking powder and salt in large bowl. Beat in water, oil, vanilla, lemon peel and egg yolks with electric mixer on low speed until smooth.

3. With clean beaters, beat egg whites and cream of tartar in large bowl with electric mixer on high speed until stiff peaks form. Gradually pour egg yolk mixture over beaten egg whites, folding in with rubber spatula just until blended. Pour into ungreased angel food cake pan (tube pan), 10 × 4 inches.

4. Bake about 1 hour 15 minutes or until top springs back when touched lightly. Immediately turn pan upside down onto heatproof funnel or bottle. Let hang about 2 hours or until cake is completely cool. Loosen side of cake with knife or long metal spatula; remove from pan.

5. Spread Lemon Glaze over top of cake, allowing some to drizzle down side.

If using self-rising flour, omit baking powder and salt.

1 Serving: Calories 295 (Calories from Fat 108); Fat 12g (Saturated 2g); Cholesterol 125mg; Sodium 360mg; Carbohydrate 42g (Dietary Fiber 1g); Protein 6g **% Daily Value:** Vitamin A 4%; Vitamin C 0%; Calcium 8%; Iron 8% **Diet Exchanges:** 2 Starch, 1 Fruit, 1 Fat

ORANGE CHIFFON CAKE: Omit vanilla. Substitute 2 tablespoons grated orange peel for the lemon peel.

Jelly Roll *Low-Fat*

Prep: 20 min; Bake: 15 min; Cool: 30 min ✳ 10 servings

If you tried to roll a regular layer cake, it would crack. This special kind of cake, called a *sponge cake*, is soft and flexible so that it can be rolled up.

3 large eggs
1 cup granulated sugar
1/3 cup water
1 teaspoon vanilla
3/4 cup all-purpose* or 1 cup cake flour
1 teaspoon baking powder
1/4 teaspoon salt
Powdered sugar
About 2/3 cup jelly or jam

1. Heat oven to 375°. Line jelly roll pan, 15 1/2 × 10 1/2 × 1 inch, with waxed paper, aluminum foil or cooking parchment paper; generously grease waxed paper or foil with shortening.

2. Beat eggs in small bowl with electric mixer on high speed about 5 minutes or until very thick and lemon colored. Pour eggs into medium bowl. Gradually beat in granulated sugar. Beat in water and vanilla on low speed. Gradually add flour, baking powder and salt, beating just until batter is smooth. Pour into pan, spreading to corners.

3. Bake 12 to 15 minutes or until toothpick inserted in center comes out clean. Immediately loosen cake from edges of pan and turn upside down onto towel generously sprinkled with powdered sugar. Carefully remove paper. Trim off stiff edges of cake if necessary. While cake is hot, carefully roll cake and towel from narrow end. Cool on wire rack at least 30 minutes.

4. Unroll cake and remove towel. Beat jelly slightly with fork to soften; spread over cake. Roll up cake. Sprinkle with powdered sugar.

If using self-rising flour, omit baking powder and salt.

1 Serving: Calories 240 (Calories from Fat 20); Fat 2g (Saturated 1g); Cholesterol 65mg; Sodium 135mg; Carbohydrate 43g (Dietary Fiber 0g); Protein 3g **% Daily Value:** Vitamin A 2%; Vitamin C 0%; Calcium 4%; Iron 4% **Diet Exchanges:** 1 Starch, 2 Fruit

CHOCOLATE CAKE ROLL: Do not use self-rising flour. Increase eggs to 4. Beat in 1/4 cup baking cocoa with the flour. If desired, fill cake with ice cream instead of jelly or jam: Spread 1 to 1 1/2 pints (2 to 3 cups) ice cream, slightly softened, over cooled cake. Roll up cake; wrap in plastic wrap. Freeze about 4 hours or until firm. Serve with Hot Fudge Sauce (page 195) if desired.

Tips for Frosting

- A good frosting is smooth and lustrous and can hold a swirl. It's soft enough to spread on the cake without running down the sides. If a creamy frosting is too thick, it can pull and tear the cake surface as you frost, leaving you with crumbs in your frosting. To make thick frosting thinner, add a few drops of water or milk.

- When testing these recipes, we found that frostings turned out best when we used butter or stick margarine. We don't recommend using vegetable oil spreads or tub margarine or tub or whipped butter because they contain more water and/or air and less fat, so frosting made with them turns out too soft (see Fats, page 16). Also, ingredients such as chocolate don't always melt or mix well with them.

- When making frosting, the recipe may list a range for the amount of ingredients, for instance 2 to 3 tablespoons milk. For better control over the consistency, start with the smallest amount, then add more if necessary.

- For step-by-step directions for using frostings, see How to Frost a Two-Layer Cake, page 109.

- How much frosting should you use? It's your call. Some like to lay it on thick, others prefer just a thin coating. See the Note for Chocolate Buttercream Frosting and Vanilla Buttercream Frosting recipes (page 110–111) for making extra frosting.

- When frosting cakes, the best and easiest tool to use is a flexible metal spatula, which allows you to spread the frosting in a larger area. Use a light touch when frosting to help prevent layers from sliding and from squishing out the filling from between layers.

- Fluffy frostings, such as White Mountain Frosting (page 112), aren't as stable as creamy frostings, so you may not want to make them in humid or rainy weather. Because of moisture in the air, you'll need to beat the frosting longer or slightly decrease the amount of water. Unfortunately, there's no rule for how much to decrease it; you'll have to experiment. Frost and serve a cake with fluffy frosting the same day.

- To drizzle a glaze with no muss or fuss, pour it into a plastic food-storage bag. Snip off a tiny corner and squeeze gently, moving the bag back and forth over the top of the cake. Make the hole bigger if you want a thicker flow of glaze.

Easy Decorating Ideas for Frosted Cakes

Cookie Cutter Designs

Outlined Designs: Press cookie cutters into frosted cake; outline markings with small candies. Or, dip cookie cutters in liquid food color; lightly press cutters into frosted cake.

Filled-in Designs: Place cookie cutters on frosted cake, sprinkle inside cutter with colored sugar, small candy sprinkles or small candies. Gently press into frosting; remove cookie cutters.

Chocolate Web Design: Drizzle round frosted or glazed cake with melted chocolate, beginning with small circle in center and encircling with larger circle 1/2 inch outside the other. Immediately draw a knife from center outward 8 times, equally spaced.

Patchwork Design: Mark servings in the frosting of a square or rectangular cake with a knife or toothpick. Fill the squares with chopped nuts; miniature candy-coated chocolate pieces; confetti candy bits; crushed candies; colored sugars; fruit-shaped candies; tinted coconut; chopped dried fruits; or small, shaped cookies, crackers or cereals to look like a patchwork quilt.

HOW TO FROST A TWO-LAYER CAKE

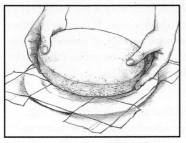

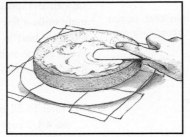

1. Brush any loose crumbs from the cooled cake layer. Place 4 strips of waxed paper around edge of cake plate. Place the layer, rounded side down, on the plate. The waxed paper will protect the plate as you frost.

2. Spread about 1/3 cup creamy frosting (1/2 cup if using a fluffy frosting such as White Mountain Frosting, page 000) over the top of the first layer to within about 1/4 inch of the edge.

3. Place second cake layer, rounded side up, on the first layer so that the 2 flat sides of the layers are together with frosting in between. Coat the side of the cake with a very thin layer of frosting to seal in the crumbs.

HOW TO COAT CAKE SIDES

HOW TO GLAZE A CAKE

4. Frost the side of the cake in swirls, making a rim about 1/4 inch high above the top of the cake so the top won't appear sloped. Spread the remaining frosting on top, just to the built-up rim. Remove waxed paper strips.

Two filled cake layers with frosted sides (not top) can be rolled in chopped nuts or candies to evenly coat the sides. Place nuts on waxed paper or cutting board. Hold cake as shown. Roll side carefully in nuts to coat.

To glaze the top of a cake, pour or drizzle glaze over top of cake. Spread with a spatula or the back of a spoon, allowing some glaze to drizzle down the side.

Fudge Frosting *Low-Fat*

Prep: 5 min; Cook: 5 min; Cool: 30 min
✱ 8 servings, about 1 1/4 cups

1/2 cup granulated sugar
1/4 cup baking cocoa
1/4 cup milk
2 tablespoons butter or stick margarine*
1 tablespoon light corn syrup
Dash of salt
1/2 to 3/4 cup powdered sugar
1/2 teaspoon vanilla

1. Mix granulated sugar and cocoa in 2-quart saucepan. Stir in milk, butter, corn syrup and salt. Heat to boiling, stirring frequently. Boil 3 minutes, stirring occasionally; cool 30 minutes.

2. Beat in powdered sugar and vanilla until smooth. Frosts 8- or 9-inch one-layer cake or 13 × 9-inch cake.

> **Note:** To fill and frost an 8- or 9-inch two-layer cake, double the ingredients and use a 3-quart saucepan.

Do not use vegetable oil spreads (page 91).

1 Serving (about 1 1/4 cup): Calories 125 (Calories from Fat 25); Fat 3g (Saturated 2g); Cholesterol 10mg; Sodium 65mg; Carbohydrate 24g (Dietary Fiber 1g); Protein 1g **% Daily Value:** Vitamin A 2%; Vitamin C 0%; Calcium 0%; Iron 2% **Diet Exchanges:** 1/2 Starch, 1 Fruit, 1/2 Fat

Chocolate Buttercream Frosting *Fast*

Prep: 15 min ✱ 12 servings, about 2 cups

3 cups powdered sugar
1/3 cup butter or stick margarine, softened*
2 teaspoons vanilla
3 ounces unsweetened baking chocolate, melted and
    cooled
3 to 4 tablespoons milk

1. Mix powdered sugar and butter in medium bowl with spoon or electric mixer on low speed. Stir in vanilla and chocolate.

2. Gradually beat in just enough milk to make frosting smooth and spreadable. If frosting is too thick, beat in more milk, a few drops at a time. If frosting becomes too thin, beat in a small amount of powdered sugar. Frosts 13 × 9-inch cake generously, or fills and frosts an 8- or 9-inch two-layer cake.

> **Note:** To fill and frost an 8-inch three-layer cake, use 4 1/2 cups powdered sugar, 1/2 cup butter or stick margarine, softened, 3 teaspoons vanilla, 4 ounces chocolate and about 1/4 cup milk.

Do not use vegetable oil spreads (page 91).

1 Serving: Calories 210 (Calories from Fat 80); Fat 9g (Saturated 6g); Cholesterol 15mg; Sodium 35mg; Carbohydrate 32g (Dietary Fiber 1g); Protein 1g **% Daily Value:** Vitamin A 4%; Vitamin C 0%; Calcium 0%; Iron 2% **Diet Exchanges:** 1 Starch, 1 Fruit, 1 1/2 Fat

CREAMY COCOA FROSTING: Substitute 1/3 cup baking cocoa for the chocolate.

MOCHA FROSTING: Add 2 1/2 teaspoons instant coffee (dry) with the powdered sugar.

WHITE CHOCOLATE FROSTING: Substitute 3/4 cup (3 ounces) white baking chips, melted and cooled, for the chocolate.

Vanilla Buttercream Frosting *Fast*

Prep: 10 min ✱ 12 servings, about 1 3/4 cups

3 cups powdered sugar
1/3 cup butter or stick margarine, softened*
1 1/2 teaspoons vanilla
1 to 2 tablespoons milk

1. Mix powdered sugar and butter in medium bowl with spoon or electric mixer on low speed. Stir in vanilla and 1 tablespoon of the milk.

2. Gradually beat in just enough remaining milk to make frosting smooth and spreadable. If frosting is too thick, beat in more milk, a few drops at a time. If frosting becomes too thin, beat in a small amount of powdered sugar. Frosts 13 × 9-inch cake generously, or fills and frosts an 8- or 9-inch two-layer cake.

Note: To fill and frost an 8-inch three-layer cake, use 4 1/2 cups powdered sugar, 1/2 cup butter or stick margarine, softened, 2 teaspoons vanilla and about 3 tablespoons milk.

Do not use vegetable oil spreads (page 91).

1 Serving: Calories 165 (Calories from Fat 45); Fat 5g (Saturated 3g); Cholesterol 15mg; Sodium 35mg; Carbohydrate 30g (Dietary Fiber 0g); Protein 0g **% Daily Value:** Vitamin A 4%; Vitamin C 0%; Calcium 0%; Iron 0% **Diet Exchanges:** 2 Fruit, 1 Fat

BROWNED BUTTER BUTTERCREAM FROSTING: Heat 1/3 cup butter (do not use margarine or spreads) over medium heat until just light brown. Watch carefully because butter can brown then burn quickly. Cool. Use browned butter instead of softened butter in recipe.

LEMON BUTTERCREAM FROSTING: Omit vanilla. Substitute lemon juice for the milk. Stir in 1/2 teaspoon grated lemon peel.

MAPLE-NUT BUTTERCREAM FROSTING: Omit vanilla. Substitute 1/2 cup maple-flavored syrup for the milk. Stir in 1/4 cup finely chopped nuts.

ORANGE BUTTERCREAM FROSTING: Omit vanilla. Substitute orange juice for the milk. Stir in 2 teaspoons grated orange peel.

PEANUT BUTTER BUTTERCREAM FROSTING: Substitute peanut butter for the butter. Increase milk to 1/4 cup, adding more if necessary, a few drops at a time.

Cream Cheese Frosting *Fast*

Prep: 10 min ✱ 12 to 16 servings, about 2 1/2 cups

Because the cream cheese will spoil if left out at room temperature, you'll need to refrigerate the frosted cake or any leftover frosting.

1 package (8 ounces) cream cheese, softened
1/4 cup butter or stick margarine*
2 to 3 teaspoons milk
1 teaspoon vanilla
4 cups powdered sugar

1. Beat cream cheese, butter, milk and vanilla in medium bowl with electric mixer on low speed until smooth.

2. Gradually beat in powdered sugar, 1 cup at a time, on low speed until smooth and spreadable. Frosts 13 × 9-inch cake generously, or fills and frosts an 8- or 9-inch two-layer cake. Store frosted cake or any remaining frosting covered in refrigerator.

Do not use vegetable oil spreads (page 91).

1 Serving: Calories 260 (Calories from Fat 90); Fat 10g (Saturated 7g); Cholesterol 30mg; Sodium 80mg; Carbohydrate 40g (Dietary Fiber 0g); Protein 2g **% Daily Value:** Vitamin A 8%; Vitamin C 0%; Calcium 2%; Iron 0% **Diet Exchanges:** 1 Starch, 1 1/2 Fruit, 2 Fat

CHOCOLATE CREAM CHEESE FROSTING: Add 2 ounces unsweetened baking chocolate, melted and cooled, with the butter.

Caramel Frosting

Prep: 10 min; Cook: 10 min; Cool: 30 min
✱ 12 servings, about 2 cups

1/2 cup butter or stick margarine*
1 cup packed brown sugar
1/4 cup milk
2 cups powdered sugar

1. Melt butter in 2-quart saucepan over medium heat. Stir in brown sugar. Heat to boiling, stirring constantly; reduce heat to low. Boil and stir 2 minutes. Stir in milk. Heat to boiling; remove from heat. Cool to lukewarm, about 30 minutes.

2. Gradually stir in powdered sugar. Place saucepan of frosting in bowl of cold water. Beat with spoon until smooth and spreadable. If frosting becomes too stiff, stir in additional milk, 1 teaspoon at a time, or heat over low heat, stirring constantly. Frosts 13 × 9-inch cake, or fills and frosts an 8- or 9-inch two-layer cake.

Do not use vegetable oil spreads (page 91).

1 Serving: Calories 225 (Calories from Fat 70); Fat 8g (Saturated 5g); Cholesterol 20mg; Sodium 60mg; Carbohydrate 38g (Dietary Fiber 0g); Protein 0g **% Daily Value:** Vitamin A 6%; Vitamin C 0%; Calcium 2%; Iron 2% **Diet Exchanges:** 2 1/2 Fruit, 1 1/2 Fat

White Mountain Frosting *Low-Fat*

Prep: 25 min; Cook: 10 min
✳ *12 to 16 servings, about 3 cups*

This fluffy white frosting is so-named because of the large peaks that it can hold after it is beaten.

1/2 cup sugar
1/4 cup light corn syrup
2 tablespoons water
2 large egg whites
1 teaspoon vanilla

1. Mix sugar, corn syrup and water in 1-quart saucepan. Cover and heat to rolling boil over medium heat. Uncover and boil 4 to 8 minutes, without stirring, to 242° on candy thermometer or until small amount of mixture dropped into cup of very cold water forms a firm ball that holds its shape until pressed. For an accurate temperature reading, tilt the saucepan slightly so mixture is deep enough for thermometer.

2. While mixture is boiling, beat egg whites in medium bowl with electric mixer on high speed just until stiff peaks form.

3. Pour hot syrup very slowly in thin stream into egg whites, beating constantly on medium speed. Add vanilla. Beat on high speed about 10 minutes or until stiff peaks form. Frosts 13 × 9-inch cake, or fills and frosts an 8- or 9-inch two-layer cake.

1 Serving: Calories 60 (Calories from Fat 0); Fat 0g (Saturated 0g); Cholesterol 0mg; Sodium 15mg; Carbohydrate 14g (Dietary Fiber 0g); Protein 1g **% Daily Value:** Vitamin A 0%; Vitamin C 0%; Calcium 0%; Iron 0% **Diet Exchanges:** 1 Fruit

BUTTERSCOTCH FROSTING: Substitute packed brown sugar for the granulated sugar. Decrease vanilla to 1/2 teaspoon.

CHERRY-NUT FROSTING: Stir in 1/4 cup cut-up candied cherries, 1/4 cup chopped nuts and, if desired, 6 to 8 drops red food color.

PEPPERMINT FROSTING: Stir in 1/3 cup coarsely crushed hard peppermint candies or 1/2 teaspoon peppermint extract.

Chocolate Glaze *Fast*

Prep: 5 min; Cook: 5 min; Cool: 10 min
✳ *12 to 16 servings, about 1/2 cup*

1/2 cup semisweet chocolate chips
2 tablespoons butter or stick margarine*
2 tablespoons corn syrup
1 to 2 teaspoons hot water

1. Heat chocolate chips, butter and corn syrup in 1-quart saucepan over low heat, stirring frequently, until chocolate chips are melted. Cool about 10 minutes.

2. Stir in hot water, 1 teaspoon at a time, until consistency of thick syrup. Glazes one 12-cup bundt cake, 10-inch angel food or chiffon cake or top of an 8- or 9-inch layer cake.

*Do not use vegetable oil spreads (page 91).

1 Serving: Calories 65 (Calories from Fat 35); Fat 4g (Saturated 2g); Cholesterol 5mg; Sodium 20mg; Carbohydrate 7g (Dietary Fiber 0g); Protein 0g **% Daily Value:** Vitamin A 2%; Vitamin C 0%; Calcium 0%; Iron 0% **Diet Exchanges:** 1/2 Fruit, 1 Fat

MILK CHOCOLATE GLAZE: Substitute milk chocolate chips for the semisweet chocolate chips.

MINT CHOCOLATE GLAZE: Substitute mint chocolate chips for the semisweet chocolate chips.

WHITE CHOCOLATE GLAZE: Substitute white baking chips for the chocolate chips.

Vanilla Glaze *Fast*

Prep: 5 min ✱ 12 to 16 servings, about 1 cup

1/3 cup butter or stick margarine*
2 cups powdered sugar
1 1/2 teaspoons vanilla or clear vanilla
2 to 4 tablespoons hot water

1. Melt butter in 1 1/2-quart saucepan over low heat; remove from heat. Stir in powdered sugar and vanilla.

2. Stir in hot water, 1 tablespoon at a time, until smooth and consistency of thick syrup. Glazes one 12-cup bundt cake, 10-inch angel food or chiffon cake or top of an 8- or 9-inch layer cake.

*Do not use vegetable oil spreads (page 91).

1 Serving: Calories 125 (Calories from Fat 45); Fat 5g (Saturated 3g); Cholesterol 15mg; Sodium 35mg; Carbohydrate 20g (Dietary Fiber 0g); Protein 0g **% Daily Value:** Vitamin A 4%; Vitamin C 0%; Calcium 0%; Iron 0% **Diet Exchanges:** 1 1/2 Fruit, 1 Fat

LEMON GLAZE: Stir 1/2 teaspoon grated lemon peel into melted butter. Substitute lemon juice for the vanilla and hot water.

ORANGE GLAZE: Stir 1/2 teaspoon grated orange peel into melted butter. Substitute orange juice for the vanilla and hot water.

Chocolate Ganache *Fast*

Prep: 5 min; Cook: 5 min; Stand: 5 min ✱ 12 to 16 servings, about 1 1/4 cups

Ganache is a very rich chocolate glaze made with semisweet chocolate and heavy cream. If you glaze the cake on a cooling rack with waxed paper underneath the rack, the ganache will drip over the side of the cake and the extra drips will fall onto the waxed paper. When the ganache hardens, you can easily and neatly transfer the cake to your serving plate.

2/3 cup whipping (heavy) cream
6 ounces semisweet baking chocolate, chopped

1. Heat whipping cream in 1-quart saucepan over low heat until hot but not boiling; remove from heat.

2. Stir in chocolate until melted. Let stand about 5 minutes. Ganache is ready to use when it mounds slightly when dropped from a spoon. It will become firmer the longer it cools.

3. Pour ganache carefully onto top center of cake; spread with large spatula so it flows evenly over top and down to cover side of cake. Glazes 13 × 9-inch cake or top of an 8- or 9-inch two-layer cake.

1 Serving: Calories 105 (Calories from Fat 70); Fat 8g (Saturated 5g); Cholesterol 15mg; Sodium 5mg; Carbohydrate 9g (Dietary Fiber 1g); Protein 1g **% Daily Value:** Vitamin A 2%; Vitamin C 0%; Calcium 0%; Iron 2% **Diet Exchanges:** 1/2 Fruit, 1 1/2 Fat

Coconut-Pecan Filling and Topping

Prep: 10 min; Cook: 12 min; Cool: 30 min ✱ 12 to 16 servings, about 3 cups

Although this filling is traditionally used for German Chocolate Cake (page 95), it is also delicious on other cakes. Frost layer cakes only between the layers and on top, leaving the sides unfrosted.

1 cup sugar
1/2 cup butter or stick margarine*
1 cup evaporated milk
1 teaspoon vanilla
3 large egg yolks
1 1/3 cups flaked coconut
1 cup chopped pecans

1. Mix sugar, butter, milk, vanilla and egg yolks in 2-quart saucepan. Cook over medium heat about 12 minutes, stirring occasionally, until thick.

2. Stir in coconut and pecans. Cool about 30 minutes, beating occasionally with spoon, until spreadable. Fills and frosts top of an 8- or 9-inch two- or three-layer cake.

*Do not use vegetable oil spreads (page 91).

1 Serving: Calories 280 (Calories from Fat 170); Fat 19g (Saturated 9g); Cholesterol 75mg; Sodium 100mg; Carbohydrate 25g (Dietary Fiber 1g); Protein 3g **% Daily Value:** Vitamin A 10%; Vitamin C 0%; Calcium 6%; Iron 2% **Diet Exchanges:** 1 Starch, 1 1/2 Fruit, 3 Fat

Lemon Filling *Low-Fat*

Prep: 5 min; Cook: 10 min; Chill: 2 hr
* *12 servings, about 1 1/4 cups*

Before squeezing juice from a lemon, roll it back and forth on a countertop, using gentle pressure, and it will release more juice. It's easier to grate the peel off whole lemons, so don't forget to grate first before juicing them.

3/4 cup sugar
3 tablespoons cornstarch
1/4 teaspoon salt
2/3 cup water
1 tablespoon butter or stick margarine*
1 teaspoon grated lemon peel
1/4 cup lemon juice
2 drops yellow food color, if desired

1. Mix sugar, cornstarch and salt in 1 1/2-quart saucepan. Gradually stir in water. Cook over medium heat, stirring constantly, until mixture thickens and boils. Boil and stir 1 minute; remove from heat.

2. Stir in butter and lemon peel until butter is melted. Gradually stir in lemon juice and food color. Press plastic wrap on filling to prevent a tough layer from forming on top. Refrigerate about 2 hours or until set. Store cakes or pastries filled with Lemon Filling covered in the refrigerator.

*Do not use vegetable oil spreads (page 91).

1 Serving: Calories 70 (Calories from Fat 10); Fat 1g (Saturated 1g); Cholesterol 5mg; Sodium 55mg; Carbohydrate 15g (Dietary Fiber 0g); Protein 0g **% Daily Value:** Vitamin A 0%; Vitamin C 0%; Calcium 0%; Iron 0% **Diet Exchanges:** 1 Fruit

Raspberry Filling *Low-Fat*

Prep: 5 min; Cook: 10 min; Cool: 30 min
* *12 servings, about 2/3 cup*

1 package (10 ounces) frozen raspberries in syrup, thawed
2 tablespoons sugar
1 tablespoon cornstarch

1. Drain raspberries, reserving 1/3 cup syrup. Mix sugar and cornstarch in 1-quart saucepan. Stir in reserved raspberry syrup.

2. Heat sugar mixture over medium-low heat, stirring constantly, until mixture thickens and boils. Boil and stir 1 minute.

3. Stir raspberries into sugar mixture. Cool completely, about 30 minutes.

1 Serving: Calories 30 (Calories from Fat 0); Fat 0g (Saturated 0g); Cholesterol 0mg; Sodium 0mg; Carbohydrate 9g (Dietary Fiber 1g); Protein 0g **% Daily Value:** Vitamin A 0%; Vitamin C 2%; Calcium 0%; Iron 0% **Diet Exchanges:** 1/2 Fruit

STRAWBERRY FILLING: Substitute 1 package (10 ounces) frozen strawberries in syrup, thawed, for the raspberries.

Pies and Pastry Basics

No one knows who first put a pie together—we're just glad they did! Times and tastes may change, but pies stay deliciously popular. Could it be because they don't require any fancy ingredients, or is it because they're so easy to tote? Or perhaps it's because even a beginner cook can make a blue-ribbon pie with just a little practice and tips like the ones you'll find in this chapter.

Pans and Preparation

Choose heat-resistant glass pie plates or dull-finish (anodized) aluminum pie pans. Never use a shiny pie pan; it reflects heat, and your pie will have a soggy bottom crust.

The most common pie size is 9 inches. Even though pie plates and pans on the market may be labeled "9 inches," their capacity can vary. Our recipes were developed with pie plates that hold about 5 cups of ingredients. However, we sometimes use up to 8 cups of fruit for a two-crust pie to give you a nice, full baked pie, because the fruit does cook down during baking.

Pastry and crusts have enough fat in them that you usually don't have to grease pie plates and pans.

Nonstick pie pans can cause an unfilled one-crust pie crust to shrink excessively during baking. To hold the pastry in place, hook it over the edge of the plate.

Mixing and Rolling Pastry

If you're using self-rising flour, don't add the salt. Pastry made with self-rising flour will be slightly different—mealy and tender instead of flaky and tender.

A pastry blender makes easy work of cutting the shortening into the flour. If you don't have one, use two knives: with the blades almost touching, move the knives back and forth in opposite directions in a parallel cutting motion. The side of a fork or a wire whisk works, too.

Easy does it. If you overwork pastry dough, it'll get tough.

For a golden color, use unbleached flour in pastry.

A nifty tip for easy rolling and shaping: After you've made the pastry dough and shaped it into a flattened round, wrap it tightly and refrigerate for at least 30 minutes. This little break lets the shortening solidify, the gluten relax and the moisture absorb evenly.

To roll out pastry, see How to Make Pastry (page 119), and pick the method that works best for you. Or try this method because the pastry won't stick to the flat surface or the rolling pin:

1. Anchor a pastry cloth or kitchen towel (not terry cloth) around a large cutting board (at least 12 × 12 inches) with masking tape, and use a cloth cover (stockinet) for your rolling pin. Rub flour into both cloths. (This prevents sticking, but won't work the flour into the pastry.) If you don't have a rolling pin cover and/or pastry cloth, rub flour on the rolling pin and your kitchen table, the countertop, a marble slab or large cutting board (at least 12 × 12 inches).

2. Place the pastry dough on the flat surface and start rolling from the center out, lifting and turning the pastry occasionally to keep it from sticking. If the pastry begins to stick, rub more flour, a little at a time, on the flat surface and rolling pin.

Baking Pies and Pastry

Pies are baked at higher temperatures (375° to 425°) than cakes so that the rich pastry dries and becomes flaky and golden brown and the filling cooks all the way through.

To prevent the pie crust and pastry edges from getting too brown, you can cover them with aluminum foil (see Preventing Excessive Browning of Pastry Edges, below). Bake as directed; remove the foil 15 minutes before the end of the bake time so the edges will brown.

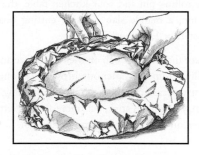

1. *Cover edge of pie with a 2- to 3-inch strip of aluminum foil, gently molding foil to edge of pie.*

2. *Fold a 12-inch square of aluminum foil into fourths; cut the open corner to round it off, making a 12-inch circle of foil. Cut a 3-inch strip from the rounded edge; discard center of foil circle. Unfold foil strip, and gently mold to edge of pie.*

To prevent an unfilled one-crust pie crust from puffing up as it bakes, prick the pastry thoroughly with a fork before baking to allow steam to escape. For one-crust pies where the filling is baked in the shell, such as pumpkin or pecan pie, *don't* prick the crust because the filling will seep under the crust during baking.

To make crumb crusts even, smooth and firm, start by pressing the crumbs down by hand. Then firmly press another pie plate of the same size into the crust.

Pie Yields and Storage

Most of the pies in this cookbook make eight servings. If a pie is really rich, it makes ten to twelve servings. An easy way to cut a pie into an even number of pieces is to cut the pie in half, then into quarters, then cut each quarter in half before removing a slice.

Keep pies that contain eggs, such as pumpkin and cream pies, in the refrigerator.

You can freeze either unbaked or baked pie crusts. Unbaked crusts will keep for 2 months in the freezer; baked crusts for 4 months. Don't thaw unbaked crusts; bake them right after taking them out of the freezer. To thaw baked pie crusts, unwrap and let stand at room temperature, or heat in the oven at 350° for about 6 minutes.

Tuck away a treat for later—freeze a fruit pie! For best results, the pie should be baked and cooled completely first. Then put it in the freezer uncovered. When it's completely frozen, wrap the pie tightly or put it in a plastic freezer bag and pop it back in the freezer. Frozen baked fruit pies will keep up to 4 months. (Do not freeze custard or cream pies.)

Pastry for Pies and Tarts

Prep: 20 min ✳ *8 servings*

Check out the information on page 115 and pictures on page 119 for additional help in making pastry. And be sure to try our flaky Buttermilk Pastry (page 121) and easy Pat-in-the-Pan Oil Pastry (page 121).

One-Crust Pie (9-inch)
1 cup all-purpose* or unbleached flour
1/2 teaspoon salt
1/3 cup plus 1 tablespoon shortening
2 to 3 tablespoons cold water

Two-Crust Pie (9-inch)
2 cups all-purpose* or unbleached flour
1 teaspoon salt
2/3 cup plus 2 tablespoons shortening
4 to 5 tablespoons cold water

1. Mix flour and salt in medium bowl. Cut in shortening, using pastry blender or crisscrossing 2 knives, until particles are size of small peas. Sprinkle with cold water, 1 tablespoon at a time, tossing with fork until all flour is moistened and pastry almost leaves side of bowl (1 to 2 teaspoons more water can be added if necessary).

2. Gather pastry into a ball. Shape into flattened round on lightly floured surface. (For Two-Crust Pie, divide pastry in half and shape into 2 rounds.) If desired, wrap flattened round of pastry in plastic wrap and refrigerate about 30 minutes to firm up the shortening slightly, which helps make the baked pastry more flaky and lets the water absorb evenly throughout the dough. If refrigerated longer, let pastry soften slightly before rolling.

3. Roll pastry on lightly floured surface, using floured rolling pin, into circle 2 inches larger than upside-down pie plate, 9 × 1 1/4 inches, or 3 inches larger than 10- or 11-inch tart pan. Fold pastry into fourths and place in pie plate; or roll pastry loosely around rolling pin and transfer to pie plate. Unfold or unroll pastry and ease into plate, pressing firmly against bottom and side and being careful not to stretch pastry, which will cause it to shrink when baked. Continue with directions below for One-Crust Pie or Two-Crust Pie.

If using self-rising flour, omit salt. Pie crusts made with self-rising flour differ in flavor and texture from those made with all-purpose flour.

1 Serving (using one crust): Calories 145 (Calories from Fat 90); Fat 10g (Saturated 3g); Cholesterol 0mg; Sodium 150mg; Carbohydrate 12g (Dietary Fiber 0g); Protein 2g **% Daily Value:** Vitamin A 0%; Vitamin C 0%; Calcium 0%; Iron 4% **Diet Exchanges:** 1 Starch, 1 1/2 Fat

Food Processor Directions: Measure 2 tablespoons water (for One-Crust Pie) or 4 tablespoons water (for Two-Crust Pie) into liquid measuring cup; set aside. Place shortening, flour and salt in food processor. Cover and process, using quick on-and-off motions, until mixture is crumbly. With food processor running, pour water all at once through feed tube just until dough leaves side of bowl (dough should not form a ball). Continue as directed in step 2.

Baked Tart Shells

Make pastry as directed for One-Crust Pie (page 117), except roll pastry into 13-inch circle. Cut into eight 4 1/2-inch circles, rerolling pastry scraps if necessary.

Heat oven to 475°. Fit circles over backs of medium muffin cups, 2 1/2 × 1 1/4 inches, or 6-ounce custard cups, making pleats so pastry will fit closely. (If using individual pie pans or tart pans, cut pastry circles 1 inch larger than upside-down pans; fit into pans.) Prick pastry thoroughly with fork to prevent puffing. Place on cookie sheet.

Bake 8 to 10 minutes or until light brown. Cool before removing from cups. Fill each shell with 1/3 to 1/2 cup of your favorite filling, pudding, fresh fruit or ice cream.

One-Crust Pie

Unbaked (for one-crust pies baked with a filling, such as pumpkin, pecan or custard pie): *For pie,* trim overhanging edge of pastry one inch from rim of pie plate. Fold and roll pastry under, even with plate; flute (see Pastry Edges, page 120). *For tart,* trim overhanging edge of pastry even with top of tart pan. Fill and bake as directed in pie or tart recipe, or partially bake crust before adding filling as directed in next paragraph.

To prevent pie crust from becoming soggy, partially bake pastry before adding filling: Heat oven to 425°. Carefully line pastry with a double thickness of aluminum foil, gently pressing foil to bottom and side of pastry. Let foil extend over edge to prevent excessive browning. Bake 10 minutes; carefully remove foil and bake 2 to 4 minutes longer or until pastry *just begins* to brown and has become set. If crust bubbles, gently push bubbles down with back of spoon. Fill and bake as directed in pie or tart recipe, adjusting oven temperature if necessary.

Baked (for one-crust pies baked completely before filling is added, such as coconut cream or lemon meringue pie): Heat oven to 475°. *For pie,* trim overhanging edge of pastry 1 inch from rim of pie plate. Fold and roll pastry under, even with plate; flute (see Pastry Edges, page 120). *For tart,* trim overhanging edge of pastry even with top of tart pan. Prick bottom and side of pastry thoroughly with fork. Bake 8 to 10 minutes or until light brown; cool on wire rack.

Two-Crust Pie

Turn desired filling into pastry-lined pie plate, 9 × 1 1/4 inches. Trim overhanging edge of pastry 1/2 inch from rim of plate. Roll other round of pastry. (Make Lattice Pie Top, page 120, if desired.) Fold pastry into fourths and cut slits so steam can escape, or cut slits in pastry and roll pastry loosely around rolling pin.

Place pastry over filling and unfold or unroll. Trim overhanging edge of top pastry 1 inch from rim of plate. Fold and roll top edge under lower edge, pressing on rim to seal; flute (see Pastry Edges, page 120). Bake as directed in pie recipe.

PASTRY CURES

Great Pastry Is

Golden brown and blistered on top

Crisp, brown undercrust

Tender, cuts easily and holds its shape when served

Flaky and crisp

Problem	Possible Cause
Pale color	• baked in shiny pan instead of in dull pan
	• underbaked
Pastry looks smooth	• dough was handled too much
Bottom crust is soggy	• baked in shiny pan instead of in dull pan
	• oven temperature too low
Tough	• too much water
	• too much flour
	• dough was mixed and handled too much
Too tender; falls apart	• too little water
	• too much shortening
Dry and mealy, not flaky	• shortening was cut in too finely
	• too little water

HOW TO MAKE PASTRY

1. Cut shortening into flour and salt, using pastry blender or crisscrossing 2 knives, until particles are the size of small peas.

2. Sprinkle with cold water and toss with fork until all flour is moistened and pastry almost leaves side of bowl.

3. Roll pastry from center to outside edge in all directions. To keep outside edge from becoming too thin, use less pressure on the rolling pin as it approaches the edge.

4. If edge of pastry splits, immediately patch it with a small piece of pastry. Occasionally lift pastry to make sure it is not sticking to the rolling surface.

5. Fold pastry into fourths and place in pie plate with point in center. Unfold and gently ease into plate, being careful not to stretch pastry, which will cause it to shrink when baked.

6. Or instead of folding pastry into fourths, roll pastry loosely around rolling pin and transfer to pie plate. Unroll pastry and ease into plate.

7. For two-crust pie, cut slits or special design in top pastry before folding. Carefully place pastry over filling by either folding it into fourths or rolling it around rolling pin. Let top pastry overhang 1 inch beyond edge of pie plate. Fold and roll overhanging pastry under edge of bottom pastry, pressing to seal.

8. After sealing the top pastry to the bottom pastry, form a stand-up rim of even thickness on edge of pie plate, continuing to press edges together. This seals the pastry and makes fluting easier (see Pastry Edges, page 120).

Lattice Pie Top

Make pastry as directed for Two-Crust Pie (page 117), except trim overhanging edge of bottom pastry one inch from rim of plate. After rolling pastry for top crust, cut into strips about 1/2 inch wide. (Use a pastry wheel to cut decorative strips.)

Place 5 to 7 strips (depending on size of pie) across filling in pie plate. Weave a cross-strip through center by first folding back every other strip of the first 5 to 7 strips. Continue weaving, folding back alternate strips before adding each cross-strip, until lattice is complete. (To save time, place second half of strips crosswise across first strips instead of weaving.) Trim ends of strips.

Fold trimmed edge of bottom crust over ends of strips, building up a high edge. A juicy fruit pie with a lattice top is more likely to bubble over than a two-crust pie, so be sure to build up a high pastry edge. Seal and flute (see Pastry Edges, right). Bake as directed in pie recipe.

Classic Lattice Top: *Place 5 to 7 strips of pastry across filling. Fold back alternate strips before adding each cross-strip.*

Easy Lattice Top: *Place 5 to 7 strips of pastry across filling. Place cross-strips over tops of first strips instead of weaving strips.*

Pastry Edges

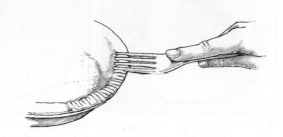

Fork Edge: *Flatten pastry evenly on rim of pie plate. Firmly press tines of fork around edge. To prevent sticking, occasionally dip fork into flour.*

Pinch Edge: *Place index finger on inside of pastry rim and thumb and index finer (or knuckles) on outside. Pinch pastry into V shape along edge. Pinch again to sharpen points.*

Rope Edge: *Place side of thumb on pastry rim at an angle. Pinch pastry by pressing the knuckle of your index finger down into pastry toward thumb.*

Buttermilk Pastry

Prep: 15 min ✳ *8 servings*

We find this pastry very easy to roll and handle, and the baked crust is very flaky. It makes enough pastry for a two-crust pie.

2 cups all-purpose flour*
1 teaspoon salt
2/3 cups shortening
3 tablespoons butter or stick margarine**
2 teaspoons vegetable oil
1/3 cup buttermilk

1. Mix flour and salt in medium bowl. Cut in shortening and butter, using pastry blender or crisscrossing 2 knives, until particles are size of small peas.

2. Mix in oil and buttermilk with fork until all flour is moistened and pastry leaves side of bowl. Divide in half; shape each half into a ball. If making one-crust pie, wrap second ball of pastry and freeze for later use.

3. Roll pastry as directed for One-Crust Pie or Two-Crust Pie on page 117. Fill and bake as directed in pie recipe. Or, for pie crust that is baked before filling is added, heat oven to 475°. Prick bottom and side of pastry thoroughly with fork. Bake 8 to 10 minutes or until light brown; cool on wire rack.

*If using self-rising flour, omit salt. Pie crusts made with self-rising flour differ in flavor and texture from those made with all-purpose flour.
**Do not use vegetable oil spreads (page 91).

1 Serving (using one crust): Calories 165 (Calories from Fat 110); Fat 12g (Saturated 3.5g); Cholesterol 5mg; Sodium 160mg; Carbohydrate 12g (Dietary Fiber 0g); Protein 2g **% Daily Value:** Vitamin A 2%; Vitamin C 0%; Calcium 0%; Iron 4% **Diet Exchanges:** 1 Starch; 2 Fat

Pat-in-the-Pan Oil Pastry

Prep: 15 min ✳ *8 servings*

This easy pastry can be used for pies that have just a bottom crust. Try it for Pumpkin Pie (page 132) as well as for pie crusts that are baked before being filled.

1 1/3 cups all-purpose* or unbleached flour
1/2 teaspoon salt
1/3 cup vegetable oil
2 tablespoons cold water

1. Mix flour, salt and oil until all flour is moistened. Sprinkle with cold water, 1 tablespoon at a time, tossing with fork until all water is absorbed.

2. Gather pastry into a ball. Press in bottom and up side of pie plate, 9 × 1 1/4 inches; flute (see Pastry Edges, page 120).

3. Fill and bake as directed in pie recipe or bake before filling is added. Heat oven to 475°. Prick bottom and side of pastry thoroughly with fork. Bake 10 to 12 minutes or until light brown; cool on wire rack.

*If using self-rising flour, omit salt.

1 Serving: Calories 150 (Calories from Fat 80); Fat 9g (Saturated 1g); Cholesterol 0mg; Sodium 150mg; Carbohydrate 16g (Dietary Fiber 1g); Protein 2g **% Daily Value:** Vitamin A 0%; Vitamin C 0%; Calcium 0%; Iron 4% **Diet Exchanges:** 1 Starch, 1 1/2 Fat

Cookie Tart Pastry **Fast**

Prep: 10 min; Bake: 12 min ✳ *8 servings*

1 1/4 cups all-purpose flour*
1/2 cup butter or stick margarine, softened**
2 tablespoons packed brown sugar
1 large egg

1. Heat oven to 400°.

2. Mix all ingredients until dough forms. Press firmly and evenly against bottom and side of ungreased 11-inch tart pan.

3. Bake 10 to 12 minutes or until light brown; cool.

*Do not use self-rising flour.
**Do not use vegetable oil spreads (page 91).

1 Serving: Calories 190 (Calories from Fat 110); Fat 12g (Saturated 7g); Cholesterol 55mg; Sodium 85mg; Carbohydrate 18g (Dietary Fiber 1g); Protein 3g **% Daily Value:** Vitamin A 10%; Vitamin C 0%; Calcium 0%; Iron 6% **Diet Exchanges:** 1 Starch, 2 1/2 Fat

Graham Cracker Crust *Fast*

Prep: 10 min; Bake: 10 min ✱ 8 servings

Baking this crust helps it hold together better when it's cut.

1 1/2 cups finely crushed regular or cinnamon graham
    crackers (about 20 squares)
1/3 cup butter or stick margarine, melted*
3 tablespoons sugar

1. Heat oven to 350°.

2. Mix all ingredients. Reserve 3 tablespoons crumb mixture for topping if desired. Press remaining mixture firmly against bottom and side of pie plate, 9 × 1 1/4 inches.

3. Bake about 10 minutes or until light brown; cool.

Spreads with at least 65% vegetable oil can be used (page 91).

1 Serving: Calories 150 (Calories from Fat 80); Fat 9g (Saturated 5g); Cholesterol 20mg; Sodium 140mg; Carbohydrate 16g (Dietary Fiber 0g); Protein 1g **% Daily Value:** Vitamin A 6%; Vitamin C 0%; Calcium 0%; Iron 2% **Diet Exchanges:** 1 Starch, 1 1/2 Fat

COOKIE CRUMB CRUST: Substitute 1 1/2 cups finely crushed chocolate or vanilla wafer cookies or gingersnaps for the graham crackers. Decrease butter to 1/4 cup; omit sugar.

Apple Pie

Prep: 45 min; Bake: 50 min; Cool: 2 hr ✱ 8 servings

There are so many good varieties of apples that are recommended for pies we can't list them all here. To help you choose, go to our apple chart on page 423.

Pastry for Two-Crust Pie (page 117) or Buttermilk
    Pastry (page 121)
1/3 to 2/3 cup sugar
1/4 cup all-purpose flour
1/2 teaspoon ground cinnamon
1/2 teaspoon ground nutmeg
Dash of salt
8 cups thinly sliced peeled tart apples (8 medium)
2 tablespoons butter or stick margarine, if desired*

1. Heat oven to 425°. Make pastry.

2. Mix sugar, flour, cinnamon, nutmeg and salt in large bowl. Stir in apples. Turn into pastry-lined pie plate. Cut butter into small pieces; sprinkle over apples. Cover with top pastry that has slits cut in it; seal and flute. Cover edge with 2- to 3-inch strip of aluminum foil to prevent excessive browning (page 116); remove foil during last 15 minutes of baking.

3. Bake 40 to 50 minutes or until crust is golden brown and juice begins to bubble through slits in crust. Cool on wire rack at least 2 hours.

Spreads with at least 65% vegetable oil can be used (page 91).

1 Serving: Calories 400 (Calories from Fat 180); Fat 20g (Saturated 3g); Cholesterol 0mg; Sodium 300mg; Carbohydrate 52g (Dietary Fiber 2g); Protein 5g **% Daily Value:** Vitamin A 0%; Vitamin C 2%; Calcium 0%; Iron 10% **Diet Exchanges:** Not Recommended

FRENCH APPLE PIE: Make pastry for One-Crust Pie (page 117). Turn apple mixture into pastry-lined pie plate. Omit butter. Sprinkle apple mixture with Crumb Topping: Mix 1 cup all-purpose flour, 1/2 cup packed brown sugar and 1/2 cup firm butter or stick margarine until crumbly. Cover topping with aluminum foil during last 10 minutes of baking to prevent excessive browning. Bake 50 minutes. Serve warm.

Apple Wrapper Pie

Apple Wrapper Pie

Prep: 40 min; Bake: 35 min; Cool: 1 hr ✱ *8 servings*

No pie plate required! The pie filling is partially wrapped in a pastry crust and baked on a cookie sheet.

Pastry for One-Crust Pie (page 117) or Buttermilk
    Pastry (page 121)
2/3 cup packed brown sugar
1/3 cup all-purpose flour
4 cups thinly sliced peeled tart apples (4 medium)
1 tablespoon butter or stick margarine
Granulated sugar, if desired

1. Heat oven to 425°. Make pastry as directed—except roll pastry into 13-inch circle. Place on large ungreased cookie sheet. Cover with plastic wrap to keep it moist while making filling.

2. Mix brown sugar and flour in large bowl. Stir in apples. Mound apple mixture on center of pastry to within 3 inches of edge. Cut butter into small pieces; sprinkle over apples. Fold edge of pastry over apples, making pleats so it lays flat on apples. Sprinkle pastry with sugar.

3. Bake 30 to 35 minutes or until crust is light golden brown. To prevent excessive browning, cover center of pie with 5-inch square of aluminum foil during last 10 to 15 minutes of baking. (See page 116.) Cool on cookie sheet on wire rack 1 hour, or serve warm if desired.

1 Serving: Calories 285 (Calories from Fat 110); Fat 12g (Saturated 4g); Cholesterol 5mg; Sodium 165mg; Carbohydrate 42g (Dietary Fiber 1g); Protein 3g **% Daily Value:** Vitamin A 0%; Vitamin C 2%; Calcium 2%; Iron 8% **Diet Exchanges:** 1 Starch, 2 Fruit, 2 Fat

Cherry Pie

Prep: 40 min; Bake: 45 min; Cool: 2 hr ✱ 8 servings

There are two groups of cherries—sweet and sour. Sour cherries are sometimes called tart cherries or tart red cherries. Sour cherries make wonderful pies, which become showpieces when topped with a lattice crust (page 120).

Pastry for Two-Crust Pie (page 117) or Buttermilk
    Pastry (page 121)
1 1/3 cup sugar
1/2 cup all-purpose flour
6 cups sour cherries, pitted
2 tablespoon butter or stick margarine, if desired

2. Mix sugar and flour in large bowl. Stir in cherries. Turn into pastry-lined pie plate. Cut butter into small pieces; sprinkle over cherries. Cover with top pastry that has slits cut in it; seal and flute. Cover edge with 2- to 3-inch strip of aluminum foil to prevent excessive browning (page 116); remove foil during last 15 minutes of baking.

3. Bake 35 to 45 minutes or until crust is golden brown and juice begins to bubble through slits in crust. Cool on wire rack at least 2 hours.

1 Serving: Calories 525 (Calories from Fat 190); Fat 21g (Saturated 6g); Cholesterol 0mg; Sodium 300mg; Carbohydrate 81g (Dietary Fiber 3g); Protein 6g **% Daily Value:** Vitamin A 2%; Vitamin C 6%; Calcium 2%; Iron 12% **Diet Exchanges:** Not Recommended

QUICK CHERRY PIE: Substitute 6 cups frozen unsweetened pitted red tart cherries, thawed and drained, or 3 cans (14 1/2 ounces each) pitted red tart cherries, drained, for the fresh cherries.

Peach Pie

Prep: 45 min; Bake: 45 min; Cool: 2 hr ✱ 8 servings

For a hint of butterscotch flavor, use packed brown sugar instead of granulated sugar in the peach filling.

Pastry for Two-Crust Pie (page 117) or Buttermilk
    Pastry (page 121)
2/3 cup sugar
1/3 cup all-purpose flour
1/4 teaspoon ground cinnamon
6 cups sliced peaches (6 to 8 medium)
1 teaspoon lemon juice
1 tablespoon butter or stick margarine, if desired

1. Heat oven to 425°. Make pastry.

2. Mix sugar, flour and cinnamon in large bowl. Stir in peaches and lemon juice. Turn into pastry-lined pie plate. Cut butter into small pieces; sprinkle over peaches. Cover with top pastry that has slits cut in it; seal and flute. Cover edge with 2- to 3-inch strip of aluminum foil to prevent excessive browning (page 116); remove foil during last 15 minutes of baking.

3. Bake about 45 minutes or until crust is golden brown and juice begins to bubble through slits in crust. Cool on wire rack at least 2 hours.

1 Serving: Calories 405 (Calories from Fat 180); Fat 20g (Saturated 6g); Cholesterol 0mg; Sodium 300mg; Carbohydrate 59g (Dietary Fiber 3g); Protein 5g **% Daily Value:** Vitamin A 6%; Vitamin C 6%; Calcium 0%; Iron 10% **Diet Exchanges:** Not Recommended

APRICOT PIE: Substitute 6 cups fresh apricot halves for the peaches.

QUICK PEACH PIE: Substitute 6 cups frozen sliced peaches, partially thawed and drained, for the fresh peaches.

Blueberry-Peach Pie (variation of Blueberry Pie)

Blueberry Pie

Prep: 30 min; Bake: 45 min; Cool: 2 hr ✳ 8 servings

Pastry for Two-Crust Pie (page 117) or Buttermilk
    Pastry (page 121)
3/4 cup sugar
1/2 cup all-purpose flour
1/2 teaspoon ground cinnamon, if desired
6 cups blueberries
1 tablespoon lemon juice
1 tablespoon butter or stick margarine, if desired

1. Heat oven to 425°. Make pastry.

2. Mix sugar, flour and cinnamon in large bowl. Stir in blueberries. Turn into pastry-lined pie plate. Sprinkle any remaining sugar mixture over blueberry mixture. Sprinkle with lemon juice. Cut butter into small pieces; sprinkle over blueberries. Cover with top pastry that has slits cut in it; seal and flute. Cover edge with 2- to 3-inch strip of aluminum foil to prevent excessive browning (page 116); remove foil during last 15 minutes of baking.

3. Bake 35 to 45 minutes or until crust is golden brown and juice begins to bubble through slits in crust. Cool on wire rack at least 2 hours.

1 Serving: Calories 465 (Calories from Fat 200); Fat 22g (Saturated 7g); Cholesterol 5mg; Sodium 320mg; Carbohydrate 64g (Dietary Fiber 3g); Protein 6g **% Daily Value:** Vitamin A 2%; Vitamin C 12%; Calcium 0%; Iron 10% **Diet Exchanges:** Not Recommended

BLACKBERRY, BOYSENBERRY, LOGANBERRY OR RASPBERRY PIE: Increase sugar to 1 cup. Substitute fresh berries for the blueberries; omit lemon juice.

BLUEBERRY-PEACH PIE: Substitute 2 1/2 cups sliced fresh peaches for 4 cups of the blueberries; omit lemon juice. Place blueberries in pastry-lined pie plate; sprinkle with half of the sugar mixture. Top with peaches; sprinkle with remaining sugar mixture. Cover with top pastry; continue as directed in step 2.

QUICK BLUEBERRY PIE: Substitute 6 cups drained canned blueberries or unsweetened frozen (thawed and drained) blueberries for the fresh blueberries.

Rhubarb Pie

Prep: 35 min; Bake: 55 min; Cool: 2 hr ✽ 8 servings

Rhubarb is very tart, so there's a lot of sugar in this pie. If you are using young rhubarb picked early in the season, the lower amount of sugar probably will be enough. Mature rhubarb needs more sugar.

Pastry for Two-Crust Pie (page 117) or Buttermilk
    Pastry (page 121)
2 to 2 1/3 cups sugar
2/3 cup all-purpose flour
1 teaspoon grated orange peel, if desired
6 cups 1/2-inch pieces rhubarb
1 tablespoon butter or stick margarine, if desired

1. Heat oven to 425°. Make pastry.

2. Mix sugar, flour and orange peel in large bowl. Stir in rhubarb. Turn into pastry-lined pie plate. Cut butter into small pieces; sprinkle over rhubarb. Cover with top pastry that has slits cut in it; seal and flute. Cover edge with 2- to 3-inch strip of aluminum foil to prevent excessive browning (page 116); remove foil during last 15 minutes of baking.

3. Bake about 55 minutes or until crust is golden brown and juice begins to bubble through slits in crust. Cool on wire rack at least 2 hours.

1 Serving: Calories 530 (Calories from Fat 180); Fat 20g (Saturated 6g); Cholesterol 0mg; Sodium 300mg; Carbohydrate 84g (Dietary Fiber 2g); Protein 6g **% Daily Value:** Vitamin A 0%; Vitamin C 4%; Calcium 18%; Iron 12% **Diet Exchanges:** Not Recommended

QUICK RHUBARB PIE: Substitute 2 bags (16 ounces each) frozen unsweetened rhubarb, completely thawed and drained, for the fresh rhubarb.

STRAWBERRY-RHUBARB PIE: Substitute 3 cups sliced strawberries for 3 cups of the rhubarb. Use 2 cups sugar.

SPECIAL TOP CRUSTS

Add a special touch to the top of your two-crust fruit pie by using one of these techniques *before* baking:

- For a shiny crust, brush crust with milk.
- For a sugary crust, moisten crust with water, then sprinkle with granulated sugar.

- For a glazed crust, brush crust lightly with a beaten egg or an egg yolk mixed with a little water. These pie crusts may brown more quickly than those without a special top treatment. If this happens, place a sheet of aluminum foil loosely on top of the pie to slow the browning.

After baking, glaze a two-crust pie with a mixture of 1/2 cup powdered sugar, 2 to 3 teaspoons milk, orange juice or lemon juice and, if desired, 2 teaspoons grated orange peel or lemon peel. Don't let the glaze run over the edge of the pie.

Upside-Down Plum-Pecan Pie

Prep: 45 min; Bake: 50 min; Cool: 30 min ✱ *8 servings*

1/4 cup butter or stick margarine, softened*
30 pecan halves (1/2 cup)
1/3 cup packed brown sugar
1 tablespoon corn syrup
Pastry for Two-Crust Pie (page 117) or Buttermilk
    Pastry (page 121)
1 1/2 pounds plums, sliced (4 cups)
1/2 cup granulated sugar
1/3 cup all-purpose flour
1 tablespoon lemon juice

1. Cut 15-inch circle from heavy-duty aluminum foil. Line pie plate, 9 × 1 1/4 inches, with foil circle, leaving 2 inches overhanging edge.

2. Spread butter over foil lining. Place pecan halves, rounded sides down, on butter. Mix brown sugar and corn syrup; drop by small spoonfuls evenly over pecans and foil.

3. Heat oven to 450°. Make pastry as directed—except roll first round of pastry into 11-inch circle. Ease into pie plate over pecans and brown sugar mixture. Mix remaining ingredients; pour into pastry-lined pie plate.

4. Roll other round of pastry into 12-inch circle. Fold into fourths; cut slits so steam can escape. Place over filling and unfold; seal and flute. Turn up overhanging foil to catch juices and to prevent crust from excessive browning. Bake 10 minutes.

5. Reduce oven temperature to 375°. Bake 35 to 40 minutes longer or until crust is brown and juice begins to bubble through slits in crust. Cool 5 minutes. Turn foil away from pastry. Place heatproof serving plate upside down onto pie plate; turn serving plate and pie plate over. Peel off foil. Cool about 25 minutes or until warm. Serve warm.

*Spreads with at least 65% vegetable oil can be used (page 91).

1 Serving: Calories 515 (Calories from Fat 260); Fat 29g (Saturated 7g); Cholesterol 0mg; Sodium 340mg; Carbohydrate 62g (Dietary Fiber 3g); Protein 5g **% Daily Value:** Vitamin A 10%; Vitamin C 6%; Calcium 2%; Iron 10% **Diet Exchanges:** Not Recommended

Cranberry-Apple Pie

Prep: 45 min; Bake: 50 min; Cool: 2 hr ✱ *8 servings*

Pastry for Two-Crust Pie (page 117) or Buttermilk
    Pastry (page 121)
1 3/4 cups sugar
1/4 cup all-purpose flour
3 cups sliced peeled tart cooking apples (3 medium)
2 cups fresh or frozen (thawed) cranberries
2 tablespoons butter or stick margarine

1. Heat oven to 425°. Make pastry.

2. Mix sugar and flour. Alternate layers of apples, cranberries and sugar mixture in pastry-lined pie plate, beginning and ending with apples. Cut butter into small pieces; sprinkle over apples. Cover with top pastry that has slits cut in it; seal and flute. Cover edge with 2- to 3-inch strip of aluminum foil to prevent excessive browning (page 116); remove foil during last 15 minutes of baking.

3. Bake 40 to 50 minutes or until crust is golden brown and juice begins to bubble through slits in crust. Cool on wire rack at least 2 hours.

1 Serving: Calories 545 (Calories from Fat 215); Fat 24g (Saturated 7g); Cholesterol 5mg; Sodium 320mg; Carbohydrate 81g (Dietary Fiber 3g); Protein 4g **% Daily Value:** Vitamin A 2%; Vitamin C 4%; Calcium 0%; Iron 10% **Diet Exchanges:** Not Recommended

Lemon Berry Tart

Lemon Berry Tart

Prep: 15 min; Bake: 12 min; Chill: 1 hr ✱ *8 servings*

Cookie Tart Pastry (page 121)

1/2 cup lemon curd

1 package (8 ounces) cream cheese, softened

3 cups berries or sliced fruits

1. Bake Cookie Tart Pastry in 11-inch tart pan or 12-inch pizza pan with 1/2-inch side.

2. Beat lemon curd and cream cheese in medium bowl with spoon or electric mixer on low speed until smooth. Spread over crust. Refrigerate at least 1 hour.

3. Arrange berries on lemon mixture just before serving. Store covered in refrigerator.

1 Serving: Calories 370 (Calories from Fat 205); Fat 23g (Saturated 14g); Cholesterol 90mg; Sodium 180mg; Carbohydrate 38g (Dietary Fiber 3g); Protein 6g **% Daily Value:** Vitamin A 18%; Vitamin C 18%; Calcium 4%; Iron 8% **Diet Exchanges:** Not Recommended

Coconut Cream Pie

Prep: 30 min; Bake: 10 min; Cook: 15 min; Chill: 2 hr ✱ *8 servings*

Try an easy Cookie Crumb Crust or Graham Cracker Crust (page 122) for any of these delicious cream pies.

Pastry for One-Crust Pie (page 117), Buttermilk Pastry (page 121) or Pat-in-the-Pan Oil Pastry (page 121)

4 large egg yolks

2/3 cup sugar

1/4 cup cornstarch

1/2 teaspoon salt

3 cups milk

2 tablespoons butter or stick margarine, softened*

2 teaspoons vanilla

1 cup flaked coconut

1 cup Sweetened Whipped Cream (page 198)

Banana Cream Pie (variation of Coconut Cream Pie)

1. Bake pastry for baked One-Crust Pie.

2. Beat egg yolks with fork in medium bowl; set aside. Mix sugar, cornstarch and salt in 2-quart saucepan. Gradually stir in milk. Cook over medium heat, stirring constantly, until mixture thickens and boils. Boil and stir 1 minute.

3. Immediately stir at least half of the hot mixture gradually into egg yolks, then stir back into hot mixture in saucepan. Boil and stir 1 minute; remove from heat. Stir in butter, vanilla and 3/4 cup of the coconut. Pour into pie crust. Press plastic wrap on filling to prevent a tough layer from forming on top. Refrigerate at least 2 hours until set.

4. Remove plastic wrap. Top pie with Sweetened Whipped Cream and remaining 1/4 cup coconut. Cover and refrigerate cooled pie until serving. Store covered in refrigerator.

*Spreads with at least 65% vegetable oil can be used (page 91).

1 Serving: Calories 425 (Calories from Fat 225); Fat 25g (Saturated 12g); Cholesterol 135mg; Sodium 390mg; Carbohydrate 43g (Dietary Fiber 0g); Protein 7g **% Daily Value:** Vitamin A 14%; Vitamin C 0%; Calcium 14%; Iron 6% **Diet Exchanges:** Not Recommended

BANANA CREAM PIE: Increase vanilla to 1 tablespoon plus 1 teaspoon; omit coconut. Cool filling slightly. Slice 2 large bananas into pie crust; pour warm filling over bananas. Continue as directed in step **3.** Garnish each serving with a dollop whipped cream, toffee bits and banana slices if desired.

CHOCOLATE CREAM PIE: Increase sugar to 1 1/2 cups and cornstarch to 1/3 cup; omit butter and coconut. Stir in 2 ounces unsweetened baking chocolate, cut up, after stirring in milk in step 2.

CHOCOLATE-BANANA CREAM PIE: Make Chocolate Cream Pie. Cool filling slightly. Slice 2 large bananas into pie crust; pour warm filling over bananas. Continue as directed in step 3. Garnish finished pie with banana slices if desired.

Lemon Meringue Pie

Lemon Meringue Pie

Prep: 30 min; Cook: 10 min; Bake: 25 min; Cool: 2 hr
✳ *8 servings*

Use the egg whites left over from separating eggs for the lemon filling to make the meringue. Letting the egg whites stand at room temperature is okay for up to 30 minutes. They'll beat up well after being out of the refrigerator for a short time.

Pastry for One-Crust Pie (page 117), Buttermilk Pastry
    (page 121) or Pat-in-the-Pan Oil Pastry (page 121)
Meringue for 9-Inch Pie (page 190)
3 large egg yolks (reserve egg whites for meringue)
1 1/2 cups sugar
1/3 cup plus 1 tablespoon cornstarch
1 1/2 cups water
3 tablespoons butter or stick margarine*
2 teaspoons grated lemon peel
1/2 cup lemon juice
2 drops yellow food color, if desired

1. Bake pastry for baked One-Crust Pie.

2. Heat oven to 350°. Complete step 2 of Meringue for 9-Inch Pie.

3. While sugar mixture for meringue is cooling, beat egg yolks with fork in small bowl; set aside. Mix sugar and cornstarch in 2-quart saucepan. Gradually stir in water. Cook over medium heat, stirring constantly, until mixture thickens and boils. Boil and stir 1 minute.

4. Immediately stir at least half of the hot mixture into egg yolks, then stir back into hot mixture in saucepan. Boil and stir 1 minute; remove from heat. Stir in butter, lemon peel, lemon juice and food color. Press plastic wrap on filling to prevent a tough layer from forming on top.

5. Complete step 3 of meringue recipe. Pour hot lemon filling into pie crust. Spoon meringue onto hot lemon filling. Spread over filling, carefully sealing meringue to edge of crust to prevent shrinking or weeping.

6. Bake 15 minutes or until meringue is light brown. Cool away from draft 2 hours. Cover and refrigerate cooled pie until serving. Store covered in refrigerator.

*Spreads with at least 65% vegetable oil can be used (page 91).

1 Serving: Calories 425 (Calories from Fat 145); Fat 16g (Saturated 6g); Cholesterol 90mg; Sodium 260mg; Carbohydrate 66g (Dietary Fiber 0g); Protein 4g **% Daily Value:** Vitamin A 6%; Vitamin C 2%; Calcium 0%; Iron 6% **Diet Exchanges:** Not Recommended

Strawberry Glacé Pie

Prep: 30 min; Bake/Cool: 30 min; Cook: 10 min; Chill: 3 hr
✳ 8 servings

Pastry for One-Crust Pie (page 117), Buttermilk Pastry (page 121) or Pat-in-the-Pan Oil Pastry (page 121)
1 1/2 quarts strawberries (3 pints)
1 cup sugar
3 tablespoons cornstarch
1/2 cup water
1 package (3 ounces) cream cheese, softened

1. Bake pastry for baked One-Crust Pie. Cool completely.

2. Mash enough strawberries to measure 1 cup. Mix sugar and cornstarch in 2-quart saucepan. Gradually stir in water and mashed strawberries. Cook over medium heat, stirring constantly, until mixture thickens and boils. Boil and stir 1 minute; cool.

3. Beat cream cheese with spoon until smooth. Spread in pie crust. Top with remaining whole strawberries. Pour cooked strawberry mixture over top. Refrigerate about 3 hours or until set. Store covered in refrigerator.

1 Serving: Calories 320 (Calories from Fat 125); Fat 14g (Saturated 5g); Cholesterol 10mg; Sodium 150mg; Carbohydrate 48g (Dietary Fiber 3g); Protein 3g **% Daily Value:** Vitamin A 4%; Vitamin C 100%; Calcium 2%; Iron 6% **Diet Exchanges:** Not Recommended

PEACH GLACÉ PIE: Substitute 5 cups sliced peaches (5 medium) for the strawberries. To prevent peaches from discoloring, use fruit protector as directed on package.

RASPBERRY GLACÉ PIE: Substitute 6 cups raspberries for the strawberries.

Key Lime Pie

Prep: 30 min; Bake: 45 min; Cool: 15 min; Chill: 2 hr
✳ 8 servings

Key limes, found in the Florida Keys, are smaller and rounder than the more familiar Persian limes. Key limes may be hard to find outside of Florida, but commercially marketed Key lime juice is available at some supermarkets and specialty stores. Or you can substitute regular lime juice for the Key lime juice.

Pastry for One-Crust Pie (page 117) or Buttermilk Pastry (page 121)
3 large eggs
1 can (14 ounces) sweetened condensed milk
1 teaspoon grated lime or lemon peel
1/2 cup Key lime juice or regular lime juice
1 1/2 cups Sweetened Whipped Cream (page 198)

1. Bake pastry for baked One-Crust Pie.

2. Heat oven to 350°.

3. Beat eggs, milk, lime peel and lime juice in medium bowl with electric mixer on medium speed about 1 minute or until well blended. Pour into pie crust.

4. Bake 30 to 35 minutes or until center is set. Cool on wire rack 15 minutes. Cover and refrigerate until chilled, at least 2 hours but no longer than 3 days. Spread with Sweetened Whipped Cream. Store covered in refrigerator.

1 Serving: Calories 480 (Calories from Fat 235); Fat 26g (Saturated 12g); Cholesterol 185mg; Sodium 270mg; Carbohydrate 52g (Dietary Fiber 0g); Protein 10g **% Daily Value:** Vitamin A 12%; Vitamin C 0%; Calcium 20%; Iron 6% **Diet Exchanges:** Not Recommended

Pumpkin Pie

Prep: 20 min; Bake: 1 hr 10 min; Cool: 2 hr ✳ 8 servings

Be sure to use canned pumpkin, not pumpkin pie mix, in this recipe. The mix has some of the additional ingredients already in it, so if you have purchased the pumpkin pie mix, follow the directions on that label. Or if you like, use 1 1/2 cups cooked pumpkin (page 504).

Pastry for One-Crust Pie (page 117), Buttermilk Pastry (page 121) or Pat-in-the-Pan Oil Pastry (page 121)
2 large eggs
1/2 cup sugar
1 teaspoon ground cinnamon
1/2 teaspoon salt
1/2 teaspoon ground ginger
1/8 teaspoon ground cloves
1 can (16 ounces) pumpkin (not pumpkin pie mix)
1 can (12 ounces) evaporated milk
Sweetened Whipped Cream (page 198), if desired

1. Heat oven to 425°. Make pastry for unbaked One-Crust Pie; before adding filling, partially bake pastry as directed on page 118 to prevent crust from becoming soggy. (Do not partially bake if using the Pat-in-the-Pan Oil Pastry.)

2. Beat eggs slightly in medium bowl with wire whisk or hand beater. Beat in remaining ingredients except Sweetened Whipped Cream.

3. Cover edge of pie crust with 2- to 3-inch strip of aluminum foil to prevent excessive browning (page 116); remove foil during last 15 minutes of baking. To prevent spilling filling, place pie plate on oven rack. Pour filling into hot pie crust.

4. Bake 15 minutes. Reduce oven temperature to 350°. Bake about 45 minutes longer or until knife inserted in center comes out clean. Cool on wire rack 2 hours. Serve with Sweetened Whipped Cream. After cooling, pie can remain at room temperature up to an additional 4 hours, then should be covered and refrigerated.

1 Serving: Calories 280 (Calories from Fat 115); Fat 13g (Saturated 6g); Cholesterol 60mg; Sodium 370mg; Carbohydrate 35g (Dietary Fiber 2g); Protein 8g **% Daily Value:** Vitamin A 100%; Vitamin C 2%; Calcium 16%; Iron 10% **Diet Exchanges:** 2 Starch, 1 Vegetable, 2 Fat

PRALINE PUMPKIN PIE: Make pie as directed—except decrease second bake time to 35 minutes. Mix 1/3 cup packed brown sugar, 1/3 cup chopped pecans and 1 tablespoon butter or stick margarine, softened. Sprinkle over pie. Bake about 10 minutes longer or until knife inserted in center comes out clean.

Impossibly Easy Pumpkin Pie

Prep: 7 min; Bake: 40 min; Cool: 2 hr ✳ 8 servings

Impossibly easy? Yes, because this pie forms a light crust as it bakes. Because there's no crust to make, it's truly a one-step pie.

1 cup canned pumpkin (not pumpkin pie mix)
1/2 cup Original or Reduced Fat Bisquick®
1/2 cup sugar
1 cup evaporated milk
1 tablespoon butter or stick margarine, softened*
1 1/2 teaspoons pumpkin pie spice
1 teaspoon vanilla
2 large eggs
Sweetened Whipped Cream (page 198), if desired

1. Heat oven to 350°. Grease pie plate, 9 × 1 1/4 inches, with shortening.

2. Mix all ingredients with fork until blended. To prevent spilling, place pie plate on oven rack. Pour filling into pie plate.

3. Bake 35 to 40 minutes or until knife inserted in center comes out clean. Cool on wire rack 2 hours. Serve with Sweetened Whipped Cream. After cooling, pie can remain at room temperature up to an additional 4 hours, then should be covered and refrigerated. Store pie covered in refrigerator.

Spreads with at least 65% vegetable oil can be used (page 91).

1 Serving: Calories 155 (Calories from Fat 45); Fat 5g (Saturated 2g); Cholesterol 60mg; Sodium 170mg; Carbohydrate 23g (Dietary Fiber 1g); Protein 5g **% Daily Value:** Vitamin A 72%; Vitamin C 0%; Calcium 12%; Iron 4% **Diet Exchanges:** 1 Starch, 1 Vegetable, 1 Fat

Custard Pie

Prep: 15 min; Bake: 45 min; Cool: 2 hr ✳ 8 servings

Pastry for One-Crust Pie (page 117) or Buttermilk
  Pastry (page 121)
4 large eggs
2/3 cup sugar
2 2/3 cups milk
1 teaspoon vanilla
1/2 teaspoon salt
1/4 teaspoon ground nutmeg

1. Heat oven to 425°. Make pastry for unbaked One-Crust Pie; before adding filling, partially bake pastry as directed on page 118 to prevent crust from becoming soggy.

2. Increase oven temperature to 450°. Beat eggs slightly in medium bowl with wire whisk or hand beater. Beat in remaining ingredients.

3. Cover edge of pie crust with 2- to 3-inch strip of aluminum foil to prevent excessive browning (page 116); remove foil during last 15 minutes of baking. To prevent spilling filling, place pie plate on oven rack. Pour filling into hot pie crust.

4. Bake 20 minutes. Reduce oven temperature to 350°. Bake 10 to 15 minutes longer or until knife inserted halfway between center and edge comes out clean. Cool on wire rack 2 hours. After cooling, pie can remain at room temperature up to an additional 4 hours, then should be covered and refrigerated.

1 Serving: Calories 290 (Calories from Fat 125); Fat 14g (Saturated 2g); Cholesterol 110mg; Sodium 220mg; Carbohydrate 33g (Dietary Fiber 0g); Protein 8g **% Daily Value:** Vitamin A 8%; Vitamin C 0%; Calcium 10%; Iron 6% **Diet Exchanges:** 2 Starch, 3 Fat

Pecan Pie

Prep: 20 min; Bake: 50 min ✳ 8 servings

Pastry for One-Crust Pie (page 117), Buttermilk Pastry
  (page 121) or Pat-in-the-Pan Oil Pastry (page 121)
2/3 cup sugar
1/3 cup butter or stick margarine, melted*
1 cup corn syrup
1/2 teaspoon salt
3 large eggs
1 cup pecan halves or broken pecans

1. Heat oven to 375°. Make pastry for unbaked One-Crust Pie.

2. Beat sugar, butter, corn syrup, salt and eggs in medium bowl with wire whisk or hand beater until well blended. Stir in pecans. Pour into pastry-lined pie plate.

3. Bake 40 to 50 minutes or until center is set.

*Spreads with at least 65% vegetable oil can be used (page 91).

1 Serving: Calories 530 (Calories from Fat 260); Fat 29g (Saturated 9g); Cholesterol 100mg; Sodium 420mg; Carbohydrate 63g (Dietary Fiber 1g); Protein 5g **% Daily Value:** Vitamin A 8%; Vitamin C 0%; Calcium 2%; Iron 6% **Diet Exchanges:** Not Recommended

KENTUCKY PECAN PIE: Add 2 tablespoons bourbon with the corn syrup. Stir in 1 bag (6 ounces) semisweet chocolate chips (1 cup) with the pecans.

Classic French Silk Pie

Prep: 30 min; Bake/Cool: 30 min; Chill: 2 hr ✳ 10 servings

We've revised the luscious filling in this pie recipe. Now made with fat-free, cholesterol-free egg product versus raw eggs, salmonella, which can be contracted from raw eggs, is no longer an issue. The egg product is safe because it's pasteurized.

Pastry for One-Crust Pie (page 117) or Buttermilk
    Pastry (page 121)
1 cup sugar
3/4 cup butter, softened*
1 1/2 teaspoons vanilla
3 ounces unsweetened baking chocolate, melted and
    cooled
3/4 cup fat-free cholesterol-free egg product
1 1/2 cups Sweetened Whipped Cream (page 198)
Chocolate curls, if desired

1. Bake pastry for baked One-Crust Pie. Cool completely.

2. Beat sugar and butter in medium bowl with electric mixer on medium speed until light and fluffy. Beat in vanilla and chocolate. Gradually beat in egg product on high speed until light and fluffy (about 3 minutes). Pour into pie crust. Refrigerate until set, at least 2 hours but no longer than 24 hours.

3. Spread with Sweetened Whipped Cream. Garnish with chocolate curls. Store covered in refrigerator.

*Do not use margarine or vegetable oil spreads.

1 Serving: Calories 460 (Calories from Fat 295); Fat 33g (Saturated 17g); Cholesterol 55mg; Sodium 260mg; Carbohydrate 37g (Dietary Fiber 1g); Protein 5g **% Daily Value:** Vitamin A 14%; Vitamin C 0%; Calcium 2%; Iron 8% **Diet Exchanges:** Not Recommended

MOCHA FRENCH SILK PIE: Beat in 1 1/2 teaspoons instant coffee (dry) with the chocolate.

Grasshopper Pie

Prep: 30 min; Chill: 4 hr 20 min ✳ 8 servings

Named after a favorite after-dinner drink, this pie is flavored with crème de menthe and crème de cacao.

Cookie Crumb Crust (page 122)
1/2 cup milk
32 large marshmallows
1/4 cup crème de menthe
3 tablespoons white crème de cacao
1 1/2 cups whipping (heavy) cream
Few drops green food color, if desired
Grated semisweet baking chocolate, if desired

1. Bake crust as directed, using chocolate wafer cookies. Reserve about 2 tablespoons crumbs to sprinkle over top of pie if desired.

2. Heat milk and marshmallows in 3-quart saucepan over low heat, stirring constantly, just until marshmallows are melted. Refrigerate about 20 minutes, stirring occasionally, until mixture mounds slightly when dropped from a spoon. (If mixture becomes too thick, place saucepan in bowl of warm water; stir mixture until proper consistency.)

3. Gradually stir in crème de menthe and crème de cacao.

4. Beat whipping cream in chilled medium bowl with electric mixer on high speed until stiff. Fold marshmallow mixture into whipped cream. Fold in food color. Spread in crust. Sprinkle with reserved cookie crumbs or grated chocolate. Refrigerate about 4 hours or until set. Store covered in refrigerator.

1 Serving: Calories 395 (Calories from Fat 205); Fat 23g (Saturated 13g); Cholesterol 60mg; Sodium 220mg; Carbohydrate 45g (Dietary Fiber 1g); Protein 3g **% Daily Value:** Vitamin A 14%; Vitamin C 0%; Calcium 6%; Iron 4% **Diet Exchanges:** Not Recommended

COFFEE CORDIAL PIE: Substitute water for the milk; add 1 tablespoon instant coffee (dry) with the water. Substitute coffee liqueur for the crème de menthe and Irish whiskey for the crème de cacao.

IRISH CREAM PIE: Substitute 1/3 cup Irish cream liqueur for the crème de menthe and white crème de cacao.

Fluffy Strawberry Pie

Prep: 30 min; Chill: 4 hr ✱ *8 servings*

Pastry for One-Crust Pie (page 117) or Buttermilk
    Pastry (page 121)
3/4 cup boiling water
1 package (4-serving size) strawberry-flavored gelatin
1 teaspoon grated lime peel
1/2 cup lime juice (2 limes)
2 cups whipping (heavy) cream
1 cup powdered sugar
2 cups strawberries, slightly crushed

1. Bake pastry for baked One-Crust Pie. Cool completely.

2. Pour boiling water on gelatin in large bowl; stir until gelatin is dissolved. Stir in lime peel and lime juice. Refrigerate about 1 hour or until very thick but not set.

3. Beat gelatin mixture with electric mixer on high speed about 4 minutes or until thick and fluffy.

4. Beat whipping cream and powdered sugar in chilled large bowl on high speed until stiff. Fold whipped cream and strawberries into gelatin mixture. Spread in pie crust. Refrigerate about 3 hours or until set. Store covered in refrigerator.

1 Serving: Calories 440 (Calories from Fat 260); Fat 29g (Saturated 14g); Cholesterol 65mg; Sodium 200mg; Carbohydrate 42g (Dietary Fiber 2g); Protein 4g **% Daily Value:** Vitamin A 14%; Vitamin C 46%; Calcium 4%; Iron 4% **Diet Exchanges:** Not Recommended

Mud Pie

Prep: 20 min; Chill: 30 min; Freeze: 3 hr ✱ *10 servings*

Recipes for mud pie can vary slightly. Ours has a chocolate crust, is filled with coffee ice cream and is topped with fudge sauce. It's wonderful with other flavors of ice cream, too, so choose your favorite to create your own special pie.

18 chocolate sandwich cookies, finely crushed
3 tablespoons butter or stick margarine, melted*
1 quart (2 pints) coffee, chocolate or other flavor ice
    cream, slightly softened
1 cup hot fudge topping
1/4 cup chopped almonds, toasted (page 177)
Sweetened Whipped Cream (page 198), if desired

1. Mix crushed cookies and butter until well blended. Press on bottom and up side of pie plate, 9 × 1 1/4 inches. Refrigerate 30 minutes.

2. Carefully spread ice cream evenly in crust. Freeze about 1 hour or until firm enough to spread with topping.

3. Spread hot fudge topping over top of pie. Sprinkle with almonds. Freeze about 2 hours or until firm. (If pie has been frozen for several hours or overnight, remove from freezer about 10 minutes before serving to soften slightly.) Top with Sweetened Whipped Cream. Store wrapped in freezer.

Spreads with at least 65% vegetable oil can be used (page 91).

1 Serving: Calories 395 (Calories from Fat 170); Fat 19g (Saturated 9g); Cholesterol 30mg; Sodium 225mg; Carbohydrate 48g (Dietary Fiber 2g); Protein 5g **% Daily Value:** Vitamin A 8%; Vitamin C 0%; Calcium 10%; Iron 8% **Diet Exchanges:** Not Recommended

Raisin-Rum Ice-Cream Pie

Prep: 20 min; Stand: 30 min; Freeze: 3 hr ✳ *8 servings*

1/2 cup rum
1/2 cup raisins
Cookie Crumb Crust (page 122)
1 quart (2 pints) vanilla ice cream, slightly softened

1. Pour rum over raisins. Let stand 30 minutes.

2. Bake crust as directed, using vanilla wafer cookies. Reserve about 2 tablespoons crumbs to sprinkle over top of pie if desired.

3. Fold raisin mixture into ice cream. Carefully spread ice cream in crust. Freeze about 3 hours or until firm. (If pie has been frozen for several hours or overnight, remove from freezer about 10 minutes before serving to soften slightly.) Store wrapped in freezer.

1 Serving: Calories 350 (Calories from Fat 160); Fat 18g (Saturated 7g); Cholesterol 30mg; Sodium 260mg; Carbohydrate 43g (Dietary Fiber 1g); Protein 4g **% Daily Value:** Vitamin A 12%; Vitamin C 0%; Calcium 10%; Iron 6% **Diet Exchanges:** Not Recommended

Blueberry Cream Tart

Prep: 30 min; Chill: 1 hr ✳ *10 servings*

Pastry for One-Crust Pie (page 117) or Buttermilk
    Pastry (page 121)
2 ounces white baking bars (white chocolate)
    (from 6-ounce package), chopped
1 cup whipping (heavy) cream
2 cups fresh blueberries

1. Make pastry as directed—except roll pastry into 13-inch circle. Bake pastry in 10-inch tart pan as directed for baked One-Crust Pie. Cool completely.

2. Melt white baking bar as directed on package; cool slightly. Gradually stir into whipping cream in large bowl. Beat cream mixture with electric mixer on medium speed until stiff. Spoon into crust.

3. Arrange blueberries on cream mixture. Refrigerate about 1 hour or until firm. Remove rim of pan before serving. Store covered in refrigerator.

1 Serving: Calories 240 (Calories from Fat 160); Fat 18g (Saturated 8g); Cholesterol 25mg; Sodium 130mg; Carbohydrate 18g (Dietary Fiber 1g); Protein 2g **% Daily Value:** Vitamin A 6%; Vitamin C 6%; Calcium 2%; Iron 4% **Diet Exchanges:** 1 Fruit, 4 Fat

Pink Lemonade Pie

Prep: 30 min; Freeze: 4 hr ✳ *8 servings*

For yellow lemonade pie, replace pink lemonade concentrate with regular lemonade concentrate and add a few drops of yellow food color.

Graham Cracker Crust (page 122)
1 quart (2 pints) vanilla ice cream, softened
1 can (6 ounces) frozen pink lemonade concentrate,
    thawed
1 container (4 ounces) frozen whipped topping, thawed
Few drops red food color, if desired

1. Bake crust as directed. Cool completely. Reserve about 2 tablespoons crumbs to sprinkle over top of pie if desired.

2. Mix ice cream, lemonade concentrate, whipped topping and food color in large bowl. Mound ice-cream mixture in crust.

3. Freeze about 4 hours or until firm. Let stand at room temperature a few minutes before cutting. (If pie has been frozen for several hours or overnight, remove from freezer about 10 minutes before serving to soften slightly.) Store wrapped in freezer.

1 Serving: Calories 345 (Calories from Fat 155); Fat 17g (Saturated 6g); Cholesterol 30mg; Sodium 250mg; Carbohydrate 45g (Dietary Fiber 0g); Protein 3g **% Daily Value:** Vitamin A 16%; Vitamin C 8%; Calcium 8%; Iron 2% **Diet Exchanges:** Not Recommended

Low-Fat = 3g or less, except main dishes with 6g or less   **Fast** = Ready in 30 minutes or less   ■ = Bread Machine directions   ● = Slow Cooker directions

Chocolate Chip Cookies (page 146)

Lighter = 1/3 fewer calories or 50% less fat

Cookie and Bar Basics

Who doesn't like homemade cookies and bars? They're fun to eat, easily portable and always a crowd pleaser. Whether chock-full of chocolate and nuts or sweet and buttery, there's a favorite cookie for everyone. Read on to learn about all the different ingredients that go into baking. The ingredients you choose will have an effect on your cookies and bars. With people's tastes changing all the time, isn't it nice to know that cookies and bars will always be favorites? Enjoy!

Ingredients

Flour

Today's flours are presifted before they are packaged, so sifting again isn't necessary. Use either bleached or unbleached all-purpose flour for most cookies. When using whole wheat flour, substitute it for one-third to one-half the amount of all-purpose flour to keep cookies from becoming too dry. Bread flour isn't recommended because cookies and bars can become tough; cake flour can result in cookies and bars that are too delicate and fragile, so they may fall apart. Use self-rising flour only when recipe directions are given for it.

To measure flour correctly, spoon it lightly into a dry-ingredient measuring cup, then level with a metal spatula or straight-edged knife. Never dip the measuring cup into the flour or tap the measuring cup to settle the flour when measuring, or you'll get too much flour. Too much flour makes cookies tough, crumbly and dry. Measuring too little flour causes cookies to spread and lose their shape.

> **Note:** Some recipes use cornstarch for a part of the flour, resulting in tender cookies that have a very fine and compact texture. Cornstarch and flour are not interchangeable cup for cup, so look for specific recipes that use cornstarch.

Oats

Quick-cooking and old-fashioned rolled oats are interchangeable unless recipes call for a specific type. Instant oatmeal products are not the same as quick-cooking and should not be used for baking (See page 150 for more about Oats). Old-fashioned oats are larger than quick-cooking oats and don't absorb as much moisture, making them more moist and chewy. Quick-cooking oats are smaller than old-fashioned oats and absorb moisture better. These two factors make quick-cooking oats especially good for nonbaked cookies because they will hold together very well.

Fats and Oils

Fats add tenderness and flavor to cookies and bars, but fats are not created equal in texture and flavor. The type of fat you choose—butter, margarine, reduced-calorie or low-fat butter or margarine, vegetable-oil spreads or shortening—depends on the kind of cookie you want. The biggest difference among these fats is how much water they contain, which affects how cookies bake and their eating texture. Cookies made with fats that have a lot of water in them will be soft, puffy and tough and will dry out quickly. We have recommended butter or stick margarine for our recipes. See page 16 for specific information on each type of fat.

SOFTENING BUTTER OR MARGARINE

Most cookie recipes call for softened butter or margarine. But how soft is it supposed to be, and how can you tell? Allow butter to soften at room temperature for 30 to 45 minutes; the time will vary, depending on the temperature of your kitchen. You can also soften it in the microwave (See Microwave Cooking and Heating Chart, page 544). Perfectly softened butter should give gently to pressure (you should be able to leave a fingerprint and slight indentation on the stick) but shouldn't be soft in appearance. Butter that is too soft or is partially melted results in dough that is too soft, causing cookies to spread too much.

LEARN WITH *Betty* — SOFTENING BUTTER

Butter Perfectly Softened   *Butter Too Soft*   *Butter Partially Melted*

Sweeteners

In addition to adding sweetness to cookies and bars, sweeteners also aid in browning and affect the texture of baked goods.

Most recipes call for granulated white sugar, brown sugar or both, but other types of sweeteners are used, such as honey or maple syrup. The higher the sugar-to-flour ratio in a recipe, the more tender and crisp the cookies will be.

Leavening

Cookies usually call for one or two types of leavening, either baking soda or baking powder, which react with liquids to form a gas that causes the cookies to rise. Baking powder and baking soda are not interchangeable. You want leaveners to be fresh, so always check the expiration dates on the containers. If the product is older than the date on the label, the leavening power is significantly decreased or completely gone, so cookies and bars made with it will be flat and dense in texture.

Eggs

Eggs add richness, moisture and structure to cookies. Yet, too many eggs can make cookies crumbly. All the recipes in this book have been tested with large eggs. Egg product substitutes, made of egg whites, can be used in place of whole eggs, but cookies made with them may be drier.

Note: Can't break the habit of nibbling on raw cookie dough? A word of caution: Salmonella, a very serious and potentially fatal food poisoning bacteria, can be contracted by eating raw whole eggs. The solution? Don't eat unbaked dough made with raw whole eggs. Or make your cookies with pasteurized raw whole eggs (if available in your area) or egg product substitutes; both are perfectly safe to eat raw. We happen to know that some cookie dough never gets baked, because you like to nibble on it while baking cookies. With these options, you can have your cookie dough and eat it, too—safely, that is!

Liquids

Liquids such as water, fruit juice, cream and milk tend to make cookies crisper by causing them to spread more. Add only as much liquid as your recipe calls for. Buttermilk can be substituted for regular milk, but if the recipe you're using doesn't have 1/4 teaspoon of baking soda already in it, add the baking soda to your dough with the flour. The reason? Without the baking soda, the leavening won't work very well.

Nuts and Peanuts

Most recipes call for walnuts, pecans, almonds or peanuts. Hazelnuts, cashews and macadamia nuts are also used. When nuts are called for in a recipe, you can use any variety of nut or peanuts instead. Nuts can easily become rancid. Rancid nuts have a very unpleasant, strong flavor that can ruin the taste of your cookies. To prevent rancidity, store nuts and peanuts tightly covered in your refrigerator or freezer for up to two years. Do not freeze cashews because they can become soggy. Before using nuts or peanuts in a recipe, do a little taste test. If they don't taste fresh, throw them out.

> **Note:** Almond brickle baking chips can also become rancid. To prevent rancidity, store them in the refrigerator or freezer up to six months. Do a taste test before using.

Pans and Preparation

Cookie Sheets

There are many types of cookie sheets to choose from, including shiny aluminum, insulated, nonstick and black surface. We recommend using shiny aluminum cookie sheets that are at least two inches narrower and shorter than the inside dimensions of your oven, so the heat will circulate around them. The sheet may be open on one to three sides. If the sheet has four sides, cookies may not brown as evenly. If cookie sheets are thin, put two sheets together for added insulation. In a pinch, the aluminum cover for a 13 × 9 × 2-inch baking pan will work, too. Having at least three or four cookie sheets to use is helpful; as you finish baking one sheet, you can get another one ready to go.

Insulated cookie sheets help prevent cookies from turning too dark on the bottom. Cookies baked on these sheets may take longer to bake, the bottoms will be light colored and cookies may not brown as much overall. Cookies may be difficult to remove from these cookie sheets because the cookie bottom is more tender.

Nonstick and black surface cookie sheets may result in cookies smaller in diameter and more rounded. The tops and especially the bottoms will be more browned, and the bottoms may be hard. Always check your cookies at the minimum bake time given in a recipe so they don't get too brown or burn. Follow the manufacturer's directions because some recommend reducing the oven temperature by 25°.

Baking Pans for Bars

Use the exact size of pan called for in a recipe. Bars baked in pans that are too big become hard and overcooked, and those baked in pans that are too small can be doughy in the center and hard on the edges. Shiny metal pans are preferred for baking bars. They reflect the heat away from the bars, preventing the crust from getting too brown and hard. Dark nonstick and glass baking pans should be used following the manufacturer's directions. These pans absorb heat easily, so reducing the oven temperature by 25° or checking for doneness 3 to 5 minutes before the minimum bake time given is usually recommended. Be careful when cutting bars baked in nonstick pans, or you may scratch the surface. Try using a plastic knife to avoid this problem. In fact, a plastic knife works best for cutting brownies and soft, sticky bars such as Lemon Bars (page 144).

Greasing Cookie Sheets and Baking Pans

Grease cookie sheets and baking pans only when a recipe calls for it. Don't grease nonstick cookie sheets even if a recipe calls for greasing; the cookies may spread too much if greasing isn't necessary. Use shortening or cooking spray to grease cookie sheets and baking pans. Do not use butter, margarine or vegetable oil for greasing; the area between the cookies will burn during baking and will be almost impossible to clean. Regrease sheets as needed during baking if cookies are sticking to them. Baking parchment paper can be used in place of shortening or cooking spray. It comes in rolls and can be found in stores near the waxed paper, aluminum foil and plastic wrap. Some stores may stock it in the baking ingredient aisle, too. If using baking parchment paper to line cookie sheets instead of greasing them, just tear off the length of parchment you need to cover your cookie sheet.

Line baking pans with aluminum foil for super-quick cleanup and to help cut bars and brownies evenly.

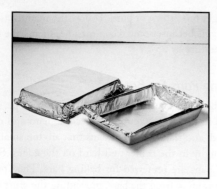

To line baking pans with aluminum foil, start by turning the pan upside down. Tear off a piece of foil longer than the pan, and shape the foil around the pan; carefully remove foil and set aside. Flip the pan over, and gently fit the shaped foil into the pan. When the bars or brownies are cool, just lift them out of the pan by the foil "handles," peel back the foil and cut the bars as directed.

Mixing Cookies and Bars

An electric mixer or spoon can be used for mixing the dough in most of our recipes. The sugars, fats and liquids usually are mixed together first until well combined. Flour and other dry ingredients are almost always stirred in by hand to avoid overmixing the dough, which can result in tougher cookies. When testing recipes, we didn't notice significant differences in the baked appearance or eating texture of cookies where the sugars, fats and liquids were mixed with an electric mixer versus a spoon.

The lighter variations for recipes in this chapter may contain reduced-fat or fat-free ingredients. Because fat helps intensify flavor but is reduced in these variations, we sometimes increased spices and flavorings in order to get the same flavor as the original recipe. The lighter doughs are usually softer and may have a slightly different texture than you're used to during mixing. If specified in a recipe, refrigerate the dough before baking.

Baking Cookies and Bars

The first step for baking is to heat your oven. This usually takes up to 10 minutes.

Bake one "test" cookie by putting the cookie dough on a greased or ungreased cookie sheet as directed in the recipe. If the cookie spreads too much, add 1 to 2 tablespoons of flour to the dough, or refrigerate the dough 1 to 2 hours before baking. If the cookie comes out too dry, add 1 to 2 tablespoons of milk to the dough. By testing the cookie dough, you can decide if any adjustments need to be made to your dough before you've baked a whole sheet of disappointing cookies.

Always scoop out cookie dough onto completely cooled cookie sheets. Cookies will spread too much if put on a hot, or even a warm, cookie sheet. A cookie sheet doesn't take long to cool to room temperature. Plus, you can cool cookie sheets quickly by popping them in the refrigerator or freezer or by running cold water over them (dry completely and grease again if needed). If you have more than one cookie sheet to work with, you can let the hot sheet cool while another sheet of cookies is baking.

Make all cookies on each cookie sheet the same size so they bake evenly. Cookies that are smaller than the others will become too brown or burn, and cookies that are bigger than the others won't be done in the center.

Bake bars in the exact size pan called for in a recipe. Bars baked in a pan that is too large will overbake and be hard. Those baked in a pan that's too small can be doughy in the center and hard on the edges.

Always bake cookies on the middle oven rack. For even baking, bake one cookie sheet at a time. If you decide to bake two sheets at once, switch the placement of the sheets halfway through baking to help the cookies bake more evenly. Also when baking two sheets at once, position the oven racks as close to the middle as possible. If racks are too close to the top of the oven, the tops of the cookies may become too brown or burn; if racks are too close to the bottom, the bottoms of the cookies may become too brown or burn.

How can you tell when your cookies are done? Each recipe gives you two ways to determine when cookies are done: a bake time and a doneness test. Check cookies at the minimum bake time listed in the recipe. Watch cookies carefully while they bake because even 1 minute can make a difference. The longer cookies bake, the more brown, crisp or hard they become. Sometimes the color of the cookie is the best test for doneness; for example, when the cookie is light brown or until its edges begin to brown. If the dough is dark, color changes are hard to see. Then the test may be until cookies are set or until almost no indentation remains when touched in center. After baking one or two sheets, you should have a feel for just the right baking time. Use that time for your first check, but always use the doneness test as your final check.

Thinner cookies that are rolled or sliced, as well as dense or very sturdy cookies, generally should be removed from cookie sheets immediately after baking to prevent sticking. Drop cookies and soft cookies generally need to cool 1 to 2 minutes to set before being removed; otherwise, they may fall apart while being transferred to a cooling rack. The larger the cookie, the longer the cooling time on the cookie sheet. Always use a pancake turner to remove cookies from a cookie sheet.

Always cool cookies on wire cooling racks to allow air to flow around the cookies, which will prevent them from becoming soggy. Cool pans of bars and brownies in the pan on a wire cooling rack. Cool cookies and bars completely before frosting them unless the recipe tells you to frost them while they're warm.

Uh-oh! If the cookies were left to cool too long on the cookie sheet, and you're having trouble getting them off without breaking them, here's what you do. Put the cookies back in the oven for about 1 to 2 minutes to warm them, and then remove them; they should come off the sheet easily.

Storing Cookies and Bars

Keep crisp cookies crisp by storing them in a loosely covered container, such as a cookie jar without a screw-on lid or sealed gasket lid (rubber ring around inside of lid). If cookies soften, heat them on a cookie sheet at 300° for 3 to 5 minutes to recrisp. Cool them on a wire cooling rack.

To keep longer, freeze cookies, tightly wrapped and labeled, up to 6 months. *Do not freeze meringue, custard-filled or cream-filled cookies.* Place delicate frosted or decorated cookies in single layers in freezer containers, and cover with waxed paper before adding another layer; freeze. Thaw most cookies, covered, in the container at room temperature for 1 to 2 hours. For crisp cookies, remove from the container to thaw.

Keep chewy and soft cookies chewy and soft by keeping them in a tightly covered container. Resealable plastic bags, plastic food containers with tight-fitting lids, metal tins and cookie jars with screw-on lids or sealed gasket lids (rubber ring around inside of lid) work best. To keep longer, freeze cookies, tightly wrapped and labeled, up to 6 months.

Allow frosted or decorated cookies to set or harden before storing; store them between layers of waxed paper, plastic wrap or aluminum foil.

Do not store crisp and chewy or soft cookies together in the same container, or the crisp cookies will become soft.

Keep different flavors and varieties of cookies in separate containers, or they will pick up the flavors of the other cookies.

Most bars can be stored tightly covered, but check the recipe for sure; some may need to be loosely covered and others need to be refrigerated.

Chocolate Brownies and Cream Cheese Brownies (page 143)

Butterscotch Brownies *Low-Fat*

Prep: 15 min; Bake: 25 min; Cool: 5 min ✱ *16 brownies*

1/4 cup butter or stick margarine*
1 cup packed brown sugar
1 teaspoon vanilla
2 tablespoons milk
1 large egg
1 cup all-purpose flour**
1/2 cup chopped nuts, if desired
1 teaspoon baking powder
1/2 teaspoon salt

1. Heat oven to 350°. Grease bottom and sides of square pan, 8 × 8 × 2 inches, with shortening.

2. Melt butter in 1 1/2-quart saucepan over low heat; remove from heat. Stir in brown sugar, vanilla, milk and egg. Stir in remaining ingredients. Spread in pan.

3. Bake about 25 minutes or until golden brown. Cool 5 minutes in pan on wire rack. For brownies, cut into 4 rows by 4 rows while warm.

*Do not use vegetable oil spreads (page 91).
**If using self-rising flour, omit baking powder and salt.

1 Brownie: Calories 110 (Calories from Fat 25); Fat 3g (Saturated 1g); Cholesterol 15mg; Sodium 150mg; Carbohydrate 20g (Dietary Fiber 0g); Protein 1g **% Daily Value:** Vitamin A 4%; Vitamin C 0%; Calcium 2%; Iron 4% **Diet Exchanges:** 1 Starch, 1/2 Fruit

Chocolate Brownies

Prep: 25 min; Bake: 45 min; Cool: 2 hr ✱ *16 brownies*

2/3 cup butter or stick margarine*
5 ounces unsweetened baking chocolate, cut into
    pieces
1 3/4 cups sugar
2 teaspoons vanilla
3 large eggs
1 cup all-purpose flour**
1 cup chopped walnuts
Chocolate Buttercream Frosting (page 110), if desired

1. Heat oven to 350°. Grease bottom and sides of square pan, 9 × 9 × 2 inches, with shortening.

2. Melt butter and chocolate in 1-quart saucepan over low heat, stirring constantly. Cool 5 minutes.

3. Beat sugar, vanilla and eggs in medium bowl with electric mixer on high speed 5 minutes. Beat in chocolate mixture on low speed, scraping bowl occasionally. Beat in flour just until blended, scraping bowl occasionally. Stir in walnuts. Spread in pan.

4. Bake 40 to 45 minutes or just until brownies begin to pull away from sides of pan. Cool completely in pan on wire rack, about 2 hours. Frost with Chocolate Buttercream Frosting. For brownies, cut into 4 rows by 4 rows.

Spreads with at least 65% vegetable oil can be used (page 91).
**Do not use self-rising flour.*

1 Brownie: Calories 300 (Calories from Fat 160); Fat 18g (Saturated 5g); Cholesterol 40mg; Sodium 115mg; Carbohydrate 32g (Dietary Fiber 2g); Protein 4g **% Daily Value:** Vitamin A 12%; Vitamin C 0%; Calcium 2%; Iron 6% **Diet Exchanges:** Not Recommended

CHOCOLATE BROWNIE PIE: Grease bottom and side of pie plate, 10 × 1 1/2 inches, with shortening. Spread batter in pie plate. Bake 35 to 40 minutes or until center is set. Cool completely in pan on wire rack. Cut into wedges. Omit frosting. Serve with ice cream and Hot Fudge Sauce (page 195) if desired. 12 servings.

CHOCOLATE-PEANUT BUTTER BROWNIES: Substitute 1/3 cup crunchy peanut butter for 1/3 cup of the butter. Omit walnuts. Before baking, arrange 16 one-inch chocolate-covered peanut butter cup candies, unwrapped, over top. Press into batter so tops of cups are even with top of batter.

Cream Cheese Brownies

Prep: 25 min; Bake: 50 min ✳ *48 brownies*

1 cup butter or stick margarine*
4 ounces unsweetened baking chocolate
Cream Cheese Filling (right)
2 cups sugar
2 teaspoons vanilla
4 large eggs
1 1/2 cups all-purpose flour**
1/2 teaspoon salt
1 cup coarsely chopped nuts

1. Heat oven to 350°. Grease bottom and sides of rectangular pan, 13 × 9 × 2 inches, with shortening.

2. Melt butter and chocolate in 1-quart saucepan over low heat, stirring frequently. Remove from heat; cool 5 minutes.

3. Make Cream Cheese Filling; set aside.

4. Beat chocolate mixture, sugar, vanilla and eggs in large bowl with electric mixer on medium speed 1 minute, scraping bowl occasionally. Beat in flour and salt on low speed 30 seconds, scraping bowl occasionally. Beat on medium speed 1 minute. Stir in nuts. Spread 1 3/4 of the batter in pan. Spread filling over batter. Drop remaining batter in mounds randomly over filling. Carefully spread to cover cream cheese layer.

5. Bake 45 to 50 minutes or until toothpick inserted in center comes out clean. Cool in pan on wire rack. For brownies, cut into 8 rows by 6 rows. Store covered in refrigerator.

Cream Cheese Filling

2 packages (8 ounces each) cream cheese, softened
1/2 cup sugar
2 teaspoons vanilla
1 large egg

Beat all ingredients until smooth.

Spreads with at least 65% vegetable oil can be used (page 91).
**If using self-rising flour, omit salt.*

1 Brownie: Calories 165 (Calories from Fat 100); Fat 11g (Saturated 4g); Cholesterol 30mg; Sodium 110mg; Carbohydrate 15g (Dietary Fiber 1g); Protein 2g **% Daily Value:** Vitamin A 8%; Vitamin C 0%; Calcium 2%; Iron 2% **Diet Exchanges:** 1 Starch, 2 Fat

Lighter Cream Cheese Brownies: For 6 grams of fat and 120 calories per serving, substitute 1/2 cup unsweetened applesauce for 1/2 cup of the butter and 2 eggs plus 4 egg whites for the 4 eggs. Decrease nuts to 1/2 cup. Use reduced-fat cream cheese (Neufchâtel), softened, in Cream Cheese Filling.

Toffee Bars

Prep: 20 min; Bake: 30 min; Cool: 30 min ✱ *32 bars*

1 cup butter or stick margarine, softened*
1 cup packed brown sugar
1 teaspoon vanilla
1 large egg yolk
2 cups all-purpose flour**
1/4 teaspoon salt
2/3 cup milk chocolate chips or 3 bars (1.55 ounces
    each) milk chocolate, broken into small pieces
1/2 cup chopped nuts

1. Heat oven to 350°.

2. Mix butter, brown sugar, vanilla and egg yolk in large bowl. Stir in flour and salt. Press dough in ungreased rectangular pan, 13 × 9 × 2 inches.

3. Bake 25 to 30 minutes or until very light brown (crust will be soft). Immediately sprinkle chocolate chips on hot crust. Let stand about 5 minutes or until soft; spread evenly. Sprinkle with nuts. Cool 30 minutes in pan on wire rack. For bars, cut into 8 rows by 4 rows while warm for easiest cutting.

Do not use vegetable oil spreads (page 91).
**If using self-rising flour, omit salt.*

1 Bar: Calories 135 (Calories from Fat 70); Fat 8g (Saturated 2g); Cholesterol 5mg; Sodium 100mg; Carbohydrate 15g (Dietary Fiber 0g); Protein 1g **% Daily Value:** Vitamin A 8%; Vitamin C 0%; Calcium 2%; Iron 2% **Diet Exchanges:** 1 Starch, 1 Fat

Lemon Bars

Prep: 10 min; Bake: 50 min ✱ *25 bars*

1 cup all-purpose flour*
1/2 cup butter or stick margarine, softened**
1/4 cup powdered sugar
1 cup granulated sugar
2 teaspoons grated lemon peel, if desired
2 tablespoons lemon juice
1/2 teaspoon baking powder
1/4 teaspoon salt
2 large eggs
Powdered sugar

1. Heat oven to 350°.

2. Mix flour, butter and 1/4 cup powdered sugar. Press in ungreased square pan, 8 × 8 × 2 or 9 × 9 × 2 inches, building up 1/2-inch edges.

3. Bake crust 20 minutes; remove from oven.

4. Beat remaining ingredients except powdered sugar with electric mixer on high speed about 3 minutes or until light and fluffy. Pour over hot crust.

5. Bake 25 to 30 minutes or until no indentation remains when touched lightly in center. Cool in pan on wire rack. Dust with powdered sugar. For bars, cut into 5 rows by 5 rows.

Self-rising flour can be used.
**Do not use vegetable oil spreads (page 91).*

1 Bar: Calories 95 (Calories from Fat 35); Fat 4g (Saturated 1g); Cholesterol 15mg; Sodium 85mg; Carbohydrate 14g (Dietary Fiber 0g); Protein 1g **% Daily Value:** Vitamin A 6%; Vitamin C 0%; Calcium 0%; Iron 2% **Diet Exchanges:** 1 Fruit, 1 Fat

LEMON-COCONUT BARS: Stir 1/2 cup flaked coconut into egg mixture in step 4.

Pumpkin-Spice Bars

Prep: 15 min; Bake: 30 min; Cool: 2 hr ✱ *49 bars*

Check labels carefully when buying canned pumpkin. Two types are available: plain pumpkin, which isn't sweetened and doesn't have any flavoring added, and pumpkin pie mix, which contains sugar and spices.

4 large eggs
2 cups sugar
1 cup vegetable oil
1 can (15 ounces) pumpkin (not pumpkin pie mix)
2 cups all-purpose flour*
2 teaspoons baking powder
2 teaspoons ground cinnamon
1 teaspoon baking soda
1/2 teaspoon salt
1/2 teaspoon ground ginger
1/4 teaspoon ground cloves
1 cup raisins, if desired
Cream Cheese Frosting (right)
1/2 cup chopped walnuts, if desired

Pumpkin-Spice Bars

1. Heat oven to 350°. Lightly grease bottom and sides of jelly roll pan, 15 1/2 × 10 1/2 × 1 inch, with shortening.

2. Beat eggs, sugar, oil and pumpkin in large bowl until smooth. Stir in flour, baking powder, cinnamon, baking soda, salt, ginger and cloves. Stir in raisins. Spread in pan.

3. Bake 25 to 30 minutes or until light brown. Cool completely in pan on wire rack, about 2 hours. Frost with Cream Cheese Frosting. Sprinkle with walnuts. For bars, cut into 7 rows by 7 rows. Store covered in refrigerator.

Cream Cheese Frosting

1 package (3 ounces) cream cheese, softened
1/3 cup butter or stick margarine, softened**
1 teaspoon vanilla
2 cups powdered sugar

Beat cream cheese, butter and vanilla in medium bowl with electric mixer on low speed until smooth. Gradually beat in powdered sugar, 1 cup at a time, on low speed until smooth and spreadable.

If using self-rising flour, omit baking powder, baking soda and salt.
**Spreads with at least 65% vegetable oil can be used (page 91).*

1 Cookie: Calories 140 (Calories from Fat 65); Fat 7g (Saturated 1g); Cholesterol 20mg; Sodium 95mg; Carbohydrate 18g (Dietary Fiber 0g); Protein 1g **% Daily Value:** Vitamin A 22%; Vitamin C 0%; Calcium 2%; Iron 2% **Diet Exchanges:** 1/2 Starch, 1 Fruit, 1 Fat

Date Bars

Prep: 30 min; Bake: 30 min; Cool: 5 min ✱ *36 bars*

Date Filling (below)
1 cup packed brown sugar
1 cup butter or stick margarine, softened*
1 3/4 cups all-purpose** or whole wheat flour
1 1/2 cups quick-cooking oats
1/2 teaspoon salt
1/2 teaspoon baking soda

1. Make Date Filling.

2. Heat oven to 400°. Grease bottom and sides of rectangular pan, 13 × 9 × 2 inches, with shortening.

3. Mix brown sugar and butter in large bowl. Stir in remaining ingredients until crumbly. Press half of the crumb mixture evenly in bottom of pan. Spread with filling. Top with remaining crumb mixture; press lightly.

4. Bake 25 to 30 minutes or until light brown. Cool 5 minutes in pan on wire rack. For bars, cut into 6 rows by 6 rows while warm.

Date Filling

3 cups cut-up pitted dates (1 pound)
1/4 cup sugar
1 1/2 cups water

Cook all ingredients in 2-quart saucepan over low heat about 10 minutes, stirring constantly, until thickened; cool 5 minutes.

Do not use vegetable oil spreads (page 91).
**If using self-rising flour, omit salt and baking soda.*

1 Bar: Calories 145 (Calories from Fat 45); Fat 5g (Saturated 1g); Cholesterol 0mg; Sodium 120mg; Carbohydrate 25g (Dietary Fiber 2g); Protein 2g **% Daily Value:** Vitamin A 6%; Vitamin C 0%; Calcium 0%; Iron 4% **Diet Exchanges:** 1 Starch, 1 Fruit

Chocolate Chip Cookies

Prep: 10 min; Bake: 8 to 10 min per sheet; Cool: 2 min
✱ *About 4 dozen*

3/4 cup granulated sugar
3/4 cup packed brown sugar
1 cup butter or stick margarine, softened*
1 teaspoon vanilla
1 large egg
2 1/4 cups all-purpose flour**
1 teaspoon baking soda
1/2 teaspoon salt
1 cup coarsely chopped nuts
1 bag (12 ounces) semisweet chocolate chips (2 cups)

1. Heat oven to 375°.

2. Beat sugars, butter, vanilla and egg in large bowl with electric mixer on medium speed, or mix with spoon. Stir in flour, baking soda and salt (dough will be stiff). Stir in nuts and chocolate chips.

3. Drop dough by rounded tablespoonfuls about 2 inches apart onto ungreased cookie sheet.

4. Bake 8 to 10 minutes or until light brown (centers will be soft). Cool 1 to 2 minutes; remove from cookie sheet to wire rack.

Spreads with at least 65% vegetable oil can be used (page 91).
**If using self-rising flour, omit baking soda and salt.*

1 Cookie: Calories 135 (Calories from Fat 70); Fat 8g (Saturated 2g); Cholesterol 5mg; Sodium 105mg; Carbohydrate 16g (Dietary Fiber 1g); Protein 1g **% Daily Value:** Vitamin A 4%; Vitamin C 0%; Calcium 2%; Iron 0% **Diet Exchanges:** 1 Starch, 1 Fat

---

FROSTING BARS

There's a handy little tool for frosting bars called an "offset spatula" (or spreader). The spreader part has a bend in it, making it ergonomically friendly and very easy to frost bars in pans. This little gem is inexpensive and can be found in large department stores or specialty cookware stores.

Lighter Chocolate Chip Cookies: For 4 grams of fat and 90 calories per serving, decrease butter to 3/4 cup and omit nuts. Substitute 1 cup miniature chocolate chips for the 12-ounce bag of chocolate chips.

CANDY COOKIES: Substitute 2 cups candy-coated chocolate candies for the chocolate chips.

CHOCOLATE CHIP BARS: Press dough in ungreased rectangular pan, 13 × 9 × 2 inches. Bake 15 to 20 minutes or until golden brown. Cool in pan on wire rack. 48 bars.

JUMBO CHOCOLATE CHIP COOKIES: Drop dough by 1/4 cupfuls or #16 cookie/ice-cream scoop about 3 inches apart onto ungreased cookie sheet. Bake 12 to 15 minutes or until edges are set (centers will be soft). Cool 1 to 2 minutes; remove from cookie sheet to wire rack. 1 1/2 dozen cookies.

COOKIE SCOOPS

A trick we use in the Betty Crocker Kitchens to make drop cookies the same size and shape is to use a spring-handled cookie or ice-cream scoop. Scoops come in various sizes and are referred to by number. (The number corresponds to the number of level scoops per quart of ice cream; the larger the number, the smaller the scoop.) Because not all manufacturers' sizes are the same, be sure to measure the volume of the scoop with water first. Use the size of scoop that drops the amount of dough called for in a recipe. Some common scoop sizes are:

1 level tablespoon = #70 scoop
1/4 cup = #16 scoop

LEARN WITH *Betty* — DIFFERENCES IN CHOCOLATE CHIP COOKIES

1. Chocolate Chip Cookies are flat and spread. Causes: Butter or margarine was too soft or partially melted (see Learn with Betty: Softening Butter on page 138 for Butter Perfectly Softened), under-measurement of flour, dough placed on hot or warm cookie sheet.

2. Chocolate Chip Cookies are slightly rounded. There are no problems with this cookie.

3. Chocolate Chip Cookies don't change shape and are hard. Causes: Over-measurement of flour (see Measuring Ingredients on page 5 for measuring flour, baking mix and sugar).

Outrageous Double Chocolate–White Chocolate Chunk Cookies and White Chocolate Chunk–Macadamia Cookies (page 149)

Outrageous Double Chocolate–White Chocolate Chunk Cookies

Prep: 15 min; Bake: 12 to 14 min per sheet; Cool: 2 min
✱ *About 2 dozen*

1 bag (24 ounces) semisweet chocolate chips (4 cups)
1 cup butter or stick margarine, softened*
1 cup packed brown sugar
1 teaspoon vanilla
2 large eggs
2 1/2 cups all-purpose flour**
1 1/2 teaspoons baking soda
1/2 teaspoon salt
1 package (6 ounces) white baking bars, cut into
    1/4- to 1/2-inch chunks
1 cup pecan or walnut halves

1. Heat oven to 350°. Heat 1 1/2 cups of the chocolate chips in 1-quart saucepan over low heat, stirring constantly, until melted. Cool to room temperature, but do not allow chocolate to become firm.

2. Beat butter, brown sugar and vanilla in large bowl with electric mixer on medium speed until light and fluffy. Beat in eggs and melted chocolate until light and fluffy. Stir in flour, baking soda and salt. Stir in remaining 2 1/2 cups chocolate chips, the white baking bar chunks and pecan halves.

3. Drop dough by level 1/4 cupfuls or #16 cookie/ice-cream scoop about 2 inches apart onto ungreased cookie sheet.

4. Bake 12 to 14 minutes or until set (centers will appear soft and moist). Cool 1 to 2 minutes; remove from cookie sheet to wire rack.

*Do not use vegetable oil spreads (page 91).
**If using self-rising flour, omit baking soda and salt.

1 Cookie: Calories 375 (Calories from Fat 200); Fat 22g (Saturated 12g); Cholesterol 40mg; Sodium 200mg; Carbohydrate 42g (Dietary Fiber 2g); Protein 4g **% Daily Value:** Vitamin A 6%; Vitamin C 0%; Calcium 4%; Iron 10% **Diet Exchanges:** Not Recommended

Chocolate Drop Cookies

Prep: 25 min; Bake: 8 to 10 min per sheet; Cool: 30 min
✱ *About 3 dozen*

Use your microwave to melt the chocolate for the cookie dough and the chocolate and butter for the frosting (page 544).

1 cup sugar
1/2 cup butter or stick margarine, softened*
1/3 cup buttermilk
1 teaspoon vanilla
1 large egg
2 ounces unsweetened baking chocolate, melted and
    cooled
1 3/4 cups all-purpose flour**
1/2 teaspoon baking soda
1/2 teaspoon salt
1 cup chopped nuts
Chocolate Frosting (below)

1. Heat oven to 400°. Grease cookie sheet with shortening or spray with cooking spray.

2. Beat sugar, butter, buttermilk, vanilla, egg and chocolate in large bowl with electric mixer on medium speed, or mix with spoon. Stir in flour, baking soda and salt. Stir in nuts.

3. Drop dough by rounded tablespoonfuls about 2 inches apart onto cookie sheet.

4. Bake 8 to 10 minutes or until almost no indentation remains when touched in center. Immediately remove from cookie sheet to wire rack. Cool completely, about 30 minutes. Frost with Chocolate Frosting.

Chocolate Frosting

2 ounces unsweetened baking chocolate
2 tablespoons butter or stick margarine*
2 cups powdered sugar
3 tablespoons hot water

Melt chocolate and butter in 2-quart saucepan over low heat, stirring occasionally; remove from heat. Stir in powdered sugar and hot water until smooth. (If frosting is too thick, add more water, 1 teaspoon at a time. If frosting is too thin, add more powdered sugar, 1 tablespoon at a time.)

Spreads with at least 65% vegetable oil can be used (page 91).
***If using self-rising flour, omit baking soda and salt.*

1 Cookie: Calories 140 (Calories from Fat 65); Fat 7g (Saturated 2g); Cholesterol 5mg; Sodium 100mg; Carbohydrate 18g (Dietary Fiber 1g); Protein 2g **% Daily Value:** Vitamin A 4%; Vitamin C 0%; Calcium 0%; Iron 2% **Diet Exchanges:** 1 Starch, 1 Fat

White Chocolate Chunk–Macadamia Cookies

Prep: 10 min; Bake: 10 to 12 min per sheet; Cool: 2 min
✱ *About 2 1/2 dozen*

These gourmet cookie-shop favorites are very rich and buttery tasting with a crisp exterior and chewy center.

1 cup packed brown sugar
1/2 cup granulated sugar
1/2 cup butter or stick margarine, softened*
1/2 cup shortening
1 teaspoon vanilla
1 large egg
2 1/4 cups all-purpose flour**
1 teaspoon baking soda
1/4 teaspoon salt
1 package (6 ounces) white baking bars, cut into
    1/4- to 1/2-inch chunks
1 jar (3 1/2 ounces) macadamia nuts, coarsely chopped

1. Heat oven to 350°.

2. Beat sugars, butter, shortening, vanilla and egg in large bowl with electric mixer on medium speed until light and fluffy, or mix with spoon. Stir in flour, baking soda and salt (dough will be stiff). Stir in white baking bar chunks and nuts.

3. Drop dough by rounded tablespoonfuls about 2 inches apart onto ungreased cookie sheet.

4. Bake 10 to 12 minutes or until light brown. Cool 1 to 2 minutes; remove from cookie sheet to wire rack.

Do not use vegetable oil spreads (page 91).
***Do not use self-rising flour.*

1 Cookie: Calories 185 (Calories from Fat 100); Fat 11g (Saturated 3g); Cholesterol 8mg; Sodium 110mg; Carbohydrate 21g (Dietary Fiber 1g); Protein 2g **% Daily Value:** Vitamin A 4%; Vitamin C 0%; Calcium 2%; Iron 4% **Diet Exchanges:** 1 Starch, 1/2 Fruit, 2 Fat

Oatmeal-Raisin Cookies

Prep: 15 min; Bake: 9 to 11 min per sheet
✳ *About 3 dozen*

Quick-cooking and old-fashioned rolled oats are interchangeable unless recipes call for a specific type. Instant oatmeal products are not the same as quick-cooking and should not be used for baking—you will get gummy or mushy results.

2/3 cup granulated sugar

2/3 cup packed brown sugar

1/2 cup butter or stick margarine, softened*

1/2 cup shortening

1 teaspoon baking soda

1 teaspoon ground cinnamon

1 teaspoon vanilla

1/2 teaspoon baking powder

1/2 teaspoon salt

2 large eggs

3 cups quick-cooking or old-fashioned oats

1 cup all-purpose flour**

1 cup raisins, chopped nuts or semisweet chocolate chips, if desired

1. Heat oven to 375°.

2. Beat all ingredients except oats, flour and raisins in large bowl with electric mixer on medium speed, or mix with spoon. Stir in oats, flour and raisins.

3. Drop dough by rounded tablespoonfuls about 2 inches apart onto ungreased cookie sheet.

4. Bake 9 to 11 minutes or until light brown. Immediately remove from cookie sheet to wire rack.

*Spreads with at least 65% vegetable oil can be used (page 91).
**If using self-rising flour, omit baking soda, baking powder and salt.

1 Cookie: Calories 120 (Calories from Fat 55); Fat 6g (Saturated 1g); Cholesterol 10mg; Sodium 115mg; Carbohydrate 15g (Dietary Fiber 1g); Protein 2g **% Daily Value:** Vitamin A 4%; Vitamin C 0%; Calcium 0%; Iron 2% **Diet Exchanges:** 1 Starch, 1 Fat

Lighter Oatmeal-Raisin Cookies: For 3 grams of fat and 95 calories per serving, substitute unsweetened applesauce for the shortening and 1/2 cup fat-free cholesterol-free egg product for the eggs. Increase cinnamon and vanilla to 1 1/2 teaspoons each.

OATMEAL-RAISIN SQUARES: Press dough in ungreased square pan, 8 × 8 × 2 inches. Bake about 25 minutes or until light brown. Cool in pan on wire rack. For squares, cut into 4 rows by 4 rows. 16 squares.

USING OATS

Measuring

Measure oats either by pouring them into a measuring cup or by dipping the measuring cup into the oats container. There are many ways to use oats, including toasting and grinding them. Toasting oats gives them a delicious, slightly nutty, rich flavor and a bit of extra crunch. Ground oats can be used for some of the flour in cookies, giving the cookies great flavor and a chewy texture.

Toasting

To toast oats, heat oven to 350°. Spread 1 to 2 cups old-fashioned or quick-cooking oats in an ungreased jelly roll pan, 15 1/2 × 10 1/2 × 1 inch, or on a large cookie sheet. Toast 15 to 20 minutes, stirring once, until light golden brown. Toasted oats can be used cup for cup in cookie and bar recipes calling for oats. They're also great sprinkled on ice cream, yogurt and fruit.

Grinding

Place about 1 1/4 cups old-fashioned or quick-cooking oats in your blender or food processor. Cover and blend on medium speed about 1 minute, stopping blender occasionally to stir oats, until they are finely ground. You'll get about 1 cup of ground oats. Ground oats can be substituted for about one-third of the amount of flour called for in a cookie or bar recipe without causing major changes in the texture.

Soft Molasses Cookies

Prep: 10 min; Bake: 9 to 11 min per sheet; Cool: 2 min
✳ *About 4 dozen*

1 cup sugar
3/4 cup sour cream
1/2 cup butter or stick margarine, softened*
1/2 cup shortening
1/2 cup molasses
1 large egg
3 cups all-purpose flour**
1 1/2 teaspoons baking soda
1 teaspoon ground cinnamon
1 teaspoon ground ginger
1/2 teaspoon salt
Sugar, if desired

1. Heat oven to 375°.

2. Beat 1 cup sugar, the sour cream, butter, shortening, molasses and egg in large bowl with electric mixer on medium speed, or mix with spoon. Stir in remaining ingredients.

3. Drop dough by rounded tablespoonfuls about 2 inches apart onto ungreased cookie sheet.

4. Bake 9 to 11 minutes or until almost no indentation remains when touched in center. Cool 1 to 2 minutes; remove from cookie sheet to wire rack. Sprinkle with sugar while warm.

*Spreads with at least 65% vegetable oil can be used (page 91).
**If using self-rising flour, omit baking soda and salt.

1 Cookie: Calories 100 (Calories from Fat 45); Fat 5g (Saturated 1g); Cholesterol 5mg; Sodium 95mg; Carbohydrate 13g (Dietary Fiber 0g); Protein 1g **% Daily Value:** Vitamin A 2%; Vitamin C 0%; Calcium 0%; Iron 2% **Diet Exchanges:** 1 Starch, 1/2 Fat

SOFT MOLASSES COOKIES WITH VANILLA FROSTING: Bake and cool coolies as directed in step 4, except omit sugar. Mix 3 cups powered sugar, 1/3 cup butter, softened, 1 1/2 teaspoons vanilla and 2 to 3 tablespoons milk until smooth and spreadable. Frost cookies.

BAKING COCOA

When a recipe calls for baking cocoa, use the unsweetened kind; do not use an instant cocoa mix that you use for hot chocolate. Two types of baking cocoa are available: nonalkalized (regular) and alkalized ("Dutch" or "European"). Alkalized cocoa goes through a "Dutching" process to neutralize the natural acids found in cocoa. The result is a darker cocoa with a more mellow chocolate flavor than regular cocoa. The two types of cocoa can be used interchangeably, but you will notice differences in color and flavor. Baked goods made with Dutch cocoa will be darker in color and a bit milder in flavor.

Coconut Cream Macaroons

Coconut Cream Macaroons

Prep: 15 min: Bake: 12 to 14 min per sheet: Cool: 30 min:
Stand: 30 min ✱ About 3 1/2 dozen

3 packages (7 ounces each) flaked coconut (7 2/3 cups)
1 cup all-purpose flour*
1/2 teaspoon salt
1 can (14 ounces) sweetened condensed milk
2/3 cup canned cream of coconut (not coconut milk)
1 tablespoon vanilla
1/4 teaspoon almond extract
1 large egg
1 bag (6 ounces) semisweet chocolate chips (1 cup), if
    desired
1 tablespoon vegetable oil, if desired

1. Heat oven to 350°. Line cookie sheet with aluminum foil or cooking parchment paper.

2. Sprinkle 1 cup of the coconut over aluminum foil. Bake 5 to 7 minutes, stirring occasionally, until golden brown; cool. Reserve aluminum foil for baking cookies.

3. Mix toasted coconut, remaining coconut, the flour and salt in large bowl. Beat milk, cream of coconut, vanilla, almond extract and egg in medium bowl until well mixed. Pour milk mixture over coconut mixture; stir until well mixed.

4. Drop mixture by heaping tablespoonfuls about 2 inches apart onto foil on cookie sheet.

5. Bake 12 to 14 minutes or until golden brown (cookies will be soft in center and set at edges). Immediately slide aluminum foil with cookies from cookie sheet to wire rack. Cool completely, about 30 minutes.

6. Heat chocolate chips and oil in 1-quart saucepan over low heat, stirring constantly, until chips are melted. Drizzle over cookies. Let stand about 30 minutes or until chocolate is set.

*If using self-rising flour, omit salt.

1 Cookie: Calories 140 (Calories from Fat 70); Fat 8g (Saturated 6g); Cholesterol 10mg; Sodium 85mg; Carbohydrate 16g (Dietary Fiber 1g); Protein 2g **% Daily Value:** Vitamin A 0%; Vitamin C 0%; Calcium 4%; Iron 2% **Diet Exchanges:** 1 Starch, 1 1/2 Fat

Granola Cookies

Prep: 10 min; Bake: 9 to 11 min per sheet; Cool: 1 min
✱ *About 3 dozen*

1/2 cup butter or stick margarine, softened*
1/3 cup granulated sugar
1/3 cup packed brown sugar
1/2 teaspoon vanilla
1 large egg
2 cups granola (any flavor), slightly crushed
1 cup all-purpose flour**
1/2 teaspoon baking soda
1/4 teaspoon baking powder
1/4 teaspoon salt

1. Heat oven to 350°.

2. Beat butter, sugars, vanilla and egg in large bowl with electric mixer on medium speed, or mix with spoon. Stir in remaining ingredients.

3. Drop dough by rounded teaspoonfuls about 2 inches apart onto ungreased cookie sheet.

4. Bake 9 to 11 minutes or until light golden brown around edges and center is set but not hard. Cool 1 minute; remove from cookie sheet to wire rack.

Do not use vegetable oil spreads (page 91).
**If using self-rising flour, omit baking soda, baking powder and salt.*

1 Cookie: Calories 80 (Calories from Fat 35); Fat 4g (Saturated 1g); Cholesterol 5mg; Sodium 75mg; Carbohydrate 10g (Dietary Fiber 0g); Protein 1g **% Daily Value:** Vitamin A 4%; Vitamin C 0%; Calcium 0%; Iron 2% **Diet Exchanges:** 1/2 Starch, 1 Fat

Chocolate-Oatmeal Chewies

Prep: 10 min; Bake: 10 to 12 min per sheet;
✱ *About 3 1/2 dozen*

1 1/2 cups sugar
1 cup butter or stick margarine, softened*
1/4 cup milk
1 large egg
2 2/3 cups quick-cooking or old-fashioned oats
1 cup all-purpose flour**
1/2 cup baking cocoa
1/2 teaspoon baking soda
1/2 teaspoon salt

1. Heat oven to 350°.

2. Beat sugar, butter, milk and egg in large bowl with electric mixer on medium speed, or mix with spoon. Stir in remaining ingredients.

3. Drop dough by rounded tablespoonfuls about 2 inches apart onto ungreased cookie sheet.

4. Bake 10 to 12 minutes or until almost no indentation remains when touched in center. Cool 1 to 2 minutes; remove from cookie sheet to wire rack.

Spreads with at least 65% vegetable oil can be used (page 91).
**If using self-rising flour, omit baking soda and salt.*

1 Cookie: Calories 100 (Calories from Fat 45); Fat 5g (Saturated 3g); Cholesterol 15mg; Sodium 75mg; Carbohydrate 13g (Dietary Fiber 1g); Protein 2g **% Daily Value:** Vitamin A 4%; Vitamin C 0%; Calcium 0%; Iron 2% **Diet Exchanges:** 1 Starch, 1/2 Fat

---

TYPES OF COCONUT

Did you know that there are different types of coconut at the grocery store? Both flaked and shredded coconut are available. Flaked coconut is cut into small pieces and is much drier than shredded coconut. In fact, if you squeeze a handful of shredded coconut, it would stick together a bit; but flaked coconut, being dry like uncooked rice kernels, would not stick together. Either type works in this macaroon recipe, but shredded coconut will make the cookies more moist and chewy. You may find unsweetened coconut available in some supermarkets, but we do not recommend it in this recipe.

Chocolate Crinkles   *Low-Fat*

Prep: 20 min; Chill: 3 hr; Bake: 10 to 12 min per sheet
✱ *About 6 dozen*

2 cups granulated sugar
1/2 cup vegetable oil
2 teaspoons vanilla
4 ounces unsweetened baking chocolate, melted and
   cooled
4 large eggs
2 cups all-purpose flour*
2 teaspoons baking powder
1/2 teaspoon salt
1 cup powdered sugar

1. Mix granulated sugar, oil, vanilla and chocolate in large bowl. Mix in eggs, one at a time. Stir in flour, baking powder and salt. Cover and refrigerate at least 3 hours.

2. Heat oven to 350°. Grease cookie sheet with shortening or spray with cooking spray.

3. Drop dough by teaspoonfuls into powdered sugar; roll around to coat. Shape into balls. Place about 2 inches apart on cookie sheet.

4. Bake 10 to 12 minutes or until almost no indentation remains when touched. Immediately remove from cookie sheet to wire rack.

*If using self-rising flour, omit baking powder and salt.

1 Cookie: Calories 70 (Calories from Fat 25); Fat 3g (Saturated 1g); Cholesterol 10mg; Sodium 35mg; Carbohydrate 10g (Dietary Fiber 0g); Protein 1g **% Daily Value:** Vitamin A 0%; Vitamin C 0%; Calcium 0%; Iron 2% **Diet Exchanges:** 1/2 Starch, 1/2 Fat

Peanut Butter Cookies

Prep: 15 min; Bake: 9 to 10 min per sheet; Cool: 5 min
✱ *About 2 1/2 dozen*

Vary the patterns on your peanut butter cookies. For a new look, try using the bottom of a cut-crystal glass, a potato masher or cookie stamp.

1/2 cup granulated sugar
1/2 cup packed brown sugar
1/2 cup peanut butter
1/4 cup shortening
1/4 cup butter or stick margarine, softened*
1 large egg
1 1/4 cups all-purpose flour**
3/4 teaspoon baking soda
1/2 teaspoon baking powder
1/4 teaspoon salt
Granulated sugar

1. Heat oven to 375°.

2. Beat 1/2 cup granulated sugar, the brown sugar, peanut butter, shortening, butter and egg in large bowl with electric mixer on medium speed, or mix with spoon. Stir in flour, baking soda, baking powder and salt.

3. Shape dough into 1 1/4-inch balls. Place about 3 inches apart on ungreased cookie sheet. Flatten in crisscross pattern with fork dipped in granulated sugar.

4. Bake 9 to 10 minutes or until light brown. Cool 5 minutes; remove from cookie sheet to wire rack.

*Spreads with at least 65% vegetable oil can be used (page 91).
**If using self-rising flour, omit baking soda, baking powder and salt.

1 Cookie: Calories 115 (Calories from Fat 55); Fat 6g (Saturated 1g); Cholesterol 5mg; Sodium 105mg; Carbohydrate 13g (Dietary Fiber 0g); Protein 2g **% Daily Value:** Vitamin A 2%; Vitamin C 0%; Calcium 0%; Iron 2% **Diet Exchanges:** 1 Starch, 1 Fat

RICH PEANUT BUTTER CHIP COOKIES: Substitute 1/2 cup packed brown sugar for 1/2 cup granulated sugar; substitute 1/4 cup butter or stick margarine, softened, for 1/4 cup shortening. After stirring in flour, baking soda, baking powder and salt, stir in 1 cup peanut butter chips. Shape dough into balls as directed. Dip tops of balls into sugar, but do not flatten. Bake as directed.

Gingersnaps *Low-Fat*

Prep: 15 min; Bake: 8 to 10 min per sheet
✳ *About 4 dozen*

After baking, these spicy cookies have a crackly top. They are very nice served with ice cream, fresh fruit, sorbet or coffee.

1 cup packed brown sugar
3/4 cup shortening
1/4 cup molasses
1 large egg
2 1/4 cups all-purpose flour*
2 teaspoons baking soda
1 teaspoon ground cinnamon
1 teaspoon ground ginger
1/2 teaspoon ground cloves
1/4 teaspoon salt
Granulated sugar

1. Heat oven to 375°.

2. Beat brown sugar, shortening, molasses and egg in large bowl with electric mixer on medium speed, or mix with spoon. Stir in remaining ingredients except granulated sugar.

3. Lightly grease cookie sheet with shortening or spray with cooking spray.

4. Shape dough by rounded teaspoonfuls into balls. Dip tops into granulated sugar. Place balls, sugared sides up, about 3 inches apart on cookie sheet.

5. Bake 10 to 12 minutes or just until set. Immediately remove from cookie sheet to wire rack.

*If using self-rising flour, decrease baking soda to 1 teaspoon and omit salt.

1 Cookie: Calories 70 (Calories from Fat 25); Fat 3g (Saturated 1g); Cholesterol 5mg; Sodium 70mg; Carbohydrate1g (Dietary Fiber 0g); Protein 1g **% Daily Value:** Vitamin A 0%; Vitamin C 0%; Calcium 0%; Iron 2% **Diet Exchanges:** 1/2 Starch, 1/2 Fat

Snickerdoodles

Prep: 10 min; Bake: 8 to 10 min per sheet
✳ *About 4 dozen*

This favorite cookie is traditionally rolled in or sprinkled with cinnamon-sugar before baking. This nonsensically named cookie originated in New England in the 1800s.

1 1/2 cups sugar
1/2 cup butter or stick margarine, softened*
1/2 cup shortening
2 large eggs
2 3/4 cups all-purpose flour**
2 teaspoons cream of tartar
1 teaspoon baking soda
1/4 teaspoon salt
1/4 cup sugar
2 teaspoons ground cinnamon

1. Heat oven to 400°.

2. Beat 1 1/2 cups sugar, the butter, shortening and eggs in large bowl with electric mixer on medium speed, or mix with spoon. Stir in flour, cream of tartar, baking soda and salt.

3. Shape dough into 1 1/4-inch balls. Mix 1/4 cup sugar and the cinnamon. Roll balls in cinnamon-sugar mixture. Place 2 inches apart on ungreased cookie sheet.

4. Bake 8 to 10 minutes or until set. Immediately remove from cookie sheet to wire rack.

*Spreads with at least 65% vegetable oil can be used (page 91).
**If using self-rising flour, omit cream of tartar, baking soda and salt.

1 Cookie: Calories 90 (Calories from Fat 35); Fat 4g (Saturated 1g); Cholesterol 10mg; Sodium 65mg; Carbohydrate 13g (Dietary Fiber 0g); Protein 1g **% Daily Value:** Vitamin A 2%; Vitamin C 0%; Calcium 0%; Iron 2% **Diet Exchanges:** 1 Starch, 1/2 Fat

---

NO-STICK MOLASSES

Before measuring molasses, spray the measuring cup with cooking spray; the molasses will come out of the cup much easier. This method also works great for maple syrup, corn syrup and honey.

Russian Tea Cakes

Prep: 20 min; Bake: 10 to 12 min per sheet; Cool: 10 min
✳ *About 4 dozen*

1 cup butter or stick margarine, softened*
1/2 cup powdered sugar
1 teaspoon vanilla
2 1/4 cups all-purpose flour**
3/4 cup finely chopped nuts
1/4 teaspoon salt
Powdered sugar

1. Heat oven to 400°.

2. Mix butter, 1/2 cup powdered sugar and the vanilla in large bowl. Stir in flour, nuts and salt until dough holds together.

3. Shape dough into 1-inch balls. Place about 1 inch apart on ungreased cookie sheet.

4. Bake 10 to 12 minutes or until set but not brown. Immediately remove from cookie sheet to wire rack; cool 5 minutes.

5. Roll warm cookies in powdered sugar; cool on wire rack 5 minutes. Roll in powdered sugar again.

Do not use vegetable oil spreads (page 91).
**Do not use self-rising flour.*

1 Cookie: Calories 75 (Calories from Fat 45); Fat 5g (Saturated 1g); Cholesterol 0mg; Sodium 65mg; Carbohydrate 7g (Dietary Fiber 0g); Protein 1g **% Daily Value:** Vitamin A 4%; Vitamin C 0%; Calcium 0%; Iron 2% **Diet Exchanges:** 1/2 Starch, 1 Fat

Thumbprint Cookies

Prep: 30 min; Bake: 10 min per sheet ✳ *About 3 dozen*

1/4 cup packed brown sugar
1/4 cup shortening
1/4 cup butter or stick margarine, softened*
1/2 teaspoon vanilla
1 large egg yolk
1 cup all-purpose flour**
1/4 teaspoon salt
1 large egg white
1 cup finely chopped nuts
About 6 tablespoons jelly or jam (any flavor)

1. Heat oven to 350°.

2. Beat brown sugar, shortening, butter, vanilla and egg yolk in medium bowl with electric mixer on medium speed, or mix with spoon. Stir in flour and salt.

3. Shape dough into 1-inch balls. Beat egg white slightly with fork. Dip each ball into egg white; roll in nuts. Place about 1 inch apart on ungreased cookie sheet. Press thumb into center of each cookie to make indentation, but do not press all the way to the cookie sheet.

4. Bake about 10 minutes or until light brown. Quickly remake indentations with end of wooden spoon if necessary. Immediately remove from cookie sheet to wire rack. Fill each thumbprint with about 1/2 measuring teaspoon of the jelly.

Do not use vegetable oil spreads (page 91).
**If using self-rising flour, omit salt.*

1 Cookie: Calories 75 (Calories from Fat 45); Fat 5g (Saturated 1g); Cholesterol 5mg; Sodium 35mg; Carbohydrate 6g (Dietary Fiber 0g); Protein 1g **% Daily Value:** Vitamin A 2%; Vitamin C 0%; Calcium 0%; Iron 2% **Diet Exchanges:** 1/2 Fruit, 1 Fat

Shortbread Cookies

Prep: 20 min; Bake: 20 min per sheet
✱ *About 2 dozen 1 1/2-inch cookies*

Serve these buttery cookies plain, or for a more festive look, dip the edges in melted chocolate and then in chopped pistachio nuts.

3/4 cup butter or stick margarine, softened*
1/4 cup sugar
2 cups all-purpose flour**

1. Heat oven to 350°.

2. Mix butter and sugar in large bowl. Stir in flour. (If dough is crumbly, mix in 1 to 2 tablespoons butter or stick margarine, softened.)

3. Roll dough 1/2 inch thick on lightly floured surface. Cut into small shapes by hand or use cookie cutters. Place 1/2 inch apart on ungreased cookie sheet.

4. Bake about 20 minutes or until set. Immediately remove from cookie sheet to wire rack.

Do not use vegetable oil spreads (page 91).
**Do not use self-rising flour.*

1 Cookie: Calories 100 (Calories from Fat 55); Fat 6g (Saturated 1g); Cholesterol 00mg; Sodium 75mg; Carbohydrate 10g (Dietary Fiber 0g); Protein 1g **% Daily Value:** Vitamin A 8%; Vitamin C 0%; Calcium 0%; Iron 2% **Diet Exchanges:** 1/2 Starch, 1 Fat

PECAN SHORTBREAD COOKIES: Stir in 1/2 cup chopped pecans, toasted if desired, with the flour.

Soft No-Roll Sugar Cookies

Prep: 20 min; Chill: 2 hr; Bake: 13 to 15 min per sheet
✱ *About 3 1/2 dozen*

1 cup granulated sugar
1 cup powdered sugar
1 cup butter or stick margarine, softened*
3/4 cup vegetable oil
2 tablespoons milk
1 tablespoon vanilla
2 eggs
4 1/4 cups all-purpose flour**
1 teaspoon baking soda
1 teaspoon cream of tartar
1/2 teaspoon salt
1/2 cup granulated sugar

1. Beat 1 cup granulated sugar, the powdered sugar, butter, oil, milk, vanilla and eggs in large bowl with electric mixer on medium speed, or mix with spoon. Stir in remaining ingredients except 1/2 cup sugar. Cover and refrigerate about 2 hours or until firm.

2. Heat oven to 350°.

3. Shape dough into 1 1/2-inch balls. Roll balls in 1/2 cup granulated sugar. Place about 3 inches apart on ungreased cookie sheet. Press bottom of drinking glass on each ball until about 1/4 inch thick. Sprinkle each cookie with a little additional sugar.

4. Bake 13 to 15 minutes or until set and edges just begin to turn brown. Immediately remove from cookie sheet to wire rack.

Do not use vegetable oil spreads (page 91).
**Do not use self-rising flour.*

1 Cookie: Calories 165 (Calories from Fat 80); Fat 9g (Saturated 3g); Cholesterol 20mg; Sodium 90mg; Carbohydrate 19g (Dietary Fiber 0g); Protein 2g **% Daily Value:** Vitamin A 4%; Vitamin C 0%; Calcium 0%; Iron 4% **Diet Exchanges:** 1 Starch, 1/2 Fruit, 1 Fat

Banana–Chocolate Chip Biscotti

Prep: 30 min; Bake: 47 min; Cool: 15 min ✳ *32 cookies*

1 cup sugar
1/2 cup butter or stick margarine, softened*
1/2 cup mashed very ripe banana (1 medium)
1 teaspoon vanilla
2 eggs
3 cups all-purpose flour**
3 teaspoons baking powder
1/4 teaspoon salt
1/2 cup miniature semisweet chocolate chips

1. Heat oven to 350°. Grease large cookie sheet.

2. Beat sugar and butter in large bowl with electric mixer on medium speed, or mix with spoon. Beat in banana, vanilla and eggs until smooth. Stir in flour, baking powder and salt. Stir in chocolate chips.

3. Divide dough in half. Shape each half into 10 × 3-inch rectangle on cookie sheet with greased hands (dough will be sticky).

4. Bake about 25 minutes or until toothpick inserted in center comes out clean. Cool on cookie sheet 15 minutes.

5. Cut crosswise into 1/2-inch slices. Turn slices cut sides down on cookie sheet. Bake 10 to 12 minutes or until golden brown and dry on top. Turn cookies. Bake about 10 minutes longer or until golden brown. Remove from cookie sheet to wire rack.

Do not use vegetable oil spreads (page 91).
**Do not use self-rising flour.*

1. Shape each half into 10 × 3-inch rectangle on cookie sheet.

2. Cut crosswise into 1/2-inch slices. Turn slices cut sides down on cookie sheet

1 Cookie: Calories 110 (Calories from Fat 35); Fat 4g (Saturated 2g); Cholesterol 20mg; Sodium 90mg; Carbohydrate 18g (Dietary Fiber 1g); Protein 2g **% Daily Value:** Vitamin A 2%; Vitamin C 0%; Calcium 2%; Iron 4% **Diet Exchanges:** 1 Starch, 1/2 Fat

Brown Sugar Refrigerator Cookies *Low-Fat*

Prep: 20 min; Chill: 2 hr; Bake: 6 to 8 min per sheet; Cool: 2 min ✳ *About 6 dozen*

You can call these refrigerator or freezer cookies. Just freeze the tightly wrapped cookie dough for up to two months, then slice and bake when you want. Just add 1 or 2 minutes to the baking time when the dough comes straight from the freezer.

1 cup packed brown sugar
1 cup butter or stick margarine, softened*
1 teaspoon vanilla
1 large egg
3 cups all-purpose flour**
1 1/2 teaspoons ground cinnamon
1/2 teaspoon baking soda
1/2 teaspoon salt
1/3 cup chopped nuts

1. Beat brown sugar, butter, vanilla and egg in large bowl with electric mixer on medium speed, or mix with spoon. Stir in remaining ingredients except nuts. Stir in nuts.

2. Shape dough into 10 × 3-inch rectangle on plastic wrap. Wrap and refrigerate about 2 hours or until firm but no longer than 24 hours.

3. Heat oven to 375°.

Buttery Spritz and Sugar Cookies (page 160)

4. Cut rectangle into 1/8-inch slices. Place 2 inches apart on ungreased cookie sheet.

5. Bake 6 to 8 minutes or until light brown. Cool 1 to 2 minutes; remove from cookie sheet to wire rack.

*Do not use vegetable oil spreads (page 91).
**If using self-rising flour, omit baking soda and salt.

1 Cookie: Calories 60 (Calories from Fat 25); Fat 3g (Saturated 1g); Cholesterol 5mg; Sodium 60mg; Carbohydrate 7g (Dietary Fiber 0g); Protein 1g **% Daily Value:** Vitamin A 4%; Vitamin C 0%; Calcium 0%; Iron 2% **Diet Exchanges:** 1/2 Starch, 1/2 Fat

Buttery Spritz *Low-Fat*

Prep: 25 min; Bake: 6 to 9 min per sheet
✳ *About 5 dozen*

1 cup butter, softened*
1/2 cup sugar
2 1/4 cups all-purpose flour**
1 teaspoon almond extract or vanilla
1/2 teaspoon salt
1 large egg
Few drops red or green food color, if desired

1. Heat oven to 400°.

2. Mix butter and sugar in large bowl. Stir in remaining ingredients.

3. Place dough in cookie press. Form desired shapes on ungreased cookie sheet.

4. Bake 6 to 9 minutes or until set but not brown. Immediately remove from cookie sheet to wire rack.

*Do not use margarine or vegetable oil spreads (page 91).
**Do not use self-rising flour.

1 Cookie: Calories 50 (Calories from Fat 25); Fat 3g (Saturated 2g); Cholesterol 10mg; Sodium 40mg; Carbohydrate 5g (Dietary Fiber 0g); Protein 1g **% Daily Value:** Vitamin A 3%; Vitamin C 0%; Calcium 0%; Iron 0% **Diet Exchanges:** 1/2 Fruit, 1/2 Fat

CHOCOLATE BUTTERY SPRITZ: Stir 2 ounces unsweetened baking chocolate, melted and cooled, into butter-sugar mixture.

Chocolaty Meringue Stars *Low-Fat*

Prep: 15 min; Bake: 25 to 30 min per sheet; Cool: 5 min ✻ *About 4 dozen*

Anyone with allergies to wheat will be grateful to have this recipe. Not only are they yummy little cookies, they are wonderfully wheat-free (and low-calorie, too).

3 large egg whites
1/2 teaspoon cream of tartar
2/3 cup sugar
2 tablespoons plus 1 teaspoon baking cocoa
About 1/3 cup ground walnuts

1. Heat oven to 275°. Line cookie sheet with aluminum foil or cooking parchment paper.

2. Beat egg whites and cream of tartar in medium bowl with electric mixer on medium speed until foamy. Beat in sugar, 1 tablespoon at a time; continue beating until stiff and glossy. Do not underbeat. Fold in cocoa. (Batter will not be mixed completely; there will be some streaks of cocoa.)

3. Place meringue in decorating bag fitted with large star tip (#4). Pipe 1 1/4-inch stars onto cookie sheet. Sprinkle lightly with walnuts; brush excess nuts from cookie sheet.

4. Bake 25 to 30 minutes or until outside is crisp and dry (meringues will be soft inside). Cool 5 minutes; remove from cookie sheet to wire rack. Store in airtight container.

1 Cookie: Calories 10 (Calories from Fat 0); Fat 0g (Saturated 0g); Cholesterol 0mg; Sodium 5mg; Carbohydrate 3g (Dietary Fiber 0g); Protein 0g **% Daily Value:** Vitamin A 0%; Vitamin C 0%; Calcium 0%; Iron 0% **Diet Exchanges:** None

Sugar Cookies *Low-Fat*

Prep: 25 min; Chill: 2 hr; Bake: 7 to 8 min per sheet ✻ *About 5 dozen 2-inch cookies*

1 1/2 cups powdered sugar
1 cup butter or stick margarine, softened*
1 teaspoon vanilla
1/2 teaspoon almond extract
1 large egg
2 1/2 cups all-purpose flour**
1 teaspoon baking soda
1 teaspoon cream of tartar
Granulated sugar

1. Beat powdered sugar, butter, vanilla, almond extract and egg in large bowl with electric mixer on medium speed, or mix with spoon. Stir in remaining ingredients except granulated sugar. Cover and refrigerate at least 2 hours.

2. Heat oven to 375°. Lightly grease cookie sheet with shortening or spray with cooking spray.

3. Divide dough in half. Roll each half 1/4 inch thick on lightly floured surface. Cut into desired shapes with 2- to 2 1/2-inch cookie cutters. Sprinkle with granulated sugar. Place about 2 inches apart on cookie sheet.

4. Bake 7 to 8 minutes or until edges are light brown. Remove from cookie sheet to wire rack.

Do not use vegetable oil spreads (page 91).
**If using self-rising flour, omit baking soda and cream of tartar.*

1 Cookie: Calories 65 (Calories from Fat 25); Fat 3g (Saturated 1g); Cholesterol 5mg; Sodium 60mg; Carbohydrate 8g (Dietary Fiber 0g); Protein 1g **% Daily Value:** Vitamin A 4%; Vitamin C 0%; Calcium 0%; Iron 0% **Diet Exchanges:** 1/2 Starch, 1/2 Fat

DECORATED SUGAR COOKIES: Omit granulated sugar. Frost cooled cookies with Vanilla Buttercream Frosting (page 110) tinted with food color if desired. Decorate with colored sugar, small candies, candied fruit or nuts if desired.

PAINTBRUSH SUGAR COOKIES: Omit granulated sugar. Cut rolled dough into desired shapes with cookie cutters. (Cut no more than 12 cookies at a time to keep them from drying out.) Mix 1 egg yolk and 1/4 teaspoon water. Divide mixture among several custard cups. Tint each with different food color to make bright colors. (If paint thickens while standing, stir in a few drops water.) Paint designs on cookies with small paintbrushes. Bake as directed in step 4.

Gingerbread Cookies *Low-Fat*

Prep: 25 min; Chill: 2 hr; Bake: 10 to 12 min per sheet; Cool: 30 min ✱ About 2 1/2 dozen 2 1/2-inch cookies

If you cut out cookies smaller or larger than 2 1/2 inches, be sure to adjust the bake time by either checking a minute or two before the minimum time for smaller cookies or adding time for larger ones.

1 cup packed brown sugar
1/3 cup shortening
1 1/2 cups dark molasses
2/3 cup cold water
7 cups all-purpose flour*
2 teaspoons baking soda
2 teaspoons ground ginger

1 teaspoon ground allspice
1 teaspoon ground cinnamon
1 teaspoon ground cloves
1/2 teaspoon salt

1. Beat brown sugar, shortening, molasses and water in large bowl with electric mixer on medium speed, or mix with spoon. Stir in remaining ingredients. Cover and refrigerate at least 2 hours.

2. Heat oven to 350°. Grease cookie sheet lightly with shortening or spray with cooking spray.

3. Roll dough 1/4 inch thick on floured surface. Cut with floured gingerbread cutter or other shaped cutter. Place about 2 inches apart on cookie sheet.

4. Bake 10 to 12 minutes or until no indentation remains when touched. Immediately remove from cookie sheet to wire rack. Cool completely, about 30 minutes. Decorate with colored frosting, colored sugar and candies if desired.

If using self-rising flour, omit baking soda and salt.

1 Cookie: Calories 195 (Calories from Fat 25); Fat 3g (Saturated 1g); Cholesterol 0mg; Sodium 135mg; Carbohydrate 40g (Dietary Fiber 1g); Protein 3g **% Daily Value:** Vitamin A 0%; Vitamin C 0%; Calcium 14%; Iron 24% **Diet Exchanges:** 1 Starch, 1 1/2 Fruit, 1/2 Fat

USING COOKIE CUTTERS

When using a cookie cutter that has one wide end and one narrow end, alternate the placement of it as you are cutting out the cookies. In other words, cut the first cookie with the wide end of the cutter toward you, then cut the next cookie with the narrow end toward you. This way, you can cut more cookies out of the dough.

Candy Basics

We all need a sweet indulgence—truffles, fudge, caramels, popcorn balls or toffee—at some time. For gifts or for enjoying at home, there's nothing like homemade candy. With the following guidelines, you'll find making candy at home surprisingly easy.

Pans and Pan Preparation

Pan size—for cooking and shaping—can make a difference.

Use the size saucepan called for in a recipe. A saucepan that's too large or too small can affect cooking time.

When you're shaping candy, if the pan is too large, the candy will be spread too thin; if it's too small, the candy will be too thick. You'll end up with the most evenly shaped pieces if you use a square or rectangular pan with straight sides.

To easily remove candy from pans, it's best to grease them with butter or margarine, not shortening (butter and margarine simply taste better), or to line them with aluminum foil.

Mixing and Cooking

Be sure to use full-fat butter or margarine—not vegetable oil spreads or tub products—so that candies will "set up" or have a nice brittle texture.

Don't double the recipe—make two batches instead. Increasing the amount of ingredients changes the cooking time.

Make candy on a cool, dry day, because heat and humidity, as well as altitude, can affect how candy turns out. If it's humid, cook candy to a temperature one degree or so higher than the recipe says.

Make sure your sugar has a chance to dissolve completely over low heat or your candy will crystallize or be grainy. So stir down any sugar grains from the side of the saucepan. Or when you start cooking the candy, cover the pan for a few minutes; the steam inside will wash down any sugar crystals from the side.

After candy has boiled, do not stir it until it has cooled to keep it from crystallizing or becoming grainy.

Determining When Candy Is Done

Using a reliable candy thermometer makes knowing when candy is done easy. Here are a few tips for using a candy thermometer:

- Check to see if it's accurate by putting the thermometer in water and then boiling the water. The thermometer should read 212°. If the reading is higher or lower, take the difference into account when making candy.

- Check an altitude table to find out the boiling point in your area, then adjust the cooking time if necessary.

- To get an accurate reading, be sure the thermometer stands upright in the candy mixture. The bulb, or tip, of the thermometer shouldn't rest on the bottom of the pan. Read the thermometer at eye level. Watch the temperature closely—after 200°, it goes up very quickly.

- If you don't have a thermometer, use the cold water test. With a clean spoon, drop a small amount of candy mixture into a cupful of very cold water. Test the hardness with your fingers (see chart below). If the candy doesn't pass the test, keep cooking.

CANDY COOKING TESTS		
Hardness	Temperature	Cold Water Test
Soft ball	234° to 240°	Forms a soft ball that flattens between fingers
Firm ball	242° to 248°	Forms a firm ball that holds its shape until pressed
Hard ball	250° to 268°	Forms a hard ball that holds its shape but is pliable
Soft crack	270° to 290°	Separates into hard but pliable threads
Hard crack	300° to 310°	Separates into hard, brittle threads that break easily

HOW TO TEST CANDY

Soft ball stage: *Forms a soft ball that flattens between fingers.*

Firm ball stage: *Forms a firm ball that holds its shape until pressed.*

Hard ball stage: *Forms a hard ball that holds its shape but is still pliable.*

Soft crack stage: *Separates into hard but pliable threads.*

Hard crack stage: *Separates into hard, brittle threads that break easily.*

Bourbon Balls *Low-Fat*

Prep: 20 min; Chill: 5 days ✱ *About 5 dozen cookies*

1 package (9 ounces) chocolate wafer cookies, finely crushed (2 1/3 cups)
2 cups finely chopped almonds, pecans or walnuts
2 cups powdered sugar
1/4 cup bourbon
1/4 cup light corn syrup
Powdered sugar

1. Mix crushed cookies, almonds and 2 cups powdered sugar in large bowl. Stir in bourbon and corn syrup.

2. Shape mixture into 1-inch balls. Roll in powdered sugar. Cover tightly and refrigerate at least 5 days before serving to blend flavors.

1 Cookie: Calories 65 (Calories from Fat 25); Fat 3g (Saturated 0g); Cholesterol 0mg; Sodium 25mg; Carbohydrate 10g (Dietary Fiber 1g); Protein 1g **% Daily Value:** Vitamin A 0%; Vitamin C 0%; Calcium 0%; Iron 2% **Diet Exchanges:** 1/2 Starch, 1/2 Fat

BRANDY BALLS: Substitute 1/4 cup brandy for the bourbon.

RUM BALLS: Substitute 1/4 cup light rum for the bourbon.

Luscious Chocolate Truffles

Prep: 20 min; Chill: 25 min; Freeze: 30 min
✱ *About 15 candies*

These truffles are as good as any you can buy! The shortening helps set the chocolate coating so it doesn't melt.

1 bag (12 ounces) semisweet chocolate chips (2 cups)*
2 tablespoons butter or stick margarine**
1/4 cup whipping (heavy) cream
2 tablespoons liqueur (almond, cherry, coffee, hazelnut, Irish cream, orange, raspberry, etc.), if desired
1 tablespoon shortening
Finely chopped nuts, if desired
1/4 cup powdered sugar, if desired
1/2 teaspoon milk, if desired

1. Line cookie sheet with aluminum foil.

2. Melt 1 cup of the chocolate chips in heavy 2-quart saucepan over low heat, stirring constantly; remove from heat. Stir in butter. Stir in whipping cream and liqueur. Refrigerate 10 to 15 minutes, stirring frequently, just until thick enough to hold a shape.

3. Drop mixture by teaspoonfuls onto cookie sheet. Shape into balls. (If mixture is too sticky, refrigerate until firm enough to shape.) Freeze 30 minutes.

4. Heat shortening and remaining 1 cup chocolate chips over low heat, stirring constantly, until chocolate is melted and mixture is smooth; remove from heat. Dip truffles, one at a time, into chocolate. Return to aluminum foil-covered cookie sheet. Immediately sprinkle some of the truffles with nuts. Refrigerate about 10 minutes or until coating is set.

5. Mix powdered sugar and milk until smooth; drizzle over some of the truffles. Refrigerate just until set. Store in airtight container in refrigerator. Serve truffles at room temperature by letting them stand out on the counter about 30 minutes before serving.

*1 cup milk chocolate chips can be substituted for the first cup of semisweet chocolate chips.
**Do not use vegetable oil spreads (page 91).

1 Truffle: Calories 145 (Calories from Fat 90); Fat 10g (Saturated 5g); Cholesterol 5mg; Sodium 25mg; Carbohydrate 14g (Dietary Fiber 1g); Protein 1g **% Daily Value:** Vitamin A 2%; Vitamin C 0%; Calcium 0%; Iron 4% **Diet Exchanges:** 1 Fruit, 2 Fat

POLKA DOT TRUFFLES: Stir 3 tablespoons chopped white baking bar into whipping cream mixture.

TOFFEE TRUFFLES: Stir 3 tablespoons chopped chocolate-covered English toffee candy into whipping cream mixture.

Chocolate Fudge *Low-Fat*

Prep: 10 min; Cook: 30 min; Cool: 2 hr; Stand: 1 to 2 hr
✱ *64 candies*

4 cups sugar
1 1/3 cups half-and-half or milk
1/4 cup corn syrup
1/4 teaspoon salt
4 ounces unsweetened baking chocolate or 2/3 cup baking cocoa
1/4 cup butter or stick margarine
2 teaspoons vanilla
1 cup coarsely chopped nuts, if desired

1. Grease bottom and sides of square pan, 8 × 8 × 2 inches, with butter.

2. Butter sides of a heavy 3-quart saucepan. Place sugar, half-and-half, corn syrup, salt and chocolate in saucepan. Cook over medium heat, stirring constantly, until chocolate is melted and sugar is dissolved. Cook, about 25 minutes, stirring occasionally, to 234° on candy thermometer or until small amount of mixture dropped into cup of very cold water forms a soft ball that flattens when removed from water; remove from heat. Drop butter on top but do not stir.

3. Cool mixture without stirring to 110°, about 2 hours. (Bottom of saucepan will be lukewarm.) Add vanilla. Beat vigorously and continuously using wooden spoon, just until fudge begins to thicken. Add nuts, continue beating 5 to 10 minutes until mixture is thick and no longer glossy. (Mixture will hold its shape when dropped from a spoon.)

4. Quickly, spread or press in pan. Let stand about 1 to 2 hours or until firm. Cut into 1-inch squares.

1 Candy: Calories 75 (Calories from Fat 20); Fat 2g (Saturated 1g); Cholesterol 5mg; Sodium 20mg; Carbohydrate 14g (Dietary Fiber 0g); Protein 0g **% Daily Value:** Vitamin A 0%; Vitamin C 0%; Calcium 0%; Iron 0% **Diet Exchanges:** 1 Fruit, 1/2 Fat

PENUCHE: Substitute 2 cups packed brown sugar for 2 cups of the granulated sugar; omit chocolate.

Super Easy Fudge   *Low-Fat*

Prep: 10 min; Chill: 1 hr 30 min ✱ 64 candies

For a deeper, richer chocolate flavor, be sure to add the unsweetened baking chocolate.

1 can (14 ounces) sweetened condensed milk
1 bag (12 ounces) semisweet chocolate chips (2 cups)
1 ounce unsweetened baking chocolate, if desired
1 1/2 cups chopped nuts, if desired
1 teaspoon vanilla

1. Grease bottom and sides of square pan, 8 × 8 × 2 inches, with butter.

2. Heat milk, chocolate chips and unsweetened chocolate in 2-quart saucepan over low heat, stirring constantly, until chocolate is melted and mixture is smooth; remove from heat.

3. Quickly stir in nuts and vanilla. Spread in pan. Refrigerate about 1 hour 30 minutes or until firm. Cut into 1-inch squares.

1 Candy: Calories 55 (Calories from Fat 20); Fat 2g (Saturated 1g); Cholesterol 5mg; Sodium 10mg; Carbohydrate 8g (Dietary Fiber 0g); Protein 1g **% Daily Value:** Vitamin A 0%; Vitamin C 0%; Calcium 2%; Iron 0% **Diet Exchanges:** 1/2 Starch, 1/2 Fat

Toffee

Prep: 15 min; Cook: 18 min; Stand: 1 hr
✱ About 36 pieces

Packaging gifts for the holidays can be as fun as making them. Wrap coffee tins with holiday paper or aluminum foil. Fill with Toffee, separating layers with colored tissue paper or waxed paper.

1 cup sugar
1 cup butter or stick margarine*
1/4 cup water
1/2 cup semisweet chocolate chips
1/2 cup finely chopped pecans

1. Heat sugar, butter and water to boiling in heavy 2-quart saucepan, stirring constantly; reduce heat to medium. Cook, about 13 minutes, stirring constantly, to 300° on candy thermometer or until small amount of mixture dropped into cup of very cold water separates into hard, brittle threads. (Watch carefully so mixture does not burn.)

2. Immediately pour toffee onto ungreased large cookie sheet. If necessary, quickly spread mixture to 1/4-inch thickness. Sprinkle with chocolate chips; let stand about 1 minute or until chips are completely softened. Spread softened chocolate evenly over toffee. Sprinkle with pecans.

3. Let stand at room temperature about 1 hour, or refrigerate if desired, until firm. Break into bite-size pieces. Store in airtight container.

*Do not use vegetable oil spreads (page 91).

1 Piece: Calories 90 (Calories from Fat 65); Fat 7g (Saturated 4g); Cholesterol 15mg; Sodium 35mg; Carbohydrate 7g (Dietary Fiber 0g); Protein 0g **% Daily Value:** Vitamin A 4%; Vitamin C 0%; Calcium 0%; Iron 0% **Diet Exchanges:** 1/2 Fruit, 1 1/2 Fat

Caramels

Prep: 5 min; Cook: 40 min; Cool: 2 hr ✱ 64 candies

Cut little rectangles of waxed paper ahead of time, so when you're ready to wrap, you're ready to go! Here's another secret—cutting the caramels with a scissors is quicker and easier than using a knife.

2 cups sugar
1/2 cup butter or stick margarine*
2 cups whipping (heavy) cream
3/4 cup light corn syrup

1. Grease bottom and sides of square baking dish, 8 × 8 × 2 or 9 × 9 × 2 inches, with butter.

2. Heat all ingredients to boiling in heavy 3-quart saucepan over medium heat, stirring constantly. Cook, about 35 minutes, stirring frequently, to 245° on candy thermometer or until small amount of mixture dropped into cup of very cold water forms a firm ball that holds its shape until pressed. Immediately spread in baking dish. Cool completely, about 2 hours.

3. Cut into 1-inch squares. Wrap individually in waxed paper or plastic wrap; store wrapped candies in airtight container.

*Do not use vegetable oil spreads (page 91).

1 Candy: Calories 70 (Calories from Fat 35); Fat 4g (Saturated 2g); Cholesterol 10mg; Sodium 25mg; Carbohydrate 9g (Dietary Fiber 0g); Protein 0g **% Daily Value:** Vitamin A 4%; Vitamin C 0%; Calcium 0%; Iron 0% **Diet Exchanges:** 1/2 Fruit, 1 Fat

CHOCOLATE CARAMELS: Heat 2 ounces unsweetened baking chocolate with the sugar mixture.

Pralines

Prep: 15 min; Cook: 20 min; Cool: 1 hr; Stand: 1 to 2 hr
✱ *About 18 candies*

Pronounced *prah-leen* or *pray-leen*, this confection originated in Louisiana, where brown sugar and pecans are in ample supply.

2 cups packed light brown sugar
1 cup granulated sugar
1 1/4 cups milk
1/4 cup light corn syrup
1/8 teaspoon salt
1 teaspoon vanilla
1 1/2 cups pecan halves (5 1/2 ounces)

1. Heat sugars, milk, corn syrup and salt to boiling in heavy 3-quart Dutch oven, stirring constantly. Reduce heat to medium. Cook, about 15 minutes, without stirring, to 236° on candy thermometer or until small amount of mixture dropped into cup of very cold water forms a soft ball that flattens when removed from water. Cool, without stirring, about 1 hour or until saucepan is cool to the touch.

2. Add vanilla and pecan halves. Beat about 1 minute or until mixture is slightly thickened and just coats pecans but does not lose its gloss. Drop mixture by spoonfuls onto waxed paper, dividing pecans equally. Let stand uncovered 1 to 2 hours or until candies are firm and no longer glossy.

3. Wrap individually in waxed paper or plastic wrap. Store in airtight container.

1 Candy: Calories 220 (Calories from Fat 55); Fat 6g (Saturated 1g); Cholesterol 0mg; Sodium 40mg; Carbohydrate 41g (Dietary Fiber 1g); Protein 1g **% Daily Value:** Vitamin A 0%; Vitamin C 0%; Calcium 4%; Iron 4% **Diet Exchanges:** 3 Fruit, 1 Fat

Peanut Brittle

Prep: 15 min; Cook: 40 min; Cool: 1 hr
✱ *About 6 dozen pieces*

1 1/2 teaspoons baking soda
1 teaspoon water
1 teaspoon vanilla
1 1/2 cups sugar
1 cup water
1 cup light corn syrup
3 tablespoons butter or stick margarine*
1 pound unsalted raw Spanish peanuts (3 cups)

1. Heat oven to 200°. Grease 2 cookie sheets, 15 1/2 × 12 inches, with butter; keep warm in oven. (Keeping the cookie sheets warm allows the candy to be spread 1/4 inch thick without it setting up.) Grease long metal spatula with butter; set aside.

2. Mix baking soda, 1 teaspoon water and the vanilla; set aside. Mix sugar, 1 cup water and the corn syrup in 3-quart saucepan. Cook over medium heat, about 25 minutes, stirring occasionally, to 240° on candy thermometer or until small amount of mixture dropped into cup of very cold water forms a soft ball that flattens when removed from water.

3. Stir in butter and peanuts. Cook, about 13 minutes, stirring constantly, to 300° or until small amount of mixture dropped into cup of very cold water separates into hard, brittle threads. (Watch carefully so mixture does not burn.) Immediately remove from heat. Quickly stir in baking soda mixture until light and foamy.

4. Pour half of the candy mixture onto each cookie sheet and quickly spread about 1/4 inch thick with buttered spatula. Cool completely, at least 1 hour. Break into pieces. Store in airtight container.

*Do not use vegetable oil spreads (page 91).

1 Piece: Calories 80 (Calories from Fat 35); Fat 4g (Saturated 1g); Cholesterol 0mg; Sodium 40mg; Carbohydrate 9g (Dietary Fiber 0g); Protein 2g **% Daily Value:** Vitamin A 0%; Vitamin C 0%; Calcium 0%; Iron 0% **Diet Exchanges:** 1/2 Starch, 1 Fat

Toffee (page 165) and Crunchy Peanut Clusters

Crunchy Peanut Clusters

Prep: 15 min; Stand: 1 hr ✻ About 6 1/2 dozen candies

Vanilla-flavored candy coating may also be called almond bark, confectionery coating or summer coating and is mainly used for candy making. The most common variety of candy coating you'll find in grocery stores are vanilla and chocolate; specialty stores, such as cake decorating shops, may carry coating in pastel colors.

1 package (24 ounces) vanilla-flavored candy coating
  (almond bark)
2/3 cup creamy peanut butter
4 cups Cheerios® cereal
2 cups miniature marshmallows
2 cups dry-roasted peanuts

1. Melt candy coating in 4-quart saucepan over medium heat, stirring frequently. Stir in peanut butter until mixture is smooth. Add remaining ingredients; stirring until completely coated.

2. Drop mixture by heaping teaspoonfuls onto waxed paper or cookie sheet. Let stand about 1 hour or until firm. Store tightly covered.

1 Candy: Calories 90 (Calories from Fat 55); Fat 6g (Saturated 2g); Cholesterol 0mg; Sodium 50mg; Carbohydrate 8g (Dietary Fiber 1g); Protein 2g **% Daily Value:** Vitamin A 2%; Vitamin C 0%; Calcium 2%; Iron 2% **Diet Exchanges:** 1/2 Starch, 1 Fat

Divinity *Low-Fat*

Prep: 20 min; Cook: 25 min; Stand: 12 hr
✱ *About 40 candies*

Here are some divinity-making tips to help ensure successful results: Drop a spoonful of the divinity mixture onto waxed paper. If it stays in a mound, it has been beaten long enough. If the mixture flattens out, beat another 30 seconds and then check again. If the mixture is too stiff to spoon, beat in a few drops of hot water at a time until a softer consistency is reached. If you make this candy on a humid day, you'll have to beat it a little longer to make it mound up.

2 2/3 cups sugar
2/3 cup light corn syrup
1/2 cup water
2 large egg whites
1 teaspoon vanilla
1 to 2 drops food color, if desired
2/3 cup coarsely chopped nuts, if desired

1. Cook sugar, corn syrup and water (use 1 tablespoon less water on humid days) in 2-quart saucepan over low heat, stirring constantly, until sugar is dissolved. Cook, about 20 minutes, without stirring, to 260° on candy thermometer or until small amount of mixture dropped into cup of very cold water forms a hard ball that holds its shape but is pliable.

2. Beat egg whites in small bowl with electric mixer on high speed until stiff peaks form. (For best results, use electric stand mixer, not a portable handheld mixer, because beating time is about 6 to 10 minutes and mixture is thick.) Gently transfer egg whites to large bowl. Continue beating constantly on medium speed while pouring hot syrup in a thin stream into egg whites. Add vanilla and food color. Beat until mixture holds its shape and becomes slightly dull, scraping bowl occasionally. (If mixture becomes too stiff for mixer, continue beating with wooden spoon.) Stir in nuts.

3. Quickly drop heaping teaspoonfuls of mixture from buttered spoon onto waxed paper. Let stand uncovered at room temperature at least 4 hours, but no longer than 12 hours until candies feel firm and are dry to the touch. Store in airtight container.

1 Candy: Calories 70 (Calories from Fat 10); Fat 1g (Saturated 0g); Cholesterol 0mg; Sodium 10mg; Carbohydrate 15g (Dietary Fiber 0g); Protein 0g **% Daily Value:** Vitamin A 0%; Vitamin C 0%; Calcium 0%; Iron 0% **Diet Exchanges:** 1 Fruit

---

STORING CANDY

Store candy tightly covered at room temperature for up to 2 weeks, unless a recipe directs you to do otherwise. Or wrap candy tightly and freeze for up to 6 months. To thaw, let the candy stand covered at room temperature for 1 to 2 hours before serving.

Desserts

Desserts

Profiteroles (page 181)

Low-Fat = *3g or less, except main dishes with 6g or less*   **Fast** = *Ready in 30 minutes or less*   ■ = *Bread Machine directions*   ● = *Slow Cooker directions*

Lighter = 1/3 fewer calories or 50% less fat

Dessert Basics

Choose the perfect finishing touch to summer picnics, weekday dinners or holiday feasts from this inviting collection of desserts that goes beyond cakes and pies or cookies and candies. Why not make one tonight?

Dessert Dress-Ups

Easier to make than you think, these "dress-ups" add pizzazz to any dessert. Sprinkling with ground cinnamon, baking cocoa or powdered sugar is a fun, easy way to dress up a dessert. Place a small amount of one of the three in a small sieve or sifter, and tap to dust over desserts or plates. Here are some ideas:

- Place a small paper doily or stencil on a plate, and dust with cinnamon, cocoa or powdered sugar. Remove the doily and arrange the piece of dessert on the plate.

- For desserts such as a piece of unfrosted cake or cheesecake, place a doily or stencil on top of the food and dust with cinnamon, cocoa or powdered sugar in a pretty design.

- Dust cinnamon, cocoa or powdered sugar onto a plate. Or, for a pretty pattern, dust cinnamon, cocoa or powdered sugar over fork tines around the plate edge.

Apple Crisp

Prep: 20 min; Bake: 30 min ✱ *6 servings*

Leftover apple crisp makes a great breakfast treat. Serve it with a dollop of plain yogurt.

4 medium tart cooking apples (Greening, Rome, Granny Smith), sliced (4 cups)
3/4 cup packed brown sugar
1/2 cup all-purpose flour*
1/2 cup quick-cooking or old-fashioned oats
1/3 cup butter or stick margarine, softened**
3/4 teaspoon ground cinnamon
3/4 teaspoon ground nutmeg
Cream or ice cream, if desired

1. Heat oven to 375°. Grease bottom and sides of square pan, 8 × 8 × 2 inches, with shortening.

2. Spread apples in pan. Mix remaining ingredients except cream; sprinkle over apples.

3. Bake about 30 minutes or until topping is golden brown and apples are tender when pierced with fork. Serve warm with cream.

*Self-rising flour can be used.
**Spreads with at least 65% vegetable oil can be used (page 91).

1 Serving: Calories 310 (Calories from Fat 100); Fat 11g (Saturated 7g); Cholesterol 25mg; Sodium 80mg; Carbohydrate 54g (Dietary Fiber 4g); Protein 2g **% Daily Value:** Vitamin A 8%; Vitamin C 4%; Calcium 4%; Iron 8% **Diet Exchanges:** Not Recommended

BLUEBERRY CRISP: Substitute 4 cups fresh or frozen (thawed and drained) blueberries for the apples.

RHUBARB CRISP: Substitute 4 cups cut-up rhubarb for the apples.

CHOOSING THE RIGHT APPLE

Many types of freshly harvested apples are available in late summer through the fall; others are available most of the year. Some are sweet, some are tart and some are better for baking than others. The recipes in this chapter work well with Newtown Pippin, Rome, Greening and Granny Smith varieties, and suitable apple types are listed in the recipes. Check the chart for Apple Varieties and Characteristics on page 423 for more choices.

Apple Dumplings

Prep: 55 min; Bake: 40 min ✱ *6 dumplings*

Pastry for Two-Crust Pie (page 117)
6 cooking apples (Golden Delicious, Braeburn, Rome),
    about 3 inches in diameter
3 tablespoons raisins
3 tablespoons chopped nuts
1/2 cup sugar
1 cup water
1/2 cup corn syrup
2 tablespoons butter or stick margarine*
1/4 teaspoon ground cinnamon
Cream or Sweetened Whipped Cream (page 198), if
    desired

1. Heat oven to 425°. Make pastry as directed—except
roll two-thirds of the pastry into 14-inch square; cut
into 4 squares. Roll remaining pastry into 14 × 7-inch
rectangle; cut into 2 squares. Peel and core apples. Place
apple on each square.

2. Mix raisins and nuts. Fill apples with raisin mixture.
Moisten corners of pastry squares. Bring 2 opposite
corners up over apple and pinch together. Repeat with
remaining corners, and pinch edges of pastry to seal.
Place dumplings in ungreased rectangular baking dish,
13 × 9 × 2 inches.

3. Heat remaining ingredients except cream to boiling
in 2-quart saucepan, stirring occasionally. Boil 3 minutes. Carefully pour around dumplings.

4. Bake about 40 minutes, spooning syrup over
dumplings 2 or 3 times, until crust is golden and apples
are tender when pierced with a small knife or toothpick. Serve warm or cool with cream.

**Spreads with at least 65% vegetable oil can be used
(page 91).*

1 Serving: Calories 680 (Calories from Fat 305); Fat 34g (Saturated
10g); Cholesterol 10mg; Sodium 450mg; Carbohydrate 93g
(Dietary Fiber 4g); Protein 5g **% Daily Value:** Vitamin A 4%;
Vitamin C 4%; Calcium 2%; Iron 12% **Diet Exchanges:** Not
Recommended

*Moisten corners of pastry squares. Bring 2 opposite corners up
over apple and pinch together. Repeat with remaining corners,
and pinch edges of pastry to seal.*

Lighter Apple Dumplings: For 7 grams of fat and
360 calories per serving, omit Pastry for Two-
Crust Pie. Cut stack of 6 sheets frozen (thawed)
phyllo (18 × 4 inches) into 14-inch square.
Discard remaining strips. Cover squares with
damp towel to prevent them from drying out.
Make 3 stacks of 2 sheets each, spraying each
lightly with butter-flavored cooking spray. Fold
each stack in half; spray top. Cut stacks in half.
Place apple on each square. Omit nuts. Continue
as directed in step 2.

Baked Apples

Prep: 10 min; Bake: 40 min ✱ *4 servings*

4 large unpeeled tart cooking apples (Rome, Granny
    Smith, Greening)
2 to 4 tablespoons granulated or packed brown sugar
4 teaspoons butter or stick margarine*
1/2 teaspoon ground cinnamon

1. Heat oven to 375°.

2. Core apples to within 1/2 inch of bottom. Peel
1-inch strip of skin around middle of each apple, or
peel upper half of each to prevent splitting. Place apples
in ungreased baking dish.

3. Place 1 teaspoon to 1 tablespoon sugar, 1 teaspoon butter and 1/8 teaspoon cinnamon in center of each apple. Sprinkle with additional cinnamon. Pour water into baking dish until 1/4 inch deep.

4. Bake 30 to 40 minutes or until apples are tender when pierced with fork. (Time will vary depending on size and variety of apple.) Spoon syrup in dish over apples several times during baking if desired.

Spreads with at least 65% vegetable oil can be used (page 91).

1 Serving: Calories 175 (Calories from Fat 45); Fat 5g (Saturated 3g); Cholesterol 10mg; Sodium 25mg; Carbohydrate 39g (Dietary Fiber 6g); Protein 0g **% Daily Value:** Vitamin A 4%; Vitamin C 10%; Calcium 2%; Iron 2% **Diet Exchanges:** 2 1/2 Fruit, 1/2 Fat

Strawberry Shortcakes

Prep: 15 min; Stand: 1 hr; Bake: 12 min ✱ *6 servings*

2 pints (4 cups) strawberries, sliced
1/2 cup sugar
1/3 cup shortening
2 cups all-purpose flour*
2 tablespoons sugar
3 teaspoons baking powder
1 teaspoon salt
3/4 cup milk
Butter or stick margarine, softened, if desired
Sweetened Whipped Cream (page 198), if desired

1. Mix strawberries and 1/2 cup sugar. Let stand about 1 hour so strawberries will become juicy.

2. Heat oven to 450°.

3. Cut shortening into flour, 2 tablespoons sugar, the baking powder and salt in medium bowl, using pastry blender or crisscrossing 2 knives, until mixture looks like fine crumbs. Stir in milk just until blended.

4. Place dough on lightly floured surface. Gently smooth into a ball. Knead 20 to 25 times. Roll or pat 1/2 inch thick. Cut with floured 3-inch cutter. Place about 1 inch apart on ungreased cookie sheet.

5. Bake 10 to 12 minutes or until golden brown.

6. Split shortcakes horizontally in half while hot. Spread butter on split sides. Fill with strawberries; replace tops. Top with strawberries and Sweetened Whipped Cream.

If using self-rising flour, omit baking powder and salt.

1 Serving: Calories 375 (Calories from Fat 115); Fat 13g (Saturated 3g); Cholesterol 5mg; Sodium 650mg; Carbohydrate 62g (Dietary Fiber 3g); Protein 6g **% Daily Value:** Vitamin A 2%; Vitamin C 96%; Calcium 18%; Iron 14% **Diet Exchanges:** Not Recommended

DROP SHORTCAKES: Make as directed—except omit step 4. Drop dough by 6 spoonfuls about 2 inches apart onto ungreased cookie sheet. Continue as directed in step 5.

PAT-IN-THE-PAN SHORTCAKE: Grease bottom and side of round pan, 8 × 1 1/2 inches, with shortening. Make as directed—except omit step 4. Pat dough in pan. Bake 15 to 20 minutes. Cut into wedges. Continue as directed in step 6.

MICROWAVING BAKED APPLES

You can make baked apples in minutes in your microwave oven. Just prepare the apples as directed, and place each one in a 10-ounce custard cup or individual microwavable casserole. Do not add water to the cups. Microwave uncovered on High 5 to 10 minutes, rotating cups 1/2 turn after 3 minutes, until apples are tender when pierced with a fork.

Chocolate-Dipped Strawberries

Chocolate-Dipped Strawberries *Low-Fat*

Prep: 20 min; Chill: 30 min ✳ *18 to 20 strawberries*

Jazz up chocolate-dipped berries with a drizzle of melted white baking chips over the chocolate.

1 pint (2 cups) medium-large strawberries (18 to 20 strawberries)
1/2 cup semisweet chocolate chips or white baking chips
1 teaspoon shortening or vegetable oil

1. Gently rinse strawberries and dry on paper towels (berries must be completely dry). Line cookie sheet with waxed paper.

2. Heat chocolate chips and shortening in 1-quart saucepan over low heat, stirring frequently, until chocolate is melted.

3. Dip lower half of each strawberry into chocolate mixture; allow excess to drip back into saucepan. Place on cookie sheet.

4. Refrigerate uncovered about 30 minutes or until chocolate is firm or until ready to serve. Store covered in refrigerator so chocolate does not soften (if made with oil, chocolate will soften more quickly at room temperature).

1 Strawberry: Calories 30 (Calories from Fat 20); Fat 2g (Saturated 1g); Cholesterol 0mg; Sodium 0mg; Carbohydrate 4g (Dietary Fiber 1g); Protein 0g **% Daily Value:** Vitamin A 0%; Vitamin C 14%; Calcium 0%; Iron 0% **Diet Exchanges:** 1 Serving is free

Pineapple Upside-Down Cake

Pineapple Upside-Down Cake

Prep: 15 min; Bake: 50 min; Cool: 15 min ✱ *9 servings*

1/4 cup butter or stick margarine*
2/3 cup packed brown sugar
1 can (20 ounces) sliced or crushed pineapple in juice, drained
Maraschino cherries without stem, if desired
1 1/3 cups all-purpose flour**
1 cup granulated sugar
1/3 cup shortening
3/4 cup milk
1 1/2 teaspoons baking powder
1/2 teaspoon salt
1 large egg
Sweetened Whipped Cream (page 198), if desired

1. Heat oven to 350°.

2. Melt butter in 10-inch ovenproof skillet or square pan, 9 × 9 × 2 inches, in oven. Sprinkle brown sugar over butter. Arrange pineapple on brown sugar, cutting one or more slices into pieces if necessary. Place cherry in center of each pineapple slice.

3. Beat remaining ingredients except Sweetened Whipped Cream with electric mixer on low speed 30 seconds, scraping bowl constantly. Beat on high speed 3 minutes, scraping bowl occasionally. Pour over pineapple.

4. Bake skillet 45 to 50 minutes, square pan 50 to 55 minutes, or until toothpick inserted in center comes out clean.

5. Immediately turn upside down onto heatproof plate. Let skillet or pan remain over cake a few minutes so brown sugar topping can drizzle over cake. Cool 15 minutes. Serve warm with Sweetened Whipped Cream.

*Spreads with at least 65% vegetable oil can be used (page 91).
**If using self-rising flour, omit baking powder and salt.

1 Serving: Calories 390 (Calories from Fat 125); Fat 14g (Saturated 6g); Cholesterol 40mg; Sodium 270mg; Carbohydrate 63g (Dietary Fiber 1g); Protein 4g **% Daily Value:** Vitamin A 6%; Vitamin C 4%; Calcium 10%; Iron 8% **Diet Exchanges:** Not Recommended

Gingerbread with Lemon Sauce (page 197)

Gingerbread

Prep: 10 min: Bake: 55 min ✱ *9 servings*

2 1/3 cups all-purpose flour*

1/2 cup shortening

1/3 cup sugar

1 cup molasses

3/4 cup hot water

1 teaspoon baking soda

1 teaspoon ground ginger

1 teaspoon ground cinnamon

3/4 teaspoon salt

1 large egg

Lemon Sauce (page 197), if desired

Sweetened Whipped Cream (page 198) or softened
   cream cheese, if desired

1. Heat oven to 325°. Grease bottom and sides of square pan, 9 × 9 × 2 inches, with shortening; lightly flour.

2. Beat all ingredients except Lemon Sauce and Sweetened Whipped Cream with electric mixer on low speed 30 seconds, scraping bowl constantly. Beat on medium speed 3 minutes, scraping bowl occasionally. Pour into pan.

3. Bake 50 to 55 minutes or until toothpick inserted in center comes out clean. Serve warm with Lemon Sauce and Sweetened Whipped Cream.

*Do not use self-rising flour.

1 Serving: Calories 350 (Calories from Fat 110); Fat 12g (Saturated 3g); Cholesterol 25mg; Sodium 360mg; Carbohydrate 58g (Dietary Fiber 1g); Protein 4g **% Daily Value:** Vitamin A 0%; Vitamin C 0%; Calcium 8%; Iron 18% **Diet Exchanges:** Not Recommended

Boston Cream Pie

Prep: 20 min; Bake: 35 min; Cool: 1 hr 10 min
✱ *8 servings*

This actually isn't a pie at all, but a cake filled with luscious custard and topped with a chocolate glaze.

1 1/4 cups all-purpose* or 1 1/2 cups cake flour
1 cup sugar
1/3 cup shortening
3/4 cup milk
1 1/2 teaspoons baking powder
1 teaspoon vanilla
1/2 teaspoon salt
1 large egg
Cream Filling (right)
Chocolate Glaze (right)

1. Heat oven to 350°. Grease bottom and side of round pan, 9 × 1 1/2 inches, with shortening; lightly flour.

2. Beat all ingredients except Cream Filling and Chocolate Glaze in large bowl with electric mixer on low speed 30 seconds, scraping bowl constantly. Beat on high speed 3 minutes, scraping bowl occasionally. Pour into pan.

3. Bake about 35 minutes or until toothpick inserted in center comes out clean. Cool 10 minutes; remove from pan to wire rack. Cool completely, about 1 hour.

4. Make Cream Filling and Chocolate Glaze. Split cake horizontally in half. Spread filling over bottom layer; top with top layer (See How to Split Cake Layers page 92). Spread glaze over top of cake. Cover and refrigerate until serving. Store covered in refrigerator.

Cream Filling

1/3 cup sugar
2 tablespoons cornstarch
1/8 teaspoon salt
1 1/2 cups milk
2 large egg yolks, slightly beaten
2 teaspoons vanilla

Mix sugar, cornstarch and salt in 2-quart saucepan. Mix milk and egg yolks; gradually stir into sugar mixture. Cook over medium heat, stirring constantly, until mixture thickens and boils. Boil and stir 1 minute; remove from heat. Stir in vanilla. Press plastic wrap on filling to prevent a layer of skin from forming on top; cool.

Chocolate Glaze

3 tablespoons butter or stick margarine**
3 ounces unsweetened baking chocolate
1 cup powdered sugar
3/4 teaspoon vanilla
About 2 tablespoons hot water

Melt butter and chocolate in 1-quart saucepan over low heat, stirring frequently; remove from heat. Stir in powdered sugar and vanilla. Stir in water, 1 teaspoon at a time, until smooth and spreadable.

If using self-rising flour, omit baking powder and salt.
**Spreads with at least 65% vegetable oil can be used (page 91).*

1 Serving: Calories 505 (Calories from Fat 200); Fat 22g (Saturated 10g); Cholesterol 95mg; Sodium 350mg; Carbohydrate 72g (Dietary Fiber 2g); Protein 7g **% Daily Value:** Vitamin A 10%; Vitamin C 0%; Calcium 16%; Iron 10% **Diet Exchanges:** Not Recommended

Hot Fudge Sundae Cake

Hot Fudge Sundae Cake

Prep: 20 min; Bake: 40 min; Cool: 10 min ✱ *9 servings*

This special dessert separates into two layers as it bakes and becomes a fudge sauce topped with cake. Serve it warm topped with ice cream.

1 cup all-purpose flour*
3/4 cup granulated sugar
2 tablespoons baking cocoa
2 teaspoons baking powder
1/4 teaspoon salt
1/2 cup milk
2 tablespoons vegetable oil
1 teaspoon vanilla
1 cup chopped nuts, if desired
1 cup packed brown sugar
1/4 cup baking cocoa
1 3/4 cups very hot water
Ice cream, if desired

1. Heat oven to 350°.

2. Mix flour, granulated sugar, 2 tablespoons cocoa, the baking powder and salt in ungreased square pan, 9 × 9 × 2 inches. Mix in milk, oil and vanilla with fork until smooth. Stir in nuts. Spread in pan.

3. Sprinkle brown sugar and 1/4 cup cocoa over batter. Pour water evenly over batter.

4. Bake about 40 minutes or until top is dry. Cool 10 minutes.

5. Spoon warm cake into dessert dishes. Top with ice cream. Spoon sauce from pan onto each serving.

*If using self-rising flour, omit baking powder and salt.

1 Serving: Calories 255 (Calories from Fat 35); Fat 4g (Saturated 1g); Cholesterol 0mg; Sodium 190mg; Carbohydrate 54g (Dietary Fiber 2g); Protein 3g **% Daily Value:** Vitamin A 0%; Vitamin C 0%; Calcium 10%; Iron 10% **Diet Exchanges:** 1 Starch, 2 1/2 Fruit, 1/2 Fat

Chocolate Mousse Brownie Dessert

Prep: 20 min; Bake: 45 min; Cool: 2 hr
❋ 12 to 16 servings

This heavenly dessert can also be baked in a 10-inch springform pan. Bake about 65 minutes. For easier cutting, use a wet knife and cut with a straight up-and-down motion.

3/4 cup whipping (heavy) cream
1 package (6 ounces) semisweet chocolate chips (1 cup)
1 package (1 pound 3.8 ounces) fudge brownie mix
Water
Vegetable oil
Eggs
3 eggs
1/3 cup sugar
Sweetened Whipped Cream (page 198), if desired

1. Heat oven to 350°. Grease bottom only of rectangular pan, 13 × 9 × 2 inches, with shortening.

2. Heat whipping cream and chocolate chips in 2-quart saucepan over low heat, stirring frequently, until chocolate is melted and mixture is smooth. Cool about 20 minutes.

3. While whipping cream mixture is cooling, make brownie mix as directed on package, using the amounts of water, oil and eggs called for on the package directions. Spread batter in pan.

4. Beat 3 eggs and sugar, using wire whisk or hand beater, until foamy; stir into whipping cream mixture. Pour evenly over brownie batter.

5. Bake about 45 minutes or until topping is set. Cool completely, about 2 hours.

6. Serve at room temperature, or cover tightly and refrigerate until chilled. For easier cutting, use wet knife and cut with straight up-and-down motion. Top each serving with Sweetened Whipped Cream. Store covered in refrigerator.

1 Serving: Calories 340 (Calories from Fat 115); Fat 13g (Saturated 7g); Cholesterol 70mg; Sodium 190mg; Carbohydrate 53g (Dietary Fiber 1g); Protein 4g **% Daily Value:** Vitamin A 4%; Vitamin C 0%; Calcium 4%; Iron 6% **Diet Exchanges:** Not Recommended

---

TOASTING NUTS, COCONUTS AND SESAME SEEDS

Toasting brings out the true flavor and adds a wonderful dimension to any recipe that calls for nuts, coconut or sesame seed. A good doneness test, along with color, is when you can smell the toasted aroma. Use it as a signal to watch them carefully so they don't burn. Remove them immediately from the hot pan or skillet so they don't continue to toast and become too dark or scorch.

Stovetop Method

Nuts: Sprinkle in an ungreased heavy skillet. Cook over medium heat 5 to 7 minutes, stirring frequently until nuts begin to brown, then stirring constantly until nuts are light brown.

Coconut: Sprinkle in an ungreased heavy skillet. Cook over medium-low heat 6 to 14 minutes, stirring frequently until browning begins, then stirring constantly until golden brown.

Sesame seed: Sprinkle in an ungreased heavy skillet over medium-low heat 5 to 7 minutes, stirring frequently until browning begins, then stirring constantly until golden brown.

Oven Method

Nuts: Spread in a ungreased shallow pan. Bake uncovered in a 350° oven 6 to 10 minutes, stirring frequently, until nuts are light brown.

Coconut: Spread in a ungreased shallow pan. Bake uncovered in 350° oven 5 to 7 minutes, stirring occasionally, until golden brown.

Sesame seed: Spread in an ungreased shallow pan. Bake uncovered in 350° oven 8 to 10 minutes, stirring occasionally, until golden brown.

Microwave Method

Nuts: Place 1 teaspoon butter or margarine and 1/2 cup nuts in a microwavable pie plate. Microwave uncovered on High (100%) 2 minutes 30 seconds to 3 minutes, stirring every 30 seconds, until nuts are light brown.

Coconut: Spread 1/2 cup in a microwavable pie plate. Microwave uncovered on High (100%) 1 minute 30 seconds, stirring every 30 seconds until golden brown.

Hot Chocolate Soufflé

Prep: 45 min; Bake: 1 hr 15 min ✱ *6 servings*

1/3 cup sugar

1/3 cup baking cocoa

1/4 cup all-purpose flour*

1 cup milk

3 large egg yolks

2 tablespoons butter or stick margarine, softened**

1 teaspoon vanilla

4 large egg whites

1/4 teaspoon cream of tartar

1/8 teaspoon salt

3 tablespoons sugar

1. Move oven rack to lowest position. Heat oven to 350°. Grease 6-cup soufflé dish with butter; lightly sugar. Make a 4-inch band of triple-thickness aluminum foil 2 inches longer than circumference of dish. Grease one side of band with butter; lightly sugar. Extend dish by securing band, buttered side in, around top outside edge.

2. Mix 1/3 cup sugar, the cocoa and flour in 1 1/2-quart saucepan. Gradually stir in milk. Heat to boiling, stirring constantly; remove from heat.

3. Beat egg yolks in large bowl with wire whisk or fork. Beat about one-third of the cocoa mixture into egg yolks. Gradually stir remaining cocoa mixture into egg yolks. Stir in butter and vanilla; cool slightly.

4. Beat egg whites, cream of tartar and salt in medium bowl with electric mixer on high speed until foamy. Beat in 3 tablespoons sugar, 1 tablespoon at a time; continue beating until stiff and glossy. Do not underbeat. (See Beating Egg Whites page 189).

5. Stir about one-fourth of the egg whites into cocoa mixture. Fold in remaining egg whites. Carefully pour into soufflé dish. Place dish in square metal pan, 9 × 9 × 2 inches, on oven rack. Pour very hot water into pan until 1 inch deep.

6. Bake 1 hour 15 minutes or until puffed in center and edges are set. Carefully remove foil band and quickly divide soufflé into sections with 2 forks. Serve immediately with whipped cream if desired.

Do not use self-rising flour.
**Spreads with at least 65% vegetable oil can be used (page 91).*

Make a 4-inch band of triple-thickness aluminum foil 2 inches longer than circumference of dish. Grease one side of band with butter; lightly sugar. Extend dish by securing band, buttered side in, around top outside edge.

1 Serving: Calories 195 (Calories from Fat 70); Fat 8g (Saturated 4g); Cholesterol 120mg; Sodium 135mg; Carbohydrate 26g (Dietary Fiber 2g); Protein 7g **% Daily Value:** Vitamin A 8%; Vitamin C 0%; Calcium 6%; Iron 6% **Diet Exchanges:** 2 Starch, 1 Fat

Tips for Cheesecakes

- To check for doneness, touch the top of the cheesecake lightly or gently shake the pan. The center may jiggle slightly, but it will set during chilling. Don't cut into the center with a knife to test for doneness because the hole could cause the cheesecake to crack.

- After baking, let the cheesecake stand at room temperature for 30 minutes or as directed before you put it in the refrigerator. Refrigerate, uncovered, 2 to 3 hours or until chilled; cover so it doesn't dry out or pick up odors. Covering warm cheesecake may cause moisture to drip onto the cheesecake top.

- If the cheesecake has a side crust, after it has cooled for 30 minutes, run a metal spatula or table knife along the side of the crust to loosen it from the pan (if the pan has a removable side, don't remove or release it yet). Loosening the crust keeps the cheesecake from pulling away. Do this again before removing the side of the pan.

- To cut cheesecake, dip the knife into water, and clean it off after every cut. Or use a piece of dental floss! Hold a length of dental floss taut and pull the floss down through the cheesecake, making a clean cut.

Turtle Cheesecake

Turtle Cheesecake

Prep: 30 min; Bake: 50 min; Cool: 1 hr; Chill: 2 hr
✻ *12 servings*

1 1/2 cups finely crushed vanilla wafer cookies (about
    40 cookies)

1/4 cup butter or stick margarine, melted*

2 packages (8 ounces each) cream cheese, softened

1/2 cup sugar

2 teaspoons vanilla

2 eggs

1/4 cup hot fudge topping

1 cup caramel topping

1/2 cup coarsely chopped pecans

1. Heat oven to 350°. Mix cookie crumbs and butter in
medium bowl. Press firmly against bottom and side of
pie plate, 9 × 1 1/4 inches.

2. Beat cream cheese, sugar, vanilla and eggs in large
bowl with electric mixer on low speed until smooth.
Pour half of the mixture into pie plate.

3. Add hot fudge topping to remaining cream cheese
mixture in bowl; beat on low speed until smooth.
Spoon over vanilla mixture in pie plate. Swirl mixtures
slightly with tip of knife.

4. Bake 40 to 50 minutes or until center is set. (Do not
insert knife into cheesecake because the hole may cause
cheesecake to crack as it cools.) Cool at room temperature 1 hour. Refrigerate at least 2 hours until chilled.
Serve with caramel topping and pecans. Store covered
in refrigerator.

**Spreads with at least 65% vegetable oil can be used
(page 91).*

1 Serving: Calories 440 (Calories from Fat 235); Fat 26g (Saturated
13g); Cholesterol 90mg; Sodium 340mg; Carbohydrate 46g
(Dietary Fiber 1g); Protein 6g **% Daily Value:** Vitamin A 16%;
Vitamin C 0%; Calcium 6%; Iron 8% **Diet Exchanges:** Not
Recommended

New York Cheesecake

Prep: 45 min; Bake: 1 hr 15 min; Cool: 1 hr; Chill: 12 hr
  ✱ *16 to 20 servings*

This rich and smooth cheesecake, made with cream cheese, is usually associated with the style of cheesecake popularized in New York. The recipe originated at Lindy's, a New York restaurant that made their cheesecake world famous.

Crust (right)
5 packages (8 ounces each) cream cheese, softened
1 3/4 cups sugar
3 tablespoons all-purpose flour*
1 tablespoon grated orange peel, if desired
1 tablespoon grated lemon peel, if desired
1/4 teaspoon salt
5 large eggs
2 large egg yolks
1/4 cup whipping (heavy) cream
3/4 cup whipping (heavy) cream
1/3 cup slivered almonds, toasted (page 177), or fresh fruit, if desired

1. Make Crust.

2. Heat oven to 475°.

3. Beat cream cheese, sugar, flour, orange peel, lemon peel and salt in large bowl with electric mixer on medium speed about 1 minute or until smooth. Beat in eggs, egg yolks and 1/4 cup whipping cream on low speed until well blended. Pour into crust.

4. Bake 15 minutes.

5. Reduce oven temperature to 200°. Bake 1 hour longer. Cheesecake may not appear to be done, but if a small area in the center seems soft, it will become firm as cheesecake cools. (Do not insert a knife to test for doneness because the hole could cause cheesecake to crack.) Turn off oven; leave cheesecake in oven 30 minutes longer. Remove from oven and cool in pan away from drafts on wire rack 30 minutes.

6. Without releasing or removing side of pan, run metal spatula carefully along side of cheesecake to loosen. Refrigerate uncovered about 3 hours or until chilled; cover and continue refrigerating at least 9 hours but no longer than 48 hours.

7. Run metal spatula along side of cheesecake to loosen again. Remove side of pan; leave cheesecake on pan bottom to serve. Beat 3/4 cup whipping cream in chilled small bowl with electric mixer on high speed until stiff. Spread whipped cream over top of cheesecake. Decorate with almonds. Store covered in refrigerator.

Crust

1 cup all-purpose flour*
1/2 cup butter or stick margarine, softened**
1/4 cup sugar
1 large egg yolk

Heat oven to 400°. Lightly grease springform pan, 9 × 3 inches, with shortening; remove bottom. Mix all ingredients with fork until dough forms; gather into a ball. Press one-third of the dough evenly on bottom of pan. Place on cookie sheet. Bake 8 to 10 minutes or until light golden brown; cool. Assemble bottom and side of pan; secure side. Press remaining dough 2 inches up side of pan.

Do not use self-rising flour in this recipe
**Do not use vegetable oil spreads (page 91).*

1 Serving: Calories 520 (Calories from Fat 340); Fat 38g (Saturated 20g); Cholesterol 200mg; Sodium 350mg; Carbohydrate 35g (Dietary Fiber 0g); Protein 9g **% Daily Value:** Vitamin A 36%; Vitamin C 0%; Calcium 8%; Iron 8% **Diet Exchanges:** Not Recommended

Lighter New York Cheesecake: For 19 grams of fat and 330 calories per serving, omit Crust. Move oven rack to lowest position. Heat oven to 425°. Lightly grease side only of springform pan, 9 × 3 inches, with shortening. Mix 3/4 cup graham cracker crumbs, 2 tablespoons margarine, melted, and 2 tablespoons sugar; press evenly in bottom of pan. Use reduced-fat cream cheese (Neufchâtel); increase flour to 1/4 cup. Substitute 1 1/4 cups fat-free cholesterol-free egg product for the 5 eggs. Omit 1/4 cup whipping cream. Continue as directed in steps 4 through 6. Omit 3/4 cup whipping cream and almonds. Serve with fresh fruit if desired.

CHOCOLATE CHIP NEW YORK CHEESECAKE: Fold 1 cup miniature semisweet chocolate chips (3 ounces) into cheese mixture before pouring into crust.

Cream Puffs

Prep: 30 min; Bake: 40 min; Cool: 1 hr
✱ *12 cream puffs*

You can make cream puffs, éclairs or profiteroles—all with this same pastry known as choux pastry.

1 cup water
1/2 cup butter or stick margarine*
1 cup all-purpose flour**
4 large eggs
Cream Filling (below) or Sweetened Whipped Cream (page 198)
Powdered sugar

1. Heat oven to 400°.

2. Heat water and butter to rolling boil in 2 1/2-quart saucepan. Stir in flour; reduce heat to low. Stir vigorously over low heat about 1 minute or until mixture forms a ball; remove from heat.

3. Beat in eggs, all at once, with spoon; continue beating until smooth. Drop dough by scant 1/4 cupfuls about 3 inches apart onto ungreased cookie sheet.

4. Bake 35 to 40 minutes or until puffed and golden. Cool away from draft, about 30 minutes. Cut off top third of each puff; pull out any strands of soft dough.

5. Fill puffs with Cream Filling; replace tops. Dust with powdered sugar. Cover and refrigerate until serving. Store remaining dessert covered in refrigerator.

Cream Filling

1/3 cup sugar
2 tablespoons cornstarch
1/8 teaspoon salt
2 cups milk
2 large egg yolks, slightly beaten
2 tablespoons butter or stick margarine, softened*
2 teaspoons vanilla

Mix sugar, cornstarch and salt in 2-quart saucepan. Gradually stir in milk. Cook over medium heat, stirring constantly, until mixture thickens and boils. Boil and stir 1 minute. Gradually stir at least half of the hot mixture into egg yolks, then stir back into hot mixture in saucepan. Boil and stir 1 minute; remove from heat. Stir in butter and vanilla. Pour into bowl. Press plastic wrap on filling to prevent a tough layer from forming on top. Refrigerate at least 1 hour until cool.

*Spreads with at least 65% vegetable oil can be used (page 91).
**Self-rising flour can be used.

1 Serving: Calories 205 (Calories from Fat 115); Fat 13g (Saturated 7g); Cholesterol 135mg; Sodium 130mg; Carbohydrate 17g (Dietary Fiber 0g); Protein 5g **% Daily Value:** Vitamin A 12%; Vitamin C 0%; Calcium 6%; Iron 4% **Diet Exchanges:** 1 Starch, 2 1/2 Fruit

CHOCOLATE ÉCLAIRS: Make as directed in steps 1, 2 and 3—except shape each scant 1/4 cupful of dough into finger shape, 4 1/2 inches long and 1 1/2 inches wide, with spatula. Continue as directed in steps 4 and 5. Fill with Cream Filling (left). Omit powdered sugar. Frost with Chocolate Frosting (below).

Chocolate Frosting

1 ounce unsweetened baking chocolate
1 teaspoon butter or stick margarine*
1 cup powdered sugar
1 to 2 tablespoons hot water

Melt chocolate and butter in 1-quart saucepan over low heat, stirring frequently; remove from heat. Stir in powdered sugar and water. Beat until smooth and spreadable.

PROFITEROLES: Make as directed in steps 1, 2 and 3—except drop dough by level tablespoonfuls about 3 inches apart onto ungreased cookie sheet. Bake 20 to 25 minutes or until puffed and golden. Cool away from draft, about 30 minutes. Cut puffs horizontally in half. Fill with ice cream; replace top half. Serve with chocolate sauce. Makes 36 profiteroles.

Bread Pudding with Whiskey Sauce

Prep: 10 min; Bake: 45 min ✱ 8 servings

Almost any bread can be used to make bread pudding, but firm breads will bake up the best. And those with a slightly softer crust, rather than a very crisp crust, work well.

2 1/4 cups milk
1/2 cup sugar
1 1/2 teaspoons ground cinnamon
2 large eggs, slightly beaten
5 cups 1/2- to 3/4-inch cubes French or other firm
    bread (8 ounces)
1/2 cup raisins, if desired
Whiskey Sauce (below)

1. Heat oven to 350°.

2. Mix milk, sugar, cinnamon and eggs in large bowl with wire whisk until well blended. Stir in bread cubes and raisins. Pour into ungreased 1 1/2-quart casserole.

3. Bake uncovered 40 to 45 minutes or until knife inserted 1 inch from edge of casserole comes out clean.

4. Make Whiskey Sauce. Serve sauce over warm bread pudding. Store remaining dessert and sauce covered in refrigerator.

Whiskey Sauce

1/2 cup butter or stick margarine, melted*
2 tablespoons water
1 large egg
1 cup sugar
2 tablespoons whiskey or bourbon or 1 teaspoon
    brandy extract

Melt butter in 1-quart saucepan over low heat; do not allow to simmer. Remove from heat; cool 10 minutes. Mix water and egg; stir into butter until blended. Stir in sugar. Cook over medium-low heat, stirring constantly, until sugar is dissolved and mixture begins to boil; remove from heat. Stir in whiskey. Cool at least 10 minutes before serving. Store covered in refrigerator.

Spreads with at least 65% vegetable oil can be used (page 91).

1 Serving: Calories 390 (Calories from Fat 145); Fat 16g (Saturated 9g); Cholesterol 115mg; Sodium 300mg; Carbohydrate 55g (Dietary Fiber 1g); Protein 7g **% Daily Value:** Vitamin A 16%; Vitamin C 0%; Calcium 12%; Iron 6% **Diet Exchanges:** Not Recommended

Lighter Bread Pudding with Whiskey Sauce: For 2 grams of fat and 280 calories per serving, use fat-free (skim) milk; substitute 1 egg plus 2 egg whites for the 2 eggs. Instead of Whiskey Sauce, stir 1 tablespoon bourbon into 1 cup caramel topping; heat if desired.

Tiramisu

Prep: 30 min; Chill: 4 hr ✱ 9 servings

A traditional tiramisu uses custard made from mascarpone cheese, a buttery-rich, slightly sweet cream cheese. This Americanized version uses regular cream cheese.

1 package (8 ounces) cream cheese, softened
1/2 cup powdered sugar
2 tablespoons light rum or 1/2 teaspoon rum extract
1 cup whipping (heavy) cream
1 package (3 ounces) ladyfingers (12 ladyfingers)
1/2 cup cold prepared espresso or strong coffee
2 teaspoons baking cocoa

1. Beat cream cheese and powdered sugar in large bowl with electric mixer on medium speed until smooth. Beat in rum on low speed; set aside.

2. Beat whipping cream in chilled small bowl on high speed until stiff peaks form. Fold into cream cheese mixture.

3. Split ladyfingers horizontally in half. Arrange half of the ladyfingers, cut sides up, on bottom of ungreased square pan, 8 × 8 × 2 inches, or round pan, 9 × 1 1/2 inches. Drizzle 1/4 cup of the espresso over ladyfingers. Spread half of the cream cheese mixture over ladyfingers.

4. Arrange remaining ladyfingers, cut sides up, on cream cheese mixture. Drizzle with remaining 1/4 cup espresso. Spread with remaining cream cheese mixture.

5. Sift or sprinkle cocoa over top. Cover and refrigerate about 4 hours or until filling is firm. Store covered in refrigerator.

1 Serving: Calories 240 (Calories from Fat 160); Fat 18g (Saturated 11g); Cholesterol 60mg; Sodium 110mg; Carbohydrate 16g (Dietary Fiber 0g); Protein 3g **% Daily Value:** Vitamin A 14%; Vitamin C 0%; Calcium 4%; Iron 4% **Diet Exchanges:** 1 Starch, 3 1/2 Fat

Lighter Tiramisu: For 9 grams of fat and 170 calories per serving, substitute reduced-fat cream cheese (Neufchâtel) for the regular cream cheese. Substitute 2 cups frozen (thawed) reduced-fat whipped topping for the beaten whipping cream.

English Trifle

Prep: 30 min; Cook: 20 min; Chill: 3 hr ✱ *10 servings*

Prepare this trifle in a pretty glass serving bowl to show off the beautiful layers of cake, fruit and cream.

1/2 cup sugar

3 tablespoons cornstarch

1/4 teaspoon salt

3 cups milk

1/2 cup dry sherry or other dry white wine or white grape juice

3 large egg yolks, beaten

3 tablespoons butter or stick margarine*

1 tablespoon vanilla

2 packages (3 ounces each) ladyfingers (24 ladyfingers)

1/2 cup strawberry preserves

1 pint (2 cups) strawberries, sliced, or 1 package (10 ounces) frozen sliced strawberries, thawed and drained

1 cup whipping (heavy) cream

2 tablespoons sugar

2 tablespoons slivered almonds, toasted (page 177)

1. Mix 1/2 cup sugar, the cornstarch and salt in 3-quart saucepan. Gradually stir in milk and sherry. Heat to boiling over medium heat, stirring constantly. Boil and stir 1 minute.

2. Gradually stir at least half of the hot mixture into egg yolks, then stir back into hot mixture in saucepan. Boil and stir 1 minute; remove from heat. Stir in butter and vanilla. Cover and refrigerate about 3 hours or until chilled.

3. Split ladyfingers horizontally in half. Spread cut sides with preserves. Layer one-fourth of the ladyfingers, cut sides up, half of the strawberries and half of the pudding in 2-quart serving bowl; repeat layers. Arrange remaining ladyfingers around edge of bowl in upright position with cut sides toward center. (It may be necessary to gently ease ladyfingers down into pudding about 1 inch so they remain upright.) Cover and refrigerate.

4. Beat whipping cream and 2 tablespoons sugar in chilled medium bowl with electric mixer on high speed until stiff. Spread over dessert. Sprinkle with almonds. Refrigerate until serving. Store covered in refrigerator.

*Spreads with at least 65% vegetable oil can be used (page 91).

1 Serving: Calories 350 (Calories from Fat 145); Fat 16g (Saturated 9g); Cholesterol 110mg; Sodium 180mg; Carbohydrate 47g (Dietary Fiber 1g); Protein 6g **% Daily Value:** Vitamin A 14%; Vitamin C 34%; Calcium 12%; Iron 6% **Diet Exchanges:** Not Recommended

---

LADYFINGERS

Ladyfingers are small, oval-shaped cakes usually found in the bakery department or freezer section of the supermarket. If they are not available, you can substitute a 1/2-inch slice of packaged pound cake (from an 8 × 4-inch loaf) for each ladyfinger. You'll need twelve slices of pound cake to substitute for a 3-ounce package of ladyfingers.

Baked Custard

Prep: 15 min; Bake: 45 min; Cool: 30 min ✻ *6 servings*

3 large eggs, slightly beaten
1/3 cup sugar
1 teaspoon vanilla
Dash of salt
2 1/2 cups very warm milk
Ground nutmeg

1. Heat oven to 350°.

2. Mix eggs, sugar, vanilla and salt in medium bowl with wire whisk or fork. Gradually stir in milk. Pour into six 6-ounce custard cups. Sprinkle with nutmeg.

3. Place cups in rectangular pan, 13 × 9 × 2 inches, on oven rack. Pour very hot water into pan to within 1/2 inch of tops of cups (see box, below).

4. Bake about 45 minutes or until knife inserted halfway between center and edge comes out clean. Remove cups from water. Cool about 30 minutes. Unmold and serve warm, or refrigerate and unmold before serving. Store covered in refrigerator.

1 Serving: Calories 135 (Calories from Fat 45); Fat 5g (Saturated 2g); Cholesterol 115mg; Sodium 120mg; Carbohydrate 16g (Dietary Fiber 0g); Protein 7g **% Daily Value:** Vitamin A 8%; Vitamin C 0%; Calcium 14%; Iron 2% **Diet Exchanges:** 1 Fat, 1 Skim Milk

CARAMEL CUSTARD (CRÈME CARAMEL): Before making custard, heat 1/2 cup sugar in heavy 1-quart saucepan over low heat 10 to 15 minutes, stirring constantly with wooden spoon, until sugar is melted and golden brown (sugar becomes very hot and could melt a plastic spoon). Immediately divide syrup among six 6-ounce custard cups before it hardens in saucepan; carefully tilt cups to coat bottoms (syrup will be extremely hot). Let syrup harden in cups about 10 minutes. Make custard as directed in step 2; pour over syrup in cups. Bake as directed in steps 3 and 4. Cool completely; cover and refrigerate until serving or up to 48 hours.

To unmold, carefully loosen side of custard with knife or small spatula. Place dessert dish on top of cup and, holding tightly, turn dish and cup upside down. Shake cup gently to loosen custard. Caramel syrup will drizzle over custard, forming a sauce.

Rich Chocolate Custard

Prep: 15 min; Bake: 25 min ✻ *8 servings*

2 1/4 cups half-and-half
1 bag (6 ounces) semisweet chocolate chips (1 cup)
4 eggs
1/2 cup sugar
1/4 teaspoon salt
Sweetened Whipped Cream (page 198), if desired

1. Heat oven to 350°.

2. Heat half-and-half and chocolate chips in 1 1/2-quart saucepan over medium heat, stirring constantly, until chocolate is melted and mixture is smooth; cool 5 minutes.

3. Mix eggs, sugar and salt in medium bowl with wire whisk or fork. Gradually stir egg mixture into chocolate mixture until blended. Pour into eight 6-ounce custard cups.

4. Place cups in rectangular pan, 13 × 9 × 2 inches, on oven rack. Carefully pour very hot water into pan to within 1/2 inch of tops of cups (see box, below).

5. Bake 20 to 25 minutes or until set. Remove cups from water. Serve custard warm or chilled with Sweetened Whipped Cream. Store covered in refrigerator.

1 Serving: Calories 290 (Calories from Fat 155); Fat 17g (Saturated 9g); Cholesterol 130mg; Sodium 135mg; Carbohydrate 29g (Dietary Fiber 1g); Protein 6g **% Daily Value:** Vitamin A 10%; Vitamin C 0%; Calcium 8%; Iron 6% **Diet Exchanges:** 1 1/2 Starch, 1/2 Skim Milk, 3 Fat

---

BAKING IN A WATER BATH

Why are these custards baked in a pan of water? This method, called a water bath, helps the custards bake gently and evenly. Without the hot water, the edges of the custard would cook too quickly. Put the custard cups in the empty pan, place the pan on the oven rack, then carefully pour hot water into the pan. When the custards are done, remove the cups from the water or they will keep cooking.

Creamy Stirred Custard

Prep: 5 min; Cook: 20 min; Cool: 30 min; Chill: 1 hr
✱ *6 to 10 servings*

The French call this creamy custard sauce *crème anglaise*. Serve it over cake, fruit or other desserts. When cooking this sauce, don't be tempted to rush or the eggs will cook too quickly and the mixture will curdle.

3 large eggs
1/3 cup sugar
Dash of salt
2 1/2 cups milk
1 teaspoon vanilla

1. Beat eggs slightly in heavy 2-quart saucepan with fork. Stir in sugar and salt. Gradually stir in milk. Cook over medium heat 15 to 20 minutes, stirring constantly, until mixture just coats a metal spoon; remove from heat. Stir in vanilla.

2. Place saucepan in bowl or sink of cold water about 30 minutes, stirring occasionally, until custard is cool. (If custard curdles, beat vigorously with hand beater until smooth.) Pour into bowl. Press plastic wrap on custard to prevent a layer of skin from forming on top. Refrigerate at least 1 hour but no longer than 48 hours. Store covered in refrigerator.

Cook over medium heat 15 to 20 minutes, stirring constantly, until mixture just coats a metal spoon.

1 Serving: Calories 135 (Calories from Fat 45); Fat 5g (Saturated 2g); Cholesterol 115mg; Sodium 120mg; Carbohydrate 16g (Dietary Fiber 0g); Protein 7g **% Daily Value:** Vitamin A 8%; Vitamin C 0%; Calcium 14%; Iron 2% **Diet Exchanges:** 1 Fat, 1 Milk

Raspberry Stirred Custard *Fast*

Prep: 5 min; Cook: 10 min **✱** *4 servings*

1 cup raspberries
1/3 cup granulated sugar
2 tablespoons cornstarch
1/4 teaspoon salt
2 cups half-and-half
1/2 teaspoon vanilla
4 teaspoons packed brown sugar

1. Divide raspberries evenly among 4 individual serving bowls.

2. Mix granulated sugar, cornstarch and salt in 2-quart saucepan. Stir in half-and-half. Heat to boiling over medium heat, stirring frequently. Stir in vanilla.

3. Spoon custard over raspberries. Sprinkle with brown sugar. Serve warm or cool. Store covered in refrigerator.

1 Serving: Calories 270 (Calories from Fat 125); Fat 14g (Saturated 9g); Cholesterol 45mg; Sodium 200mg; Carbohydrate 34g (Dietary Fiber 2g); Protein 4g **% Daily Value:** Vitamin A 12%; Vitamin C 14%; Calcium 14%; Iron 2% **Diet Exchanges:** 2 Fruit, 1/2 Skim Milk, 2 1/2 Fat

Chocolate Mousse

Chocolate Mousse

Prep: 25 min; Chill: 2 hr ✱ *8 servings*

For a special touch, garnish with fresh fruit or chocolate curls.

4 large egg yolks
1/4 cup sugar
1 cup whipping (heavy) cream
1 package (6 ounces) semisweet chocolate chips (1 cup)
1 1/2 cups whipping (heavy) cream

1. Beat egg yolks in small bowl with electric mixer on high speed about 3 minutes or until thick and lemon colored. Gradually beat in sugar.

2. Heat 1 cup whipping cream in 2-quart saucepan over medium heat just until hot.

3. Gradually stir at least half of the hot cream into egg yolk mixture, then stir back into hot cream in saucepan. Cook over low heat about 5 minutes, stirring constantly, until mixture thickens (do not boil).

4. Stir in chocolate chips until melted. Cover and refrigerate about 2 hours, stirring occasionally, just until chilled.

5. Beat 1 1/2 cups whipping cream in chilled medium bowl on high speed until stiff. Fold chocolate mixture into whipped cream. Pipe or spoon mixture into dessert dishes or stemmed glasses. Refrigerate until serving. Store covered in refrigerator.

1 Serving: Calories 390 (Calories from Fat 290); Fat 32g (Saturated 19g); Cholesterol 190mg; Sodium 30mg; Carbohydrate 22g (Dietary Fiber 1g); Protein 4g **% Daily Value:** Vitamin A 20%; Vitamin C 0%; Calcium 6%; Iron 4% **Diet Exchanges:** Not Recommended

Lighter Chocolate Mousse: For 13 grams of fat and 225 calories per serving, substitute 2 eggs for the 4 egg yolks, half-and-half for the 1 cup whipping cream and 3 cups frozen (thawed) reduced-fat whipped topping for the whipped 1 1/2 cups whipping cream.

WHITE CHOCOLATE MOUSSE: Substitute white baking chips for the chocolate chips.

Crème Brûlée

Prep: 15 min: Cook: 15 min: Chill: 3 hr ✱ *4 servings*

This unbaked version of *brûlée* has a puddinglike texture with a caramelized topping. It's delicious all on its own or spooned over fruit or slices of angel food cake or pound cake. Before spooning over fruit or cake, break up the delicious caramelized topping with a few taps of a spoon.

4 large egg yolks
3 tablespoons granulated sugar
2 cups whipping (heavy) cream
1 teaspoon vanilla
1/3 cup packed brown sugar

1. Beat egg yolks in medium bowl with electric mixer on high speed about 3 minutes or until thick and lemon colored. Gradually beat in granulated sugar.

2. Heat whipping cream in 2-quart saucepan over medium heat just until hot.

3. Gradually stir at least half of the hot cream into egg yolk mixture, then stir back into hot cream in saucepan. Cook over low heat 5 to 8 minutes, stirring constantly, until mixture thickens (do not boil). Stir in vanilla.

4. Pour custard into four 6-ounce ceramic ramekins* or ungreased ceramic pie plate, 9 × 1 1/4 inches.* Cover and refrigerate at least 2 hours but no longer than 24 hours. Custard must be completely chilled before broiling with brown sugar on top to keep custard from overheating.

5. Set oven control to broil. Sprinkle brown sugar evenly over custard. Broil with tops about 5 inches from heat about 3 minutes or until sugar is melted and forms a glaze. Serve immediately (mixture will be runny), or refrigerate 1 to 2 hours or until slightly firm. Store covered in refrigerator.

*Do not use glass custard cups or glass pie plates; they cannot withstand the heat from broiling and may break.

1 Serving: Calories 610 (Calories from Fat 380); Fat 42g (Saturated 24g); Cholesterol 340mg; Sodium 60mg; Carbohydrate 54g (Dietary Fiber 2g); Protein 6g **% Daily Value:** Vitamin A 36%; Vitamin C 36%; Calcium 16%; Iron 4% **Diet Exchanges:** Not Recommended

Rice Pudding *Low-Fat*

Prep: 30 min: Bake: 45 min: Stand: 15 min ✱ *8 servings*

Two cups of leftover cooked rice can be used for the rice in this recipe; increase the bake time by about 5 minutes because the rice will be cold.

1/2 cup uncooked regular long-grain rice
1 cup water
2 large eggs or 4 large egg yolks
1/2 cup sugar
1/2 cup raisins or chopped dried apricots
2 1/2 cups milk
1 teaspoon vanilla
1/4 teaspoon salt
Ground cinnamon or nutmeg
Raspberry Sauce (page 197) or Sweetened Whipped
    Cream (page 198), if desired

1. Heat rice and water to boiling in 1 1/2-quart saucepan, stirring once or twice; reduce heat to low. Cover and simmer 14 minutes (do not lift cover or stir). All water should be absorbed.

2. Heat oven to 325°.

3. Beat eggs in ungreased 1 1/2-quart casserole with wire whisk or fork. Stir in sugar, raisins, milk, vanilla, salt and hot rice. Sprinkle with cinnamon.

4. Bake uncovered 45 minutes, stirring every 15 minutes. Top of pudding will be very wet and not set (overbaking may cause pudding to curdle).

5. Stir well; let stand 15 minutes. Enough liquid will be absorbed while standing to make pudding creamy. Serve warm, or cover and refrigerate about 3 hours or until chilled. Serve with Raspberry Sauce. Store covered in refrigerator.

1 Serving (about 2/3 cup): Calories 265 (Calories from Fat 25); Fat 3g (Saturated 1g); Cholesterol 60mg; Sodium 130mg; Carbohydrate 54g (Dietary Fiber 1g); Protein 7g **% Daily Value:** Vitamin A 6%; Vitamin C 0%; Calcium 12%; Iron 10% **Diet Exchanges:** 2 Starch, 1 1/2 Fruit, 1/2 Fat

Vanilla Pudding

Prep: 10 min; Cook: 10 min; Chill: 1 hr ✳ 4 servings

1/3 cup sugar
2 tablespoons cornstarch
1/8 teaspoon salt
2 cups milk
2 large egg yolks, slightly beaten
2 tablespoons butter or stick margarine, softened*
2 teaspoons vanilla

1. Mix sugar, cornstarch and salt in 2-quart saucepan. Gradually stir in milk. Cook over medium heat, stirring constantly, until mixture thickens and boils. Boil and stir 1 minute.

2. Gradually stir at least half of the hot mixture into egg yolks, then stir back into hot mixture in saucepan. Boil and stir 1 minute; remove from heat. Stir in butter and vanilla.

3. Pour pudding into dessert dishes. Cover and refrigerate about 1 hour or until chilled. Store covered in refrigerator.

*Spreads with at least 65% vegetable oil can be used (page 91).

1 Serving: Calories 230 (Calories from Fat 100); Fat 11g (Saturated 6g); Cholesterol 130mg; Sodium 180mg; Carbohydrate 27g (Dietary Fiber 0g); Protein 6g **% Daily Value:** Vitamin A 14%; Vitamin C 0%; Calcium 16%; Iron 2% **Diet Exchanges:** 1 Fruit, 1 1/2 Fat, 1 Milk

BUTTERSCOTCH PUDDING: Substitute 2/3 cup packed brown sugar for the granulated sugar; decrease vanilla to 1 teaspoon.

CHOCOLATE PUDDING: Increase sugar to 1/2 cup; stir 1/3 cup baking cocoa into sugar mixture. Omit butter.

Orange Bavarian

Prep: 45 min; Chill: 5 hr ✳ 6 to 8 servings

1 cup boiling water
1 package (4-serving size) orange-flavored gelatin
1/2 cup sugar
1 tablespoon grated orange peel
1 cup orange juice
1 cup whipping (heavy) cream

1. Pour boiling water on gelatin in medium bowl; stir until gelatin is dissolved. Stir in sugar, orange peel and orange juice. Refrigerate, stirring occasionally, until mixture is slightly thickened and mounds when dropped from a spoon. (Refrigeration time will vary and may take up to 1 hour.)

2. Beat whipping cream in chilled medium bowl with electric mixer on high speed until stiff. Beat gelatin mixture until foamy.

3. Carefully fold gelatin mixture into whipped cream. Pour into 4-cup mold or serving dish or individual dessert dishes. Cover and refrigerate about 4 hours or until firm. Unmold if desired.

Refrigerate, stirring occasionally, until mixture is slightly thickened and mounds when dropped from a spoon.

1 Serving: Calories 255 (Calories from Fat 110); Fat 12g (Saturated 8g); Cholesterol 45mg; Sodium 50mg; Carbohydrate 35g (Dietary Fiber 0g); Protein 2g **% Daily Value:** Vitamin A 10%; Vitamin C 12%; Calcium 2%; Iron 0% **Diet Exchanges:** 1 Starch, 1 1/2 Fruit, 2 Fat

Lighter Orange Bavarian: For 1 gram of fat and 160 calories per serving, substitute 2 cups frozen (thawed) reduced-fat whipped topping for the beaten whipping cream. Do not pour into a mold or try to unmold from dishes.

Tips for Meringues

- Meringue, a froth of egg white, sugar and air, can make a melt-in-your-mouth soft topping for pies, such as Lemon Meringue Pie (page 130), or a hard, crispy shell to cradle cream fillings, fruit or ice cream, such as for Lemon Meringue Torte (page 191). Here are tips for making successful meringues every time:

- Pick a cool, dry day to make meringue. If it's humid or rainy, the sugar in the meringue will absorb moisture from the air and make the meringue sticky and spongy. The meringue also may get beads, or drops, of sugar syrup on the surface.

- Start with cold eggs. You'll want to separate them very carefully, because even a speck of yolk in the whites will keep the whites from fluffing up fully during beating. To prevent contamination from the outside of the shell, don't pass the egg yolk back and forth between the shell halves. To separate eggs, use an egg separator (page 9).

- So that the egg whites will really fluff up during beating, let them stand at room temperature for 30 minutes before beating. Or put the whites in a microwavable bowl and microwave uncovered on High for about 10 seconds per egg white to bring them to room temperature. Don't heat them for more time in the microwave; if you heat them too long they'll cook through.

- Beat in sugar slowly, about 1 tablespoon, at a time so that your meringue will be smooth and not gritty. Continue beating until the meringue stands in stiff, glossy peaks when you lift the beaters out of the mixture.

Soft Meringue

- Spread the meringue over the hot pie filling right up to the crust all the way around so that it will "seal." If the meringue is sealed, it won't shrink or weep, or ooze, liquid after baking. With a table knife or metal spatula, swirl the meringue into points to make it look light, fluffy and pretty.

- So the meringue won't shrink as it cools, make sure the pie isn't placed in a draft.

Hard Meringue

- A hard meringue shell should be thoroughly dry after baking. If not baked long enough, it will be limp and gummy.

- Cool hard meringue shells in the oven—with the heat turned off—for as long as the recipe suggests so they will be dry and crisp. To keep them crisp, store meringue shells in a container with a tight-fitting lid.

- Fill hard meringue shells just before serving so they don't absorb moisture from the filling and become chewy, unless the recipe gives other directions.

BEATING EGG WHITES

Egg whites will not beat up if even a trace of fat is present. Because there is fat in egg yolks, there cannot be even the smallest amount of yolk with the whites. The beaters and bowl must be clean and dry. Separate the eggs very carefully, one egg at a time, into a small bowl. Then add that egg white to the mixing bowl. Discard any egg white that does not separate completely from the yolk, and start with another clean small bowl for the next egg. If you separate eggs directly into the mixing bowl, one speck of yolk will mean that the entire amount will not beat up.

Meringue for 9-Inch Pie *Low-Fat*

Prep: 20 min ✳ 8 servings

This meringue has a special method: making a syrup with sugar, cornstarch and water. It makes a meringue that clings to a filling, does not shrink and cuts beautifully. It's well worth the small bit of extra effort.

1/2 cup sugar
4 teaspoons cornstarch
1/2 cup cold water
4 large egg whites
1/8 teaspoon salt

1. Heat oven to 350°.

2. Mix sugar and cornstarch in 1-quart saucepan. Stir in water. Cook over medium heat, stirring constantly, until mixture thickens and boils. Boil and stir 1 minute; remove from heat. Cool completely while making filling for pie recipe. (To cool more quickly, place in freezer about 10 minutes.)

3. Beat egg whites and salt in large bowl with electric mixer on high speed until soft peaks *just begin* to form. *Very gradually* beat in sugar mixture until stiff peaks form.

4. Spoon meringue onto hot pie filling. Spread over filling, carefully sealing meringue to edge of crust to prevent shrinking. Bake about 15 minutes or until meringue is light brown. Cool away from drafts.

Spoon meringue onto hot pie filling. Spread over filling, carefully sealing meringue to edge of crust to prevent shrinking.

1 Serving: Calories 65 (Calories from Fat 0); Fat 0g (Saturated 0g); Cholesterol 0mg; Sodium 65mg; Carbohydrate 14g (Dietary Fiber 0g); Protein 2g **% Daily Value:** Vitamin A 0%; Vitamin C 0%; Calcium 0%; Iron 0% **Diet Exchanges:** 1 Starch

Meringue Shell *Low-Fat*

Prep: 15 min; Bake: 2 1/2 hr; Cool: 2 hr ✳ 8 servings

3 large egg whites
1/4 teaspoon cream of tartar
3/4 cup sugar

1. Heat oven to 275°. Line cookie sheet with cooking parchment paper or heavy brown paper.

2. Beat egg whites and cream of tartar in medium bowl with electric mixer on high speed until foamy. Beat in sugar, 1 tablespoon at a time; continue beating until stiff peaks form and mixture is glossy. Do not underbeat. Shape meringue on cookie sheet into 9-inch circle with back of spoon, building up side.

3. Bake 1 1/2 hours. Turn off oven; leave meringue in oven with door closed 1 hour. Finish cooling at room temperature, about 2 hours.

Beat egg whites and sugar until stiff peaks form and mixture is glossy.

Shape meringue with back of spoon into desired shape, building up side.

1 Serving: Calories 80 (Calories from Fat 0); Fat 0g (Saturated 0g); Cholesterol 0mg; Sodium 20mg; Carbohydrate 19g (Dietary Fiber 0g); Protein 1g **% Daily Value:** Vitamin A 0%; Vitamin C 0%; Calcium 0%; Iron 0% **Diet Exchanges:** 1 Starch

INDIVIDUAL MERINGUES: Drop meringue by 1/3 cupfuls onto paper-lined cookie sheet. Shape into circles, building up sides. Bake 1 hour. Turn off oven; leave meringues in oven with door closed 1 1/2 hours. Finish cooling at room temperature, about 2 hours. Fill with ice cream and drizzle with Hot Fudge Sauce (page 195) or Butterscotch Sauce (page 196). 8 to 10 meringues.

Lemon Meringue Torte

Prep: 35 min; Bake: 2 1/2 hr; Cool: 2 hr; Chill: 12 hr
✱ *8 to 10 servings*

This recipe sometimes is called a *Schaum torte*, which is a German term describing the meringue part of the recipe.

Meringue Shell (page 190)
3/4 cup sugar
3 tablespoons cornstarch
1/4 teaspoon salt
3/4 cup water
3 large egg yolks, slightly beaten
1 tablespoon butter or stick margarine*
1 teaspoon grated lemon peel
1/3 cup lemon juice
1 cup whipping (heavy) cream

1. Bake and cool Meringue Shell.

2. Mix sugar, cornstarch and salt in 2-quart saucepan. Gradually stir in water. Cook over medium heat, stirring constantly, until thickens and boils. Boil and stir 1 minute.

3. Gradually stir at least half of the hot mixture into egg yolks, then stir back into hot mixture in saucepan. Boil and stir 1 minute; remove from heat.

4. Stir in butter, lemon peel and lemon juice. Press plastic wrap on filling to prevent a tough layer from forming on top. Cool to room temperature. Spoon into shell. Cover and refrigerate at least 12 hours but no longer than 24 hours.

5. Beat whipping cream in chilled medium bowl with electric mixer on high speed until soft peaks form. Spread over filling. Store covered in refrigerator.

Spreads with at least 65% vegetable oil can be used (page 91).

1 Serving: Calories 295 (Calories from Fat 115); Fat 13g (Saturated 7g); Cholesterol 115mg; Sodium 120mg; Carbohydrate 42g (Dietary Fiber 0g); Protein 3g **% Daily Value:** Vitamin A 10%; Vitamin C 4%; Calcium 2%; Iron 2% **Diet Exchanges:** 1 Starch, 2 Fruit, 2 Fat

Lighter Lemon Meringue Torte: For 6 grams of fat and 245 calories per serving, substitute 2 cups frozen (thawed) reduced-fat whipped topping for the whipping cream.

Cherry-Berries on a Cloud

Cherry-Berries on a Cloud

Prep: 30 min; Bake: 1 1/2 hr; Cool: 2 hr; Chill: 12 hr
* ***** *15 servings*

6 large egg whites
1/2 teaspoon cream of tartar
1/4 teaspoon salt
1 1/2 cups sugar
2 cups whipping (heavy) cream
2 packages (3 ounces each) cream cheese, softened
1/2 cup sugar
1 teaspoon vanilla
2 cups miniature marshmallows
Cherry-Berries Topping (right)

1. Heat oven to 275°. Butter rectangular pan, 13 × 9 × 2 inches.

2. Beat egg whites, cream of tartar and salt in large bowl with electric mixer on high speed until foamy. Beat in 1 1/2 cups sugar, 1 tablespoon at a time; continue beating until stiff and glossy. Do not underbeat. (See page 190.) Spread in pan.

3. Bake 1 1/2 hours. Turn off oven; leave meringue in oven with door closed at least 2 hours.

4. Beat whipping cream in chilled large bowl on high speed until soft peaks form.

5. Beat cream cheese, 1/2 cup sugar and the vanilla until blended. Gently fold cream cheese mixture and marshmallows into whipped cream. Spread over meringue. Cover and refrigerate at least 12 hours. Cut into serving pieces; top with Cherry-Berries Topping. Store covered in refrigerator.

Cherry-Berries Topping

2 cups sliced strawberries or 1 bag (16 ounces) frozen strawberries, thawed and drained
1 can (21 ounces) cherry pie filling
2 teaspoons lemon juice

Mix all ingredients.

1 Serving: Calories 310 (Calories from Fat 125); Fat 14g (Saturated 9g); Cholesterol 45mg; Sodium 110mg; Carbohydrate 44g (Dietary Fiber 1g); Protein 3g **% Daily Value:** Vitamin A 10%; Vitamin C 22%; Calcium 4%; Iron 2% **Diet Exchanges:** Not Recommended

Tips for Ice Cream

Although store-bought ice cream is delicious, making ice cream in an old-fashioned hand-crank freezer somehow tastes even better. It's great family entertainment, too. As you take turns on the crank, tell stories and catch up on family news. Or if time's short, use an electric freezer; the results still are a special treat. Following are tips for making wonderful ice cream, frozen yogurt, sherbet or sorbet at home:

- Every ice cream freezer is different, so follow the manufacturer's instructions for freezing the ice cream.
- Get all your supplies ready—ingredients, plenty of ice, salt. Be sure to clear a big enough space in your freezer!
- Eggs are an ingredient in most ice creams and must be cooked so the ice cream will be safe to eat. If you're using a recipe that calls for raw eggs, you'll need to revise it or find a different one. The ice cream recipe in this book features cooked eggs.

Vanilla Ice Cream

Prep: 10 min; Cook: 10 min; Chill: 3 hr; Freeze: Time will vary ✱ *1 quart ice cream*

3 large egg yolks, slightly beaten
1/2 cup sugar
1 cup milk
1/4 teaspoon salt
2 cups whipping (heavy) cream
1 tablespoon vanilla

1. Mix egg yolks, sugar, milk and salt in 2-quart saucepan. Cook just to boiling over medium heat, stirring constantly (do not boil). Pour into chilled bowl. Refrigerate uncovered 2 to 3 hours, stirring occasionally, until room temperature. At this point, mixture can be refrigerated up to 24 hours before completing recipe if desired.

2. Stir whipping cream and vanilla into milk mixture. Pour into 1-quart ice-cream freezer and freeze according to manufacturer's directions.

1 Serving (about 1/2 cup): Calories 265 (Calories from Fat 190); Fat 21g (Saturated 13g); Cholesterol 150mg; Sodium 110mg; Carbohydrate 16g (Dietary Fiber 0g); Protein 3g **% Daily Value:** Vitamin A 18%; Vitamin C 0%; Calcium 8%; Iron 0% **Diet Exchanges:** 1 Starch, 4 Fat

CHOCOLATE ICE CREAM: Increase sugar to 1 cup. Beat 2 ounces unsweetened baking chocolate, melted and cooled, into milk mixture before cooking. Decrease vanilla to 1 teaspoon.

FRESH PEACH ICE CREAM: Decrease vanilla to 1 teaspoon. Mash 4 or 5 peaches with potato masher or in food processor until slightly chunky (not pureed) to make 2 cups. Stir an additional 1/2 cup sugar into peaches; stir into milk mixture after adding vanilla.

FRESH STRAWBERRY ICE CREAM: Decrease vanilla to 1 teaspoon. Mash 1 pint (2 cups) strawberries and an additional 1/2 cup sugar with potato masher or in food processor until slightly chunky (not pureed); stir into milk mixture after adding vanilla. Stir in a few drops of red food color if desired.

Fresh Lemon Sherbet

Prep: 10 min; Freeze: Time will vary ✱ *1 quart sherbet*

1 1/4 cups sugar
2 cups half-and-half
1/3 cup lemon juice
1 to 2 tablespoons grated lemon peel
1 or 2 drops yellow food color

1. Mix all ingredients until sugar is dissolved.

2. Pour into 1-quart ice-cream freezer and freeze according to manufacturer's directions.

1 Serving (about 1/2 cup): Calories 210 (Calories from Fat 65); Fat 7g (Saturated 4g); Cholesterol 20mg; Sodium 25mg; Carbohydrate 35g (Dietary Fiber 0g); Protein 2g **% Daily Value:** Vitamin A 6%; Vitamin C 6%; Calcium 6%; Iron 0% **Diet Exchanges:** 2 Fruit, 1 Fat, 1/2 Skim Milk

Fresh Berry Frozen Yogurt *Low-Fat*

Prep: 15 min; Freeze: Time will vary
✱ *5 cups frozen yogurt*

1 pint (2 cups) strawberries or raspberries
1/4 cup sugar
4 cups vanilla yogurt

1. Mash strawberries with sugar in medium bowl. Stir in yogurt.

2. Pour into 1-quart ice-cream freezer and freeze according to manufacturer's directions.

1 Serving (about 1/2 cup): Calories 115 (Calories from Fat 10); Fat 1g (Saturated 1g); Cholesterol 5mg; Sodium 50mg; Carbohydrate 23g (Dietary Fiber 1g); Protein 4g **% Daily Value:** Vitamin A 0%; Vitamin C 26%; Calcium 14%; Iron 0% **Diet Exchanges:** 1 Fruit, 1/2 Skim Milk

BANANA FROZEN YOGURT: Substitute 1 1/2 cups mashed ripe bananas (3 medium) for the strawberries.

Lemonade Sorbet *Low-Fat*

Prep: 10 min; Freeze: 4 hr **✱** *4 servings*

1 1/2 cups cold water
1 cup frozen (thawed) lemonade concentrate (from 12-ounce can)
3 tablespoons honey
Lemon slices, if desired
Blueberries, if desired

1. Place water, lemonade concentrate and honey in blender or food processor. Cover and blend on low speed until smooth. Pour into square baking dish, 8 × 8 × 2 inches.

2. Freeze about 4 hours, stirring several times to keep mixture smooth, until firm. Garnish with lemon slices and blueberries.

1 Serving: Calories 185 (Calories from Fat 0); Fat 0g (Saturated 0g); Cholesterol 0mg; Sodium 5mg; Carbohydrate 47g (Dietary Fiber 0g); Protein 0g **% Daily Value:** Vitamin A 0%; Vitamin C 22%; Calcium 0%; Iron 2% **Diet Exchanges:** 3 Fruit

Tips for Dessert Sauces

A yummy sauce can turn something simple such as sliced fruit into a satisfying dessert. Let your imagination create delicious combinations, such as Butterscotch Sauce (page 196) over sliced fresh fruit or Hot Fudge Sauce (page 195) over a thick, chewy brownie. Here are some fresh sauce ideas.

- Sauce doesn't have to be served over a dessert, it can be under it, too.
- With a spoon, a plastic bag with one corner trimmed off or an inexpensive plastic squeeze bottle (such as a red ketchup or yellow mustard bottle), you can drizzle dramatic designs on serving plates before adding the dessert.
- Keep the color of the plate as well as the color of the dessert and sauce in mind. Contrasting colors will make your design especially eye-catching.

Try your hand at one of these dessert sauce designs:

Spider Web: Drizzle a small ring of sauce in the center of a plate. Make a larger ring around the smaller ring, about one inch apart, then add a third and larger ring. Starting at the center and moving to the outside ring, draw a knife or toothpick through the sauce rings toward the outside edge of the plate; repeat, making a web design.

Chevron: Spoon sauce onto a plate. Drizzle three lines of a contrasting sauce across the first sauce. Immediately draw a knife or toothpick back and forth across the lines.

Wispy Heart: Spoon sauce onto a plate. Drop dots of a contrasting sauce in a circle 1 inch from the edge of the first sauce and again in a smaller circle in the center. Draw a knife or toothpick through the dots to make heart shapes.

Sunburst: Spoon sauce onto a plate. Drizzle semicircular lines of a contrasting sauce across the first sauce, about one inch apart. Starting at the smallest semicircle, draw a knife or toothpick across the lines toward the edge of the plate.

Dessert Sauces: choose from Hot Fudge, Glossy Chocolate (page 196), Divine Caramel (page 196) and Raspberry (page 197)

Hot Fudge Sauce

Prep: 5 min; Cook: 5 min; Cool: 30 min ✱ 3 cups

Pour this lavish sauce over your favorite ice cream, and top it off with colored sprinkles, chopped toffee candy bars, chopped nuts, miniature chocolate chips or cherries—the list is endless!

1 can (12 ounces) evaporated milk
1 package (12 ounces) semisweet chocolate chips
    2 cups)
1/2 cup sugar
1 tablespoon butter or stick margarine*
1 teaspoon vanilla

1. Heat milk, chocolate chips and sugar to boiling in 2-quart saucepan over medium heat, stirring constantly; remove from heat.

2. Stir in butter and vanilla until mixture is smooth and creamy. Cool about 30 minutes or until sauce begins to thicken. Serve warm. Store remaining sauce covered in refrigerator up to 4 weeks. Sauce becomes firm when refrigerated; heat slightly before serving (sauce will become thin if overheated).

Spreads with at least 65% vegetable oil can be used (page 91).

1 Tablespoon: Calories 60 (Calories from Fat 25); Fat 3g (Saturated 2g); Cholesterol 0mg; Sodium 10mg; Carbohydrate 7g (Dietary Fiber 0g); Protein 1g **% Daily Value:** Vitamin A 0%; Vitamin C 0%; Calcium 2%; Iron 0% **Diet Exchanges:** 1/2 Starch, 1/2 Fat

Glossy Chocolate Sauce

Fast & Low-Fat

Prep: 15 min ✱ *About 1 1/2 cups*

1 1/2 cups light corn syrup
3 ounces unsweetened baking chocolate, cut into
    pieces
1 tablespoon butter or stick margarine*
3/4 teaspoon vanilla

1. Heat corn syrup and chocolate over low heat, stirring frequently, until chocolate is melted; remove from heat.

2. Stir in butter and vanilla. Serve warm or cold. Store covered in refrigerator up to 10 days. Reheat slightly before serving if desired.

Spreads with at least 65% vegetable oil can be used (page 91).

1 Tablespoon: Calories 90 (Calories from Fat 25); Fat 3g (Saturated 2g); Cholesterol 0mg; Sodium 30mg; Carbohydrate 17g (Dietary Fiber 1g); Protein 0g **% Daily Value:** Vitamin A 0%; Vitamin C 0%; Calcium 0%; Iron 0% **Diet Exchanges:** 1 Fruit, 1/2 Fat

Divine Caramel Sauce

Prep: 5 min; Cook: 40 min; Cool: 30 min ✱ *4 cups*

This sauce bubbles up as it cooks, so be sure to make it in a large pan.

2 cups sugar
3/4 cup butter or stick margarine*
2 cups whipping (heavy) cream
1 cup light corn syrup
Dash of salt
1 teaspoon vanilla

1. Heat all ingredients except vanilla to boiling in heavy 4-quart Dutch oven over medium heat, stirring constantly; reduce heat slightly. Boil about 30 minutes, stirring frequently, until sugar is dissolved and mixture is caramel colored.

2. Stir in vanilla. Cool about 30 minutes. Serve warm. Store covered in refrigerator up to 2 months. Reheat slightly before serving if desired.

Do not use vegetable oil spreads (page 91).

1 Tablespoon: Calories 75 (Calories from Fat 35); Fat 4g (Saturated 3g); Cholesterol 15mg; Sodium 30mg; Carbohydrate 10g (Dietary Fiber 0g); Protein 0g **% Daily Value:** Vitamin A 2%; Vitamin C 0%; Calcium 0%; Iron 0% **Diet Exchanges:** 1/2 Fruit, 1 Fat

Butterscotch Sauce

Prep: 10 min; Cook: 5 min; Cool: 20 min
✱ *About 1 3/4 cups*

A blend of brown sugar and butter creates this wonderful butterscotch flavor.

1/2 cup granulated sugar
1/2 cup packed brown sugar
6 tablespoons butter or stick margarine*
1/2 cup whipping (heavy) cream
1/2 cup light corn syrup
1/2 teaspoon salt
1 teaspoon vanilla

1. Mix all ingredients except vanilla in 2-quart saucepan. Cook over low heat, stirring constantly, until butter is melted and sugars are dissolved.

2. Increase heat to medium; heat to boiling, stirring constantly. Boil gently 5 minutes, stirring occasionally; remove from heat. Cool 20 minutes.

3. Stir in vanilla. Serve sauce warm or cool. Store covered in refrigerator up to 10 days. Sauce becomes firm when refrigerated; heat slightly before serving (sauce will become thin if overheated).

Spreads with at least 65% vegetable oil can be used (page 91).

1 Tablespoon: Calories 85 (Calories from Fat 35); Fat 4g (Saturated 2g); Cholesterol 10mg; Sodium 70mg; Carbohydrate 12g (Dietary Fiber 0g); Protein 0g **% Daily Value:** Vitamin A 2%; Vitamin C 0%; Calcium 0%; Iron 0% **Diet Exchanges:** 1 Starch

Lemon Sauce *Fast & Low-Fat*

Prep: 5 min; Cook: 10 min ✱ 1 1/4 cups

1/2 cup sugar

2 tablespoons cornstarch

3/4 cup water

1 tablespoon grated lemon peel

1/4 cup lemon juice

2 tablespoons butter or stick margarine*

1. Mix sugar and cornstarch in 1-quart saucepan. Gradually stir in water. Cook over medium heat, stirring constantly, until mixture thickens and boils. Boil and stir 1 minute; remove from heat.

2. Stir in remaining ingredients. Serve warm or cool. Store covered in refrigerator up to 10 days.

Spreads with at least 65% vegetable oil can be used (page 91).

1 Tablespoon: Calories 35 (Calories from Fat 10); Fat 1g (Saturated 1g); Cholesterol 5mg; Sodium 10mg; Carbohydrate 6g (Dietary Fiber 0g); Protein 0g **% Daily Value:** Vitamin A 0%; Vitamin C 0%; Calcium 0%; Iron 0% **Diet Exchanges:** 1/2 Fruit

Raspberry Sauce *Low-Fat*

Prep: 5 min; Cook: 5 min ✱ About 1 cup

3 tablespoons sugar

2 teaspoons cornstarch

1/3 cup water

1 package (10 ounces) frozen raspberries in syrup, thawed and undrained

1. Mix sugar and cornstarch in 1-quart saucepan. Stir in water and raspberries. Cook over medium heat, stirring constantly, until mixture thickens and boils. Boil and stir 1 minute.

2. Strain sauce through a strainer to remove seeds if desired. Serve sauce warm or cool. Store covered in refrigerator up to 10 days.

1 Tablespoon: Calories 50 (Calories from Fat 0); Fat 0g (Saturated 0g); Cholesterol 0mg; Sodium 0mg; Carbohydrate 15g (Dietary Fiber 2g); Protein 0g **% Daily Value:** Vitamin A 0%; Vitamin C 10%; Calcium 0%; Iron 0% **Diet Exchanges:** 1 Fruit

Orange Sauce *Fast & Low-Fat*

Prep: 10 min; Cook: 15 min ✱ About 2 1/3 cups sauce

1 cup sugar

2 tablespoons cornstarch

1 tablespoon all-purpose flour

1/4 teaspoon salt

1 1/4 cups orange juice

1/2 cup water

1/4 cup lemon juice

1 tablespoon butter or stick margarine*

1 teaspoon grated orange peel

1 teaspoon grated lemon peel

1. Mix sugar, cornstarch, flour and salt in 1 1/2 quart saucepan. Gradually stir in orange juice, water and lemon juice. Cook over medium heat, stirring constantly, until mixture thickens and boils. Boil and stir 3 minutes; remove from heat.

2. Stir in remaining ingredients. Serve warm. Store covered in refrigerator.

Spreads with at least 65% vegetable oil can be substituted (page 91).

1 Tablespoon: Calories 30 (Calories from Fat 0); Fat 0g (Saturated 0g); Cholesterol 0mg; Sodium 20mg; Carbohydrate 7g (Dietary Fiber 0g); Protein 0g **% Daily Value:** Vitamin A 0%; Vitamin C 2%; Calcium 0%; Iron 0% **Diet Exchanges:** 1/2 Fruit

---

STOP THE SPATTER

Beating whipping cream can be a bit messy. Since you are beating at such a high speed, before the cream begins to thicken, it may spatter out of the bowl onto the kitchen counter. To help control the mess, make a shield from waxed paper to cover the top of the bowl. Pull off a piece of waxed paper just slightly bigger than your bowl, and cut a slit in the middle. Place the beaters into the slit and then into the mixer. As you beat, the waxed paper stops the spatters from flying out of the bowl and all over your counter.

Sweetened Whipped Cream

Prep: 5 min

Well-chilled cream will whip the best, so keep it refrigerated until ready to use. When the cream begins to thicken as you beat it, reduce the mixer speed so you can watch carefully and beat just until soft peaks form. Overbeaten cream will look curdled.

FOR 1 CUP WHIPPED CREAM: Beat 1/2 cup whipping (heavy) cream and 1 tablespoon granulated or powdered sugar in chilled small bowl with electric mixer on high speed until soft peaks form.

FOR 1 1/2 CUPS WHIPPED CREAM: Beat 3/4 cup whipping (heavy) cream and 2 tablespoons granulated or powdered sugar in chilled small bowl with electric mixer on high speed until soft peaks form.

FOR 2 CUPS WHIPPED CREAM: Beat 1 cup whipping (heavy) cream and 2 tablespoons granulated or powdered sugar in chilled medium bowl with electric mixer on high speed until soft peaks form.

2 Tablespoons: Calories 55 (Calories from Fat 45); Fat 5g (Saturated 3g); Cholesterol 15mg; Sodium 5mg; Carbohydrate 2g (Dietary Fiber 0g); Protein 0g **% Daily Value:** Vitamin A 4%; Vitamin C 0%; Calcium 0%; Iron 0% **Diet Exchanges:** 1 Fat

FLAVORED SWEETENED WHIPPED CREAM: Beat 1 cup whipping (heavy) cream, 3 tablespoons granulated or powdered sugar and **one** of the following ingredients in chilled medium bowl with electric mixer on high speed until soft peaks form.

1 teaspoon grated lemon or orange peel
1 teaspoon vanilla
1/2 teaspoon ground cinnamon
1/2 teaspoon ground ginger
1/2 teaspoon ground nutmeg
1/2 teaspoon almond extract
1/2 teaspoon peppermint extract
1/2 teaspoon rum extract
1/4 teaspoon maple extract

FREEZING SWEETENED WHIPPED CREAM: Place waxed paper or aluminum foil on cookie sheet. Drop whipped cream by spoonfuls onto waxed paper. Freeze uncovered at least 2 hours. Place frozen mounds of whipped cream in a freezer container. Cover tightly and freeze no longer than 2 months.

LEARN WITH *Betty* — BEATING WHIPPING CREAM

Softly Beaten Cream. This whipped cream was not beaten long enough to form soft peaks and is best used as a dessert topping. It is too soft to be used in desserts that must set up and become firm enough to cut into serving pieces.

Perfectly Beaten Cream. This whipped cream was beaten long enough to form soft peaks. It can be used as a dessert topping and is stiff enough to be used in dessert recipes that call for the cream to be beaten "until soft peaks form."

Overbeaten Cream. This whipped cream was beaten too long and has begun to curdle and separate. Continued beating will turn it into butter. We do not recommend using this in recipes, but it may be used as a dessert topping if you don't mind the appearance.

CHAPTER 7

Eggs & Cheese

Eggs & Cheese

Eggs Benedict (page 204)

Low-Fat = *3g or less, except main dishes with 6g or less*   **Fast** = *Ready in 30 minutes or less*   ■ = *Bread Machine directions*   ● = *Slow Cooker directions*

Lighter = 1/3 fewer calories or 50% less fat

Egg Basics

Eggs are powerful package of nutrition and versatility. Packed inside each egg is lots of protein, vitamins and minerals, some fat and cholesterol, not much sodium and only 80 calories. In cooking, 1 or 2 incredible eggs give structure, create lightness, add richness and texture, and bind other ingredients together. On top of that, they're just plain tasty, whether eaten hard-cooked with a little salt and pepper or as part of an airy soufflé.

Chicken eggs are most commonly used in American cooking; other cuisines include the eggs of ducks, geese, quail and other poultry.

The egg white contains water and about half the egg's protein; the yolk contains the rest of the protein and all of the fat, cholesterol, vitamins and minerals and most of the calories. People at risk for heart disease may want to limit the number of whole eggs they eat. As a general guide for cooking, use 2 egg whites in place of 1 whole egg.

Buying Eggs

Eggs are marketed according to size, grade and color. The U.S. Department of Agriculture sets size and grade standards.

Size: The most popular egg size is large; sizes range from jumbo to peewee. We tested the recipes in this cookbook with large eggs.

Grade: The grade is based on an egg's quality, both inside and out. The three grades are AA, A and B. There's little difference in quality between Grades AA and A, and the nutrition content is the same for all three grades. Almost no Grade B eggs find their way to the supermarket. High-grade eggs have thick whites, compact and rounded yolks and a small air pocket. As eggs get older, the white gradually thins and the yolk flattens.

Color: Eggshell colors (white or brown) and yolk colors (pale or deep yellow) vary with the breed and diet of the hen. White eggs are most in demand, but brown are preferred in some parts of the country; brown eggs tend to be more expensive. Flavor, nutrition content and cooking performance are the same for white and brown eggs.

Handling and Storing Eggs Safely

Recently, raw eggs contaminated with salmonella have caused some outbreaks of illness. How eggs become contaminated is unclear, but scientists are working to find a solution to the problem. By storing, handling and cooking eggs safely, you can prevent the growth of potentially harmful bacteria.

Buy eggs only from the refrigerated case, and put them in the refrigerator (at a temperature no higher than 40°) as soon as you get home. You don't need to wash eggs before storing or using because washing is a routine part of commercial egg processing.

Look for eggs that are clean and not cracked. Before buying them, open the carton and gently move each egg to be sure it hasn't cracked and stuck to the carton. If an egg cracks on the way home, throw it away.

Although you may have an egg storage area on the door of your refrigerator, it's best to keep eggs in their carton on a shelf to be sure they stay good and cold. If desired, store eggs with the large end up to keep the yolk centered for more attractive hard- and soft-cooked eggs.

Wash your hands, utensils, equipment and work area with hot, soapy water before and after they come in contact with raw eggs and dishes where eggs are the main ingredient, such as quiches and baked custards.

Handle colored hard-cooked eggs carefully if you plan to eat them after using them as decoration, in children's baskets or for egg hunts. Follow these guidelines:

- If eggs won't be colored right after cooking them, store them in their egg cartons in the refrigerator.
- Wash hands thoroughly before cooking and each handling step, such as cooling, dyeing, arranging, hiding and regathering them.
- Don't use or color cracked raw eggs.
- Use only food color or specially made food-grade dyes for eggs.
- If not using colored eggs for decoration, baskets or egg hunts right after they've been colored, store them in their egg cartons in the refrigerator until ready to use.

- Eggs cannot be out of the refrigerator for more than 2 hours without the risk of food poisoning. If you plan on using eggs for decoration that will be out of the refrigerator longer than 2 hours or for several days, just cook and refrigerate extra eggs for eating and throw out the ones used for decoration.
- When hiding eggs, avoid areas where they may come in contact with pets, wild animals, birds, insects and lawn chemicals. Once the eggs are found, refrigerate them right away.

Egg whites may stand safely at room temperature for up to 30 minutes. Egg whites at room temperature will beat up fluffier for recipes such as meringue.

Refrigerate raw eggs and cooked eggs. Uncooked eggs in the shell will keep up to 5 weeks when properly stored (check the carton for an expiration date); hard-cooked eggs in the shell will keep up to 1 week. Store leftover raw egg whites in a tightly covered container in the refrigerator up to 4 days. Unbroken egg yolks store best when covered with a small amount of water in a tightly covered container; store up to 2 days.

You can freeze eggs, too, but not in the shell. One way is to freeze raw egg whites in a plastic ice-cube tray; once they're frozen, transfer them to a plastic freezer bag for storage. Thaw frozen egg whites in the refrigerator. When you use them, note that 2 tablespoons thawed egg white is equal to 1 fresh egg white.

Eggs yolks require some special treatment before freezing. If using the yolks in savory dishes such as scrambled eggs, add 1/8 teaspoon salt for each 1/4 cup of egg yolks (about 4 yolks). If using the yolks in sweet dishes such as custards, add 1 1/2 teaspoons sugar or 1 1/2 teaspoons corn syrup for each 1/4 cup of egg yolks. Be sure to label them with the number of egg yolks and whether you've added salt or sugar.

Freezing hard-cooked eggs is only half-successful: the yolks freeze well, the whites become tough and watery.

Note: For more information on handling eggs safely, call the USDA Meat and Poultry Hotline at 1-800-535-4555; in Washington, D.C., call 202-720-3333; TTY 1-800-256-7072. Recorded information is available 24 hours; to speak to a specialist, call Monday through Friday, 10 A.M. to 4 P.M. eastern standard time. Or check out the USDA's food safety Web site at www.fsis.usda.gov.

Cooking Eggs

Avoid eating raw eggs and foods containing raw eggs. This includes favorite homemade foods such as ice cream, eggnog and mayonnaise, unless the recipes call for cooking the eggs. Commercial versions of these foods are safe to eat because they contain pasteurized eggs; pasteurization destroys salmonella bacteria.

For 1 cup of raw egg, you need 5 large eggs, 7 large whites or 14 yolks.

Cook eggs over medium to low heat, except for omelets, which can handle medium heat. If the heat is too high and the eggs are overcooked, the whites will shrink and become tough and rubbery; the yolks become tough, and their surface may turn green.

Cook eggs until both the yolk and white are firm, not runny, to kill any bacteria.

When you're making egg dishes such as Cheesy Vegetable Strata (page 214) or Quiche Lorraine (page 213), don't let the dishes stand at room temperature before baking.

Serve cooked eggs and dishes containing eggs immediately. Refrigerate leftovers as soon as possible, and use them within 2 days.

After taking egg-rich desserts such as cream or custard pies and cheesecakes out of the oven, let them stand at room temperature for no more than 6 hours before chilling in the refrigerator.

If you're making a "do-ahead" recipe with eggs, refrigerate the unbaked mixture no longer than 24 hours before baking.

Determining Egg Doneness

Cook eggs until both the yolk and white are firm, not runny. An egg is cooked when it reaches 160°. Timings and doneness tests for our recipes reflect this requirement.

EGGS COOKING CHART

Eggs need to be cooked until the whites and yolks are firm, not runny, to eliminate the food safety issue of contracting salmonella from eating raw or undercooked eggs..

Type	Other Ingredients	Directions	Success Tips
Soft-Cooked		Not recommended, see note above.	
Hard-Cooked	Cold water at least 1 inch above egg(s)	Heat to boiling in saucepan; remove from heat. Cover and let stand 18 minutes. Immediately cool briefly in cold water to prevent further cooking. Tap egg to crack shell; roll egg between hands to loosen shell, then peel.	If shell is hard to peel, hold egg in cold water while peeling.
Poached	1 1/2 to 2 inches water	Heat water to boiling in skillet or saucepan; reduce to simmering. Break each egg into custard cup or saucer. Carefully slip egg into water. Cook about 5 minutes or until whites and yolks are firm not runny. Remove with slotted spoon.	• Hold cup or saucer close to surface of water for best shape and to avoid splashing. • Use a large enough pan so eggs do not touch while cooking. • Substitute chicken or beef broth for the water if desired.
Fried	Butter, margarine or bacon fat	Melt enough butter in heavy skillet over over medium heat until 1/8 inch deep and hot. Break each egg into custard cup or saucer. Carefully slip egg into skillet. Immediately reduce heat to low. Cook 5 to 7 minutes, spooning butter over eggs, until whites are set a film forms over top and whites and yolks are firm, not runny.	Lighter Fried Eggs: Use a non-stick skillet; spray skillet with cooking spray. Cook eggs over low heat about 1 minute or until edges turn white. Add 2 teaspoons water for each egg. Cover and cook about 5 minutes longer or until a film forms over top and whites and yolks are firm, not runny.
Baked (Shirred)	Butter or margarine, softened	Heat oven to 325°. Grease custard cups with butter. Carefully break 1 egg into each cup. Sprinkle with salt and pepper. Top each with 1 tablespoon milk or half-and-half. Dot with butter. Bake 15 to 18 minutes or until whites and yolks are firm, not runny.	Instead of dotting with butter, sprinkle egg with 1 tablespoon shredded Cheddar or grated Parmesan cheese if desired.

Break each egg into custard cup or saucer. Carefully slip egg into simmering water.

Break each egg into custard cup or saucer. Carefully slip egg into skillet.

Scrambled Eggs *Fast*

Prep: 5 min; Cook: 10 min ✱ *4 servings*

Want to scramble only an egg or two? Using a 6- or 8-inch skillet, cook them the same way using this recipe, adjust the liquid, using about 1 tablespoon milk, half-and-half or water for each egg. Add salt and pepper to taste.

6 large eggs
1/3 cup milk, half-and-half or water
1/4 teaspoon salt
1/8 teaspoon pepper, if desired
1 tablespoon butter or stick margarine

1. Beat eggs, milk, salt and pepper thoroughly with fork or wire whisk until well mixed.

2. Heat butter in 10-inch skillet over medium heat just until butter begins to sizzle. Pour egg mixture into skillet.

3. As mixture begins to set at bottom and side, gently lift cooked portions with metal spatula so that thin, uncooked portion can flow to bottom. Avoid constant stirring. Cook 3 to 4 minutes or until eggs are thickened throughout but still moist.

1 Serving: Calories 140 (Calories from Fat 90); Fat 10g (Saturated 3g); Cholesterol 320mg; Sodium 280mg; Carbohydrate 2g (Dietary Fiber 0g); Protein 10g **% Daily Value:** Vitamin A 14%; Vitamin C 0%; Calcium 6%; Iron 4% **Diet Exchanges:** 1 1/2 Medium-Fat Meat, 1/2 Fat

SCRAMBLED EGGS AND POTATOES: Increase butter to 1/4 cup. Cook 1 cup refrigerated diced potatoes with onion or frozen hash brown potatoes, 1 small zucchini, chopped (1 cup), and 1 medium tomato, seeded and chopped (3/4 cup), in butter in 10-inch skillet over medium-high heat, stirring occasionally, until hot. Pour egg mixture over potato mixture; continue as directed in step 3.

MEXICAN SCRAMBLED EGGS: Cook 1/2 pound chorizo sausage links, cut lengthwise in half and then sliced, 1 small green or red bell pepper, chopped (1/2 cup), and 1 medium onion, chopped (1/2 cup), in 10-inch skillet over medium-high heat about 5 minutes, stirring frequently, until sausage is no longer pink; drain. Add sausage mixture to eggs before cooking the last 3 to 4 minutes in step 3. Serve egg mixture wrapped in flour tortillas and topped with salsa, shredded cheese and sour cream if desired.

LEARN WITH *Betty* — SCRAMBLE EGGS

Undercooked Eggs. Cause: Eggs were not cooked long enough so stay wet and runny.

Perfectly scrambled eggs. There are no problems with these eggs; they are fluffy, soft and tender.

Overcooked Eggs. Cause: Eggs were cooked too long and stirred too frequently so become dry and crumbly.

French Omelet *Fast*

Prep: 10 min ✻ 1 serving

Serving an omelet on a warm plate is a nice touch. Just rinse the serving plate with hot water to warm it, then dry it thoroughly.

2 teaspoons butter or stick margarine
2 large eggs, beaten

1. Heat butter in 8-inch omelet pan or skillet over medium-high heat just until butter is hot and sizzling. As butter melts, tilt pan to coat bottom.

2. Quickly pour eggs into pan. While rapidly sliding pan back and forth over heat, quickly stir with fork to spread eggs continuously over bottom of pan as they thicken. Let stand over heat a few seconds to lightly brown bottom of omelet. Do not overcook—omelet will continue to cook after folding.

3. Tilt pan and run fork under edge of omelet, then jerk pan sharply to loosen eggs from bottom of pan. Fold portion of omelet just to center. Allow for a portion of the omelet to slide up side of pan. Turn omelet onto warm plate, flipping folded portion of omelet over so it rolls over the bottom. Tuck sides of omelet under if necessary.

1 Serving: Calories 180 (Calories from Fat 125); Fat 14g (Saturated 4g); Cholesterol 425mg; Sodium 170mg; Carbohydrate 1g (Dietary Fiber 0g); Protein 13g **% Daily Value:** Vitamin A 18%; Vitamin C 0%; Calcium 4%; Iron 6% **Diet Exchanges:** 2 Medium-Fat Meat, 1 Fat

Lighter French Omelet: For 8 grams of fat and 80 calories per serving, substitute 1/2 cup fat-free cholesterol-free egg product for the eggs.

CHEESE OMELET: Before folding omelet, sprinkle with 1/4 cup shredded Cheddar, Monterey Jack or Swiss cheese or 1/4 cup crumbled blue cheese.

DENVER OMELET: Before adding eggs to pan, cook 2 tablespoons chopped fully cooked ham, 1 tablespoon finely chopped bell pepper and 1 tablespoon finely chopped onion in butter about 2 minutes, stirring frequently. Continue as directed in step 2.

Tilt pan and run spatula under edge of omelet, then jerk pan sharply to loosen eggs from bottom of pan. Fold portion of omelet just to center. Allow for a portion of the omelet to slide up side of pan.

Turn omelet onto warm plate, flipping folded portion of omelet over so it rolls over the bottom.

Puffy Omelet with Italian Tomato sauce (page 436)

Eggs Benedict

Prep: 30 min ✱ 6 servings

This classic brunch dish was created years ago and named after Mr. and Mrs. LeGrand Benedict, patrons of Delmonico's Restaurant in New York, after they complained there was nothing new on the lunch menu.

Hollandaise Sauce (page 440)
3 English muffins
3 tablespoons butter or stick margarine, softened
1 teaspoon butter or stick margarine
6 thin slices Canadian-style bacon or fully cooked ham
6 Poached Eggs (page 201)
Paprika, if desired

1. Make Hollandaise Sauce; keep warm.

2. Split English muffins; toast. Spread each muffin half with some of the 3 tablespoons butter; keep warm.

3. Melt 1 teaspoon butter in 10-inch skillet over medium heat. Cook bacon in butter until light brown on both sides; keep warm.

4. Make Poached Eggs.

5. Place 1 slice bacon on each muffin half. Top with egg. Spoon warm Hollandaise Sauce over eggs. Sprinkle with paprika, if desired.

1 Serving: Calories 390 (Calories from Fat 280); Fat 31g (Saturated 14g); Cholesterol 370mg; Sodium 780mg; Carbohydrate 14g (Dietary Fiber 1g); Protein 15g **% Daily Value:** Vitamin A 30%; Vitamin C 0%; Calcium 8%; Iron 10% **Diet Exchanges:** 1 Starch, 2 High-Fat Meat, 2 1/2 Fat

Puffy Omelet *Fast*

Prep: 15 min; Bake: 15 min ✳ 2 servings

After beating the egg whites, you can use the same beaters—without washing them—to beat the egg yolks.

4 large eggs, separated
1/4 cup water
1/4 teaspoon salt
1/8 teaspoon pepper
1 tablespoon butter or stick margarine
Italian Tomato Sauce (page 436), salsa or spaghetti
   sauce, heated, if desired

1. Heat oven to 325°.

2. Beat egg whites, water and salt in medium bowl with electric mixer on high speed until stiff but not dry. Beat egg yolks and pepper on high speed about 3 minutes or until very thick and lemon colored. Fold egg yolks into egg whites.

3. Melt butter in 10-inch ovenproof skillet over medium heat. As butter melts, tilt skillet to coat bottom. Pour egg mixture into skillet. Gently level surface; reduce heat to low. Cook about 5 minutes or until puffy and bottom is light brown. (Carefully lift omelet at edge to judge color.)

4. Bake uncovered 12 to 15 minutes or until knife inserted in center comes out clean.

5. Tilt skillet and slip pancake turner or metal spatula under omelet to loosen. Fold omelet in half, being careful not to break it. Slip onto warm serving plate. Serve with Italian Tomato Sauce.

1 Serving: Calories 180 (Calories from Fat 125); Fat 14g (Saturated 4g); Cholesterol 425mg; Sodium 470mg; Carbohydrate 1g (Dietary Fiber 0g); Protein 13g **% Daily Value:** Vitamin A 18%; Vitamin C 0%; Calcium 4%; Iron 6% **Diet Exchanges:** 2 Medium-Fat Meat, 1/2 Fat

Huevos Rancheros

Prep: 45 min; Cook: 15 min ✳ 6 servings

Huevos rancheros is Spanish for "ranch-style" or "rancher's eggs." It's a hearty combination of fried eggs, sausage, salsa and tortillas. When buying tortillas, check for freshness. They should not look dry or cracked around the edges.

1 1/4 cups Tomato Salsa (page 456) or prepared salsa
1/2 pound bulk chorizo or pork sausage
Vegetable oil
6 corn tortillas (6 or 7 inches in diameter)
6 Fried Eggs (page 201)
1 1/2 cups shredded Cheddar cheese (6 ounces)

1. Make Tomato Salsa.

2. Cook sausage in 8-inch skillet over medium heat, stirring occasionally, until no longer pink; drain. Cover and keep warm.

3. Heat 1/8 inch oil in 8-inch skillet over medium heat just until hot. Cook tortillas, one at a time, in oil about 1 minute, turning once, until crisp; drain.

4. Heat salsa in 1-quart saucepan, stirring occasionally, until hot.

5. Make Fried Eggs.

6. Spread 1 tablespoon salsa over each tortilla to soften. Place egg on each tortilla. Top with salsa, sausage, additional salsa and cheese.

1 Serving: Calories 455 (Calories from Fat 295); Fat 33g (Saturated 14g); Cholesterol 275mg; Sodium 1,010mg; Carbohydrate 16g (Dietary Fiber 2g); Protein 25g **% Daily Value:** Vitamin A 20%; Vitamin C 8%; Calcium 24%; Iron 12% **Diet Exchanges:** 1 Starch, 3 High-Fat Meat, 1 1/2 Fat

---

HUEVOS RANCHEROS SHORTCUT

Save some time by using prepared salsa, as suggested. Place it in a 4-cup glass microwavable measuring cup and microwave on High about 2 minutes or until hot; stir. Use purchased crisp tortilla shells, and heat them as directed on the package instead of cooking them in oil as directed in step 3.

Savory Italian Frittata

Savory Italian Frittata *Fast*

Prep: 10 min; Cook: 16 min ✱ 6 servings

8 large eggs

1 tablespoon chopped fresh or 1/2 teaspoon dried
    basil leaves

1 tablespoon chopped fresh or 1/2 teaspoon dried
    mint leaves

1 tablespoon chopped fresh or 1/2 teaspoon dried sage
    leaves

1 tablespoon freshly grated Parmesan cheese

1/2 teaspoon salt

1/8 teaspoon pepper

1/4 cup diced fully cooked ham or prosciutto
    (2 ounces)

1 tablespoon butter or stick margarine

1 small onion, finely chopped (1/4 cup)

1. Beat all ingredients except ham, butter and onion thoroughly with fork or wire whisk until well mixed. Stir in ham.

2. Melt butter in 10-inch nonstick skillet over medium-high heat. Cook onion in butter 4 to 5 minutes, stirring frequently, until crisp-tender; reduce heat to medium-low.

3. Pour egg mixture into skillet. Cover and cook 9 to 11 minutes or until eggs are set around edge and light brown on bottom. Cut into wedges.

1 Serving: Calories 130 (Calories from Fat 80); Fat 9g (Saturated 3g); Cholesterol 290mg; Sodium 390mg; Carbohydrate 2g (Dietary Fiber 0g); Protein 10g **% Daily Value:** Vitamin A 10%; Vitamin C 0%; Calcium 4%; Iron 4% **Diet Exchanges:** 1 1/2 Medium-Fat Meat, 1/2 Vegetable

Lighter Savory Italian Frittata: For 2 grams of fat and 60 calories per serving, substitute 2 cups fat-free cholesterol-free egg product for the eggs. Use fully cooked turkey ham.

Fresh Spinach and New Potato Frittata

Prep: 15 min; Cook: 20 min ✱ *4 servings*

Purchase spinach that has already been washed to speed preparation for this tasty breakfast, lunch or dinner dish.

6 eggs
2 tablespoons milk
1/4 teaspoon dried marjoram leaves
1/4 teaspoon salt
2 tablespoons butter or stick margarine*
6 or 7 small red potatoes, thinly sliced (2 cups)
1/4 teaspoon salt
1 cup firmly packed bite-size pieces spinach
1/4 cup oil-packed sun-dried tomatoes, drained and sliced
3 medium green onions, cut into 1/4-inch pieces
1/2 cup shredded Swiss cheese (2 ounces)

1. Beat eggs, milk, marjoram and 1/4 teaspoon salt; set aside.

2. Melt butter in 10-inch nonstick skillet over medium heat. Add potatoes to skillet; sprinkle with 1/4 teaspoon salt. Cover and cook 8 to 10 minutes, stirring occasionally, until potatoes are tender.

3. Stir in spinach, tomatoes and onions. Cook, stirring occasionally, just until spinach is wilted; reduce heat to low.

4. Carefully pour egg mixture over potato mixture. Cover and cook 6 to 8 minutes or just until top is set. Sprinkle with cheese. Cover and cook about 1 minute or until cheese is melted.

Spreads with at least 65% vegetable oil can be used (page 91).

1 Serving: Calories 305 (Calories from Fat 170); Fat 19g (Saturated 6g); Cholesterol 330mg; Sodium 530mg; Carbohydrate 20g (Dietary Fiber 2g); Protein 16g **% Daily Value:** Vitamin A 28%; Vitamin C 16%; Calcium 20%; Iron 12% **Diet Exchanges:** 1 Starch, 1 1/2 High-Fat Meat, 1 Vegetable, 1 Fat

WHAT'S A FRITTATA?

Frittata is an Italian word for omelet, and it differs from a classic French omelet in several ways. The ingredients are cooked with the eggs instead of being folded inside the omelet. Frittatas are also cooked over a lower heat for a longer period of time than regular omelets. Additional ingredients, such as herbs or tomatoes, may be sprinkled on top.

Cheese Basics

There's a great big world of cheese out there. Exploring the varieties of domestic and imported cheeses can be a taste adventure with myriad flavors, textures, colors and shapes to choose from that brings excitement to both eating and cooking.

Legend has it that cheese was "discovered" by an Arab merchant crossing the desert who was pleased to find that the milk he'd carried all day in a pouch had transformed into dinner: thin, watery whey and thick curds. Although cheese making is a little more scientific today, the process is similar.

It's the different ways milk is processed that accounts for the major differences among cheeses, along with their fat contents. Today you'll find reduced-fat and low-fat cheeses on the market, and many are just fine for eating. For cooking, keep in mind that lower-fat cheeses don't melt well; they also become rubbery, and the flavor may change.

All cheeses fall into four categories: natural, pasteurized process cheese, cheese food and pasteurized cheese spread.

Kinds of Cheese

Cheeses are made from the milk (whole, skim or sometimes raw) or cream of cows, sheep or goats. The milk is treated with heat, smoke, bacteria or other agents to make it curdle; then the curds (solids) are separated from the whey (liquid). The curds may or may not be aged or ripened. Some fresh, or unripened, cheeses are cottage cheese and cream cheese; some aged, or ripened, cheeses are Cheddar and Parmesan. Both ripened and unripened cheeses may have ingredients such as herbs, spices and even bits of fruit added. Ripened cheese is processed further by being shaped, coated in wax or colored. Then it's left to ripen until it reaches its distinct flavor and texture.

Natural cheeses have so many variations—from the kind of milk they're made from to their flavor and texture to the cheesemaking process used—that categorizing them is difficult. In the chart Varieties of Natural Cheese (page 210), we've grouped them according to hardness.

Pasteurized process cheese is a blend of one or more varieties of natural cheese that is ground and heated. The process stops the ripening, so the flavor doesn't change and they keep well. American is probably the most famous of these cheeses. Pasteurized process cheese often is flavored with herbs, spices and even bits of fruit, vegetables and meat.

Cheese food is one or more varieties of natural cheeses made without heat (coldpack) or with heat (pasteurized process cheese). Dairy products such as cream, milk, skim milk or whey are added, so cheese food has a higher percentage of moisture than natural or pasteurized process cheese. Cheese food is usually sold in tubs or jars and is often flavored.

Pasteurized cheese spread is similar to pasteurized process cheese except it's spreadable at room temperature. It's also higher in moisture and lower in fat than cheese food. One example is cheese in aerosol cans.

Handling and Storing Cheese

For appetizers or snacks, serve ripened cheeses at room temperature to bring out their full flavor. Take the cheese out of the refrigerator, and let stand covered about 30 minutes before serving. Or microwave firm cheese uncovered on Medium-Low (30%) about 30 seconds for 8 ounces of cheese, rotating a half turn after half the time. Let stand a few minutes before serving.

For cooking, use cheese right from the refrigerator.

To keep cheese from drying out, wrap all cheeses tightly in plastic wrap or aluminum foil, then store in the refrigerator. Ripened cheese will continue to age during storage; hard cheeses will keep for 3 to 4 weeks, softer cheeses will keep from 1 to 2 weeks. Large pieces tend to keep longer than smaller ones.

Moldy cheese? It looks yucky, but it's harmless. Before using, trim away 1/2 inch of cheese on all sides of the mold; use the remaining cheese as quickly as possible. If mold appears on blue cheese (besides the natural blue veining), throw it out. You can reduce mold growth by changing the wrapping each time you use the cheese.

Unripened cheeses, such as cottage cheese and cream cheese, have a higher water content and are more perishable than hard cheeses. They don't improve with age and should be used by the use-by date on the package.

Cheeses from very soft to very hard shred easier if they're cold. Shred cheese right from the refrigerator or put in the freezer for 30 minutes before shredding with a grater or food processor. For very soft cheese, use a grater with large holes, or finely chop it instead.

Mold-ripened or blue-veined cheeses are a little on the sticky and crumbly side. Here's a cutting tip: Use a length of dental floss or heavy thread. Or freeze them for easier handling.

Most hard cheeses can be frozen, but their texture will change, so crumble or shred thawed cheese as a topping or blend it into other uncooked dishes. Some tips for freezing hard cheeses: Freeze in pieces that are 1/2 pound or less; use moistureproof and airtight wrapping; freeze at 0° for 2 months; thaw frozen cheese in the refrigerator; and use as soon as possible after thawing.

Cooking with Cheese

Four ounces of most shredded, crumbled or grated cheese equals 1 cup.

Two tips for cheese cooking success: Keep cooking temps low; keep cooking times short. Cooking on too high a heat and for too long make cheese tough and stringy.

Cheese melts and blends better with other ingredients if you shred it or cut it into small pieces.

Add a cheese topping to casseroles during the last 5 to 10 minutes of baking for perfect melting. When broiling cheese-topped dishes, keep a close eye on them— the cheese melts really fast!

Use cheeses with similar flavor and texture interchangeably.

Cheese microwaves well, but use lower power settings. To soften cream cheese, remove the foil wrapper and microwave uncovered on Medium (50%) until softened: 30 to 45 seconds for a 3-ounce package, 60 to 90 seconds for an 8-ounce one.

CREATING A CHEESE TRAY

To create an interesting and balanced cheese tray, choose three to five varieties of cheese with different shapes, textures and flavors. See the chart Varieties of Natural Cheese (page 210) for ideas.

- Plan on 2 to 3 ounces of cheese per person.
- Separate sharp and strong-flavored cheeses from mild cheeses.

- Serve most cheeses at room temperature to maximize their flavor and aroma.
- Flag or label cheeses so guests can identify types and preferences.

VARIETIES OF NATURAL CHEESE

Texture	Flavor	Use
Very Hard (grating)		
Asiago	Sharp, slightly fruity	Cooking, seasoning
Parmesan	Sharp, salty	Cooking, pasta, salad, seasoning
Romano	Sharp, piquant, salty	Cooking, pasta, seasoning
Hard		
Cheddar	Rich, nutty, from mild to full-bodied bite	Cooking, dessert, with fruit
Cheshire	Tangy, salty	Cooking, with fruit
Edam, Gouda	Milky and nutty to sharp and salty	Appetizer, dessert
Gjetost	Sweet, fudgelike, caramely with a hint of condensed milk	Sandwich, snack
Gruyère	Mellow and buttery with a nutlike flavor	Cooking, dessert
Jarlsberg	Slightly sweet, nutty	Appetizer, sandwich, cooking
Nökkelost	Spiced with cloves, buttery	Appetizer, sandwich, cooking
Swiss	Mild, very fruity, mouth-tingling tang	Appetizer, cooking, dessert, sandwich
Semisoft		
Blue	Rich, robust, salty with a lingering tanginess	Appetizer, dessert, salad
Brick	From mild and sweet to savory with a spicy tang	Appetizer, sandwich
Colby	Mild and milky	Cooking, sandwich
Curds	Mild and milky, rubbery	Appetizer, snack
Feta	Very sharp, salty	Cooking, salad
Fontina	Delicate, nutty with a hint of honey	Appetizer, cooking
Gorgonzola	Earthy, rich, spicy	Dessert, salad
Havarti	Creamy, mild, smooth	Appetizer, cooking
Monterey Jack	Mild to mellow	Appetizer, cooking, sandwich
Mozzarella	Delicate, vaguely sweet and stringy	Appetizer, cooking, pizza
Muenster	Strong tasting and smelling, tangy, spicy	Appetizer, dessert, sandwich

VARIETIES OF NATURAL CHEESE (cont.)

Texture	Flavor	Use
Semisoft, continued		
Port du Salut	Nutty, almost meaty	Appetizer, dessert, sandwich
Provolone	Creamy, firm, slightly smoky	Cooking, sandwich
Reblochon	Mild with flavor of fresh-crushed walnuts	Appetizer, dessert
Roquefort	Rich, melt-in-your-mouth texture with a clean, sharp, lingering tang	Appetizer, dessert, salad
Stilton	Rich, spicy with a blended flavor of blue and Cheddar cheeses	Dessert, salad, snack
Taleggio	Full-bodied, creamy with a hint of asparagus	Appetizer, cooking
Soft		
Bel Paese	Rich, sweet, creamy, robust	Cooking, dessert
Boursin	Mild, rich, often seasoned with herbs or pepper	Appetizer
Brie	Mild, creamy, slight flavor of mushrooms	Appetizer, dessert
Bucheron	Mild, fresh, tangy	Cooking, dessert
Camembert	Creamy, slightly tangy, earthy	Appetizer, dessert, sandwich
Cottage, dry or creamed	Very bland, sometimes flavored	Cooking, salad
Cream	Rich, slightly tangy	Appetizer, dessert, salad
Farmer	Mild, fresh with a faintly sour tinge	Cooking
Liederkranz	Full-flavored, pungent, almost honeylike consistency	Appetizer, dessert
Limburger	Tangy, gamy and strong-smelling	Appetizer, snack
Mascarpone	Very soft, mild, sweet, almost like whipped cream	Dessert
Montrachet	Creamy, fresh, mildly tangy	Appetizer, cooking
Neufchâtel	Mild, rich with a hint of salt	Appetizer, dessert, salad, spread
Ricotta	Bland, slightly sweet	Cooking, dessert, pasta

CHEESES

Fontina

Cheshire

arlesberg

Gruyère

Nökkelost (Kuminost)

Gouda

Harvarti

Gjetost

Blue

Port du Salut

Stilton

Cream

Gorgonzola

Brie

Limburger

Provolone

Bel Paese

Taleggio

Asiago

Parmesan

Reblochon

Feta

Camembert

Romano

Boursin

Cottage

Roquefort

Curds

Mascarpone

Ricotta

CHEESES

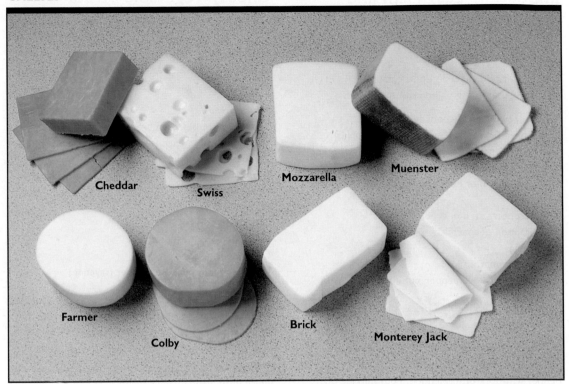

Cheddar — Swiss — Mozzarella — Muenster

Farmer — Colby — Brick — Monterey Jack

Quiche Lorraine

Prep: 25 min; Bake: 45 min; Stand: 10 min ✱ *6 servings*

Serve this flavorful egg dish with crusty French bread and a crisp mixed-greens salad with Italian dressing.

Pastry for 9-Inch One-Crust Pie (page 117)
8 slices bacon, crisply cooked and crumbled
1 cup shredded natural Swiss cheese (4 ounces)
1/3 cup finely chopped onion
4 large eggs
2 cups whipping (heavy) cream or half-and-half
1/4 teaspoon salt
1/4 teaspoon pepper
1/8 teaspoon ground red pepper (cayenne)

1. Heat oven to 425°.

2. Make pastry. Fold pastry into fourths; place in quiche dish, 9 × 1 1/2 inches, or pie plate, 9 × 1 1/4 inches. Unfold and ease into dish, pressing firmly against bottom and side.

3. Sprinkle bacon, cheese and onion in pastry-lined quiche dish. Beat eggs slightly in large bowl with fork or wire whisk. Beat in remaining ingredients. Pour into quiche dish. Bake 15 minutes.

4. Reduce oven temperature to 300°. Bake about 30 minutes longer or until knife inserted in center comes out clean. Let stand 10 minutes before cutting.

1 Serving: Calories 600 (Calories from Fat 460); Fat 51g (Saturated 25g); Cholesterol 255mg; Sodium 550mg; Carbohydrate 20g (Dietary Fiber 1g); Protein 16g **% Daily Value:** Vitamin A 26%; Vitamin C 0%; Calcium 24%; Iron 8% **Diet Exchanges:** 1 Starch, 1 1/2 High-Fat Meat, 1 Vegetable, 8 Fat

SEAFOOD QUICHE: Substitute 1 cup chopped cooked crabmeat (pat dry), shrimp, seafood sticks (imitation crabmeat) or salmon for the bacon, use green onions and increase salt to 1/2 teaspoon.

Impossibly Easy Ham and Swiss Pie

Prep: 9 min; Bake: 40 min; Stand: 5 min
✳ 6 to 8 servings

Here's a simplified version of the traditional Quiche Lorraine because there's no crust to prepare.

1 1/2 cups cut-up fully cooked ham
1 cup shredded natural Swiss cheese (4 ounces)
1/4 cup chopped green onions (4 medium) or other
    chopped onion
1/2 cup Original or Reduced Fat Bisquick®
1 cup milk
1/4 teaspoon salt, if desired
1/8 teaspoon pepper
2 large eggs
1 medium tomato, sliced
1 medium green bell pepper, cut into rings

1. Heat oven to 400°. Grease pie plate, 9 × 1 1/4 inches, with shortening.

2. Sprinkle ham, cheese and onions in pie plate.

3. Beat remaining ingredients except tomato and bell pepper with fork until blended. Pour into pie plate.

4. Bake 35 to 40 minutes or until knife inserted in center comes out clean. Let stand 5 minutes before cutting. Garnish with tomato and bell pepper.

1 Serving: Calories 215 (Calories from Fat 110); Fat 12g (Saturated 6g); Cholesterol 110mg; Sodium 740mg; Carbohydrate 11g (Dietary Fiber 1g); Protein 17g **% Daily Value:** Vitamin A 10%; Vitamin C 18%; Calcium 26%; Iron 6% **Diet Exchanges:** 1/2 Starch, 2 Medium-Fat Meat, 1 Vegetable

IMPOSSIBLY EASY HAM AND BROCCOLI PIE: Decrease ham to 1 cup, use 1/2 cup shredded Cheddar cheese for the Swiss cheese and add 2 cups frozen broccoli cuts, thawed and drained; sprinkle in pie plate with the onions. Decrease milk to 1/4 cup; add 1 cup small curd creamed cottage cheese to the egg mixture. Bake about 30 minutes. Sprinkle 1/2 cup shredded Cheddar cheese evenly over top. Bake about 5 minutes or until cheese is melted. Let stand 5 minutes. Omit tomato and bell pepper.

Cheesy Vegetable Strata

Prep: 15 min; Chill: 2 hr; Bake: 1hr 15 min; Stand: 10 min
✳ 8 servings

Make this easy strata the evening before you plan to serve it. It's a make-ahead dish that's ready to bake without any last-minute fuss.

8 slices bread
1 bag (16 ounces) frozen broccoli, green beans, pearl
    onions and red peppers (or other combination),
    thawed and drained
2 cups shredded sharp Cheddar cheese (8 ounces)
8 large eggs
4 cups milk
1 teaspoon salt
1 teaspoon ground mustard
1/4 teaspoon pepper
1/4 teaspoon ground red pepper (cayenne)

1. Cut each bread slice diagonally into 4 triangles. Arrange half of the bread triangles in ungreased rectangular pan, 13 × 9 × 2 inches. Top with vegetables. Sprinkle with cheese. Top with remaining bread.

2. Beat remaining ingredients with hand beater or wire whisk until blended; pour evenly over bread. Cover and refrigerate at least 2 hours but no longer than 24 hours.

3. Heat oven to 325°. Cover and bake 30 minutes. Uncover and bake about 45 minutes longer or until knife inserted in center comes out clean. Let stand 10 minutes before cutting.

1 Serving: Calories 325 (Calories from Fat 160); Fat 18g (Saturated 9g); Cholesterol 250mg; Sodium 440mg; Carbohydrate 23g (Dietary Fiber 2g); Protein 20g **% Daily Value:** Vitamin A 26%; Vitamin C 22%; Calcium 36%; Iron 10% **Diet Exchanges:** 1 Starch, 2 High-Fat Meat, 2 Vegetable

Lighter Cheesy Vegetable Strata: For 3 grams of fat and 185 calories per serving, substitute 2 cups fat-free cholesterol-free egg product for the eggs. Use reduced-fat Cheddar cheese and fat-free (skim) milk.

CHEESY VEGETABLE-HAM STRATA: Sprinkle 1 cup chopped fully cooked turkey ham over the vegetables in step 1. Decrease salt to 1/2 teaspoon.

Chilies Rellenos Bake

Prep: 10 min; Bake: 45 min ✱ *8 servings*

This version of the Mexican dish *chiles rellenos* omits the extra work of stuffing and frying whole chilies.

8 large eggs
1 cup sour cream
1/4 teaspoon salt
2 drops red pepper sauce
2 cups shredded Monterey Jack cheese (8 ounces)
2 cups shredded Cheddar cheese (8 ounces)
2 cans (4 ounces each) chopped green chilies, undrained
Fresh Cilantro Salsa (below)
Black Bean and Corn Salsa (below)

1. Heat oven to 350°. Grease rectangular baking dish, 13 × 9 × 2 inches, with shortening.

2. Beat eggs, sour cream, salt and pepper sauce in large bowl with wire whisk. Stir in cheeses and chilies. Pour into baking dish.

3. Bake uncovered about 45 minutes or until golden brown and set in center.

4. While casserole is baking, make Fresh Cilantro Salsa and Black Bean and Corn Salsa. Serve salsas with casserole.

Fresh Cilantro Salsa

1 cup salsa
2 tablespoons chopped fresh cilantro

Mix salsa and cilantro.

Black Bean and Corn Salsa

1 cup salsa
1/2 cup canned black beans, rinsed and drained
1/2 cup frozen (thawed) or canned (drained) whole
   kernel corn

Mix salsa, beans and corn.

1 Serving: Calories 390 (Calories from Fat 260); Fat 29g (Saturated 16g); Cholesterol 285mg; Sodium 770mg; Carbohydrate 12g (Dietary Fiber 3g); Protein 23g **% Daily Value:** Vitamin A 32%; Vitamin C 26%; Calcium 44%; Iron 10% **Diet Exchanges:** 3 High-Fat Meat, 2 Vegetable, 1 Fat

Lighter Chilies Rellenos Bake: For 4 grams of fat and 195 calories per serving, substitute 2 cups fat-free cholesterol-free egg product for the eggs and 2 cups cooked rice for the Monterey Jack cheese. Use reduced-fat sour cream and Cheddar cheese.

Southwestern Egg Bake

Prep: 8 min; Bake: 28 min ✱ *6 servings*

With this make-ahead recipe, brunch time will be extra relaxing. Prepare the stuffing mixture (step 2) and refrigerate up to a day in advance. Add the eggs just before baking.

2 cups corn bread stuffing crumbs
1 can (15 1/4 ounces) whole kernel corn, drained
1 can (4 ounces) chopped green chilies, undrained
1/2 cup sour cream
7 large eggs
1 cup shredded Monterey Jack cheese (4 ounces)
Salsa, if desired

1. Heat oven to 400°. Spray rectangular baking dish, 13 × 9 × 2 inches, with cooking spray.

2. Mix stuffing, corn, chilies, sour cream and 1 egg. Spread evenly in baking dish.

3. Make 6 indentations in stuffing mixture with back of spoon. Break 1 egg into each indentation. Pierce yolk of each egg with fork.

4. Bake uncovered 20 to 25 minutes or until egg whites and yolks are firm, not runny. Sprinkle cheese over stuffing mixture. Bake 2 to 3 minutes longer or until cheese is melted. Serve with salsa.

1 Serving: Calories 300 (Calories from Fat 115); Fat 13g (Saturated 6g); Cholesterol 265mg; Sodium 740mg; Carbohydrate 32g (Dietary Fiber 2g); Protein 16g **% Daily Value:** Vitamin A 16%; Vitamin C 16%; Calcium 18%; Iron 12% **Diet Exchanges:** 2 Starch, 1 1/2 High-Fat Meat

Santa Fe Brunch Bake

Prep: 15 min; Chill: 2 hr; Bake: 1 hr ✱ *6 to 8 servings*

If you use 1 cup frozen stir-fry bell peppers and onions (from a 16-ounce bag) in place of the onion and bell pepper, this dish will be ready in the blink of an eye.

4 cups frozen southern-style hash brown potatoes
1 cup frozen whole kernel corn
1 medium onion, chopped (1/2 cup)
1 small bell pepper, chopped (1/2 cup)
1 can (15 ounces) black beans, rinsed and drained
2 cups shredded Colby-Monterey Jack cheese
    (8 ounces)
2 tablespoons chopped fresh cilantro
8 large eggs
1 1/4 cups milk
1/2 teaspoon salt
1/4 teaspoon ground red pepper (cayenne)

1. Spray rectangular baking dish, 11 × 7 × 1 1/2 inches, with cooking spray.

2. Mix potatoes, corn, onion, bell pepper and beans in baking dish. Sprinkle with cheese and cilantro.

3. Beat remaining ingredients with hand beater or wire whisk until well blended; pour evenly over potato mixture. Cover and refrigerate at least 2 hours but no longer than 24 hours.

4. Heat oven to 350°. Bake uncovered 55 to 60 minutes or until knife inserted in center comes out clean. Let stand 5 minutes before cutting.

1 Serving: Calories 500 (Calories from Fat 190); Fat 21g (Saturated 11g); Cholesterol 325mg; Sodium 1,190mg; Carbohydrate 57g (Dietary Fiber 8g); Protein 29g **% Daily Value:** Vitamin A 22%; Vitamin C 20%; Calcium 38%; Iron 18% **Diet Exchanges:** 3 Starch, 3 Medium-Fat Meat, 2 Vegetable

Sausage and Egg Breakfast Pizza *Fast*

Prep: 6 min; Cook: 6 min; Bake: 12 min ✱ *4 servings*

Customize your pizzas by adding ingredients such as chopped tomato, green bell pepper or mushrooms before topping with the second cheese layer.

1 package (8 ounces) brown-and-serve pork sausage
    links, cut into 1/2-inch pieces
6 large eggs, beaten
2 packages (8 ounces each) ready-to-serve pizza crusts
    or 4 pita breads (6 inches in diameter)
1 1/2 cups shredded Cheddar cheese (6 ounces)

1. Heat oven to 400°. Spray 10-inch nonstick skillet with cooking spray; heat over medium heat.

2. Cook sausage in skillet about 3 minutes, stirring occasionally, until brown. Remove sausage from skillet; drain.

3. Pour eggs into skillet. As mixture begins to set at bottom and side, gently lift cooked portions with spatula so that thin, uncooked portion can flow to bottom. Do not stir. Cook 4 to 5 minutes or until eggs are thickened throughout but still moist.

4. Place pizza crusts on ungreased cookie sheets. Sprinkle with half of the cheese. Top with eggs and sausage. Sprinkle with remaining cheese. Bake 10 to 12 minutes or until cheese is melted.

1 Serving: Calories 680 (Calories from Fat 425); Fat 47g (Saturated 21g); Cholesterol 415mg; Sodium 1,180mg; Carbohydrate 30g (Dietary Fiber 1g); Protein 35g **% Daily Value:** Vitamin A 18%; Vitamin C 0%; Calcium 32%; Iron 16% **Diet Exchanges:** 2 Starch, 4 High-Fat Meat, 3 Fat

Deviled Eggs *Fast*

Prep: 15 min ✱ 12 servings

These versatile eggs are welcome as an appetizer, snack, and even for breakfast.

6 Hard-Cooked Eggs (page 201)
3 tablespoons mayonnaise, salad dressing or
   half-and-half
1/2 teaspoon ground mustard
1/8 teaspoon salt
1/8 teaspoon pepper

1. Peel eggs. Cut lengthwise in half. Slip out yolks and mash with fork.

2. Stir mayonnaise, mustard, salt and pepper into yolks. Fill whites with egg yolk mixture, heaping it lightly. Cover and refrigerate up to 24 hours.

1 Serving: Calories 55 (Calories from Fat 45); Fat 5g (Saturated 1g); Cholesterol 110mg; Sodium 75mg; Carbohydrate 0g (Dietary Fiber 0g); Protein 3g **% Daily Value:** Vitamin A 4%; Vitamin C 0%; Calcium 0%; Iron 2% **Diet Exchanges:** 1/2 High-Fat Meat

> **Lighter Deviled Eggs:** For 1 gram of fat and 25 calories per serving, mash only 6 yolk halves in step 1 (reserve remaining yolks for another purpose or discard). Use fat-free mayonnaise. Stir in 1/3 cup finely chopped zucchini.

DEVILED EGGS AND CHEESE: Add 1/2 cup finely shredded cheese (2 ounces) to egg yolk mixture.

DEVILED EGGS WITH OLIVES: Omit mustard. Mix 1/4 cup finely chopped ripe or pimiento-stuffed olives and 1/4 teaspoon curry powder into egg yolk mixture.

ZESTY DEVILED EGGS: Mix 1 to 2 tablespoons chopped fresh parsley and 1 teaspoon prepared horseradish into egg yolk mixture.

Classic Cheese Soufflé

Prep: 25 min; Bake: 1 hr ✱ 4 servings

Have your family seated and ready to eat when you take the soufflé out of the oven so they can see how wonderful it looks. It will lose its puffiness once it is on the table, but it still tastes delicious.

1/4 cup butter or stick margarine
1/4 cup all-purpose flour
1/2 teaspoon salt
1/4 teaspoon ground mustard
Dash of ground red pepper (cayenne)
1 cup milk
1 cup shredded Cheddar cheese (4 ounces)
3 large eggs, separated
1/4 teaspoon cream of tartar

1. Heat oven to 350°. Butter 1-quart soufflé dish or casserole. Make a 4-inch-wide band of triple-thickness aluminum foil 2 inches longer than circumference of dish. Butter one side of foil. Secure foil band, buttered side in, around top edge of dish.

2. Melt butter in 2-quart saucepan over medium heat. Stir in flour, salt, mustard and red pepper. Cook over medium heat, stirring constantly, until smooth and bubbly; remove from heat. Stir in milk. Heat to boiling, stirring constantly. Boil and stir 1 minute. Stir in cheese until melted; remove from heat.

3. Beat egg whites and cream of tartar in medium bowl with electric mixer on high speed until stiff but not dry; set aside. Beat egg yolks on high speed about 3 minutes or until very thick and lemon colored; stir into cheese mixture. Stir about one-fourth of the egg whites into cheese mixture. Fold cheese mixture into remaining egg whites. Carefully pour into soufflé dish.

4. Bake 50 to 60 minutes or until knife inserted halfway between center and edge comes out clean. Carefully remove foil band and quickly divide soufflé into sections with 2 forks. Serve immediately.

1 Serving: Calories 315 (Calories from Fat 215); Fat 24g (Saturated 10g); Cholesterol 195mg; Sodium 670mg; Carbohydrate 10g (Dietary Fiber 0g); Protein 15g **% Daily Value:** Vitamin A 26%; Vitamin C 0%; Calcium 24%; Iron 6% **Diet Exchanges:** 1 High-Fat Meat, 3 Fat, 1 Skim Milk

Cheese Fondue

Cheese Fondue

Prep: 10 min: Cook: 30 min ✱ *5 servings*

Fondue is French for "melted." Be patient when making cheese fondue, and allow each addition of cheese to completely melt into the wine before adding more. Serve with a tossed green salad to make a meal.

2 cups shredded natural Swiss cheese (8 ounces)
2 cups shredded Gruyère cheese (8 ounces)*
2 tablespoons all-purpose flour
1 clove garlic, cut in half
1 cup dry white wine or nonalcoholic white wine
1 tablespoon lemon juice
3 tablespoons kirsch, dry sherry, brandy or
    nonalcoholic white wine
1 loaf (1 pound) French bread, cut into 1-inch pieces

1. Place cheeses and flour in resealable plastic bag. Shake until cheese is coated with flour.

2. Rub garlic on bottom and side of fondue pot, heavy saucepan or skillet; discard garlic. Add wine. Heat over simmer setting or low heat just until bubbles rise to surface (do not boil). Stir in lemon juice.

3. Gradually add cheese mixture, about 1/2 cup at a time, stirring constantly with wooden spoon over low heat, until melted. Stir in kirsch.

4. Keep warm over simmer setting. If prepared in saucepan or skillet, pour into a fondue pot or heatproof serving bowl and keep warm over low heat. Fondue must be served over heat to maintain its smooth, creamy texture.

5. Spear bread with fondue forks; dip and swirl in fondue with stirring motion. If fondue becomes too thick, stir in 1/4 to 1/2 cup heated wine.

*2 cups shredded natural Swiss cheese (8 ounces) can be substituted for the Gruyère cheese to total 4 cups Swiss cheese.

1 Serving: Calories 575 (Calories from Fat 245); Fat 27g (Saturated 16g); Cholesterol 80mg; Sodium 760mg; Carbohydrate 53g (Dietary Fiber 3g); Protein 33g **% Daily Value:** Vitamin A 14%; Vitamin C 0%; Calcium 90%; Iron 18% **Diet Exchanges:** 3 Starch, 3 Medium-Fat Meat, 1 1/2 Fat, 1/2 Milk

Meats

Meats

Low-Fat = *3g or less, except main dishes with 6g or less*　　**Fast** = *Ready in 30 minutes or less*　　■ = *Bread Machine directions*　　● = *Slow Cooker directions*

Peach- and Mustard-Glazed Pork Tenderloin (page 255)　　　　Lighter = *1/3 fewer calories or 50% less fat*

Meat Basics

Chops and cutlets, sirloin, short loin and top loin, roasts and ribs, beef, veal, pork and lamb. Standing in front of the meat case at your local supermarket can be overwhelming. But we're here to help! With more than sixty cuts of beef available, knowing what you're looking for before you buy really helps. Not only will the information in this chapter help you be a savvy shopper, it'll help you cook any kind of meat like an expert.

Today's meat is leaner and lower in fat and calories than ever before. That's great, but it does mean you have to be mindful when you are preparing it so as not to overcook it.

How to buy meat and how to cook it are just a couple of the tips you'll pick up from this chapter. We've included the latest information and recommendations for storing, seasoning and handling, too.

Grades of Meat

Meat inspection and meat grading are two different steps. As required by law, meat is inspected for wholesomeness and cleanliness. Meat grading is an optional practice and is not required by law. Meats are graded for quality by the U.S. Department of Agriculture (USDA).

There are eight USDA grades; the ones you'll find in your supermarket are Choice and Select, the second and third highest grades. Prime, the highest grade, usually is reserved for restaurant use but can be found in some meat stores and in some supermarkets. Grading gives you an idea about the meat's tenderness, flavor and overall quality. You've probably seen the USDA's shield-shaped stamp of approval, especially on beef.

Meat Marbling

Ever examine a piece of meat and see the little specks and streaks of white fat through the lean? That's marbling, and it's an indicator of how juicy the meat will be when cooked. The more marbling, the more tender and juicy the meat, but also the more fat and calories per serving. The amount of marbling will affect how you cook a cut of meat and for how long. The timetables

throughout the chapter take the guesswork out of cooking all different kinds and cuts of meat.

Tips for Buying Fresh Meats

- Choose wrapped packages without any tears, holes or leaks. There should be little or no liquid in the bottom of the tray.

- Make sure the package is cold and feels firm. Avoid buying packages that are stacked too high in the meat case because they may not have been kept cold enough.

- Check the sell-by date. This shows the last day the product should be sold, but the meat will be fresh if cooked and eaten within 2 days of the date.

- Put packages of meat in plastic bags before putting them in your grocery cart so that any bacteria present in the juices doesn't drip on and contaminate other foods, especially those that won't be cooked.

- Don't buy or use any meat that has turned gray, has an off odor or feels slippery.

- Put meat in the refrigerator as soon as you get home from shopping. If you're running a lot of errands, save shopping until last, then scoot right home if you've got fresh or frozen meat in your grocery bags.

Reading a Meat Label

A lot of information is squeezed onto the little label on a package of meat, information that will help you make the right selection for your recipe and even help you know how the meat should be cooked. Label information is standardized, so no matter what kind of meat you're buying or where you live, everyone has the same information.

- The kind of meat: beef, pork, veal, lamb.

- The primal or wholesale cut (where it comes from on the animal): chuck, rib, loin, etc.

- The retail cut (where it comes from on the primal cut): blade roast, loin chops, etc.

- The weight, the price per pound, the total price and sell-by date.

Serving Size

When buying meats, you'll want to consider the cost per serving. The number of servings per pound varies depending on the type of meat when it's cooked and the amount of bone and fat waste removed. The average serving is 2 1/2 to 3 1/2 ounces of cooked meat. You may want to plan on more meat per serving for heartier appetites. Below is a general guide to use for determining the number of servings you'll get per pound of meat. To figure cost per serving, divide the price per pound of meat by the number of servings per pound.

SERVINGS PER POUND

Type of Meat	Servings per Pound
Boneless cuts (ground, boneless chops, loin, tenderloin)	3 to 4
Bone-in cuts (rib roasts, pot roasts, country-style ribs)	2 to 3
Very bony cuts (back ribs, spareribs, short ribs, shanks)	1 to 1 1/2

Storing and Handling Meat

Tips for Storing Meat

Follow these tips and timetable to keep meat fresh before cooking:

- If meat is purchased at the meat counter, it will be wrapped in butcher paper. Once you bring it home, unwrap it and repackage tightly in moisture- and vapor-resistant materials such as plastic wrap, aluminum foil or plastic freezer bags.
- You don't need to rewrap meat packaged in clear plastic wrap on a plastic or Styrofoam tray, but you may want to put it a plastic bag in case the original packaging leaks.
- Store meat immediately in the meat compartment or coldest part of your refrigerator, or freeze it as soon as possible. Ground meat is more perishable than other cuts, so use it within 2 days.
- Cook or freeze meat within 2 days of the sell-by date.

TIMETABLE FOR STORING MEATS

Cut of Meat	Refrigerator (36° to 40°)	Freezer (0° or colder)
Ground meats	1 to 2 days	3 to 4 months
Meat cuts		
Beef	3 to 4 days	6 to 12 months
Veal	1 to 2 days	6 to 9 months
Pork	2 to 3 days	6 months
Lamb	3 to 5 days	6 to 9 months
Variety meats (liver, heart, tongue, etc.)	1 to 2 days	3 to 4 months
Leftover cooked meats	3 to 4 days	2 to 3 months

Handling Raw Meat

Cooking meat to the recommended doneness destroys any bacteria present in the meat. To avoid foodborne illnesses and cross-contamination when preparing raw meat for cooking, follow these tips and see also Food Safety Basics, page 531:

- Wash your hands in hot, soapy water before and after handling meat.
- Wash all surfaces and utensils in hot, soapy water after contact with raw meat.
- Use disposable paper towels when working with raw meat or cleaning up afterward. If you use a dishcloth, throw it in the washer with hot water and detergent before using again.
- Never serve cooked meat on the unwashed platter that was used to carry it to the grill. The same goes for using unwashed knives and cutting boards for cooked meats that were first used with raw meats.
- Keep hot foods hot (about 140°) and cold foods cold (below 40°). Refrigerate leftovers as soon as possible after cooking.
- Cook meat in one step, so bacteria don't get a head start in growing. If you're "combination" cooking, meaning first partially cooking meat in the microwave then using a grill to finish, be sure the grill is ready so the partially cooked meat can be grilled immediately.

Cutting Raw Meat

Need to cut raw meat into cubes, thin slices or strips? Here's a handy tip: Put the meat in the freezer first! Leave the meat in the freezer until it's firm but not frozen, 30 to 60 minutes, depending on the size of the piece. It's a snap to slice, even paper thin!

Thawing Meat

Thaw meat slowly in the refrigerator or quickly in the microwave following the manufacturer's directions. Don't thaw meat on the countertop because bacteria thrive at room temperature.

If the meat was frozen when you bought it or you froze it right after you brought it home, keep the thawed meat in the refrigerator for the number of days listed in the Timetable for Storing Meats, page 220. If the meat was refrigerated several days *before* freezing, use it the same day you thaw it.

To thaw meat in the refrigerator, placed the wrapped meat in a dish, baking pan with sides or plastic bag to catch any drips during thawing. Thaw according to the following chart:

REFRIGERATOR THAWING METHOD

Amount of Frozen Meat	Thawing Time in Refrigerator
Large roast (4 pounds or larger)	4 to 7 hours per pound
Small roast (under 4 pounds)	3 to 5 hours per pound
Steak or chops (1 inch thick)	12 to 14 hours total
Ground beef (1 pound)	12 to 24 hours total

Cooking Meat

Where the meat comes from on an animal will determine the methods you use to cook it. With the right cooking method, time and temperature, every cut of meat can be tender and flavorful.

- **Tender cuts** come from muscles that aren't exercised much because of their location or because the animal is very young. The rib and loin are two tender cuts. Use dry cooking methods—those with no added liquid—such as roasting, broiling, panbroiling, grilling, panfrying, stir-frying and deep-frying.

- **Less-tender cuts** come from muscles that are exercised more, so they're tougher but also more flavorful. The shoulder, rump and cuts from the legs are less-tender cuts. Use moist heat methods—those using steam or added liquid—such as braising, slow-cookers and stewing. Long, slow, moist cooking will both tenderize the meat and develop the flavor.

Most tender cuts of meat and some less-tender cuts such as top sirloin and some round steaks, can be cooked using either a dry or moist method, depending on their quality and the cooking time and temp. You'll find the cooking methods we recommend for meat cuts in the charts on pages 228, 243, 249 and 263.

Determining Doneness

Different types or cuts of meat must be cooked to certain degrees of doneness in order to kill bacteria in the meat. No meat should be cooked to less than medium-rare; veal and pork to no less than medium. You can always cook meat so it's *more* done, but it will be chewier and less juicy. Keep in mind that the cooking times are *approximate*. Lots of factors can affect them: your oven, the color of the pan, the part of the country you live in and the individual animal. So, let the internal temperature be your guide for doneness and the recipe's cooking time your guide for when to start checking if it is done.

IS IT DONE YET?

Cooking meat to just the right doneness not only ensures that it will taste great but that it will be safe to eat, too. For larger pieces of meat such as roasts and ground meat mixtures such as burgers and meat loaf, it's best to use a meat thermometer to tell if meat is done. For smaller pieces or cuts, cut a small slit in the center of boneless cuts or in the center near the bone of bone-in cuts and check the color. The Recommended Meat Doneness Chart, page 222, helps you in determining when meat is done. (See example for Steak Doneness on page 334).

RECOMMENDED MEAT DONENESS

Meat	Thermometer Reading After Cooking	Color of Cooked Meat When Small Cut Is Made
Beef		
Roasts	140° (for medium-rare)*	Does not apply
	155° (for medium)*	Does not apply
Other Beef Cuts	145° (medium-rare)	Very pink in center and slightly brown toward exterior
	160° (medium)	Light pink in center and brown toward exterior
Ground Beef	170° (well)	No longer pink in center and juices run clear
Loaves	160° (medium)	Does not apply
Patties	160° (medium)	No longer pink in center and juices run clear
Veal		
Roasts	155° (for medium)*	Does not apply
Other Veal Cuts	160° (medium)	Slightly pink in center
Pork		
Roasts	155° (for medium)*	Does not apply
	165° (for well)*	Does not apply
Other Pork Cuts	160° (medium)	Slightly pink in center
	170° (well)	No longer pink in center
Ground Pork	170° (well)	No longer pink in center
Ham, fully cooked	135°*	Heated through
Lamb		
Roasts	140° (for medium-rare)*	Does not apply
	155° (for medium)*	Does not apply
Other Lamb Cuts	145° (medium-rare)	Pink in center
	160° (medium)	Light pink in center

*Roasts and hams will continue to cook after being removed from oven, so the temperature will rise about 5°. Pork should reach a final temperature (after standing) at 160°. Also see Roasting Beef, page 226; Roasting Veal, page 243; Roasting Pork, page 248; Roasting Ham, page 252; or Roasting Lamb, page 263.

Microwaving Meats

Ground meat, bacon, hot dogs and sausages cook great in the microwave. Other meats, though, aren't so microwave-friendly because they tend to become tough. Here are some quick microwaving tips:

- Use microwavable dishes.
- Microwave on High power.
- For most types of meat, stir, rearrange or rotate meat after about halfway through the cooking time.

TIMETABLE FOR MICROWAVING MEATS

Type of Meat	Amount	Power Level	Time	Doneness
Ground Meat Directions: Place ground meat in 1-quart microwavable dish; place meatballs or patties on microwavable rack or in shallow microwavable dish. Cover with plastic wrap, folding one edge or corner back 1/4 inch to vent steam, or cover with waxed paper.				
Ground				
crumbled	1 pound	High (100%)	3 1/2 to 4 1/2 minutes, stirring once	Until brown
uncooked, meatballs (24)	1 pound	Medium-High (70%)	6 to 8 minutes, rearranging after 3 minutes	Until no longer pink in center and juice is clear
uncooked, patties (3/4 inch thick)	1 pound	Medium-High (70%)	6 to 8 minutes, rearranging after 3 minutes	Until no longer pink in center and juice is clear
Bacon Directions: Place bacon slices on microwavable plate or microwavable rack lined with paper towels. Place paper towels between layers; cover with paper towels.				
Bacon	1 slice	High (100%)	30 to 90 seconds	Until crisp
	2 slices	High (100%)	1 to 2 minutes	Until crisp
	4 slices	High (100%)	2 to 3 minutes	Until crisp
	6 slices	High (100%)	3 to 5 minutes	Until crisp
	8 slices	High (100%)	4 to 6 minutes	Until crisp
Hot Dog and Sausages (Precooked) Directions: Place hot dogs or sausages on microwavable plate lined with paper towel. Pierce several times with fork. Cover with paper towel or napkin.				
Hot Dogs (10 per pound)	1	High (100%)	20 to 30 seconds	Let stand 3 minutes
	2	High (100%)	40 to 50 seconds	Let stand 3 minutes
	3	High (100%)	50 to 60 seconds	Let stand 3 minutes
	4	High (100%)	1 minute 10 seconds to 1 minute 30 seconds	Let stand 3 minutes
Sausages (cooked) bratwurst, Italian (6 per pound)	2	High (100%)	1 minute 10 seconds to 1 minute 30 seconds	Let stand 3 minutes
	4	High (100%)	2 1/2 to 3 minutes, rearranging once	Let stand 3 minutes

continues

TIMETABLE FOR MICROWAVING MEATS (cont.)

Type of Meat	Amount	Power Level	Time	Doneness
Sausages (Uncooked) Directions: Place sausages in microwavable dish; add 1/2 cup water. Cover with vented plastic wrap or waxed paper.				
Sausages (uncooked) bratwurst, Polish (6 per pound)	1	High (100%)	3 to 4 minutes	Until no longer pink in center (180° on microwavable meat thermometer)
	2	High (100%)	4 to 6 minutes	Until no longer pink in center (180° on microwavable meat thermometer)
	4	High (100%)	Increase water to 1 cup; 6 to 8 minutes, rearranging once	Until no longer pink in center (180° on microwavable meat thermometer)
Ham Slice Directions: Place ham slice in microwavable dish. Cover with vented plastic wrap.				
Ham Slice (fully cooked, smoked)	1 pound (1/4 to 1/2 inch thick)	Medium (50%)	6 to 8 minutes	Until hot

USING A THERMOMETER

A thermometer designed for meat is the best way to tell if meat is done. Use it along with the temperatures in the Recommended Meat Doneness chart, page 222. For an accurate reading, insert the thermometer in the thickest part of the meat and not touching bone or fat. Several types of thermometers are available. These are the most common:

- **Meat thermometer:** Also called a meat and poultry thermometer or roast-yeast thermometer, it's designed to be inserted into meat or poultry and left in during cooking. It usually has both a temperature gauge and markings indicating doneness. We recommend reading the gauge.

- **Instant-read thermometer.** Also called an instant or rapid-response thermometer, it's designed to take an almost immediate temperature reading of the food (within 1 minute of insertion.) Because it's made with plastic, this type can't be left in the oven. It's great for taking the temp of grilled, broiled and panfried meats, especially burgers and steaks.

Seasoning Meats

What are the ways to season meat? There are many answers to that question because of all of the wonderful options. Start with a grind of black pepper, then go from there. For more seasoning ideas, see Chapter 16, Sauces, Seasonings & Accompaniments, beginning on page 435.

So what do you do with these seasonings? You can sprinkle them on, brush them on, rub them on or let them soak into the meat.

- To help sprinkled seasonings stick, spritz the meat with a bit of cooking spray first.

- Brush sauces on before, during and after cooking.

- A rub is a blend of seasonings such as herbs, spices, crushed garlic or mustard. You literally rub the mixture onto the meat before cooking.

- A marinade is a blend of ingredients that not only flavor but also tenderize meat. For more about marinades, see Tips for Marinades and Marinating, page 453.

To Salt or Not to Salt

The rule is to salt most cuts of meat *after* cooking to keep their juiciness—except for roasts (rules are meant to be broken!). But salting a roast actually adds flavor as it cooks without drying it out.

Beef Basics

Selecting Beef

Lean, fresh beef should be bright red in color; ground beef should be cherry red. A darker, purplish red is typical for beef that's vacuum packaged, as well as for the inside of ground beef. Once it's exposed to air, beef will turn its familiar bright red. After purchasing beef, use it within the time recommended in the timetable on page 220.

Ground beef is made from the primal cuts of beef: chuck, round and sirloin. Leanness varies from 70% to more than 90%. We tested our recipes using ground beef that's 80% lean. On average, 1 pound of ground beef makes 12 ounces of cooked beef.

Cooking Beef

Cook beef—except for ground beef—to medium-rare or medium doneness for the best flavor and texture and to kill any bacteria present in the meat. Ground beef should be cooked thoroughly. Also see Recommended Meat Doneness, page 222.

Cooking Ground Beef

Ground beef is handled frequently and touches many surfaces during grinding, making it easy prey for bacteria. So it's important to cook it thoroughly. Meat loaf and all other ground meats must reach 160° in the center of the thickest portion to be safe to eat.

> Note: Due to the natural nitrate content of certain ingredients often used in meat loaves, such as onions, celery and bell peppers, meat loaves may remain pink even though beef is cooked to 160°. Always check meat loaf with a thermometer to make sure it has reached 160° in the center of the thickest portion.

Unlike regular ground beef, which has enough fat in it to keep it from sticking during cooking, very lean ground beef needs a little help. To keep it from sticking, spritz the skillet with a little cooking spray. Lean ground beef loses moisture during cooking, so it's somewhat drier than ground beef with a higher percentage of fat.

Do not overmix ground beef when making burgers, meatballs or meat loaves because the meat can become compact and tough, so use a gentle touch.

Roasting Beef

Beef is roasted in the oven with literally no water, so start with a tender cut of meat such as boneless rump roast or a rib roast. Check the Timetable for Roasting Beef (page 226) to determine the right oven temperatures and times for each cut. Follow these steps for roasted beef that's well browned on the outside and moist and tender inside:

1. Choose one of the beef cuts from the Timetable for Roasting Beef.

2. Place beef—right from the refrigerator—fat side up, on a rack in a shallow roasting pan. (For easy cleanup, line the pan with aluminum foil first.) As the fat melts, it bastes the beef, making other basting during cooking unnecessary.

3. If you like, season the beef with herbs, spices or other seasonings before, during or after cooking. Sprinkling the roast with salt *before* cooking adds flavor.

4. Insert a meat thermometer so the tip is centered in the thickest part of the roast and not resting in fat or touching bone. Don't cover the roast or add water.

5. Using the chart as a guide, roast at the recommended oven temp until the meat thermometer registers the "Meat Thermometer Reading (after roasting)" temperature. The roast will continue to cook after you take it out of the oven.

6. Take the roast out of the oven and cover it loosely with a foil tent. Let stand for 15 to 20 minutes or until it reaches the "Final Meat Thermometer Reading (after standing)" temperature. After standing, the roast also will be easier to carve. Avoid covering the roast tightly because doing so will create steam, which will soften the surface of the beef.

TIMETABLE FOR ROASTING BEEF

Beef Cut	Approximate Weight (pounds)	Oven Temperature	Meat Thermometer Reading (after roasting)	Final Meat Thermometer Reading (after standing)	Approximate Cooking Time (minutes per pound)**
Eye Round	2 to 3	325°	140°	145° (medium-rare)	20 to 22
Rib* (small end)	4 to 6	325°	140°	145° (medium-rare)	25 to 30
			155°	160° (medium)	30 to 34
	6 to 8	325°	140°	145° (medium-rare)	23 to 26
			155°	160° (medium)	27 to 32
Rib Eye (small end)	4 to 6	350°	140°	145° (medium-rare)	18 to 20
			155°	160° (medium)	20 to 22
Round Tip Sirloin Tip (high quality)	2 1/2 to 4	325°	140°	145° (medium-rare)	30 to 35
			155°	160° (medium)	35 to 40
	4 to 6	325°	140°	145° (medium-rare)	25 to 30
			155°	160° (medium)	30 to 35
	8 to 10	325°	140°	145° (medium-rare)	18 to 22
			155°	160° (medium)	23 to 25
Tenderloin (whole)	4 to 6	425°	140°	145° (medium-rare)	45 to 60 (total time)
(half)	2 to 3	425°	140°	145° (medium-rare)	35 to 45 (total time)
Tri-Tip (bottom sirloin)	1 1/2 to 2	425°	140°	145° (medium-rare)	30 to 40

*Ribs that measure 6 to 7 inches from chine bone to tip of rib.
**Smaller roasts require more minutes per pound than larger roasts.

How to Carve a Standing Rib Roast

Place roast, large side down, on carving board. Remove slice from the large end, so roast will stand firmly. Insert mea fork below top rib. Slice from outside of roast toward rib side.

After making several slices, cut along inner side of rib bone with tip of knife. As each slice is released, slide knife under and lift to plate.

Broiling or Grilling Beef

Broiling and grilling are great ways to cook tender cuts of beef, such as steaks or ground beef patties. Less-tender cuts broil and grill best if they're marinated first (see Tips for Marinades and Marinating, page 453). The tips below use direct heat. For more information about using your grill, check out the instruction booklet that came with your grill or the Grilling Basics, page 331. Check the Timetable for Broiling or Grilling Beef, below, to determine the right oven temperatures and times for each cut.

1. Choose a cut good for broiling or grilling from Timetable for Broiling or Grilling Beef (below). If you like, marinate the beef first.

2. **To Broil:** Set oven to broil. Check your oven manual for whether the oven door should be open or closed during broiling.

   To Grill: Heat the coals or gas grill to medium; spread the coals to a single layer.

3. Remove any excess fat before cooking to avoid flare-ups.

4. **To Broil:** Place beef on the rack in the broiler pan. (For easy cleanup, line the pan with aluminum foil first.) Position the pan so the top of the beef is the distance from the heat recommended in the chart.

   To Grill: Place beef on the grill the distance from the heat recommended in the chart.

TIMETABLE FOR BROILING OR GRILLING BEEF

Beef Cut	Approximate Thickness or Weight	Inches from Heat	Approximate Total Broiling Time (minutes)		Approximate Total Grilling Time (minutes)	
			145° (medium-rare)	160° (medium)	145° (medium-rare)	160° (medium)
Rib and Rib Eye Steaks	3/4 to 1 inch	2 to 4	8	15	7	12
Top Loin Steak (boneless)	3/4 to 1 inch	2 to 4	8	17	7	12
Porterhouse and T-Bone Steaks	1 inch	3 to 4	10	15	10	14
Sirloin Steak (boneless)	3/4 to 1 inch	2 to 4	10	21	12	16
Sirloin Cubes (kabobs)	1 to 1 1/4 inches	3 to 4	9	12	8	11
Tenderloin Steak	1 inch	2 to 3	10	15	11	13
Tri-Tip Roast* (bottom sirloin)	1 1/2 to 2 pounds	4 to 5	25	30	30	35
Chuck Shoulder Steak** (boneless)	1 inch	3 to 4	14	18	14	20
Eye Round Steak	1 inch	2 to 3	9	11	9	12
Top Round Steak**	1 inch	3 to 4	15	18	12	14
Flank Steak**	1 to 1 1/2 pounds	2 to 3	12	14	12	15
Ground Beef Patties	1/2 inch	3 to 4	†	10	†	7 to 9
	3/4 inch	3 to 4	†	13	†	10 to 11

Cover roast with tent of aluminum foil and let stand 15 to 20 minutes before carving. Temperature will continue to rise about 5° and roast will be easier to carve as juices set up.
**Marinate beef 6 to 8 hours to tenderize.*
† *Not recommended*

5. Broil or grill the beef for about half the recommended time or until it's brown on one side.

6. Turn the beef, and continue broiling or grilling until it's done to your liking. To see if it's done, cut a small slit in the center of boneless cuts or in the center near the bone of bone-in cuts. Medium-rare is very pink in the center; medium is light pink in the center; and well-done is brown all the way through. Burgers must be cooked until a thermometer inserted in the center of the thickest portion reads 160°. If you like, season the beef after it's done.

Panbroiling Beef

Panbroiling is a quick, fat-conscious way to cook beef because drippings are poured off as they form. In other words, the meat doesn't stew in its own juices or need additional fat to cook. Panbroiling is a great way to cook steaks and burgers. Check the Timetable for Panbroiling Beef, below, to determine the right oven temperatures and times for each cut.

1. Choose one of the cuts for panbroiling from the Timetable for Panbroiling Beef.

2. Use a heavy nonstick skillet, or coat a regular skillet with a film of vegetable oil or cooking spray. Heat the skillet for 5 minutes over medium heat.

3. Place the beef in the skillet; don't cover and don't add oil or water.

4. Cook for the time recommended in the chart, turning once. Occasionally turn cuts that are 1-inch thick. Drain excess drippings from the skillet as they form. To see if the beef is done, cut a small slit in the center of boneless cuts or in the center near the bone of bone-in cuts. Medium-rare is very pink in the center; medium is light pink in the center; and well-done is brown all the way through. Burgers must be cooked until a thermometer inserted in the center of the thickest portion reads 160°. If you like, season the meat after it's done.

TIMETABLE FOR PANBROILING BEEF

Beef Cut	Approximate Thickness (inches)	Stove-top Temperature	Approximate Total Cooking Time (minutes) 145° to 160° (medium-rare to medium)
Rib Eye Steak	1/2	Medium-High	3 to 5
Top Loin Steak	1/4	Medium-High	2 to 3
Eye Round Steak	1	Medium	8 to 10
Tenderloin	3/4 to 1	Medium	6 to 9
Round Tip	1/8 to 1/4	Medium-High	1
Sirloin (boneless)	3/4 to 1	Medium-Low to Medium	10 to 12
Top Round	1	Medium	13 to 16
Ground Beef Patties	1/2	Medium	7 to 8*

*USDA recommends cooking ground beef to 160°.

Beef

RETAIL CUTS

Where They Come From
How To Cook Them

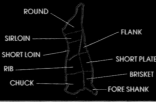

ROUND

SIRLOIN

SHORT LOIN

RIB

CHUCK

FLANK

SHORT PLATE

BRISKET

FORE SHANK

Round Steak
Braise, Panfry

Top Round Roast
Roast

Top Round Steak
Broil, Panbroil, Panfry

Boneless Rump Roast
Roast, Braise

Bottom Round Roast
Braise, Roast

Tip Roast, Cap Off
Roast, Braise

Eye Round Roast
Braise, Roast

Tip Steak
Broil, Panbroil, Panfry

ROUND

Sirloin Steak, Flat Bone
Broil, Panbroil, Panfry

Sirloin Steak, Round Bone
Broil, Panbroil, Panfry

Top Sirloin Steak
Broil, Panbroil Panfry

SIRLOIN

Shank Cross Cut
Braise, Cook in Liquid

Brisket, Whole
Braise, Cook in Liquid

Corned Brisket, Point Half
Braise, Cook in Liquid

Brisket, Flat Half
Braise

FORESHANK & BRISKET

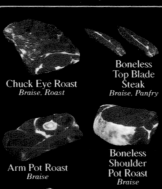

Chuck Eye Roast
Braise, Roast

Boneless Top Blade Steak
Braise, Panfry

Arm Pot Roast
Braise

Boneless Shoulder Pot Roast
Braise

Cross Rib Pot Roast
Braise

Mock Tender
Braise

Under Blade Pot Roast
Braise, Roast

Blade Roast
Braise

Short Ribs
Braise, Cook in Liquid

7-Bone Pot Roast
Braise

Flanken-Style Ribs
Braise, Cook in Liquid

CHUCK

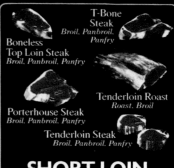

Boneless Top Loin Steak
Broil, Panbroil, Panfry

T-Bone Steak
Broil, Panbroil, Panfry

Porterhouse Steak
Broil, Panbroil, Panfry

Tenderloin Roast
Roast, Broil

Tenderloin Steak
Broil, Panbroil, Panfry

SHORT LOIN

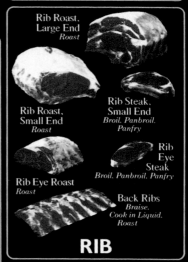

Rib Roast, Large End
Roast

Rib Roast, Small End
Roast

Rib Steak, Small End
Broil, Panbroil, Panfry

Rib Eye Roast
Roast

Rib Eye Steak
Broil, Panbroil, Panfry

Back Ribs
Braise, Cook in Liquid, Roast

RIB

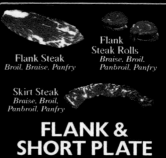

Flank Steak
Broil, Braise, Panfry

Flank Steak Rolls
Braise, Broil, Panbroil, Panfry

Skirt Steak
Braise, Broil, Panbroil, Panfry

FLANK & SHORT PLATE

Ground Beef
Broil, Panfry, Panbroil, Roast (Bake)

Cubed Steak
Panfry, Braise

Beef for Stew
Braise, Cook in Liquid

Cubes for Kabobs
Broil, Braise

OTHER CUTS

Roast Beef *Low-Fat*

Prep: 5 min; Roast: 2 hr ✱ 6 servings

A sharp knife with a straight edge or an electric knife works best to cut even slices of roast beef. To keep beef in place while cutting, hold it with a two-tined meat fork.

Beef roast*
Oven-Browned Potatoes or Yorkshire Pudding (below),
    if desired
Pan Gravy (page 442), if desired

1. Pick the type of beef roast you want to make from those listed in Timetable for Roasting Beef on page 226.

2. Follow steps for Roasting Beef on page 225.

3. Make Oven-Browned Potatoes and Pan Gravy, or spoon hot beef drippings over carved beef.

If making Yorkshire Pudding, use a rib roast or rib eye roast because they will provide enough of the fat drippings you will need to make the recipe.

1 Serving: Calories 110 (Calories from Fat 25); Fat 3g (Saturated 1g); Cholesterol 55mg; Sodium 150mg; Carbohydrate 0g (Dietary Fiber 0g); Protein 20g **% Daily Value:** Vitamin A 0%; Vitamin C 0%; Calcium 0%; Iron 10% **Diet Exchanges:** 3 Very Lean Meat

Oven-Browned Potatoes

About 1 1/2 hours before beef roast is done, prepare and boil 6 medium potatoes as directed on page 503. For decorative potatoes, make crosswise cuts almost through whole potatoes to make thin slices and decrease boiling time to 10 minutes. Place potatoes in beef drippings in pan, turning each potato to coat completely; or brush potatoes with melted butter or margarine and place on rack with beef. Continue cooking about 1 1/4 hours, turning potatoes once, until golden brown. Sprinkle with salt and pepper if desired.

Yorkshire Pudding

1 cup all-purpose flour
1 cup milk
1/2 teaspoon salt
2 large eggs
Melted shortening, if necessary

Thirty minutes before rib roast or rib eye roast is done, mix all ingredients except shortening with hand beater just until smooth. Heat square pan, 9 × 9 × 2 inches, in oven. Remove beef from oven. Spoon off drippings and add enough melted shortening to drippings, if necessary, to measure 2 tablespoons.

Increase oven temperature to 425°. Return beef to oven. Place hot drippings in heated square pan. Pour batter into pan. Bake beef and pudding 20 minutes. Remove beef from oven. Bake pudding 5 to 10 minutes longer or until deep golden brown (pudding will puff during baking but will deflate shortly after being removed from oven). Cut pudding into squares; serve with beef.

New England Pot Roast

Prep: 30 min; Cook: 3 hr 30 min ✱ 8 servings

This pot roast has a secret ingredient—horseradish! No, the roast doesn't taste hot or spicy or like horseradish. During the cooking, the horseradish just blends right in and mellows, leaving behind an utterly delicious flavor you can't quite put your finger on.

4-pound beef arm, blade or cross rib pot roast*
1 to 2 teaspoons salt
1 teaspoon pepper
1 jar (8 ounces) prepared horseradish
1 cup water
8 small potatoes, cut in half
8 medium carrots, cut into fourths
8 small onions
Pot Roast Gravy (right)

1. Cook beef in 4-quart Dutch oven over medium heat until brown on all sides; reduce heat to low.

2. Sprinkle beef with salt and pepper. Spread horseradish over all sides of beef. Add water to Dutch oven. Heat to boiling; reduce heat. Cover and simmer 2 hours 30 minutes.

3. Add potatoes, carrots and onions to Dutch oven. Cover and simmer about 1 hour or until beef and vegetables are tender.

4. Remove beef and vegetables to warm platter; keep warm. Make Pot Roast Gravy. Serve gravy with beef and vegetables.

Pot Roast Gravy

1/2 cup cold water
1/4 cup all-purpose flour

Skim excess fat from broth in Dutch oven. Add enough water to broth to measure 2 cups. Shake 1/2 cup cold water and the flour in tightly covered container; gradually stir into broth. Heat to boiling, stirring constantly. Boil and stir 1 minute.

*3-pound beef bottom round, rolled rump, tip or chuck eye roast can be substituted; decrease salt to 3/4 teaspoon.

Place roast on carving board or platter. With meat fork in meat to hold meat in place, cut between muscles and around bones. Remove one section of meat at a time. Turn section so meat grain runs parallel to carving board. Cut meat across grain into 1/4-inch slices.

1 Serving: Calories 385 (Calories from Fat 100); Fat 11g (Saturated 4g); Cholesterol 85mg; Sodium 690mg; Carbohydrate 40g (Dietary Fiber 6g); Protein 37g **% Daily Value:** Vitamin A 94%; Vitamin C 22%; Calcium 6%; Iron 26% **Diet Exchanges:** 2 Starch, 4 Very Lean Meat, 2 Vegetable, 1 Fat

Slow Cooker Directions: Cook beef in 12-inch skillet over medium heat until brown on all sides. Place potatoes, carrots and onions in 4- to 6-quart slow cooker. Place beef on vegetables. Mix horseradish, salt and pepper; spread evenly over beef. Pour water into slow cooker. Cover and cook on low heat setting 8 to 10 hours or until beef and vegetables are tender.

BARBECUE POT ROAST: Decrease pepper to 1/2 teaspoon. Omit horseradish and water. Prepare Smoky Barbecue Sauce (page 337). After browning beef in step 1, pour Smoky Barbecue Sauce over beef. Omit Pot Roast Gravy. Skim fat from sauce after removing beef and vegetables in step 4. Spoon sauce over beef and vegetables or serve sauce with beef and vegetables.

CREAM GRAVY POT ROAST: For roast—substitute 1 can (10 1/2 ounces) condensed beef broth for the 1 cup water. For gravy—add enough half-and-half or milk, instead of water, to the broth (from the roast) to measure 2 cups. Substitute 1/2 cup half-and-half or milk for the water.

GARLIC-HERB POT ROAST: Decrease pepper to 1/2 teaspoon. Omit horseradish. After browning beef in step 1, sprinkle with 1 tablespoon chopped fresh or 1 teaspoon dried marjoram leaves, 1 tablespoon chopped fresh or 1 teaspoon dried thyme leaves, 2 teaspoons chopped fresh or 1/2 teaspoon dried oregano leaves and 4 cloves garlic, crushed. Substitute 1 can (10 1/2 ounces) condensed beef broth for the 1 cup water.

Corned Beef and Cabbage

Prep: 20 min; Cook: 2 hr 15 min ✱ 6 servings

Corned beef is beef brisket that has been cured in brine to give a distinct flavor; it should not be confused with the plain cut of meat called *brisket*. Corned beef is sold in a sealed plastic bag with the brine. Because salt is added during the curing process, there's no need to add salt while cooking.

2-pound well-trimmed beef corned brisket, undrained
1 medium onion, cut into 6 wedges
1 clove garlic, finely chopped
1 small head cabbage, cut into 6 wedges

1. Place beef in 4-quart Dutch oven. Add enough cold water just to cover beef. Add onion and garlic.

2. Heat to boiling; reduce heat. Cover and simmer about 2 hours or until beef is tender.

3. Remove beef to warm platter; keep warm. Skim fat from broth.

4. Add cabbage to broth. Heat to boiling; reduce heat. Simmer uncovered about 15 minutes or until cabbage is tender. Serve cabbage with beef.

1 Serving: Calories 385 (Calories from Fat 100); Fat 11g (Saturated 4g); Cholesterol 85mg; Sodium 690mg; Carbohydrate 40g (Dietary Fiber 6g); Protein 37g **% Daily Value:** Vitamin A 94%; Vitamin C 22%; Calcium 6%; Iron 26% **Diet Exchanges:** 2 Starch, 4 Very Lean Meat, 2 Vegetable, 1 Fat

Slow Cooker Directions: Place beef in 3 1/2- to 6-quart slow cooker. Add enough cold water just to cover beef. Add onion and garlic. Top with cabbage. Cover and cook on low heat setting 7 to 8 hours or until beef and vegetables are tender.

NEW ENGLAND BOILED DINNER: Omit 1 medium onion. Decrease simmer time of beef in step 2 to 1 hour 40 minutes. Skim fat from broth. Add 6 small onions, 6 medium carrots, 3 medium potatoes, cut in half, and, if desired, 3 turnips, cut into cubes, to broth. Cover and simmer 20 minutes. Remove beef to warm platter; keep warm. Add cabbage to broth. Heat to boiling; reduce heat. Simmer uncovered about 15 minutes or until vegetables are tender.

Roasted Beef Tenderloin

Prep: 15 min; Bake: 50 min; Stand: 15 min ✱ 6 servings

1 beef tenderloin (about 2 1/2 pounds)
1 tablespoon olive or vegetable oil
1/2 teaspoon coarsely ground pepper
1/2 teaspoon dried marjoram leaves
1/4 teaspoon coarse kosher salt, coarse sea salt or regular salt

1. Heat oven to 425°.

2. Turn small end of beef under about 6 inches. Tie turned-under portion of beef with string at about 1 1/2-inch intervals. Place in shallow roasting pan. Brush with oil. Sprinkle with pepper, marjoram and salt. Insert meat thermometer so tip is in thickest part of beef.

3. Bake uncovered 40 to 50 minutes or until thermometer reads at least 140°. Cover beef with aluminum foil and let stand until thermometer reads 145°. (Temperature will continue to rise about 5°, and beef will be easier to carve.) Remove string from beef before carving.

1 Serving: Calories 230 (Calories from Fat 110); Fat 12g (Saturated 4g); Cholesterol 80mg; Sodium 170mg; Carbohydrate 0g (Dietary Fiber 0g); Protein 30g **% Daily Value:** Vitamin A 0%; Vitamin C 0%; Calcium %;0 Iron 14% **Diet Exchanges:** 4 Lean Meat

Swiss Steak

Prep: 15 min; Cook: 1 hr 50 min ✱ 6 servings

1 1/2-pound beef boneless round, tip or chuck steak, about 3/4 inch thick
3 tablespoons all-purpose flour
1 teaspoon ground mustard
1/2 teaspoon salt
2 tablespoons vegetable oil
1 can (14 1/2 ounces) whole tomatoes, undrained
2 cloves garlic, finely chopped
1 cup water
1 large onion, sliced
1 large green bell pepper, sliced

Swiss Steak

1. Cut beef into 6 serving pieces. Mix flour, mustard and salt. Sprinkle half of the flour mixture over 1 side of beef; pound in with meat mallet. Turn beef; pound in remaining flour mixture.

2. Heat oil in 10-inch skillet over medium heat. Cook beef in oil about 15 minutes, turning once, until brown.

3. Add tomatoes and garlic, breaking up tomatoes with a fork or snipping with kitchen scissors. Heat to boiling; reduce heat. Cover and simmer about 1 1/4 hours, spooning sauce occasionally over beef, until beef is tender.

4. Add water, onion and bell pepper. Heat to boiling; reduce heat. Cover and simmer 5 to 8 minutes or until vegetables are tender.

1 Serving: Calories 205 (Calories from Fat 70); Fat 8g (Saturated 2g); Cholesterol 60mg; Sodium 360mg; Carbohydrate 11g (Dietary Fiber 2g); Protein 24g **% Daily Value:** Vitamin A 6%; Vitamin C 30%; Calcium 4%; Iron 16% **Diet Exchanges:** 3 Lean Meat, 2 Vegetable

Slow Cooker Directions: Omit water. Cut beef into 6 pieces. Mix flour, mustard and salt; coat beef (do not pound in). Heat oil in 10-inch skillet over medium heat. Cook beef in oil until brown on both sides. Place beef in 3 1/2- to 6-quart slow cooker. Top with onion and bell pepper. Mix tomatoes and garlic; pour over beef and vegetables. Cover and cook on low heat setting 7 to 9 hours or until beef is tender.

Southwestern Cheese Steak Supper

Southwestern Cheese Steak Supper

Prep: 20 min; Cook: 25 min ✳ *4 servings*

1 pound beef boneless sirloin steak, 3/4 inch thick
1 1/2 cups mild salsa
1 1/2 cups water
1 1/2 cups uncooked rotini pasta (5 ounces)
8 ounces process cheese spread loaf, cut into cubes
    (1 cup)

1. Spray 12-inch skillet with cooking spray; heat over medium heat. Cut beef into 4 serving pieces. Cook beef in skillet about 4 minutes, turning once, until brown. Remove beef from skillet.

2. Add salsa and water to skillet. Heat to boiling. Stir in pasta. Place beef in pasta mixture. Cover and cook over medium heat 12 to 15 minutes, stirring occasionally, until pasta is tender.

3. Stir in cheese until melted.

1 Serving: Calories 500 (Calories from Fat 200); Fat 22g (Saturated 12g); Cholesterol 105mg; Sodium 1,100mg; Carbohydrate 40g (Dietary Fiber 3g); Protein 39g **% Daily Value:** Vitamin A 20%; Vitamin C 16%; Calcium 34%; Iron 24% **Diet Exchanges:** 2 Starch, 4 Lean Meat, 2 Vegetable, 2 Fat

Fajitas

Prep: 30 min; Marinate: 8 hr; Broil: 16 min ✳ *6 servings*

Fajita Marinade (page 455)
1 1/2-pound beef boneless top sirloin steak,
    1 1/2 inches thick
12 flour tortillas (8 to 10 inches in diameter)
2 tablespoons vegetable oil
2 large onions, sliced
2 medium green or red bell peppers, cut into 1/4-inch
    strips
1 jar (8 ounces) picante sauce (1 cup)
1 cup shredded Cheddar or Monterey Jack cheese
    (4 ounces)
1 1/2 cups Guacamole (page 23) or prepared
    guacamole
3/4 cup sour cream

Fajitas

1. Make Fajita Marinade in small bowl.

2. Remove fat from beef. Pierce beef with fork in several places. Place beef in resealable plastic food-storage bag or shallow glass or plastic dish. Pour marinade over beef; turn beef to coat with marinade. Cover and refrigerate at least 8 hours but no longer than 24 hours, turning beef occasionally.

3. Heat oven to 325°.

4. Wrap tortillas in aluminum foil. Heat in oven about 15 minutes or until warm. Remove tortillas from oven; keep wrapped.

5. Set oven control to broil.

6. Remove beef from marinade; reserve marinade. Place beef on rack in broiler pan. (For easy cleanup, line broiler pan with aluminum foil before placing beef on rack.) Broil beef with top about 3 inches from heat about 8 minutes or until brown. Turn; brush beef with marinade. Broil 7 to 8 minutes longer for medium-rare to medium. (Also see Recommended Meat Doneness, page 222.) Discard any remaining marinade.

7. While beef is broiling, heat oil in 10-inch skillet over medium-high heat. Cook onions and bell peppers in oil 6 to 8 minutes, stirring frequently, until crisp-tender.

8. Cut beef across grain into very thin slices. For each fajita, place a few slices of beef, some of the onion mixture, 1 heaping tablespoonful each picante sauce and cheese, about 2 tablespoons Guacamole and 1 tablespoon sour cream on center of tortilla. Fold 1 end of tortilla up about 1 inch over filling; fold right and left sides over folded end, overlapping. Fold remaining end down.

1 Serving: Calories 735 (Calories from Fat 360); Fat 40g (Saturated 12g); Cholesterol 90mg; Sodium 1,080mg; Carbohydrate 66g (Dietary Fiber 8g); Protein 36g **% Daily Value:** Vitamin A 26%; Vitamin C 60%; Calcium 28%; Iron 34% **Diet Exchanges:** 4 Starch, 3 Medium-Fat Meat, 1 Vegetable, 4 Fat

Lighter Fajitas: For 15 grams of fat and 510 calories per serving, omit vegetable oil and spray skillet with cooking spray; use fat-free tortillas and reduced-fat cheese and sour cream. Omit Guacamole.

Beef Stroganoff

Prep: 20 min; Cook: 30 min ✱ *6 servings*

1 1/2 pounds beef tenderloin or boneless top loin
      steak, about 1/2 inch thick
2 tablespoons butter or stick margarine
1 1/2 cups beef broth
2 tablespoons ketchup
1 teaspoon salt
1 small clove garlic, finely chopped
3 cups sliced mushrooms (8 ounces)
1 medium onion, chopped (1/2 cup)
3 tablespoons all-purpose flour
1 cup sour cream or plain yogurt
Hot cooked noodles or rice (page 390 or 348),
      if desired

1. Cut beef across grain into about 1 1/2 × 1/2-inch strips. (Beef is easier to cut if partially frozen, 30 to 60 minutes.)

2. Melt butter in 10-inch skillet over medium-high heat. Cook beef in butter, stirring occasionally, until brown.

3. Reserve 1/3 cup of the broth. Stir remaining broth, the ketchup, salt and garlic into skillet. Heat to boiling; reduce heat. Cover and simmer about 10 minutes or until beef is tender.

4. Stir in mushrooms and onion. Cover and simmer about 5 minutes or until onion is tender.

5. Shake reserved broth and the flour in tightly covered container; gradually stir into beef mixture. Heat to boiling, stirring constantly. Boil and stir 1 minute; reduce heat to low.

6. Stir in sour cream; heat until hot. Serve over noodles.

1 Serving (about 1 cup): Calories 380 (Calories from Fat 250); Fat 28g (Saturated 13g); Cholesterol 100mg; Sodium 800mg; Carbohydrate 9g (Dietary Fiber 1g); Protein 24g **% Daily Value:** Vitamin A 8%; Vitamin C 2%; Calcium 6%; Iron 14% **Diet Exchanges:** 3 Lean Meat, 2 Vegetable, 4 Fat

---

PICKING MUSHROOMS

Be picky when picking mushrooms. Look for those with smooth, firm caps without major blemishes. Their surface should be dry but not dried out or shriveled.

Pepper Steak

Prep: 15 min; Cook: 30 min ✱ *6 servings*

1 1/2 pounds beef top round or sirloin steak, 3/4 to 1
      inch thick
3 tablespoons vegetable oil
1 cup water
1 medium onion, cut into 1/4-inch slices
1 clove garlic, finely chopped
1/2 teaspoon finely chopped gingerroot or 1/4 tea-
      spoon ground ginger
2 medium green bell peppers, cut into 3/4-inch strips
1 tablespoon cornstarch
2 teaspoons sugar, if desired
2 tablespoons soy sauce
2 medium tomatoes
6 cups hot cooked rice (page 348)

1. Remove fat from beef. Cut beef into 2 × 1/4-inch strips. (Beef is easier to cut if partially frozen, 30 to 60 minutes.)

2. Heat oil in 12-inch skillet over medium-high heat. Cook beef in oil about 5 minutes, turning frequently, until brown.

3. Stir in water, onion, garlic and gingerroot. Heat to boiling; reduce heat. Cover and simmer 12 to 15 minutes for round steak, 5 to 8 minutes for sirloin steak, adding bell peppers during last 5 minutes of simmering, until beef is tender and peppers are crisp-tender.

4. Mix cornstarch, sugar and soy sauce; stir into beef mixture. Cook, stirring constantly, until mixture thickens and boils. Boil and stir 1 minute; reduce heat to low.

5. Cut each tomato into 8 wedges; place on beef mixture. Cover and cook over low heat about 3 minutes or just until tomatoes are heated through. Serve with rice.

1 Serving (about 2 cups): Calories 405 (Calories from Fat 100); Fat 11g (Saturated 2g); Cholesterol 55mg; Sodium 350mg; Carbohydrate 52g (Dietary Fiber 2g); Protein 26g **% Daily Value:** Vitamin A 4%; Vitamin C 36%; Calcium 2%; Iron 24% **Diet Exchanges:** 3 Starch, 2 Medium-Fat Meat, 1 Vegetable

Lighter Pepper Steak: For 4 grams of fat and 350 calories per serving, omit oil and use nonstick skillet. Spray cold skillet with cooking spray before heating in step 2.

Beef with Pea Pods

Prep: 20 min; Cook: 30 min ✳ *8 servings*

2 pounds beef round steak, 3/4 to 1 inch thick

2 tablespoons vegetable oil

1 clove garlic, finely chopped

1/2 teaspoon salt

Dash of pepper

1 can (10 1/2 ounces) condensed beef broth

2 tablespoons cornstarch

1/4 cup water

1 tablespoon soy sauce

1/4 teaspoon finely chopped gingerroot or
　　1/8 teaspoon ground ginger

4 ounces fresh snow (Chinese) pea pods or 1 package
　　(6 ounces) frozen snow (Chinese) pea pods, thawed
　　and drained

8 cups hot cooked rice (page 348)

1. Remove fat from beef. Cut beef with grain into 2-inch strips; cut strips lengthwise into 1/4-inch slices. (Beef is easier to cut if partially frozen, 30 to 60 minutes.)

2. Heat wok or 10-inch skillet over high heat. Add oil; rotate wok to coat side. Add beef and garlic; stir-fry about 3 minutes or until beef is brown. Sprinkle with salt and pepper.

3. Stir in broth. Heat to boiling; reduce heat. Simmer uncovered 10 to 15 minutes or until beef is tender. (If liquid evaporates, add small amount of water.)

4. Mix cornstarch, water and soy sauce; stir into beef mixture. Cook, stirring constantly, until mixture thickens and boils. Boil and stir 1 minute. (Sauce will be thin.)

5. Stir in gingerroot and pea pods. Cook about 5 minutes, stirring occasionally, until pea pods are crisp-tender. Serve over rice.

To remove tips and strings from pea pods, snap off the stem end of pea pod and pull the string across the pea pod to remove it.

1 Serving (about 2 cups): Calories 385 (Calories from Fat 65); Fat 7g (Saturated 2g); Cholesterol 55mg; Sodium 500mg; Carbohydrate 53g (Dietary Fiber 1g); Protein 28g **% Daily Value:** Vitamin A 0%; Vitamin C 8%; Calcium 2%; Iron 26% **Diet Exchanges:** 3 Starch, 2 Lean Meat, 2 Vegetable

Lighter Beef with Pea Pods: For 4 grams of fat and 345 calories per serving, omit oil and use nonstick skillet or wok. Spray cold skillet or wok with cooking spray before heating in step 2.

Stuffed Peppers

Prep: 15 min; Cook: 15 min; Bake: 1 hr ✱ *6 servings*

6 large bell peppers (any color)
1 pound lean ground beef
2 tablespoons chopped onion
1 cup cooked rice (page 348)
1 teaspoon salt
1 clove garlic, finely chopped
1 can (15 ounces) tomato sauce
3/4 cup shredded mozzarella cheese (3 ounces)

1. Cut thin slice from stem end of each bell pepper to remove top of pepper. Remove seeds and membranes; rinse peppers. Cook peppers in enough boiling water to cover in 4-quart Dutch oven about 5 minutes; drain.

2. Cook beef and onion in 10-inch skillet over medium heat 8 to 10 minutes, stirring occasionally, until beef is brown; drain. Stir in rice, salt, garlic and 1 cup of the tomato sauce; cook until hot.

3. Heat oven to 350°.

4. Stuff peppers with beef mixture. Stand peppers upright in ungreased square baking dish, 8 × 8 × 2 inches. Pour remaining tomato sauce over peppers.

5. Cover and bake 45 minutes. Uncover and bake about 15 minutes longer or until peppers are tender. Sprinkle with cheese.

1 Serving: Calories 290 (Calories from Fat 125); Fat 14g (Saturated 6g); Cholesterol 50mg; Sodium 930mg; Carbohydrate 24g (Dietary Fiber 4g); Protein 21g **% Daily Value:** Vitamin A 18%; Vitamin C 100%; Calcium 14%; Iron 16% **Diet Exchanges:** 1 Starch, 2 Medium-Fat Meat, 2 Vegetable

Lighter Stuffed Peppers: For 3 grams of fat and 190 calories per serving, substitute ground turkey breast for the ground beef; use reduced-fat cheese.

Hamburger Stroganoff

Prep: 10 min; Cook: 25 min ✱ *4 servings*

1 pound lean ground beef
1 medium onion, chopped (1/2 cup)
1 clove garlic, finely chopped
1 can (10 3/4 ounces) condensed cream of mushroom soup
1 can (4 ounces) mushroom pieces and stems, drained
1/2 teaspoon salt
1 cup sour cream or plain yogurt
Hot cooked noodles or rice (page 390 or 348), if desired

1. Cook beef, onion and garlic in 10-inch skillet over medium heat 8 to 10 minutes, stirring occasionally, until beef is brown; drain.

2. Stir soup, mushrooms and salt into beef. Simmer uncovered 10 minutes; reduce heat to low.

3. Stir in sour cream; heat until hot. Serve over noodles.

1 Serving (about 1 cup): Calories 425 (Calories from Fat 290); Fat 32g (Saturated 14g); Cholesterol 105mg; Sodium 1,020mg; Carbohydrate 11g (Dietary Fiber 1g); Protein 24g **% Daily Value:** Vitamin A 8%; Vitamin C 2%; Calcium 10%; Iron 14% **Diet Exchanges:** 1 Starch, 3 Medium-Fat Meat, 2 Fat

Lighter Hamburger Stroganoff: For 10 grams of fat and 280 calories per serving, substitute ground turkey breast for the ground beef; use reduced-fat sour cream or yogurt.

Cabbage Rolls

Prep: 20 min; Bake: 45 min ✲ *4 servings*

Cabbage leaves will separate easily if you first remove the core from the head of cabbage and let the cabbage stand in cold water for 10 minutes.

12 cabbage leaves
1 pound lean ground beef
1/2 cup uncooked instant rice
1 can (15 ounces) tomato sauce
1/2 teaspoon salt
1/8 teaspoon pepper
1 medium onion, chopped (1/2 cup)
1 clove garlic, finely chopped
1 can (4 ounces) mushroom pieces and stems,
    undrained
1 teaspoon sugar
1/2 teaspoon lemon juice
1 tablespoon cornstarch
1 tablespoon water

1. Cover cabbage leaves with boiling water. Cover and let stand about 10 minutes or until leaves are limp. Remove leaves; drain.

2. Heat oven to 350°.

3. Mix beef, rice, 1/2 cup of the tomato sauce, the salt, pepper, onion, garlic and mushrooms.

4. Place about 1/3 cup beef mixture at stem end of each leaf. Roll leaf around beef mixture, tucking in sides. Place cabbage rolls, seam sides down, in ungreased square baking dish, 8 × 8 × 2 inches.

5. Mix remaining tomato sauce, the sugar and lemon juice; pour over cabbage rolls.

6. Cover and bake about 45 minutes or until beef mixture is no longer pink in center.

7. Remove cabbage rolls to platter. Pour liquid in baking dish into 1-quart saucepan. Mix cornstarch and water; stir into liquid. Heat to boiling, stirring constantly. Boil and stir 1 minute. Pour sauce over cabbage rolls.

1 Serving: Calories 355 (Calories from Fat 155); Fat 17g (Saturated 6g); Cholesterol 65mg; Sodium 1,120mg; Carbohydrate 30g (Dietary Fiber 4g); Protein 25g **% Daily Value:** Vitamin A 10%; Vitamin C 32%; Calcium 6%; Iron 20% **Diet Exchanges:** 1 Starch, 2 Medium-Fat Meat, 3 Vegetable, 1 Fat

Lighter Cabbage Rolls: For 2 grams of fat and 245 calories per serving, substitute ground turkey breast for the ground beef.

CORNED BEEF CABBAGE ROLLS: Substitute 1 pound chopped cooked corned beef for the ground beef.

Mexican Beef and Bean Casserole

Prep: 10 min; Cook: 10 min; Bake: 50 min ✲ *4 servings*

1 pound lean ground beef
2 cans (15 to 16 ounces each) pinto or kidney beans,
    rinsed and drained
1 can (8 ounces) tomato sauce
1/2 cup thick-and-chunky salsa
1 teaspoon chili powder
1 cup shredded Monterey Jack cheese (4 ounces)

1. Heat oven to 375°.

2. Cook beef in 10-inch skillet over medium heat 8 to 10 minutes, stirring occasionally, until brown; drain.

3. Mix beef, beans, tomato sauce, salsa and chili powder in ungreased 2-quart casserole.

4. Cover and bake 40 to 45 minutes, stirring once or twice, until hot and bubbly. Sprinkle with cheese. Bake uncovered about 57 minutes or until cheese is melted.

1 Serving (about 1 1/2 cups): Calories 585 (Calories from Fat 235); Fat 26g (Saturated 12g); Cholesterol 90mg; Sodium 1,030mg; Carbohydrate 62g (Dietary Fiber 20g); Protein 46g **% Daily Value:** Vitamin A 18%; Vitamin C 16%; Calcium 34%; Iron 46% **Diet Exchanges:** 3 Starch, 3 High-Fat Meat, 3 Vegetable

Meat Loaf

Prep: 20 min; Bake: 1 hr 15 min; Stand: 5 min
✱ *6 servings*

1 1/2 pounds lean ground beef
1 cup milk
1 tablespoon Worcestershire sauce
1 teaspoon chopped fresh or 1/4 teaspoon dried sage
    leaves
1/2 teaspoon salt
1/2 teaspoon ground mustard
1/4 teaspoon pepper
1 clove garlic, finely chopped, or 1/8 teaspoon garlic
    powder
1 large egg
3 slices bread, torn into small pieces*
1 small onion, chopped (1/4 cup)
1/2 cup ketchup, chili sauce or barbecue sauce

1. Heat oven to 350°.

2. Mix all ingredients except ketchup. Spread mixture in ungreased loaf pan, 8 1/2 × 4 1/2 × 2 1/2 or 9 × 5 × 3 inches, or shape into 9 × 5-inch loaf in ungreased rectangular pan, 13 × 9 × 2 inches. Spread ketchup over top.

3. Insert meat thermometer so tip is in center of loaf. Bake uncovered 1 hour to 1 hour 15 minutes or until beef is no longer pink in center, juice is clear and thermometer reads at least 160°. (Also see Recommended Meat Doneness, page 222.)** Drain meat loaf.

4. Let stand 5 minutes; remove from pan.

*1/2 cup dry bread crumbs or 3/4 cup quick-cooking oats can be substituted for the 3 slices bread.
**Due to the natural nitrate content of certain ingredients often used in meat loaf such as onions, celery and bell peppers, meat loaf may remain pink even though beef is cooked to 160° doneness. Always check meat loaf with a thermometer to make sure it's reached 160° in the center.

1 Serving: Calories 320 (Calories from Fat 160); Fat 18g (Saturated 7g); Cholesterol 105mg; Sodium 610mg; Carbohydrate 15g (Dietary Fiber 1g); Protein 25g **% Daily Value:** Vitamin A 4%; Vitamin C 4%; Calcium 8%; Iron 14% **Diet Exchanges:** 1 Starch, 3 Medium-Fat Meat, 1/2 Fat

Lighter Meat Loaf: For 2 grams of fat and 195 calories per serving, substitute ground turkey breast for the ground beef and 1/4 cup fat-free cholesterol-free egg product for the egg. Use fat-free (skim) milk. Bake uncovered 1 hour to 1 hour 15 minutes or until turkey is no longer pink in center and thermometer reads 165°.

INDIVIDUAL MEAT LOAVES: Grease 12 medium muffin cups, 2 1/2 × 1 1/4 inches, with shortening, or spray with cooking spray. Divide beef mixture evenly among cups (cups will be very full). Brush individual loaves with about 1/4 cup ketchup. Place muffin pan on cookie sheet in oven (to catch any spillover). Bake about 30 minutes or until loaves are no longer pink in center and thermometer reads 160° when inserted in center of loaves in middle of muffin pan (outer loaves will be done sooner). Immediately remove from cups.

MEXICAN MEAT LOAF: Omit sage. Substitute 2/3 cup milk and 1/3 cup salsa for the 1 cup milk. Stir in 1/2 cup shredded Colby–Monterey Jack cheese (2 ounces) and 1 can (4 ounces) chopped green chilies, drained, in step 2. Substitute 2/3 cup salsa for the ketchup.

Skillet Hash

Prep: 10 min; Cook: 15 min ✱ *4 servings*

To make this a speedy skillet hash, substitute 2 cups frozen diced hash browns, partially thawed, for the potatoes.

2 cups chopped cooked lean beef or corned beef
4 small potatoes, cooked and chopped (2 cups)
1 medium onion, chopped (1/2 cup)
1 tablespoon chopped fresh parsley
1/2 teaspoon salt
1/8 teaspoon pepper
2 to 3 tablespoons vegetable oil

1. Mix beef, potatoes, onion, parsley, salt and pepper.

2. Heat oil in 10-inch skillet over medium heat. Spread beef mixture evenly in skillet. Cook 10 to 15 minutes, turning frequently, until brown.

1 Serving (about 1 cup): Calories 260 (Calories from Fat 80); Fat 9g (Saturated 2g); Cholesterol 55mg; Sodium 340mg; Carbohydrate 24g (Dietary Fiber 3g); Protein 24g **% Daily Value:** Vitamin A 0%; Vitamin C 12%; Calcium 2%; Iron 18% **Diet Exchanges:** 1 Starch, 3 Very Lean Meat, 2 Vegetable, 1 Fat

OVEN HASH: Heat oven to 350°. Grease square baking dish, 8 × 8 × 2 inches, with shortening. Omit oil. Spread beef mixture evenly in baking dish. Bake uncovered about 20 minutes or until hot.

RED FLANNEL SKILLET HASH: Use 1 1/2 cups chopped cooked corned beef and 3 small potatoes, cooked and chopped (1 1/2 cups). Mix in 1 can (15 ounces) diced or shoestring beets, drained.

Meatballs

Prep: 15 min; Bake: 25 min ✱ *4 or 5 servings*

To save time, instead of shaping beef mixture into balls, pat mixture into a 9 × 3-inch rectangle in ungreased rectangular pan, 13 × 9 × 2 inches. Cut into 1 1/2-inch squares; separate slightly. Bake uncovered 25 to 30 minutes. You can also use an ice cream scoop to form meatballs.

1 pound lean ground beef
1/2 cup dry bread crumbs
1/4 cup milk
1/2 teaspoon salt
1/2 teaspoon Worcestershire sauce
1/4 teaspoon pepper
1 small onion, chopped (1/4 cup)
1 large egg

1. Heat oven to 400°.

2. Mix all ingredients. Shape mixture into twenty 1 1/2-inch meatballs. Place in ungreased rectangular pan, 13 × 9 × 2 inches, or on rack in broiler pan.

3. Bake uncovered 20 to 25 minutes or until no longer pink in center and juice is clear.

1 Serving: Calories 315 (Calories from Fat 170); Fat 19g (Saturated 7g); Cholesterol 120mg; Sodium 490mg; Carbohydrate 12g (Dietary Fiber 1g); Protein 25g **% Daily Value:** Vitamin A 2%; Vitamin C 0%; Calcium 6%; Iron 16% **Diet Exchanges:** 1 Starch, 3 Medium-Fat Meat

COCKTAIL MEATBALLS: Shape beef mixture into 1-inch meatballs. Bake 15 to 20 minutes. 3 dozen appetizers.

SKILLET MEATBALLS: Cook meatballs in 10-inch skillet over medium heat about 20 minutes, turning occasionally, until no longer pink in center and juice is clear.

TURKEY OR CHICKEN MEATBALLS: Substitute 1 pound ground turkey or chicken for the ground beef. (If using ground chicken, decrease milk to 2 tablespoons.) To bake, grease rectangular pan with shortening. To panfry, heat 1 tablespoon vegetable oil in 10-inch skillet over medium heat before adding meatballs.

Beef Enchiladas

Prep: 15 min; Cook: 20 min; Bake: 20 min ✱ 4 servings

1 pound lean ground beef
1 medium onion, chopped (1/2 cup)
1/2 cup sour cream
1 cup shredded Cheddar cheese (4 ounces)
2 tablespoons chopped fresh parsley
1/4 teaspoon pepper
1/3 cup chopped green bell pepper
2/3 cup water
1 tablespoon chili powder
1 1/2 teaspoons chopped fresh or 1/2 teaspoon dried
    oregano leaves
1/4 teaspoon ground cumin
2 whole green chilies, chopped, if desired
1 clove garlic, finely chopped
1 can (15 ounces) tomato sauce
8 corn tortillas (5 or 6 inches in diameter)
Shredded cheese, sour cream and chopped onions, if
    desired

1. Heat oven to 350°.

2. Cook beef in 10-inch skillet over medium heat 8 to 10 minutes, stirring occasionally, until brown; drain. Stir in onion, sour cream, 1 cup cheese, the parsley and pepper. Cover and remove from heat.

3. Heat bell pepper, water, chili powder, oregano, cumin, chilies, garlic and tomato sauce to boiling in 2-quart saucepan, stirring occasionally; reduce heat. Simmer uncovered 5 minutes. Pour into ungreased pie plate, 9 × 1 1/4 inches.

4. Dip each tortilla into sauce in pie plate to coat both sides. Spoon about 1/4 cup beef mixture onto each tortilla; roll tortilla around filling. Place seam side down in ungreased rectangular baking dish, 11 × 7 × 1 1/2 inches. Pour remaining sauce over enchiladas.

5. Bake uncovered about 20 minutes or until bubbly. Garnish with shredded cheese, sour cream and chopped onions.

1 Serving: Calories 670 (Calories from Fat 380); Fat 42g (Saturated 22g); Cholesterol 140mg; Sodium 1,160mg; Carbohydrate 38g (Dietary Fiber 6g); Protein 41g **% Daily Value:** Vitamin A 36%; Vitamin C 26%; Calcium 44%; Iron 24% **Diet Exchanges:** 2 Starch, 4 Medium-Fat Meat, 2 Vegetable, 4 Fat

Lighter Enchiladas: For 6 grams of fat and 485 calories per serving, substitute ground turkey breast for the ground beef; use fat-free flour tortillas and reduced-fat sour cream and cheese.

Pepperoni Pizza– Hamburger Pie

Prep: 20 min; Bake: 30 min; Stand: 5 min ✱ 6 servings

1 pound lean ground beef
1/3 cup dry bread crumbs
1 1/2 teaspoons chopped fresh or 1/2 teaspoon dried
    oregano leaves
1/4 teaspoon salt
1 large egg
1/2 cup sliced mushrooms
1 small green bell pepper, chopped (1/2 cup)
1/3 cup chopped pepperoni (2 ounces)
1/4 cup sliced ripe olives
1 cup spaghetti sauce
1 cup shredded mozzarella cheese (4 ounces)

1. Heat oven to 400°.

2. Mix beef, bread crumbs, oregano, salt and egg. Press mixture evenly against bottom and side of ungreased pie plate, 9 × 1 1/4 inches.

3. Sprinkle mushrooms, bell pepper, pepperoni and olives into beef-lined plate. Pour spaghetti sauce over toppings.

4. Bake uncovered about 25 minutes or until beef is no longer pink in center and juice is clear; carefully drain. Sprinkle with cheese. Bake about 5 minutes longer or until cheese is light brown. Let stand 5 minutes before cutting.

1 Serving: Calories 335 (Calories from Fat 190); Fat 21g (Saturated 8g); Cholesterol 95mg; Sodium 740mg; Carbohydrate 14g (Dietary Fiber 1g); Protein 24g **% Daily Value:** Vitamin A 8%; Vitamin C 14%; Calcium 18%; Iron 14% **Diet Exchanges:** 3 Medium-Fat Meat, 3 Vegetable, 1 Fat

Veal Basics

Selecting Veal

Very young beef, 1 to 3 months old, is classified as veal. Veal is lean with a mild, delicate flavor. When buying veal, let color be your guide: Veal should be light pink and the fat should be white. Meat that's red in color indicates the animal is older, and the meat won't be quite as mild in flavor or as tender.

Cooking Veal

Because it's so low in fat, all cuts are cooked at low temperatures or with moist-heat methods to prevent them from drying out. Sauces and coatings also help to retain veal's natural juices and enhance its delicate flavor. Cook veal to 160° (medium). Also see Recommended Meat Doneness, page 222.

Roasting Veal

Roasting is best for larger veal cuts from the loin, sirloin and rib, although roasting a boneless veal shoulder arm, eye round or rump roast works well, too. Check the Timetable for Roasting Veal, below, to determine the right oven temperatures and times for each cut.

1. Choose one of the roasts from the Timetable for Roasting Veal.

2. Place the veal—right from the refrigerator—fat side up, on a rack in a shallow roasting pan. (For easy cleanup, line the pan with aluminum foil first.) As the fat melts, it bastes the veal, making basting during cooking unnecessary.

3. If you like, season the veal with herbs, spices or other seasonings before, during or after cooking. Sprinkling the roast with salt *before* cooking adds flavor.

4. Insert a meat thermometer so the tip is centered in the thickest part of the roast and not resting in fat or touching bone. Don't cover the roast or add water.

5. Roast at 325° for the time recommended in the chart until the meat thermometer reads 155°. The roast will continue to cook after you take it out of the oven.

6. Take the roast out of the oven and cover it loosely with a foil tent. Let stand for 15 to 20 minutes or until the temperature rises to 160°. After standing, the roast also will be easier to carve. Avoid covering the roast tightly because doing so will create steam, which will soften the surface of the veal.

TIMETABLE FOR ROASTING VEAL*

Veal Cut	Approximate Weight (pounds)	Approximate Cooking Time (minutes)**
Rump (boneless)	2 to 3	33 to 35
Shoulder (boneless)	2 1/2 to 3	31 to 34
Loin		
(bone in)	3 to 4	34 to 36
(boneless)	2 to 3	18 to 20
Rib	4 to 5	25 to 27
Crown (12 to 14 ribs)	7 1/2 to 9 1/2	19 to 21

*Oven temperature 325°
**Smaller roasts require more minutes per pound than larger roasts.

Veal

RETAIL CUTS
Where They Come From
How To Cook Them

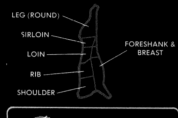

LEG (ROUND)
SIRLOIN
LOIN
RIB
SHOULDER
FORESHANK & BREAST

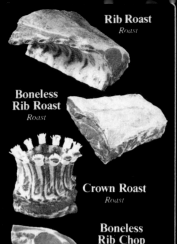

Rib Roast
Roast

Boneless Rib Roast
Roast

Crown Roast
Roast

Boneless Rib Chop
Braise. Panfry. Broil

Rib Chop
Braise. Panfry. Broil

Short Ribs
Braise. Cook in Liquid

RIB

Blade Roast
Braise. Roast

Arm Roast
Braise. Roast

Blade Steak
Braise. Panfry

Arm Steak
Braise. Panfry

Boneless Shoulder Arm Roast
Braise. Roast

Boneless Shoulder Eye Roast
Braise. Roast

SHOULDER

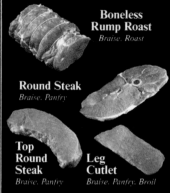

Boneless Rump Roast
Braise. Roast

Round Steak
Braise. Panfry

Top Round Steak
Braise. Panfry

Leg Cutlet
Braise. Panfry. Broil

LEG (ROUND)

Breast
Braise. Roast

Boneless Breast Roast
Braise. Roast

Cross Cut Shank
Braise. Cook in Liquid

Riblet
Braise. Cook in Liquid

Shank
Braise. Cook in Liquid

FORESHANK & BREAST

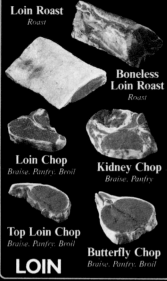

Loin Roast
Roast

Boneless Loin Roast
Roast

Loin Chop
Braise. Panfry. Broil

Kidney Chop
Braise. Panfry

Top Loin Chop
Braise. Panfry. Broil

Butterfly Chop
Braise. Panfry. Broil

LOIN

Sirloin Roast
Roast

Boneless Sirloin Roast
Roast

Sirloin Steak
Braise. Panfry. Broil

Top Sirloin Steak
Braise. Panfry. Broil

SIRLOIN

Veal for Stew
Braise. Cook in Liquid

Ground Veal
Panfry. Broil

Cubes for Kabobs
Braise

Cubed Steak
Braise. Panfry

OTHER CUTS

Broiling or Grilling Veal

Broiling and grilling are great ways for cooking bone-in and boneless veal rib or loin chops or ground veal. Less-tender cuts, such as blade or arm steaks, broil and grill best if they're marinated first (see Tips for Marinades and Marinating, page 453). The tips below use direct heat. For more information on using your grill, check out the instruction booklet that came with your grill or Grilling Basics, page 331. Check the Timetable for Broiling or Grilling Veal, below, to determine the right oven temperatures and times for each cut.

1. Choose a cut of veal from the Timetable for Broiling or Grilling Veal. If you like, marinate the veal first.

2. **To Broil:** Set oven to broil. Check your oven manual for whether the oven door should be open or closed during broiling.

   To Grill: Heat the coals or gas grill to medium; spread the coals to a single layer.

3. **To Broil:** Place veal on the rack in the broiler pan. (For easy cleanup, line the pan with aluminum foil first.) Position the pan so the top of the veal is the distance from the heat recommended in the chart.

   To Grill: Place veal on the grill the distance from the heat recommended in the chart.

4. Broil or grill the veal for about half the recommended time or until it's brown on one side.

5. Turn the veal, and continue broiling or grilling until it's done to your liking. To see if it's done, cut a small slit in the center of boneless cuts or in the center near the bone of bone-in cuts.

Medium-rare is very pink in the center; medium is light pink in the center; and well-done is brown all the way through. If you like, season the veal after it's done.

Panbroiling Veal

Panbroiling is a quick, fat-conscious way to cook veal because drippings are poured off as they form. In other words, the meat doesn't stew in its own juices. Panbroiling is a great way to cook veal chops and patties. Check the Timetable for Panbroiling Veal, page 246, to determine the right oven temperatures and times for each cut.

1. Choose one of the cuts for panbroiling from the Timetable for Panbroiling Veal, page 246.

2. Use a heavy nonstick skillet, or coat a regular skillet with a film of vegetable oil or cooking spray. Heat the skillet for 5 minutes over medium-low to medium heat if the veal is 5/8 inch to 1 inch thick, medium-high for cuts 1/4 to 1/2 inch thick.

3. Put the veal in the skillet; don't cover and don't add oil or water.

4. Cook for the time recommended in the chart, turning once. Occasionally turn cuts that are thicker than 1/2 inch. Drain excess drippings from the skillet as they form. Cook until veal is brown on both sides and slightly pink in the center. To see if the veal is done, cut a small slit in the center of boneless cuts or in the center near the bone of bone-in cuts. If you like, season the veal after it's done.

TIMETABLE FOR BROILING OR GRILLING VEAL

Veal Cut	Approximate Thickness	Inches from Heat	Approximate Total Broiling Time (minutes) 160° (medium)	Approximate Total Grilling Time (minutes) 160° (medium)
Loin or Rib Chops	1 inch	4	14 to 16	12 to 14
Arm or Blade Steaks*	3/4 inch	4	14 to 15	16 to 18
Ground Veal Patties	1/2 inch	4	8 to 10	10 to 12

Marinate at least 6 hours but no longer than 24 hours to tenderize.

TIMETABLE FOR PANBROILING VEAL

Veal Cut	Approximate Thickness (inches)	Stove-top Temperature	Approximate Total Cooking Time (minutes) 160° (medium)
Loin or Rib Chops	3/4 to 1	Medium-Low to Medium	10 to 12
Arm or Blade Steaks*	3/4	Medium to Medium-High	13 to 14
Ground Veal Patties	1/2	Medium-Low to Medium	6 to 7

*Marinate at least 6 hours but no longer than 24 hours to tenderize.

Veal Scallopini *Fast*

Prep: 10 min; Cook: 20 min ✱ 4 servings

1/2 cup all-purpose flour
2 teaspoons garlic salt
1 pound veal for scallopini*
1/4 cup vegetable oil
2 tablespoons butter or stick margarine
1/4 cup dry white wine, nonalcoholic white wine or
    chicken broth
2 tablespoons lemon juice
1/2 lemon, cut into 4 wedges

1. Mix flour and garlic salt. Coat veal with flour mixture.

2. Heat 2 tablespoons of the oil in 10-inch skillet over medium-high heat. Cook half of the veal in oil about 5 minutes, turning once, until brown. Remove veal; keep warm. Repeat with remaining oil and veal. Drain any remaining oil and overly browned particles from skillet.

3. Add butter, wine and lemon juice to skillet. Heat to boiling, scraping any remaining brown particles from skillet. Boil until liquid is reduced by about half and mixture has thickened slightly. Pour over veal. Serve with lemon wedges.

1 pound veal round steak can be substituted for the veal for scallopini. Cut veal into 8 pieces. Place each piece between sheets of plastic wrap or waxed paper. Lightly pound with flat side of meat mallet until 1/4 inch thick.

1 Serving: Calories 300 (Calories from Fat 170); Fat 19g (Saturated 7g); Cholesterol 90mg; Sodium 460mg; Carbohydrate 13g (Dietary Fiber 0g); Protein 19g **% Daily Value:** Vitamin A 4%; Vitamin C 2%; Calcium 2%; Iron 8% **Diet Exchanges:** 1 Starch, 2 Medium-Fat Meat, 2 Fat

Lighter Veal Scallopini: For 14 grams of fat and 255 calories per serving, decrease oil to 2 tablespoons and cook half of the veal at a time in 1 tablespoon oil in nonstick skillet. Decrease butter to 1 tablespoon.

Osso Buco

Prep: 40 min; Cook: 2 hr 30 min ✱ 6 servings

4 pounds veal or beef shanks
1/2 teaspoon salt
1/4 teaspoon pepper
1/4 cup all-purpose flour
2 tablespoons olive or vegetable oil
1/3 cup dry white wine or apple juice
1 can (10 1/2 ounces) condensed beef broth
1 clove garlic, finely chopped
1 bay leaf
2 tablespoons chopped fresh parsley
1 teaspoon grated lemon peel
6 cups hot cooked spaghetti
Grated Romano cheese, if desired

1. Remove fat from veal. Sprinkle with salt and pepper; coat with flour.

2. Heat oil in 4-quart Dutch oven over medium heat. Cook veal in oil about 20 minutes, turning occasionally, until brown on all sides.

3. Stir in wine, broth, garlic and bay leaf. Heat to boiling; reduce heat. Cover and simmer 1 hour 30 minutes to 2 hours or until veal is tender. Remove veal; place on serving platter. Skim fat from broth; remove bay leaf. Pour broth over veal; sprinkle with parsley and lemon peel. Serve veal with spaghetti and cheese.

1 Serving: Calories 630 (Calories from Fat 170); Fat 19g (Saturated 6g); Cholesterol 260mg; Sodium 660mg; Carbohydrate 45g; (Dietary Fiber 1g); Protein 71g **% Daily Value:** Vitamin A 0%; Vitamin C 2%; Calcium 8mg; Iron 28mg **Diet Exchanges:** 9 Very Lean Meat, 3 Starch, 2 Fat

Veal Parmigiana

Prep: 1 hr 5 min; Cook: 10 min; Bake: 25 min ✱ *6 servings*

2 cups Italian Tomato Sauce (page 436) or spaghetti
　　sauce
1 large egg
2 tablespoons water
2/3 cup dry bread crumbs
1/3 cup grated Parmesan cheese
1 1/2 pounds veal for scallopini*
1/4 cup olive or vegetable oil
2 cups shredded mozzarella cheese (8 ounces)

1. Make Italian Tomato Sauce; heat oven to 350°.

2. Mix egg and water. Mix bread crumbs and Parmesan cheese. Dip veal into egg mixture, then coat with bread crumb mixture.

3. Heat oil in 12-inch skillet over medium heat. Cook half of the veal at a time in oil about 5 minutes, turning once, until light brown; drain. Repeat with remaining veal, adding 1 or 2 tablespoons oil if necessary.

4. Place half of the veal in ungreased rectangular baking dish, 11 × 7 × 1 1/2 inches, overlapping slices slightly. Spoon half of the sauce over veal. Sprinkle with 1 cup of the mozzarella cheese. Repeat with remaining veal, sauce and cheese.

5. Bake uncovered about 25 minutes or until sauce is bubbly and cheese is light brown.

*1 1/2 pounds veal round steak can be substituted for the veal for scallopini. Cut veal into 12 pieces. Place each piece between sheets of plastic wrap or waxed paper. Lightly pound with flat side of meat mallet until 1/4 inch thick.

1 Serving: Calories 440 (Calories from Fat 205); Fat 23g (Saturated 8g); Cholesterol 120mg; Sodium 840mg; Carbohydrate 26g (Dietary Fiber 1g); Protein 33g **% Daily Value:** Vitamin A 12%; Vitamin C 10%; Calcium 38%; Iron 12% **Diet Exchanges:** 1 Starch, 4 Medium-Fat Meat, 2 Vegetable

CHICKEN PARMIGIANA: Substitute 8 boneless, skinless chicken breast halves (about 2 pounds) for the veal. Place each chicken breast half between sheets of plastic wrap or waxed paper. Lightly pound with flat side of meat mallet until 1/4 inch thick.

Pork Basics

Selecting Pork

Lean and flavorful, fresh pork should be fine-grained and pale pink with white fat. Pork is available in a variety of cuts, from roasts to chops to tenderloins. When buying pork, keep in mind that an average serving is 3 ounces of cooked pork; 4 ounces of uncooked boneless pork will give you 3 ounces cooked. You can cook pork lots of different ways: stew it, grill it, sauté it, roast it. The secret to cooking tender, juicy pork is to think pink. When cooked to an internal temp of 160°, pork has just a hint of pink. Modern feeding practices have made the age-old fear of trichinosis unfounded today. Trichinae are very rare. Even in the highly unlikely event they were present, trichinae are killed at 137°—well below the recommended 160°. Because pork has little fat, overcooking pork (over 160°) will make it tough and dry.

Ham, cured meat from the hind legs of hogs, should be firm, plump, fine-grained, rosy pink and without excess moisture. Any fat should be firm and white. You may notice a rainbowlike appearance on the surface of ham—don't worry, it's perfectly safe. It's called *iridescence* and is caused by the refraction of light on the cut ends of the muscle fibers.

Curing gives ham its salty flavor; exposure to wood smoke or smoke-flavored liquids gives ham its smoky flavor. Smoking and curing also can darken the color of the meat. Ham is available bone-in, semi-boneless, boneless, canned and country style. Bone-in hams may be sold as whole hams, shank and rump halves, shank and rump (butt) portions and center slices. Plan on four servings per pound of fully cooked boneless ham, two servings per pound of bone-in.

The most popular ham is fully cooked, brine cured and spiral cut. Fully cooked hams are ready to eat; to warm, heat to 140° (see Roasting Ham, page 252). Hams labeled "cook before eating" must be cooked to an internal temperature of 160°. If you aren't sure what kind of ham you've bought, cook it to 160° to be safe.

Country or country-style hams have been dry cured and smoked and are often quite salty, the opposite of wet-cured hams, or "city hams" as some people call the ham most of us are familiar with. Look for them bone-in, boneless or sliced. To get rid of the excess salt before serving these hams, if you like, soak them in cold water for 24 to 72 hours. Refrigerate the ham immediately after soaking if you won't be serving it cold right away or if you're not ready to serve it hot. To serve it hot, heat to an internal temperature of 140° (see Roasting Ham, page 252).

Turkey ham is skinless, boneless turkey thigh meat that has been cured and smoked to taste like ham. Turkey ham may be lower in calories and fat than regular ham, but check the label. Turkey hams are available in large, boneless pieces or as cold cuts. The large pieces, like fully cooked hams, can be eaten cold or warm by heating to an internal temperature of 140°.

How to Carve a Pork Loin Roast

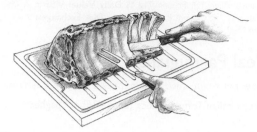

Place roast on carving board or platter; remove backbone from ribs for easy carving. Place roast with rib side toward you. With meat fork inserted in roast to keep the meat from moving, cut slices on each side of rib bones. (Every other slice will contain a bone.)

TIMETABLE FOR ROASTING PORK*

Pork Cut	Approximate Weight (pounds)	Meat Thermometer Reading (after roasting)	Final Meat Thermometer Reading (after standing)	Approximate Cooking Time (minutes per pound)
Loin Center (bone in)	3 to 5	155°	160° (medium)	20
Tenderloin (450°)	1/2 to 1	155°	160° (medium)	20
Blade Loin or Sirloin (boneless, tied)	2 1/2 to 3 1/2	155°	160° (medium)	20
Rib (boneless)	2 to 4	155°	160° (medium)	20
Top Loin Double (boneless)	3 to 4	155°	160° (medium)	20
Top Loin (boneless)	2 to 4	155°	160° (medium)	20
Crown	6 to 10	155°	160° (medium)	20
Boston Butt (boneless)	3 to 6	155°	160° (medium)	45
				Total Cooking Time
Back Ribs			Until tender	1 1/2 to 2 hours
Country-Style Ribs	1-inch slices			1 1/2 to 1 3/4 hours
Spareribs			Until tender	1 1/2 to 2 hours

Oven temperature 350°, except where indicated.

Roasting Pork

Pork is roasted in the oven with no water, so start with a tender cut such as a top loin. Check the Timetable for Roasting Pork (page 248) to determine the right oven temperatures and times for each cut. Follow these steps for roasted pork that's well browned on the outside and moist and tender inside:

1. Choose one of the cuts from the Timetable for Roasting Pork.

2. Place the pork—right from the refrigerator—fat side up (if present), on a rack in a shallow roasting pan. (For easy cleanup, line the pan with aluminum foil first.) As the fat melts, it bastes the pork, making basting during cooking unnecessary.

3. If you like, season the pork with herbs, spices or other seasonings before, during or after cooking.

Sprinkling the roast with salt *before* cooking adds flavor.

4. Insert a meat thermometer so the tip is centered in the thickest part of the roast and not resting in fat or touching bone. Don't cover the roast or add water.

5. Roast at 350°. Roast ribs until tender; for all other cuts, use the chart as a guide and roast for the recommended time until the meat thermometer reads the "Meat Thermometer Reading (after roasting)" temperature. The roast will continue to cook after you take it out of the oven.

6. Take the roast out of the oven and cover it loosely with a foil tent. Let stand for 15 to 20 minutes or until it reaches the "Final Meat Thermometer Reading (after standing)" temp. After standing, the roast also will be easier to carve. Avoid covering the

TIMETABLE FOR BROILING OR GRILLING PORK

Pork Cut	Approximate Thickness or Weight	Inches from Heat	Meat Doneness	Approximate Total Broiling Time (minutes)	Approximate Total Grilling Time (minutes)
Loin or Chops (bone in)	3/4 inch	3 to 4	160° (medium)	8 to 11	6 to 8
	1 1/2 inches	3 to 4	160° (medium)	19 to 22	12 to 16
Loin Chop (boneless)	1 inch	3 to 4	160° (medium)	11 to 13	8 to 10
Blade Chop (bone in)	3/4 inch	3 to 4	170° (well)	13 to 15	11 to 13
	1 1/2 inches	3 to 4	170° (well)	26 to 29	19 to 22
Arm Chop (bone in)	3/4 inch	3 to 4	170° (well)	16 to 18	13 to 15
	1 inch	3 to 4	170° (well)	18 to 20	15 to 18
Cubes for Kabobs	1-inch pieces	3 to 4	160° (medium)	9 to 11	10 to 20
Loin or Leg Tenderloin	1-inch pieces	3 to 4	160° (medium)	12 to 14	13 to 21
Ground Pork Patties	1/2 inch thick	3 to 4	170° (well)	7 to 9	7 to 9
Country-Style Ribs	1-inch slices	5	160° (medium)	45 to 60	1 1/2 to 2 hours*
Spareribs		5	160° (medium)	45 to 60	1 1/2 to 2 hours*
Backribs		5	160° (medium)	45 to 55	1 1/2 to 2 hours*

Grill over indirect heat.

roast tightly because doing so will create steam, which will soften the surface of the pork.

Broiling or Grilling Pork

Broiling and grilling are great ways for cooking roasts, ribs, tenderloin, chops and patties. Less-tender cuts, such as ribs and roasts, grill best if they're marinated first (see Tips for Marinades and Marinating, page 453) and cooked over indirect heat. The tips below use direct heat. For more information on using your grill, check out the instruction booklet that came with your grill or the Grilling Basics, page 331. Check the Timetable for Broiling or Grilling Pork to determine the right oven temperatures and times for each cut.

1. Choose a cut of pork from the Timetable for Broiling or Grilling Pork (page 249). If you like, marinate the pork first.

2. **To Broil:** Set oven to broil. Check your oven manual for whether the oven door should be open or closed during broiling.

   To Grill: Heat the coals or gas grill to medium; spread the coals to a single layer.

3. **To Broil:** Place pork on the rack in the broiler pan. (For easy cleanup, line the pan with aluminum foil first.) Position the pan so the top of the pork is the distance from the heat recommended in the chart.

To Grill: Place pork on the grill the distance from the heat recommended in the chart.

4. Broil or grill the pork for about half the recommended time or until it's brown on one side.

5. Turn the pork, and continue broiling or grilling until the doneness shown in the chart on page 249 for the cut you're using. To see if it's done, cut a small slit in the center of boneless cuts or in the center near the bone of bone-in cuts. Medium pork is slightly pink in the center, well-done pork is creamy-tan all the way through. If you like, season the pork after it's done.

Panbroiling Pork

Panbroiling is a quick, fat-conscious way to cook pork because drippings are poured off as they form. In other words, the meat doesn't stew in its own juices. Panbroiling is a great way to cook pork chops and patties. Check the Timetable for Panbroiling Pork, below, to determine the right oven temperatures and times for each cut.

1. Choose one of the cuts for panbroiling from the Timetable for Panbroiling Pork.

2. Use a heavy nonstick skillet, or coat a regular skillet with a film of vegetable oil or cooking spray. Heat the skillet for 5 minutes over medium heat.

3. Put the pork in the skillet; don't cover and don't add oil or water.

TIMETABLE FOR PANBROILING PORK*

Pork Cut	Approximate Thickness (inches)	Meat Doneness	Approximate Total Grilling Time (minutes)
Loin or Rib Chops (bone in)	1/2	160° (medium)	7 to 8
	1	160° (medium)	12 to 14
Loin Chops (boneless)	1/2	160° (medium)	7 to 8
	1	160° (medium)	10 to 12
Butterflied Chops	1/2	160° (medium)	8 to 9
	1	160° (medium)	12 to 14
Ground Pork Patties	1/2	170° (well)	7 to 9

*Medium heat

Pork

RETAIL CUTS
Where They Come From
How To Cook Them

LEG

SIDE

LOIN

ARM SHOULDER

BLADE SHOULDER

LEG/HAM

Leg Cutlet
Panfry, Braise, Broil, Panbroil

Top Leg (Inside) Roast
Roast, Braise

Smoked Ham
Roast

Smoked Ham Shank Portion
Roast

Smoked Ham Center Slice
Broil, Panbroil, Panfry, Roast

Smoked Ham Rump Portion
Roast

Canned Ham
Roast

Sliced Ham
Panfry, Panbroil, Braise

Boneless Smoked Ham
Roast

SHOULDER

Blade Roast
Roast, Braise

Blade Steak
Braise, Broil, Panbroil, Panfry

Boneless Blade Roast
Roast, Braise

Boneless Arm Picnic Roast
Roast, Braise

Smoked Shoulder Roll
Roast, Cook in Liquid

Smoked Hocks
Braise, Cook in Liquid

Smoked Picnic
Roast, Cook in Liquid

LOIN

Country-Style Ribs
Roast, Braise, Broil, Cook in Liquid

Sirloin Cutlet
Braise, Broil, Panbroil, Panfry

Back Ribs
Roast, Broil, Braise, Cook in Liquid

Center Rib Roast
Roast

Tenderloin
Roast, Braise, (Slices: Panfry, Braise)

Top Loin Roast (Double)
Roast

Blade Roast
Roast, Braise

Boneless Blade Roast
Roast, Braise

Sirloin Roast
Roast

Crown Roast
Roast

Center Loin Roast
Roast

Boneless Sirloin Roast
Roast

Smoked Loin Chop
Roast, Broil, Panbroil, Panfry

Canadian-Style Bacon
Roast, Broil, Panbroil, Panfry

Blade Chop
Braise, Broil, Panbroil, Panfry

Rib Chop
Broil, Panbroil, Panfry, Braise

Top Loin Chop
Broil, Panbroil, Panfry, Braise

Loin Chop
Broil, Panbroil, Panfry, Braise

Sirloin Chop
Braise

Butterfly Chop
Broil, Panbroil, Panfry, Braise

SIDE

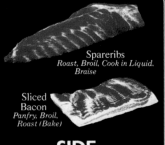

Spareribs
Roast, Broil, Cook in Liquid, Braise

Sliced Bacon
Panfry, Broil, Roast (Bake)

OTHER CUTS

Cubed Steak
Braise, Panbroil, Panfry

Pork Pieces
Braise, Cook in Liquid

Cubes for Kabobs
Broil, Braise

Ground Pork
Broil, Panbroil, Panfry, Roast (Bake)

Sausage Links
Braise, Panfry, Roast

4. Cook for the time recommended in the chart, turning occasionally, until the pork is brown on both sides and reaches the doneness shown in the chart on page 250 for the cut you're using. Drain excess drippings from the skillet as they form. To see if the pork is done, cut a small slit in the center of boneless cuts or in the center near the bone of bone-in cuts. Medium pork is slightly pink in the center; well-done pork is creamy-tan all the way through. If you like, season the pork after it's done.

Roasting Ham

Ham is roasted in the oven with no water. Check the Timetable for Roasting Ham, below, to determine the right oven temperatures and times for the type of ham you've chosen. (See also Glazed Baked Ham, page 261.) Follow these steps for roasted ham that's well-browned on the outside and moist inside:

1. Choose one of the types of ham from the Timetable for Roasting Ham.

2. Place ham—right from the refrigerator—fat side up (if present), on a rack in a shallow roasting pan. There is no need to season ham with salt, pepper, herbs or spices. (For easy cleanup, line the pan with aluminum foil first.) As the fat melts, it bastes the ham, making other basting unnecessary.

3. Insert a meat thermometer so the tip is centered in the thickest part of the ham and not resting in fat or touching bone. Don't cover the roast or add water.

4. Roast at 325°; preheat the oven for hams weighing less than 2 pounds. Roast as directed in the chart until the thermometer reads 135°. The ham will continue to cook after you take it out of the oven.

5. Take the ham out of the oven and cover it loosely with a foil tent. Let stand for 15 to 20 minutes or until it reaches 140°. After standing, the ham also will be easier to carve.

How to Carve a Whole Ham

1. Place ham, fat side up, shank to your right, on carving board or platter. (Face shank to your left if you are left-handed.) Cut a few slices from thin side. Turn ham, cut side down, so it rests firmly.

TIMETABLE FOR ROASTING HAM*

Fully Cooked Smoked Cut	Approximate Weight (pounds)	Approximate Roasting Time (minutes per pound)
Boneless Ham (Cook in covered pan with 1/2 cup water.)	1 1/2 to 2	29 to 33
	3 to 4	19 to 23
	6 to 8	16 to 20
	9 to 11	12 to 16
Bone-in Ham (Cook in covered pan with no water.)	6 to 8	13 to 17
	14 to 16	11 to 14
Canned Ham (Cook uncovered with can juices.)	1 1/2 to 2	23 to 25
	3	21 to 23
	5	17 to 20

*Oven temperature 325°

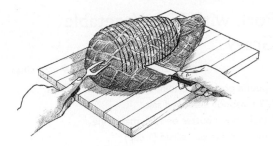

2. Make vertical slices down the leg bone, then cut horizontally along bone to release slices.

Broiling, Panbroiling and Panfrying Ham

Broiling

1. Choose one of the types of ham from the Timetable for Broiling, Panbroiling and Panfrying Ham, below.

2. Set oven to broil. Check your oven manual for whether the oven door should be open or closed during broiling.

3. Place ham on the rack in the broiler pan. (For easy cleanup, line the pan with aluminum foil first.) Position the pan so the top of the ham is four to five inches from the heat.

4. Broil for the time shown in the chart, turning once.

Panbroiling

1. Choose one of the types of ham from the Timetable for Broiling, Panbroiling and Panfrying Ham, below.

2. Use a heavy nonstick skillet, or coat a regular skillet with a film of vegetable oil or cooking spray. Heat the skillet for 5 minutes over medium heat.

3. Put the ham in the skillet; don't cover and don't add oil or water.

4. Cook for the time recommended in the chart, turning occasionally, until the ham is hot. Drain excess drippings from the skillet as they form.

Panfrying

1. Choose one of the types of ham from the Timetable for Broiling, Panbroiling and Panfrying Ham, below.

2. Heat a small amount of vegetable oil in a heavy skillet over medium heat.

3. Cook the ham, uncovered, in the oil, turning occasionally, until it's hot.

TIMETABLE FOR BROILING, PANBROILING AND PANFRYING HAM

Fully Cooked Smoked Cut	Approximate Thickness	Total Broiling Time	Approximate Total Panbroiling or Panfrying Time (minutes)
Ham Cubes for Kabobs	1-inch pieces	7 to 8	*
Ham Slice	1/4 inch	6 to 7	3 to 4
	1/2 inch	8 to 10	5 to 6

Panbroiling or panfrying is not recommended for kabobs.

Pork Crown Roast with Mushroom Stuffing

Prep: 20 min; Roast: 3 hr 20 min; Stand: 20 min ✳ *12 servings*

This special roast may be on hand at your supermarket during the holidays, but call the meat department ahead of time to make sure. Those fancy paper frills usually come with the roast.

7 1/2- to 8-pound pork crown roast (about 20 ribs)
2 teaspoons salt
1 teaspoon pepper
Mushroom Stuffing (page 281)

1. Sprinkle pork with salt and pepper. Place pork, bone ends up, on rack in shallow roasting pan. Wrap bone ends in aluminum foil to prevent excessive browning. Insert meat thermometer so tip is in thickest part of meat and does not touch bone or rest in fat. Place small heatproof bowl or crumpled aluminum foil in crown to hold shape of roast evenly. Do not add water. Do not cover.

2. Roast in 350° oven (preheating oven is not necessary) 2 hours 30 minutes to 3 hours or until thermometer reads 155°. (Also see Recommended Meat Doneness, page 222.)

3. While pork is roasting, make Mushroom Stuffing. 1 hour before pork is done, remove bowl and fill center of crown with stuffing. Cover stuffing with aluminum foil only for first 30 minutes. Remove aluminum foil and finish baking.

4. Remove pork from oven, cover with tent of aluminum foil and let stand 15 to 20 minutes or until thermometer reads 160°. (Temperature will continue to rise about 5°, and pork will be easier to carve.)

5. Remove foil wrapping; place paper frills on bone ends. To serve, spoon stuffing into bowl and cut pork between ribs.

1 Serving: Calories 680 (Calories from Fat 250); Fat 28g (Saturated 8g); Cholesterol 110mg; Sodium 1,500mg; Carbohydrate 61g (Dietary Fiber 3g); Protein 49g **% Daily Value:** Vitamin A 14%; Vitamin C 2%; Calcium 20%; Iron 36% **Diet Exchanges:** 4 Starch, 5 Medium-Fat Meat

Pork with Rich Vegetable Gravy

Prep: 20 min; Cook: 30 min ✳ *4 servings*

1-pound pork tenderloin, cut into 1/4-inch slices
1/2 teaspoon seasoned salt
1 tablespoon butter or stick margarine
2 medium carrots, sliced (1 cup)
1 medium onion, chopped (1/2 cup)
1 medium stalk celery, sliced (1/2 cup)
1 cup sliced mushrooms (4 ounces)
1 can (14 1/2 ounces) ready-to-serve beef broth
2 tablespoons all-purpose flour
1 tablespoon ketchup
2 tablespoons dry sherry, if desired
1/4 teaspoon dried thyme leaves
Hot cooked noodles (page 390), if desired

1. Spray 12-inch skillet with cooking spray; heat over medium-high heat. Sprinkle pork with seasoned salt. Cook pork in skillet 4 to 6 minutes, turning once, until brown. Remove pork from skillet.

2. Add butter, carrots, onion and celery to skillet. Cook 4 to 5 minutes, stirring occasionally, until vegetables are crisp-tender. Stir in mushrooms. Cook 2 minutes.

3. Mix broth and flour until smooth. Stir broth mixture, ketchup, sherry and thyme into vegetable mixture. Cook uncovered about 10 minutes, stirring occasionally, until vegetables are tender.

4. Stir in pork. Cook 4 to 5 minutes or until pork is no longer pink in center. Serve with noodles.

1 Serving: Calories 215 (Calories from Fat 70); Fat 8g (Saturated 3g); Cholesterol 75mg; Sodium 780mg; Carbohydrate 11g (Dietary Fiber 2g); Protein 27g **% Daily Value:** Vitamin A 50%; Vitamin C 6%; Calcium 2%; Iron 12% **Diet Exchanges:** 3 Lean Meat, 2 Vegetable

Peach- and Mustard-Glazed Pork Tenderloin

Prep: 10 min; Marinate: 1 hr; Bake: 30 min; Stand: 15 min; Cook: 2 min ✳ 6 servings

1/2 cup peach preserves
2 tablespoons Dijon mustard
2 teaspoons vegetable oil
1/4 teaspoon dried thyme leaves
1/4 teaspoon salt
2 pork tenderloins (about 3/4 pound each)

1. Mix all ingredients except pork. Place pork in resealable plastic food-storage bag or shallow glass or plastic dish. Pour preserves mixture over pork; turn pork to coat with preserves mixture. Seal bag or cover dish and refrigerate at least 1 hour but no longer than 8 hours, turning pork occasionally.

2. Heat oven to 450°.

3. Remove pork from marinade; reserve marinade in 1-quart saucepan. Place pork in shallow roasting pan. Insert meat thermometer so tip is in thickest part of pork.

4. Bake uncovered 25 to 30 minutes or until thermometer reads 155°. Cover pork with aluminum foil and let stand 10 to 15 minutes, brushing once with reserved marinade, until thermometer reads 160°. (Temperature will continue to rise about 5°, and pork will be easier to carve.)

5. Heat marinade to boiling. Boil 1 minute, stirring constantly. Cut pork into slices. Serve with marinade.

1 Serving: Calories 220 (Calories from Fat 55); Fat 6g (Saturated 2g); Cholesterol 65mg; Sodium 220mg; Carbohydrate 18g (Dietary Fiber 0g); Protein 24g **% Daily Value:** Vitamin A 0%; Vitamin C 2%; Calcium 0%; Iron 8% **Diet Exchanges:** 3 1/2 Very Lean Meat, 1 Fruit, 1 Fat

Italian Roasted Pork Tenderloin

Prep: 10 min; Bake: 30 min; Stand: 15 min ✳ 6 servings

1 teaspoon olive or vegetable oil
1/2 teaspoon salt
1/2 teaspoon fennel seed, crushed
1/4 teaspoon pepper
1 clove garlic, finely chopped
2 pork tenderloins, about 3/4 pound each

1. Heat oven to 450°. Spray shallow roasting pan with cooking spray.

2. Mash all ingredients except pork into a paste. Rub paste on pork. Place pork in pan. Insert meat thermometer so tip is in thickest part of pork.

3. Bake uncovered 25 to 30 minutes or until thermometer reads 155°. Cover pork with aluminum foil and let stand 10 to 15 minutes or until thermometer reads 160°. (Temperature will continue to rise about 5°, and pork will be easier to carve.)

1 Serving: Calories 140 (Calories from Fat 45); Fat 5g (Saturated 2g); Cholesterol 65mg; Sodium 240mg; Carbohydrate 0g (Dietary Fiber 0g); Protein 24g **% Daily Value:** Vitamin A 0%; Vitamin C 0%; Calcium 0%; Iron 6% **Diet Exchanges:** 3 lean meat

Saucy Ribs

Prep: 10 min; Bake: 2 hr 15 min ✱ *6 servings*

Spicy Barbecue Sauce, Molasses-Mustard Sauce or
   Sweet-Savory Sauce (below)
4 1/2 pounds pork loin back ribs, pork spareribs or
   beef short ribs or 3 pounds pork country-style ribs

1. Heat oven to 350°.

2. Make desired sauce. Use sauce as directed in chart on
page 257.

3. Cut ribs into serving pieces. Place meaty sides up in
pan listed in chart.

4. Cook as directed in chart.

Spicy Barbecue Sauce

1/3 cup butter or stick margarine
2 tablespoons white or cider vinegar
2 tablespoons water
1 teaspoon sugar
1/2 teaspoon garlic powder
1/2 teaspoon onion powder
1/2 teaspoon pepper
Dash of ground red pepper (cayenne)

Heat all ingredients in 1-quart saucepan over medium
heat, stirring frequently, until butter is melted.

Molasses-Mustard Sauce

1/2 cup molasses
1/3 cup Dijon mustard
1/3 cup cider or white vinegar

Mix molasses and mustard. Stir in vinegar.

Using sharp knife or kitchen scissors, cut pork ribs into serving-size pieces.

Sweet-Savory Sauce

1 cup chili sauce
3/4 cup grape jelly
1 tablespoon plus 1 1/2 teaspoons dry red wine or
   beef broth
1 teaspoon Dijon mustard

Heat all ingredients in 1-quart saucepan over medium
heat, stirring occasionally, until jelly is melted.

1 Serving: Calories 735 (Calories from Fat 540); Fat 60g (Saturated
25g); Cholesterol 225mg; Sodium 220mg; Carbohydrate 1g
(Dietary Fiber 0g); Protein 48g **% Daily Value:** Vitamin A 8%;
Vitamin C 0%; Calcium 8%; Iron 16% **Diet Exchanges:** 7 High-Fat
Meat, 1 Fat

Slow Cooker Directions: Reduce amount of ribs to
3 1/2 pounds. Cut ribs into 2- or 3-rib portions. Place
ribs in 5- to 6-quart slow cooker. Sprinkle with 1/2 teaspoon salt and 1/4 teaspoon pepper. Pour 1/2 cup water
into slow cooker. Cover and cook on low heat setting
8 to 9 hours or until tender. Remove ribs. Drain and
discard liquid from slow cooker. Make desired sauce;
pour into bowl. Dip ribs into sauce to coat. Place ribs
in slow cooker. Pour any remaining sauce over ribs.
Cover and cook on low heat setting 1 hour.

HIGH ON THE HOG

Pork is 50 percent leaner than it
was twenty years ago. The
leanest pork cuts, in descending
order, are:

- Boneless loin roast and chops
- Top loin roast
- Tenderloin
- Top loin chops

- Loin chops
- Boneless ham
- Canadian-style bacon

SAUCY RIBS COOKING CHART

Kind of Ribs	Pan	Cooking Directions	Serving Tips
Pork Loin, Back Ribs	Rack in shallow roasting pan	Bake uncovered 1 hour 30 minutes; brush with sauce. Bake uncovered about 45 minutes longer, brushing frequently with sauce, until tender.	Heat any remaining sauce to boiling, stirring constantly; boil and stir 1 minute. Serve sauce with ribs.
Pork, Spareribs	Rack in shallow roasting pan	Bake uncovered 1 hour; brush with sauce. Bake uncovered about 45 minutes longer, brushing frequently with sauce, until tender.	Heat any remaining sauce to boiling, stirring constantly; boil and stir 1 minute. Serve sauce with ribs.
Pork, Country-Style Ribs	Rectangular pan, 13 × 9 × 2 inches	Cover and bake about 2 hours or until tender; drain. Pour sauce over ribs. Bake uncovered 30 minutes longer.	Spoon sauce from pan over ribs.
Beef Short Ribs	Rectangular pan, 13 × 9 × 2 inches	Pour sauce over ribs. Cover and bake about 2 hours 30 minutes or until tender.	Spoon sauce from pan over ribs.

Spicy Asian Pork Ribs

Prep: 5 min; Bake: 1 hr 30 min; Cook: 2 min
✱ *4 to 6 servings*

Serve these luscious ribs on a pretty platter, and garnish with fresh orange wedges and parsley.

4 pounds pork loin back ribs
1/4 cup orange marmalade
2 tablespoons hoisin sauce
1 tablespoon soy sauce
1/4 teaspoon ground mustard

1. Heat oven to 350°.

2. Cut ribs into serving pieces. Place meaty sides up in shallow roasting pan.

3. Mix remaining ingredients in 1-quart saucepan. Brush pork generously with some of the marmalade mixture.

4. Cover and bake 1 hour. Brush with marmalade mixture. Cover and bake 15 to 30 minutes longer or until pork is tender.

5. Heat remaining marmalade mixture to boiling. Boil 1 minute, stirring constantly. Serve with pork.

1 Serving: Calories 920 (Calories from Fat 600); Fat 67g (Saturated 24g); Cholesterol 265mg; Sodium 570mg; Carbohydrate 16g (Dietary Fiber 1g); Protein 64g **% Daily Value:** Vitamin A 2%; Vitamin C 2%; Calcium 10%; Iron 24% **Diet Exchanges:** 1 Starch, 9 Medium-Fat Meat, 4 Fat

Caramelized Pork Slices **Fast**

Prep: 10 min; Cook: 13 min ✱ *4 servings*

Serve this slightly sweet pork with corn and baked or mashed sweet potatoes.

1 pound pork tenderloin
2 cloves garlic, finely chopped
2 tablespoons packed brown sugar
1 tablespoon orange juice
1 tablespoon molasses or maple-flavored syrup
1/2 teaspoon salt
1/4 teaspoon pepper

1. Cut pork into 1/2-inch slices. Spray 10-inch non-stick skillet with cooking spray; heat over medium-high heat.

2. Cook pork and garlic in skillet 6 to 8 minutes, turning occasionally, until pork is slightly pink in center. Drain if necessary.

3. Stir in remaining ingredients. Cook about 2 to 5 minutes, stirring occasionally, until mixture thickens and coats pork.

1 Serving: Calories 175 (Calories from Fat 35); Fat 4g (Saturated 2g); Cholesterol 65mg; Sodium 350mg; Carbohydrate 11g (Dietary Fiber 0g); Protein 24g **% Daily Value:** Vitamin A 0%; Vitamin C 2%; Calcium 2%; Iron 10% **Diet Exchanges:** 3 lean meat, 1/2 fruit

Chili-Orange Country-Style Ribs

Chili-Orange Country-Style Ribs

Prep: 15 min; Bake: 2 hr ✱ *4 servings*

3 to 4 pounds pork boneless country-style ribs
1/2 teaspoon salt
1/2 teaspoon dried marjoram leaves
1/4 teaspoon pepper
1 cup chili sauce
1/4 cup orange marmalade
2 tablespoons Worcestershire sauce
1 teaspoon ground mustard
2 tablespoons chopped fresh chives, if desired

1. Heat oven to 350°.

2. Place ribs in rectangular pan, 13 × 9 × 2 inches. Sprinkle both sides with salt, marjoram and pepper. Cover tightly with aluminum foil.

3. Bake 1 hour 30 minutes to 1 hour 45 minutes or until tender; drain.

4. While ribs are baking, mix chili sauce, marmalade, Worcestershire sauce and mustard in 1-quart saucepan. Cook over medium-low heat 5 minutes, stirring occasionally, or until flavors are blended. Stir in chives. Brush sauce over ribs.

5. Bake uncovered 15 minutes. Brush again with sauce. Bake 10 to 15 minutes longer or until ribs are glazed. Serve with remaining sauce.

1 Serving: Calories 485 (Calories from Fat 200); Fat 22g (Saturated 8g); Cholesterol 115mg; Sodium 1,260mg; Carbohydrate 33g (Dietary Fiber 1g); Protein 40g **% Daily Value:** Vitamin A 6%; Vitamin C 10%; Calcium 2%; Iron 12% **Diet Exchanges:** 5 Lean Meat, 1 Vegetable, 2 Fruit, 1 1/2 Fat

Pork Chop and Potato Skillet

Prep: 15 min; Cook: 45 min ✳ *6 servings*

6 pork loin or rib chops, 1/2 inch thick (about 1 1/2
  pounds)
1 can (10 3/4 ounces) condensed cream of mushroom
  soup
1 can (4 ounces) mushroom pieces and stems,
  undrained
1/4 cup water
2 tablespoons dry white wine or apple juice
3/4 teaspoon chopped fresh or 1/4 teaspoon dried
  thyme leaves
1/2 teaspoon garlic powder
1/2 teaspoon Worcestershire sauce
6 medium new potatoes (about 1 1/2 pounds), cut into
  fourths
1 tablespoon diced pimiento
1 package (10 ounces) frozen green peas, rinsed and
  drained

1. Spray 10-inch nonstick skillet with cooking spray;
heat over medium-high heat. Cook pork in skillet,
turning once, until brown.

2. Mix soup, mushrooms, water, wine, thyme, garlic
powder and Worcestershire sauce; pour over pork. Heat
to boiling, stirring occasionally; reduce heat. Cover and
simmer 15 minutes.

3. Add potatoes. Cover and simmer 15 minutes. Stir in
pimiento and peas. Cover and simmer about 10 minutes, stirring occasionally, until peas are tender and
pork is slightly pink when cut near bone.

1 Serving: Calories 275 (Calories from Fat 100); Fat 11g (Saturated
4g); Cholesterol 65mg; Sodium 520mg; Carbohydrate 21g (Dietary
Fiber 4g); Protein 27g **% Daily Value:** Vitamin A 4%; Vitamin C 8%;
Calcium 4%; Iron 14% **Diet Exchanges:** 1 Starch, 3 Lean Meat, 1
Vegetable

Slow Cooker Directions: Drain mushrooms. Omit
water. Cut potatoes into eighths. Place potatoes in
3 1/2- to 6-quart slow cooker. Mix soup, mushrooms,
wine, thyme, garlic powder, Worcestershire sauce and
3 tablespoons all-purpose flour; spoon half of soup
mixture over potatoes. Place pork on potatoes; cover
with remaining soup mixture. Cover and cook on low
heat setting 6 to 7 hours or until pork is tender.
Remove pork; keep warm. Stir pimiento and green peas
into slow cooker. Cover and cook on low heat setting
15 minutes.

Sweet-and-Sour Pork

Prep: 25 min; Cook: 30 min ✳ *8 servings*

2 pounds pork boneless top loin
Vegetable oil
1/2 cup all-purpose flour
1/4 cup cornstarch
1/2 cup cold water
1/2 teaspoon salt
1 large egg
1 can (20 ounces) pineapple chunks in syrup, drained
  and syrup reserved
1/2 cup packed brown sugar
1/2 cup white vinegar
1/2 teaspoon salt
2 teaspoons soy sauce
2 medium carrots, cut into thin diagonal slices
1 clove garlic, finely chopped
2 tablespoons cornstarch
2 tablespoons cold water
1 medium green bell pepper, cut into 3/4-inch pieces
8 cups hot cooked rice (page 348)

1. Remove fat from pork. Cut pork into 3/4-inch
pieces. Heat 1 inch oil in deep fryer or 4-quart Dutch
oven to 360°.

2. Beat flour, 1/4 cup cornstarch, 1/2 cup cold water,
1/2 teaspoon salt and the egg in large bowl with hand
beater until smooth. Stir pork into batter until well
coated.

3. Add pork pieces, one at a time, to oil. Fry about 20
pieces at a time about 5 minutes, turning 2 or 3 times,
until golden brown. Drain on paper towels; keep warm.

4. Add enough water to reserved pineapple syrup to
measure 1 cup. Heat syrup mixture, brown sugar, vinegar, 1/2 teaspoon salt, the soy sauce, carrots and garlic
to boiling in Dutch oven; reduce heat. Cover and simmer about 6 minutes or until carrots are crisp-tender.

5. Mix 2 tablespoons cornstarch and 2 tablespoons cold
water; stir into sauce. Add pork, pineapple and bell
pepper. Heat to boiling, stirring constantly. Boil and
stir 1 minute. Serve with rice.

1 Serving (about 2 cups): Calories 540 (Calories from Fat 100);
Fat 11g (Saturated 3g); Cholesterol 80mg; Sodium 420mg;
Carbohydrate 87g (Dietary Fiber 2g); Protein 25g **% Daily Value:**
Vitamin A 26%; Vitamin C 16%; Calcium 4%; Iron 20% **Diet
Exchanges:** 3 Starch, 1 1/2 Lean Meat, 2 Vegetable, 2 Fruit, 1 Fat

Corn Bread- and Bacon-Stuffed Pork Chops

Corn Bread- and Bacon-Stuffed Pork Chops

Prep: 20 min; Cook: 10 min; Bake: 1 hr ✳ *6 servings*

6 pork rib or loin chops, 1 to 1 1/4 inches thick (about 4 pounds)
4 slices bacon, cut into 1/2-inch pieces
1 medium onion, chopped (1/2 cup)
1 small green bell pepper, chopped (1/2 cup)
1 cup corn bread stuffing crumbs
1/2 cup water
1/2 cup shredded Cheddar cheese (2 ounces)
1/2 teaspoon seasoned salt
1/2 teaspoon dried marjoram leaves
1/4 teaspoon pepper

1. Heat oven to 350°.

2. Make a pocket in each pork chop by cutting into side of chop toward the bone.

3. Cook bacon in 12-inch skillet over medium heat, stirring occasionally, until crisp. Stir in onion and bell pepper. Cook 2 to 3 minutes, stirring occasionally, until vegetables are crisp-tender; remove from heat. Drain. Stir in stuffing crumbs and water until well mixed. Stir in cheese.

4. Sprinkle both sides of pork with seasoned salt, marjoram and pepper. Fill pockets with about 1/3 cup corn bread mixture. Cook pork in same skillet over medium heat, turning once, until brown. Place pork in ungreased rectangular pan, 13 × 9 × 2 inches. Cover tightly with aluminum foil.

5. Bake 45 minutes. Uncover and bake about 15 minutes longer or until pork is slightly pink when cut near bone.

1 Serving: Calories 335 (Calories from Fat 180); Fat 20g (Saturated 7g); Cholesterol 90mg; Sodium 550mg; Carbohydrate 15g (Dietary Fiber 1g); Protein 25g **% Daily Value:** Vitamin A 10%; Vitamin C 10%; Calcium 12%;Iron 8% **Diet Exchanges:** 1 Starch, 3 Medium-Fat Meat, 1 Fat

Make a pocket in each chop by cutting into side of chop toward the bone

Glazed Baked Ham

Prep: 10 min; Bake: 1 hr 30 min; Stand: 15 min
✻ *20 servings*

6-pound fully cooked smoked bone-in ham
Brown Sugar–Orange Glaze or Pineapple Glaze (below)

1. Heat oven to 325°. Place ham on rack in shallow roasting pan. Insert meat thermometer in thickest part of ham. Bake uncovered 1 hour 30 minutes or until thermometer reads 135° to 140°.

2. Make desired glaze. Brush glaze over ham during last 45 minutes of baking. (Also see Recommended Meat Doneness, page 222.)

3. Remove ham from oven, cover with tent with aluminum foil and let stand 10 to 15 minutes for easier carving.

Brown Sugar–Orange Glaze

1/2 cup packed brown sugar
2 tablespoons orange or pineapple juice
1/2 teaspoon ground mustard

Mix all ingredients.

Pineapple Glaze

1 cup packed brown sugar
1 tablespoon cornstarch
1/4 teaspoon salt
1 can (8 ounces) crushed pineapple in syrup, undrained
2 tablespoons lemon juice
1 tablespoon yellow mustard

Mix brown sugar, cornstarch and salt in 1-quart saucepan. Stir in pineapple, lemon juice and mustard. Cook over medium heat, stirring constantly, until mixture thickens and boils. Boil and stir 1 minute.

1 Serving: Calories 125 (Calories from Fat 35); Fat 4g (Saturated 1g); Cholesterol 40mg; Sodium 890mg; Carbohydrate 7g (Dietary Fiber 0g); Protein 15g **% Daily Value:** Vitamin A 0%; Vitamin C 0%; Calcium 0%; Iron 6% **Diet Exchanges:** 2 Lean Meat, 1/2 Fruit

*Nutrition run calculated on a 6-pound bone-in ham.

Ham Loaf

Prep: 15 min; Bake: 1 hr 30 minutes; Stand: 5 min
✻ *8 servings*

Either Whipped Horseradish Sauce (page 439) or Molasses Mustard Sauce (page 256) would taste great with this ham loaf.

1 1/2 pounds ground fully cooked ham
1 small onion, finely chopped (1/4 cup)
1/2 cup dry bread crumbs
1/4 cup finely chopped green bell pepper
1/2 cup milk
1/2 teaspoon ground mustard
1/4 teaspoon pepper
2 large eggs

1. Heat oven to 350°.

2. Mix all ingredients. Spread mixture in ungreased loaf pan, 9 × 5 × 3 or 8 1/2 × 4 1/2 × 2 1/2 inches.

3. Insert meat thermometer so tip is in center of loaf. Bake uncovered about 1 hour 30 minutes or until thermometer reads 170°.

4. Let stand 5 minutes; remove from pan.

1 Serving: Calories 205 (Calories from Fat 90); Fat 10g (Saturated 3g); Cholesterol 105mg; Sodium 1,360mg; Carbohydrate 7g (Dietary Fiber 0g); Protein 22g **% Daily Value:** Vitamin A 2%; Vitamin C 4%; Calcium 4%; Iron 10% **Diet Exchanges:** 1/2 Starch, 3 Lean Meat

Lighter Ham Loaf: For 5 grams of fat and 155 calories per serving, use reduced-fat ham; substitute 1/2 cup fat-free cholesterol-free egg product for the eggs.

Lamb Basics

Selecting Lamb

A lean, tender and usually delicate-flavored meat, lamb comes from animals six to eight months old. Once lamb reaches one year of age, it is referred to as "mutton," which has a much stronger flavor. When buying lamb, let color be your guide: Look for lamb that's pinkish red with a velvety texture and a thin, firm layer of white fat surrounding it. The darker the meat, the older the animal and stronger the flavor. The thin, paperlike covering on larger cuts of lamb is called *fell*. Don't remove the fell because it helps these cuts keep their shape and retain juices during cooking. (The fell usually has been trimmed from smaller cuts at the store.) Trim excess fat before cooking to avoid a stronger flavor. For best flavor and juiciness, cook lamb to medium-rare (145°) or medium (160°). Also see Recommended Meat Doneness, page 222.

Roasting Lamb

Lamb is roasted in the oven with no water. Because lamb is tender, it's a natural for roasting. Check the Timetable for Roasting Lamb, page 263, to determine the right oven temperatures and times for each cut. Follow these steps for roasted lamb that's well browned on the outside and moist and tender inside:

1. Choose one of the cuts from the Timetable for Roasting Lamb.

2. Place lamb—right from the refrigerator—fat side up, on a rack in a shallow roasting pan. (For easy cleanup, line the pan with aluminum foil first.) Don't remove the fell; it helps the roast keep its shape and holds in juices. As the fat melts during roasting, it bastes the lamb, making basting during cooking unnecessary.

3. If you like, season the lamb with herbs, spices or other seasonings before, during or after cooking. Sprinkling the roast with salt *before* cooking adds flavor.

4. Insert a meat thermometer so the tip is centered in the thickest part of the roast and not resting in fat or touching bone. Don't cover the roast or add water.

5. Roast at 325°. Use the chart as a guide and roast for the recommended time until the meat thermometer reads the "Meat Thermometer Reading (after roasting)" temperature. The roast will continue to cook after you take it out of the oven.

6. Take the roast out of the oven and cover it loosely with a foil tent. Let stand for 15 to 20 minutes or until it reaches the "Final Meat Thermometer Reading (after standing)" temp. After standing, the roast also will be easier to carve. Avoid covering the roast tightly because doing so will create steam, which will soften the surface of the lamb.

How to Carve a Leg of Lamb

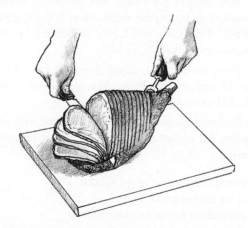

Place leg, shank bone to your right, on carving board or platter. (Place shank bone to your left if you are left-handed.) Cut a few lengthwise slices from thin side. Turn leg, cut side down, so it rests firmly. Make vertical slices to the leg bone, then cut horizontally along bone to release slices.

TIMETABLE FOR ROASTING LAMB*

Lamb Cut	Approximate Weight (pounds)	Meat Thermometer Reading (after roasting)	Final Meat Thermometer Reading (after standing)	Approximate Cooking Time (minutes per pound)
Leg Roast, Whole (bone in)	12	140°	145° (medium-rare)	15 to 20
		155°	160° (medium)	20 to 25
	5 to 7	140°	145° (medium-rare)	20 to 25
		155°	160° (medium)	25 to 30
Leg Roast, Whole (boneless)	4 to 7	140°	145° (medium-rare)	25 to 30
		155°	160° (medium)	30 to 35
Leg Roast, Shank half	3 to 4	140°	145° (medium-rare)	30 to 35
		155°	160° (medium)	40 to 45
Leg Roast, Sirloin	3 to 4	140°	145° (medium-rare)	25 to 30
		155°	160° (medium)	35 to 40
Shoulder Roast (boneless)	3 1/2 to 5	140°	145° (medium-rare)	30 to 35
		155°	160° (medium)	35 to 40
(bone in)	3 1/2 to 5	140°	145° (medium-rare)	35 to 40
(presliced)		155°	160° (medium)	40 to 45

*Oven temperature 325°

Lamb

RETAIL CUTS
Where They Come From
How To Cook Them

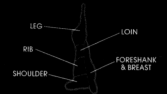

LEG — LOIN
RIB
SHOULDER
FORESHANK & BREAST

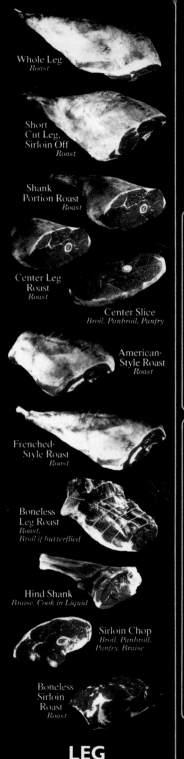

Whole Leg
Roast

Short Cut Leg, Sirloin Off
Roast

Shank Portion Roast
Roast

Center Leg Roast
Roast

Center Slice
Broil, Panbroil, Panfry

American-Style Roast
Roast

Frenched-Style Roast
Roast

Boneless Leg Roast
Roast, Broil if butterflied

Hind Shank
Braise, Cook in Liquid

Sirloin Chop
Broil, Panbroil, Panfry, Braise

Boneless Sirloin Roast
Roast

LEG

Loin Roast
Roast

Loin Chop
Broil, Panbroil, Panfry

Double Loin Chop
Broil, Panbroil, Panfry

LOIN

Shank
Braise, Cook in Liquid

Spareribs
Braise, Broil, Roast

Boneless Rolled Breast
Roast, Braise

Riblets
Braise, Cook in Liquid. Broil

FORESHANK & BREAST

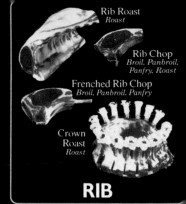

Rib Roast
Roast

Rib Chop
Broil, Panbroil, Panfry, Roast

Frenched Rib Chop
Broil, Panbroil, Panfry

Crown Roast
Roast

RIB

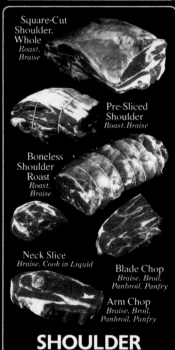

Square-Cut Shoulder, Whole
Roast, Braise

Pre-Sliced Shoulder
Roast, Braise

Boneless Shoulder Roast
Roast, Braise

Neck Slice
Braise, Cook in Liquid

Blade Chop
Braise, Broil, Panbroil, Panfry

Arm Chop
Braise, Broil, Panbroil, Panfry

SHOULDER

Lamb for Stew
Braise, Cook in Liquid

Cubes for Kabobs
Broil, Braise

Ground Lamb
Broil, Panbroil, Roast (Bake)

OTHER CUTS

Broiling or Grilling Lamb

Broiling and grilling are great ways for cooking bone-in and boneless cuts of lamb, such as chops and patties. Less-tender cuts grill best if they're marinated first (see Tips for Marinades and Marinating, page 453). Other lamb cuts can be grilled over indirect heat. The tips below use direct heat. For more information on using your grill, check out the instruction booklet that came with your grill or the Grilling Basics, page 331. Check the Timetable for Broiling or Grilling Lamb, below, to determine the right oven temperatures and times for each cut.

1. Choose a cut of lamb from the Timetable for Broiling or Grilling Lamb. If you like, marinate the lamb first.

2. **To Broil:** Set oven to broil. Check your oven manual for whether the oven door should be open or closed during broiling.

   To Grill: Heat coals or gas grill to medium; spread the coals to a single layer.

3. Remove any excess fat before broiling or grilling.

4. **To Broil:** Place lamb on the rack in the broiler pan. (For easy cleanup, line the pan with aluminum foil first.) Position the pan so the top of the lamb is the distance from the heat recommended in the chart.

   To Grill: Place lamb on the grill the distance from the heat recommended in the chart.

5. Broil or grill the lamb for about half the recommended time or until it's brown on one side.

6. Turn the lamb, and continue broiling or grilling until the doneness shown in the chart below for the cut you're using. To see if it's done, cut a small slit in the center of boneless cuts or in the center near the bone of bone-in cuts. Medium-rare lamb is pink in the center, medium is light pink. If you like, season the lamb after it's done.

TIMETABLE FOR BROILING OR GRILLING LAMB

Lamb Cut	Approximate Thickness or Weight	Inches from Heat	Approximate Total Broiling Time (minutes)		Approximate Total Grilling Time (minutes)	
			145° (medium-rare)	160° (medium)	145° (medium-rare)	160° (medium)
Shoulder Chop*	3/4 to 1 inch	3 to 4	5 to 9	7 to 11	9 to 12	12 to 14
Loin or Rib Chop	1 inch	3 to 4	5 to 9	7 to 11	7 to 9	9 to 11
	1 1/2 inches	4 to 5	12 to 17	15 to 19	14 to 17	17 to 20
Sirloin Chop	3/4 to 1 inch	3 to 4	10 to 13	12 to 15	15 to 17	17 to 21
Butterflied Leg (sirloin removed, boneless)	4 pounds	5 to 7	40 to 46	47 to 53	33 to 53	40 to 60
Leg Steak	3/4 to 1 inch	3 to 4	11 to 15	14 to 18	15 to 18	17 to 21
Cubes for Kabobs	1 to 1 1/2 inch	4 to 5	6 to 10	8 to 12	7 to 9	9 to 20
Ground Lamb Patties	1/2 inch	3	3 to 6	5 to 8	3 to 5	5 to 7

Marinate at least 6 hours but no longer than 24 hours to tenderize.

Apricot-Rosemary Marinated Leg of Lamb

Prep: 20 min; Marinate: 8 hr; Bake: 2 hr; Cook: 5 min; Stand: 15 min ✱ 8 servings

5-pound bone-in leg of lamb
16 slices garlic (2 or 3 cloves)
16 small rosemary sprigs (2 tablespoons)
1 can (15 to 16 ounces) apricot halves in light syrup, drained and syrup reserved
1/2 cup dry red wine or nonalcoholic red wine
1/4 cup olive or vegetable oil
2 tablespoons honey
1/4 teaspoon salt
1 teaspoon chopped fresh rosemary leaves

1. Make about 16 small slits, each about 1/4 inch wide and 1/2 inch deep, over surface of lamb. Place slice of garlic and sprig of rosemary in each slit. Place lamb in large resealable plastic food-storage bag or shallow glass or plastic dish.

2. Mix reserved apricot syrup, the wine, oil, 1 tablespoon of the honey and the salt; pour over lamb. Seal bag or cover dish and refrigerate at least 8 hours but no longer than 24 hours, turning lamb occasionally.

3. Heat oven to 325°.

4. Remove lamb from marinade; reserve marinade. Place lamb, fat side up, in shallow roasting pan. Insert meat thermometer so tip is in thickest part of lamb and does not touch bone or rest in fat.

5. Bake uncovered about 2 hours, brushing once or twice with marinade, until thermometer reads 140°. Cover with aluminum foil and let stand 10 to 15 minutes. (Temperature will continue to rise about 5°, and lamb will be easier to carve.)

6. Place apricots in food processor or blender. Cover and process until smooth. Mix apricots, 1/4 cup of the reserved marinade, remaining 1 tablespoon honey and the chopped rosemary in 1-quart saucepan. Heat to boiling. Boil 1 to 2 minutes, stirring occasionally. Serve sauce with lamb.

Make about 16 small slits, each about 1/4 inch wide and 1/2 inch deep, over surface of lamb. Place slice of garlic and sprig of rosemary in each slit.

1 Serving: Calories 400 (Calories from Fat 180); Fat 20g (Saturated 5g); Cholesterol 125mg; Sodium 170mg; Carbohydrate 16g (Dietary Fiber 1g); Protein 40g **% Daily Value:** Vitamin A 4%; Vitamin C 2%; Calcium 2%; Iron 18% **Diet Exchanges:** 6 Lean Meat, 1 Fruit

Greek Lamb Chops

Prep: 15 min; Cook: 25 min ✳ *4 servings*

4 lamb shoulder, arm or loin chops, about 1/2 inch
    thick (about 6 ounces each)
1 teaspoon dried oregano leaves
1/4 teaspoon salt
1/4 teaspoon pepper
4 cloves garlic, finely chopped (1 tablespoon)
1 tablespoon olive or vegetable oil
1/2 cup chicken broth
1 tablespoon lemon juice
1 tablespoon butter or stick margarine
1/4 cup sliced pitted Kalamata or ripe olives
2 tablespoons chopped fresh parsley
2 tablespoons crumbled feta cheese

1. Sprinkle both sides of lamb with oregano, salt and
pepper. Press garlic into lamb. Heat oil in 12-inch skillet over medium-high heat. Cook lamb in oil 4 to 6
minutes, turning once, until brown.

2. Add broth to skillet; reduce heat to medium-low.
Cover and cook 8 to 10 minutes, turning once, until
lamb is tender. Remove lamb from skillet; keep warm.

3. Heat liquid in skillet to boiling. Boil 1 to 2 minutes
or until slightly reduced. Stir in lemon juice and butter.
Cook and stir just until slightly thickened. Stir in olives
and parsley. Spoon sauce over lamb. Top with cheese.

1 Serving: Calories 210 (Calories from Fat 110); Fat 12g (Saturated
5g); Cholesterol 85mg; Sodium 480mg; Carbohydrate 2g (Dietary
Fiber 1g); Protein 24g **% Daily Value:** Vitamin A 4%; Vitamin C 4%;
Calcium 4%; Iron 14% **Diet Exchanges:** 4 Lean Meat Lamb

Liver and Onions *Fast*

Prep: 10 min; Cook: 15 min ✳ *4 servings*

Serve this favorite sprinkled with crumbled crisply
cooked bacon, and add mashed potatoes on the side.

3 tablespoons butter or stick margarine
2 medium onions, thinly sliced
1 pound beef, veal or pork liver, 1/2 to 3/4 inch thick
All-purpose flour
3 tablespoons vegetable oil or shortening
Salt and pepper to taste

1. Melt butter in 10-inch skillet over medium-high
heat. Cook onions in butter 4 to 6 minutes, stirring frequently, until light brown. Remove onions from skillet;
keep warm.

2. Coat liver with flour. Heat oil in same skillet over
medium heat. Cook liver in oil 2 to 3 minutes on each
side or until brown on outside and slightly pink in center, returning onions to skillet during last minute of
cooking. Sprinkle with salt and pepper.

1 Serving: Calories 310 (Calories from Fat 180); Fat 20g (Saturated
8g); Cholesterol 350mg; Sodium 705mg; Carbohydrate 11g
(Dietary Fiber 1g); Protein 22g **% Daily Value:** Vitamin A 100%;
Vitamin C 18%; Calcium 2%; Iron 32% **Diet Exchanges:** 3 Medium-
Fat Meat, 2 Vegetable, 1 Fat

Lighter Liver and Onions: For 8 grams of fat
and 200 calories per serving, omit butter and
decrease oil to 1 tablespoon. Use nonstick skillet.
Spray cold skillet with cooking spray before
cooking onions in step 1.

Game Basics

Low in fat and high in protein, game meats typically have a more robust flavor than beef, veal, pork or lamb. Game found in meat markets, supermarkets and restaurants is farm-raised and federally inspected. Wild game is leaner, stronger tasting and often tougher than commercially raised meats. Marinating wild game will tenderize it and mask some of the unique, gamy flavor without overpowering the flavor of the meat. Cooking also affects the tenderness and flavor; match the cut of game to a similar cut of beef when choosing how to cook it. The secret to cooking large cuts of game? Cook it slowly over low heat and don't overcook!

Rabbit and venison are popular farm-raised game. Wild game includes antelope, armadillo, bear, boar, caribou, deer, elk, kangaroo, opossum, porcupine, raccoon, reindeer, squirrel, wild goats and wild sheep.

Rabbit

Rabbit tastes similar to chicken, and it can be used in most recipes calling for chicken. Some supermarkets and meat markets carry rabbit in the freezer case, or you may have to order it from them a few days in advance. Farm-raised rabbit is sold cut up in ready-to-cook parts. If it's frozen, thaw it in the refrigerator, and use within 2 days.

The lean, mild-flavored meat will darken when marinated and cooked. Typically, a rabbit will weigh 2 1/2 to 3 pounds. A 3-ounce serving of rabbit contains about 130 calories. It's most flavorful and tender if cooked with moist-heat methods. Smaller, more tender rabbits (under 2 pounds) can be broiled or roasted. Always cook rabbit until well done, never medium or rare. Cook whole rabbits until thermometer reaches 180° and rabbit pieces until thermometer reaches 170°. (See Where Do I Put the Thermometer and I Don't Have a Thermometer on page 275.) Because the meat is lean, it dries out quickly during cooking, so be careful not to overcook it.

Venison

Venison isn't a type of animal, it's a term used for deer, elk, moose, antelope, reindeer and caribou. Farm-raised venison, whether fresh or frozen, is available in cuts similar to beef or pork; look for it at specialty stores, meat markets that carry game, game farms and venison farms.

Venison is very lean meat with a rich, full-bodied flavor. Like most game, it will become tough if overcooked. Before cooking, remove the silvery membrane from the meat, and trim off as much of the fat as possible because the fat has a concentration of gamy flavor, congeals quickly and is unpleasant to eat. Game fat can also become rancid quickly. To tenderize fresh venison, marinate it in the refrigerator overnight.

Because venison is so lean, you may need to add fat when cooking it. You can "lard" venison or other lean game by inserting slivers of uncooked salt pork or bacon with a skewer or ice pick all over the meat. Or to add fat for extra moisture and added flavor, try one of these ideas before cooking:

- Place uncooked slices of bacon over the venison
- Rub venison with salt pork, beef suet or bacon fat
- Rub venison with butter, margarine, olive oil or vegetable oil

While cooking venison, basting with the fatty pan drippings will also help to keep the meat more moist. Grill or broil steaks and chops, and braise or roast larger cuts.

Roast large cuts of venison to 160° to destroy bacterial contamination or parasites that might be present. For an accurate reading, insert a meat thermometer so the tip is centered in the thickest part of the meat and not touching bone or fat. If the roast is boneless, insert the thermometer in the center of the roast.

Rabbit Italiano

Prep: 15 min; Cook: 1 hr 20 min ✳ *6 servings*

1/2 cup olive or vegetable oil
1 medium onion, sliced
2 1/2- to 3-pound domestic rabbit, cut up
1/2 cup all-purpose flour
1/2 teaspoon salt
1/2 teaspoon pepper
1 cup dry white wine or chicken broth
2 cups sliced mushrooms (about 5 ounces)
1/2 cup chicken broth
1 can (14 1/2 ounces) whole tomatoes, drained
1 can (6 ounces) small pitted ripe olives, drained

1. Heat oil in 4-quart Dutch oven over medium-high heat. Cook onion in oil, stirring frequently, until tender. Reduce heat to medium.

2. Coat rabbit with flour. Cook rabbit in onion mixture, turning occasionally, until brown. Sprinkle with salt and pepper. Stir in wine. Cook uncovered until liquid has evaporated and juice of rabbit is no longer pink when centers of thickest pieces are cut.

3. Stir in remaining ingredients, breaking up tomatoes with a fork or snipping with kitchen scissors. Cover and simmer about 1 hour or until rabbit is tender.

1 Serving: Calories 455 (Calories from Fat 235); Fat 26g (Saturated 5g); Cholesterol 105mg; Sodium 690mg; Carbohydrate 16g (Dietary Fiber 2g); Protein 41g **% Daily Value:** Vitamin A 4%; Vitamin C 8%; Calcium 8%; Iron 28% **Diet Exchanges:** 1 Starch, 5 1/2 Lean Meat, 2 Fat

Venison with Rosemary Sauce

Prep: 15 min; Cook: 25 min ✳ *4 servings*

8 venison chops or steaks, 1/2 inch thick
    (about 1 3/4 pounds)
1/2 teaspoon salt
1/2 teaspoon pepper
1/4 cup butter or stick margarine
1 tablespoon chopped fresh or 1 teaspoon dried
    rosemary leaves, crumbled
2 cloves garlic, cut in half
1/4 cup Chianti, dry red wine or beef broth
1/4 cup whipping (heavy) cream

1. Remove fat from venison. Sprinkle venison with salt and pepper.

2. Melt butter in 12-inch skillet over medium heat. Cook rosemary and garlic in butter, stirring frequently, until garlic is golden. Add venison. Cook uncovered 10 minutes, turning once, until venison is brown.

3. Stir in wine and whipping cream; reduce heat to low. Cover and cook about 10 minutes or until venison is tender.

1 Serving: Calories 420 (Calories from Fat 200); Fat 22g (Saturated 12g); Cholesterol 245mg; Sodium 470mg; Carbohydrate 1g (Dietary Fiber 0g); Protein 54g **% Daily Value:** Vitamin A 12%; Vitamin C 0%; Calcium 2%; Iron 44% **Diet Exchanges:** 7 1/2 Lean Meat

Venison with Cranberry-Wine Sauce

Venison with Cranberry-Wine Sauce

Prep: 20 min; Marinate: 2 hr; Cook: 15 min ✳ *4 servings*

1/2 cup dry red wine or nonalcoholic red wine

1 tablespoon Dijon mustard

4 venison tenderloin steaks, about 1 inch thick
    (1 1/4 pounds)

1/4 teaspoon salt

1/4 teaspoon coarsely ground pepper

1 tablespoon olive or vegetable oil

1/2 cup beef broth

1/2 cup dried cranberries

2 tablespoons currant or apple jelly

1 tablespoon butter or stick margarine

2 medium green onions, sliced (2 tablespoons)

1. Mix wine and mustard until well blended. Place venison in resealable plastic food-storage bag or shallow glass or plastic dish. Pour wine mixture over venison; turn venison to coat with wine mixture. Seal bag or cover dish and refrigerate at least 2 hours but no longer than 4 hours, turning venison occasionally.

2. Remove venison from marinade; reserve marinade. Sprinkle venison with salt and pepper. Heat oil in 12-inch nonstick skillet over medium-high heat. Cook venison in oil about 4 minutes, turning once, until brown.

3. Add broth to skillet; reduce heat to low. Cover and cook about 10 minutes, turning venison once, until venison is tender and desired doneness. (Don't overcook or venison will become tough.)

4. Remove venison from skillet; keep warm. Stir marinade into skillet. Heat to boiling, scraping up any bits from bottom of skillet; reduce heat to medium. Cook about 5 minutes until mixture is slightly reduced. Stir in cranberries, jelly, butter and onions. Cook 1 to 2 minutes, stirring occasionally, until butter is melted and mixture is hot. Serve sauce with venison.

1 Serving: Calories 255 (Calories from Fat 80); Fat 9g (Saturated 3g); Cholesterol 100mg; Sodium 400mg; Carbohydrate 23g (Dietary Fiber 6g); Protein 27g **% Daily Value:** Vitamin A 2%; Vitamin C 14%; Calcium 2%; Iron 24% **Diet Exchanges:** 3 Lean Meat, 2 Vegetable, 1 Fruit

Poultry

Low-Fat = *3g or less, except main dishes with 6g or less*   **Fast** = *Ready in 30 minutes or less*   ■ = *Bread Machine directions*   ● = *Slow Cooker directions*

Zesty Italian Chicken (page 287)

Lighter = 1/3 fewer calories or 50% less fat

Poultry Basics

It's hard to go wrong when you serve chicken and turkey! Especially when there's a lot to love about it. Poultry is so versatile that it always earns an A for cooperation in the kitchen. You can serve it any way you choose—sandwiches, stir-fries and salads are just a start—and it's adaptable to just about any flavoring. Plus, it fits well into today's healthful eating because both chicken and turkey are relatively low in fat and calories.

Buying Poultry

Choosing the freshest poultry is easy if you follow these guidelines.

Label and Package

- Check the sell-by date on the label (product dating is not a federal requirement). This shows the last day the product should be sold, but the product still will be fresh if cooked and eaten within 2 days of this date.
- Package trays or bags should have very little or no liquid in the bottom.
- Avoid torn and leaking packages.
- Avoid packages that are stacked too high in the refrigerator case. They may not have been kept cold enough, which shortens shelf life.
- Frozen poultry should be hard to the touch and free of freezer burn and tears in the packaging.

Odor and Appearance

- Check for a fresh odor (you can usually smell off odors through the plastic). If you smell anything unusual, the product isn't fresh.
- Choose whole birds and cut-up pieces that are plump and meaty with smooth, moist-looking skin.
- Boneless, skinless products should look plump and moist.
- The color of chicken skin doesn't indicate quality. Skin color can range from yellow to white, depending on what the chicken was fed. Turkey, however, should have cream-colored skin.

- The cut ends of the poultry bones should be pink to red in color; if they are gray, it's not as fresh.
- Avoid poultry with traces of feathers. It may not have been handled properly, and the feathers don't add anything to a cooked dish!

Storing Poultry

In the Refrigerator

Uncooked Poultry: Refrigerate poultry in its original wrapping in the coldest part of the fridge (40° or below) for no longer than 2 days. If poultry products were wrapped in meat-market paper, rewrap them the following way before storing. First, rinse these products with cold water, then pat them dry with paper towels. Repackage in either heavy-duty plastic bags, several layers of plastic wrap (put poultry in a dish or baking pan with sides to prevent leakage on refrigerator shelves during storage) or food-storage containers with tight-fitting lids.

Cooked Poultry: Cut into small pieces, cover or wrap tightly and refrigerate no longer than 2 days. Store leftover cooked stuffing up to 4 days and gravy 1 to 2 days. Place giblets, stuffing and gravy in separate containers to store in refrigerator. Be sure to thoroughly reheat leftovers. Keep leftovers moist while reheating by covering them; covering also will ensure that they are thoroughly heated in the center. Before serving leftover gravies and marinades, bring them to a rolling boil and boil 1 minute, stirring constantly.

In the Freezer

Uncooked Poultry: Freeze cut-up chicken and turkey for up to 9 months, whole chicken and turkey for up to 12 months. Wrap the poultry tightly in moisture- and vapor-resistant freezer wrap, heavy-duty plastic freezer bags or heavy-duty aluminum foil. Store giblets separately. Press as much air as possible out of the package before sealing it to prevent ice crystals from forming and freezer burn. Mark the package with the date and contents before freezing.

Cooked Poultry: Wrap tightly in moisture- and vapor-resistant freezer wrap, heavy-duty plastic freezer bags or heavy-duty aluminum foil, and freeze for up to 1 month. Store poultry, giblets, stuffing and gravy in separate containers. Mark the package with the date and contents before freezing.

Thawing Poultry

Frozen cooked and uncooked poultry can be thawed safely in the refrigerator, in cold water or in your microwave. Never thaw chicken or turkey at room temperature on your countertop because these temperatures provide the perfect environment for bacteria to grow. If your poultry was frozen when you bought it or you froze it right after you brought it home, it will keep in the refrigerator for 2 days after thawing. On the other hand, if the fresh poultry was refrigerated several days before freezing, use it the same day you thaw it.

Refrigerator Method: Thaw frozen uncooked chicken or turkey gradually in your refrigerator. Place poultry in a dish or baking pan with sides to prevent it from leaking on refrigerator shelves during thawing.

Thaw frozen cooked poultry slowly in the refrigerator. Allow approximately 3 to 9 hours for 1 pound cubed, chopped or shredded pieces and up to 24 hours for whole pieces (bone-in or boneless).

Cold Water Method: Frozen uncooked chicken and turkey also can be safely thawed in cold water. Don't be tempted to use hot water as it is a food safety concern—cold water works very well and keeps everything at a safe temperature using the guidelines that follow: Place poultry in its original wrap or in a resealable heavy-duty plastic bag in cold water. Allow 30 minutes per pound to thaw, and change the water often

POULTRY THAWING (REFRIGERATOR METHOD)

Poultry Cut	Approximate Weight (pounds)	Thawing Time in Refrigerator
Whole Chicken	3 to 4	24 hours
Whole Turkey	8 to 12	1 to 2 days
	12 to 16	2 to 3 days
	16 to 20	3 to 4 days
	20 to 24	4 to 5 days
Chicken or Turkey, cut-up pieces	Up to 4	3 to 9 hours

to make sure it stays cold. If you're not going to use the poultry immediately, store it in the refrigerator as directed above; do not refreeze.

Microwave Method: Frozen uncooked and cooked poultry can be thawed in the microwave oven following the manufacturer's directions for your oven.

Seasoning Poultry

The beauty of poultry is that its mild flavor makes it a perfect partner for just about any herb or seasoning. Give poultry a seasoned rub, brush or soak before cooking to enhance the flavor. For ideas, consult the herbs, spices and seasonings charts in Chapter 16 (pages 446 to 452). Or try marinating poultry for deep, cooked-in flavors (see Tips for Marinades and Marinating, page 453).

CUTTING BONELESS POULTRY INTO PIECES

Here's a nifty trick that makes cutting boneless poultry into cubes, thin slices or strips easier: Freeze it for 30 to 60 minutes or until firm and partially frozen. Get the best results— safely—by using a sharp knife or poultry shears.

CUTTING UP A WHOLE CHICKEN

1. Place chicken, breast up, on cutting board. Remove wing from body by cutting into wing joint with sharp knife, rolling knife to let the blade follow through at the curve of the joint as shown. Repeat with remaining wing.

2. Cut off each leg by cutting skin between the thigh and body of the chicken; continue cutting through the meat between the tail and hip joint, cutting as closely as possible to the backbone. Bend leg back until hip joint pops out as shown.

3. Continue cutting around bone and pulling leg from body until meat is separated from bone as shown. Cut through remaining skin. Repeat on other side.

4. Separate thigh and drumstick by cutting about 1/8 inch from the fat line toward the drumstick side as shown. (A thin white fat line runs crosswise at joint between drumstick and thigh.) Repeat with remaining leg.

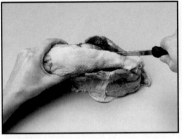

5. Separate back from breast by holding body, neck end down, and cutting downward along each side of backbone through the rib joints.

6. Bend breast halves back to pop out the keel bone; remove keel bone (for more detail, see step 2 on page 274. Using poultry shears or knife, cut breast into halves through wishbone; cut each breast half into halves.

HOW TO BONE A CHICKEN BREAST

1. Bend breast halves back to pop out the keel bone; remove keel bone.

2. Loosen keel bone and white cartilage by running the tip of the index finger around both sides. Pull out bone in one or two pieces.

3. Working with one side of the breast, insert tip of knife under long rib bone. Resting knife against bones, use steady and even pressure to gradually trim meat away from bones. Cut rib cage away from breast, cutting through shoulder joint to remove entire rib cage; repeat.

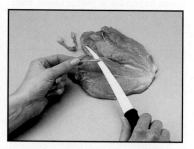

4. Turn chicken breast over and cut away wishbone. Slip knife under white tendons on either side of breast; loosen and pull out tendons (grasp end of tendons with paper towel if tendons are slippery). Remove skin if desired. Cut breasts into halves.

HOW TO FLATTEN CHICKEN BREASTS

1. Place chicken breast between pieces of plastic wrap or waxed paper. Using flat side of meat mallet, pounder or a rolling pin, gently pound chicken breasts until they are 1/4 inch thick.

2. Place chicken breast between pieces of plastic wrap or waxed paper. Using the heel of your hand, apply firm pressure (pounding lightly, if necessary) to chicken breasts, pressing until they are 1/4 inch thick.

Cooking Poultry

Always cook chicken and turkey until well done, never medium or rare. Don't stop cooking poultry partway through and then finish cooking it again later, because partial cooking may encourage bacteria growth before cooking is complete. The U.S. Department of Agriculture recommends using a meat thermometer when cooking whole chicken or turkey. When using a meat thermometer, the internal temperature should reach:

- **180°** for whole birds
- **170°** for whole turkey breasts, bone-in pieces, boneless pieces
- **165°** for center of stuffing

Where Do I Put the Thermometer?

Whole Chicken or Turkey: Insert meat thermometer so tip is in the thickest part of the inside thigh muscle and does not touch bone.

Whole Turkey Breast: Insert meat thermometer so tip is in the thickest part of the breast muscle and does not touch bone.

Boneless Turkey Breast: Insert meat thermometer so tip is in center of the thickest part of breast muscle.

I Don't Have a Thermometer

If you don't have a meat thermometer, check if poultry is done with a sharp knife or fork. Poultry is done when:

Whole Chicken and Turkey: Juice is no longer pink when center of thigh is cut and drumstick (leg) moves easily when lifted or twisted.

Whole Turkey Breast: Juice is no longer pink when center is cut.

Cut-up Broiler-Fryers or Bone-in Pieces: Juice is no longer pink when centers of thickest pieces are cut.

Boneless Pieces: Juice is no longer pink when centers of thickest pieces are cut.

Small Pieces (for stir-fry, fajitas or chicken tenders): No longer pink in center.

Ground: No longer pink.

Poultry Cooked in a Sauce or with Other Ingredients: When checking for doneness, be sure you are checking that the juice of the poultry is no longer pink, not any other liquids being cooked with the poultry.

All of our recipes include directions on how to tell when the dish is properly cooked, which may include time, temperature, appearance or any combination of these. And on the following pages, you'll find charts and tips for the different methods of cooking poultry: Roasting Poultry, page 276; Broiling or Grilling Poultry, page 277; and Microwaving Poultry, page 279. Keep in mind that the cooking times are *approximate*, so be sure to check doneness as indicated in each chart.

Cooked Poultry Yields

If a recipe calls for 1 cup cubed cooked chicken, how much chicken or turkey should you cook? We've pulled that information together for you in the chart below. In any recipe calling for cooked chicken or turkey, it's okay to use convenience products such as canned or frozen cooked chicken or poultry from the deli.

COOKED POULTRY YIELDS

Poultry Type	Weight of Uncooked Poultry (pounds)	Approximate Yield of Chopped, Cubed or Shredded Cooked Poultry
Chicken		
Broiler-fryer, whole	3 to 3 1/2	2 1/2 to 3 cups
Whole breast, bone in	1 1/2	2 cups
Boneless, skinless breast halves	1 1/2	3 cups
Legs (thighs and drumsticks)	1 1/2	1 3/4 cups
Turkey		
Whole turkey	6 to 8	7 to 10 cups
Whole breast, bone in	1 1/2	2 1/2 cups
Tenderloins	1 1/2	3 cups

Roasting Poultry

1. Remove the giblets (gizzard, heart and neck) if present, and rinse the cavity of the bird. Rub the cavity lightly with salt, if you like; however, do not salt the cavity if the bird will be stuffed.

2. If you're going to stuff the bird, do it just before roasting (in other words, don't prestuff the bird as a timesaving measure). This prevents any bacteria in the raw poultry from contaminating the stuffing. You'll need about 3/4 cup stuffing per pound of poultry; don't be tempted to overfill the bird. The stuffing will expand while it cooks. Fill the wishbone area with stuffing first. For turkey, fasten the neck skin to the back with a skewer (this isn't necessary for chicken). Fold the wings across the back with the tips touching. Fill the cavity lightly—don't pack it—because the stuffing will expand during roasting. For chicken, tie or skewer the drumsticks (legs) to the tail. For turkey, tuck drumsticks under the band of skin at the tail, or tie or skewer to the tail.

3. Place the bird, breast side up, on a rack in a shallow roasting pan. Brush it with melted butter or margarine. Do not add water. Do not cover. Insert an ovenproof meat thermometer (not the instant-read type, which isn't ovenproof) so the tip is in the thickest part of the inside thigh muscle and does not touch bone. Use the following table for approximate roasting times, but use the temperature as the final doneness guide. For turkey, place a tent of aluminum foil loosely over the turkey when it begins to turn golden. When two-thirds done, cut the band or remove the tie or skewer holding the legs.

4. Roast the bird until the thermometer temperature reaches 180° and the juice is no longer pink when you cut the center of a thigh. The drumsticks should move easily when lifted and twisted. If the bird is stuffed, the center of the stuffing must reach an internal temperature of 165°; the same is true for prestuffed store-bought poultry. When done, remove the bird from the oven and let it stand about 15 minutes for easiest carving. This resting period allows the meat to become more firm, so carving smooth, even slices is easier.

TIMETABLE FOR ROASTING POULTRY

Ready-to-Cook Weight (pounds)	Oven Temperature	Approximate Roasting Time* (hours)
Whole Chicken (stuffed)		
3 to 3 1/2	325°	2 to 2 1/2
Whole Chicken (not stuffed)		
3 to 3 1/2	375°	1 3/4 to 2
Duck		
3 1/2 to 4	350°	2
5 to 5 1/2	350°	3
Goose		
7 to 9	350°	2 1/2 to 3
9 to 11	350°	3 to 3 1/2
11 to 13	350°	3 1/2 to 4
Pheasant		
2 to 3	350°	1 1/4 to 1 1/2
Rock Cornish Hen		
1 to 1 1/2	350°	1 to 1 1/4
Whole Turkey (stuffed)		
8 to 12	325°	3 to 3 1/2
12 to 14	325°	3 1/2 to 4
14 to 18	325°	4 to 4 1/4
18 to 20	325°	4 1/4 to 4 3/4
20 to 24	325°	4 3/4 to 5 1/4
Whole Turkey (not stuffed)		
8 to 12	325°	2 3/4 to 3
12 to 14	325°	3 to 3 3/4
14 to 18	325°	3 3/4 to 4 1/4
18 to 20	325°	4 1/4 to 4 1/2
20 to 24	325°	4 1/2 to 5
Turkey Breast (bone in)		
2 to 4	325°	1 1/2 to 2
3 to 5	325°	1 1/2 to 2 1/2
5 to 7	325°	2 to 2 1/2

Times given are for unstuffed birds unless noted. Stuffed birds other than turkey require 15 to 30 minutes longer. Begin checking turkey doneness about 1 hour before end of recommended roasting time. For prestuffed turkeys purchased at your grocer or meat market, follow package directions very carefully—do not use this timetable.

Broiling or Grilling Poultry

Broiling and grilling are quick and delicious ways to cook poultry. Chicken pieces are usually grilled over direct heat and whole chicken and turkey over indirect heat. Follow the instructions that came with your grill, or see Grilling Basics, page 331.

1. Marinate poultry, if you like. (See Tips for Marinades and Marinating, page 453.)
2. **To Broil:** Brush rack of broiler pan with vegetable oil or spritz with cooking spray. Set oven to "broil."

Place poultry on rack in broiler pan. (For easy cleanup, line the pan with aluminum foil first.) For whole chicken, turkey or Rock Cornish hens, insert an ovenproof meat thermometer in thickest part of inside thigh muscle so that it doesn't touch the bone.

3. **To Grill:** *Before turning grill on or lighting coals,* brush grill rack with vegetable oil or spritz with cooking spray. Start the grill using heat setting given in the recipe or wait until coals are covered with ash (medium heat).

(continues)

TIMETABLE FOR BROILING OR GRILLING POULTRY

Poultry Type	Approximate Weight (pounds)	Approximate Total Broiling Time	Approximate Grilling Time (minutes)	Doneness
Chicken				
Cut-up chicken pieces	3 to 3 1/2	Skin sides down 30 minutes; turn. Broil 15 to 25 minutes longer (7 to 9 inches from heat).	35 to 40 (dark meat may take longer to cook)	Cook until juice of chicken is no longer pink when centers of thickest pieces are cut.
Breast halves (bone in)	2 1/2 to 3	25 to 35 minutes (7 to 9 inches from heat)	20 to 25	Cook until juice of chicken is no longer pink when centers of thickest pieces are cut.
Breast halves (boneless)	1 1/4	15 to 20 minutes, turning once (4 to 6 inches from heat)	15 to 20	Cook until juice of chicken is no longer pink when centers of thickest pieces are cut.
Wings	3 to 3 1/2	10 minutes, turning once (5 to 7 inches from heat)	12 to 18	Cook until juice of chicken is no longer pink when centers of thickest pieces are cut.
Ground turkey chicken patties (1/2 inch thick)	1	6 minutes on each side (3 inches from heat)	15 to 20	Cook until no longer pink in center.
Turkey				
Tenderloins	1 to 1 1/2	8 to 12 minutes on each side (6 inches from heat)	20 to 30	Cook until juice of turkey is no longer pink when centers of thickest pieces are cut.
Breast slices	1 to 1 1/2	7 minutes, turning once (4 inches from heat)	8 to 10	Cook until turkey is no longer pink in center.
Rock Cornish Hens*	2 to 3 (two hens)	30 to 40 minutes (4 to 6 inches from heat)	30 to 40	Cook until meat thermometer reads 180° and juice of hen is no longer pink when center of thigh is cut.

Cut hens in half before broiling or grilling for best results.

(continued)

Place poultry on grill 4 to 6 inches from heat. For even cooking, put meatier poultry pieces in the center of the grill rack, smaller pieces around the edges. For whole chicken, turkey or Rock Cornish hens, insert ovenproof meat thermometer in thickest part of inside thigh muscle, not touching bone.

4. Broil or grill as directed in the Timetable for Broiling or Grilling Poultry (page 277), turning pieces frequently with tongs. Prevent poultry from getting too brown or burning by brushing sauces on during the last 15 to 20 minutes of grilling, especially sauces made with tomato or sugar because they burn easily.

Food safety reminder: Never put cooked poultry on the same unwashed platter that raw poultry had been on.

Carving a Whole Cooked Chicken and Turkey

Carving is easier if the bird is allowed to stand for 15 to 20 minutes before cutting. This resting period allows the meat to become more firm, so carving smooth, uniform slices is easier. When carving poultry, get the best results—safely—by using a sharp knife and a meat fork. A carving knife works best because it has a long, curved blade. A meat fork has a long handle and two tines. Carve poultry on a stable cutting surface, such as a cutting board or meat carving board to catch the juices.

How to Carve Chicken and Turkey

1. Place bird, breast up, with legs to carver's right if right-handed and to the left if left-handed. Remove ties or skewers.

2. While gently pulling leg and thigh away from body, cut through joint between leg and body. Separate drumstick (leg) and thigh by cutting down through connecting joint.

3. Make a deep horizontal cut into breast just above wing. Insert fork in top of breast, and starting halfway up breast, carve thin slices down to the horizontal cut, working from outer edge of bird to the center.

4. Now repeat steps 1 through 3 on the other side of the bird.

Special Note for Turkey: *Remove and separate drumstick (leg) and thigh as directed above, and serve them whole or carve them. To carve, remove meat from drumstick (leg) by slicing at an angle, and slice thigh by cutting even slices parallel to the bone.*

Microwaving Poultry

1. Marinate poultry, if you like. (See Tips for Marinades and Marinating, page 453.)

2. Arrange poultry pieces—with the skin sides up and thickest parts to the outside edge—in a microwavable dish that's big enough to hold the pieces in a single layer.

3. Cover with plastic wrap, folding back one corner to vent steam. Microwave on High as directed in the Timetable for Microwaving Poultry, page 279.

TIMETABLE FOR MICROWAVING POULTRY

Poultry Type	Amount	Power Level	Time	Doneness
Chicken				
Broiler-fryer (cut up)	3 to 3 1/2	Medium-High (70%)	18 to 22 minutes, rearranging once; let stand 5 minutes	Cook until juice of chicken is no longer pink when centers of thickest pieces are cut.
Breast halves (bone in)	2 (1 to 1 1/2 pounds)	Medium (60%)	14 to 16 minutes; let stand 5 minutes	Cook until juice of chicken is no longer pink when centers of thickest pieces are cut.
	4 (2 to 2 1/2 pounds)	Medium-High (70%)	18 to 22 minutes; let stand 5 minutes	
Breast halves (boneless)	4 (1 to 1 1/2 pounds)	Medium (60%)	14 to 16 minutes; let stand 5 minutes	Cook until juice of chicken is no longer pink when centers of thickest pieces are cut.
Drummies/Wings	1 1/2 to 2 pounds	High (100%)	10 to 12 minutes, rearranging once; let stand 5 minutes	Cook until juice of chicken is no longer pink when centers of thickest pieces are cut.
Legs or thighs	1 to 1 1/2 pounds	High (100%)	9 to 11 minutes; let stand 5 minutes	Cook until juice of chicken is no longer pink when centers of thickest pieces are cut.
Ground turkey or chicken	1 pound	High (100%)	4 to 6 minutes, stirring once	Cook until no longer pink.
Ground chicken or turkey patties (1/2 inch thick)	1 pound	Medium-High (70%)	6 to 8 minutes, rearranging once; let stand 5 minutes	Cook until no longer pink in center.
Turkey				
Tenderloins	1 to 1 1/2 pounds	Medium (50%)	6 to 8 minutes; let stand 3 minutes	Cook until juice of turkey is no longer pink when centers of thickest pieces are cut.
Breast slices	1 to 1 1/2	Medium-High (70%)	Roll up slices; place seam side down in dish. Microwave 8 to 10 minutes; let stand 3 minutes	Cook until turkey is no longer pink in center.
Rock Cornish Hens	2 hens (1 1/2 pounds each)	Medium-High (70%)	30 to 35 minutes, rearranging once; let stand 5 minutes	Cook until meat thermometer reads 180° and juice of hen is no longer pink when center of thigh is cut.
To Thaw Frozen				
Chicken Breast Halves, boneless, skinless (6 to 7 ounces each)	1	Medium (50%)	1 1/2 to 2 minutes, turning over once	Center still will be icy.
	2	Medium (50%)	3 to 4 minutes, turning over once	Center still will be icy.
	3	Medium (50%)	5 to 6 minutes, turning over once	Center still will be icy.
	4	Medium (50%)	6 to 7 minutes, turning over once	Center still will be icy.

Tips for Stuffing Poultry

- Just about any kind of bread makes great stuffing! The traditional stuffing bread is white, but for a change of pace, try whole grain, sourdough, rye, herb or corn bread, and you can mix and match bread varieties, if you like. And if time's short, go ahead and use packaged croutons or convenience stuffing mix.

- Stuffing's great because it lets you use up stale bread. Stale bread actually is best because it's easier to cut and doesn't get soft and mushy during baking so your stuffing will have a nice texture.

- When trying to decide on amount to serve, figure 3/4 cup stuffing per pound of poultry.

- Always stuff the poultry cavity loosely, so the stuffing can expand and cook all the way through. **The center of the stuffing must reach 165° to avoid any food safety issues.**

- To avoid overpacking the bird's cavity, place extra stuffing in a covered casserole dish alongside the poultry. Many people love stuffing this way because during the last 30 to 45 minutes of baking, they remove the cover from the stuffing so the top can get nicely crisp, crunchy and golden brown.

- Always remove stuffing from the bird before carving—never keep it inside the poultry because it won't cool quickly enough, which can allow bacteria to grow more easily. Put it in a separate container.

- Never prestuff a chicken or turkey and then put it in the refrigerator or freezer for later roasting; always stuff it just before cooking. This will help prevent any bacteria from contaminating the stuffing.

Stuffing doesn't have to be made with bread. Some people add just a couple of quartered onions and a clove or two of garlic to the cavity; others add wedges of fresh lemon or orange and fresh herbs.

Bread Stuffing

Prep: 15 min; Cook: 5 min ✱ *5 cups*

3/4 cup butter or stick margarine
2 large stalks celery (with leaves), chopped (1 1/2 cups)
1 large onion, chopped (1 cup)
9 cups soft bread cubes (about 15 slices bread)
1 1/2 teaspoons chopped fresh or 1/2 teaspoon dried thyme leaves
1 teaspoon salt
1/2 teaspoon ground sage
1/4 teaspoon pepper

1. Melt butter in 4-quart Dutch oven over medium-high heat. Cook celery and onion in butter, stirring occasionally, until tender; remove from heat.

2. Toss celery mixture and remaining ingredients. Use to stuff one 10 to 12 pound turkey. See Roasting Poultry (page 276), Timetable for Roasting Poultry (page 276) and Tips for Stuffing Poultry (left) for specific directions.

1 Serving (about 1/2 cup): Calories 215 (Calories from Fat 135); Fat 15g (Saturated 9g); Cholesterol 40mg; Sodium 510mg; Carbohydrate 18g (Dietary Fiber 1g); Protein 3g **% Daily Value:** Vitamin A 10%; Vitamin C 2%; Calcium 4%; Iron 6% **Diet Exchanges:** 1 Starch, 3 Fat

> **Lighter Bread Stuffing:** For 6 grams of fat and 135 calories per serving, decrease butter to 1/4 cup. Heat butter and 1/2 cup chicken broth to boiling in Dutch oven over medium-high heat. Cook celery and onion in broth mixture.

APPLE-RAISIN STUFFING: Increase salt to 1 1/2 teaspoons. Add 3 cups finely chopped apples and 3/4 cup raisins with the remaining ingredients. 15 servings, 1/2 cup each.

CORN BREAD STUFFING: Substitute corn bread cubes for the soft bread cubes.

GIBLET STUFFING: Simmer heart, gizzard and neck from chicken or turkey in water seasoned with salt and pepper 1 to 2 hours or until tender. Add liver during the last 15 minutes of cooking. Drain giblets. Remove meat from neck and finely chop with giblets; add with the remaining ingredients. 12 servings, 1/2 cup each.

MUSHROOM STUFFING: Cook 2 cups sliced mushrooms (about 5 ounces) with the celery and onion. 10 servings, 1/2 cup each.

OYSTER STUFFING: Add 2 cans (8 ounces each) oysters, drained and chopped, or 2 cups shucked oysters, drained and chopped, with the remaining ingredients. 12 servings, 1/2 cup each.

SAUSAGE STUFFING: Omit salt. Cook 1 pound bulk pork sausage in 10-inch skillet over medium heat, stirring occasionally, until no longer pink; drain, reserving drippings. Substitute drippings for part of the butter. Add cooked sausage with the remaining ingredients. 12 servings, 1/2 cup each.

Rice Stuffing *Fast*

Prep: 20 min; Cook: 5 min ✱ 8 servings

2 tablespoons butter or stick margarine
1 medium stalk celery, chopped (1/2 cup)
1 small onion, chopped (1/4 cup)
1/2 teaspoon salt
1/8 teaspoon pepper
2 cups cooked rice (page 348)
1/2 cup chopped walnuts
1/3 cup raisins
1/4 teaspoon paprika
4 slices bacon, crisply cooked and crumbled

1. Melt butter in 10-inch skillet over medium-high heat. Cook celery, onion, salt and pepper in butter, stirring occasionally, until vegetables are tender; remove from heat.

2. Toss celery mixture and remaining ingredients.

1 Serving (about 1/2 cup): Calories 165 (Calories from Fat 80); Fat 9g (Saturated 3g); Cholesterol 10mg; Sodium 220mg; Carbohydrate 19g (Dietary Fiber 1g); Protein 3g **% Daily Value:** Vitamin A 2%; Vitamin C 0%; Calcium 2%; Iron 4% **Diet Exchanges:** 1 Starch, 1 Vegetable, 1 1/2 Fat

WILD RICE STUFFING: Substitute 1 cup cooked wild rice (page 348) for 1 cup of the cooked rice. Substitute pecans for the walnuts. Omit raisins and paprika.

Apricot–Wild Rice Stuffing *Fast*

Prep: 10 min ✱ 12 servings

Wild rice is actually an aquatic grass native to North America. It is more expensive than other types of rice because of its limited supply.

1 cup hot water
1 cup cooked wild rice (page 348)
1/2 cup chopped pecans
1/2 cup chopped dried apricots
1/4 cup butter or stick margarine, melted
1 large onion, chopped (1 cup)
1 package (6 ounces) stuffing mix for chicken

Mix all ingredients in large bowl.

1 Serving (about 1/2 cup): Calories 130 (Calories from Fat 55); Fat 6g (Saturated 1g); Cholesterol 0mg; Sodium 130mg; Carbohydrate 17g (Dietary Fiber 1g); Protein 3g **% Daily Value:** Vitamin A 6%; Vitamin C 0%; Calcium 2%; Iron 4% **Diet Exchanges:** 1 Starch/Bread, 1 Fat

CRANBERRY–WILD RICE STUFFING: Substitute 1/2 cup dried cranberries for the dried apricots.

Chicken Basics

Nowadays, there are so many chicken choices in the grocery store. Should you buy a fryer or a roaster, whole or cut-up pieces, frozen or fresh? Listed below are some facts about different types of chicken and the different ways chickens are grown.

Broiler-Fryer Chickens: This all-purpose chicken weighs from 3 to 3 1/2 pounds, with the best bargain being the whole bird versus buying it cut-up. Larger birds will have a higher ratio of meat to bone. Allow about 3/4 pound (bone-in) per serving.

Cut-up Pieces: Cut-up chicken and boneless chicken parts, such as breasts and thighs, cost more per pound, but they can make getting dinner on the table faster and easier!

Drummettes: Perfect for appetizers, drummettes or drummies are just the meatier first section of the chicken wing. 2 pounds should give you about 24 pieces, but this can vary.

Roaster Chickens: This chicken is a little older and larger than the broiler-fryer chicken, weighing 4 to 6 pounds. Even though these are larger than broiler-fryer chickens, they are still tender and moist enough to roast. Allow 3/4 pound (bone-in) per serving.

Stewing Chickens: This chicken (also called a "hen") weighs 4 1/2 to 6 pounds and provides a generous amount of meat. It's a mature, less-tender bird and is best cooked in stew and soup recipes. Allow 3/4 pound (bone-in) per serving.

Rock Cornish Hens: These small, young, specially bred chickens (also called "game hens") weigh 1 to 1 1/2 pounds and have only white meat. Allow 1/2 to 1 whole hen per person. Look for them in the freezer case.

Amish, Free-Range, Organic and Kosher Chickens: These names refer to the ways the chickens are raised or processed. With Amish, free-range and organic chickens, the emphasis is on raising the chickens without using antibiotics and feeding them a diet free of pesticides and herbicides. They tend to be more expensive than commercially raised chickens. Kosher chickens are processed according to stringent guidelines.

Substituting Chicken Parts

Are you partial to particular parts? No problem. Use your favorite chicken pieces in any of the recipes in this book that call for a cut-up broiler-fryer chicken. Just substitute 3 to 3 1/2 pounds breasts, thighs, drumsticks (legs) or wings for the cut-up broiler-fryer. If you choose to use all breasts or thighs, which are thicker and meatier than other pieces, you may need to increase the cooking time.

Thyme-Baked Chicken with Vegetables

Prep: 15 min; Bake: 1 hr 45 min ✱ *6 servings*

3- to 3 1/2-pound whole broiler-fryer chicken
6 medium carrots, cut into 1-inch pieces
4 medium stalks celery, cut into 1-inch pieces
3 medium baking potatoes, cut into 1 1/2-inch pieces
2 medium onions, cut into wedges
2 tablespoons butter or stick margarine, melted
4 teaspoons chopped fresh or 1 teaspoon dried thyme leaves

1. Heat oven to 375°.

2. Fold wings of chicken across back with tips touching. Tie or skewer drumsticks to tail. Place chicken, breast side up, in shallow roasting pan. Insert meat thermometer so tip is in thickest part of inside thigh muscle and does not touch bone.

3. Bake uncovered 45 minutes. Arrange carrots, celery, potatoes and onions around chicken. Mix butter and thyme; drizzle over chicken and vegetables.

4. Cover and bake 45 to 60 minutes or until thermometer reads 180° and juice of chicken is no longer pink when center of thigh is cut.

1 Serving: Calories 355 (Calories from Fat 155); Fat 17g (Saturated 6g); Cholesterol 95mg; Sodium 160mg; Carbohydrate 26g (Dietary Fiber 4g); Protein 29g **% Daily Value:** Vitamin A 100%; Vitamin C 14%; Calcium 6%; Iron 14% **Diet Exchanges:** 1 Starch, 3 Medium-Fat Meat, 2 Vegetable

Spicy Jamaican Chicken and Potatoes

Prep: 15 min; Bake: 1 hr 15 min; Stand: 15 min
✱ *6 servings*

Jamaican Jerk Seasoning (page 453)
3- to 3 1/2-pound whole broiler-fryer chicken
2 tablespoons vegetable oil
3 medium baking potatoes, cut lengthwise into fourths

1. Make Jamaican Jerk Seasoning.

2. Heat oven to 375°. Line roasting pan with aluminum foil.

3. Place chicken, breast side up, on rack in roasting pan. Brush 1 tablespoon of the oil over chicken. Rub 2 tablespoons of the seasoning into chicken skin. Insert meat thermometer in chicken so tip is in thickest part of inside thigh muscle and does not touch bone.

4. Brush remaining 1 tablespoon oil over potatoes. Sprinkle with remaining seasoning mix. Place potatoes on rack around chicken.

5. Roast uncovered 1 hour to 1 hours 15 minutes or until potatoes are tender, thermometer reads 180° and juice of chicken is no longer pink when center of thigh is cut. Let chicken stand about 15 minutes for easiest carving.

1 Serving: Calories 325 (Calories from Fat 170); Fat 18g (Saturated 4g); Cholesterol 85mg; Sodium 280mg; Carbohydrate 12g (Dietary Fiber 1g); Protein 28g **% Daily Value:** Vitamin A 4%; Vitamin C 6%; Calcium 2%; Iron 10% **Diet Exchanges:** 1 Starch, 3 Medium-Fat

Skillet-Fried Chicken

Prep: 10 min; Cook: 45 min ✱ *6 servings*

1/2 cup all-purpose flour
1 tablespoon paprika
1 1/2 teaspoons salt
1/2 teaspoon pepper
3- to 3 1/2-pound cut-up broiler-fryer chicken
Vegetable oil

1. Mix flour, paprika, salt and pepper. Coat chicken with flour mixture.

2. Heat oil (1/4 inch) in 12-inch nonstick skillet over medium-high heat. Cook chicken in oil about 10 minutes or until light brown on all sides; reduce heat to low. Turn chicken skin side up.

3. Simmer uncovered about 20 minutes, without turning, until juice of chicken is no longer pink when centers of thickest pieces are cut.

1 Serving: Calories 350 (Calories from Fat 205); Fat 23g (Saturated 5g); Cholesterol 85mg; Sodium 670mg; Carbohydrate 9g (Dietary Fiber 1g); Protein 28g **% Daily Value:** Vitamin A 10%; Vitamin C 0%; Calcium 2%; Iron 10% **Diet Exchanges:** 1/2 Starch, 4 Medium-Fat Meat

> **Lighter Skillet-Fried Chicken:** For 11 grams of fat and 250 calories per serving, remove skin from chicken before cooking. Use 2 tablespoons oil in step 2.

BUTTERMILK FRIED CHICKEN: Increase flour to 1 cup. Dip chicken into 1 cup buttermilk before coating with flour mixture.

Crunchy Oven-Fried Chicken

Oven-Fried Chicken

Prep: 10 min; Bake: 1 hr ✱ *6 servings*

1/4 cup butter or stick margarine
1/2 cup all-purpose flour
1 teaspoon paprika
1/2 teaspoon salt
1/4 teaspoon pepper
3- to 3 1/2-pound cut-up broiler-fryer chicken

1. Heat oven to 425°. Melt butter in rectangular pan, 13 × 9 × 2 inches, in oven.

2. Mix flour, paprika, salt and pepper. Coat chicken with flour mixture. Place chicken, skin side down, in pan.

3. Bake uncovered 30 minutes. Turn chicken; bake about 30 minutes longer or until juice is no longer pink when centers of thickest pieces are cut.

1 Serving: Calories 320 (Calories from Fat 180); Fat 20g (Saturated 8g); Cholesterol 100mg; Sodium 320mg; Carbohydrate 7g (Dietary Fiber 0g); Protein 28g **% Daily Value:** Vitamin A 12%; Vitamin C 0%; Calcium 2%; Iron 10% **Diet Exchanges:** 1/2 Starch, 4 Medium-Fat Meat

Lighter Oven-Fried Chicken: For 11 grams of fat and 235 calories per serving, remove skin from chicken before cooking. Do not melt butter in pan; spray pan with cooking spray. Decrease butter to 2 tablespoons; drizzle over chicken after turning in step 3.

CHICKEN FINGERS: Substitute 1 1/2 pounds boneless, skinless chicken breast halves, cut crosswise into 1 1/2-inch strips, for the broiler-fryer. Decrease butter to 2 tablespoons. After coating chicken with flour mixture in step 2, toss with melted butter in pan. Bake uncovered 15 minutes. Turn strips; bake 10 to 15 minutes longer or until no longer pink in center.

CRUNCHY OVEN-FRIED CHICKEN: Substitute 1 cup cornflake crumbs for the 1/2 cup flour. Dip chicken into 1/4 cup butter or stick margarine, melted, before coating with crumb mixture.

Chicken and Dumplings

Prep: 20 min; Cook: 2 hr 45 min ✷ *4 to 6 servings*

3- to 3 1/2-pound stewing or broiler-fryer chicken,
    cut up
2 medium stalks celery (with leaves), cut up
1 medium carrot, sliced
1 small onion, sliced
2 tablespoons chopped fresh parsley or 2 teaspoons
    parsley flakes
1 teaspoon salt
1/8 teaspoon pepper
5 cups water
2 1/2 cups Original Bisquick®
2/3 cup milk

1. Remove excess fat from chicken. Place chicken, giblets (except liver), neck, celery, carrot, onion, parsley, salt, pepper and water in 4-quart Dutch oven. Cover and heat to boiling; reduce heat. Simmer about 2 hours or until juice of chicken is no longer pink when centers of thickest pieces are cut.

2. Remove chicken and vegetables from Dutch oven. Discard giblets and neck. Skim 1/2 cup fat from broth; reserve. Transfer broth to large bowl; reserve 4 cups.

3. Heat reserved fat in Dutch oven over low heat. Stir in 1/2 cup of the Bisquick. Cook, stirring constantly, until mixture is smooth and bubbly; remove from heat.

4. Stir in reserved broth. Heat to boiling, stirring constantly. Boil and stir 1 minute. Add chicken and vegetables to Dutch oven; reduce heat to low; heat until hot.

5. Mix remaining 2 cups Bisquick and the milk until soft dough forms. Drop dough by spoonfuls onto hot chicken mixture (do not drop directly into liquid). Cook uncovered over low heat 10 minutes. Cover and cook 10 minutes longer.

1 Serving: Calories 635 (Calories from Fat 280); Fat 31g (Saturated 9g); Cholesterol 130mg; Sodium 1,820mg; Carbohydrate 51g (Dietary Fiber 2g); Protein 47g **% Daily Value:** Vitamin A 32%; Vitamin C 4%; Calcium 22%; Iron 24% **Diet Exchanges:** 3 Starch, 5 Medium-Fat Meat, 1 Vegetable

---

TESTING CHICKEN FOR DONENESS—DON'T OVERDO IT

Keep the juices in and the cook time to a minimum for moist, tender chicken. Don't test too often for doneness, only once or twice, so the juices of the chicken stay in the chicken. To test for doneness, use a knife to cut into the center of the thickest part of the chicken to see if the juice is no longer pink. Do not pierce the chicken with a thick, multi-tined fork or the chicken will lose an excessive amount of juices. Avoid overcooking your chicken by testing after the minimum cook time given in a recipe.

Coq au Vin

Coq au Vin

Prep: 10 min: Cook: 55 min ✱ *6 servings*

Small whole onions, also called pearl onions, are sold in the frozen vegetable section of the grocery store.

1/2 cup all-purpose flour

1 teaspoon salt

1/4 teaspoon pepper

3- to 3 1/2-pound cut-up broiler-fryer chicken

8 slices bacon

3/4 cup frozen small whole onions (from 16-ounce bag)

3 cups sliced mushrooms (8 ounces)

1 cup chicken broth

1 cup dry red wine or non-alcoholic red wine

1/2 teaspoon salt

4 medium carrots, cut into 2-inch pieces

1 clove garlic, finely chopped

Bouquet garni*

1. Mix flour, 1 teaspoon salt and the pepper. Coat chicken with flour mixture.

2. Cook bacon in 12-inch skillet over medium heat until crisp. Remove bacon with slotted spoon and drain on paper towels; set aside. Cook chicken in bacon fat over medium heat about 15 minutes or until brown on all sides.

3. Move chicken to one side of skillet; add onions and mushrooms to other side. Cook over medium-high heat, stirring occasionally, until mushrooms are tender. Drain fat from skillet.

4. Crumble bacon. Stir bacon and remaining ingredients into vegetables. Heat to boiling; reduce heat. Cover and simmer about 35 minutes or until juice of chicken is no longer pink when centers of thickest pieces are cut. Remove bouquet garni; skim off excess fat.

*Tie 1/2 teaspoon dried thyme leaves, 2 large sprigs fresh parsley and 1 bay leaf in cheesecloth bag or place in tea ball. This classic trio of herbs hails from France and is used frequently in many types of recipes.

1 Serving: Calories 380 (Calories from Fat 160); Fat 18g (Saturated 5g); Cholesterol 90mg; Sodium 960mg; Carbohydrate 23g (Dietary Fiber 3g); Protein 34g **% Daily Value:** Vitamin A 66%; Vitamin C 8%; Calcium 4%; Iron 16% **Diet Exchanges:** 1 Starch, 4 Lean Meat, 2 Vegetable, 1 Fat

Slow Cooker Directions: Remove skin from chicken. Decrease flour to 1/3 cup. Cut carrots into 1/2-inch slices. Cook, drain and crumble bacon; refrigerate. Brown chicken as directed. Place carrots in 3 1/2- to 6-quart slow cooker. Top with chicken. Mix remaining ingredients except mushrooms and bacon; pour over chicken. Cover and cook on low heat setting 4 to 6 hours or until juice of chicken is no longer pink when centers of thickest pieces are cut. Stir in mushrooms and bacon. Cover and cook on high heat setting 30 minutes. Remove bouquet garni; skim off excess fat

Roasted Chicken and New Potatoes

Prep: 8 min; Bake: 1 hr ✱ *4 servings*

New potatoes are young red or brown potatoes that are about 1 1/2 inches in diameter. Their texture is velvety, their skins very tender and they hold their shape better than baking potatoes, which are starchy and more mealy. These potatoes are usually not peeled.

1 1/2 to 2 pounds broiler-fryer chicken pieces, skin removed
1 pound new potatoes, cut into fourths
2 tablespoons chopped fresh or 2 teaspoons dried basil leaves
1 tablespoon chopped fresh or 1/2 teaspoon dried thyme leaves
3 tablespoons olive or vegetable oil
1 teaspoon garlic salt

1. Heat oven to 375°.

2. Place chicken and potatoes in ungreased rectangular pan, 13 × 9 × 2 inches. Mix remaining ingredients; sprinkle over chicken and potatoes.

3. Cover and bake 30 minutes. Turn chicken and potatoes. Bake uncovered 20 to 30 minutes longer or until juice of chicken is no longer pink when centers of thickest pieces are cut.

1 Serving: Calories 305 (Calories from Fat 135); Fat 15g (Saturated 3g); Cholesterol 60mg; Sodium 310mg; Carbohydrate 23g (Dietary Fiber 2g); Protein 21g **% Daily Value:** Vitamin A 2%; Vitamin C 10%; Calcium 2%; Iron 12% **Diet Exchanges:** 1 1/2 Starch, 2 Medium-Fat Meat, 1 Fat

Zesty Italian Chicken

Prep: 5 min; Bake: 1 hr ✱ *6 servings*

3- to 3 1/2-pound cut-up broiler-fryer chicken
1/4 cup mayonnaise or salad dressing
1/4 cup zesty Italian dressing
2 tablespoons chopped fresh basil
1 tablespoon chopped fresh oregano
1 teaspoon chopped fresh rosemary

1. Heat oven to 375°. Place chicken, skin sides down, in ungreased rectangular pan, 13 × 9 × 2 inches.

2. Mix remaining ingredients; brush half of mayonnaise mixture on chicken. Cover and bake 30 minutes. Turn chicken; brush with remaining mayonnaise mixture. Bake uncovered about 30 minutes longer or until juice of chicken is no longer pink when centers of thickest pieces are cut. (If chicken browns too quickly, cover with aluminum foil.)

1 Serving: Calories 375 (Calories from Fat 245); Fat 27g (Saturated 6g); Cholesterol 105mg; Sodium 220mg; Carbohydrate 2g (Dietary Fiber 0g); Protein 31g **% Daily Value:** Vitamin A 6%; Vitamin C 0%; Calcium 2%; Iron 8% **Diet Exchanges:** 4 Medium-Fat Meat, 1 1/2 Fat

ZESTY ITALIAN CHICKEN WITH SWEET POTATOES: Peel 4 medium sweet potatoes; cut into 1 1/2-inch pieces. Increase mayonnaise and zesty Italian dressing to 1/3 cup each. Continue as directed in steps 1 and 2; except, after backing chicken 30 minutes, turn chicken and arrange sweet potatoes around chicken. Brush chicken and sweet potatoes with remaining mayonnaise mixture. Bake uncovered about 30 minutes longer or until potatoes are tender and juice of chicken is no longer pink when centers of thickest pieces are cut. (If chicken browns too quickly, cover with aluminum foil.)

Indonesian Peanut Chicken

Indonesian Peanut Chicken

Prep: 10 min; Cook: 50 min ✳ 6 servings

Serve this with or over Chinese noodles or rice.

3- to 3 1/2-pound cut-up broiler-fryer chicken
3/4 teaspoon salt
1/2 teaspoon pepper
2 tablespoons vegetable oil
1 medium onion, chopped (1/2 cup)
1/3 cup peanut butter
1/4 cup chili sauce
1/2 teaspoon ground red pepper (cayenne)
1 cup water
1/4 cup chopped salted peanuts
1/4 cup chopped red bell pepper

1. Sprinkle chicken with salt and pepper.

2. Heat oil in 12-inch skillet or 4-quart Dutch oven over medium heat. Cook chicken in oil about 15 minutes, turning occasionally, until brown on all sides. Cover and cook over low heat about 20 minutes or until juice is no longer pink when centers of thickest pieces are cut. Remove chicken from skillet with tongs.

3. Drain all but 1 tablespoon drippings from skillet; heat over medium heat. Cook onion in drippings, stirring occasionally, until tender; reduce heat. Stir in peanut butter, chili sauce and red pepper. Gradually stir in water, stirring constantly, until peanut butter is melted.

4. Add chicken. Spoon sauce over chicken. Heat to boiling; reduce heat. Simmer uncovered about 5 minutes, spooning sauce frequently over chicken, until sauce is slightly thickened. Serve sauce over chicken. Sprinkle with peanuts and bell pepper.

1 Serving: Calories 400 (Calories from Fat 245); Fat 27g (Saturated 6g); Cholesterol 85mg; Sodium 580mg; Carbohydrate 9g (Dietary Fiber 2g); Protein 32g **% Daily Value:** Vitamin A 10%; Vitamin C 12%; Calcium 2%; Iron 10% **Diet Exchanges:** 1/2 Starch, 4 Medium-Fat Meat, 1 Fat

Slow Cooker Directions: Remove skin from chicken. Omit oil. Decrease water to 1/3 cup. Sprinkle chicken with salt and pepper; place half of the chicken in 3 1/2- to 6-quart slow cooker. Mix remaining ingredients except peanuts and bell pepper; spoon half of mixture over chicken. Add remaining chicken; top with remaining peanut butter mixture. Cover and cook on low heat setting 4 to 6 hours or until juice of chicken is no longer pink when centers of thickest pieces are cut. Remove chicken. Cook sauce uncovered over high heat setting about 10 minutes or until slightly thickened. Serve sauce over chicken. Sprinkle with peanuts and bell pepper.

Smoked Gouda- and Spinach-Stuffed Chicken

Prep: 20 min; Bake: 55 min ✱ *4 servings*

Smoked Gouda and Spinach Stuffing (right)
4 bone-in, skin-on chicken breast halves (2 1/2 to 3 pounds)
2 teaspoons butter or stick margarine, melted
1/2 teaspoon salt
1/4 teaspoon pepper

1. Heat oven to 375°. Grease square pan, 9 × 9 × 2 inches.

2. Make Smoked Gouda and Spinach Stuffing.

3. Loosen skin from chicken by inserting fingers between skin and meat; gently separate in center, but leave skin attached at sides. Spread one-fourth of the stuffing evenly between meat and skin of each chicken breast. Smooth skin over breasts, tucking under loose areas.

4. Place chicken, skin sides up, in pan. Brush with butter. Sprinkle with salt and pepper.

5. Bake uncovered 45 to 55 minutes or until juice of chicken is no longer pink when centers of thickest pieces are cut.

Smoked Gouda and Spinach Stuffing

1/2 package (10-ounce size) frozen chopped spinach, thawed
1 package (3 ounces) cream cheese, softened
1/2 cup shredded smoked Gouda or Swiss cheese (2 ounces)
1/4 teaspoon ground nutmeg

Squeeze spinach to drain; spread on paper towels and pat dry. Mix remaining ingredients. Stir in spinach.

1 Serving: Calories 325 (Calories from Fat 190); Fat 21g (Saturated 10g); Cholesterol 115mg; Sodium 590mg; Carbohydrate 2g (Dietary Fiber 1g); Protein 33g **% Daily Value:** Vitamin A 32%; Vitamin C 2%; Calcium 16%; Iron 8% **Diet Exchanges:** 5 Lean Meat, 1 Fat

APPLE-HAZELNUT STUFFED CHICKEN: Omit Smoked Gouda and Spinach Stuffing. Mix 1/4 cup chopped hazelnuts (filberts); 1 medium apple, chopped (1 cup) and 1 package (3 ounces) cream cheese, softened. Continue as directed in 3.

WHAT'S NEW WITH CHICKEN BREASTS

In an effort to make boneless, skinless chicken breasts more moist and tender, producers are injecting the chicken with a salt-water solution. This method also increases the sodium content, so if you're watching your sodium intake, be sure to check the package label. Two types of this new generation of chicken breasts are now available—you'll find them both in the fresh-meat case or in the freezer case as bags of individually frozen breasts.

Chicken Cacciatore

Prep: 20 min; Cook: 1 hr ✱ 6 servings

3- to 3 1/2-pound cut-up broiler-fryer chicken
1/2 cup all-purpose flour
1/4 cup vegetable oil
1 medium green bell pepper
2 medium onions
1 can (14 1/2 ounces) diced tomatoes, undrained
1 can (8 ounces) tomato sauce
1 cup sliced mushrooms (3 ounces)
1 1/2 teaspoons chopped fresh or 1/2 teaspoon dried
    oregano leaves
1 teaspoon chopped fresh or 1/4 teaspoon dried basil
    leaves
1/2 teaspoon salt
2 cloves garlic, finely chopped
Grated Parmesan cheese, if desired

1. Coat chicken with flour. Heat oil in 12-inch skillet over medium-high heat. Cook chicken in oil 15 to 20 minutes or until brown on all sides; drain.

2. Cut bell pepper and onions crosswise in half; cut each half into fourths.

3. Stir bell pepper, onions and remaining ingredients except cheese into chicken in skillet. Heat to boiling; reduce heat. Cover and simmer 30 to 40 minutes or until juice of chicken is no longer pink when centers of thickest pieces are cut. Serve with cheese.

1 Serving: Calories 365 (Calories from Fat 180); Fat 20g (Saturated 5g); Cholesterol 85mg; Sodium 620mg; Carbohydrate 19g (Dietary Fiber 3g); Protein 30g **% Daily Value:** Vitamin A 14%; Vitamin C 30%; Calcium 6%; Iron 14% **Diet Exchanges:** 4 Medium-Fat Meat, 4 Vegetable

Slow Cooker Directions: Remove skin from chicken. Decrease flour to 1/3 cup. Omit oil and tomato sauce. Use 1 can (4 ounces) sliced mushrooms, drained. Brown chicken as directed. Cut bell pepper and onions crosswise in half; cut each half into fourths. Place half of the chicken in 3 1/2- to 6-quart slow cooker. Mix bell pepper, onions and remaining ingredients except cheese; spoon half of mixture over chicken. Add remaining chicken; top with remaining vegetable mixture. Cover and cook on low heat setting 4 to 6 hours or until juice of chicken is no longer pink when centers of thickest pieces are cut. Serve with cheese.

Tomato-Feta Chicken with Orzo

Prep: 10 min; Cook: 1 hr 20 min ✱ 6 servings

2 tablespoons olive or vegetable oil
3- to 3 1/2-pound cut-up broiler-fryer chicken
1 tablespoon olive or vegetable oil
1 3/4 cups frozen small whole onions (from 16-ounce
    bag)
2 cloves garlic, finely chopped
1/2 cup white wine or apple juice
2 tablespoons chopped fresh cilantro or parsley
1 tablespoon chopped fresh or 1 teaspoon dried
    oregano leaves
1/8 teaspoon pepper
2 cans (14 1/2 ounces each) stewed tomatoes, drained
3 cups hot cooked rosamarina (orzo) pasta (page 390)
    or rice (page 348)
1/4 cup crumbled feta cheese (2 ounces)

1. Heat 2 tablespoons oil in 12-inch skillet or 4-quart Dutch oven over medium heat. Cook chicken in oil about 15 minutes, turning occasionally, until brown on all sides. Remove chicken from skillet with tongs.

2. Add 1 tablespoon oil to drippings in skillet. Heat over medium-low heat. Cook onions in oil mixture about 6 minutes, stirring occasionally, until golden brown. Stir in garlic. Cook and stir about 30 seconds or until garlic is light golden brown.

3. Stir in remaining ingredients except pasta and cheese, breaking up tomatoes with a fork or snipping with kitchen scissors. Add chicken. Heat to boiling; reduce heat. Cover and simmer about 20 minutes or until juice of chicken is no longer pink when centers of thickest pieces are cut.

4. Serve tomato mixture over chicken and pasta. Sprinkle with cheese and, if desired, additional chopped fresh cilantro.

1 Serving: Calories 400 (Calories from Fat 180); Fat 20g (Saturated 5g); Cholesterol 75mg; Sodium 340mg; Carbohydrate 30g (Dietary Fiber 3g); Protein 28g **% Daily Value:** Vitamin A 12%; Vitamin C 18%; Calcium 10%; Iron 16% **Diet Exchanges:** 1 Starch, 4 Lean Meat, 3 Vegetable, 1 Fat

Chicken with Curry Sour Cream Sauce

Prep: 10 min; Cook: 35 min ✱ *4 servings*

Go all out! Serve this succulent chicken with little bits of dry-roasted peanuts, chopped green onions, chopped fresh cilantro, shredded coconut and mandarin orange sections to sprinkle on each serving.

2 tablespoons vegetable oil
4 chicken breast halves (2 1/2 to 3 pounds)
1/2 teaspoon salt
1 medium onion, chopped (1/2 cup)
2 tablespoons water
1/4 cup water
2 teaspoons curry powder
1/8 teaspoon ground ginger
1/8 teaspoon ground cumin
1 cup sour cream
4 cups hot cooked rice (page 348)
1/2 cup Golden Fruit Chutney (page 457) or prepared
    chutney

1. Heat oil in 12-inch skillet or 4-quart Dutch oven over medium heat. Cook chicken in oil about 15 minutes, turning occasionally, until brown on all sides. Drain fat from skillet.

2. Sprinkle chicken with salt. Add onion and 2 tablespoons water to chicken in skillet. Heat to boiling; reduce heat. Cover and simmer about 20 minutes or until juice of chicken is no longer pink when centers of thickest pieces are cut.

3. Remove chicken from skillet; keep warm.

4. Add 1/4 cup water, curry, ginger and cumin to skillet. Heat to boiling, scraping up any browned bits from bottom of skillet. Reduce heat to low; stir in sour cream just until hot.

5. Pour sauce over chicken and rice. Serve with Golden Fruit Chutney.

1 Serving: Calories 395 (Calories from Fat 135); Fat 15g (Saturated 6g); Cholesterol 75mg; Sodium 220mg; Carbohydrate 41g (Dietary Fiber 1g); Protein 25g **% Daily Value:** Vitamin A 6%; Vitamin C 2%; Calcium 6%; Iron 12% **Diet Exchanges:** 2 Starch, 2 Medium-Fat Meat, 2 Vegetable, 1 Fat

Crunchy Garlic Chicken

Prep: 30 min; Bake: 25 min ✱ *6 servings*

2 tablespoons butter or stick margarine, melted
2 tablespoons milk
1 tablespoon chopped fresh chives or parsley
1/2 teaspoon salt
1/2 teaspoon garlic powder
2 cups cornflakes cereal, crushed (1 cup)
3 tablespoons chopped fresh parsley
1/2 teaspoon paprika
6 boneless, skinless chicken breast halves
    (1 3/4 pounds)
2 tablespoons butter or stick margarine, melted

1. Heat oven to 425°. Grease rectangular pan, 13 × 9 × 2 inches.

2. Mix 2 tablespoons butter, the milk, chives, salt and garlic powder. Mix cornflakes, parsley and paprika. Dip chicken into milk mixture, then coat lightly and evenly with cornflakes mixture. Place in pan. Drizzle with 2 tablespoons butter.

3. Bake uncovered 20 to 25 minutes or until chicken is no longer pink when centers of thickest pieces are cut.

1 Serving: Calories 205 (Calories from Fat 100); Fat 11g (Saturated 6g); Cholesterol 80mg; Sodium 350mg; Carbohydrate 5g (Dietary Fiber 0g); Protein 22g **% Daily Value:** Vitamin A 12%; Vitamin C 4%; Calcium 2%; Iron 12% **Diet Exchanges:** 1/2 Starch, 3 Lean Meat

Baked Chicken Kiev

Prep: 20 min; Freeze: 30 min; Bake: 35 min ❋ 6 servings

1/4 cup butter or stick margarine, softened
1 tablespoon chopped fresh chives or parsley
1 clove garlic, finely chopped
6 boneless, skinless chicken breast halves (about
    1 3/4 pounds)
12 toothpicks
3 cups cornflakes cereal, crushed (1 1/2 cups)
2 tablespoons chopped fresh parsley
1/2 teaspoon paprika
1/4 cup buttermilk or milk

1. Mix butter, chives and garlic. Shape mixture into 3 × 2-inch rectangle. Cover and freeze about 30 minutes or until firm.

2. Heat oven to 425°. Grease square pan, 9 × 9 × 2 inches.

3. Place each chicken breast half between sheets of plastic wrap or waxed paper. Lightly pound chicken, using flat side of meat mallet, until 1/4 inch thick (see page 274).

4. Cut butter mixture crosswise into 6 pieces. Place 1 piece on center of each chicken breast half. Fold long sides of chicken over butter. Fold ends up and secure each end with toothpick.

5. Mix cornflakes, parsley and paprika. Dip chicken into buttermilk, then coat evenly with cornflakes mixture. Place chicken, seam sides down, in pan.

6. Bake uncovered about 35 minutes or until chicken is no longer pink in center (when checking for doneness, be careful not to pierce all the way through chicken so butter mixture will not run out). Remove toothpicks.

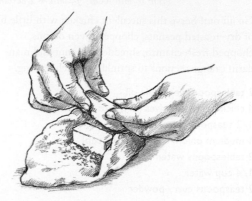

Place 1 piece of butter on center of each chicken breast half. Fold long sides of chicken over butter. Fold ends up and secure each end with toothpick.

1 Serving: Calories 265 (Calories from Fat 110); Fat 12g (Saturated 6g); Cholesterol 95mg; Sodium 280mg; Carbohydrate 13g (Dietary Fiber 1g); Protein 28g **% Daily Value:** Vitamin A 18%; Vitamin C 6%; Calcium 2%; Iron 30% **Diet Exchanges:** 1 Starch, 3 1/2 Lean Meat

BAKED CHICKEN CORDON BLEU: Omit butter, chives, garlic and step 1. In step 4, top each piece of chicken with 1 thin slice fully cooked smoked ham and 1 thin slice Swiss cheese, each about the same shape as the piece of chicken. Roll up carefully, beginning at narrow end; secure each end with toothpick.

THE SKINNY ON SKIN

Cooking chicken with the skin on adds to the flavor, not the fat. Research has found that the fat does not transfer to the meat during cooking. So go ahead and leave the skin on—it helps keep the juices in, creates moister, more tender meat and boosts the flavor. Then, once the chicken is cooked, remove the skin and throw it away if you want to save on fat, calories and cholesterol.

Two-Mustard Chicken

Two-Mustard Chicken

Prep: 6 min; Bake: 35 min ✱ 8 servings

Mustard is made from the ground seeds of the mustard plant. Dijon mustard has the addition of white wine. Coarse-grain mustard contains whole mustard seeds and has a strong mustard and nutty flavor and a slightly chewy texture.

1/2 cup Dijon mustard
1/4 cup coarse-grained mustard
1/4 cup honey
8 boneless, skinless chicken breast halves (about
    2 1/2 pounds)

1. Heat oven to 375°.

2. Grease rectangular pan, 13 × 9 × 2 inches. Mix mustards and honey; spread on both sides of chicken. Place in pan.

3. Bake uncovered 25 to 35 minutes or until juice is no longer pink when centers of thickest pieces are cut.

1 Serving: Calories 195 (Calories from Fat 45); Fat 5g (Saturated 1g); Cholesterol 75mg; Sodium 360mg; Carbohydrate 10g (Dietary Fiber 1g); Protein 28g **% Daily Value:** Vitamin A 0%; Vitamin C 0%; Calcium 2%; Iron 8% **Diet Exchanges:** 1/2 Starch, 4 Very Lean Meat

Chicken Satay with Peanut Sauce

Prep: 15 min; Marinate: 2 hr; Broil: 9 min ✱ *4 servings*

3 tablespoons lime juice
1 teaspoon curry powder
2 teaspoons honey
1/2 teaspoon ground coriander
1/2 teaspoon ground cumin
1/8 teaspoon salt
2 cloves garlic, finely chopped
1 pound boneless, skinless chicken breast halves, cut into 1-inch cubes
Peanut Sauce (below)

1. Mix all ingredients except chicken and Peanut Sauce. Place chicken in resealable plastic food-storage bag or shallow glass or plastic dish. Pour lime juice mixture over chicken; stir chicken to coat with lime juice mixture. Cover and refrigerate 2 hours, stirring occasionally.

2. Make Peanut Sauce.

3. Set oven control to broil. Spray rack in broiler pan with cooking spray. Remove chicken from marinade; reserve marinade. Thread chicken on eight 8-inch skewers,* leaving space between each piece. Place skewers on rack in broiler pan.

4. Broil with tops about 3 inches from heat 4 minutes. Turn; brush with marinade. Broil 4 to 5 minutes longer or until chicken is no longer pink in center. Discard any remaining marinade. Serve chicken with sauce.

Peanut Sauce

2/3 cup vanilla yogurt
1/4 cup creamy peanut butter
1/4 cup coconut milk (not cream of carrot)
1 tablespoon soy sauce
1/4 to 1/2 teaspoon red pepper sauce

Beat all ingredients with wire whisk.

*If using bamboo skewers, soak in water at least 30 minutes before using to prevent burning.

1 Serving: Calories 285 (Calories from Fat 125); Fat 14g (Saturated 5g); Cholesterol 50mg; Sodium 470mg; Carbohydrate 17g (Dietary Fiber 2g); Protein 25g **% Daily Value:** Vitamin A 0%; Vitamin C 2%; Calcium 8%; Iron 8% **Diet Exchanges:** 3 1/2 Lean Meat, 1 Fruit, 1 Fat

Tandoori Chicken and Chutney

Prep: 5 min; Marinate: 1 hr; Cook: 20 min ✱ *4 servings*

Entertain your friends with an Indian meal by serving this dish with traditional condiments: coconut, raisins, peanuts and chopped hard-cooked egg.

Spicy Yogurt Marinade (below)
4 boneless, skinless chicken breast halves (about 1 1/4 pounds)
1/2 cup Golden Fruit Chutney (page 457) or mango chutney
Hot cooked basmati rice (page 348), if desired

1. Make Spicy Yogurt Marinade.

2. Place chicken in resealable plastic food-storage bag or shallow glass or plastic dish. Pour marinade over chicken; turn chicken to coat with marinade. Seal bag or cover dish and refrigerate 1 hour.

3. Cook chicken and marinade in 12-inch skillet over medium-high heat 15 to 20 minutes, turning chicken once, until juice of chicken is no longer pink when centers of thickest pieces are cut. Top with chutney. Serve with rice.

Spicy Yogurt Marinade

1/2 cup plain yogurt
1 tablespoon lemon juice
2 teaspoons grated gingerroot
1/2 teaspoon paprika
1/2 teaspoon ground coriander
1/2 teaspoon salt
1/4 teaspoon ground red pepper (cayenne)
1/8 teaspoon ground cloves

Mix all ingredients.

1 Serving: Calories 215 (Calories from Fat 45); Fat 5g (Saturated 1g); Cholesterol 75mg; Sodium 400mg; Carbohydrate 14g (Dietary Fiber 0g); Protein 28g **% Daily Value:** Vitamin A 4%; Vitamin C 2%; Calcium 6%; Iron 6% **Diet Exchanges:** 4 Very Lean Meat, 1 Fruit

Smothered Chicken

Prep: 20 min; Cook: 20 min ✴ 4 servings

4 boneless, skinless chicken breast halves (about
   1 1/4 pounds)
1 teaspoon dried oregano leaves
1/2 teaspoon salt
1/2 teaspoon garlic powder
1/4 teaspoon pepper
1/4 teaspoon ground red pepper (cayenne)
1 tablespoon butter or stick margarine
1 medium green bell pepper, thinly sliced
1 medium onion, thinly sliced
1 cup sliced mushrooms (4 ounces)
1/2 cup shredded mozzarella cheese (2 ounces)
1/2 cup shredded Cheddar cheese (2 ounces)

1. Spray 12-inch nonstick skillet with cooking
spray; heat over medium heat. Sprinkle both sides of
chicken with oregano, salt, garlic powder, pepper and
red pepper. Cook in skillet 8 to 10 minutes, turning
once, until juice is no longer pink when centers of
thickest pieces are cut. Remove chicken from skillet;
keep warm.

2. Melt butter in skillet over medium heat. Cook bell
pepper and onion in butter about 5 minutes, stirring
occasionally, until crisp-tender. Stir in mushrooms.
Cook 3 to 5 minutes, stirring occasionally, until vegetables are tender.

3. Place chicken in skillet; spoon vegetables over
chicken. Sprinkle cheeses over chicken and vegetables;
remove from heat. Cover and let stand until cheese
is melted.

1 Serving: Calories 285 (Calories from Fat 125); Fat 14g (Saturated
7g); Cholesterol 105mg; Sodium 540mg; Carbohydrate 6g (Dietary
Fiber 1g); Protein 35g **% Daily Value:** Vitamin A 10%; Vitamin C
24%; Calcium 20%; Iron 8% **Diet Exchanges:** 4 1/2 Lean Meat,
1 Vegetable

Summer Garden Chicken Stir-Fry *Low-Fat*

Prep: 15 min; Cook: 13 min ✴ 4 servings

To save time, you can use 4 to 5 cups of your favorite
fresh vegetables from the salad bar for the vegetable
combination used in this recipe. Or use a package of
precut stir-fry vegetables available in the produce
department.

1 pound boneless, skinless chicken breast
   halves, cut into 1-inch pieces
2 cloves garlic, finely chopped
2 teaspoons finely chopped gingerroot
1 medium onion, cut into thin wedges
1 cup baby-cut carrots, cut lengthwise in half
1 cup chicken broth
3 tablespoons soy sauce
2 to 3 teaspoons sugar
2 cups broccoli flowerets
1 cup sliced mushrooms (3 ounces)
1/2 cup diced red bell pepper
2 teaspoons cornstarch
Hot cooked rice (page 348), if desired

1. Spray 12-inch nonstick skillet with cooking spray;
heat over medium-high heat. Add chicken, garlic
and gingerroot; stir-fry 2 to 3 minutes or until
chicken is brown.

2. Add onion, carrots, 3/4 cup of the broth, the soy
sauce and sugar. Cover and cook over medium heat 5
minutes, stirring occasionally.

3. Add broccoli, mushrooms and bell pepper. Cover
and cook about 5 minutes, stirring occasionally, until
chicken is no longer pink in center and vegetables are
crisp-tender.

4. Mix cornstarch and remaining 1/4 cup broth; stir
into chicken mixture. Cook, stirring frequently, until
sauce is thickened. Serve over rice.

1 Serving (about 1 1/4 cups): Calories 165 (Calories from Fat
25); Fat 3g (Saturated 1g); Cholesterol 50mg; Sodium 1,020mg;
Carbohydrate 16g (Dietary Fiber 4g); Protein 23g **% Daily Value:**
Vitamin A 66%; Vitamin C 84%; Calcium 6%; Iron 12% **Diet
Exchanges:** 2 1/2 Very Lean Meat, 3 Vegetable

Fiesta Taco Casserole

Prep: 15 min; Bake: 30 min ✳ *4 servings*

1 pound ground chicken or turkey
1 can (15 to 16 ounces) spicy chili beans in sauce,
    undrained
1 cup salsa
2 cups coarsely broken tortilla chips
1/2 cup sour cream
4 medium green onions, sliced (1/4 cup)
1 medium tomato, chopped (3/4 cup)
1 cup shredded Cheddar or Monterey Jack cheese
    (4 ounces)
Tortilla chips, if desired
Shredded lettuce, if desired
Salsa, if desired

1. Heat oven to 350°. Cook chicken in 10-inch skillet over medium heat 8 to 10 minutes, stirring occasionally, until no longer pink; drain. Stir in beans and 1 cup salsa. Heat to boiling, stirring occasionally.

2. Place broken tortilla chips in ungreased 2-quart casserole. Top with chicken mixture. Spread with sour cream. Sprinkle with onions, tomato and cheese.

3. Bake uncovered 20 to 30 minutes or until hot and bubbly. Arrange tortilla chips around edge of casserole. Serve with lettuce and salsa.

1 Serving (about 1 1/4 cups): Calories 430 (Calories from Fat 215); Fat 24g (Saturated 9g); Cholesterol 80mg; Sodium 1,010mg; Carbohydrate 32g (Dietary Fiber 6g); Protein 27g **% Daily Value:** Vitamin A 18%; Vitamin C 18%; Calcium 18%; Iron 20% **Diet Exchanges:** 1 Starch, 3 Medium-Fat Meat, 3 Vegetable, 1 Fat

> **Lighter Fiesta Taco Casserole:** For 13 grams of fat and 345 calories per serving, use ground turkey breast and reduced-fat sour cream and Cheddar cheese.

Chicken à la King *Fast*

Prep: 20 min; Cook: 10 min ✳ *5 servings*

1/2 cup butter or stick margarine
1 small green bell pepper, chopped (1/2 cup)
1 cup sliced mushrooms (3 ounces)*
1/2 cup all-purpose flour
1/2 teaspoon salt
1/4 teaspoon pepper
1 1/2 cups milk
1 1/4 cups chicken broth
2 cups cut-up cooked chicken or turkey
1 jar (2 ounces) diced pimientos, drained
3 cups hot cooked rice (page 348) or 12 triangles
    toasted bread

1. Melt butter in 3-quart saucepan over medium-high heat. Cook bell pepper and mushrooms in butter, stirring occasionally, until bell pepper is crisp-tender.

2. Stir in flour, salt and pepper. Cook over medium heat, stirring constantly, until bubbly; remove from heat. Stir in milk and broth. Heat to boiling, stirring constantly. Boil and stir 1 minute. Stir in chicken and pimientos; cook until hot. Serve over rice.

*1 can (4 ounces) mushroom pieces and stems, drained, can be substituted for the fresh mushrooms.

1 Serving (about 1 1/2 cups): Calories 485 (Calories from Fat 225); Fat 25g (Saturated 14g); Cholesterol 105mg; Sodium 700mg; Carbohydrate 42g (Dietary Fiber 1g); Protein 24g **% Daily Value:** Vitamin A 24%; Vitamin C 20%; Calcium 12%; Iron 16% **Diet Exchanges:** 2 Starch, 1 Medium-Fat Meat, 1 Vegetable, 1/2 Milk, 4 Fat

TUNA À LA KING: Substitute 1 can (12 ounces) tuna, drained, for the chicken.

Chicken Pot Pie

Prep: 40 min; Bake: 35 min ✴ *6 servings*

Make putting this all-time favorite together a snap by purchasing a ready-to-use pie crust.

1 package (10 ounces) frozen peas and carrots
1/3 cup butter or stick margarine
1/3 cup all-purpose flour
1/3 cup chopped onion
1/2 teaspoon salt
1/4 teaspoon pepper
1 3/4 cups chicken broth
2/3 cup milk
2 1/2 to 3 cups cut-up cooked chicken or turkey
Pastry for 9-Inch Two-Crust Pie (page 117)

1. Rinse frozen peas and carrots in cold water to separate; drain.

2. Melt butter in 2-quart saucepan over medium heat. Stir in flour, onion, salt and pepper. Cook, stirring constantly, until mixture is bubbly; remove from heat. Stir in broth and milk. Heat to boiling, stirring constantly. Boil and stir 1 minute. Stir in chicken and peas and carrots; remove from heat.

3. Heat oven to 425°.

4. Make pastry. Roll two-thirds of the pastry into 13-inch square. Ease into ungreased square pan, 9 × 9 × 2 inches. Pour chicken mixture into pastry-lined pan.

5. Roll remaining pastry into 11-inch square. Cut out designs with 1-inch cookie cutter. Place square over chicken mixture. Arrange cutouts on pastry. Turn edges of pastry under and flute. (See page 120 for Pastry Edges.)

6. Bake about 35 minutes or until golden brown.

1 Serving (about 1 cup): Calories 685 (Calories from Fat 425); Fat 47g (Saturated 16g); Cholesterol 80mg; Sodium 1,050mg; Carbohydrate 44g (Dietary Fiber 3g); Protein 24g **% Daily Value:** Vitamin A 48%; Vitamin C 4%; Calcium 6%; Iron 20% **Diet Exchanges:** 2 Starch, 2 Medium-Fat Meat, 3 Vegetable, 6 Fat

TUNA POT PIE: Substitute 1 can (12 ounces) tuna, drained, for the chicken.

Chicken Club Salad with Hot Bacon Dressing *Fast*

Prep: 15 min; Cook: 8 min ✴ *4 servings*

6 cups bite-size pieces leaf lettuce
1/2 pint (1 cup) cherry tomatoes, cut in half
2 teaspoons vegetable oil
4 boneless, skinless chicken breast halves
    (about 1 1/4 pounds), cut into 1-inch strips
8 slices bacon
1 medium onion, chopped (1/2 cup)
2 teaspoons sugar
1/2 teaspoon ground mustard
1/2 teaspoon pepper
1/2 cup cider vinegar
1/2 cup flavored croutons
1/4 cup shredded Swiss cheese (1 ounce)

1. Mix lettuce and tomatoes in large bowl.

2. Heat oil in 10-inch skillet over medium-high heat. Cook chicken in oil 6 to 8 minutes, stirring occasionally, until no longer pink in center. Arrange chicken on lettuce mixture.

3. Cook bacon in same skillet over low heat 8 to 10 minutes, turning occasionally, until crisp and brown. Remove bacon from skillet, reserving 2 tablespoons fat in skillet. Drain bacon on paper towels. Crumble bacon; sprinkle over salad.

4. Cook onion in bacon fat over medium heat about 2 minutes, stirring occasionally, until crisp-tender. Stir in sugar, mustard, pepper and vinegar. Cook about 2 minutes, stirring occasionally, until hot.

5. Pour onion mixture over salad; toss. Top with croutons and cheese. Serve warm.

1 Serving: Calories 190 (Calories from Fat 100); Fat 11g (Saturated 4g); Cholesterol 30mg; Sodium 270mg; Carbohydrate 12g (Dietary Fiber 2g); Protein 13g **% Daily Value:** Vitamin A 16%; Vitamin C 34%; Calcium 10%; Iron 8% **Diet Exchanges:** 1 1/2 Medium-Fat Meat, 2 Vegetable, 1 Fat

Turkey Basics

Turkey isn't just for Thanksgiving. It's an any-meal, any-day, any-time-of-year kind of bird! And no wonder, when you can choose from whole turkey, turkey breast, ground turkey, turkey sausage, turkey bacon, turkey ham, turkey cutlets, turkey tenderloins and, don't forget, those jumbo turkey drumsticks that are just made for grilling. Use turkey as you would chicken. It's just as versatile and nutritious.

Buying a whole bird? Whole ready-to-cook turkeys can range in size from 8 to 24 pounds, and there's no difference in quality between fresh and frozen. Store whole frozen turkeys in your freezer at 0° for up to 12 months. Keep fresh whole turkeys in the refrigerator and use within 1 to 2 days after buying them. How much should you buy? Whether it's your first turkey or your tenth, that's always the question! Allow about 1 pound of uncooked whole turkey per serving. That makes enough for a feast—and leftovers, too!

Maple-Glazed Turkey Breast

Prep: 5 min; Bake: 45 min ✱ *4 servings*

1 package (6 ounces) seasoned long-grain and wild rice
1 1/2 cups water
1 boneless turkey breast (about 1 pound)
3 tablespoons maple-flavored syrup
1/2 cup chopped walnuts
1/2 teaspoon ground cinnamon

1. Heat oven to 350°.

2. Mix uncooked rice, seasoning packet from rice and water in ungreased square baking dish, 8 × 8 × 2 inches. Place turkey breast, skin side up, on rice mixture. Drizzle with maple syrup. Sprinkle with walnuts and cinnamon.

3. Cover and bake about 45 minutes or until rice is tender and juice of turkey is no longer pink when center is cut.

1 Serving: Calories 305 (Calories from Fat 90); Fat 10g (Saturated 1g); Cholesterol 75mg; Sodium 170mg; Carbohydrate 25g (Dietary Fiber 1g); Protein 30g **% Daily Value:** Vitamin A 0%; Vitamin C 0%; Calcium 2%; Iron 12% **Diet Exchanges:** 1 1/2 Starch, 4 Very Lean Meat, 1 Fat

Slow Cooker Directions: Decrease water to 1 1/4 cups. Increase maple-flavored syrup to 1/4 cup. Mix uncooked rice, seasoning packet from rice and water in 3 1/2- to 6-quart slow cooker. Place turkey breast, skin side up, on rice mixture. Drizzle with maple syrup. Sprinkle with walnuts and cinnamon. Cover and cook on low heat setting 4 to 5 hours or until juice of turkey is no longer pink when center is cut.

Turkey with Lemon Rice

Fast & Low-Fat

Prep: 15 min; Cook: 9 min ✱ *6 servings*

16 medium green onions, chopped (1 cup)
2 cloves garlic, finely chopped
1 cup chicken broth
1 1/2 pounds uncooked turkey breast slices, cut into
    3 × 1/4-inch strips
3 cups cooked brown or white rice (page 348)
2 teaspoons grated lemon peel
1/3 cup lemon juice
1 tablespoon capers, rinsed and drained
1/4 teaspoon pepper
3 tablespoons chopped fresh parsley

1. Heat onions, garlic and broth to boiling in 12-inch skillet. Boil 3 minutes, stirring occasionally, until onions are tender. Reduce heat to medium; stir in turkey. Cook 3 minutes.

2. Stir in remaining ingredients except parsley. Cook about 3 minutes or until rice is hot and turkey is no longer pink in center; remove from heat. Stir in parsley.

1 Serving: Calories 215 (Calories from Fat 20); Fat 2g (Saturated 1g); Cholesterol 60mg; Sodium 260mg; Carbohydrate 26g (Dietary Fiber 2g); Protein 25g **% Daily Value:** Vitamin A 2%; Vitamin C 8%; Calcium 4%; Iron 10% **Diet Exchanges:** 1 Starch, 2 1/2 Very Lean Meat, 2 Vegetable

Brandied Turkey with Cheese

Brandied Turkey with Cheese *Fast*

Prep: 5 min: Cook: 4 min: Stand: 2 min ✳ *4 servings*

Serve turkey a whole new way using quick-cooking turkey breast slices. Serve with sweet potatoes and cranberry sauce.

4 uncooked turkey breast slices, about 1/4 inch thick
   (from 1 1/4 pound package)
1/4 teaspoon salt
1/4 teaspoon pepper
1/4 cup all-purpose flour
1/4 cup butter or stick margarine
1/4 cup brandy or chicken broth
4 thin slices (1 ounce each) Fontina or provolone
   cheese

1. Sprinkle turkey with salt and pepper. Coat turkey with flour.

2. Melt butter in 12-inch skillet over medium heat. Cook turkey in butter about 2 minutes on each side or until brown.

3. Add brandy. Cook uncovered until liquid has evaporated and turkey is no longer pink in center. Top turkey slices with cheese; remove from heat. Cover and let stand about 2 minutes or until cheese is melted.

1 Serving: Calories 320 (Calories from Fat 155); Fat 17g (Saturated 10g); Cholesterol 135mg; Sodium 370mg; Carbohydrate 6g (Dietary Fiber 0g); Protein 36g **% Daily Value:** Vitamin A 14%; Vitamin C 0%; Calcium 12%; Iron 12% **Diet Exchanges:** 1/2 Starch, 5 Lean Meat

Turkey Divan

Prep: 35 min; Broil: 3 min ✻ 6 servings

1 1/2 pounds broccoli*
1/4 cup butter or stick margarine
1/4 cup all-purpose flour
1/8 teaspoon ground nutmeg
1 1/2 cups chicken broth
1 cup grated Parmesan cheese
1/2 cup whipping (heavy) cream
2 tablespoons dry white wine or chicken broth
6 large slices cooked turkey or chicken breast, 1/4 inch
   thick (3/4 pound)

1. Cut broccoli lengthwise into 1/2-inch-wide spears. Heat 1 inch water (salted if desired) to boiling in 2-quart saucepan. Add broccoli. Heat to boiling. Boil uncovered 5 minutes; drain.

2. Melt butter in same saucepan over medium heat. Stir in flour and nutmeg. Cook, stirring constantly, until smooth and bubbly; remove from heat. Stir in broth. Heat to boiling, stirring constantly. Boil and stir 1 minute; remove from heat. Stir in 1/2 cup of the cheese, the whipping cream and wine.

3. Place hot broccoli in ungreased rectangular baking dish, 11 × 7 × 1 1/2 inches. Top with turkey. Pour cheese sauce over turkey. Sprinkle with remaining 1/2 cup cheese.

4. Set oven control to broil. Broil with top 3 to 5 inches from heat about 3 minutes or until cheese is bubbly and light brown.

*2 packages (10 ounces each) frozen broccoli spears, cooked and drained, can be substituted for the fresh broccoli.

1 Serving: Calories 290 (Calories from Fat 170); Fat 19g (Saturated 11g); Cholesterol 90mg; Sodium 610mg; Carbohydrate 9g (Dietary Fiber 2g); Protein 23g **% Daily Value:** Vitamin A 20%; Vitamin C 54%; Calcium 24%; Iron 10% **Diet Exchanges:** 3 Lean Meat, 2 Vegetable, 2 Fat

Duckling with Orange Sauce

Prep: 20 min; Roast: 2 hr 30 min; Cook: 5 min;
Stand: 15 min ✻ 4 servings

Piercing the duck skin is commonly done because it lets a lot of the unwanted fat drain away. Using a fork, pierce the skin all over, especially at the breast, but do not pierce the flesh.

4- to 5-pound duckling
2 teaspoons grated orange peel
1/2 cup orange juice
1/4 cup currant jelly
1 tablespoon lemon juice
1/8 teaspoon ground mustard
1/8 teaspoon salt
1 tablespoon cold water
1 1/2 teaspoons cornstarch
1 orange, peeled and sectioned
1 tablespoon orange-flavored liqueur, if desired

1. Heat oven to 350°.

2. Fasten neck skin of duckling to back with skewer. Fold wings across back with tips touching. Place duckling, breast side up, on rack in shallow roasting pan. Pierce skin all over with fork. Loosely tie legs to the tail, if desired, to better hold an even shape during cooking. Insert meat thermometer so tip is in thickest part of inside thigh muscle and does not touch bone.

3. Roast uncovered about 2 hours 30 minutes or until thermometer reads 180° and juice is no longer pink when center of thigh is cut. Place tent of aluminum foil loosely over breast during last hour to prevent excessive browning. Place duckling on heated platter. Let stand 15 minutes for easier carving.

4. Meanwhile, heat orange peel, orange juice, jelly, lemon juice, mustard and salt to boiling in 1-quart saucepan. Mix water and cornstarch; stir into sauce. Cook over medium heat, stirring constantly, until mixture thickens and boils. Boil and stir 1 minute.

5. Stir in orange sections and liqueur. Brush duckling with some of the orange sauce. Serve with remaining sauce.

1 Serving: Calories 490 (Calories from Fat 215); Fat 24g (Saturated 7g); Cholesterol 155mg; Sodium 230mg; Carbohydrate 20g (Dietary Fiber 1g); Protein 49g **% Daily Value:** Vitamin A 9%; Vitamin C 26%; Calcium 4%; Iron 14% **Diet Exchanges:** 7 Lean Meat, 1 1/2 Fat

Roast Goose with Apple Stuffing

Prep: 1 hr 30 min; Roast: 3 hr 30 min; Stand: 15 min;
Cook: 10 min ✱ 8 servings

For easy cleanup, line the roasting pan with aluminum foil before placing the goose on the rack in the roasting pan.

8- to 10-pound goose
2 cups water
1 small onion, sliced
3/4 teaspoon salt
6 cups soft bread crumbs (about 9 slices bread)
1/4 cup butter or stick margarine, melted
1 1/2 teaspoons chopped fresh or 1/2 teaspoon dried
    sage leaves
3/4 teaspoon chopped fresh or 1/4 teaspoon dried
    thyme leaves
1/2 teaspoon salt
1/4 teaspoon pepper
3 medium tart apples, chopped (3 cups)
2 medium stalks celery (with leaves), chopped (1 cup)
1 medium onion, chopped (1/2 cup)
1/4 cup all-purpose flour

1. Remove excess fat from goose.

2. Heat giblets, water, sliced onion and 3/4 teaspoon salt to boiling in 1-quart saucepan; reduce heat. Cover and simmer about 1 hour or until giblets are tender. Strain broth; cover and refrigerate.

3. Remove meat from neck and finely chop with giblets. Toss giblets and remaining ingredients except flour in large bowl.

4. Heat oven to 350°.

5. Fill wishbone area of goose with stuffing first. Fasten neck skin to back with skewer. Fold wings across back with tips touching. Fill body cavity lightly. (Do not pack—stuffing will expand while cooking.) Fasten opening with skewers, and lace with string. Pierce skin all over with fork.

6. Place goose, breast side up, on rack in shallow roasting pan. Insert meat thermometer so tip is in thickest part of inside thigh muscle and does not touch bone.

7. Roast uncovered 3 hours to 3 hours 30 minutes (if necessary, place tent of aluminum foil loosely over goose during last hour to prevent excessive browning), removing excess fat from pan occasionally, until thermometer reads 180° and juice of goose is no longer pink when center of thigh is cut. The center of the stuffing should be 165°. Place goose on heated platter. Let stand 15 minutes for easier carving.

8. Pour drippings from pan into bowl; skim off fat. Return 1/4 cup drippings to pan (discard remaining drippings). Stir in flour. Cook over medium heat, stirring constantly, until smooth and bubbly; remove from heat.

9. Add enough water to reserved broth, if necessary, to measure 2 cups. Stir into flour mixture. Heat to boiling, stirring constantly. Boil and stir 1 minute. Serve goose with apple stuffing and gravy.

1 Serving: Calories 800 (Calories from Fat 485); Fat 54g (Saturated 19g); Cholesterol 210mg; Sodium 490mg; Carbohydrate 25g (Dietary Fiber 3g); Protein 57g **% Daily Value:** Vitamin A 8%; Vitamin C 4%; Calcium 6%; Iron 40% **Diet Exchanges:** 1 Starch, 8 Medium-Fat Meat, 1 Fruit, 1 Fat

Pheasant with Rosemary Cream Sauce

Prep: 30 min; Cook: 10 min; Bake: 1 hr 30 min
✳ *4 servings*

2 pheasants (about 2 1/2 to 3 pounds each)
1/2 cup all-purpose flour
1/2 teaspoon seasoned salt
1/4 teaspoon pepper
2 tablespoons vegetable oil
1 package (8 ounces) whole mushrooms
2 cups baby-cut carrots
1 tablespoon butter or stick margarine
1 cup half-and-half
1/2 cup chicken broth
2 tablespoons dry sherry or chicken broth
1 tablespoon chopped fresh or 1/2 teaspoon dried
    rosemary leaves

1. Heat oven to 350°.

2. Cut each pheasant in half along backbone and breastbone from tail to neck with kitchen scissors.

3. Mix flour, seasoned salt and pepper in shallow bowl. Coat pheasant generously with flour mixture. Reserve remaining flour mixture.

4. Heat oil in 12-inch skillet over medium-high heat. Cook pheasant in oil 3 to 4 minutes on each side or until well-browned. Place in ungreased rectangular pan, 13 × 9 × 3 inches, or in shallow roaster. Top and surround pheasant with mushrooms and carrots.

5. Melt butter in 2-quart saucepan over medium heat. Add enough additional flour to remaining flour mixture to make 2 tablespoons. Stir flour mixture into butter. Cook, stirring constantly, until mixture is smooth and bubbly; remove from heat. Gradually stir in half-and-half and broth. Heat to boiling, stirring constantly. Boil and stir 1 minute. Stir in sherry and rosemary. Pour evenly over pheasant.

6. Bake uncovered 1 hour 15 minutes to 1 hour 30 minutes, spooning sauce in pan over pheasant once, until pheasant is tender and juice is no longer pink when centers of thickest pieces are cut. Remove pheasant from pan with slotted spoon. Stir sauce until smooth. Serve sauce with pheasant.

1 Serving: Calories 910 (Calories from Fat 460); Fat 51g (Saturated 18g); Cholesterol 285mg; Sodium 650mg; Carbohydrate 21g (Dietary Fiber 3g); Protein 95g **% Daily Value:** Vitamin A 100%; Vitamin C 12%; Calcium 22%; Iron 100% **Diet Exchanges:** 1 Starch, 13 Lean Meat, 1 Vegetable, 2 Fat

Pheasant Stew

Prep: 15 min; Cook: 1 hr 15 min **✳** *4 servings*

1/4 cup butter or stick margarine
6 slices bacon, cut into 1-inch pieces
1 large onion, thinly sliced
2 pheasants (about 2 1/2 to 3 pounds each), cut
    into fourths
1 cup dry white wine or chicken broth
1 teaspoon salt
1/2 teaspoon pepper
1 cup chicken broth
2 tablespoons chopped fresh or 2 teaspoons dried
    sage leaves
2 tablespoons chopped fresh or 1 teaspoon dried
    rosemary leaves
2 medium carrots, thinly sliced (1 cup)

1. Melt butter in 12-inch skillet over medium-high heat. Cook bacon and onion in butter, stirring frequently, until bacon is crisp.

2. Cook pheasant in bacon mixture over medium-high heat, turning occasionally, until pheasant is brown. Add wine. Cook uncovered until liquid has evaporated.

3. Sprinkle with salt and pepper. Stir in remaining ingredients. Cover and cook over low heat about 1 hour or until pheasants are tender and juice is no longer pink when centers of thickest pieces are cut.

1 Serving: Calories 870 (Calories from Fat 470); Fat 52g (Saturated 20g); Cholesterol 295mg; Sodium 1370mg; Carbohydrate 8g (Dietary Fiber 1g); Protein 93g **% Daily Value:** Vitamin A 70%; Vitamin C 6%; Calcium 16%; Iron 100% **Diet Exchanges:** 13 Lean Meat, 2 Vegetable, 2 Fat

Low-Fat = 3g or less, except main dishes with 6g or less   **Fast** = Ready in 30 minutes or less   ■ = Bread Machine directions   ● = Slow Cooker directions

Shrimp Scampi with Fettucine (page 321)

Lighter = 1/3 fewer calories or 50% less fat

Fish Basics

Cooking fish, eating fish and even catching fish are more popular than ever. It's no wonder. Fish is healthful, flavorful, and versatile. With the advent of more varieties of farm-raised fish, such as catfish, salmon and trout, fresh or freshly frozen fish is available almost everywhere. Nutrition-wise, fish has a lot going for it. It's naturally rich in high-quality protein, yet low in fat, saturated fat, cholesterol and calories. So, if your facts on fish aren't up to speed, here are all the basics to help you get in the swim of cooking fish.

Selecting Fish

When buying fish, put your senses of sight, smell and touch into action.

Fresh Whole Fish, Fillets or Steaks

- Eyes should be bright, clear and slightly bulging; only a few fish such as walleye have naturally cloudy eyes.
- Gills should be bright pink to red and have no slime on them.
- Scales should be bright with a sheen. Avoid fish with any darkening around the edges or brown or yellowish discoloration.
- Flesh should be shiny, firm and elastic. It will spring back when touched.
- Fish should smell fresh and mild, not fishy or like ammonia.

Frozen Fish

- Package should be tightly wrapped and frozen solid with little or no gap between packaging and fish.
- There should be no dark, icy or dry spots—these are signs of freezer burn.
- The package should be odor free.

How Much Fish to Buy?

How much fish is enough? That depends on what form you're using, how many you're serving and how hungry they are. These general guidelines can help.

Whole fish is just as it comes from the water. Allow about 1 pound per serving.

Drawn fish is whole with only the internal organs removed, and the head and tail are still intact. Allow about 3/4 pound per serving.

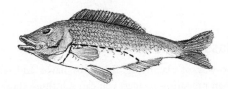

Pan-dressed fish is scaled with the internal organs, head, tail and fins removed. Allow about 1/2 pound per serving.

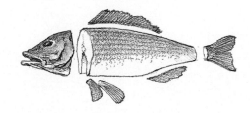

Fish steaks are the cross-section slices of a large pan-dressed fish. Steaks are 3/4 to 1 1/2 inches thick. Allow 1/4 to 1/3 pound per serving.

Fish fillets are the sides of a fish, cut lengthwise from the fish. They're available with or without skin. You may also find butterfly fillets, which are two fillets held together by the uncut flesh and skin of the belly. Fillets are usually boneless; however, small bones called *pins* may be present. Allow 1/4 to 1/3 pound per serving.

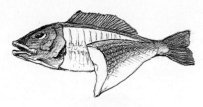

Classifying Fish

One way of classifying fish is by flavor and texture. When preparing recipes, you can substitute those with the same characteristics for one another.

CLASSIFICATION OF FISH

Mild Flavor	Moderate Flavor	Full Flavor
Delicate Texture		
Alaska Pollock	Lingcod	Butterfish
Catfish	Salmon, Pink	Herring/ Sardines Smelt
Flounder	Whitefish	
Orange Roughy	Whiting	
Skate		
Sole		
Walleye Pike		
Medium-Firm Texture		
Cod	Amberjack	Bluefish
Cusk	Buffalo	Carp
Grouper	Drum	Mackerel
Haddock	Mahimahi	Sablefish
Sea Bass		Salmon (Atlantic, King, Sockeye)
Snapper	Ocean Perch	Wahoo
Tilapia	Pompano	
Tilefish	Porgy/Scup	
	Redfish	
	Rockfish	
	Shad	
	Trout, Rainbow	
Firm Texture		
Halibut	Shark	Marlin
Monkfish	Sturgeon	Swordfish
		Tuna

Cooking Fish

There are almost as many ways to cook fish as there are kinds of fish. Baking, broiling, frying, grilling and steaming are just a few. As a general guide for how long to cook fish, measure it at its thickest point, then cook 8 to 10 minutes per inch of thickness for fresh fish or 20 minutes per inch of thickness if the fish is frozen.

Determining When Fish Is Done

Fish is delicate and tender; overcooking makes it dry and tough. Fish is done when you can flake it easily with a fork. Test this by inserting a fork at an angle into the thickest part of the fish and twisting gently. The flesh and any juices should be opaque. For food safety reasons, we recommend cooking fish to an internal temperature of 160°.

Microwaving Fish

Microwaves and fish were made for each other. Fish cooks quickly and gently in the microwave. For the best microwaved fish:

1. Arrange fish fillets or steaks with thickest parts to outside edge in shallow microwavable dish that's large enough to hold fish in a single layer. (Fold thin ends of fillets under for more even thickness.)

2. Cover with plastic wrap, folding one edge or corner back about 1/4 inch to vent steam.

3. Microwave on Medium-High (70%) as directed below, rotating dish once if microwave does not have turntable, until fish flakes easily with fork.

Orange-Almond Trout *Fast*

Prep: 10 min; Cook: 15 min ✳ 4 servings

1 pound trout, salmon or other medium-firm fish fillets,
about 3/4 inch thick
1/4 cup butter or stick margarine
1/4 cup sliced almonds
1 medium onion, sliced
1/2 cup all-purpose flour
1 teaspoon salt
1/2 teaspoon paprika
1/8 teaspoon pepper
2 oranges, peeled and sectioned (page 9)

1. If fish fillets are large, cut into 5 serving pieces.

2. Melt butter in 10-inch skillet over medium heat. Cook almonds and onion in butter, stirring occasionally, until onion is tender. Remove almonds and onion with slotted spoon; keep warm.

3. Mix flour, salt, paprika and pepper. Coat fish with flour mixture. Cook fish in same skillet over medium heat 6 to 10 minutes, turning once, until fish is brown and flakes easily with fork.

4. Top fish with almonds and onion. Garnish with orange sections.

1 Serving: Calories 320 (Calories from Fat 160); Fat 18g (Saturated 6g); Cholesterol 75mg; Sodium 550mg; Carbohydrate 19g (Dietary Fiber 3g); Protein 24g **% Daily Value:** Vitamin A 8%; Vitamin C 60%; Calcium 8%; Iron 12% **Diet Exchanges:** 3 Lean Meat, 1 Vegetable, 1 Fruit, 2 Fat

TIMETABLE FOR MICROWAVING FISH

Type	Approximate Weight	Microwave Time	Stand Time
Fillets	12 ounces	4 to 5 minutes	3 minutes
	1 1/2 pounds	7 to 9 minutes	3 minutes
Steaks (1 inch thick)	12 ounces	4 to 5 minutes	3 minutes
	1 1/2 pounds	7 to 9 minutes	3 minutes

Panfried Fish *Fast*

Prep: 10 min; Cook: 10 min per batch ✳ *6 servings*

Place the completed panfried fish on a heatproof serving platter and keep warm in a 250 ° oven while you fry the remaining fish.

Vegetable oil or shortening
1 1/2 pounds perch, snapper or other medium-firm fish fillets, about 3/4 inch thick
Salt
Pepper
1 large egg
1 tablespoon water
2/3 cup all-purpose flour, cornmeal or fine dry bread crumbs

1. Heat oil (1/8 inch) in 10-inch skillet over medium heat.

2. Cut fish into 6 serving pieces. Sprinkle both sides of fish with salt and pepper.

3. Beat egg and water with fork or wire whisk until blended. Dip fish into egg, then coat with flour.

4. Fry fish in batches in oil 6 to 10 minutes, turning once, until fish flakes easily with fork and is brown on both sides. Fish cooks very quickly; be careful not to overcook. Remove with slotted spoons, drain on paper towels.

1 Serving: Calories 165 (Calories from Fat 55); Fat 6g (Saturated 1g); Cholesterol 75mg; Sodium 280mg; Carbohydrate 8g (Dietary Fiber 0g); Protein 20g **% Daily Value:** Vitamin A 2%; Vitamin C 0%; Calcium 2%; Iron 4% **Diet Exchanges:** 1/2 Starch, 3 Very Lean Meat, 1/2 Fat

Lighter Panfried Fish: For 2 grams of fat and 140 calories per serving, omit vegetable oil. Spray 10-inch nonstick skillet with cooking spray; heat over medium heat.

Oven-Fried Fish *Fast*

Prep: 15 min; Bake: 10 min ✳ *4 servings*

1 pound cod, haddock or other medium-firm fish fillets, about 3/4 inch thick
1/4 cup cornmeal
1/4 cup dry bread crumbs
3/4 teaspoon chopped fresh or 1/4 teaspoon dried dill weed
1/2 teaspoon paprika
1/4 teaspoon salt
1/8 teaspoon pepper
1/4 cup milk
3 tablespoons butter or stick margarine, melted

1. Move oven rack to position slightly above middle of oven. Heat oven to 500°.

2. Cut fish into 2 × 1 1/2-inch pieces. Mix cornmeal, bread crumbs, dill weed, paprika, salt and pepper. Dip fish into milk, then coat with cornmeal mixture.

3. Place fish in ungreased rectangular pan, 13 × 9 × 2 inches. Drizzle butter over fish. Bake uncovered about 10 minutes or until fish flakes easily with fork.

1 Serving: Calories 200 (Calories from Fat 90); Fat 10g (Saturated 2g); Cholesterol 55mg; Sodium 390mg; Carbohydrate 9g (Dietary Fiber 1g); Protein 20g **% Daily Value:** Vitamin A 14%; Vitamin C 0%; Calcium 4%; Iron 4% **Diet Exchanges:** 1/2 Starch, 3 Lean Meat

Baked Fish Fillets *Fast*

Prep: 5 min; Bake: 20 min ✱ *4 servings*

1 pound sole, orange roughy or other delicate fish
    fillets, about 3/4 inch thick
2 tablespoons butter or stick margarine, melted
1 tablespoon lemon juice
1/4 teaspoon salt
1/4 teaspoon paprika

1. Heat oven to 375°. Spray rectangular pan, 13 × 9 × 2 inches, with cooking spray.

2. Cut fish into 4 serving pieces; place in pan. If fish has skin, place skin sides down. Tuck under any thin ends for more even cooking.

3. Mix remaining ingredients; drizzle over fish.

4. Bake uncovered 15 to 20 minutes or until fish flakes easily with fork. Remove skin from fish before serving if desired.

Check fish for doneness by placing a fork in the thickest part of the fish, then gently twisting the fork. The fish will flake easily when it's done.

1 Serving: Calories 130 (Calories from Fat 65); Fat 7g (Saturated 1g); Cholesterol 45mg; Sodium 300mg; Carbohydrate 0g (Dietary Fiber 0g); Protein 17g **% Daily Value:** Vitamin A 8%; Vitamin C 0%; Calcium 2%; Iron 2% **Diet Exchanges:** 2 1/2 Lean Meat

Flounder with Mushrooms and Wine *Fast*

Prep: 10 min; Bake: 20 min ✱ *4 servings*

1 pound flounder, sole or other delicate fish fillets,
    about 3/4 inch thick
1/2 teaspoon paprika
1/2 teaspoon salt
1/8 teaspoon pepper
1 tablespoon butter or stick margarine
1/2 cup sliced mushrooms
1/3 cup sliced leeks
1/3 cup dry white wine or chicken broth
1/4 cup sliced almonds
1 tablespoon grated Parmesan cheese

1. Heat oven to 375°.

2. If fish fillets are large, cut into 4 serving pieces. Arrange in ungreased square baking dish, 8 × 8 × 2 inches. Sprinkle with paprika, salt and pepper.

3. Melt butter in 10-inch skillet over medium heat. Cook mushrooms and leeks in butter, stirring occasionally, until leeks are tender. Stir in wine. Pour mushroom mixture over fish. Sprinkle with almonds and cheese.

4. Bake uncovered 15 to 20 minutes or until fish flakes easily with fork.

1 Serving: Calories 170 (Calories from Fat 70); Fat 8g (Saturated 3g); Cholesterol 60mg; Sodium 420mg; Carbohydrate 3g (Dietary Fiber 1g); Protein 20g; **%Daily Value:** Vitamin A 2%; Vitamin C 2%; Calcium 6%; Iron 6%; **Diet Exchanges:** 3 Very Lean Meat, 1 Vegetable, 1 Fat

---

BAKING FISH WITH SKIN ON IT

Baking fish with the skin on helps to hold delicate fish fillets together. Removing the skin after the fish has been cooked is much easier than removing it before cooking. When fish is done, carefully insert a metal spatula between the skin and the flesh, starting at the tail end if the fillet happens to have one. While holding onto a small piece of skin, slide the fish off of the skin.

Broiled Fish Fillets (variation of Broiled Fish Steaks)

Broiled Fish Steaks *Fast*

Prep: 5 min; Broil: 11 min ✳ *4 servings*

Simply broiled, fresh fish can be enjoyed with just a squeeze of fresh lime or lemon.

4 small salmon, trout or other medium-firm fish steaks, about 3/4 inch thick (1 1/2 pounds)
Salt
Pepper
2 tablespoons butter or stick margarine, melted

1. Set oven control to broil.

2. Sprinkle both sides of fish with salt and pepper. Brush with half of the butter.

3. Place fish on rack in broiler pan. Broil with tops about 4 inches from heat 5 minutes. Brush with butter. Carefully turn fish; brush with butter. Broil 4 to 6 minutes longer or until fish flakes easily with fork.

1 Serving: Calories 240 (Calories from Fat 115); Fat 13g (Saturated 3g); Cholesterol 95mg; Sodium 440mg; Carbohydrate 0g (Dietary Fiber 0g); Protein 31g **% Daily Value:** Vitamin A 10%; Vitamin C 2%; Calcium 2%; Iron 6% **Diet Exchanges:** 4 Lean Meat

BROILED FISH FILLETS: Substitute 1 pound fish fillets, cut into 4 serving pieces, for the fish steaks. Broil with tops about 4 inches from heat 5 to 6 minutes or until fish flakes easily with fork (do not turn).

Beer Batter–Fried Fish

Fast & Low-Fat

Prep: 15 min; Cook: 4 min per batch ✳ *4 servings*

Vegetable oil
1 pound walleye pike, sole or other delicate fish fillets, about 3/4 inch thick
3 to 4 tablespoons Original Bisquick
1 cup Original Bisquick
1/2 cup beer or nonalcoholic beer
1 egg
1/2 teaspoon salt
Tartar Sauce (page 438), if desired

1. Heat oil (1 1/2 inches) in 4-quart Dutch oven or deep fryer to 350°. Cut fish into 8 serving pieces. Lightly coat fish with 3 to 4 tablespoons Bisquick.

2. Mix remaining ingredients except Tartar Sauce with hand beater until smooth. (If batter is too thick, stir in additional beer, 1 tablespoon at a time, until desired consistency.) Dip fish into batter, letting excess drip into bowl.

3. Fry fish in batches in oil about 4 minutes, turning once, until golden brown. Remove with slotted spoon; drain on paper towels. Serve hot with Tartar Sauce.

1 Serving: Calories 210 (Calories from Fat 55); Fat 6g (Saturated 2g); Cholesterol 80mg; Sodium 510mg; Carbohydrate 20g (Dietary Fiber 1g); Protein 20g **% Daily Value:** Vitamin A 2%; Vitamin C 0%; Calcium 6%; Iron 6% **Diet Exchanges:** 1 Starch, 2 1/2 Lean Meat

Sole Amandine

Prep: 15 min; Bake: 20 min ✱ *6 servings*

A French term, *amandine* means "garnished with almonds" and is often misspelled as "almondine." A shallow oval-shaped baking dish (au gratin dish) also can be used to bake this classic dish.

1 1/2 pounds sole, orange roughy or other delicate fish fillets, about 3/4 inch thick
1/2 cup sliced almonds
1/4 cup butter or stick margarine, softened
2 tablespoons grated lemon peel
1/2 teaspoon salt
1/2 teaspoon paprika
2 tablespoons lemon juice

1. Heat oven to 375°. Spray rectangular baking dish, 11 × 7 × 1 1/2 inches, with cooking spray.

2. Cut fish into 6 serving pieces. Place in baking dish. If fish has skin, place skin sides down. Tuck under any thin ends for more even cooking

3. Mix almonds, butter, lemon peel, salt and paprika; spoon over fish. Sprinkle with lemon juice.

4. Bake uncovered 15 to 20 minutes or until fish flakes easily with fork.

1 Serving: Calories 180 (Calories from Fat 100); Fat 11g (Saturated 2g); Cholesterol 45mg; Sodium 350mg; Carbohydrate 2g (Dietary Fiber 1g); Protein 19g **% Daily Value:** Vitamin A 8%; Vitamin C 2%; Calcium 4%; Iron 2% **Diet Exchanges:** 3 Very Lean Meat, 1 1/2 Fat

Lighter Sole Amandine: For 5 grams of fat and 115 calories per serving, decrease almonds to 2 tablespoons and butter to 2 tablespoons.

Tuna with Pesto *Fast*

Prep: 5 min; Cook: 15 min ✱ *4 servings*

1 pound yellowfin tuna, swordfish or halibut fillets, 3/4 inch thick
1 teaspoon olive or vegetable oil
2 medium green onions, sliced (2 tablespoons)
1/2 cup pesto
2 tablespoons lemon juice

1. If fish fillets are large, cut into 4 serving pieces. Heat oil in 10-inch nonstick skillet over medium heat. Cook onions in oil 2 to 3 minutes, stirring occasionally, until crisp-tender.

2. Stir in pesto and lemon juice. Top with fish. Heat to boiling; reduce heat to low. Cover and cook 5 to 10 minutes or until fish flakes easily with fork.

1 Serving: Calories 325 (Calories from Fat 205); Fat 23g (Saturated 5g); Cholesterol 45mg; Sodium 300mg; Carbohydrate 2g (Dietary Fiber 1g); Protein 29g **% Daily Value:** Vitamin A 72%; Vitamin C 2%; Calcium 12%; Iron 10% **Diet Exchanges:** 4 Medium-Fat Meat, 1/2 Fat

Seafood-Stuffed Whitefish

Prep: 35 min: Bake: 1 hr ✱ *6 servings*

Present this masterpiece on a long shallow platter, and garnish with salad greens and orange slices.

Seafood-Rice Stuffing (below)
2- to 2 1/2-pound pan-dressed whitefish or other delicate fish
3 tablespoons butter or stick margarine, melted
1 tablespoon grated orange peel

1. Make Seafood-Rice Stuffing.

2. Heat oven to 350 °.

3. Loosely stuff fish with stuffing. Close opening with skewers; lace with string.

4. Place fish in shallow roasting pan. Mix butter and orange peel. Brush half of the butter mixture over fish.

5. Bake uncovered 50 to 60 minutes, brushing occasionally with butter mixture, until fish flakes easily with fork. Remove skewers and string. See How to Carve a Whole Fish (right).

Seafood-Rice Stuffing

1/2 cup uncooked parboiled (converted) white or brown rice
1 1/3 cups orange juice
1/4 cup chopped pecans
1 medium stalk celery, thinly sliced (1/2 cup)
4 medium green onions, chopped (1/4 cup)
1 can (4 to 4 1/4 ounces) tiny shrimp, rinsed and drained

Cook rice as directed on package, using orange juice instead of the water called for in the directions. Mix cooked rice and remaining ingredients.

*Bake any extra stuffing separately in a small casserole. Cover with lid or aluminum foil and refrigerate until about 20 minutes before fish is done. Bake covered about 30 minutes or until hot. Or heat in microwave until hot.

1 Serving: Calories 380 (Calories from Fat 160); Fat 18g (Saturated 3g); Cholesterol 110mg; Sodium 190mg; Carbohydrate 23g (Dietary Fiber 1g); Protein 33g **% Daily Value:** Vitamin A 12%; Vitamin C 18%; Calcium 4%; Iron 16% **Diet Exchanges:** 1 Starch, 3 1/2 Lean Meat, 2 Vegetable, 1 Fat

How to Carve a Whole Fish

Using a sharp knife, cut the top side of fish into serving pieces, just down to the bone. Carefully remove pieces from the rib bones.

Carefully remove bones and discard. Cut the lower portion into serving pieces.

Potato-Crusted Salmon *Fast*

Prep: 10 min; Cook: 6 min ✱ *4 servings*

In this recipe, the crispy-coated fish tastes like it's deep-fried but uses only 2 tablespoons of oil for cooking.

1 pound salmon, trout or other medium-firm fish fillets,
    about 3/4 inch thick
1 egg, slightly beaten
1 tablespoon water
1/3 cup mashed potato mix (dry)
2 teaspoons cornstarch
1 teaspoon paprika
1 teaspoon lemon pepper
2 tablespoons vegetable oil

1. Cut fish into 4 serving pieces. Beat egg and water with fork. Mix potato mix, cornstarch, paprika and lemon pepper. Dip just the top and sides of fish into egg, then press into potato mixture.

2. Heat oil in 10-inch skillet over medium-high heat. Cook fish, potato sides down, in oil 3 minutes. Carefully turn fish with wide slotted spatula. Reduce heat to medium. Cook about 3 minutes longer or until fish flakes easily with fork.

3. If fish has skin, carefully slide cooked fish off of the skin with wide spatula.

1 Serving: Calories 215 (Calories from Fat 110); Fat 12g (Saturated 3g); Cholesterol 115mg; Sodium 160mg; Carbohydrate 5g (Dietary Fiber 0g); Protein 22g **% Daily Value:** Vitamin A 8%; Vitamin C 2%; Calcium 2%; Iron 6% **Diet Exchanges:** 3 Lean Meat, 1 Vegetable, 1/2 Fat

Salmon Patties with Sour Cream–Dill Sauce *Fast*

Prep: 20 min; Cook: 8 min ✱ *4 servings*

Sour Cream–Dill Sauce (below)
1 large egg
2 tablespoons milk
1 can (14 3/4 ounces) red or pink salmon, drained, skin
    and bones removed and salmon flaked
2 medium green onions, chopped (2 tablespoons)
1 cup soft bread crumbs (about 1 1/2 slices bread)
1/4 teaspoon salt
1 tablespoon vegetable oil

1. Make Sour Cream–Dill Sauce; refrigerate.

2. Beat egg and milk in medium bowl with spoon. Stir in remaining ingredients except oil. Shape mixture into 4 patties, about 4 inches in diameter

3. Heat oil in 10-inch nonstick skillet over medium heat. Cook patties in oil about 8 minutes, turning once, until golden brown. Serve with sauce.

Sour Cream–Dill Sauce

1/3 cup sour cream
3 tablespoons mayonnaise or salad dressing
3/4 teaspoon dried dill weed

Mix all ingredients.

1 Serving: Calories 415 (Calories from Fat 225); Fat 25g (Saturated 6g); Cholesterol 130mg; Sodium 1,050mg; Carbohydrate 21g (Dietary Fiber 1g); Protein 27g **% Daily Value:** Vitamin A 6%; Vitamin C 0%; Calcium 32%; Iron 16% **Diet Exchanges:** 1 Starch, 3 Lean Meat, 1 Vegetable, 3 Fat

Tuna-Pasta Casserole

Tuna-Pasta Casserole

Prep: 20 min; Bake: 30 min ✱ *6 servings*

Crumb Topping (right) or 2/3 cup crushed potato chips
1 1/4 cups uncooked medium pasta shells or elbow
    macaroni (about 5 ounces)
2 tablespoons butter or stick margarine
2 tablespoons all-purpose flour
3/4 teaspoon salt
2 cups milk
1 cup shredded sharp process American or Cheddar
    cheese (4 ounces)
2 cups cooked broccoli flowerets or 1 cup frozen
    (thawed) green peas
2 cans (6 ounces each) tuna in water, drained

1. Heat oven to 350°. Make Crumb Topping; set aside.

2. Cook and drain pasta as directed on package.

3. While pasta is cooking, melt butter in 1 1/2-quart
saucepan over low heat. Stir in flour and salt. Cook over
medium heat, stirring constantly, until smooth and

bubbly; remove from heat. Gradually stir in milk. Heat
to boiling, stirring constantly. Boil and stir 1 minute.
Stir in cheese until melted.

4. Mix pasta, broccoli, tuna and sauce in ungreased
2-quart casserole. Cover and bake about 25 minutes or
until hot and bubbly. Sprinkle with topping. Bake
uncovered about 5 minutes or until topping is toasted.

Crumb Topping

2/3 cup crushed cereal (Wheaties®, Cheerios or
    Country Corn Flakes®) or dry bread crumbs
1 tablespoon butter or stick margarine, melted

Mix ingredients.

1 Serving: Calories 360 (Calories from Fat 125); Fat 14g (Saturated
6g); Cholesterol 35mg; Sodium 600mg; Carbohydrate 33g (Dietary
Fiber 3g); Protein 29g **% Daily Value:** Vitamin A 28%; Vitamin C
18%; Calcium 24%; Iron 24% **Diet Exchanges:** 2 Starch, 3 Lean
Meat, 1 Fat

SALMON-PASTA CASSEROLE: Substitute 1 can
(14 3/4 ounces) red or pink salmon, drained, skin
and bones removed and salmon flaked, for the tuna.

Cold Poached Salmon with Herb Mayonnaise

Prep: 25 min; Cook: 19 min; Chill: 2 hr ✱ 6 servings

Because the salmon is chilled until served, you'll have time to make the delicious herb-spiked mayonnaise.

2 cups water
1 cup dry white wine, nonalcoholic white wine or apple juice
1 teaspoon salt
1/4 teaspoon dried thyme leaves
1/4 teaspoon dried oregano leaves
1/8 teaspoon ground red pepper (cayenne)
1 small onion, sliced
4 black peppercorns
4 sprigs cilantro
2 pounds salmon or other medium-firm fish fillets
Herb Mayonnaise (below)
Lemon wedges, if desired

1. Heat all ingredients except fish, Herb Mayonnaise and lemon wedges to boiling in 12-inch skillet; reduce heat to low. Cover and simmer 5 minutes.

2. Cut fish into 6 serving pieces. Place fish in skillet; add water to cover if necessary. Heat to boiling; reduce heat to low. Simmer uncovered about 14 minutes or until fish flakes easily with fork.

3. Carefully remove fish with slotted spatula; drain on wire rack. Cover and refrigerate about 2 hours or until chilled.

4. Make Herb Mayonnaise. Serve fish with Herb Mayonnaise and lemon wedges.

Herb Mayonnaise

3/4 cup mayonnaise or salad dressing
1 1/2 tablespoons chopped fresh or 1 1/2 teaspoons dried dill weed or tarragon leaves
1 tablespoon chopped fresh chives
1 tablespoon chopped fresh parsley
1 tablespoon lemon juice
1 1/2 teaspoons Dijon mustard
Dash of ground red pepper (cayenne)

Mix all ingredients. Cover and refrigerate until serving.

1 Serving: Calories 375 (Calories from Fat 260); Fat 29g (Saturated 5g); Cholesterol 100mg; Sodium 350mg; Carbohydrate 1g (Dietary Fiber 0g); Protein 28g **% Daily Value:** Vitamin A 6%; Vitamin C 2%; Calcium 2%; Iron 6% **Diet Exchanges:** 4 Medium-Fat Meat, 1 1/2 Fat

Crispy Baked Catfish **Fast**

Prep: 10 min; Bake: 18 min ✱ 4 servings

1 pound catfish, trout or other medium-firm fish fillets
1/4 cup yellow cornmeal
1/4 cup dry bread crumbs
1 teaspoon chili powder
1/2 teaspoon paprika
1/2 teaspoon garlic salt
1/4 teaspoon pepper
1/4 cup French or ranch dressing

1. Heat oven to 450°. Spray broiler pan rack with cooking spray.

2. If fish fillets are large, cut into 4 serving pieces. Mix remaining ingredients except dressing. Lightly brush dressing on all sides of fish. Coat fish with cornmeal mixture.

3. Place fish on rack in broiler pan. Bake uncovered 15 to 18 minutes or until fish flakes easily with fork.

1 Serving: Calories 220 (Calories from Fat 70); Fat 8g (Saturated 1g); Cholesterol 60mg; Sodium 410mg; Carbohydrate 14g (Dietary Fiber 1g); Protein 24g **% Daily Value:** Vitamin A 4%; Vitamin C 0%; Calcium 6%; Iron 6% **Diet Exchanges:** 1 Starch, 3 Lean Meat

Lighter Crispy Baked Catfish: For 2 grams of fat and 175 calories per serving, use fat-free French or ranch dressing.

Pecan-Crusted Fish Fillets

Pecan-Crusted Fish Fillets *Fast*

Prep: 15 min; Cook: 10 min ✳ *4 servings*

1 cup finely chopped pecans (not ground)
1/4 cup dry bread crumbs
2 teaspoons grated lemon peel
1 egg
1 tablespoon milk
1 pound sole, orange roughy, walleye pike or other
    delicate fish fillets, about 1/2 inch thick
1/2 teaspoon salt
1/4 teaspoon pepper
2 tablespoons vegetable oil
Lemon wedges

1. Mix pecans, bread crumbs and lemon peel in shallow bowl. Beat egg and milk with wire whisk or fork in another shallow bowl.

2. Cut fish into 4 serving pieces. Sprinkle both sides of fish with salt and pepper. Coat fish with egg mixture, then coat well with pecan mixture, pressing slightly into fish.

3. Heat oil in 12-inch nonstick skillet over medium heat. Add fish. Reduce heat to medium-low. Cook 6 to 10 minutes, turning once carefully with 2 pancake turners, until fish flakes easily with fork and is brown. Serve with lemon wedges.

1 Serving: Calories 350 (Calories from Fat 235); Fat 26g (Saturated 3g); Cholesterol 105mg; Sodium 450mg; Carbohydrate 10g (Dietary Fiber 2g); Protein 21g **% Daily Value:** Vitamin A 2%; Vitamin C 0%; Calcium 4%; Iron 8% **Diet Exchanges:** 1/2 Starch, 3 Very Lean Meat, 3 Fat

Sea Bass with Vegetable Melange

Sea Bass with Vegetable Melange

Prep: 30 min; Bake: 25 min ✷ *4 servings*

1 tablespoon butter or stick margarine

1 medium onion, chopped (1/2 cup)

2 medium carrots, cut into 2 × 1/4 × 1/4-inch strips (1 cup)

1 medium red bell pepper, cut into 1/4-inch strips

1 small zucchini, cut into 2 × 1/4 × 1/4-inch strips (1 cup)

1 teaspoon grated lemon peel

1/4 teaspoon salt

1/8 teaspoon dried tarragon leaves, if desired

1 pound sea bass, tilapia, snapper or other medium-firm fish fillets, 3/4 to 1 inch thick

1 tablespoon butter or stick margarine, melted

2 tablespoons chopped fresh parsley

1 teaspoon grated lemon peel

1 tablespoon lemon juice

1. Heat oven to 425°.

2. Melt 1 tablespoon butter in 10-inch nonstick skillet over medium-high heat. Cook onion and carrots in butter 2 minutes, stirring frequently. Stir in bell pepper. Cook 1 minute, stirring frequently. Stir in zucchini, 1 teaspoon lemon peel, the salt and tarragon. Cook 1 minute, stirring frequently; remove from heat.

3. Cut fish into 4 serving pieces (skin can be left on). If fish has skin, place fish skin side down in ungreased rectangular baking dish, 11 × 7 × 1 1/2 inches. Mix remaining ingredients; spread over fish. Spoon vegetable mixture around fish.

4. Bake uncovered 20 to 25 minutes or until fish flakes easily with fork. Remove skin from fish before serving if desired.

1 Serving: Calories 200 (Calories from Fat 90); Fat 10g (Saturated 5g); Cholesterol 65mg; Sodium 260mg; Carbohydrate 9g (Dietary Fiber 3g); Protein 21g **% Daily Value:** Vitamin A 74%; Vitamin C 58%; Calcium 4%; Iron 10% **Diet Exchanges:** 3 Lean Meat, 2 Vegetable

Fish en Papillote *Low-Fat*

Prep: 25 min; Bake: 25 min ✳ *4 servings*

En papillote is a French term describing food baked inside a wrapping of parchment paper. The packet puffs during baking as the food lets off steam. For a dramatic presentation, slit the packet at the table, being careful to avoid the hot steam that is released when the packet is cut.

1 pound grouper, sea bass or other medium-firm
   fish fillets
4 teaspoons chopped fresh or 1 teaspoon dried
   oregano
1/4 teaspoon salt
1/8 teaspoon pepper
1 small onion, thinly sliced
1 small tomato, thinly sliced
1 small zucchini, thinly sliced
1/4 cup sliced ripe olives

1. Heat oven to 400°.

2. Cut four 12-inch circles of cooking parchment paper or aluminum foil. Cut fish into 4 serving pieces. Place each piece of fish on half of each parchment circle. Sprinkle fish with oregano, salt and pepper. Layer onion, tomato, zucchini and olives on fish.

3. Fold other half of circle over fish and vegetables. Beginning at one end, seal edge by turning up and folding tightly 2 or 3 times. Twist each end several times to secure. Place on ungreased cookie sheet.

4. Bake 20 to 25 minutes or until vegetables are crisp-tender and fish flakes easily with fork. To serve, cut a large X in top of each packet; carefully fold back points to avoid the steam that is released.

1 Serving: Calories 110 (Calories from Fat 20); Fat 2g (Saturated 0g); Cholesterol 55mg; Sodium 310mg; Carbohydrate 5g (Dietary Fiber 2g); Protein 20g **% Daily Value:** Vitamin A 4%; Vitamin C 6%; Calcium 6%; Iron 8% **Diet Exchanges:** 2 1/2 Very Lean Meat, 1 Vegetable

Sweet-Sour Fish Bake *Low-Fat*

Prep: 10 min; Cook: 5 min; Bake: 25 min
✳ *4 servings*

1 can (8 ounces) pineapple chunks in juice, drained and
   juice reserved
3 tablespoons sugar
1/4 cup cider vinegar
1 teaspoon soy sauce
1/4 teaspoon salt
1 small clove garlic, finely chopped
2 tablespoons cornstarch
2 tablespoons cold water
1 small green bell pepper, cut into 1/2-inch strips
1 pound halibut, swordfish or other firm fish steaks,
   1/2 to 3/4 inch thick
1/4 teaspoon salt
1 tomato, cut into 8 wedges

1. Heat oven to 350°.

2. Add enough water to reserved pineapple juice to measure 1 cup. Heat pineapple juice, sugar, vinegar, soy sauce, 1/4 teaspoon salt and garlic to boiling in 2-quart saucepan. Mix cornstarch and water; stir into sauce. Heat to boiling, stirring constantly. Boil and stir 1 minute. Stir in pineapple chunks and bell pepper.

3. Place fish steaks in ungreased square baking dish, 8 × 8 × 2 inches. Sprinkle with 1/4 teaspoon salt. Pour pineapple mixture over fish.

4. Bake uncovered 20 to 25 minutes or until fish flakes easily with fork. Add tomato wedges during last 5 minutes of baking.

1 Serving: Calories 180 (Calories from Fat 10); Fat 1g (Saturated 0g); Cholesterol 50mg; Sodium 450mg; Carbohydrate 26g (Dietary Fiber 1g); Protein 18g **% Daily Value:** Vitamin A 4%; Vitamin C 22%; Calcium 2%; Iron 4% **Diet Exchanges:** 2 Very Lean Meat, 2 Vegetable, 1 Fruit

Shellfish Basics

The colors, flavors and shapes of shellfish add variety—and a taste of the sea—to a wonderful array of dishes. Check out the selection of shellfish at your local supermarket or seafood market for both fresh and frozen shellfish; it's best to buy shellfish from a vendor you know. For the best ocean-fresh flavor, buy and eat shellfish the same day. Shellfish can be grouped into three main categories:

Crustaceans have long bodies with soft, jointed shells and legs. Crabs, crayfish, lobster and shrimp are crustaceans.

Mollusks have soft bodies with no spinal column and are covered by a shell in one or more pieces. Examples are abalone, clams, mussels, oysters, scallops, snails, octopus and squid.

Imitation seafood products such as imitation crab legs and lobster bites often are less expensive than shellfish but provide similar taste and texture in recipes. Imitation seafood is made from pollock, a mild white-fleshed fish. To flavor it, real shellfish, a shellfish extract or artificial shellfish flavoring is added. So if you have a shellfish allergy, check labels carefully.

Selecting Shellfish

Live clams, oysters, mussels and scallops should have tightly closed shells and a mild odor. Shells should not be cracked, chipped or broken. If a shell is open, test to see if the shellfish is still alive by tapping on the shell. Live shellfish will close when tapped. If shellfish are not alive, don't use them.

Shucked clams, oysters and mussels—those with their shells removed—should be plump and surrounded by a clear, slightly opalescent liquid. Clams range in color from pale to deep orange. Oysters are typically creamy white but may also be tinted green, red, brown or pink. Mussels can be light tan to deep orange.

Shucked scallops are available in two sizes: the larger sea scallops, which are about two inches in diameter, and the tiny bay scallops, about 1/2 inch in diameter. Sweet and moist, scallops should have a mild, sweet odor and look moist, but they should not be standing in liquid or in direct contact with ice. Sea scallops are usually creamy white and may be tinted light orange or pink. Bay scallops are also creamy white and may be tinted light tan or pink.

Live lobsters and crabs should have hard shells and be moving their legs. For food safety reasons, lobster must be cooked live or killed immediately before cooking. To test if a lobster is alive, pick it up—it should tightly curl its tail under. Discard dead lobsters or crabs. Use lobsters and crabs the day you buy them. Lobster meat and crabmeat also are available fresh, frozen and canned.

Shrimp are sold either raw—"green"— with the heads on; raw in the shell without the heads; raw and peeled and deveined, or cleaned; cooked in the shell; or cooked, peeled and deveined. Shrimp also are available frozen and canned. Fresh shrimp may have descriptive market names, such as "jumbo" or "large," but they're usually sold by count, or number per pound. In general, the smaller the shrimp, the higher the count per pound; the larger the shrimp, the lower the count—and higher the price. Because the market names can vary, look over the sizes, ask the fish manager for suggestions and buy shrimp by the count. Following is an approximate guide to the number, or count, per pound of raw shrimp in shells, along with some common market names:

Shrimp Market Name	Count (Number) Per Pound
Super/Extra Colossal	Less than 10
Super/Extra Jumbo	16 to 20
Jumbo	21 to 25
Extra Large	26 to 30
Large	31 to 35
Medium Large	36 to 40
Medium	41 to 45
Small	51 to 60
Extra Small to Tiny	61 to 100

Squid, also known as calamari, should be cream colored with reddish brown spots. As squid ages, the skin will turn pinkish. Buy fresh squid that's whole with clear eyes and a clean sea odor. It's also available cleaned. Cleaned squid should be in juices, and the meat should be firm.

> **Note:** For more information about shellfish handling, safety and nutrition, call the FDA's Center for Food Safety and Applied Nutrition, 1-800-332-4010. Recorded information is available 24 hours; to speak to a specialist, call Monday through Friday, 12–4 eastern standard time. Or check the FDA's Web site at www.fda.gov.

How Much Shellfish to Buy

Live clams, oysters and mussels: About 6 small hard-shell clams, 3 large hard-shell clams, 18 soft-shell clams, 6 oysters, or 18 mussels per serving.

Shucked clams, oysters, mussels and scallops: About 1/4 pound per serving.

Crab and lobsters: About 1 1/4 pounds live or 1/4 pound cooked meat per serving.

Raw shrimp: About 1 pound whole shrimp, 1/2 pound headless unpeeled shrimp or 1/4 pound headless peeled shrimp per serving.

Squid: About 1/2 pound whole squid or 1/4 pound cleaned squid per serving.

Determining When Shellfish Is Done

When done just right, cooked shellfish is a delight: moist, slightly chewy and delicious. Overcooked, and it's tough and rubbery. These are the clues to watch for when determining when cooked shellfish is done.

Live clams, oysters and mussels will open their shells as they are done.

Shucked clams, oysters and mussels will become plump and opaque. Oyster edges will start to curl.

Crabs and lobsters will turn bright red.

Scallops turn white or opaque and become firm. Cooking time depends on the size.

Raw shrimp will turn pink and become firm. Cooking time depends on the size.

Microwaving Shellfish

Shrimp and scallops are two varieties of shellfish that cook well in the microwave. For best results:

1. Cut large scallops in half. Rinse shrimp. Arrange shellfish in circle in shallow microwavable dish that's large enough to hold shellfish in a single layer.
2. Cover with plastic wrap, folding one edge or corner back about 1/4 inch to vent steam.
3. Microwave on High (100%) as directed in chart below, rotating dish once if microwave does not have turntable, until shrimp are pink and firm or until scallops are white.

TIMETABLE FOR MICROWAVING SHELLFISH

Type	Approximate Weight	Microwave Time	Stand Time
Scallops, sea	1 pound	6 to 9 minutes, stirring after 4 minutes	3 minutes
Shrimp, peeled and deveined	1 pound	6 to 8 minutes, stirring after 3 minutes	3 minutes
Shrimp in the shell	1 pound	5 to 7 minutes, stirring after 3 minutes	3 minutes

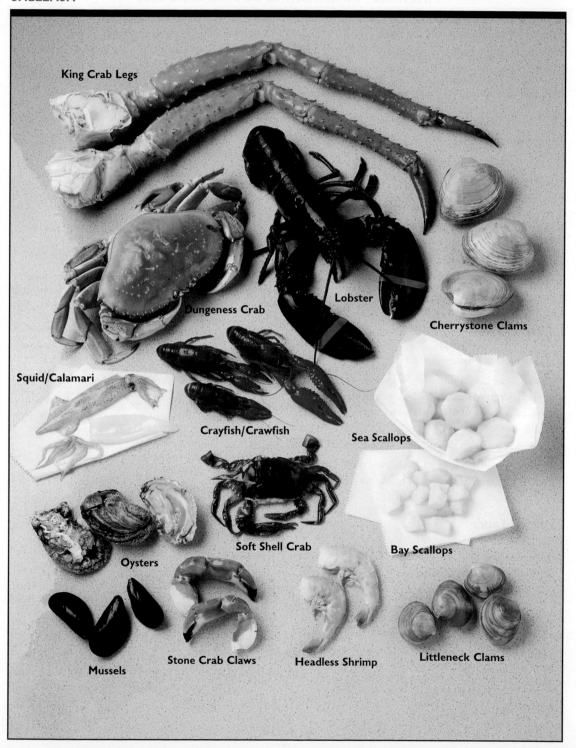

King Crab Legs

Lobster

Cherrystone Clams

Dungeness Crab

Squid/Calamari

Crayfish/Crawfish

Sea Scallops

Oysters

Soft Shell Crab

Bay Scallops

Mussels

Stone Crab Claws

Headless Shrimp

Littleneck Clams

TIMETABLE FOR REHEATING COOKED CRAB LEGS

Type	Approximate Weight	Microwave Time	Stand Time
Frozen cooked crab legs	2 pounds	10 to 12 minutes, rearranging *legs once*	5 minutes
Thawed cooked crab legs	2 pounds	5 to 6 minutes	5 minutes

Crab legs reheat well in the microwave. Here's how:

1. Cut crab legs to fit 8-inch square microwavable dish.

2. Cover with plastic wrap, folding one edge or corner back about 1/4 inch to vent steam.

3. Microwave on Medium-High (70%) as directed in chart above, rotating dish once if microwave does not have turntable, until hot.

Boiled Shrimp *Low-Fat*

Prep: 30 min; Cook: 5 min ✱ *4 servings*

Cocktail Sauce (below), if desired
4 cups water
1 pound uncooked medium shrimp in shells

1. Make Cocktail Sauce.

2. Heat water to boiling in 3-quart saucepan. Add shrimp. Cover and heat to boiling; reduce heat. Simmer uncovered 3 to 5 minutes or until shrimp are pink and firm; drain.

3. Peel shrimp, leaving tails on. Make a shallow cut lengthwise down back of each shrimp; wash out vein (see How to Devein Shrimp, right). Serve shrimp with Cocktail Sauce.

Cocktail Sauce

1 cup ketchup
4 teaspoons prepared horseradish
1 teaspoon Worcestershire sauce
2 or 3 drops red pepper sauce

Mix all ingredients. Stir in 1 to 2 teaspoons additional horseradish, if desired, until sauce has desired flavor. Cover and refrigerate until serving.

1 Serving: Calories 55 (Calories from Fat 10); Fat 1g (Saturated 0g); Cholesterol 105mg; Sodium 120mg; Carbohydrate 0g (Dietary Fiber 0g); Protein 11g **% Daily Value:** Vitamin A 3%; Vitamin C 0%; Calcium 2%; Iron 8% **Diet Exchanges:** 1 1/2 Very-Lean Meat

How to Devein Shrimp

Using a small, pointed knife or shrimp deveiner, make a shallow cut along the center back of each shrimp, and wash out vein.

Deep-Fried Shrimp

Prep: 35 min; Cook: 1 min per batch ✱ *4 servings*

The number of medium-size shrimp per pound is normally 41 to 50. This number may vary, however, depending on where the shrimp are purchased.

1 pound uncooked medium shrimp in shells
Vegetable oil
1/2 cup all-purpose flour
1 teaspoon salt
1/2 teaspoon pepper
2 large eggs, slightly beaten
3/4 cup dry bread crumbs

1. Peel shrimp, leaving tails on. Make a shallow cut lengthwise down back of each shrimp; wash out vein (see How to Devein Shrimp, above).

2. Heat oil (2 to 3 inches) in deep fryer or Dutch oven to 350°.

3. Mix flour, salt and pepper. Coat shrimp with flour mixture. Dip shrimp into eggs, then coat with bread crumbs.

4. Fry 4 or 5 shrimp at a time in oil about 1 minute, turning once, until golden brown. Drain on paper towels.

1 Serving: Calories 340 (Calories from Fat 160); Fat 18g (Saturated 3g); Cholesterol 210mg; Sodium 830mg; Carbohydrate 26g (Dietary Fiber 1g); Protein 19g **% Daily Value:** Vitamin A 6%; Vitamin C 0%; Calcium 8%; Iron 22% **Diet Exchanges:** 2 Starch, 2 Lean Meat, 1 1/2 Fat

DEEP-FRIED OYSTERS OR CLAMS: Substitute 3/4 pound shucked oysters or clams, drained, for the shrimp.

DEEP-FRIED SEA SCALLOPS: Substitute 3/4 pound shucked sea scallops, drained, for the shrimp. Fry 3 to 4 minutes or until golden brown. Bay scallops, which are smaller, will cook more quickly.

Shrimp Scampi *Low-Fat*

Prep: 30 min: Cook: 3 min ✻ 6 servings

Scampi is a term often used in restaurants to describe a dish made with large shrimp that are prepared with garlic, oil or butter, then broiled in a shallow ramekin. This easy version is cooked in a skillet.

1 1/2 pounds uncooked medium shrimp in shells
2 tablespoons olive or vegetable oil
1 tablespoon chopped fresh parsley
2 tablespoons lemon juice
1/4 teaspoon salt
2 medium green onions, thinly sliced (2 tablespoons)
2 cloves garlic, finely chopped
Grated Parmesan cheese, if desired

1. Peel shrimp, removing tails. Make a shallow cut lengthwise down back of each shrimp; wash out vein (see How to Devein Shrimp, page 320).

2. Heat oil in 10-inch skillet over medium heat. Cook shrimp and remaining ingredients except cheese in oil 2 to 3 minutes, stirring frequently, until shrimp are pink and firm; remove from heat. Sprinkle with cheese.

1 Serving: Calories 95 (Calories from Fat 45); Fat 5g (Saturated 1g); Cholesterol 105mg; Sodium 220mg; Carbohydrate 1g (Dietary Fiber 0g); Protein 12g **% Daily Value:** Vitamin A 4%; Vitamin C 4%; Calcium 2%; Iron 10% **Diet Exchanges:** 2 Lean Meat

SHRIMP SCAMPI WITH FETTUCCINE: Cook and drain 8 ounces uncooked fettuccine as directed on package. Serve shrimp mixture over fettucine; sprinkle with cheese.

Shrimp Creole

Prep: 30 min: Cook: 30 min ✻ 6 servings

2 pounds uncooked medium shrimp in shells
1/4 cup butter or stick margarine
3 medium onions, chopped (1 1/2 cups)
2 medium green bell peppers, finely chopped (2 cups)
2 medium stalks celery, finely chopped (1 cup)
2 cloves garlic, finely chopped
1 cup water
2 teaspoons chopped fresh parsley
1 1/2 teaspoons salt
1/4 teaspoon ground red pepper (cayenne)
2 bay leaves
1 can (15 ounces) tomato sauce
6 cups hot cooked rice (page 348)

1. Peel shrimp. Make a shallow cut lengthwise down back of each shrimp; wash out vein (see How to Devein Shrimp, page 320). Cover and refrigerate.

2. Melt butter in 3-quart saucepan over medium heat. Cook onions, bell peppers, celery and garlic in butter about 10 minutes, stirring occasionally, until onions are tender.

3. Stir in remaining ingredients except rice and shrimp. Heat to boiling; reduce heat to low. Simmer uncovered 10 minutes.

4. Stir in shrimp. Heat to boiling; reduce heat to medium. Cover and cook 4 to 6 minutes, stirring occasionally, until shrimp are pink and firm. Remove bay leaves. Serve shrimp mixture over rice.

1 Serving: Calories 385 (Calories from Fat 80); Fat 9g (Saturated 2g); Cholesterol 140mg; Sodium 1,110mg; Carbohydrate 58g (Dietary Fiber 4g); Protein 22g **% Daily Value:** Vitamin A 24%; Vitamin C 42%; Calcium 8%; Iron 28% **Diet Exchanges:** 3 Starch, 1 1/2 Lean Meat, 2 Vegetable

> **Lighter Shrimp Creole:** For 3 grams of fat and 335 calories per serving, decrease butter to 1 tablespoon; use nonstick saucepan.

Shrimp and Scallops with Wine and Vegetables

Shrimp and Scallops with Wine and Vegetables *Fast*

Prep: 20 min; Cook: 10 min ✱ *4 servings*

1 pound uncooked medium shrimp in shells

2 tablespoons olive or vegetable oil

1 clove garlic, finely chopped

2 medium green onions, sliced (2 tablespoons)

2 medium carrots, thinly sliced (1 cup)

1 tablespoon chopped fresh parsley or 1 teaspoon parsley flakes

1 pound sea scallops, cut in half

1/2 cup dry white wine or chicken broth

1 tablespoon lemon juice

1/4 to 1/2 teaspoon crushed red pepper

1. Peel shrimp. Make a shallow cut lengthwise down back of each shrimp; wash out vein (see How to Devein Shrimp, page 320). Cover and refrigerate.

2. Heat oil in 12-inch nonstick skillet over medium heat. Cook garlic, onions, carrots and parsley in oil about 5 minutes, stirring occasionally, until carrots are crisp-tender.

3. Stir in shrimp and remaining ingredients. Cook 4 to 5 minutes, stirring frequently, until shrimp are pink and firm and scallops are white.

1 Serving: Calories 190 (Calories from Fat 70); Fat 8g (Saturated 1g); Cholesterol 125mg; Sodium 290mg; Carbohydrate 6g (Dietary Fiber 1g); Protein 25g **% Daily Value:** Vitamin A 54%; Vitamin C 6%; Calcium 10%; Iron 20% **Diet Exchanges:** 3 Lean Meat, 1 Vegetable

Shrimp Fondue

Prep: 30 min; Cook: 2 min per shrimp ✱ *6 servings*

Mustard Tartar Sauce (right)

Chili Cocktail Sauce (right)

2 pounds uncooked peeled medium or large shrimp, thawed if frozen

3 cans (14 1/2 ounces each) ready-to-serve chicken broth

2 tablespoons lemon juice

2 cloves garlic, thinly sliced

1. Make Mustard Tartar Sauce and Chili Cocktail Sauce. Devein shrimp (see How to Devein Shrimp, page 320). Cover and refrigerate.

2. Mix broth, lemon juice and garlic in 2-quart saucepan. Heat to boiling. Pour into fondue pot. Keep warm over medium heat.

3. Arrange shrimp on serving plate. Spear shrimp with fondue forks; dip into simmering broth to cook. Cook medium shrimp about 1 minute, large shrimp 1 1/2 to 2 minutes, or until pink and firm. Serve with sauces.

Mustard Tartar Sauce

1/2 cup mayonnaise or salad dressing
1/4 cup dill pickle relish
2 tablespoons yellow mustard
2 teaspoons sugar
1 teaspoon ground mustard
2 medium green onions, chopped (2 tablespoons)

Mix all ingredients. Cover and refrigerate until serving.

Chili Cocktail Sauce

1/2 cup chili sauce
2 tablespoons apricot preserves
1 teaspoon chili powder
1 teaspoon cider vinegar
1/8 teaspoon ground red pepper (cayenne)

Mix all ingredients. Cover and refrigerate until serving.

1 Serving: Calories 260 (Calories from Fat 145); Fat 16g (Saturated 2g); Cholesterol 150mg; Sodium 1,010mg; Carbohydrate 14g (Dietary Fiber 1g); Protein 16g **% Daily Value:** Vitamin A 10%; Vitamin C 4%; Calcium 4%; Iron 14% **Diet Exchanges:** 1 Starch, 2 Lean Meat, 2 Fat

Steamed Clams *Low-Fat*

Prep: 10 min; Stand: 30 min; Cook: 8 min ✱ 4 servings

4 pounds soft-shell clams in shells (steamers)
6 cups water
1/3 cup white vinegar
1/2 cup boiling water
Butter or stick margarine, melted, if desired

1. Discard any broken-shell or open (dead) clams. Place remaining clams in large container. Cover with 6 cups water and the vinegar. Let stand 30 minutes; drain. Scrub clams in cold water.

2. Place clams in steamer* with boiling water. Cover and steam 5 to 8 minutes or until clams open at least 1 inch, removing clams as they open. Discard any unopened clams.

3. Serve hot clams in shells with butter.

If steamer is not available, place clams in 6-quart Dutch oven. Add 1 inch boiling water; cover tightly.

1 Serving: Calories 55 (Calories from Fat 10); Fat 1g (Saturated 0g); Cholesterol 25mg; Sodium 40mg; Carbohydrate 2g (Dietary Fiber 0g); Protein 9g **% Daily Value:** Vitamin A 6%; Vitamin C 6%; Calcium 2%; Iron 52% **Diet Exchanges:** 1 Lean Meat

How to Open Raw Clams

Hold a clam with the hinged side against a heavy cloth or oven mitt. Insert a blunt-tipped knife between shell halves. Be sure to work over a bowl or plate to catch juices.

Holding the clam firmly, move a sharp knife around the clam, cutting the muscle at the hinge. Gently twist the knife to pry open the shell. Cut the clam meat from the shell.

Steamed Mussels *Low-Fat*

Prep: 20 min; Cook: 5 min per batch ✱ 4 servings

4 pounds mussels in shells
1/2 cup boiling water
Butter or stick margarine, melted, if desired

1. Discard any broken-shell or open (dead) mussels. Scrub remaining mussels in cold water, removing any barnacles with a dull paring knife. Follow directions below to remove beards.

2. Place mussels in large container. Cover with cool water. Agitate water with hand, then drain and discard water. Repeat several times until water runs clear; drain.

3. Place half of the mussels in steamer* with boiling water. Cover and steam 3 to 5 minutes, removing mussels as they open. Discard any unopened mussels. Repeat with remaining mussels.

4. Serve hot mussels in shells with butter.

*If steamer is not available, place mussels in 6-quart Dutch oven. Add 1 inch boiling water; cover tightly.

Pull beard by giving it a tug (using a kitchen towel may help). If you have trouble removing it, use a pliers to grip and pull gently.

1 Serving: Calories 90 (Calories from Fat 10); Fat 1g (Saturated 0g); Cholesterol 45mg; Sodium 370mg; Carbohydrate 3g (Dietary Fiber 0g); Protein 17g **% Daily Value:** Vitamin A 10%; Vitamin C 14%; Calcium 6%; Iron 100% **Diet Exchanges:** 2 Lean Meat

STEAMED OYSTERS: Substitute oysters for the mussels. Clean as directed in step 1 (oysters do not have beards). Omit step 2. Continue as directed. Steam 5 to 8 minutes.

Crabmeat Roll-Ups

Prep: 20 min; Bake: 25 min ✱ 5 servings

1 can (6 ounces) crabmeat, drained and cartilage removed
1/2 cup shredded Swiss or Monterey Jack cheese (2 ounces)
1 small zucchini, shredded (1/2 cup)
1/4 cup finely chopped celery
1 small onion, finely chopped (1/4 cup)
3 tablespoons chili sauce
1/2 teaspoon salt
10 slices white sandwich bread
3 tablespoons butter or stick margarine, melted
Avocado Sauce (below)

1. Heat oven to 350°.

2. Mix crabmeat, cheese, zucchini, celery, onion, chili sauce and salt.

3. Remove crusts from each bread slice. Roll each slice to about 1/4-inch thickness. Spoon crabmeat mixture across center of each slice. Bring sides of bread up over crabmeat mixture; secure with toothpicks.

4. Place roll-ups, seam sides down, in ungreased rectangular baking dish, 13 × 9 × 2 inches. Brush with butter. Bake uncovered about 25 minutes or until golden brown and hot.

5. While roll-ups are baking, make Avocado Sauce. Serve sauce over roll-ups.

Avocado Sauce

1/2 cup sour cream
1/4 teaspoon salt
1 medium tomato, seeded, chopped and drained
1 medium avocado, chopped

Heat sour cream and salt in 1-quart saucepan over low heat, stirring occasionally, just until warm. Gently stir in tomato. Heat 1 minute; remove from heat. Gently stir in avocado.

1 Serving: Calories 380 (Calories from Fat 200); Fat 22g (Saturated 10g); Cholesterol 75mg; Sodium 950mg; Carbohydrate 34g (Dietary Fiber 4g); Protein 16g **% Daily Value:** Vitamin A 16%; Vitamin C 10%; Calcium 22%; Iron 14% **Diet Exchanges:** 2 Starch, 1 Medium-Fat Meat, 2 Vegetable, 2 Fat

Boiled Hard-Shell Blue Crabs   *Low-Fat*

Prep: 20 min; Cook: 10 min per batch ✳ *4 servings*

Blue crab is the most familiar hard-shell crab. It is usually four to six inches in diameter and often has red claw tips.

4 quarts water
16 live hard-shell blue crabs
Cocktail Sauce (page 320), if desired

1. Heat water to boiling in stockpot or canner. Drop 4 crabs at a time into water. Cover and heat to boiling; reduce heat to low. Simmer 10 minutes; drain. Repeat with remaining crabs.

2. Follow directions below to remove meat. Serve with Cocktail Sauce

1 Serving: Calories 100 (Calories from Fat 20); Fat 2g (Saturated 0g); Cholesterol 105mg; Sodium 290mg; Carbohydrate 0g (Dietary Fiber 0g); Protein 21g **% Daily Value:** Vitamin A 0%; Vitamin C 2%; Calcium 10%; Iron 4% **Diet Exchanges:** 3 Very Lean Meat

---

HARD-SHELL AND SOFT-SHELL BLUE CRABS

Atlantic hard-shell and soft-shell blue crabs are the same species, except the soft-shell crabs have been caught immediately after shedding their old hard shells. They stay soft for only a couple of hours. When their new shells harden, they are known as hard-shell blue crabs.

HOW TO REMOVE CRABMEAT

Place crab on its back. Using thumb, pry up the tail flap, twist off and discard. Turn crab right side up, and pry up the top shell. Pull it away from the body and discard.

Using a small knife (or fingers), cut the gray-white gills (called "devil's fingers") from both sides of the crab. Discard gills and internal organs.

To remove meat, twist off the crab claws and legs. Use a nutcracker to crack shells at the joints. Remove meat with a small cocktail fork or nutpick. Break the body and remove any remaining meat in the deeper pockets.

Crab Cakes

Crab Cakes *Fast*

Prep: 15 min: Cook: 10 min ✱ *6 servings*

1/4 cup mayonnaise or salad dressing

1 large egg

1 1/4 cups soft bread crumbs (about 2 slices bread)

1 teaspoon ground mustard

1/4 teaspoon salt

1/8 teaspoon pepper

2 medium green onions, chopped (2 tablespoons)

2 cans (6 ounces each) crabmeat, drained, cartilage removed and flaked*

2 tablespoons vegetable oil

1/4 cup dry bread crumbs

1. Mix mayonnaise and egg in medium bowl. Stir in remaining ingredients except oil and dry bread crumbs. Shape mixture into 6 patties, about 3 inches in diameter.

2. Heat oil in 12-inch skillet over medium heat. Coat each patty with dry bread crumbs. Cook in oil over medium heat about 10 minutes, turning once, until golden brown and hot in center. Reduce heat if crab cakes become brown too quickly.

*3/4 pound cooked crabmeat, flaked, can be substituted for the canned crabmeat.

1 Serving: Calories 195 (Calories from Fat 115); Fat 13g (Saturated 2g); Cholesterol 90mg; Sodium 440mg; Carbohydrate 8g (Dietary Fiber 0g); Protein 14g **% Daily Value:** Vitamin A 2%; Vitamin C 2%; Calcium 8%; Iron 6% **Diet Exchanges:** 1/2 Starch, 2 Very Lean Meat, 2 Fat

Boiled Lobsters *Low-Fat*

Prep: 20 min; Cook: 12 min ✳ 2 servings

2 to 4 quarts water
2 live lobsters (about 1 pound each)
Butter or stick margarine, melted, if desired
Lemon wedges, if desired

1. Fill 6-quart Dutch oven or stockpot one-third full of water. Heat to boiling. Plunge lobsters headfirst into water. Cover and heat to boiling; reduce heat to low. Simmer 10 to 12 minutes or until lobsters turn bright red; drain.

2. Follow directions below to remove meat. Serve with butter and lemon wedges.

1 Serving: Calories 115 (Calories from Fat 10); Fat 1g (Saturated 0g); Cholesterol 85mg; Sodium 450mg; Carbohydrate 2g (Dietary Fiber 0g); Protein 24g **% Daily Value:** Vitamin A 2%; Vitamin C 0%; Calcium 6%; Iron 2% **Diet Exchanges:** 3 Very Lean Meat

Lobster Newburg *Fast*

Prep: 10 min; Cook: 15 min ✳ 6 servings

Instead of being served over rice, Lobster Newburg is also delicious served over Fried Polenta (page 354), hot Popovers (page 58) or baked pastry shells.

1/4 cup butter or stick margarine
3 tablespoons all-purpose flour
1/2 teaspoon salt
1/2 teaspoon ground mustard
1/4 teaspoon pepper
2 cups milk
2 cups cut-up cooked lobster
2 tablespoons dry sherry or apple juice
6 cups hot cooked rice (page 348)

1. Melt butter in 3-quart saucepan over medium heat. Stir in flour, salt, mustard and pepper. Cook, stirring constantly, until smooth and bubbly; remove from heat.

2. Stir in milk. Heat to boiling, stirring constantly. Boil and stir 1 minute. Stir in lobster and sherry; heat through. Serve over rice.

1 Serving: Calories 365 (Calories from Fat 90); Fat 10g (Saturated 2g); Cholesterol 40mg; Sodium 520mg; Carbohydrate 53g (Dietary Fiber 1g); Protein 17g **% Daily Value:** Vitamin A 16%; Vitamin C 0%; Calcium 14%; Iron 12% **Diet Exchanges:** 3 Starch, 1 Lean Meat, 1 Fat, 1/2 Skim Milk

CRAB NEWBURG: Substitute 2 cups chopped cooked crabmeat or imitation crabmeat for the lobster.

HOW TO REMOVE LOBSTER MEAT

Separate tail from body by breaking shell in half where tail and body meet.

Cut away the membrane on the tail to expose meat. Discard the intestinal vein that runs through the tail and the small sac near the head of the lobster. Serve the green tomalley (liver) and coral roe (only in females) if you like.

Twist the large claws away from the body of the lobster. Using a nutcracker, break open the claws. Remove meat from claws, tail and body.

Coquilles Saint Jacques

Prep: 45 min; Cook: 15 min; Broil: 5 min ✱ 6 servings

Coquilles is French for "shell" and can also mean "scallop." Oven-to-table scallop shells (either authentic shells or porcelain reproductions) are available in kitchenware or gourmet food shops, and add a pretty touch.

1 1/2 pounds bay scallops*
1 cup dry white wine, nonalcoholic white wine or
    chicken broth
1/4 cup chopped fresh parsley
1/2 teaspoon salt
2 tablespoons butter or stick margarine
6 ounces mushrooms, sliced (2 cups)
2 shallots or green onions, chopped
3 tablespoons butter or stick margarine
3 tablespoons all-purpose flour
1/2 cup half-and-half
1/2 cup shredded Swiss cheese (2 ounces)
1 cup soft bread crumbs (about 1 1/2 slices bread)
2 tablespoons butter or stick margarine, melted

1. Lightly grease six 4-inch baking shells or ramekins with butter. Place in jelly roll pan, 15 1/2 × 10 1/2 × 1 inch.

2. Place scallops, wine, parsley and salt in 3-quart saucepan. Add just enough water to cover scallops. Heat to boiling; reduce heat to low. Simmer uncovered about 6 minutes or until scallops are white.

3. Remove scallops with slotted spoon; reserve liquid. Heat reserved liquid to boiling. Boil until reduced to 1 cup. Strain and reserve.

4. Melt 2 tablespoons butter in same saucepan over medium heat. Cook mushrooms and shallots in butter 5 to 6 minutes, stirring occasionally, until mushrooms are tender. Remove from saucepan.

5. Melt 3 tablespoons butter in same saucepan over medium heat. Stir in flour. Cook, stirring constantly, until smooth and bubbly; remove from heat. Gradually stir in reserved liquid. Heat to boiling, stirring constantly; cook and stir 1 minute. Stir in half-and-half, scallops, mushroom mixture and 1/4 cup of the cheese; heat through.

6. Toss bread crumbs and 2 tablespoons melted butter. Divide scallop mixture among baking shells. Sprinkle with remaining 1/4 cup cheese and the bread crumbs.

7. Set oven control to broil. Broil baking shells with tops 5 inches from heat 3 to 5 minutes or until crumbs are toasted.

*2 packages (12 ounces each) frozen scallops, thawed, can be substituted for the fresh scallops.

1 Serving: Calories 335 (Calories from Fat 180); Fat 20g (Saturated 7g); Cholesterol 45mg; Sodium 690mg; Carbohydrate 21g (Dietary Fiber 1g); Protein 19g **% Daily Value:** Vitamin A 24%; Vitamin C 4%; Calcium 22%; Iron 20% **Diet Exchanges:** 1 Starch, 2 Lean Meat, 1 Vegetable, 3 Fat

Thai Scallops and Noodles *Fast*

Prep: 10 min; Cook: 16 min ✱ 6 servings

If you can't find bay scallops at your supermarket or seafood shop, the larger sea scallops will work equally well—just cut them into fourths.

1 package (7 ounces) spaghetti, broken in half
5 cups broccoli pieces or 1 bag (16 ounces) frozen cut
    broccoli, thawed
3/4 pound bay scallops or quartered sea scallops
1/2 cup peanut butter
1/4 cup soy sauce
1/4 cup rice vinegar
1 teaspoon red pepper sauce
2 tablespoons dry-roasted peanuts, finely chopped

1. Cook spaghetti as directed on package—except add broccoli and scallops during last 4 minutes of cooking. Scallops are done when they turn white.

2. While spaghetti, broccoli and scallops are cooking, beat peanut butter, soy sauce, vinegar and red pepper sauce with wire whisk until smooth.

3. Drain spaghetti mixture; return to saucepan. Add peanut butter mixture; toss gently to coat. Sprinkle with peanuts.

1 Serving: Calories 320 (Calories from Fat 90); Fat 10g (Saturated 2g); Cholesterol 10mg; Sodium 600mg; Carbohydrate 41g (Dietary Fiber 4g); Protein 20g; **% Daily Value:** Vitamin A 8%; Vitamin C 46%; Calcium 8%; Iron 20%; **Diet Exchanges:** 2 starch, 1 1/2 lean meat, 2 vegetable, 1 fat

Hearty Seafood Stew

Prep: 20 min; Cook: 40 min ✱ *7 servings*

1/4 pound uncooked fresh or frozen medium shrimp in
    shells
2 tablespoons vegetable oil
2 medium carrots, thinly sliced (1 cup)
2 medium stalks celery, sliced (1 cup)
1 large onion, chopped (1 cup)
1 clove garlic, finely chopped
1 can (14 1/2 ounces) stewed tomatoes, undrained
2 cups water
2 teaspoons beef bouillon granules
1 medium potato, cut into 1/2-inch pieces (1 cup)
1/2 pound catfish or other medium-firm fish fillets, cut
    into 1-inch pieces
1 can (15 to 16 ounces) great northern beans, rinsed
    and drained
1 small zucchini, cut lengthwise in half, then cut cross-
    wise into slices (1 cup)
1 teaspoon chopped fresh or 1/4 teaspoon dried
    thyme leaves
Chopped fresh parsley, if desired

1. Peel shrimp. Make a shallow cut lengthwise down back of each shrimp; wash out vein (see How to Devein Shrimp, page 320). Set aside.

2. Heat oil in 4-quart Dutch oven over medium-high heat. Cook carrots, celery, onion and garlic in oil, stirring frequently, until vegetables are tender. Stir in tomatoes, water, bouillon granules and potato. Heat to boiling; reduce heat. Cover and simmer 20 minutes, stirring occasionally.

3. Stir in shrimp, catfish, beans, zucchini and thyme. Heat to boiling; reduce heat. Cover and simmer 6 to 10 minutes or until fish flakes easily with fork and shrimp are pink and firm. Serve topped with parsley.

1 Serving: Calories 200 (Calories from Fat 45); Fat 5g (Saturated 1g); Cholesterol 40mg; Sodium 600mg; Carbohydrate 28g (Dietary Fiber 6g); Protein 16g **% Daily Value:** Vitamin A 30%; Vitamin C 10%; Calcium 10%; Iron 18% **Diet Exchanges:** 1 Starch, 1 Lean Meat, 3 Vegetable

Seafood Chilaquiles Casserole

Prep: 10 min; Cook: 12 min; Bake: 20 min ✱ *6 servings*

1/2 cup vegetable oil
10 flour or corn tortillas (6 or 8 inches in diameter),
    cut into 1/2-inch strips
1/4 cup butter or stick margarine
8 medium green onions, sliced (1/2 cup)
1/4 cup all-purpose flour
1/2 teaspoon salt
1/4 teaspoon pepper
2 cups half-and-half
1 canned chipotle chile in adobo sauce, finely chopped
1 pound bay scallops
1 pound uncooked peeled deveined medium shrimp,
    thawed if frozen
4 slices bacon, crisply cooked and crumbled

1. Heat oil in 10-inch skillet over medium-high heat. Cook tortilla strips in oil 30 to 60 seconds, stirring occasionally, until light golden brown. Remove with slotted spoon and drain on paper towels.

2. Melt butter in 3-quart saucepan over low heat. Cook onions in butter, stirring occasionally, until tender. Stir in flour, salt and pepper. Cook, stirring constantly, until mixture is bubbly; remove from heat. Stir in half-and-half. Heat to boiling, stirring constantly. Boil and stir 1 minute; reduce heat to medium.

3. Stir chile, scallops and shrimp into sauce. Cook over medium heat about 9 minutes, stirring frequently, just until shrimp are pink and firm and scallops are white.

4. Heat oven to 350°. Grease 3-quart casserole.

5. Arrange half of the tortilla strips in bottom of casserole. Top with half of the seafood mixture. Repeat with remaining tortilla strips and seafood mixture. Top with bacon. Bake uncovered 15 to 20 minutes or until hot and bubbly.

1 Serving: Calories 625 (Calories from Fat 335); Fat 37g (Saturated 14g); Cholesterol 135mg; Sodium 890mg; Carbohydrate 49g (Dietary Fiber 3g); Protein 27g **% Daily Value:** Vitamin A 18%; Vitamin C 6%; Calcium 24%; Iron 28% **Diet Exchanges:** 3 Starch, 2 High-Fat Meat, 1 Vegetable, 4 Fat

Seafood Paella

Prep: 1 hr 30 min; Bake: 25 min ✳ *6 servings*

A Spanish dish made with saffron-flavored rice, paella can include other meats such as chicken, pork and sausage. The dish takes its name from the pan in which it was made, a 14-inch shallow metal pan (traditionally copper) with two handles.

12 mussels in shells
6 medium clams in shells
1/2 pound uncooked fresh or frozen (thawed) medium
    shrimp in shells
1/4 cup olive or vegetable oil
1/2 pound bay scallops
1/2 pound squid or octopus, cleaned and cut into
    1/4-inch rings, if desired
1 medium onion, chopped (1/2 cup)
2 cloves garlic, finely chopped
1 can (14 1/2 ounces) whole tomatoes, undrained
2 cups water
1 cup uncooked regular long-grain rice
1 teaspoon salt
3 or 4 threads saffron or 1/2 teaspoon ground
    turmeric
1/4 teaspoon pepper
1/2 cup frozen green peas
1 jar (2 ounces) sliced pimientos, drained
Lemon wedges, if desired

1. Clean mussels as directed for Steamed Mussels, steps 1 and 2 (page 324), and clean clams as directed for Steamed Clams, step 1 (page 323). Peel shrimp. Make a shallow cut lengthwise down back of each shrimp; wash out vein (see How to Devein Shrimp, page 320).

2. Heat oil in 14-inch metal paella pan or 4-quart ovenproof Dutch oven over medium heat. Cook shrimp in oil about 2 minutes, stirring occasionally, just until pink and firm; remove with slotted spoon. Cook scallops in oil 1 to 2 minutes, stirring occasionally, until slightly firm; remove with slotted spoon. Cover and refrigerate shrimp and scallops. Cook squid in oil about 2 minutes, stirring occasionally, until rings begin to shrink; remove with slotted spoon.

3. Add 1 or 2 tablespoons more oil to pan if necessary. Cook onion and garlic in oil over medium heat, stirring occasionally, until onion is tender. Stir in squid and tomatoes, breaking up tomatoes with a fork or snipping with kitchen scissors. Heat to boiling; reduce heat to low. Simmer uncovered 20 minutes, stirring occasionally.

4. Stir in shrimp, scallops, water, rice, salt, saffron and pepper. Heat to boiling; reduce heat to low. Simmer uncovered 10 minutes, stirring occasionally.

5. Heat oven to 350°.

6. Arrange mussels, clams and peas on rice mixture. Cover loosely with aluminum foil. Bake about 25 minutes in paella pan, 40 minutes in Dutch oven, or until liquid is absorbed. Discard any unopened mussels or clams. Sprinkle pimientos over paella. Garnish with lemon wedges.

1 Serving: Calories 330 (Calories from Fat 100); Fat 11g (Saturated 2g); Cholesterol 135mg; Sodium 720mg; Carbohydrate 37g (Dietary Fiber 2g); Protein 23g **% Daily Value:** Vitamin A 14%; Vitamin C 24%; Calcium 10%; Iron 54% **Diet Exchanges:** 2 Starch, 2 Medium-Fat Meat, 1 Vegetable

Grilling

Grilling

Low-Fat = *3g or less, except main dishes with 6g or less*   *Fast* = *Ready in 30 minutes or less*   ■ = *Bread Machine directions*   ● = *Slow Cooker directions*

Lighter = 1/3 fewer calories or 50% less fat

Texas T-Bones (page 334)

Grilling Basics

Nothing is more tantalizing than the irresistible aroma of grilled food filling the air! As more and more people are grilling in all seasons, this once-summertime treat is being enjoyed any time of year. And grilling is so convenient with little cleanup. Outdoor grilling not only puts great-tasting food on the table, it also can turn a meal into a special event. Visiting with family, friends and neighbors while heating the grill and cooking the food makes mealtime a party. Here are some guidelines to make grilling fun and easy.

Fueling the Fire

Charcoal Grilling

Charcoal is a porous compound made from burned hardwood that's usually compacted and made into the very popular pillow-shaped briquettes or sold in small lumps. Henry Ford is credited with its invention in 1923. Single-use charcoal bags are a premeasured convenience because you light the entire bag.

Keep your charcoal dry. Damp charcoal can take forever to start, and it burns unevenly. To keep charcoal from becoming damp, store it in a dry place. In humid climates, store charcoal in a tightly closed plastic bag.

When lighting charcoal, follow the manufacturer's directions. Most suggest lighting charcoal 30 to 45 minutes before you start to cook so the coals will be hot enough.

Use enough briquettes to form a solid bed under the grilling area that is a little larger than the area the food will cover. Charcoal produces lots of heat, and a little goes a long way. About thirty briquettes are needed to grill 1 pound of meat. (Each pound of charcoal contains about fifteen to twenty briquettes.) Any food that grills longer than 1 hour will require about ten additional briquettes per hour. When adding extra briquettes, place them around the edges so that they touch the already burning coals, or give them a head start by lighting them separately (in a can or charcoal chimney starter) before adding them to the grill.

WHEN ARE COALS READY?

When the coals are 80 percent ashy gray in daylight, they are ready for grilling. (After dark, coals are ready when they have an even red glow.) Bright red coals are too hot, black coals are too cool and a mix of red and black coals gives off uneven heat. Coals that are too cool can cause the food to have an off-flavor from charcoal lighter that has not vaporized.

Check the temperature of the coals by placing your hand, palm side down, near but not touching the cooking grill rack. If you can keep your hand there for 2 seconds (one-thousand one, one-thousand two), the temperature is high; 3 seconds is medium-high; 4 seconds is medium; 5 seconds is low.

Gas Grilling

For a gas grill, follow the manufacturer's directions for heating it for direct- or indirect-heat grilling. Gas grills usually heat up in 5 to 10 minutes.

Control the Heat

Charcoal Grilling

Keep the heat as even as possible throughout the grilling time. If the food does not sizzle as it cooks, the fire may be too cool.

Raise the heat by raking the coals closer together and knocking off a bit of the ash, lowering the cooking grill rack or opening the vents.

Lower the heat by doing the opposite: spread and separate the coals, raise the cooking grill rack or close the vents halfway.

Occasional flare-ups from the fat burning as it drips onto the coals are a normal part of grilling. Control flare-ups (which can cook your food unevenly) by spacing out the coals or covering the grill. Or keep a spray bottle filled with water handy for spraying; take care not to soak the coals.

Gas Grilling

Adjust the heat control, reposition the grill rack or cover the grill.

Most gas grills have faster and slower cooking areas, which can be used effectively when grilling foods to different donenesses. Take the time to learn where these areas are on your grill.

Lava rock in a gas grill can be used over and over. When lava rock becomes extremely greasy, however, it contributes to flare-ups. Avoid flare-ups and lengthen the life of lava rock by turning the rock over every once in a while (between grilling times) to burn off the grease that accumulates from cooking meat with fat. If flare-ups occur, do not use water on a gas grill. Just close the hood and reduce the heat until it subsides.

Direct- and Indirect-Heat Grilling

Direct-Heat Grilling: Food is cooked on the grill rack directly over the heat source.

Indirect-Heat Grilling: Food is cooked on the grill rack away from the heat. This is the preferred method for longer-cooking foods, such as whole poultry, whole turkey breasts and roasts. Place a drip pan (to catch fats and liquids) directly under the grilling area, and arrange the coals around the edge of the grill. For a dual-burner grill, heat only one side and place food over the burner that is not lit. For a single-burner grill, place food in an aluminum-foil tray or on several layers of aluminum foil and use low heat.

Food Safety Tips for Grilling

- Trim visible fat from meat to avoid flare-ups.
- Always marinate foods in the refrigerator—never by leaving them on the kitchen counter—and use a nonmetal container.
- Use a long-handled brush for adding sauces or marinades to food before or during grilling. To prevent transferring any bacteria, do not use the same brush on raw meat that you use on cooked meat. Wash the brush in hot, soapy water, and dry thoroughly.
- Before using a marinade in which raw meat was placed as a sauce for the cooked meat, be sure to heat the marinade to boiling and then boil 1 minute, stirring constantly, before serving.
- Always serve grilled meat on a clean platter. Never serve cooked meat on the same unwashed platter on which raw meat was carried to the grill. For example, do not carry raw hamburgers to the grill on a platter and then serve the cooked hamburgers on the same unwashed platter. Dangerous bacteria can be transferred to the cooked meat from the juices of the raw meat.
- Consume perishable food within 2 hours; 1 hour if the outside temperature is over 90°.
- In case of a flare-up, raise the grill cooking rack and spread the coals to lower the temperature. If using a charcoal grill, you also can spray water on the flare-up, remembering to first remove food from the cooking rack so that clumps of ash don't fly onto the food.
- Open food packets of aluminum foil carefully and facing away from you to let out the steam. Steam burns can be painful!

Fire and Fuel Safety Tips

- Place the grill in a well-ventilated area, away from buildings, dry leaves or brush. The grill can become hot enough to ignite flammable materials.
- Grilling on a wooden deck requires extra precautions. Place a metal sheet or several sheets of heavy-duty aluminum foil under the grill to catch any hot ashes that might fall through an open vent.
- Never add more liquid charcoal lighter after a charcoal fire has started; the liquid can catch fire as you pour it and be extremely dangerous. If needing to add more charcoal to heated coals, start three or four more charcoal briquettes separately in a can or on a piece of heavy-duty aluminum foil and then add them using tongs.
- Extinguish coals completely after removing food and grilling is finished. Close the vents on a covered grill to cut off the supply of oxygen. If there is no cover, spread the coals or let them burn completely and then cool. Coals can be doused with a heavy layer of ash or water, but clean the grill as

soon as it is cool if water was used so that the inside of the grill doesn't rust. After partially used coals are completely dry, they can be reused.

- Dispose of ashes properly. A covered metal pail works best just in case there is one live coal.

- Don't wear long-sleeved or loose-fitting clothing when grilling.

- Refillable gas tanks of fuel for gas grills have the potential to cause explosions and fires. Fill a portable gas tank to only 80-percent capacity for maximum efficiency and safety. Take care to secure the tank when transporting it so that it can't tip over. Be careful not to tip the tank when it's connected to the regulator. When attaching a refill tank, check the connection by rubbing it with a liquid detergent. If bubbles appear, there is a leak.

- Never store spare gas tanks under the grill or in the house.

How Weather Affects Grilling

Check the manufacturer's use-and-care manual for your grill for tips and hints on grilling in different climates and weather conditions. These general tips may be helpful:

- Place the grill out of the wind. If in the wind, neither the grill nor the food will stay as hot as it should.

- Charcoal grilling times will be faster on hot, calm days and slower on chilly, windy ones. Grilling in cold weather requires more charcoal, a longer time to heat the coals and longer grilling times.

- Gas grilling will need slightly longer heating times as well as a higher heat setting to speed the cooking if the weather is cool or windy.

Backyard Grilling Secrets

All grills are not created equal! Read the use-and-care manual for your grill for the best tips and recommendations.

- Get to know your grill, including where any hot spots are and how long the grill takes to heat, especially in chilly or windy weather.

- Brush the grill rack with vegetable oil or spray with cooking spray to prevent food from sticking and make cleaning the grill easier. Always brush or spray *before* heating the grill, which is safer because the grill is not hot.

- Keep the heat as even as possible throughout the grilling time. For more even cooking, place thicker foods on the center of the grill rack and smaller pieces on the edges.

- Check the food and fire often. The type of grill, outdoor temperature and wind, position of food on the grill and temperature of the coals all can affect cooking times.

- If the food isn't sizzling, the fire might not be hot enough. Increase the heat by raking the coals together, opening the vents, lowering the grill rack and/or adjusting the control on a gas or electric grill.

- If the food is browning too quickly on the outside but the middle is not cooked, the fire is too hot. Spread the coals, close the vents halfway, raise the grill rack and/or adjust the control on a gas or electric grill. Covering the grill also will help control the heat.

- Add a smoky flavor to grilled foods by adding wood chips or chunks to the coals. If you have a gas grill, check the owner's manual or recipe booklet for how to use wood chips or chunks. Covering the grill allows the aroma to penetrate the food.

- Use long-handled barbecue tools to allow for a safe distance between you and the intense heat of the grill.

- Turn foods with tongs, instead of piercing them with a fork, to retain food juices.

- Brush sauces on foods during the last 15 to 20 minutes of cooking to prevent overbrowning or burning, especially sauces that contain tomato or sugar.

- Use stainless-steel, flat-bladed skewers because foods on rounded-bladed skewers tend to spin around on the skewers when they're turned. Wooden skewers can be used, but they must be soaked in water at least 30 minutes before using to prevent burning.

Texas T-Bones *Fast*

Prep: 10 min; Grill: 14 min ✳ *4 servings*

To crush peppercorns, place in a heavy-duty resealable plastic bag and use a rolling pin to crush them into smaller pieces. Grilled mushrooms are terrific with steak, see our Fresh Vegetable Grilling Chart on page 505 for directions.

4 beef T-bone steaks, 1 inch thick (about 1 pound)
2 cloves garlic, cut in half
4 teaspoons black peppercorns, crushed
1/4 cup butter or stick margarine, softened
1 tablespoon Dijon mustard
1/2 teaspoon Worcestershire sauce
1/4 teaspoon lime juice
Salt and pepper, if desired

1. Heat coals or gas grill for direct heat (page 332).

2. Trim fat on beef steaks to 1/4-inch thickness. Rub garlic on beef. Press peppercorns into beef. Mix remaining ingredients except salt and pepper; set aside.

3. Cover and grill beef 4 to 5 inches from medium heat 10 to 14 minutes for medium doneness, turning once. Sprinkle with salt and pepper. Serve with butter mixture.

1 Serving: Calories 260 (Calories from Fat 190); Fat 21g (Saturated 6g); Cholesterol 50mg; Sodium 180mg; Carbohydrate 1g (Dietary Fiber 0g); Protein 17g **% Daily Value:** Vitamin A 10%; Vitamin C 0%; Calcium 0%; Iron 8% **Diet Exchanges:** 2 1/2 High-Fat Meat

Barbecued Chuck Roast

Prep: 15 min; Marinate: 8 hr; Grill: 1 hr 15 min
✳ *6 to 8 servings*

California Marinade (right)
3- to 4-pound beef chuck roast, 2 1/2 to 3 inches thick

1. Make California Marinade.

2. Place beef in resealable plastic food-storage bag or shallow glass or plastic dish. Pour marinade over beef; turn beef to coat with marinade. Seal bag or cover dish and refrigerate at least 8 hours but no longer than 24 hours, turning beef frequently.

3. Brush grill rack with vegetable oil. Heat coals or gas grill for direct heat (page 332).

4. Remove beef from marinade; reserve marinade. Insert barbecue meat thermometer so tip is in center of beef and does not touch bone. Place marinade in heatproof container. Heat marinade mixture on grill, stirring occasionally, until heated through; brush over beef.

5. Grill beef uncovered 4 to 5 inches from medium heat 1 hour to 1 hour 15 minutes, turning and brushing every 10 minutes with hot marinade, until thermometer reads 155° (medium doneness). Discard any remaining marinade.

LEARN WITH *Betty* — BEEF STEAK DONENESS GUIDE

Medium Rare (internal temperature 145°) steak will be very pink in the center and slightly brown toward the exterior.

Medium (internal temperature 160°) steak will be light pink in the center and brown toward exterior.

Well Done (internal temperature 170°) steak will be uniformly brown throughout.

Italian Burgers

California Marinade

1/4 cup olive or vegetable oil

1/4 cup red wine or cider vinegar

1/4 cup sherry or apple juice

1 tablespoon chopped fresh or 1 teaspoon dried rosemary leaves, crumbled

2 tablespoons ketchup

2 teaspoons soy sauce

1/2 teaspoon ground mustard

2 cloves garlic, finely chopped

Mix all ingredients.

1 Serving: Calories 475 (Calories from Fat 340); Fat 38g (Saturated 14g); Cholesterol 105mg; Sodium 170mg; Carbohydrate 3g (Dietary Fiber 0g); Protein 30g **% Daily Value:** Vitamin A 0%; Vitamin C 0%; Calcium 2%; Iron 16% **Diet Exchanges:** 4 High-Fat Meat, 1 1/2 Fat

Italian Burgers *Low-Fat*

Prep: 10 min; Grill: 15 min ✳ *4 burgers*

Spice it up! Substitute 1/2 pound of the ground beef with hot or mild bulk Italian sausage.

1 pound lean ground beef

1/3 cup spaghetti sauce

3 tablespoons finely chopped red onion

4 slices (1 ounce each) provolone cheese, cut in half

4 lettuce leaves

4 hamburger buns, split

4 slices red onion

Spaghetti sauce, warmed, if desired

1. Heat coals or gas grill for direct heat (page 332).

2. Mix beef, spaghetti sauce and chopped onion. Shape mixture into 4 patties, about 3/4 inch thick.

3. Cover and grill patties 4 to 6 inches from medium heat 10 to 15 minutes, turning once, until no longer pink in center and juice is clear. Top with cheese. Place lettuce on bottoms of buns; top with burgers, sliced onion and tops of buns. Serve with spaghetti sauce.

1 Serving: Calories 475 (Calories from Fat 245); Fat 27g (Saturated 12g); Cholesterol 90mg; Sodium 670mg; Carbohydrate 28g (Dietary Fiber 2g); Protein 32g **% Daily Value:** Vitamin A 8%; Vitamin C 4%; Calcium 28%; Iron 20% **Diet Exchanges:** 2 Starch, 4 Medium-Fat Meat

Italian Mixed Grill

Italian Mixed Grill

Prep: 15 min; Stand: 1 hr; Microwave: 12 min;
Grill: 25 min ✱ *8 servings*

Herbed Lemon Oil (right)
4 fresh Italian sausages (about 1 pound)
1/2 cup water
1 small onion, chopped (1/4 cup)
4 boneless, skinless chicken breast halves or thighs
    (about 1 1/4 pounds)
1-pound beef boneless top loin steak, about 1 inch
    thick

1. Make Herbed Lemon Oil.

2. Place sausages, water and onion in 2-quart microwavable casserole. Cover and microwave on High 5 minutes; rearrange sausages. Re-cover and microwave on Medium (50%) 5 to 7 minutes or until sausages are no longer pink in center. Remove sausages; discard onion and water.

3. Brush grill rack with vegetable oil. Heat coals or gas grill for direct heat (page 332).

4. Brush all sides of chicken, beef and sausages with oil mixture.

5. Grill meats uncovered 4 to 5 inches from medium heat, brushing frequently with oil mixture and turning occasionally. Grill beef 5 minutes. Add chicken and grill beef and chicken 5 minutes. Add sausages. Grill beef, chicken and sausages 4 to 15 minutes or until each are done according to the following guidelines. Cook beef to desired doneness (about 18 to 25 minutes total grilling time). Chicken is done when centers of thickest pieces are cut (about 14 to 16 minutes total grilling time), sausages are done when no longer pink in center (about 12 to 14 minutes total grilling time). Discard any remaining oil mixture.

6. To serve, cut sausages and chicken pieces in half, and cut beef into slices, if desired.

Herbed Lemon Oil

1/2 cup olive or vegetable oil
3 tablespoons lemon juice
3 tablespoons chopped fresh parsley
1 tablespoon chopped fresh or 1 teaspoon dried
    rosemary leaves
2 teaspoons chopped fresh or 1/2 teaspoon dried
    thyme leaves
1/2 teaspoon salt
1/4 teaspoon pepper
2 large cloves garlic, finely chopped

Mix all ingredients. Cover and let stand at least 1 hour to blend flavors.

1 Serving: Calories 370 (Calories from Fat 245); Fat 27g (Saturated 8g); Cholesterol 95mg; Sodium 440mg; Carbohydrate 2g (Dietary Fiber 0g); Protein 30g **% Daily Value:** Vitamin A 0%; Vitamin C 2%; Calcium 2%; Iron 12% **Diet Exchanges:** 4 Medium-Fat Meat, 1 Fat

Pork Ribs with Smoky Barbecue Sauce

Prep: 10 min; Grill: 70 min; Cook: 20 min ✳ *4 servings*

Because these smoky ribs are not precooked, they'll be winners for folks who like their ribs chewy and firm.

4 pounds pork loin back ribs (not cut into serving
    pieces)
1 tablespoon vegetable oil
4 teaspoons chopped fresh or 1 1/2 teaspoons dried
    thyme leaves
Smoky Barbecue Sauce (right)

1. Brush grill rack with vegetable oil. Heat coals or gas grill for indirect heat (page 332).

2. Brush meaty sides of pork with oil. Sprinkle with thyme.

3. Cover and grill pork, meaty sides up, over drip pan and 4 to 5 inches from medium heat 60 to 70 minutes or until no longer pink when cut near bone.

4. While pork is grilling, make Smoky Barbecue Sauce. Brush sauce over pork 2 or 3 times during the last 15 minutes of grilling. Heat any remaining sauce to boiling; boil and stir 1 minute.

5. To serve, cut pork into serving pieces. Serve with sauce.

Smoky Barbecue Sauce

1/2 cup ketchup
1/4 cup water
3 tablespoons packed brown sugar
2 tablespoons white vinegar
2 teaspoons celery seed
1/4 teaspoon liquid smoke
1/4 teaspoon red pepper sauce

Heat all ingredients to boiling in 1-quart saucepan; reduce heat. Simmer uncovered 15 minutes, stirring occasionally.

1 Serving: Calories 910 (Calories from Fat 605); Fat 67g (Saturated 24g); Cholesterol 265mg; Sodium 440mg; Carbohydrate 13g (Dietary Fiber 0g); Protein 64g **% Daily Value:** Vitamin A 2%; Vitamin C 2%; Calcium 10%; Iron 24% **Diet Exchanges:** 8 1/2 High-Fat Meat, 1 Fruit

Teriyaki Pork Tenderloins

Prep: 10 min; Marinate: 8 hr; Grill: 30 min ✳ *6 servings*

Teriyaki Marinade (page 455)
2 pork tenderloins (each about 3/4 pound)

1. Make Teriyaki Marinade in small bowl.

2. Fold thin end of each pork tenderloin under so that pork is an even thickness; secure with toothpicks. Place pork in resealable plastic food-storage bag or shallow glass or plastic dish. Pour marinade over pork; turn pork to coat with marinade. Seal bag or cover dish and refrigerate at least 8 hours but no longer than 24 hours, turning pork occasionally.

3. Brush grill rack with vegetable oil. Heat coals or gas grill for indirect heat (page 332).

4. Remove pork from marinade; reserve marinade. Cover and grill pork over drip pan and 4 to 5 inches from medium heat 25 to 30 minutes, brushing occasionally with marinade and turning once, until pork is slightly pink in center. Discard any remaining marinade.

5. Remove toothpicks. To serve, cut pork across grain into thin slices.

1 Serving: Calories 160 (Calories from Fat 55); Fat 6g (Saturated 2g); Cholesterol 70mg; Sodium 5mg; Carbohydrate 1g (Dietary Fiber 0g); Protein 25g **% Daily Value:** Vitamin A 0%; Vitamin C 0%; Calcium 0%; Iron 8% **Diet Exchanges:** 4 Very Lean Meat, 1/2 Fat

Honey-Mustard Pork Chops

Honey-Mustard Pork Chops *Fast*

Prep: 10 min; Grill: 16 min ✳ *4 servings*

The sweet honey glaze on these chops browns easily, so watch the chops carefully and make sure the coals aren't too hot. Grilled onion slices would taste great with these chops, check our Fresh Vegetable Grilling Chart on page 505 for directions.

Honey-Mustard Glaze (right)
4 pork boneless loin chops, 1 inch thick (about 1 pound)

1. Brush grill rack with vegetable oil. Heat coals or gas grill for direct heat (page 332).

2. Make Honey-Mustard Glaze.

3. Cover and grill pork 4 to 5 inches from medium heat 14 to 16 minutes, brushing occasionally with glaze and turning once, until slightly pink in center. Discard any remaining glaze.

Honey-Mustard Glaze

1/4 cup honey
2 tablespoons Dijon mustard
1 tablespoon orange juice
1 teaspoon chopped fresh or 1/4 teaspoon dried tarragon leaves
1 teaspoon balsamic or cider vinegar
1/2 teaspoon white or regular Worcestershire sauce
Dash of onion powder

Mix all ingredients.

1 Serving: Calories 270 (Calories from Fat 115); Fat 13g (Saturated 5g); Cholesterol 70mg; Sodium 105mg; Carbohydrate 15g (Dietary Fiber 0g); Protein 23g **% Daily Value:** Vitamin A 0%; Vitamin C 0%; Calcium 0%; Iron 4% **Diet Exchanges:** 3 Lean Meat, 1 Fruit, 1 Fat

Zesty Pork Chops *Fast*

Prep: 5 min; Grill: 15 min ✳ *6 servings*

For a complete grilled meal, cut zucchini lengthwise in half, brush with oil, sprinkle with salt and pepper and grill, seasoned sides down, with the pork chops. Add buttered French bread to the grill during the last 3 to 5 minutes, turning occasionally.

2/3 cup packed brown sugar
1/4 cup prepared horseradish
1 tablespoon lemon juice
6 fully cooked smoked pork chops, about 1/2 inch
    thick (about 1 1/4 pounds)

1. Heat coals or gas grill for direct heat (page 332).

2. Heat brown sugar, horseradish and lemon juice to boiling in 1-quart saucepan, stirring constantly. Brush on pork.

3. Cover and grill pork 4 to 5 inches from medium heat 15 minutes, turning once, until hot. Serve remaining sauce with pork.

1 Serving: Calories 215 (Calories from Fat 55); Fat 6g (Saturated 2g); Cholesterol 40mg; Sodium 1,020mg; Carbohydrate 25g (Dietary Fiber 0g); Protein 15g **% Daily Value:** Vitamin A 0%; Vitamin C 2%; Calcium 2%; Iron 8% **Diet Exchanges:** 2 Lean Meat, 1 1/2 Fruit

Rack of Lamb

Prep: 15 min; Grill: 45 min ✳ *8 servings*

We've called for dried marjoram leaves in this recipe because in our testing, we found that fresh marjoram burned.

3-pound rack of lamb
2 teaspoons dried marjoram leaves (not fresh)
1 teaspoon salt
1 clove garlic
2 tablespoons olive or vegetable oil
Wine Mop (right)

1. Have butcher saw backbone between center rib bones of lamb so lamb can be cut apart for serving. Remove excess fat.

2. Brush grill rack with vegetable oil. Heat coals or gas grill for direct heat (page 332).

3. Grind marjoram, salt and garlic in a mortar with pestle or small bowl with back of spoon; add oil to make a paste. Rub marjoram mixture on cut surfaces of lamb. Insert barbecue meat thermometer so tip is in center of lamb and does not touch bone.

4. Make Wine Mop.

5. Grill lamb, fat side down, uncovered about 4 inches from hot heat 25 minutes, mopping or brushing frequently with wine mixture. Turn lamb; grill uncovered 15 to 20 minutes longer or until thermometer reads 160° (medium doneness). Discard any remaining wine mixture.

6. To serve, cut lamb apart between ribs.

Wine Mop

3/4 cup dry red wine, nonalcoholic red wine or apple
    cider
2 tablespoons lemon juice
2 tablespoons Worcestershire sauce

Mix all ingredients.

1 Serving: Calories 340 (Calories from Fat 260); Fat 29g (Saturated 12g); Cholesterol 90mg; Sodium 390mg; Carbohydrate 1g (Dietary Fiber 0g); Protein 19g **% Daily Value:** Vitamin A 0%; Vitamin C 0%; Calcium 2%; Iron 8% **Diet Exchanges:** 3 High-Fat Meat, 1 Fat

---

KEEPING BURGERS MOIST AND FLAVORFUL

Don't press down on a hamburger patty with your spatula while it's cooking (even though it may be tempting). If you do, you'll squeeze out too much of the great-tasting juices that also make the burgers nice and moist!

Grilled Citrus Chicken with Easy Grilled Vegetables (page 343)

Grilled Citrus Chicken

Prep: 10 min; Marinate: 2 hr; Grill: 20 min ✱ *6 servings*

Citrus Marinade (right)
6 boneless, skinless chicken breast halves (about 1 3/4 pounds)

1. Make Citrus Marinade.

2. Place chicken in resealable plastic food-storage bag or shallow glass or plastic dish. Pour marinade over chicken; turn chicken to coat with marinade. Seal bag or cover dish and refrigerate at least 2 hours but no longer than 24 hours, turning chicken occasionally.

2. Heat coals or gas grill for direct heat (page 332).

3. Remove chicken from marinade; reserve marinade. Cover and grill chicken 4 to 6 inches from medium heat 15 to 20 minutes, turning and brushing with marinade occasionally, until juice of chicken is no longer pink when centers of thickest pieces are cut.

4. Heat remaining marinade to boiling; boil and stir 1 minute. Serve with chicken.

Citrus Marinade

1/2 cup frozen (thawed) orange juice concentrate
1/4 cup vegetable oil
1/4 cup lemon juice
2 tablespoons grated orange peel
1/2 teaspoon salt
1 clove garlic, finely chopped

Mix all ingredients.

1 Serving: Calories 245 (Calories from Fat 100); Fat 11g (Saturated 2g); Cholesterol 75mg; Sodium 70mg; Carbohydrate 10g (Dietary Fiber 0g); Protein 27g **% Daily Value:** Vitamin A 0%; Vitamin C 30%; Calcium 2%; Iron 6% **Diet Exchanges:** 4 Very Lean Meat, 1 Fruit, 1 Fat

Chicken Breasts Teriyaki

Prep: 5 min; Marinate: 1 hr; Grill: 35 min ✱ 4 servings

1/4 cup soy sauce
1/4 cup dry sherry or orange juice
1 tablespoon sugar
1 tablespoon vegetable oil
1 teaspoon grated gingerroot or 1/4 teaspoon ground
    ginger
1 clove garlic, crushed
4 chicken breast halves (about 1 1/2 pounds)

1. Mix all ingredients except chicken. Place chicken in resealable plastic food-storage bag or shallow glass or plastic dish. Pour soy sauce mixture over chicken; turn chicken to coat with soy sauce mixture. Seal bag or cover dish and refrigerate at least 1 hour but no longer than 24 hours, turning chicken occasionally.

2. Heat coals or gas grill for direct heat (page 332).

3. Remove chicken from marinade; reserve marinade. Cover and grill chicken, skin sides up, 5 to 6 inches from medium heat about 15 minutes or until golden brown. Turn chicken. Cover and grill 10 to 20 minutes longer, turning and brushing 2 or 3 times with marinade, until juice of chicken is no longer pink when centers of thickest pieces are cut. Discard any remaining marinade.

1 Serving: Calories 220 (Calories from Fat 90); Fat 10g (Saturated 2g); Cholesterol 75mg; Sodium 790mg; Carbohydrate 4g (Dietary Fiber 0g); Protein 28g **% Daily Value:** Vitamin A 2%; Vitamin C 0%; Calcium 2%; Iron 6% **Diet Exchanges:** 4 Lean Meat

---

KEEPING GRILLED CHICKEN MOIST

For extra-moist grilled chicken, use a pair of tongs instead of a fork to turn the pieces. A fork will pierce the meat and let too many of the juices run out, thereby drying out the chicken.

Grilled Caesar Chicken and Vegetables with Pasta

Prep: 15 min; Marinate: 30 min; Grill: 1 hr ✱ 6 servings

3- to 3 1/2-pound cut-up broiler-fryer chicken
2/3 cup Caesar dressing
1 medium red bell pepper, cut into 1-inch pieces
2 medium zucchini or yellow summer squash, cut into
    1-inch pieces
1 medium red onion, cut into wedges
3 cups uncooked rotelle pasta (8 ounces)
Salt and pepper to taste

1. Place chicken in resealable plastic food-storage bag or shallow glass or plastic dish. Pour 1/3 cup of the dressing over chicken; turn chicken to coat with dressing. Seal bag or cover dish and refrigerate at least 30 minutes but no longer than 24 hours, turning chicken occasionally.

2. Heat coals or gas grill for direct heat (page 332).

3. Remove chicken from dressing; reserve dressing. Cover and grill chicken, skin sides up, 4 to 5 inches from medium heat 15 to 20 minutes. Turn chicken. Cover and grill 20 to 40 minutes longer, turning and brushing 2 or 3 times with dressing, until juice of chicken is no longer pink when centers of thickest pieces are cut. While chicken is grilling, continue with step 4.

4. Thread bell pepper, zucchini and onion alternately on each of four 10-inch metal skewers, leaving 1/4-inch space between each piece. Brush with remaining 1/3 cup dressing. Cover and grill vegetables 4 to 5 inches from medium heat 15 to 20 minutes, turning and brushing twice with dressing, until vegetables are crisp-tender. Discard any remaining dressing. While chicken and vegetables are grilling, continue with step 5.

5. Cook and drain pasta as directed on package. Remove vegetables from skewers. Toss vegetables and pasta, adding additional dressing if desired. Sprinkle with salt and pepper. Serve with chicken.

1 Serving: Calories 545 (Calories from Fat 205); Fat 23g (Saturated 5g); Cholesterol 90mg; Sodium 330mg; Carbohydrate 53g (Dietary Fiber 4g); Protein 35g **% Daily Value:** Vitamin A 18%; Vitamin C 36%; Calcium 4%; Iron 22% **Diet Exchanges:** 3 Starch, 3 Medium-Fat Meat, 1 Vegetable, 1 Fat

Herbed Seafood

Mexican Chicken Burgers *Fast*

Prep: 10 min; Grill: 18 min ✳ *4 servings*

1 pound ground chicken or turkey
1 envelope (1 1/4 ounces) taco seasoning mix
4 slices (1 ounce each) Monterey Jack cheese
4 hamburger buns, split
1 medium avocado, sliced
1/4 cup thick-and-chunky salsa

1. Heat coals or gas grill for direct heat (page 332).

2. Mix chicken and taco seasoning mix. Shape mixture into 4 patties, about 3/4 inch thick.

3. Cover and grill patties 4 to 6 inches from medium heat 14 to 16 minutes, turning once, until chicken is no longer pink in center and juices of patties run clear. Top each patty with cheese slice. Grill 1 to 2 minutes or until cheese begins to melt. Place patties on bottoms of buns; top with avocado, salsa and tops of buns.

1 Serving: Calories 470 (Calories from Fat 215); Fat 24g (Saturated 9g); Cholesterol 100mg; Sodium 900mg; Carbohydrate 32g (Dietary Fiber 4g); Protein 36g **% Daily Value:** Vitamin A 22%; Vitamin C 8%; Calcium 30%; Iron 18% **Diet Exchanges:** 2 Starch, 4 Medium-Fat Meat

Herbed Seafood *Fast*

Prep: 20 min; Grill: 10 min ✳ *4 servings*

1/2 pound sea or bay scallops
1/2 pound orange roughy fillets, cut into 1-inch pieces
1/2 pound uncooked fresh or frozen large shrimp, peeled and deveined (page 320)
2 tablespoons chopped fresh or 2 teaspoons dried marjoram leaves
1/2 teaspoon grated lemon peel
1/8 teaspoon white pepper
3 tablespoons butter or stick margarine, melted
2 tablespoons lemon juice
4 cups hot cooked pasta (page 390) or rice (page 348)

1. Heat coals or gas grill for direct heat (page 332).

2. If using sea scallops, cut each in half.

3. Spray 18-inch square of heavy-duty aluminum foil with cooking spray. Arrange scallops, fish and shrimp on foil, placing shrimp on top. Sprinkle with marjoram, lemon peel and white pepper. Drizzle with butter and lemon juice. Bring corners of foil up to center and seal loosely.

4. Cover and grill foil packet 4 inches from medium heat 8 to 10 minutes or until scallops are white, fish flakes easily with fork and shrimp are pink and firm.

5. Serve seafood mixture over pasta.

1 Serving: Calories 355 (Calories from Fat 80); Fat 9g (Saturated 2g); Cholesterol 140mg; Sodium 270mg; Carbohydrate 41g (Dietary Fiber 2g); Protein 30g **% Daily Value:** Vitamin A 12%; Vitamin C 0%; Calcium 6%; Iron 24% **Diet Exchanges:** 3 Starch, 3 Very Lean Meat

Easy Grilled Fish Fillets *Fast*

Prep: 5 min; Grill: 14 min ✱ 4 servings

1 pound fish fillets or steaks, 3/4 to 1 inch thick
Salt and pepper to taste
2 tablespoons butter or stick margarine, melted

1. Heat coals or gas grill for direct heat (page 332).

2. Cut fish into 4 serving pieces. Sprinkle both sides of fish with salt and pepper. Brush both sides with butter.

3. Cover and grill fish 4 to 6 inches from medium heat 10 to 14 minutes or until fish flakes easily with fork.

1 Serving: Calories 140 (Calories from Fat 65); Fat 7g (Saturated 1g); Cholesterol 50mg; Sodium 160mg; Carbohydrate 0g (Dietary Fiber 0g); Protein 19g **% Daily Value:** Vitamin A 8%; Vitamin C 0%; Calcium 2%; Iron 0% **Diet Exchanges:** 2 1/2 Lean Meat

Easy Grilled Vegetables

Prep: 10 min; Marinate: 1 hr; Grill: 15 min ✱ 6 servings

12 pattypan squash, about 1 inch in diameter
2 medium red or green bell peppers, each cut into 6 pieces
1 large red onion, cut into 1/2-inch slices
1/3 cup Italian dressing
Freshly ground pepper, if desired

1. Place squash, bell peppers and onion in rectangular baking dish, 13 × 9 × 2 inches. Pour dressing over vegetables. Cover and let stand 1 hour to blend flavors.

2. Heat coals or gas grill for direct heat (page 332).

3. Remove vegetables from marinade; reserve marinade. Cover and grill squash and bell peppers 4 to 5 inches from medium heat 5 minutes.

4. Add onion. Cover and grill 5 to 10 minutes, turning and brushing vegetables with marinade 2 or 3 times, until tender. Sprinkle with pepper.

1 Serving: Calories 70 (Calories from Fat 35); Fat 4g (Saturated 1g); Cholesterol 0mg; Sodium 85mg; Carbohydrate 9g (Dietary Fiber 3g); Protein 2g **% Daily Value:** Vitamin A 26%; Vitamin C 72%; Calcium 2%; Iron 4% **Diet Exchanges:** 2 Vegetable, 1/2 Fat

---

MAKING A FOIL GRILL COVER

If your grill doesn't have a cover, shape two sheets of heavy-duty aluminum foil into a dome shape the same size as the grill rack. You can form the foil over bent coat hangers to keep the shape and to reuse. If you like, fashion a handle out of the hangers, and poke it through the foil at the top of the dome.

Smokey Cheddar Potatoes

Smokey Cheddar Potatoes

Prep: 10 min; Grill: 1 hr ✻ 4 servings

4 medium potatoes, cut into 1-inch chunks

1/2 teaspoon salt

2 tablespoons butter or stick margarine

1 cup shredded smoked or regular Cheddar cheese (4 ounces)

2 tablespoons bacon flavor bits or chips

2 medium green onions, sliced (2 tablespoons)

1. Heat coals or gas grill for direct heat (page 332).

2. Place potato chunks on 30 × 18-inch piece of heavy-duty aluminum foil. Sprinkle with salt. Dot with butter. Sprinkle with cheese and bacon bits.

3. Wrap foil securely around potatoes; pierce top of foil once or twice with fork to vent steam. Cover and grill foil packet, seam side up, 4 to 6 inches from medium heat 45 to 60 minutes or until potatoes are tender. Sprinkle with onions.

1 Serving: Calories 310 (Calories from Fat 145); Fat 16g (Saturated 7g); Cholesterol 30mg; Sodium 620mg; Carbohydrate 33g (Dietary Fiber 3g); Protein 11g **% Daily Value:** Vitamin A 14%; Vitamin C 14%; Calcium 16%; Iron 12% **Diet Exchanges:** 2 Starch, 1 Vegetable, 3 Fat

Rice, Grains & Beans

Low-Fat = *3g or less, except main dishes with 6g or less*   **Fast** = *Ready in 30 minutes or less*   ■ = *Bread Machine directions*   ● = *Slow Cooker directions*

Risotto (page 352)

Lighter = 1/3 fewer calories or 50% less fat

Grains Basics

Every culture and every cuisine of the world uses grains in cooking. And for good reason: grains are versatile, offer a wealth of nutrients (including fiber and protein and are low in fat and have zero cholesterol), provide texture, are economical and can be used in just about any dish for any meal. Grains aren't just a meat substitute, they're a whole exciting way of cooking. Classic dishes such as polenta, risotto and pilaf a just part of the repertoire. This chapter features grains usually cooked as a side dish. If you're just learning about grains, you'll find the information right here: what they look and taste like, how to cook them and what recipes to use them in.

Selecting Grains

You'll find a wonderful selection of grains in your local supermarket, ethnic food markets, health food stores and food co-ops. They're available packaged as well as in bulk, plain and in seasoned dry mixes, frozen and refrigerated and in many forms from whole kernels to finely ground flours.

Storing Grain

Uncooked: Most grains will keep indefinitely but are best when used within 1 to 2 years. Store them in their original packaging or in airtight glass or plastic containers; label the container with the date you filled it.

Store in a cool (60° or less), dry place. All grains can be refrigerated or frozen, which is a good idea if you live in a hot, humid climate. Whole grains that contain oil (brown rice, stone-ground or whole-grain cornmeal, wheat berries, wheat germ and whole wheat flour) can become rancid and *must be stored in the refrigerator or freezer;* store up to 6 months.

Cooked: Tightly cover cooked grains and put in the refrigerator for up to 5 days. Freeze them in airtight containers for up to 6 months. Leftover long-grain rice will become firmer when refrigerated, making it perfect to use in fried rice. But for other uses, you will want to reheat and soften it using one of these methods:

- In a microwavable container, add 1 tablespoon water per cup of cooked grain, tightly cover and microwave on High for 1 to 2 minutes.

- In a covered saucepan, add 2 tablespoons water per cup of cooked grain, and heat over low heat.

- Place frozen or refrigerated cooked grain in a colander, and pouring boiling water over it until warm.

Grains Glossary

White Rice:

- **Regular long-grain rice:** Has been milled to remove the hull, germ and most of the bran. About 90 percent of the rice produced in the United States is enriched. It's available in both long and short grains. The shorter the grain, the stickier the cooked rice will be; therefore, long grain is a better all-purpose rice.

- **Converted (parboiled) rice:** Is steamed and pressure cooked before being milled and polished. This process retains more nutrients but hardens the grain, so it takes longer to cook than regular rice. It also removes excess starch, so the grains stay separate after cooking.

- **Instant (precooked) rice:** Is commercially cooked, rinsed and dried before packaging, resulting in a very short cooking time. White, brown and wild rice all are available in this form.

- **Arborio (Italian or risotto) rice:** Is shorter, fatter and has a higher starch content than regular short-grain rice. Originally from northern Italy, Arborio is preferred for making risotto, a classic rice dish. As it cooks, the rice releases starch to give the dish its distinctive creamy texture.

- **Aromatic rices:** Contain a natural ingredient that gives them their nutty or perfumy smell and taste. The quality of the fragrance can differ from year to year; it also intensifies as the rice ages. Aromatic rices include basmati, wild pecan rice, Wehani rice and popcorn rice. Texmati, a cross between long-grain and basmati rices; Kalijiara, a rice one-third the size of basmati; and jasmine, similar to basmati but much less expensive.

GRAINS

Bulgar

Barley

Quinoa

Kasha

Cornmeal

Jasmine Rice

Wheat Berries

Basmati Rice

Arborio Rice

Millet

Brown Rice

Wild Rice

White Rice (Regular & Long Grain)

Amaranth

Brown rice: Unpolished rice with only the outer hull removed. It has a slightly firm texture and nutlike flavor, and it takes longer to cook than regular long-grain rice. If you're in a hurry, you'll be glad to know that instant brown rice is available, too. Because the germ and outer hull haven't been removed, brown rice has more fiber and other nutrients.

Wild rice: The seed of a grass that grows in marshes and rivers. Very dark greenish brown in color, it has a distinctive nutlike flavor and chewy texture. It's often found in rice mixtures with white or brown rice.

Other Grains

- **Barley:** One of the first grains ever cultivated. Pearl barley, the most common variety, has been steamed and polished; it's good in soups, stews and served as a side dish like rice is. Barley is available in both regular and quick-cooking varieties.

- **Bulgur and cracked wheat:** Made from whole wheat kernels. To make bulgur, wheat kernels are steamed, dried and crushed into coarse fragments. Cracked wheat is from kernels that are cleaned, then cracked or cut into fine fragments. Bulgur and cracked wheat are often used as breakfast cereals, and they appear in many Middle Eastern dishes.

- **Cornmeal:** Crushed dried corn kernels that can be blue, yellow or white, depending on the variety of corn used. It may be either commercially or stone ground; stone ground is more nutritious because it still contains some of the hull and germ of the corn. Although cornmeal is available in fine, medium and coarse textures, only one type is generally available in most supermarkets. Grits is a very coarse-ground cornmeal.

- **Kasha:** Also called *buckwheat groats*, it is the kernel inside the buckwheat seed. It's roasted for a toasty, nutty flavor, then coarsely ground.

- **Millet:** A small, round, yellow seed that looks like whole mustard seed. Rich in protein, this tiny grain has a chewy texture and mild flavor similar to brown rice. It's good whole as a hot cereal and is the base for dishes such as pilaf. It's also ground as a flour for puddings, cakes and breads.

- **Quinoa** (keen-wa): An ancient grain native to South America where the Incas called it "the mother grain." Quinoa is higher in protein than any other grain and is actually a complete protein. This creamy white, tiny, bead-shaped grain has a light texture and delicate flavor. Look for quinoa in larger supermarkets and health food stores.

- **Triticale:** A cross between wheat and rye. It's more nutritious than either wheat or rye and is a blend of wheat's nutlike flavor and rye's chewy texture. It's available in berries, flakes and flour. Whole triticale can be cooked as cereal and used in casseroles and pilafs.

- **Wheat berries:** Hulled whole kernels of wheat. Presoaking is necessary so they'll be tender enough to eat. Because they contain the entire wheat kernel, they take longer to cook and are high in nutritional value. They're eaten as a breakfast cereal and as a replacement for beans in chili, salads and baked dishes. They're also sprouted. Look for wheat berries in health food stores.

Basic Directions for Cooking Rice and Other Grains

1. Use 1 cup uncooked grain, and rinse only if directed to on the package. Be sure to use an extra-fine mesh strainer for tiny grains, such as quinoa.

2. Use a 2-quart saucepan for 1 cup of uncooked grain.

3. For liquid besides water, try broth (chicken, beef, vegetable) or half vegetable or fruit juice. Add salt, if desired, using 1/2 teaspoon per 1 cup of grain.

4. Cook or soak as directed in the chart on page 348. Do not remove lid or stir during cooking.

5. After cooking, fluff with fork, lifting grains to release steam.

6. For more information, see page 348.

Note: Grains lose moisture with age, so more or less liquid than the recipe calls for may be needed. If all the liquid is absorbed but the grain isn't quite tender, add a little more liquid and cook longer. If the grain is tender but all the liquid hasn't been absorbed, just drain.

RICE AND OTHER GRAINS COOKING CHART (1 CUP UNCOOKED)

Type	Cooking Liquid (in cups)	Directions	Approximate Simmer Time (in minutes)	Approximate Yield (in cups)
Rice				
White Rice				
Regular long grain	2	Heat rice and liquid to boiling. Reduce heat to low. Cover and simmer.	15	3
Parboiled (converted)	2 1/2	Heat liquid to boiling. Stir in rice. Reduce heat to low. Cover and simmer. Remove from heat. Let stand covered 5 minutes.	20 to 25	3 to 4
Precooked (instant)	1	Heat liquid to boiling. Stir in rice. Cover and remove from heat. Let stand covered 5 minutes.	0	2
Brown Rice				
Regular long grain	2 3/4	Heat rice and liquid to boiling. Reduce heat to low. Cover and simmer.	45 to 50	4
Precooked (instant)	1 1/4	Heat liquid to boiling. Stir in rice. Reduce heat to low. Cover and simmer.	10	2
Aromatic Rice				
Basmati	1 1/2	Heat rice and liquid to boiling. Reduce heat to low. Cover and simmer.	15 to 20	3
Jasmine	1 3/4	Heat rice and liquid to boiling. Reduce heat to low. Cover and simmer.	15 to 20	3
Texmati	1 3/4	Heat rice and liquid to boiling. Reduce heat to low. Cover and simmer	15 to 20	3
Wild Rice	2 1/2	Heat rice and liquid to boiling. Reduce heat to low. Cover and simmer.	40 to 50	3
Other Grains—Cooking				
Barley				
Quick-cooking	2	Heat liquid to boiling. Stir in barley. Reduce heat to low. Cover and simmer. Let stand covered 5 minutes.	10 to 12	3
Regular	4	Heat liquid to boiling. Stir in barley. Reduce heat to low. Cover and simmer.	45 to 50	4
Millet	2 1/2	Heat millet and liquid to boiling. Reduce heat to low. Cover and simmer.	15 to 20	4
Quinoa	2	Heat quinoa and liquid to boiling. Reduce heat to low. Cover and simmer.	15	3 to 4
Wheat Berries	2 1/2	Heat wheat berries and liquid to boiling. Reduce heat to low. Cover and simmer.	50 to 60	2 3/4 to 3

Type	Cooking Liquid (in cups)	Directions	Approximate Simmer Time (in minutes)	Approximate Yield (in cups)
Other Grains—Soaking				
Bulgur	3	Pour boiling liquid over bulgur. Cover and soak (do not cook). Drain if needed. Or cook as directed on package.	Soak 30 to 60 minutes	3
Kasha (roasted buckwheat groats/kernels)	2	Pour boiling liquid over kasha. Cover and soak (do not cook). Drain if needed. Or cook as directed on package.	Soak 10 to 15 minutes	4

Tips for Cooking Rice

- For perfect rice, measure the water and rice carefully.

- Rinse rice only if directed to on the package or instructed in the recipe.

- Stirring makes for sticky and starchy rice. So don't stir rice during cooking, unless of course you are making risotto—this is the exception!

- Add flavor to rice and grains by cooking them in beef, chicken or vegetable broth, or apple, orange, pineapple or tomato juice. Use half water and half flavored liquid of the amount of liquid called for.

- If rice is going to be cooked again, such as in a casserole, you can make a firmer rice by decreasing the liquid (by 2 to 4 tablespoons) and cooking time. For softer rice, add more liquid (2 to 3 tablespoons) and cook a few minutes longer. Or let the rice stand covered for 10 minutes after cooking.

- If rice is still wet after cooking, cook it uncovered over low heat for a few minutes.

- Fluff rice after cooking with a fork to separate the grains. Stirring it with a spoon can make it sticky.

- For easy cleanup, fill the saucepan with cold water and let it soak.

- Both electric and nonelectric rice cookers are available and becoming more popular for cooking rice. Follow the manufacturer's directions.

- You can cook rice in the microwave, but it's no time-saver. Follow the manufacturer's instructions or the microwave directions on the rice package.

LEARN WITH *Betty* — COOKING RICE

Undercooked Rice. Cause: Rice not cooked long enough and has a hard, white center.

Perfectly Cooked Rice. There are no problems with this rice; the grains remain fluffy and separate and are tender but still firm to the bite.

Overcooked Rice. Cause: Cooking rice too long causes the grains to split open or fall apart, and the texture becomes mushy.

Rice Pilaf

Prep: 10 min; Cook: 20 min; Stand: 5 min ✱ *4 servings*

2 tablespoons butter or stick margarine
1 small onion, chopped (1/4 cup)
1 cup uncooked regular long-grain rice
2 cups chicken broth
1/4 teaspoon salt

1. Melt butter in 3-quart saucepan over medium heat. Cook onion in butter about 3 minutes, stirring occasionally, until tender.

2. Stir in rice. Cook 5 minutes, stirring frequently. Stir in broth and salt.

3. Heat to boiling, stirring once or twice; reduce heat to low. Cover and simmer 16 minutes (do not lift cover or stir); remove from heat. Let stand covered 5 minutes.

1 Serving (about 3/4 cup): Calories 245 (Calories from Fat 65); Fat 7g (Saturated 4g); Cholesterol 15mg; Sodium 1,250mg; Carbohydrate 41g (Dietary Fiber 1g); Protein 6g **% Daily Value:** Vitamin A 4%; Vitamin C 0%; Calcium 2%; Iron 10% **Diet Exchanges:** 2 Starch, 2 Vegetable, 1 Fat

CURRY PILAF: Stir in 1/2 cup diced dried fruit and raisin mixture, 1/4 teaspoon ground allspice, 1/4 teaspoon ground turmeric and 1/4 teaspoon curry powder with the broth and salt in step 2.

MUSHROOM PILAF: Stir in 1 can (4 ounces) mushroom pieces and stems, drained, with the broth and salt in step 2.

Spanish Rice *Low-Fat*

Prep: 15 min; Cook: 35 min ✱ *6 servings*

2 tablespoons vegetable oil
1 cup uncooked regular long-grain rice
1 medium onion, chopped (1/2 cup)
2 1/2 cups water
1 1/2 teaspoons salt
3/4 teaspoon chili powder
1/8 teaspoon garlic powder
1 small green bell pepper, chopped (1/2 cup)
1 can (8 ounces) tomato sauce

1. Heat oil in 10-inch skillet over medium heat. Cook rice and onion in oil about 5 minutes, stirring frequently, until rice is golden brown and onion is tender.

2. Stir in remaining ingredients. Heat to boiling; reduce heat. Cover and simmer about 30 minutes, stirring occasionally, until rice is tender.

1 Serving (about 2/3 cup): Calories 175 (Calories from Fat 45); Fat 5g (Saturated 1g); Cholesterol 0mg; Sodium 820mg; Carbohydrate 32g (Dietary Fiber 2g); Protein 3g **% Daily Value:** Vitamin A 6%; Vitamin C 14%; Calcium 2%; Iron 8% **Diet Exchanges:** 2 Starch, 1/2 Fat

Curried Rice

Prep: 10 min; Cook: 25 min ✱ *4 servings*

Curry powder is not a single spice, as many believe, but a blend of up to twenty spices. Hot, mild and Madras are the types commonly available at most large supermarkets.

1 cup uncooked regular long-grain rice
2 cups water
2 tablespoons butter or stick margarine
1 tablespoon finely chopped onion
1/2 to 1 teaspoon curry powder
1/4 teaspoon salt
1/4 teaspoon pepper
1/4 cup slivered almonds, toasted (page 177)
1/4 cup chopped pimiento-stuffed or ripe olives

1. Heat rice and water to boiling in 2-quart saucepan; reduce heat. Cover and simmer about 15 minutes or until rice is tender and liquid is absorbed. Fluff rice with fork; set aside.

2. Melt butter in 10-inch skillet over medium heat. Cook onion in butter about 2 minutes, stirring occasionally, until tender. Stir in curry powder, salt and pepper.

3. Stir onion mixture into hot rice. Sprinkle with almonds and olives.

1 Serving (about 3/4 cup): Calories 280 (Calories from Fat 100); Fat 11g (Saturated 4g); Cholesterol 15mg; Sodium 410mg; Carbohydrate 42g (Dietary Fiber 2g); Protein 5g **% Daily Value:** Vitamin A 4%; Vitamin C 0%; Calcium 4%; Iron 12% **Diet Exchanges:** 2 Starch, 2 Vegetable, 2 Fat

Pork Fried Rice *Fast*

Prep: 15 min: Cook: 10 min ✱ 4 servings

Using cold, slightly dried-out rice (day-old rice is perfect) is essential for successful fried rice because it allows the grains to stay separate during frying—no mushy fried rice!

1 cup bean sprouts
2 tablespoons vegetable oil
1 cup sliced mushrooms (3 ounces)
3 cups cold cooked regular long-grain rice (page 348)
1 cup cut-up cooked pork
2 medium green onions, sliced (2 tablespoons)
2 large eggs, slightly beaten
3 tablespoons soy sauce
Dash of white pepper

1. Rinse bean sprouts with cold water; drain.

2. Heat 1 tablespoon of the oil in 10-inch skillet over medium heat; rotate skillet until oil covers bottom. Cook mushrooms in oil about 1 minute, stirring frequently, until coated.

3. Add bean sprouts, rice, pork and onions. Cook over medium heat about 5 minutes, stirring and breaking up rice, until hot.

4. Move rice mixture to side of skillet. Add the remaining 1 tablespoon oil to other side of skillet. Cook eggs in oil over medium heat, stirring constantly, until eggs are thickened throughout but still moist. Stir eggs into rice mixture. Stir in soy sauce and white pepper.

1 Serving (about 1 cup): Calories 345 (Calories from Fat 125); Fat 14g (Saturated 3g); Cholesterol 135mg; Sodium 740mg; Carbohydrate 37g (Dietary Fiber 1g); Protein 19g **% Daily Value:** Vitamin A 4%; Vitamin C 2%; Calcium 4%; Iron 16% **Diet Exchanges:** 2 Starch, 2 Medium-Fat Meat, 1 Vegetable

Lighter Pork Fried Rice: For 7 grams of fat and 265 calories per serving, decrease pork to 1/2 cup and finely chop. Use nonstick skillet and omit oil in step 4. Substitute 1/2 cup fat-free cholesterol-free egg product for the eggs.

Cheesy Broccoli-Rice Bake

Prep: 15 min: Bake: 35 min ✱ 8 servings

2 tablespoons butter or stick margarine
1 large onion, chopped (1 cup)
16 ounces process cheese spread loaf, cut into cubes
1 can (10 3/4 ounces) condensed cream of mushroom soup
2/3 cup milk
1/4 teaspoon pepper, if desired
2 cups 1/2-inch pieces broccoli flowerets
3 cups cooked rice (page 348)
1 cup fine soft bread crumbs (about 1 1/2 slices bread)
2 tablespoons butter or stick margarine, melted

1. Heat oven to 350°. Grease rectangular baking dish, 13 × 9 × 2 inches.

2. Melt 2 tablespoons butter in 10-inch skillet over medium-high heat. Cook onion in butter, stirring occasionally, until crisp-tender; reduce heat to medium. Stir in cheese, soup, milk and pepper. Cook, stirring frequently, until cheese is melted.

3. Stir in broccoli and rice. Spoon into baking dish. Mix bread crumbs and 2 tablespoons melted butter; sprinkle over rice mixture. Bake uncovered 30 to 35 minutes or until light brown on top and bubbly around edges.

1 Serving: Calories 445 (Calories from Fat 245); Fat 27g (Saturated 16g); Cholesterol 70mg; Sodium 1,250mg; Carbohydrate 34g (Dietary Fiber 2g); Protein 18g **% Daily Value:** Vitamin A 24%; Vitamin C 18%; Calcium 38%; Iron 12% **Diet Exchanges:** 2 Starch, 1 1/2 Medium-Fat Meat, 1 Vegetable, 3 Fat

Baked Rice with Green Chilies

Prep: 5 min; Cook: 20 min; Bake: 30 min
✳ *6 servings*

1 cup uncooked regular long-grain rice
2 cups water
1 cup sour cream
1/2 cup shredded Monterey Jack cheese (2 ounces)
1/2 cup shredded Cheddar cheese (4 ounces)
1 teaspoon salt
2 cans (4 ounces each) chopped green chilies, drained
1/2 cup shredded Cheddar cheese (4 ounces)

1. Heat rice and water to boiling in 2-quart saucepan; reduce heat to low. Cover and simmer 15 minutes (do not lift cover or stir) or until rice is tender and liquid is absorbed. Fluff rice with fork.

2. Heat oven to 350°.

3. Mix all ingredients except 1/2 cup of the Cheddar cheese in ungreased 2-quart casserole. Bake uncovered about 30 minutes or until heated through. During last 5 minutes of baking, sprinkle with remaining cheese. Bake until cheese is melted.

1 Serving: Calories 280 (Calories from Fat 125); Fat 14g (Saturated 8g); Cholesterol 45mg; Sodium 600mg; Carbohydrate 30g (Dietary Fiber 1g); Protein 9g **% Daily Value:** Vitamin A 14%; Vitamin C 22%; Calcium 16%; Iron 8% **Diet Exchanges:** 2 Starch, 3 Fat

Risotto

Prep: 10 min; Cook: 30 min ✳ *6 servings*

2 tablespoons butter or stick margarine
1 medium onion, coarsely chopped (1/2 cup)
1/2 cup dry white wine or apple juice
1 1/2 cups uncooked Arborio or other short-grain white rice
2 cups chicken broth
1 cup water
1/4 cup finely shredded Parmesan cheese
Freshly ground pepper
Chopped fresh parsley, if desired

1. Melt butter in 12-inch skillet or 4-quart Dutch oven over medium-high heat. Cook onion in butter, stirring frequently, until tender; reduce heat to medium.

2. Add wine to onion mixture in skillet; cook until liquid has evaporated. Stir in rice. Cook uncovered over medium heat, stirring frequently, until rice begins to brown.

3. Mix broth and water; pour 1/2 cup broth mixture over rice. Cook uncovered, stirring occasionally, until liquid is absorbed. Repeat with remaining broth mixture, 1/2 cup at a time, until rice is tender and creamy. Sprinkle with cheese, pepper and parsley.

1 Serving: Calories 370 (Calories from Fat 55); Fat 6g (Saturated 3g); Cholesterol 15mg; Sodium 440mg; Carbohydrate 68g (Dietary Fiber 1g); Protein 10g **% Daily Value:** Vitamin A 2%; Vitamin C 0%; Calcium 8%; Iron 18% **Diet Exchanges:** 4 Starch, 2 Vegetable

RISOTTO WITH PEAS: Just before serving, stir in 1 package (10 ounces) frozen green peas, cooked and drained.

LEARN WITH *Betty* — COOKING RISOTTO

Undercooked Risotto. Cause: Risotto not cooked long enough so stays soupy or watery, not creamy.

Perfectly Cooked Risotto. There are no problems with this risotto; it is thickened and creamy.

Mediterranean Risotto

Prep: 10 min; Cook: 25 min ✱ *6 servings*

Broccoli is added at the last minute in this recipe to retain its color, flavor and nutrients. Its crisp-tender texture goes nicely with the creamy richness of the rice. If you don't have feta cheese on hand, sprinkle the risotto with shredded Parmesan cheese.

4 3/4 cups chicken broth

4 cloves garlic, finely chopped

1 1/2 cups uncooked Arborio or other short-grain
    white rice

2 cups broccoli flowerets

3/4 cup crumbled feta cheese

1/2 cup oil-packed sun-dried tomatoes, drained and
    chopped

1 teaspoon dried oregano leaves

1 can (2 1/4 ounces) sliced ripe olives, drained

1. Heat 1/4 cup of the broth and the garlic to boiling in 12-inch nonstick skillet over medium-high heat. Stir in rice. Cook 1 minute, stirring constantly.

2. Pour 1/2 cup of the broth over rice mixture. Cook uncovered over medium heat, stirring occasion-ally, until liquid is absorbed. Continue cooking 15 to 20 minutes, adding broth 1/2 cup at a time and stirring occasionally, until rice is creamy and almost tender.

3. Stir in remaining ingredients. Cook 1 minute.

1 Serving: Calories 295 (Calories from Fat 70); Fat 8g (Saturated 4g); Cholesterol 15mg; Sodium 1160mg; Carbohydrate 46g (Dietary Fiber 2g); Protein 12g **% Daily Value:** Vitamin A 6%; Vitamin C 26%; Calcium 14%; Iron 16% **Diet Exchanges:** 2 Starch, 3 Vegetable, 1 Fat

---

BEYOND WATER: FLAVOR-PACKED RICE AND GRAINS

Using water for cooking rice and grains is only one of many possibilities. Other liquids can add interesting flavor to your finished dish. Some high-acid liquids, such as tomato juice and wine, should be combined with water because the amount of acid may increase the cook time. Be sure the flavored liquid you use to cook rice and grains goes well with the dish to which you will add it or with which it is served. Try one of the following "liquid assets" in place of water in your recipe:

• Fruit Juice: Replace half or all of the amount of water with apple or orange juice or fruit juice blends such as pineapple-orange or apple-cranberry. This makes an easy side dish or a flavorful addition to a salad or dessert.

• Vegetable Juice: Replace half of the amount of water with tomato, spicy eight-vegetable, carrot or other vegetable juice. This is good as a side dish or in casseroles, soups and salads.

• Wine: Replace half of the amount of water with white or red wine. A sweeter white wine is good for salads and dessert dishes; a hearty red wine is great in casseroles and soups.

• Broth: A good-quality canned or homemade vegetable broth can be used for cooking any rice or grain. It can replace all of the water in your recipe.

• Milk: Replace half or all of the amount of water with milk when cooking rice and grains. This can make a rich, hearty hot cereal or a base for a side dish or dessert. Unsweetened canned coconut milk also can be used. For a rich-er flavor, use all coconut milk. Rice and grains cooked in coconut milk can be used as a side dish or dessert.

Fried Polenta (Polenta variation)

Polenta *Fast & Low-Fat*

Prep: 10 min; Cook: 20 min ✱ *6 servings*

1 cup yellow cornmeal
3/4 cup water
3 1/4 cups boiling water
1 1/2 teaspoons salt

1. Mix cornmeal and 3/4 cup water in 2-quart saucepan. Stir in 3 1/4 cups boiling water and the salt. Cook, stirring constantly, until mixture thickens and boils; reduce heat.

2. Cover and simmer about 10 minutes, stirring occasionally, until very thick; remove from heat. Stir until smooth.

1 Serving (about 3/4 cup): Calories 72 (Calories from Fat 0); Fat 0g (Saturated 0g); Cholesterol 0mg; Sodium 590mg; Carbohydrate 18g (Dietary Fiber 2g); Protein 2g **% Daily Value:** Vitamin A 0%; Vitamin C 0%; Calcium 0%; Iron 4% **Diet Exchanges:** 1 Starch

FRIED POLENTA: Grease loaf pan, 9 × 5 × 3 inches, with shortening. After simmering polenta 10 minutes in step 2, spread in loaf pan. Cover and refrigerate at least 12 hours until firm. Turn pan upside down to unmold. Cut into 1/2-inch slices. Coat slices with flour. Melt 2 tablespoons butter or stick margarine in 10-inch skillet over low heat. Cook slices in butter about 5 minutes on each side or until brown. Serve with molasses, jam, maple-flavored syrup, sour cream or spaghetti sauce if desired.

For faster Fried Polenta, spread polenta in greased rectangular pan, 13 × 9 × 2 inches; refrigerate uncovered about 3 hours or until firm. Cut into 6 squares. (Cut squares diagonally into triangles if desired.) Cook in butter as directed.

Barley and Asparagus

Barley and Asparagus *Low-Fat*

Prep: 15 min; Cook: 20 min ✳ 8 servings

2 tablespoons butter or stick margarine

1 medium onion, chopped (1/2 cup)

1 medium carrot, chopped (1/2 cup)

1 cup uncooked quick-cooking barley

2 cans (14 1/2 ounces each) ready-to-serve chicken
    broth, heated

8 ounces asparagus (8 to 10 stalks), cut into 1-inch
    pieces

2 tablespoons shredded Parmesan cheese

1/4 teaspoon dried marjoram or thyme leaves

1/8 teaspoon pepper

1. Melt butter in 12-inch skillet over medium heat.
Cook onion and carrot in butter 1 to 2 minutes, stirring
occasionally, until crisp-tender. Stir in barley. Cook and
stir 1 minute.

2. Pour 1 cup of the hot broth over barley mixture. Cook
uncovered about 5 minutes, stirring occasionally, until
liquid is absorbed. Stir in asparagus. Cook 15 to 20

minutes longer, adding broth 1 cup at a time and stirring
frequently, until barley is tender and liquid is absorbed;
remove from heat. Stir in remaining ingredients.

*Break off tough ends of asparagus stalks where they snap
easily while gently bending stalk; discard.*

1 Serving (about 1/2 cup): Calories 130 (Calories from Fat 35);
Fat 4g (Saturated 2g); Cholesterol 10mg; Sodium 520mg;
Carbohydrate 23g (Dietary Fiber 5g); Protein 6g **% Daily Value:**
Vitamin A 14%; Vitamin C 4%; Calcium 4%; Iron 6% **Diet
Exchanges:** 1 Starch, 2 Vegetable

Cheese Grits

Prep: 20 min; Bake: 40 min; Stand: 10 min ✱ *8 servings*

As American as apple pie, grits are traditional Southern cuisine. Grits are the product of coarsely ground corn and are eaten as a cereal or side dish.

2 cups milk
2 cups water
1/2 teaspoon salt
1/4 teaspoon pepper
1 cup uncooked white hominy quick grits
1 1/2 cups shredded Cheddar cheese (6 ounces)
2 medium green onions, sliced (2 tablespoons)
2 large eggs, slightly beaten
1 tablespoon butter or stick margarine
1/4 teaspoon paprika

1. Heat oven to 350°. Grease bottom and side of 1 1/2-quart casserole with shortening.

2. Heat milk, water, salt and pepper to boiling in 2-quart saucepan. Gradually add grits, stirring constantly; reduce heat. Simmer uncovered about 5 minutes, stirring frequently, until thickened. Stir in cheese and onions.

3. Stir 1 cup of the grits mixture into eggs, then stir back into remaining grits in saucepan. Pour into casserole. Cut butter into small pieces; sprinkle over grits. Sprinkle with paprika.

4. Bake uncovered 35 to 40 minutes or until set. Let stand 10 minutes before serving.

1 Serving: Calories 220 (Calories from Fat 100); Fat 11g (Saturated 7g); Cholesterol 85mg; Sodium 620mg; Carbohydrate 19g (Dietary Fiber 0g); Protein 11g **% Daily Value:** Vitamin A 10%; Vitamin C 0%; Calcium 20%; Iron 6% **Diet Exchanges:** 1 Starch, 1 High-Fat Meat, 1 Fat

Bulgur Pilaf

Prep: 15 min; Cook: 25 min ✱ *6 servings*

2 tablespoons butter or stick margarine
1/2 cup slivered almonds
1 medium onion, chopped (1/2 cup)
1 medium carrot, chopped (1/2 cup)
1 can (14 1/2 ounces) ready-to-serve chicken broth
1 cup uncooked bulgur
1/4 teaspoon lemon pepper seasoning salt or pepper
1/4 cup chopped fresh parsley

1. Melt 1 tablespoon of the butter in 12-inch skillet over medium-high heat. Cook almonds in butter 2 to 3 minutes, stirring constantly, until golden brown. Remove almonds from skillet.

2. Add remaining 1 tablespoon butter, the onion and carrot to skillet. Cook about 3 minutes, stirring occasionally, until vegetables are crisp-tender.

3. Stir in broth, bulgur and lemon pepper seasoning salt. Heat to boiling; reduce heat. Cover and simmer about 15 minutes or until bulgur is tender and liquid is absorbed. Stir in almonds and parsley.

1 Serving (about 1/2 cup): Calories 170 (Calories from Fat 70); Fat 8g (Saturated 2g); Cholesterol 10mg; Sodium 340mg; Carbohydrate 23g (Dietary Fiber 6g); Protein 7g **% Daily Value:** Vitamin A 18%; Vitamin C 4%; Calcium 4%; Iron 6% **Diet Exchanges:** 1 Starch, 2 Vegetable, 1 Fat

Legumes Basics

Good things come in small packages. Despite their tiny size, legumes are packed with protein, fiber, vitamins and minerals. Virtually fat-free, they contain no cholesterol but lots of calcium and iron. To make a good thing even better, they're available in a colorful array of varieties—dried, canned and frozen—and they're economical, to boot. Extremely versatile, beans have a mild flavor that makes them perfect partners with spices and herbs.

Beans also contain complex sugars that when eaten tend to cause flatulence (gas). You can lessen this effect by discarding the water after soaking beans for uncooked and cooked dried beans, rinsing canned beans, adding a little vinegar near the end of cooking or using a few drops of over-the-counter products.

Selecting Legumes

Look for legumes at your supermarket, farmers' market, ethnic foods and gourmet markets as well as health food stores and food co-ops for more unusual varieties.

- Fresh, high-quality beans are bright in color with smooth, unbroken seed coats.
- Legumes of the same size will cook more evenly.
- Rinse legumes in a colander before cooking, and pick out any stones or shriveled, small or damaged beans.

Storing Legumes

Dried Legumes: Most legumes will keep indefinitely but are best when used within 1 to 2 years. Store them in their original packaging or in airtight glass or plastic containers; label the container with the date you filled it. Store in a cool (60° or less), dry place.

Cooked Legumes: *Refrigerator:* Cover and store cooked legumes in the refrigerator for 2 to 3 days. *Freezer:* Freeze cooked legumes in airtight containers for up to 6 months.

Legumes Glossary

Adzuki Beans: Small, oval, reddish brown beans with a light, nutty flavor. They originated in China and Japan. They taste similar to kidney beans and can replace them in recipes.

Anasazi Beans: Kidney-shaped, red-and-white speckled beans; the spots disappear when cooked. The name is Navajo and means "ancient ones." Their sweet, full flavor makes them excellent for Mexican dishes.

Black Beans: Also called *turtle beans,* black beans are found in the cuisines of Mexico, South and Central America as well as the Caribbean. Dark and tasty, they stand up well to bold seasonings.

Black-Eyed Peas: Also called *cowpeas* and *black-eyed suzies,* black-eyed peas are creamy colored with a small, dark brown to black spot on one side. They don't require presoaking and cook quickly. Found in traditional southern recipes, black-eyed peas pair well with strong-flavored greens such spinach, chard and kale.

Butter Beans: Large, cream-colored lima beans with a smooth, buttery texture and mild flavor. They're often served as a vegetable side dish or added to soups, main dishes and salads for color and texture interest.

Cannellini Beans: Large white kidney beans that originated in South America. Adopted by Italy, they are often mixed with pasta and added to soups and salads.

Cranberry Beans: Pink with dark red streaks, these beans fade during cooking but retain their nutty flavor. They're a favorite in Italian cooking and are also known as *Roman beans.*

Fava Beans: Large flat beans with an earthy flavor that appear brown and wrinkled when dried. They are the bean of choice for the Middle Eastern specialty *falafel.*

Garbanzo Beans: Tan, bumpy and round, garbanzo beans need long, slow cooking. Also called *chickpeas,* they are used in the popular Middle Eastern dip Hummus (page 25). Their firm texture makes them a good addition to soups, stews, casseroles and salads.

LEGUMES

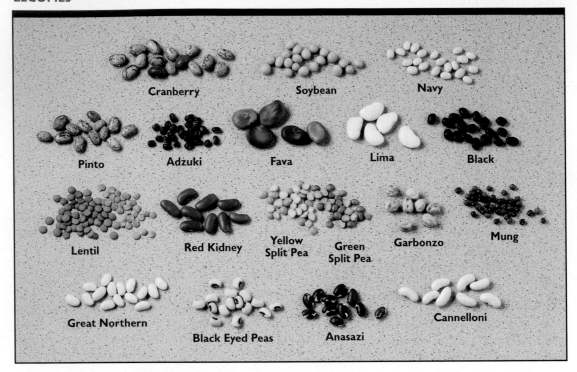

Great Northern Beans: Kidney-shaped white beans that resemble lima beans, as well as their cousin, navy beans. Can be used in any dish calling for white beans, such as casseroles and soups. Cannellini beans are a good substitute, although they're smaller.

Kidney Beans: Available in dark and light red, they add color and texture to many dishes. A favorite in Cincinnati-Style Chili (page 466) as well as in Red Beans and Rice (page 363).

Lentils: The familiar small, grayish green lentil is only one of the many types and colors of lentils used around the world. Also available in white, yellow, red and black, dried lentils do not require presoaking, and they cook in a short time.

Lima Beans: The choice of regular and baby sizes make them a wonderful addition to multibean salads, soups and casseroles. (Also see Butter Beans.)

Marrow Beans: The largest and roundest of the white beans, marrow beans are typically served as a side dish.

Mung Beans: Called *grams*, or when hulled, *moong dal*, this sweet-flavored bean is native to India and is also popular in China. Americans know its sprouted form as bean sprouts. Use them in place of lentils or peas in recipes.

Navy Beans: Also known as *pea beans*, these small, white beans are so named because they've been a staple of sailors' diets since the early 1800s. You'll find navy beans in commercially canned pork and beans, and they're the bean of choice for homemade Old-Fashioned Baked Beans (page 361).

Pink Beans: Popular in the cooking of the western United States, these reddish-brown beans are interchangeable with pinto beans in recipes.

Pinto Beans: Speckled pink and brown when dried, they fade to a uniform pinkish brown when cooked. Their full-bodied, earthy flavor makes them a staple of southwestern and Mexican cooking.

Red Beans: A dark red bean that's popular in Mexican, southwestern United States and Caribbean cooking. Use them interchangeably with kidney beans.

Soybeans: Soybeans are becoming very popular! They're incorporated into energy and nutrition bars, salt-crunchy snacks and are being used just like any other type of bean in all sorts of recipes. Check out our Soybeans and Rice recipe on page 364. Much of the soybean harvest is processed into oil or tofu (bean curd) and tempeh, often used in meatless dishes.

Split Peas: Available green or yellow, split peas are used mostly in soups. They don't need presoaking and cook in less time than beans. When cooked, they turn into a soft mush, making them perfect for soups and stews, as well as for *dal*, a spicy Indian dish.

Soaking Dried Legumes Before Cooking

With the exception of black-eyed peas, lentils and split peas, dried legumes need to be soaked before cooking to soften and plump them. Soaking also makes beans more digestible by dissolving some of the sugars that cause intestinal gas. After soaking dried beans, discard the water and cook the beans in clean, cold water. And don't forget: Most legumes rehydrate to triple their dry size, so start with a pot that's big enough.

There are two methods for soaking legumes:

- **Quick-Soak Method:** Place dried legumes in a large saucepan; add enough water to cover them. Heat to boiling; boil 2 minutes. Remove from the heat, cover and let stand for at least 1 hour before cooking. Drain, then cook in clean, cold water.
- **Long-Soak Method:** Place dried legumes in a large saucepan or bowl; add enough cold water to cover them. Let stand 8 to 24 hours. Drain, then cook in clean, cold water.

Tips for Cooking Dried Legumes

- If dried legumes haven't been rehydrated, they'll double or triple in volume as they cook, so be sure to use a large enough saucepan or casserole.
- Use legumes of similar size and cooking times interchangeably in recipes.
- To reduce foaming and boilovers during cooking, add 1 tablespoon butter, margarine, olive oil or vegetable oil to the cooking water; drain legumes and rinse. If the water does foam, skim it off once or twice.
- Simmer—rather than boil—beans, stirring them *gently* or the skins may burst.
- Go ahead and add seasoning such as garlic, onion, oregano, parsley or thyme during cooking. Just don't add salt or acidic ingredients. Salt and acid toughen beans, so add salt and ingredients such as lemon juice, vinegar, wine and tomatoes (whole, sauce, paste or juice) only after beans are soft and tender.
- To test if beans are done, bite into one or two. They should be tender but not mushy. Not only does overcooking ruin the texture, it reduces the nutrients.
- If legumes aren't quite tender but they've absorbed all the water, add a little more water and cook longer.

DRIED BEAN YIELDS

Dried beans double or triple in volume as they cook, so be sure to use a large enough pan or casserole. When buying or cooking beans, use this chart as a guide.

This amount	Equals
8 ounces dried beans	1 cup uncooked
1 cup dried beans	2 to 3 cups cooked
1 pound dried beans	2 cups uncooked
2 cups dried beans	4 to 6 cups cooked
1 can (15 to 16 ounces) cooked beans, drained	1 1/2 to 2 cups

- Legumes continue to dry with age, so you may need to add more water than a recipe calls for and they may take longer to cook. If the legumes are really old, they may never soften completely.

- High altitude or hard water may increase cooking times.

- You can cook legumes in the microwave, but it's no time-saver because microwaving can take 1 hour to 1 hour 30 minutes. For best results, cook legumes slowly for a long time in lots of water.

- We don't recommend cooking legumes in a pressure cooker because they can foam during cooking and clog the pressure valve, causing a sudden release of pressure and possibly forcing the lid off.

Basic Directions for Cooking Dried Legumes

1. Sort legumes, discarding any stones or shriveled, small or damaged beans; rinse and drain. Place 1 cup legumes in 3- to 4-quart saucepan. (Lentils do not require soaking or precooking.)

2. Add enough cold water (about 3 to 4 cups) to cover legumes.

3. Heat to boiling. Boil uncovered 2 minutes.

4. Reduce heat to low. Cover and simmer (do not boil or legumes will burst), stirring occasionally, for amount of simmer time in chart or until tender.

DRIED LEGUMES COOKING CHART
(1 CUP DRIED LEGUMES)

Type	Approximate Simmer time	Approximate Yield
Adzuki Beans Lentils	30 to 45 minutes	2 to 3 cups
Mung Beans Split Peas	45 to 60 minutes	2 to 2 1/4 cups
Black-Eyed Peas Butter Beans Cannellini Beans Great Northern Beans Lima Beans Navy Beans Pinto Beans	1 hour to 1 hour 30 minutes	2 to 2 1/2 cups
Anasazi Beans Black Beans Fava Beans Kidney Beans	1 to 2 hours	2 cups
Garbanzo Beans	2 hours to 2 hours 30 minutes	2 cups
Soybeans	3 to 4 hours	2 cups

UNLEADED BEANS

Flatulence, commonly known as intestinal gas, can result from eating beans. Gas is caused by the digestive system's inability to digest the complex sugars found in beans.

You can reduce this effect by draining the soaking liquid used to hydrate dried beans before cooking or by rinsing and draining canned beans. In case you were wondering, minimal nutrition is lost by draining dried or canned beans.

You may also want to check out the over-the-counter products available in liquid and tablet form to help minimize gas.

When adding more beans to your diet, add them gradually over a period of several weeks to allow your digestive system time to adjust. Sudden consumption of large amounts of beans can cause bloating and gas.

Old-Fashioned Baked Beans

Old-Fashioned Baked Beans *Low-Fat*

Prep: 20 min; Bake: 6 hr 15 min ✳ *10 servings*

Many fond memories, as well as pride, often center around a particular cook's recipe for baked beans. Here's a recipe that will stir up warm memories for you and your family.

2 cups dried navy beans (1 pound), sorted and rinsed
10 cups water
1/2 cup packed brown sugar
1/4 cup molasses
1 teaspoon salt
6 slices bacon, crisply cooked and crumbled
1 medium onion, chopped (1/2 cup)
3 cups water

1. Heat oven to 350°.

2. Heat beans and 10 cups water to boiling in 4-quart Dutch oven. Boil uncovered 2 minutes. Stir in remaining ingredients except 3 cups water.

3. Cover and bake 4 hours, stirring occasionally.

4. Stir in 3 cups water. Bake uncovered 2 hours to 2 hours 15 minutes longer, stirring occasionally, until beans are tender and desired consistency.

1 Serving (about 1/2 cup): Calories 200 (Calories from Fat 20); Fat 2g (Saturated 1g); Cholesterol 5mg; Sodium 300mg; Carbohydrate 42g (Dietary Fiber 6g); Protein 10g **% Daily Value:** Vitamin A 0%; Vitamin C 0%; Calcium 10%; Iron 16% **Diet Exchanges:** 2 Starch, 2 Vegetable

Slow Cooker Directions: Place beans and 5 cups water in 3 1/2- to 6-quart slow cooker. Cover and cook on high heat setting 2 hours. Turn off heat; let stand 8 to 24 hours. Stir in brown sugar, molasses, salt, bacon and onion. Cover and cook on low heat setting 10 to 12 hours or until beans are very tender and most of liquid is absorbed.

Easy Skillet Baked Beans

Prep: 15 min; Cook: 25 min ✳ 4 servings

Great cooks have been doctoring up convenience foods for a long time, creating their own personal touch. We've done it here with canned beans—it's so easy!

3 slices bacon, cut into 1-inch pieces
1 medium onion, chopped (1/2 cup)
2 cans (15 ounces each) pork and beans
1/4 cup chili sauce
1 teaspoon yellow mustard

1. Cook bacon and onion in 10-inch skillet over medium heat, stirring occasionally, until bacon is crisp.

2. Stir in remaining ingredients. Heat to boiling; reduce heat. Simmer uncovered 15 to 20 minutes, stirring occasionally, until liquid is absorbed.

1 Serving (about 1 cup): Calories 255 (Calories from Fat 45); Fat 5g (Saturated 2g); Cholesterol 20mg; Sodium 1,290mg; Carbohydrate 51g (Dietary Fiber 12g); Protein 14g **% Daily Value:** Vitamin A 4%; Vitamin C 8%; Calcium 8%; Iron 14% **Diet Exchanges:** 3 Starch, 1 Vegetable

EASY OVEN BAKED BEANS: Heat oven to 350°. After boiling mixture in step 2, pour into ungreased 1 1/2-quart casserole. Bake uncovered about 40 minutes.

Three-Bean Casserole

Prep: 20 min; Bake: 45 min ✳ 8 servings

You know you have a winning recipe when it shows up again and again, no matter where you are or what the occasion. So it is with this terrific bean recipe that's perfect for potlucks and other gatherings.

1 pound bulk pork sausage
2 medium stalks celery, sliced (1 cup)
1 medium onion, chopped (1/2 cup)
1 large clove garlic, finely chopped
2 cans (21 ounces each) baked beans in tomato sauce
1 can (15 to 16 ounces) lima or butter beans, drained
1 can (15 to 16 ounces) kidney beans, drained
1 can (8 ounces) tomato sauce
1 tablespoon ground mustard
2 tablespoons honey or packed brown sugar
1 tablespoon white or cider vinegar
1/4 teaspoon red pepper sauce

1. Heat oven to 400°.

2. Cook sausage, celery, onion and garlic in 10-inch skillet over medium heat about 10 minutes, stirring occasionally, until sausage is no longer pink; drain.

3. Mix sausage mixture and remaining ingredients in ungreased 3-quart casserole. Bake uncovered about 45 minutes, stirring once, until hot and bubbly.

1 Serving (about 1 1/3 cups): Calories 255 (Calories from Fat 45); Fat 5g (Saturated 2g); Cholesterol 20mg; Sodium 1,290mg; Carbohydrate 51g (Dietary Fiber 12g); Protein 14g **% Daily Value:** Vitamin A 4%; Vitamin C 8%; Calcium 8%; Iron 14% **Diet Exchanges:** 3 Starch, 1 Vegetable

Slow Cooker Directions: Substitute 1/2 cup ketchup for the tomato sauce. Decrease honey to 1 tablespoon. Cook sausage, celery, onion and garlic in 10-inch skillet over medium heat about 10 minutes, stirring occasionally, until sausage is no longer pink; drain. Mix sausage mixture and remaining ingredients in 3 1/2- to 6-quart slow cooker. Cover and cook on high heat setting 2 hours to 2 hours 30 minutes to blend flavors.

Red Beans and Rice *Low-Fat*

Prep: 10 min; Cook: 1 hr 45 min; Stand: 5 min
✱ *8 servings*

Dried beans are usually simmered, rather than boiled, during the longest part of the cooking time because boiling the beans for too long can cause them to fall apart.

1 cup dried kidney beans (8 ounces), sorted and rinsed*
3 cups water
2 ounces salt pork (with rind), diced, or 3 slices bacon, cut up
1 medium onion, chopped (1/2 cup)
1 medium green bell pepper, chopped (1 cup)
1 cup uncooked regular long-grain rice
1 teaspoon salt

1. Heat beans and water to boiling in 3-quart saucepan. Boil uncovered 2 minutes; reduce heat. Cover and simmer 1 hour to 1 hour 15 minutes or until tender (do not boil or beans will fall apart).

2. Drain beans, reserving liquid. Cook salt pork in 10-inch skillet over medium heat, stirring occasionally, until crisp. Stir in onion and bell pepper. Cook, stirring occasionally, until onion is tender.

3. Add enough water to bean liquid, if necessary, to measure 2 cups. Add bean liquid, salt pork mixture, rice and salt to beans in 3-quart saucepan. Heat to boiling, stirring once or twice; reduce heat. Cover and simmer 14 minutes (do not lift cover or stir); remove from heat. Fluff with fork. Cover and let steam 5 to 10 minutes.

One can (15 to 16 ounces) red kidney beans (drained and liquid reserved) can be substituted for the dried kidney beans. Omit water and step 1.

1 Serving (about 3/4 cup): Calories 150 (Calories from Fat 35); Fat 4g (Saturated 2g); Cholesterol 5mg; Sodium 360mg; Carbohydrate 27g (Dietary Fiber 2g); Protein 4g **% Daily Value:** Vitamin A 0%; Vitamin C 14%; Calcium 2%; Iron 8% **Diet Exchanges:** 1 Starch, 2 Vegetable, 1/2 Fat

Slow Cooker Directions: Increase water to 3 1/4 cups. Use 1 1/3 cups uncooked instant rice. Mix all ingredients except rice in 3 1/2- to 6-quart slow cooker. Cover and cook on high heat setting 3 hours 30 minutes to 4 hours 30 minutes or until beans are tender. Stir in rice. Cover and cook on high heat setting 15 minutes. Stir well.

HOPPIN' JOHN: Substitute 1 cup dried black-eyed peas for the kidney beans. Omit bell pepper.

Savory Black-Eyed Peas with Bacon

Prep: 20 min; Cook: 1 hr 15 min ✱ *4 servings*

4 slices bacon, cut into 1-inch pieces
2 1/2 cups chicken broth
1 cup dried black-eyed peas (8 ounces), sorted and rinsed
2 medium stalks celery, sliced (1 cup)
1 large onion, chopped (1 cup)
1 1/2 tablespoons chopped fresh or 1 1/2 teaspoons dried savory leaves
1 clove garlic, finely chopped
3 medium carrots, thinly sliced (1 1/2 cups)
1 large green bell pepper, cut into 1-inch pieces
1/2 cup shredded Monterey Jack cheese with jalapeño peppers (2 ounces)

1. Cook bacon in 10-inch skillet over medium heat, stirring occasionally, until crisp. Remove bacon with slotted spoon; drain. Drain fat from skillet.

2. Heat broth, black-eyed peas, celery, onion, savory and garlic to boiling in same skillet. Boil uncovered 2 minutes; reduce heat. Cover and simmer about 40 minutes, stirring occasionally, until peas are almost tender (do not boil or peas will fall apart).

3. Stir in carrots and bell pepper. Heat to simmering. Cover and simmer about 13 minutes, stirring occasionally, until vegetables are tender; stir. Sprinkle with cheese and bacon.

1 Serving: Calories 260 (Calories from Fat 80); Fat 9g (Saturated 4g); Cholesterol 20mg; Sodium 890mg; Carbohydrate 37g (Dietary Fiber 11g); Protein 19g **% Daily Value:** Vitamin A 78%; Vitamin C 38%; Calcium 18%; Iron 24% **Diet Exchanges:** 2 Starch, 1 1/2 Lean Meat, 1 Vegetable

Soybeans and Rice

Soybeans and Rice *Low-Fat*

Prep: 15 min; Stand 1 hr; Cook: 3 hr ✳ *12 servings*

1 cup uncooked soybeans (8 ounces), sorted and rinsed
2 cups water
1 tablespoon olive or vegetable oil
1 medium onion, chopped (1/2 cup)
1 small green bell pepper, chopped (1/2 cup)
1 clove garlic, finely chopped
1 can (14 1/2 ounces) ready-to-serve chicken broth
1/4 teaspoon dried oregano leaves
1/8 teaspoon ground red pepper (cayenne)
2 bay leaves
3/4 cup uncooked regular long-grain rice
1 can (14 1/2 ounces) diced tomatoes, undrained

1. Heat soybeans and enough water just to cover beans to boiling in 4-quart saucepan or Dutch oven. Boil uncovered 2 minutes; remove from heat. Cover and let stand 1 hour; drain.

2. Stir in 2 cups water. Heat to boiling; reduce heat to medium-low. Cover and cook 2 hours to 2 hours 30 minutes or until soybeans are tender (do not boil or beans will fall apart); drain.

3. Heat oil in 12-inch skillet over medium-high heat. Cook onion, bell pepper and garlic in oil 2 to 3 minutes, stirring occasionally, until vegetables are crisp-tender. Stir in broth, oregano, red pepper and bay leaves. Heat to boiling. Stir in rice; reduce heat. Cover and simmer 15 to 20 minutes or until liquid is absorbed.

4. Stir in soybeans and tomatoes. Cook, stirring occasionally, until heated through and liquid is absorbed. Remove bay leaves.

1 Serving (about 1/2 cup): Calories 150 (Calories from Fat 55); Fat 6g (Saturated 1g); Cholesterol 0mg; Sodium 210mg; Carbohydrate 17g (Dietary Fiber 3g); Protein 10g **% Daily Value:** Vitamin A 2%; Vitamin C 10%; Calcium 6%; Iron 16% **Diet Exchanges:** 1 Starch, 1 Medium-Fat Meat

Low-Fat = 3g or less, except main dishes with 6g or less   **Fast** = Ready in 30 minutes or less   ■ = Bread Machine directions   ● = Slow Cooker directions

California Black Bean Burgers (page 381)

Lighter = 1/3 fewer calories or 50% less fat

Vegetarian Basics

Both vegetarianism and including more meatless meals in our everyday diet have become more popular. By definition, vegetarians do not include beef, pork, chicken, fish or seafood in their diets. Luckily, there are many delicious foods to choose from whether you're a vegetarian or just eating more meatless meals. The variety includes legumes, grains, pasta, vegetables and fruits. If you're like many families, you may have many types of eaters pulling a chair up to the supper table, so keep on reading for more information and great recipes!

Vegetarian Health and Nutrition Benefits

What we choose to eat has direct effects on our health, depending upon our specific food choices. Choosing a vegetarian way of eating, namely diets that are low in fat and saturated fat and high in fiber, has been shown to provide health and nutrition benefits.

Strong research data supports that vegetarians are at less risk for the following disorders: obesity, constipation, lung cancer, alcoholism, high blood pressure, heart disease, Type II (adult-onset) diabetes and gallstones. Some data support a reduced risk for breast cancer, diverticular disease, colon cancer, kidney stones (calcium), osteoporosis, dental erosion and dental cavities.

Reduced risk of certain diseases indeed may be due to a combination of both lifestyle and dietary practices. Of course, there are ongoing studies to determine the true benefits for vegetarians and whether they can translate to the entire U.S. population.

Types of Vegetarians

Many people call themselves vegetarians, yet each can sit down to a meal that is extremely different. Some popular styles of vegetarianism are described below.

Ovo-Lacto Vegetarian

This is the most popular style of vegetarianism in the United States. The diet includes eggs (ovo) and dairy products (lacto), but eliminates meat, poultry, fish and seafood. This diet provides a wide variety of food choices, so eating away from home isn't usually a problem.

Do Eat: Vegetables, fruits, grains, legumes, nuts, seeds, eggs and dairy products such as milk and milk-based foods.

Do Not Eat: Meat, poultry, fish or seafood. Vast majority do not consume animal-based broths such as chicken, beef, fish or seafood

Lacto-Vegetarian

This is probably the most popular style worldwide. Many vegetarians choose it because they're cutting eggs from their diet to reduce cholesterol.

Do Eat: Vegetables, fruits, grains, legumes, nuts, seeds and dairy products such as milk and milk-based foods.

Do Not Eat: Eggs, meat, poultry, fish or seafood. Vast majority do not consume animal-based broths such as chicken, beef, fish or seafood.

Vegan Vegetarian

This is the strictest style of vegetarianism because the diet includes no animal products or by-products. It is more difficult to eat away from home when following a vegan diet.

Do Eat: Vegetables, fruits, grains, legumes, nuts and seeds.

Do Not Eat: Meat, poultry, fish, seafood, eggs, dairy products such as milk and milk-based foods or products containing animal products such as chicken, beef, fish or seafood broth, lard or gelatin. Vegans may not use animal products or animal by-products such as honey, beeswax, leather, fur, silk, wool, cosmetics or soaps.

Semi-Vegetarian

This is a term that has become very trendy although it doesn't fit the standard definition of vegetarianism. It usually refers to people who include a lot of meatless meals in their diet but who still occasionally eat fish, poultry and meat. It also includes those who eat fish and poultry but who have eliminated meat from their diet. Overall, people eating this way include more vegetables, fruits, pasta, grains and legumes in their diet, which is a more healthful lifestyle. This generally does not create problems for choosing foods when eating away from home.

Do Eat: Vegetables, fruits, grains, legumes, nuts, seeds, eggs and dairy products such as milk and milk-based foods. Many include poultry, fish and seafood but usually limit these foods to occasional use.

Do Not Eat: Usually avoid red meat.

Vegetarian Teens

Teens make up the fastest-growing segment of the U.S. population that is interested in becoming or choosing to become vegetarians. Panic is often the first reaction nonvegetarian parents have when teens make this announcement. Nutrition and meal planning are primary concerns for many parents as this may be brandnew territory!

Fear not, the majority of vegetarian diets are healthful and incorporate the principles of the U.S. Department of Agriculture (USDA) and U.S. Department of Health and Human Services (USDHHS) Food Guide Pyramid with its emphasis on eating plenty of grains, legumes, vegetables and fruit. The key to a healthful, successful vegetarian diet is variety. And with some minor alterations, only one family meal needs to be made rather than cooking separate, highly specialized meals for your vegetarian teens.

Encourage your teens to come up with ideas for their own recipe creations, and let them to shop for the ingredients and make the recipe for the family. If your teens are very strict about what they eat, they may want to help prepare their own part of the family meal. Allowing that type of initiative and creativity to shine through will make the transition to vegetarianism easier for everyone.

Nutrition Guidelines

Most teenagers' diets could use a bit of fine-tuning, and because teens are still growing, they require extra nutrients and calories. Here are some nutrition guidelines to follow to ensure a healthful vegetarian diet.

IRON

Teenage girls and women in general, even nonvegetarians, have some difficulty getting enough iron in their diets. The RDA for iron for adult women is 18 milligrams. Taking an iron supplement is the best way to get the iron you need if you are not eating any animal-source foods. The body absorbs nonanimal iron sources more easily when eaten with vitamin C, such as in an orange or orange juice.

13 BEST NONANIMAL IRON SOURCES

Food	Amount	Iron (milligrams)
Ready-to-eat cereals (fortified)	1 cup	4.5 to 8.1
Quinoa	1 cup cooked	5.3
Spinach	1 cup cooked	4.0
Black-eyed peas	1/2 cup cooked	3.8
Lentils	1/2 cup cooked	3.4
Swiss chard	1 cup cooked	3.2
Lima beans	1/2 cup cooked	2.9
Prunes	10 dried	2.4
Blackstrap molasses	1 tablespoon	2.3
Millet	1 cup cooked	2.2
Raisins	1/2 cup	1.7
Winter squash (acorn, buttercup, butternut, Hubbard)	1 cup cooked	1.4
Brewer's yeast	1 tablespoon	1.4

CALCIUM

Teenage girls and women in general, even nonvegetarians, have difficulty getting enough calcium in their diets. Before the age of 25, the RDA for calcium is 1,200 milligrams; for those over the age of 25, the RDA is 800 milligrams.

If you take a calcium supplement, follow these three guidelines to get the most out of this nutrient:

- Limit doses to 600 milligrams at one time, so the body can absorb it more easily.
- Take it with meals, to help with absorption.
- If not taking multivitamins, look for calcium tablets containing vitamin D, which helps with absorption.

15 BEST CALCIUM SOURCES

Food	Amount	Calcium (milligrams)
Milk (fat-free and low-fat)	1 cup	300
Tofu (calcium-fortified)	1/2 cup	258
Yogurt	1 cup	250
Orange juice (calcium-fortified)	1 cup	240
Ready-to-eat cereals (calcium-fortified)	1 cup	200
Mozzarella cheese (part-skim)	1 ounce	183
Canned salmon with bones	3 ounces	181
Collards	1/2 cup cooked	179
Ricotta cheese (part-skim)	1/4 cup	169
Bread (calcium-fortified)	2 slices	160
Cottage cheese (1 percent fat)	1 cup	138
Parmesan cheese	2 tablespoons grated	138
Navy beans	1 cup cooked	128
Turnips	1/2 cup cooked	125
Broccoli	1 cup cooked	94

PROTEIN

The fact is, American meat eaters are getting more protein than they need. Eliminating meat protein from your diet will decrease protein intake, but vegetarian diets usually meet or even exceed the Recommended Dietary Allowance (RDA). The recommended amounts of protein are 44 grams for girls fifteen to eighteen years old, 59 grams for boys fifteen to eighteen years old, 50 grams for adult women and 63 grams for adult men. Recent studies confirm that as long as you eat a variety of foods each day, you'll most likely eat enough protein to meet your needs. Vegetarians not eating protein from animal sources rely on protein found in combinations of legumes, grains, pastas, cereals, breads, nuts and seeds.

VITAMIN B_{12}

Vitamin B_{12} is necessary for all body cells to function properly. It occurs naturally only in animal foods but can be found in supplements. Vegans are the only vegetarians who need to supplement their diets with B_{12}. A deficiency of B_{12} can lead to anemia and nerve damage.

Vegetarian Ingredient Glossary

Meatless eating is growing in popularity—and it's growing fast! With this new interest, more new and unfamiliar ingredients are popping up in the supermarket, in articles about food and on restaurant menus. The following glossary will help you become more knowledgeable about these ingredients and foods.

Agar-Agar: A thickening agent made from sea vegetation. It is often used in place of unflavored gelatin, which is made from animal products.

Arborio Rice: Arborio is shorter, fatter and has a higher starch content than regular white rice. Hailing from Italy, this rice is the preferred ingredient in risotto, where its starch contributes to the creamy texture.

Arrowroot: This powdery starch comes from the tropical root of the same name. It is a substitute for unflavored gelatin.

Barley Malt Syrup: A sweetener made from sprouted whole barley. It has a mild caramel flavor and is not as sweet as sugar or honey.

Basmati Rice: A long-grain, finely textured, highly aromatic and nutty-flavored rice. It is often used in Indian and Middle Eastern cuisines.

Brewer's Yeast: This yeast has no leavening power and is used in making beer. It is a good source of vitamin B and is widely used as a nutritional supplement.

Brown Rice Syrup: A cultured sweetener made from brown rice, water and an enzyme. It has a light flavor that is less sweet than sugar.

Carob: Carob is the dried pulp from the pods of the tropical carob tree. It is generally sold ground and used as a substitute for baking cocoa. Carob doesn't contain caffeine.

Chipotle Chilies in Adobo Sauce: Chipotles are smoked jalapeño chilies and are sold either dried or canned in a tomato-based sauce called adobo sauce. They add a rich, smoky, complex flavor to foods.

Cilantro: Also known as Mexican or Chinese parsley or fresh coriander. This herb looks like flat-leaf parsley, but the flavor is very different: strong, fresh and tangy.

Coconut Milk: An unsweetened liquid made from a mixture of coconut flesh that has been steeped in water, then strained. Its consistency can range from thin to quite thick and creamy. Do not confuse it with cream of coconut which is quite sweet and used primarily in tropical drinks and desserts.

Cumin: The quintessential flavor in chili con carne and in many popular Tex-Mex and southwestern foods. It is also used in making curries. Cumin has a strong, warm, complex flavor.

Egg Replacer: Egg replacer is cholesterol-free and is made from starches and leavening ingredients that act similar to fresh eggs. Do not confuse it with fat-free cholesterol-free egg substitute products, which are made with egg whites.

Falafel: This Middle-Eastern specialty is a combination of ground garbanzo beans and spices. The mixture is formed into balls or patties and deep-fried, then served in pita bread with a yogurt sauce.

Kelp: Also known as kombu, it is an algae harvested from the ocean. It is available in dried sheets and powdered, a form used as a salt substitute.

Lupini Pasta: A pasta made from the ground beans of the lupin plant, which has been harvested for thousands of years. It contains more protein and fiber than wheat pasta, and because of its low starch content, it doesn't stick together during cooking.

Meat Analogs: Meat substitutes made generally from soybeans and sometimes tofu. They come in many different forms: burgers, sausages, crumbles, hot dogs, ready-made meal mixes (such as chili) and in frozen dinners.

Miso: A fermented paste made from soybeans and grain such as barley or rice. Ranging in color from yellow to red to brown, this paste is primarily used as a flavoring ingredient in place of chicken or beef granules.

Nori: Seaweed that has been dried in paper-thin sheets. Generally, it is used for wrapping sushi and rice balls.

Seitan: Wheat gluten made by combining whole-wheat flour and water. After the dough is mixed, it is repeatedly kneaded and rinsed while immersed in water to remove all of its starch. The resulting dough is then simmered in vegetable stock and used as a meat substitute. It has a chewy meatlike texture.

Soba: Also known as Japanese noodles, soba is made from buckwheat flour and is dark brown in color.

Soy Cheese: Made from tofu or soymilk, it tastes similar to cheese made with cow's milk. Although soy cheeses do contain fat, they are cholesterol-free.

Soy Milk: Made by pressing ground cooked soybeans. It is higher in protein than cow's milk. Because it's a nondairy product, it's a common substitute for those with milk allergies.

Soy Yogurt: Made from cultured soy milk and is available in many flavors. Soy yogurt is lactose-free and cholesterol-free.

Tahini: Also known as sesame seed paste, it comes from the Middle East and is made from ground sesame seed. It is the critical ingredient in hummus, a classic Middle Eastern dip of pureed garbanzo beans.

Tamari: This soybean product is very similar in flavor to soy sauce, but it is subtler and a little bit thicker.

Tempeh: Is made from fermented soybeans. It has a chewy texture and a mild flavor similar to fresh mushrooms. It is available flavored and unflavored in refrigerated and frozen forms.

Texturized Soy Protein (also known as TSP): TSP is soy flour that has been compressed until the protein fibers change in structure. It is available in a dried granular form and requires rehydration. It has a texture similar to ground beef. It can be used to replace part or all of the ground meat in some recipes. Chunk-size pieces also are available to replace stew meat.

Tofu: Also known as soybean curd or bean curd, tofu is made from soybeans. The soybeans are soaked, cooked, ground and then mixed with a curdling ingredient. The resulting curds are drained and pressed into cakes, which are tofu. It is very mildly flavored with a taste similar to a very mild cheese. Because it is so mild, it

easily absorbs the flavors of the herbs, spices and foods it is cooked with.

Tofu and Tempeh Know-How!

Tofu and tempeh are two of the many by-products of soybeans. These protein-packed foods, which are high in B vitamins and low in sodium, provide a healthful protein alternative for those who prefer a meatless diet.

Know Your Tofu

Tofu, also known as soybean curd, is made with soybeans that are soaked, cooked, ground and then mixed with a curdling ingredient. This ends up forming curds, which are drained and then pressed into a solid block. A staple in Asian diets, tofu is made fresh and sold daily in small shops. In our supermarkets, tofu commonly is sold in water-filled tubs, vacuum packs or aseptic packages. Look for tofu in the produce, dairy or deli section.

SOY

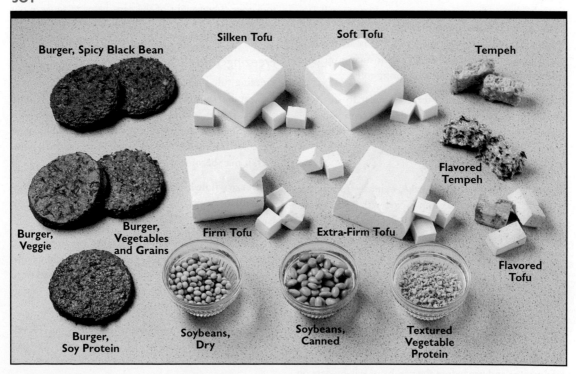

Burger, Spicy Black Bean · Silken Tofu · Soft Tofu · Tempeh · Burger, Veggie · Burger, Vegetables and Grains · Firm Tofu · Extra-Firm Tofu · Flavored Tempeh · Flavored Tofu · Burger, Soy Protein · Soybeans, Dry · Soybeans, Canned · Textured Vegetable Protein

TYPES OF TOFU

Firm or **Extra-Firm** tofu is solid, dense and a little coarse in appearance. Because it has a sturdy texture, it's great for marinating before cooking, in stir-fries, on the grill or in any dish where you want to keep the shape of the tofu. This type of tofu is the best type for freezing. Firm or extra-firm tofu is higher in protein, fat and calcium than other types of tofu.

Soft tofu can be used in recipes such as meat loaf and chili or used in cream pie fillings. Its delicate texture allows it to be used in many ways.

Silken tofu comes in soft and firm varieties and is processed in a slightly different way, giving it a creamy, perfectly smooth, custardlike appearance. It's best when used in blended or pureed dishes, in dips, as an egg substitute, in salad dressings and cheesecake. Pureed in a blender, it can be substituted in recipes for part of mayonnaise, sour cream, cream cheese and ricotta cheese ingredients.

Flavored tofu (marinated baked tofu) is packaged in a variety of flavored marinades. This type of tofu is very firm, having a chewy, meaty texture. Flavors will vary with different brands and may include Asian, Italian, sloppy joe and barbecue. Flavored tofu is an excellent choice for sautéing and stir-frying or dicing up for a filling ingredient in egg rolls or spring rolls.

Fat-Reduced tofu, with a texture similar to soft tofu, also is available for those looking to trim fat. The reduced-fat content results in a somewhat soft tofu.

All About Tempeh

Tempeh, a chunky soybean cake, is made from whole soybeans. The beans are often mixed with a grain, such as rice or millet, then fermented into a cake. The result is a tender yet chewy bean cake with a smoky, mushroom or nutty flavor. Tempeh can be crumbled and used like ground meat, marinated and grilled or added to soups, stews, casseroles and chili. Flavored tempeh also is available. Look for tempeh in the freezer case.

Storing Tofu and Tempeh

Unless tofu is aseptically packaged, keep it in the refrigerator and use before the use-by or sell-by date on the label.

Once tofu is opened, rinse the leftovers and cover with fresh water that you change every day. Keep covered in the refrigerator, and use within 1 week.

Throw out tofu that smells sour.

Keep tempeh in the freezer for up to 2 months or in the refrigerator for up to 10 days. As with other aged or fermented products, like cheese, a little mold may form on the surface. Once you remove the mold, you can eat the tempeh.

Draining Tofu

Draining the excess water in tofu helps prevent it from spattering when it's fried and lets marinades soak in more easily. The fastest way to drain it is to place the whole block or cut-up tofu on several layers of paper towels, then gently but firmly press the tofu with more paper towels to blot even more excess liquid. When you have more time, put paper towels on a cutting board and put the whole block or cut-up tofu on the towels, then cover the tofu with more paper towels and weight it with something such as canned vegetables, fruit or tomatoes. The weight of the cans helps to squeeze out excess liquid.

Freezing Tofu

Freezing tofu makes it more chewy and "meaty" in texture, and it will absorb flavors more easily. Because thawed frozen tofu is sturdier in texture, it's great for recipes that are marinated or grilled. Freezing changes the color from white to beige, yellow or caramel; however, it may become white again as it thaws.

To freeze whole blocks: Drain tofu, and wrap it tightly in plastic wrap or place in resealable plastic freezer bag. Freeze up to 5 months.

To freeze pieces: Drain tofu, and cut into slices, chunks or cubes. Arrange pieces—not touching—on cookie sheet, and freeze until hard. Remove pieces from cookie sheet, and pop into a resealable plastic freezer bag. Freeze up to 5 months.

To thaw: Thaw in refrigerator. Press or squeeze out excess liquid before using.

Tofu and Tempeh Ideas

- Add cubes of firm tofu or tempeh to soups, stews and chilies.
- Substitute the "egg" in egg salad sandwiches with firm tofu.
- Crumble soft tofu into meat loaf or casseroles. Prepare recipe as directed.
- Use silken tofu for some of the mayonnaise, sour cream or cream cheese in recipes.
- Marinate cubes of firm or extra-firm tofu or tempeh in teriyaki sauce, Italian dressing or barbecue sauce. Thread on skewers and grill.
- Use soft or silken tofu in milk or fruit shakes.
- Substitute soft tofu for ricotta cheese or cottage cheese in lasagna.
- Grill or panfry sliced tofu or tempeh and eat as is or use instead of a burger for sandwiches, adding your favorite toppings.

VEGETARIAN SUBSTITUTIONS

If you want to replace meat or an animal by-product with a vegetarian ingredient, the list below will be helpful.

For	Substitute
Meat, poultry, fish or seafood	Cheese, eggs, legumes, mushrooms, nut butters (almond, cashew, peanut, sesame), nuts, seeds, seitan, tempeh, texturized soy protein, tofu
Meat, poultry, fish or seafood broth	Miso, fruit juices, vegetable juices, vegetable broth, wine
Gelatin	Agar-agar, arrowroot, ground nuts, ground peanuts, ground seeds
Cheese	Soy cheeses
Eggs	Tofu
Milk	Soy milk, nut milk, rice milk

HAMBURGER SUBSTITUTES

Many great-tasting vegetarian patties are available to replace the familiar hamburger. Eat them as a meal all by themselves or tucked into a bun with all the burger toppings you love. Most vegetarian burgers work well on the grill if they are marinated first or brushed with a little vegetable oil to help prevent sticking. Vegetarian products that don't grill well are the low-fat or fat-free products because either they become rubbery or they crumble.

Legume Burgers: These burgers can be a combination of beans, lentils, vegetables, grains and tofu. Build a terrific burger by starting with California Black Bean Burgers, page 381, or Italian Bean Cakes, page 380. Look for plain or flavored legume burgers in the freezer section of the supermarket. Just follow the package directions to heat and eat.

Vegetable Burgers: Some patties are a combination of chopped vegetables with no added cheese, legumes, grains or tofu. Some combinations might be mushroom, carrot, ripe olive, onion and bell pepper. They are found in the freezer section of most supermarkets.

Cooked portabella mushrooms and thick eggplant slices also make tasty "patties" on whole-grain buns or bread. Jazz them up by topping with pesto, cheese or fresh vegetables.

Meat Analog Burgers: Meat analog patties are nonmeat and often made from soy protein or tofu. Other ingredients include vegetables or grains. Some have beef, chicken, pork or fish flavors added, so they taste more like meat. You can find them in the freezer section of most supermarkets. Natural-foods stores and food cooperatives usually carry a wide variety of these patties.

Chunky Vegetable Lasagna

Chunky Vegetable Lasagna

Prep: 35 min; Bake: 40 min; Stand: 10 min ✱ *8 servings*

12 uncooked lasagna noodles (about 12 ounces)
3 cups frozen broccoli flowerets, thawed
3 large carrots, coarsely shredded (2 cups)
1 can (14 1/2 ounces) diced tomatoes, drained
1 medium red bell pepper, cut into thin strips
1 medium green bell pepper, cut into thin strips
3/4 cup Pesto (page 438) or prepared pesto
1/4 teaspoon salt
1 container (15 ounces) ricotta cheese
1/2 cup grated Parmesan cheese
1/4 cup chopped fresh parsley
1 large egg
3 tablespoons butter or stick margarine
1 clove garlic, finely chopped
3 tablespoons all-purpose flour
2 cups milk
3 cups shredded mozzarella cheese (12 ounces)

1. Cook and drain noodles as directed on package.

2. Mix broccoli, carrots, tomatoes, bell peppers, Pesto and salt. Mix ricotta cheese, Parmesan cheese, parsley and egg.

3. Melt butter in 2-quart saucepan over medium heat. Cook garlic in butter about 2 minutes, stirring frequently, until garlic is golden. Stir in flour. Cook over medium heat, stirring constantly, until mixture is smooth and bubbly; remove from heat. Stir in milk. Heat to boiling, stirring constantly. Boil and stir 1 minute.

4. Heat oven to 350°.

5. Place 3 noodles in ungreased rectangular pan, 13 × 9 × 2 inches. Spread half of the cheese mixture over noodles. Top with 3 noodles; spread with half of the vegetable mixture. Sprinkle with 1 cup of the mozzarella cheese. Top with 3 noodles; spread with remaining cheese mixture. Top with 3 noodles; spread with remaining vegetable mixture. Pour sauce evenly over top. Sprinkle with remaining 2 cups mozzarella cheese.

Teriyaki Noodles

6. Bake uncovered 35 to 40 minutes or until hot in center. Let stand 10 minutes before cutting.

1 Serving: Calories 540 (Calories from Fat 270); Fat 30g (Saturated 13g); Cholesterol 80mg; Sodium 740mg; Carbohydrate 45g (Dietary Fiber 6g); Protein 28g **% Daily Value:** Vitamin A 86%; Vitamin C 68%; Calcium 64%; Iron 18% **Diet Exchanges:** 2 Starch, 2 High-Fat Meat, 3 Vegetable, 2 Fat

Teriyaki Noodles *Fast*

Prep: 20 min: Cook: 9 min ✱ *4 servings*

1 cup hot water

6 dried Chinese black or shiitake mushrooms (1/2 ounce)

8 ounces uncooked soba (buckwheat) noodles or whole wheat spaghetti

1 tablespoon vegetable oil

1 large onion, sliced

1 package (8 ounces) sliced mushrooms (3 cups)

8 ounces fresh shiitake, crimini or baby portabella mushrooms, sliced

1/3 cup teriyaki sauce

1/4 cup chopped fresh cilantro

1. Pour water over dried mushrooms in small bowl. Let stand about 20 minutes or until soft; drain. Rinse with warm water; drain. Squeeze out excess moisture from mushrooms. Remove and discard stems; cut caps into 1/2-inch strips.

2. Cook and drain noodles as directed on package.

3. Heat oil in 12-inch skillet or wok over medium-high heat. Add onion; stir-fry 3 minutes. Add all mushrooms; stir-fry 3 minutes. Stir in teriyaki sauce; reduce heat. Partially cover and simmer about 2 minutes or until vegetables are tender. Stir in noodles, cilantro and, if desired, 1 tablespoon toasted sesame seed.

1 Serving (about 2 cups): Calories 285 (Calories from Fat 55); Fat 6g (Saturated 1g); Cholesterol 0mg; Sodium 930mg; Carbohydrate 52g (Dietary Fiber 7g); Protein 13g **% Daily Value:** Vitamin A 0%; Vitamin C 4%; Calcium 4%; Iron 20% **Diet Exchanges:** 3 Starch, 1 Vegetable, 1/2 Fat

TOFU TERIYAKI MUSHROOM NOODLES: Cut a 1-pound block of firm tofu into 1/4-inch pieces and add with the mushrooms in step 2.

Spaghetti and Spicy Rice Balls

Spaghetti and Spicy Rice Balls *Fast*

Prep: 12 min; Cook: 15 min ✱ *6 servings*

Rice and oats replace ground beef in these "meatballs." The balls are rolled in a small amount of wheat germ to give them a golden-brown color and just a bit of crunch. Because wheat germ contains oil, it can turn rancid, so it is best to store it in the refrigerator.

1 package (16 ounces) uncooked spaghetti
2 cups cooked white rice
1/2 cup quick-cooking oats (do not use instant oatmeal)
1 medium onion, chopped (1/2 cup)
1/4 cup dry bread crumbs
1/4 cup milk
1 tablespoon chopped fresh or 1 teaspoon dried basil leaves
2 teaspoons chopped fresh or 1/2 teaspoon dried oregano leaves
1/4 teaspoon ground red pepper (cayenne)

1 large egg, beaten
1/2 cup wheat germ
1 tablespoon vegetable oil
2 cups spaghetti sauce
Finely shredded Parmesan cheese, if desired

1. Cook spaghetti as directed on package.

2. While spaghetti is cooking, mix rice, oats, onion, bread crumbs, milk, basil, oregano, red pepper and egg. Shape mixture into 12 balls. Roll balls in wheat germ.

3. Heat oil in 10-inch skillet over medium heat. Cook balls in oil about 10 minutes, turning occasionally, until light golden brown.

4. Drain spaghetti. Heat spaghetti sauce until hot. Serve sauce and rice balls over spaghetti. Sprinkle with cheese.

1 Serving: Calories 565 (Calories from Fat 90); Fat 10g (Saturated 2g); Cholesterol 35mg; Sodium 470mg; Carbohydrate 107g (Dietary Fiber 7g); Protein 19g **% Daily Value:** Vitamin A 8%; Vitamin C 12%; Calcium 8%; Iron 32% **Diet Exchanges:** 6 Starch, 3 Vegetable

Rice Noodles with Peanut Sauce *Fast*

Prep: 15 min ✳ *4 servings*

Rice stick noodles are white and translucent and have a very delicate flavor and texture, making them perfect for soaking up whatever flavors they're mixed with. Look for them in the ethnic-foods section of the supermarket.

8 ounces rice stick noodles
1/2 cup creamy peanut butter
2 tablespoons soy sauce
1 teaspoon grated gingerroot
1/2 teaspoon crushed red pepper
1/2 cup vegetable or chicken broth
4 ounces bean sprouts
1 small red bell pepper, cut into 1/4-inch strips
2 medium green onions, sliced (2 tablespoons)
2 tablespoons chopped fresh cilantro, if desired

1. Heat 2 quarts water to boiling in 3-quart saucepan. Break noodles in half and pull apart slightly; drop into boiling water. Cook uncovered 1 minute; drain. Rinse with cold water; drain.

2. Beat peanut butter, soy sauce, gingerroot and crushed red pepper in small bowl, using wire whisk, until smooth. Gradually beat in broth.

3. Place noodles in large bowl. Add peanut butter mixture, bean sprouts, bell pepper and onions; toss. Sprinkle with cilantro.

1 Serving (1 cup): Calories 375 (Calories from Fat 160); Fat 18g (Saturated 4g); Cholesterol 0mg; Sodium 740mg; Carbohydrate 42g (Dietary Fiber 3g); Protein 14g **% Daily Value:** Vitamin A 14%; Vitamin C 34%; Calcium 4%; Iron 14% **Diet Exchanges:** 2 Starch, 1/2 High-Fat Meat, 2 Vegetable, 2 Fat

Easy Vegetable Chow Mein *Fast*

Prep: 5 min; Cook: 10 min ✳ *4 servings*

1 cup vegetable or chicken broth
2 tablespoons cornstarch
2 tablespoons oyster sauce*
1/4 teaspoon red pepper sauce
2 tablespoons vegetable oil
2 cloves garlic, finely chopped
1 bag (16 ounces) frozen snap peas, carrots, onions and mushrooms
2 1/2 cups coleslaw mix
4 cups chow mein noodles

1. Mix broth, cornstarch, oyster sauce and pepper sauce; set aside.

2. Heat oil in 12-inch nonstick skillet over medium-high heat. Cook garlic and frozen vegetables in oil about 5 minutes, stirring frequently, until vegetables are crisp-tender.

3. Stir in coleslaw mix and broth mixture. Cook, stirring constantly, until thickened. Serve over noodles.

*1 tablespoon soy sauce can be substituted for the oyster sauce.

1 Serving (about 1 1/2 cups): Calories 365 (Calories from Fat 190); Fat 21g (Saturated 3g); Cholesterol 0mg; Sodium 570mg; Carbohydrate 43g (Dietary Fiber 6g); Protein 7g **% Daily Value:** Vitamin A 74%; Vitamin C 28%; Calcium 6%; Iron 20% **Diet Exchanges:** 2 Starch, 3 Vegetable, 3 Fat

---

VEGETARIAN MUNCHIES TO HAVE ON HAND

- Assorted raw vegetables
- Cheese and whole-grain crackers
- Chips and salsa
- Dips and spreads
- Dried fruit
- Fresh fruit
- Fruit-filled breakfast bars
- Popcorn
- Popcorn or rice cakes
- Pretzels
- Yogurt
- Hummus

Roasted Vegetable Stew

Prep: 15 min; Roast: 15 min; Cook: 20 min ✻ *6 servings*

Loading up a soup or stew with vegetables and pasta makes it a very substantial meatless meal. Easy Garlic-Cheese Biscuits (page 56) and Mandarin Salad (page 412) would be perfect to add to this meal.

5 small red potatoes (3/4 pound), cut into fourths
1 large onion, cut into fourths
1 medium red bell pepper, cut into fourths and seeded
1 medium green bell pepper, cut into fourths and seeded
1 medium carrot, cut into 1/4-inch diagonal slices
1 small zucchini, cut into 1/2-inch slices
1/4 pound medium whole mushrooms
2 cloves garlic, finely chopped
2 tablespoons olive or vegetable oil
1 can (14 1/2 ounces) ready-to-serve vegetable or chicken broth
2 cans (14 1/2 ounces each) Italian-style stewed tomatoes, undrained
1 1/4 cups uncooked rotini pasta (4 ounces)
2 tablespoons chopped fresh parsley
Freshly ground pepper, if desired

1. Set oven control to broil. Toss potatoes, onion, bell peppers, carrot, zucchini, mushrooms, garlic and oil. Spread vegetable mixture, skin sides up, in ungreased jelly roll pan, 15 1/2 × 10 1/2 × 1 inch.

2. Broil with tops 4 to 6 inches from heat 10 to 15 minutes or until roasted. Remove vegetables as they become soft; cool. Remove skins from peppers. Coarsely chop potatoes, onion and peppers.

3. Mix vegetables, broth, tomatoes and pasta in 4-quart Dutch oven. Heat to boiling; reduce heat. Cover and simmer about 15 minutes, stirring occasionally, until pasta is tender. Sprinkle with parsley and pepper.

1 Serving (about 1 1/2 cups): Calories 285 (Calories from Fat 55); Fat 6g (Saturated 1g); Cholesterol 0mg; Sodium 700mg; Carbohydrate 55g (Dietary Fiber 6g); Protein 9g **% Daily Value:** Vitamin A 34%; Vitamin C 72%; Calcium 6%; Iron 18% **Diet Exchanges:** 2 Starch, 5 Vegetable

Eggplant Parmigiana

Prep: 1 hr 5 min; Cook: 10 min; Bake: 25 min ✻ *6 servings*

2 cups Italian Tomato Sauce (page 436) or spaghetti sauce
2 small unpeeled eggplants (about 1 pound each)
1 large egg
2 tablespoons water
2/3 cup dry bread crumbs
1/3 cup grated Parmesan cheese
1/4 cup olive or vegetable oil
2 cups shredded mozzarella cheese (8 ounces)

1. Make Italian Tomato Sauce.

2. Heat oven to 350°.

3. Cut eggplants into 1/4-inch slices. Mix egg and water. Mix bread crumbs and Parmesan cheese. Dip eggplant into egg mixture, then coat with bread crumb mixture.

4. Heat oil in 12-inch skillet over medium heat. Cook half of the eggplant at a time in oil about 5 minutes, turning once, until light brown; drain. Repeat with remaining eggplant, adding 1 or 2 tablespoons oil if necessary.

5. Place half of the eggplant in ungreased rectangular baking dish, 11 × 7 × 1 1/2 inches, overlapping slices slightly. Spoon half of the sauce over eggplant. Sprinkle with 1 cup of the mozzarella cheese. Repeat with remaining eggplant, sauce and cheese.

6. Bake uncovered about 25 minutes or until sauce is bubbly and cheese is light brown.

1 Serving: Calories 350 (Calories from Fat 200); Fat 22g (Saturated 7g); Cholesterol 60mg; Sodium 690mg; Carbohydrate 26g (Dietary Fiber 5g); Protein 17g **% Daily Value:** Vitamin A 14%; Vitamin C 18%; Calcium 38%; Iron 12% **Diet Exchanges:** 1 High-Fat Meat, 5 Vegetable, 3 Fat

Cheese Enchiladas

Prep: 15 min; Cook: 8 min; Bake: 20 min ✱ *4 servings*

2 cups shredded Monterey Jack cheese (8 ounces)
1 cup shredded Cheddar cheese (4 ounces)
1/2 cup sour cream
2 tablespoons chopped fresh parsley
1/4 teaspoon pepper
1 medium onion, chopped (1/2 cup)
1 small green bell pepper, chopped (1/2 cup)
2/3 cup water
1 tablespoon chili powder
1 1/2 teaspoons chopped fresh or 1/2 teaspoon dried
    oregano leaves
1/4 teaspoon ground cumin
2 whole green chilies, seeded and chopped, if desired
1 clove garlic, finely chopped
1 can (15 ounces) tomato sauce
8 corn tortillas (5 or 6 inches in diameter)

1. Heat oven to 350°.

2. Mix cheeses, sour cream, parsley, pepper and onion; set aside.

3. Heat remaining ingredients except tortillas to boiling in 2-quart saucepan, stirring occasionally; reduce heat. Simmer uncovered 5 minutes. Pour into ungreased pie plate, 9 × 1 1/4 inches.

4. Dip each tortilla into sauce to coat both sides. Spoon about 1/4 cup cheese mixture onto each tortilla; roll tortilla around filling. Place seam side down in ungreased rectangular baking dish, 11 × 7 × 1 1/2 inches. Pour remaining sauce over enchiladas.

5. Bake uncovered about 20 minutes or until bubbly. Garnish with additional shredded cheese, sour cream and chopped onion if desired.

1 Serving: Calories 550 (Calories from Fat 305); Fat 34g (Saturated 20g); Cholesterol 100mg; Sodium 1,290mg; Carbohydrate 40g (Dietary Fiber 6g); Protein 27g **% Daily Value:** Vitamin A 70%; Vitamin C 62%; Calcium 70%; Iron 16% **Diet Exchanges:** 2 Starch, 2 High-Fat Meat, 2 Vegetable, 3 Fat

Lighter Cheese Enchiladas: For 16 grams of fat and 430 calories per serving, use reduced-fat cheeses and sour cream.

Cheesy Polenta Bake

Prep: 5 min; Cook: 20 min; Bake: 20 min ✱ *6 servings*

1 cup yellow cornmeal
3/4 cup water
3 1/4 cups boiling water
1 1/2 teaspoons salt
1 teaspoon butter or stick margarine
2/3 cup grated Parmesan cheese
1/3 cup shredded Swiss cheese

1. Heat oven to 350°. Grease 1 1/2-quart casserole.

2. Mix cornmeal and 3/4 cup water in 2-quart saucepan. Stir in 3 1/4 cups boiling water and the salt. Cook, stirring constantly, until mixture thickens and boils; reduce heat.

3. Cover and simmer about 10 minutes, stirring occasionally, until very thick; remove from heat. Stir until smooth.

4. Spread one-third of the polenta in casserole; dot with butter. Sprinkle with 1/3 cup of the Parmesan cheese. Spread with another third of polenta; sprinkle with remaining 1/3 cup Parmesan cheese. Spread with remaining third of polenta; sprinkle with Swiss cheese. Bake uncovered 15 to 20 minutes or until hot and bubbly.

1 Serving (about 3/4 cup): Calories 135 (Calories from Fat 45); Fat 5g (Saturated 3g); Cholesterol 15mg; Sodium 780mg; Carbohydrate 18g (Dietary Fiber 2g); Protein 7g **% Daily Value:** Vitamin A 2%; Vitamin C 0%; Calcium 18%; Iron 6% **Diet Exchanges:** 1 Starch, 1/2 High-Fat Meat

Brown Rice and Lentils

Prep: 15 min; Cook: 55 min ✳ *4 servings*

2 tablespoons butter or stick margarine
1 small onion, chopped (1/4 cup)
1 clove garlic, finely chopped
1/2 cup dried lentils (4 ounces), sorted and rinsed
1/2 cup uncooked brown rice
1 can (14 1/2 ounces) ready-to-serve vegetable or
    chicken broth
1/4 cup water
1/4 teaspoon red pepper sauce
1 medium green bell pepper, coarsely chopped (1 cup)
1/2 cup shredded mozzarella cheese (2 ounces)

1. Melt butter in 2-quart saucepan over medium heat. Cook onion and garlic in butter about 3 minutes, stirring occasionally, until onion is tender.

2. Stir in lentils, rice, broth, water and pepper sauce. Heat to boiling; reduce heat. Cover and simmer about 50 minutes, adding water if necessary, until rice is tender and liquid is absorbed.

3. Stir in bell pepper; sprinkle with cheese.

1 Serving (about 1 cup): Calories 260 (Calories from Fat 90); Fat 10g (Saturated 5g); Cholesterol 25mg; Sodium 470mg; Carbohydrate 36g (Dietary Fiber 7g); Protein 14g **% Daily Value:** Vitamin A 8%; Vitamin C 24%; Calcium 14%; Iron 16% **Diet Exchanges:** 2 Starch, 1 Medium-Fat Meat, 1 Vegetable

Three-Alarm Spaghetti and Pinto Bean Chili

Prep: 10 min; Cook: 25 min ✳ *4 servings*

This chili recipe is based on the well-known Cincinnati-Style Chili (page 466), which is traditionally served over spaghetti. We've cooked the spaghetti right along with this spicy chili.

1 tablespoon vegetable oil
1 large onion, chopped (1 cup)
1 medium green bell pepper, chopped (1 cup)
3 cups water
1/2 cup taco sauce
2 teaspoons chili powder
1/2 teaspoon salt
1/4 teaspoon ground cinnamon
2 cans (10 ounces each) diced tomatoes and green
    chilies, undrained
4 ounces uncooked spaghetti, broken into thirds
    (1 1/2 cups)
1 can (15 to 16 ounces) pinto beans, rinsed and drained
Sour cream, if desired
Jalapeño chilies, if desired

1. Heat oil in 4-quart Dutch oven over medium-high heat. Cook onion and bell pepper in oil 3 to 5 minutes, stirring occasionally, until crisp-tender.

2. Stir in water, taco sauce, chili powder, salt, cinnamon and tomatoes. Heat to boiling; reduce heat to medium-low. Simmer uncovered 5 minutes, stirring occasionally.

3. Stir in spaghetti and beans. Heat to boiling; reduce heat to medium. Cook uncovered 8 to 10 minutes, stirring occasionally, until spaghetti is tender. Garnish each serving with sour cream and jalapeño chilies.

1 Serving (about 1 1/4 cups): Calories 315 (Calories from Fat 45); Fat 5g (Saturated 1g); Cholesterol 0mg; Sodium 940mg; Carbohydrate 67g (Dietary Fiber 15g); Protein 15g **% Daily Value:** Vitamin A 10%; Vitamin C 44%; Calcium 12%; Iron 28% **Diet Exchanges:** 4 Starch, 1 Vegetable

Meatless Meatball Pizza

Meatless Meatball Pizza *Fast*

Prep: 12 min; Bake: 20 min ✳ 6 servings

Do you have meat-lovers and vegetarians to please? You won't miss the sausage when you make "mini-meatballs" using Italian-flavored frozen vegetable burgers. This tastes just like Italian sausage pizza!

1 package (16 ounces) ready-to-serve pizza crust
   (12 to 14 inches in diameter)
2 frozen Italian-style vegetable burgers, thawed
1 can (8 ounces) pizza sauce
2 tablespoons sliced ripe olives
1 cup shredded mozzarella cheese (4 ounces)
1 cup shredded provolone cheese (4 ounces)

1. Heat oven to 425°.

2. Place pizza crust on ungreased cookie sheet. Shape burgers into 1/2-inch balls. Spread pizza sauce over crust. Top with burger balls and olives. Sprinkle with cheeses.

3. Bake 18 to 20 minutes or until cheese is melted and light golden brown.

1 Serving: Calories 425 (Calories from Fat 135); Fat 15g (Saturated 6g); Cholesterol 25mg; Sodium 990mg; Carbohydrate 55g (Dietary Fiber 3g); Protein 21g **% Daily Value:** Vitamin A 10%; Vitamin C 6%; Calcium 30%; Iron 22% **Diet Exchanges:** 3 Starch, 1 High-Fat Meat, 2 Vegetable, 1 Fat

MUSHROOM MEATLESS MEATBALL PIZZA: Arrange 1 jar (6 ounces) sliced mushrooms, drained, with burger balls and olives in step 2.

Italian Bean Cakes *Fast*

Prep: 10 min; Cook: 10 min ✳ 6 servings

Bean patties are more delicate than ground beef patties, so use a gentle touch when turning them over with a spatula. These bean patties make great California burgers. Serve on hamburger buns topped with slices of crunchy raw onion, creamy avocado, crispy lettuce, juicy tomato slices and mayonnaise.

2 cans (15 to 16 ounces each) great northern or can-
    nellini beans, rinsed and drained
1/2 cup Italian-style dry bread crumbs
1/4 cup chopped fresh or 1 teaspoon dried basil leaves
3/4 teaspoon garlic salt
1 large egg, beaten
2 tablespoons olive or vegetable oil
Spaghetti sauce, heated, if desired

1. Mash beans in large bowl. Stir in remaining ingredients except oil and spaghetti sauce. Shape mixture into 6 patties, each about 1/2 inch thick.

2. Heat oil in 12-inch nonstick skillet over medium heat. Cook patties in oil 8 to 10 minutes, turning once, until golden brown.

3. Serve patties with spaghetti sauce.

1 Serving: Calories 250 (Calories from Fat 55); Fat 6g (Saturated 1g); Cholesterol 35mg; Sodium 210mg; Carbohydrate 42g (Dietary Fiber 9g); Protein 16g **% Daily Value:** Vitamin A 2%; Vitamin C 0%; Calcium 16%; Iron 32% **Diet Exchanges:** 2 Starch, 1 Very Lean Meat, 2 Vegetable

---

THE NEIGHBORHOOD CO-OP STORE

Whether you call them cooperatives, natural-foods stores or whole-foods stores, one thing is for certain: these stores are fun, interesting and informative! If your vision of a co-op is a throwback to the 1960s, disorganized and a little too laid-back, you should revisit one.

These types of food stores are a great boon to a variety of people with a variety of needs. Not only do the stores serve the vegetarian community, but they also cater to people with special diets, allergies, health problems, environmental concerns, a preference for organic foods, the desire to buy in bulk and the need to buy foods that can be purchased in very small quantities. Memberships

are offered at many stores, giving you a discount on your purchases, but you do not need to be a member to shop at these stores.

Just take a look at a sampling of what your friendly neighborhood co-op is likely to offer:

- Full line of groceries, including produce, canned goods, refrigerated foods, frozen foods, delis, toiletries and household cleaning products. Vegetarian pet foods and cosmetics not tested on animals or containing all natural ingredients can be found, too!

- Bulk grains, pastas, flours, beans, legumes, dried fruits, herbs, spices, teas, oils, syrups and many other ingredients.

- Specialty foods to meet many dietary needs, including vegetarianism and allergies (egg-free, wheat-free, gluten-free, yeast-free, lactose-free, salt-free and sugar-free, to name some).

- Nutritional supplements, natural remedies, wellness and medicinal remedies and ingredients, homeopathic products and pharmaceutical products.

- Natural and environmentally friendly household cleaning and lawn-care products.

- Information pamphlets, magazines, newsletters and classes that address food, ingredients, health, environment, gardening and a wide variety of other subjects.

California Black Bean Burgers *Fast*

Prep: 15 min; Cook: 10 min ✻ 6 sandwiches

Coating the patties with cornmeal gives them a delicious crispy coating.

1 can (15 ounces) black beans, undrained
1 can (4 ounces) chopped green chilies, undrained
1 cup plain dry bread crumbs
1 teaspoon chili powder
1 large egg, beaten
1/4 cup yellow cornmeal
2 tablespoons vegetable oil
6 hamburger buns, toasted
1 tablespoon mayonnaise or salad dressing
1 1/4 cups shredded lettuce
3 tablespoons thick-and-chunky salsa

1. Place beans in food processor or blender. Cover and process until slightly mashed; remove from food processor. Mix beans, chilies, bread crumbs, chili powder and egg. Shape mixture into 6 patties, each about 1/2 inch thick. Coat each patty with cornmeal.

2. Heat oil in 10-inch skillet over medium heat. Cook patties in oil 5 to 10 minutes, turning once, until crisp and thoroughly cooked on both sides.

3. Spread bottom halves of buns with mayonnaise. Top with lettuce, patties, salsa and tops of buns.

1 Sandwich: Calories 360 (Calories from Fat 90); Fat 10g (Saturated 0g); Cholesterol 35mg; Sodium 750mg; Carbohydrate 60g (Dietary Fiber 7g); Protein 14g **% Daily Value:** Vitamin A 4%; Vitamin C 12%; Calcium 16%; Iron 26% **Diet Exchanges:** 3 Starch, 3 Vegetable, 1 Fat

Italian Grinders *Fast*

Prep: 12 min; Cook: 10 min ✻ 4 sandwiches

Can't resist the aroma and flavor of a meatball sandwich slathered in spaghetti sauce and adorned with peppers and onions? The solution is at hand. Frozen vegetable burgers mixed with just a few ingredients create memorable meatless "meatballs."

4 frozen vegetable burgers, thawed and crumbled
3 tablespoons grated Parmesan cheese
1 teaspoon Italian seasoning
4 teaspoons olive or vegetable oil
1 small onion, cut in half and sliced
1 small red bell pepper, cut into 1/4-inch strips
1 small green bell pepper, cut into 1/4-inch strips
1/2 cup spaghetti sauce
4 hot dog buns, split

1. Mix burgers, cheese and Italian seasoning. Shape mixture into 16 balls.

2. Heat 2 teaspoons of the oil in 10-inch nonstick skillet over medium heat. Cook burger balls in oil, turning frequently, until brown. Remove from skillet; keep warm.

3. Heat remaining 2 teaspoons oil in same skillet over medium heat. Cook onion and bell peppers in oil, stirring frequently, until crisp-tender. Heat spaghetti sauce until hot.

4. Place 4 burger balls in each bun. Top with vegetable mixture. Serve with spaghetti sauce.

1 Sandwich: Calories 315 (Calories from Fat 115); Fat 13g (Saturated 3g); Cholesterol 5mg; Sodium 960mg; Carbohydrate 35g (Dietary Fiber 3g); Protein 17g **% Daily Value:** Vitamin A 14%; Vitamin C 48%; Calcium 14%; Iron 16% **Diet Exchanges:** 2 Starch, 1 Medium-Fat Meat, 1 Vegetable, 1 Fat

Tofu and Sweet Potato Jambalaya

Prep: 20 min; Cook: 35 min ✱ *4 servings*

1 package (14 ounces) firm tofu
1 tablespoon olive or vegetable oil
1 large sweet potato, peeled and cut into 1/2-inch
    cubes (2 cups)
2 cloves garlic, finely chopped
1 can (14 1/2 ounces) ready-to-serve vegetable or
    chicken broth
3/4 cup uncooked regular long-grain rice
2 tablespoons Worcestershire sauce
1/4 teaspoon ground red pepper (cayenne)
1 can (15 ounces) black beans, rinsed and drained
12 medium green onions, sliced (3/4 cup)

1. Drain tofu; cut into 3/4-inch cubes. Carefully press cubes between paper towels to remove as much water as possible.

2. Heat oil in 12-inch skillet over medium heat. Cook tofu in oil 6 to 8 minutes, turning frequently, until light golden brown. Remove tofu from skillet; set aside.

3. Add sweet potato and garlic to skillet. Cook 2 to 3 minutes, stirring occasionally, just until sweet potato begins to brown. Stir in broth, rice, Worcestershire sauce and red pepper. Heat to boiling; reduce heat. Cover and simmer 10 minutes.

4. Stir in beans. Cover and cook 8 to 10 minutes, stirring occasionally, until rice is tender and liquid is absorbed. Stir in tofu and onions. Cook 1 to 2 minutes or until heated through.

1 Serving (about 1 1/2 cups): Calories 390 (Calories from Fat 65); Fat 7g (Saturated 1g); Cholesterol 0mg; Sodium 940mg; Carbohydrate 74g (Dietary Fiber 10g); Protein 18g **% Daily Value:** Vitamin A 100%; Vitamin C 14%; Calcium 18%; Iron 44% **Diet Exchanges:** 4 Starch, 3 Vegetable

Niçoise Tofu Skillet Supper

Prep: 15 min; Cook: 27 min ✱ *4 servings*

2 tablespoons olive or vegetable oil
1/2 cup coarsely chopped red onion
4 or 5 small red potatoes, sliced (2 cups)
1 cup frozen cut green beans
1/2 teaspoon Italian seasoning
1/2 teaspoon garlic salt
1/2 package (14-ounce size) firm tofu, cut into 1/2-inch
    cubes
2 roma (plum) tomatoes, thinly sliced
1 Hard-Cooked Egg (page 201), chopped

1. Heat oil in 12-inch skillet over medium-high heat. Cook onion in oil 2 minutes, stirring frequently. Stir in potatoes; reduce heat to medium-low. Cover and cook 10 to 12 minutes, stirring occasionally, until potatoes are tender.

2. Stir in green beans, Italian seasoning and garlic salt. Cover and cook 6 to 8 minutes, stirring occasionally, until beans are tender and potatoes are light golden brown.

3. Stir in tofu and tomatoes. Cook 3 to 5 minutes, stirring occasionally and gently, just until hot. Sprinkle each serving with egg.

1 Serving: Calories 245 (Calories from Fat 100); Fat 11g (Saturated 2g); Cholesterol 55mg; Sodium 160mg; Carbohydrate 29g (Dietary Fiber 5g); Protein 12g **% Daily Value:** Vitamin A 4%; Vitamin C 14%; Calcium 14%; Iron 40% **Diet Exchanges:** 1 Starch, 1/2 Medium-Fat Meat, 3 Vegetable, 1 Fat

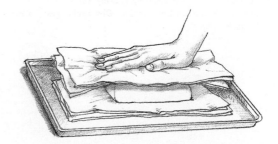

Place several layers of paper towels on cookie sheet. Place whole block or cut-up tofu on paper towels. Place several more layers of paper towels on tofu; gently but firmly press the tofu to blot excess liquid.

Tempeh Stir-Fry with Yogurt Peanut Sauce

Tempeh Stir-Fry with Yogurt Peanut Sauce

Prep: 20 min: Cook: 20 min ✳ 4 servings

Tempeh (TEHM-pay), also spelled "tempe," is fermented, high-protein soybean cake with a chewy texture and slightly nutty flavor.

1/4 cup creamy peanut butter

1/4 cup vanilla yogurt

3.tablespoons teriyaki marinade

1 tablespoon honey

2 tablespoons vegetable oil

1 package (8 ounces) tempeh, cut into 2 × 1/4 × 1/4-inch strips

1 medium onion, cut into thin wedges

3 medium carrots, cut into 2 × 1/4 × 1/4-inch strips (1 1/2 cups)

8 ounces green beans, cut in half (1 1/2 cups)

1/4 cup water

1 medium red bell pepper, cut into thin strips

1/4 cup chopped fresh cilantro

1. Beat peanut butter, yogurt, teriyaki marinade and honey, using wire whisk, until smooth; set aside.

2. Heat 1 tablespoon of the oil in 12-inch skillet over medium heat. Cook tempeh in oil 5 to 6 minutes, turning frequently, until light golden brown. Remove tempeh from skillet; set aside.

3. Add remaining 1 tablespoon oil and the onion to skillet. Cook 1 minute, stirring occasionally. Stir in carrots, green beans and water. Cover and cook 5 minutes. Stir in bell pepper. Cook 2 to 3 minutes, stirring occasionally, until vegetables are crisp-tender.

4. Stir in tempeh and peanut butter mixture until well mixed. Cook 1 to 2 minutes, stirring occasionally, until heated through. Sprinkle with cilantro.

1 Serving (about 1 1/4 cups): Calories 350 (Calories from Fat 180); Fat 20g (Saturated 3g); Cholesterol 0mg; Sodium 630mg; Carbohydrate 34g (Dietary Fiber 10g); Protein 18g **% Daily Value:** Vitamin A 78%; Vitamin C 28%; Calcium 12%; Iron 14% **Diet Exchanges:** 2 Starch, 1 High-Fat Meat, 1 Vegetable, 1 1/2 Fat

THE VEGETARIAN PANTRY

Going vegetarian or meatless? Now is the time to consider what to stock in your pantry, refrigerator and freezer to make meal preparation easier. This list is just a beginning; we're sure you will add your own favorites to it, as well.

On the Shelf

Canned or jarred sauces: chutney, mustards, pasta sauces, pesto, relishes, salsa

Canned tomato products: plain and seasoned

Canned vegetarian baked beans, chili beans and refried beans

Canned vegetarian soups and broth

Canned whole beans: black, butter, cannellini, great northern, kidney, navy, pinto

Dried fruit: apricots, dates, diced dried fruits, raisins

Dried legumes: beans, lentils, split peas

Grains: barley, oats, rice, roasted buckwheat groats (also known as kasha)

Nuts: almonds, cashews, pecans, sunflower nuts, walnuts

Pasta

Peanut butter

Peanuts

Prebaked pizza crusts or shells

Ready-to-eat cereals

Spices and herbs

Texturized soy protein (TSP) mixes: chili, sloppy Joes, soup

Whole-grain breads and rolls

Whole-grain crackers

In the Refrigerator

Cheeses

Flour and corn tortillas

Fresh fruit

Fresh herbs

Fresh vegetables

Hummus

Milk

Yogurt

In the Freezer

Cheese or vegetable pizza

Fruit and vegetable juices

Fruits

Meat substitutes: vegetable burgers, vegetarian hot dogs and breakfast meats

Vegetables

Pasta

Pasta

Low-Fat = 3g or less, except main dishes with 6g or less   **Fast** = Ready in 30 minutes or less   ■ = Bread Machine directions   ● = Slow Cooker directions

Vermicelli with Fresh Herbs (page 396)

Lighter = 1/3 fewer calories or 50% less fat

Pasta Basics

Pasta is an American favorite. What makes it so popular is that it's convenient to store, it's easy to fix and it's good for you. Check out the Food Guide Pyramid (page 531); you'll find pasta in the broad bottom band, the band that calls for six to eleven servings per day. One-half cup of cooked pasta contains about 100 calories, 0.5 grams of fat and less than 5 milligrams of sodium.

But there's more to pasta than convenience and good nutrition: It's just plain fun to cook with. Who can resist a cool salad made with radiator-shaped pasta or a hearty soup dotted with shell-shaped pasta? You can bake pasta and fill it, toss it in a salad, stir-fry it, layer it or smother it in sauce.

And if you are looking for flavors, pasta has it! Pasta flavors range from the common—spinach, tomato and whole wheat—to the exotic—beet, lemon, herb, garlic, hot chili, red wine, chocolate, fruit and squid ink.

So how is pasta made? Dried pasta, the most common kind, is made from semolina flour, which is ground from durum wheat. The flour is mixed with water, or sometimes egg, to form a dough. The dough is kneaded, then pushed through a metal disk with holes in it to create the incredible variety of pasta shapes. Then the pasta is dried. Whether made at a pasta factory or in your own kitchen, the process is the same.

Picking Out Pasta

Pasta is available in three forms: dried, fresh and frozen. Dried pasta is usually found packaged or in self-serve bulk bins. Look for fresh pasta in the refrigerated section of your supermarket. Some varieties of frozen pasta are lasagna noodles, egg noodles and filled tortellini and ravioli.

When buying pasta, keep these tips in mind:

- **Dried pasta:** Look for unbroken pieces. Avoid dried pasta with a marbled surface (many fine lines); this indicates a drying problem, and the pasta may fall apart during cooking.

- **Fresh pasta:** Look for smooth, evenly colored, unbroken pieces. Fresh pasta will look dry, but it shouldn't be brittle or crumbly. Avoid packages with moisture droplets or liquid, because the pasta may be moldy or mushy.

- **Frozen pasta:** Avoid packages with the pieces frozen together in a solid block, as well as those with ice crystals or freezer burn, which looks like dry, white spots.

Pasta Glossary

From twists to ribbons to wagon wheels, check out all the "pastabilities" for shapes and sizes at your supermarket. The endings on some Italian names give you a hint on pasta size: "oni" means large; "elle," "ina," and "iti" mean small. Here are just some of the pastas, with serving suggestions too, to choose from:

Acini de Pepe: Spaghetti cut to the size of peppercorns. Top with any sauce, or add to a casserole.

Agnolotti: Small, crescent-shaped, stuffed pasta that resembles priests' caps. Usually served with light sauces to let the flavor of the filling shine through.

Anelli: Tiny rings of pasta. Excellent for soups, salads.

Bucatini: Long, hollow noodles that resemble drinking straws. This pasta originates in Naples, and the word *bucato* means "with a hole." Break into thirds, if desired, and serve with any sauce.

Capellini/Angel Hair: "Fine hairs" of pasta, the thinnest of spaghettis. Legend has it that Parmesan cheese clings to this pasta like gold clings to an angel's hair. Takes just minutes to cook because it's so thin. Serve with more delicate sauces, or break in half for stir-fries.

Cappelletti: Small, stuffed pasta similar to tortellini but with the ends pinched together in the shape of "little hats."

Cavatappi: Corkscrew-shaped pasta with a hollow middle, making it perfect for thick and creamy vegetable, meat and seafood sauces.

PASTA

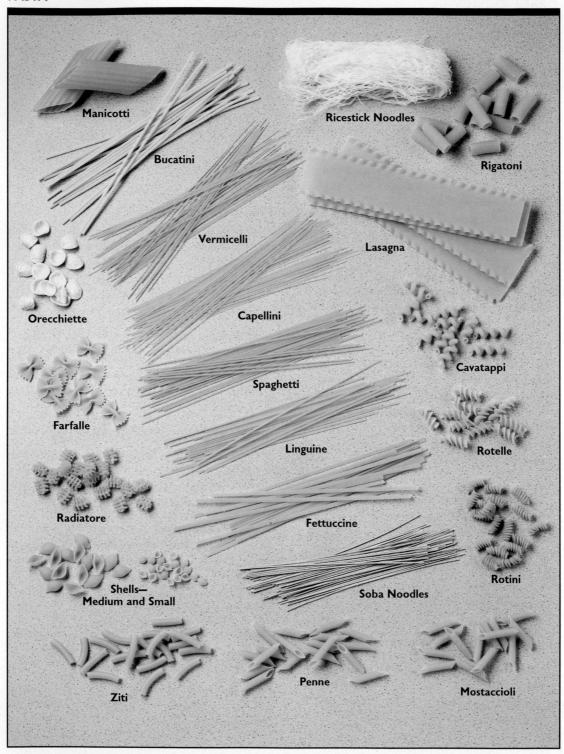

Manicotti

Ricestick Noodles

Bucatini

Rigatoni

Vermicelli

Lasagna

Orecchiette

Capellini

Cavatappi

Spaghetti

Farfalle

Linguine

Rotelle

Radiatore

Fettuccine

Rotini

Shells—
Medium and Small

Soba Noodles

Ziti

Penne

Mostaccioli

PASTA

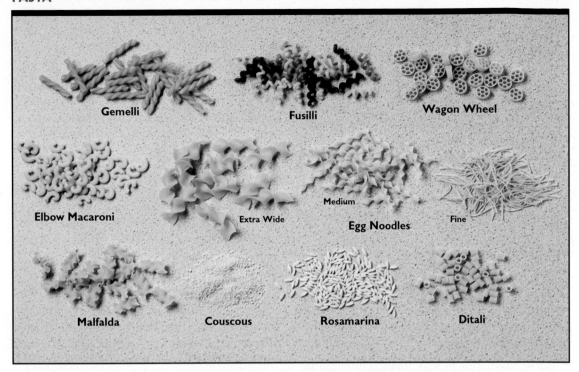

Gemelli Fusilli Wagon Wheel

Elbow Macaroni Extra Wide Medium Egg Noodles Fine

Malfalda Couscous Rosamarina Ditali

Cellophane: Also called *bean threads* or *glass noodles*, these noodles are made from the starch of mung beans, which we know as bean sprouts. These dried, translucent noodles must be presoaked before using in most recipes unless they are added directly to soups or simmering liquids. The dry noodles also can be deep-fried; they puff up instantly and dramatically to a size many times larger than when dry. You can substitute rice sticks if you can't find cellophane noodles.

Chinese Egg Noodles: A type of wheat-egg noodle that closely resembles Italian pasta and is available either dried or fresh. Noodles range in thickness from very thin to thick and round. If you like, you may substitute narrow egg noodles, spaghetti or linguine.

Couscous: The tiniest pasta, it's made from granular semolina and is a staple of North African and some Middle Eastern cuisines. Often used as an alternative to rice. Available in regular, precooked (which cooks in just 5 minutes) and flavored varieties.

Ditali/Ditalini: Very tiny, very short tubes. In Italian, they're "little thimbles." Available in two varieties:

grooved and smooth. Top with any sauce, toss into soup or bake in casseroles.

Egg Noodles: Flat or curly short pasta strips usually made with eggs or egg yolks; there's also an eggless variety. Top with sauces, or serve as a side dish.

Elbow Macaroni: Curved, short, hollow "elbows" of pasta. Perfect for soups, salads, casseroles and, of course, macaroni and cheese!

Farfalle: The bow-tie or butterfly pasta; its mini version is *tripolini*. This shape adds interest to soups and salads and is also wonderful with colorful sauces.

Fettuccine: Long, flat, narrow, "little ribbon" noodles. Perfect for heavier cheese and meat sauces. Available in many flavors, including plain and spinach.

Fusilli: A long or short spring-shaped pasta from southern Italy. Hailing originally from Naples, it is also known as *eliche*, or "propellers," for its quality of trapping some of the sauce and propelling the flavor.

Gemelli/Twist: A short, twisted pasta that resembles two strands of spaghetti wound together. Like fusilli, it adds interest to salads and also works well with sauces.

Japanese Curly Noodles: Quick-cooking, wavy, thin, long noodles sold in rectangular "bricks." Toss in stir-fries, or top with stir-fried meat and vegetables.

Lasagna: Flat noodle, about two inches wide, with ruffled or straight edges. It's great for layering with sauces, such as the Italian Sausage Lasagna (page 398). Look for fresh, dried, frozen and precooked lasagna.

Linguine: Long, flat, thin noodle, usually 1/8 inch wide. Italians call it "little tongues" because its original shape resembled the thickness of a songbird's tongue. A good shape for all sauces.

Mafalda: Mini lasagna noodles—short, flat with ruffled edges. Popular used with seafood sauces and for casseroles.

Manicotti/Cannelloni: A large, four-inch tubular noodle usually stuffed and baked. Derived from the word *canna*, it means "hollow cane."

Mostaccioli: A short cut pasta about two inches long. These tubular "mustaches" have slanted cuts at both ends. Mostaccioli can have a smooth or grooved finish.

Noodles: Noodles can be fresh, frozen or dried and are made with or without eggs. This flat pasta comes in a variety of lengths and widths, including extra-wide, wide, medium, fine, ribbons and dumpling.

Novelty Pasta Shapes: Fun, funky new pasta shapes are popping up in larger supermarkets and gourmet stores everywhere. You can find pasta in the shape of pumpkins, trees, rabbits, hearts, states, cars, birthday cakes, alphabets, grape clusters and garlic bulbs. Beyond shapes, how about unique flavors: smoked salmon, porcini mushroom and more.

Orecchiette: The name means "little ears." This tiny disk-shaped pasta is great with chunky vegetable or meat sauces.

Penne: A short cut pasta, about 1 1/4 inches long. Tubular in shape with slanted cuts at both ends, penne can have a smooth or grooved finish; it is narrower than mostaccioli. The word *penne* means "feather," indicating either the lightness of the noodle or the shape that resembles the wing of a bird. It is excellent with tomato and vegetable sauces.

Radiatore: Shaped like old-fashioned home-heating radiators or air conditioners; the ruffled edges help catch all the flavors in the sauce or dressing. An interesting shape for sauces, salads and soups.

Ramen Noodles: These are instant, deep-fried noodles sold in cellophane packages with a broth mixture and sometimes little bits of vegetables. The noodles can be cooked or used dry as a crunchy addition to salads. Some brands bake rather than deep-fry the noodles, so they are lower in fat.

Ravioli: Pillow-shaped pasta, usually made with a stuffing of cheese, meat or spinach, that's popular in several Italian regions. Ravioli also can be filled with less traditional ingredients such as crabmeat or pumpkin. Typically served with butter or Parmesan, this pasta is delicious with tomato and meat sauces.

Rice Noodles/Rice Sticks: These noodles are opaque white in color and sold fresh or dried. Dried rice noodles are the most widely available and usually come in the form of very thin strands. Rice sticks are often fried, but when cooked, they have a creamy, soft texture. Angel hair or linguine can be used in place of rice sticks.

Rigatoni: Short cut, wide tubular pasta with lengthwise grooves, about one inch long. It suits most chunky sauces and meat sauces.

Rosamarina/Orzo: Looks like large, fat grains of rice. Terrific in salads, side dishes and soups and is a great substitute for rice.

Rotelle: A wide, corkscrew-shaped pasta. Its curves are great for catching any kind of sauce.

Rotini: A skinny version of rotelle, it's plain or tricolored. Rotini is a favorite for pasta salads.

Soba: Slightly wider than somen noodles, soba noodles are made from buckwheat flour. They have a chewy texture and nutty flavor and can be round or flat. They make a great addition to soups and stews or can be topped with a delicate sauce. Use whole wheat spaghetti if soba noodles are unavailable.

Somen: These noodles are made from wheat flour and formed into very thin strands. In a pinch, you can substitute vermicelli or angel hair pasta.

Shells: Shells are available in jumbo, medium and small sizes. Jumbo shells are great stuffed; medium and small shells are more suited to thick sauces, soups and salads. Conchiglie and conchiglioni are the Italian names for shells, or "conches."

Spaghetti: Means "little strings" in Italian. These long, thin strands of pasta are round and solid. Whole-wheat spaghetti, high in fiber and flavor, is increasingly popular.

Tortellini: Little rings of pasta filled with cheese, originally from the city of Bologna. The fresh, refrigerated products are offered in many flavors with a variety of fillings such as Italian sausage and chicken. Tortellini usually is served with a tomato or cream sauce. It's also well-suited to soups and salads.

Udon: Fat and slippery noodles made from wheat flour. They can be flat, square or round and are available both dried and fresh. Substitute fettuccine or linguine if udon noodles are unavailable.

Vermicelli: A long, very thin pasta. "Little worms" is the original meaning of this word, so named for the squirming motion the noodles undergo when surrounded by sauce and twirled around a fork. It was the original pasta for spaghetti and meatballs. Use vermicelli with lighter sauces and in soups.

Wagon Wheel/Ruote: Called wagon wheel pasta because its shape resembles a spoked wheel. A fun pasta to add to casseroles, soups and salads, especially when you want to boost the kid appeal. Some brands may also label this pasta *rotelle*.

Ziti: Medium-size tubular pasta that's perfect for chunky sauces and meat dishes. In Italian, it means "bridegrooms."

Storing Pasta

Dried

Keep dried pasta in a cool (60° or less), dry place. You can leave it in its original package or transfer it to airtight glass or plastic containers. Label the containers with the date you filled them. Although dried pasta can be stored indefinitely, use it within 1 to 2 years for the best quality and flavor.

Fresh

Fresh pasta is perishable, so keep it in the refrigerator and use it by the "use by" or expiration date on the package. Store opened, uncooked pasta in a tightly covered container for no more than 3 days.

Frozen

Store unopened pasta in its original package in the freezer until ready to cook. Put unused amounts in airtight containers to avoid freezer burn. Freeze unopened pasta up to 9 months, opened pasta up to 3 months.

Homemade Pasta

If it's completely dried, you can store homemade pasta like dried pasta. Refrigerate freshly made pasta in a tightly covered container for up to 3 days or freeze in an airtight package for up to 1 month.

Tips for Cooking Pasta

- Here's an easy way to measure 4 ounces of long pasta such as spaghetti: Make a circle about the size of a quarter with your thumb and index finger, and fill it with pasta.

- Pasta shapes can be substituted for one another, as long as they're similar in size.

- Use plenty of water, at least 1 quart (4 cups) water for every 4 ounces of pasta. Be sure the water is boiling vigorously before adding the pasta which helps to prevent it from sticking together as soon as it's put in.

- Do not add oil to the cooking water. It isn't necessary and sauces will not cling to oil-coated pasta. Keep pasta from sticking to the pan by adding it gradually to rapidly boiling water, then stir frequently during cooking.

- To salt or not to salt? The answer is, it's up to you. Salt isn't necessary for cooking, but it does enhance the flavor. As a guide, use 1/2 teaspoon salt for every 8 ounces of pasta. For a slightly different flavor, add a tablespoon of dried herbs or lemon juice into the water during cooking.

- Follow the package directions for cooking times, or refer to the Pasta Cooking Chart on right. If using the pasta in a baked dish or casserole, slightly undercook the pasta; it should be flexible but still firm. (It is a good idea to begin testing the pasta after 5 minutes of cooking.) While the pasta bakes in the oven, it will become more tender as it soaks up the sauce.

- Taste the pasta to tell if it's done. Perfectly cooked pasta should be *al dente*, tender but firm to the bite, without any raw flavor. Another way to check for doneness is to cut several pieces with a fork against the side of the pan. There should be some resistance, but the pasta should cut easily. Overcooked pasta is mushy and watery and loses its flavor.

- Do not rinse pasta after draining unless the recipe says to do so, or sauces will not cling to the pasta. Pasta usually is rinsed only when it is to be used in a cold salad.

Pasta Yields

When preparing pasta, allow 1/2 to 3/4 cup cooked pasta per side-dish or appetizer serving. If you plan to make pasta your main dish, allow 1 1/4 to 1 1/2 cups per serving.

Two ounces (2/3 cup) dried pasta will yield approximately 1 cup of cooked pasta. This yield will vary slightly depending on the shape, type and size of pasta.

To measure 4 ounces of spaghetti easily, make a circle with your thumb and index finger, about the size of a quarter, and fill it with pasta.

Uncooked	Cooked	Servings
Short Pastas		
Macaroni, Penne, Rotini, Shells, Wagon Wheels		
6 to 7 ounces (2 cups)	4 cups	4 to 6
Long Pastas		
Capellini, Linguine, Spaghetti, Vermicelli		
7 to 8 ounces	4 cups	4 to 6
Noodles		
8 ounces	4 to 5 cups	4 to 6

Storing and Reheating Cooked Pasta

Storing options:

- Toss the cooked pasta with a small amount of vegetable or olive oil (1 to 2 teaspoons per pound of pasta) to prevent sticking during storage.

- Store in an airtight container or plastic bag in the refrigerator up to 5 days or in the freezer up to 2 months. Store pasta and sauce separately.

Reheating options:

- Place pasta in rapidly boiling water for up to 2 minutes. Drain, then serve immediately.

- Place pasta in a colander, and pour boiling water over it until heated through. Drain, then serve immediately.

- Place pasta in microwavable dish or container. Cover and microwave on High for 1 to 2 minutes per 2 cups of pasta or until heated through. Serve immediately.

Pasta Cooking Guide

You'll find cooking directions right on pasta packages, but if you've bought the pasta in bulk or stored it in a different container, this reference chart gives you *approximate* cooking times for the most popular types and shapes of pasta.

Making Fresh Pasta

In Italian, pasta means "paste," and the paste is made from wheat flour and water. Flour is at the heart of pasta. Wheat, which is ground into flour, gives pasta its structure and texture. Although you can make pasta from just about any type of flour, we've found some flours work better than others.

Semolina flour: Semolina flour is made from durum wheat, which is a variety of wheat particularly high in protein. Semolina flour doesn't produce satisfactory baked goods, but it makes excellent pasta. With its springy texture, pasta made from durum wheat is less likely to become starchy or sticky when cooked than

PASTA COOKING CHART

Type of Pasta	CookingTime (minutes)	Type of Pasta	CookingTime (minutes)
Dried Pasta		Rosamarina (orzo)	8 to 10
		Rotelle	10 to 12
Acini de pepe	5 to 6	Rotini	8 to 10
Capellini	5 to 6	Shells, jumbo	12 to 15
Egg noodles, regular	8 to 10	Shells, medium and small	9 to 11
Egg noodles, extra wide	10 to 12	Soba noodles	6 to 7
Elbow macaroni	8 to 10	Spaghetti	8 to 10
Farfalle	13 to 15	Vermicelli	5 to 7
Fettuccine	11 to 13	Wagon wheel	10 to 12
Fusilli	11 to 13	Ziti	14 to 15
Japanese curly noodles	4 to 5	**Refrigerated Packaged Fresh Pasta**	
Lasagna noodles	12 to 15		
Linguine	9 to 13	Capellini	1 to 2
Mafalda	8 to 10	Farfalle	2 to 3
Manicotti	10 to 12	Fettuccine	1 to 2
Mostaccioli	12 to 14	Lasagna	2 to 3
Penne	9 to 13	Linguine	1 to 2
Radiatore	9 to 11	Ravioli	6 to 8
Rigatoni	12 to 15	Tortellini	8 to 10

pasta made from all-purpose flour. The dried pasta you buy at the store is made from durum wheat.

Semolina flour is more coarsely ground than most flour and looks similar to yellow cornmeal but is paler in color. Semolina flour may be difficult to find, but it is likely to be available in most large supermarkets, gourmet shops and Italian markets or through mail-order sources. Pasta dough made with semolina is slightly drier and stiffer than dough made with other flours because it absorbs liquid more easily.

All-purpose flour: All-purpose flour, as its name implies, can be used for making all types of baked goods, as well as pasta. This flour is a blend of hard and soft wheat varieties, not durum wheat. Because of the types of wheat used in all-purpose flour, pasta dough made with it is easy to work with. You will notice how smooth and elastic the dough is when made with all-purpose flour.

Unbleached flour: Unbleached flour is more cream colored than all-purpose flour (most all-purpose flour is whitened by a bleaching process), and it has a slightly higher protein content. Unbleached flour will yield the same results as all-purpose flour and can be used interchangeably in scratch pasta recipes that call for all-purpose or semolina flour.

Whole wheat flour: Whole wheat flour is made from the whole grain of wheat, with the outer covering of the grain left intact. Whole wheat flour may be coarsely ground or finely ground. Pasta made from whole wheat flour will have a slightly heavier texture and nuttier flavor than pasta made from semolina, all-purpose or unbleached flour. If the dough seems dry and difficult to work with, add a little extra water (1 to 2 teaspoons) to help make it more manageable. Because whole wheat flour has a higher fat content than other flours, it can become rancid more quickly. It is best to store this flour tightly wrapped in the refrigerator or freezer.

Homemade Pasta

Spaetzle *Fast & Low-Fat*

Prep: 10 min; Cook: 15 min ✱ *6 servings*

These tiny noodles or dumplings are usually served as a side dish, like potatoes or rice, and are often served with a sauce or gravy. If you find yourself making this often, look for a spaetzle maker in your kitchenware store, which fits over your pot and makes quick work of making the dumplings.

2 large eggs, beaten
1/4 cup milk or water
1 cup all-purpose flour*
1/4 teaspoon salt
Dash of pepper
1 tablespoon butter or stick margarine

1. Mix eggs, milk, flour, salt and pepper (batter will be thick).

2. Fill 4-quart Dutch oven half full with water; heat to boiling.

3. Press a few tablespoons of the batter at a time through colander (preferably one with large holes) into boiling water. Stir once or twice to prevent sticking.

4. Cook about 5 minutes or until spaetzle rise to surface and are tender; drain. Toss with butter.

*Do not use self-rising flour.

1 Serving (about 1/2 cup): Calories 120 (Calories from Fat 35); Fat 4g (Saturated 2g); Cholesterol 75mg; Sodium 140mg; Carbohydrate 17g (Dietary Fiber 1g); Protein 5g **% Daily Value:** Vitamin A 4%; Vitamin C 0%; Calcium 2%; Iron 6% **Diet Exchanges:** 1 Starch, 1 Fat

Lighter Spaetzle: For 2 grams of fat and 100 calories per serving, substitute 1/2 cup fat-free cholesterol-free egg product for the eggs.

Homemade Pasta *Low-Fat*

Prep: 30 min; Roll/Cut: 40 min; Stand: 30 min;
Cook: 15 min ✱ *8 servings*

A large wooden board or laminated plastic surface
works best for rolling out pasta dough. Cold surfaces,
such as metal or marble, do not work as well because
the dough has a tendency to stick.

2 cups all-purpose flour*
1/2 teaspoon salt
2 large eggs
1/4 cup water
1 tablespoon olive or vegetable oil

1. Mix flour and salt in medium bowl. Make a well in
center of flour mixture. Add eggs, water and oil to well;
mix thoroughly. (If dough is too dry, mix in enough
water to make dough easy to handle. If dough is too
sticky, gradually add flour when kneading.)

2. Gather dough into a ball. Knead on lightly floured
surface 5 to 10 minutes or until smooth and elastic.
Cover with plastic wrap or aluminum foil. Let stand 15
minutes.

3. Divide dough into 4 equal parts. Roll one-fourth of
dough at a time into rectangle, 1/16 to 1/8 inch thick,
on lightly floured surface (keep remaining dough covered). Loosely fold rectangle lengthwise into thirds.
Cut crosswise into 2-inch strips for lasagna, 1/4-inch
strips for fettuccine or 1/8-inch strips for linguine.
Unfold and gently shake out strips. Hang pasta on
pasta drying rack or arrange in single layer on lightly
floured towels; let stand 30 minutes or until dry. (If
using pasta machine, pass dough through machine
until 1/16 inch thick.)

4. Heat 4 quarts water (salted if desired) to boiling
in 6- to 8-quart saucepan; add pasta. Boil uncovered 2
to 5 minutes, stirring occasionally, until firm but tender.
Begin testing for doneness when pasta rises to surface
of water. Drain pasta.

*Cut crosswise into 2-inch strips for lasagna, 1/4-inch strips for
fettuccine or 1/8-inch strips for linguine.*

*Unfold and gently shake out strips. Hang pasta on pasta drying
rack or arrange in single layer on lightly floured towels.*

*If using self-rising flour, omit salt.

1 Serving (about 3/4 cup): Calories 140 (Calories from Fat 25);
Fat 3g (Saturated 1g); Cholesterol 55mg; Sodium 160mg;
Carbohydrate 24g (Dietary Fiber 1g); Protein 5g **% Daily Value:**
Vitamin A 2%; Vitamin C 0%; Calcium 0%; Iron 8% **Diet
Exchanges:** 1 1/2 Starch, 1/2 Fat

HERB PASTA: Add 1 tablespoon chopped fresh or 1
teaspoon dried herb leaves, crumbled, to the flour
mixture before adding eggs.

LEMON PASTA: Add 2 to 3 teaspoons finely shredded
lemon peel to the flour mixture before adding eggs.

POPPY OR SESAME SEED PASTA: Add 1 tablespoon
poppy or sesame seed to the flour mixture before
adding eggs.

Egg Noodles *Low-Fat*

Prep: 15 min; Stand: 30 min; Cook: 15 min ✱ 6 servings

2 cups all-purpose* or whole wheat flour
1 teaspoon salt
3 large egg yolks
1 large egg
1/3 to 1/2 cup water

1. Mix flour and salt in medium bowl. Make a well in center of flour mixture. Add egg yolks, egg and water to well; mix thoroughly. (If dough is too dry, mix in enough water to make dough easy to handle. If dough is too sticky, mix in enough flour to make dough easy to handle.)

2. Divide dough into 4 equal parts. Roll one-fourth of dough at a time into rectangle, 1/16 to 1/8 inch thick, on lightly floured surface (keep remaining dough covered). Loosely fold rectangle lengthwise into thirds. Cut crosswise into 1/8-inch strips for narrow noodles, 1/4-inch strips for medium noodles or 1/2-inch strips for wide noodles. Unfold and gently shake out strips. Hang pasta on pasta drying rack or arrange in single layer on lightly floured towels; let stand 30 minutes or until dry. (If using pasta machine, pass dough through machine until 1/16 inch thick.)

3. Break strips into smaller pieces. Heat 4 quarts water (salted if desired) to boiling in 6- to 8-quart saucepan; add pasta. Boil uncovered 5 to 7 minutes, stirring occasionally, until firm but tender. Begin testing for doneness when pasta rises to surface of water. Drain pasta.

*If using self-rising flour, omit salt.

1 Serving (about 3/4 cup): Calories 190 (Calories from Fat 35); Fat 4g (Saturated 1g); Cholesterol 140mg; Sodium 410mg; Carbohydrate 32g (Dietary Fiber 1g); Protein 7g **% Daily Value:** Vitamin A 5%; Vitamin C 0%; Calcium 2%; Iron 12% **Diet Exchanges:** 2 Starch, 1/2 Fat

CORNMEAL NOODLES: Substitute 1/2 cup cornmeal for 1/2 cup of the flour.

Noodles Romanoff *Fast*

Prep: 10 min; Cook: 20 min ✱ 8 servings

4 cups uncooked wide noodles (8 ounces) or Egg
    Noodles (left)
2 cups sour cream
1/4 cup grated Parmesan cheese
1 tablespoon chopped fresh chives
1/2 teaspoon salt
1/8 teaspoon pepper
1 large clove garlic, finely chopped
2 tablespoons butter or stick margarine, melted
1/4 cup grated Parmesan cheese

1. Cook noodles as directed on package or in recipe.

2. While noodles are cooking, mix sour cream, 1/4 cup cheese, the chives, salt, pepper and garlic.

3. Drain noodles. Stir butter into noodles. Stir in sour cream mixture. Place on warm platter. Sprinkle with 1/4 cup cheese.

1 Serving (about 2/3 cup): Calories 230 (Calories from Fat 145); Fat 16g (Saturated 10g); Cholesterol 70mg; Sodium 290mg; Carbohydrate 16g (Dietary Fiber 1g); Protein 6g **% Daily Value:** Vitamin A 12%; Vitamin C 0%; Calcium 12%; Iron 4% **Diet Exchanges:** 1 Starch, 1/2 High-Fat Meat, 2 Fat

Lighter Noodles Romanoff: For 7 grams of fat and 190 calories per serving, use reduced-fat sour cream and grated fat-free Parmesan cheese topping. Decrease butter to 1 tablespoon.

CRACKING EGGS

If you find yourself always picking bits of eggshell out of the dish you're making, read on. Eggshells are less likely to splinter if they are cracked on a flat surface rather than on the edge of the mixing bowl. Try it the next time you need to crack open raw eggs.

Fettuccine Alfredo

Fettuccine Alfredo *Fast*

Prep: 10 min; Cook: 15 min ✳ *4 servings*

A rich northern Italian dish named after restaurateur Alfredo di Lello, who created it. Fettuccine Alfredo can be served as a side dish as well as a main dish. Note that freshly grated Parmesan cheese will result in a thinner sauce than when canned grated cheese is used.

8 ounces uncooked fettuccine
Alfredo Sauce (right)
Chopped fresh parsley

1. Cook fettuccine as directed on package.

2. While fettuccine is cooking, make Alfredo Sauce.

3. Drain fettuccine. Pour sauce over fettuccine; toss until fettuccine is well coated. Sprinkle with parsley.

Alfredo Sauce

1/2 cup butter or stick margarine
1/2 cup whipping (heavy) cream
3/4 cup grated Parmesan cheese
1/2 teaspoon salt
Dash of pepper

Heat butter and whipping cream in 10-inch skillet over medium heat, stirring frequently, until butter is melted and mixture starts to bubble. Reduce heat to low, simmer 6 minutes, stirring frequently, until slightly thickened. Remove from heat; stir in cheese, salt and pepper.

1 Serving (about 1 cup): Calories 550 (Calories from Fat 350); Fat 39g (Saturated 25g); Cholesterol 155mg; Sodium 750mg; Carbohydrate 38g (Dietary Fiber 2g); Protein 14g **% Daily Value:** Vitamin A 28%; Vitamin C 0%; Calcium 24%; Iron 14% **Diet Exchanges:** 2 1/2 Starch, 1 High-Fat Meat, 5 1/2 Fat

Lighter Fettuccine Alfredo: For 17 grams of fat and 370 calories per serving, decrease butter to 1/4 cup and Parmesan cheese to 1/2 cup; substitute evaporated milk for the whipping cream.

Pasta Primavera

Prep: 15 min; Cook: 20 min ✱ *4 servings*

8 ounces uncooked fettuccine or linguine
1 tablespoon olive or vegetable oil
1 cup broccoli flowerets
1 cup cauliflowerets
2 medium carrots, thinly sliced (1 cup)
1 cup frozen green peas, rinsed to separate
1 small onion, chopped (1/4 cup)
Alfredo Sauce (page 395)
1 tablespoon grated Parmesan cheese

1. Cook fettuccine as directed on package.

2. While fettuccine is cooking, heat oil in 12-inch skillet over medium-high heat. Cook broccoli, cauliflowerets, carrots, peas and onion in oil 6 to 8 minutes, stirring frequently, until vegetables are crisp-tender. Remove from heat; keep warm.

3. Make Alfredo Sauce. Stir sauce into vegetable mixture.

4. Drain fettuccine. Stir fettuccine into sauce mixture; heat through. Sprinkle with cheese.

1 Serving (about 1 3/4 cups): Calories 635 (Calories from Fat 385); Fat 43g (Saturated 24g); Cholesterol 155mg; Sodium 530mg; Carbohydrate 50g (Dietary Fiber 6g); Protein 18g **% Daily Value:** Vitamin A 78%; Vitamin C 28%; Calcium 30%; Iron 20% **Diet Exchanges:** 3 Starch, 1 High-Fat Meat, 1 Vegetable, 6 Fat

Pasta with Pesto *Fast*

Prep: 10 min; Cook: 15 min ✱ *4 servings*

Pesto is a specialty of Genoa, Italy, whose people claim to grow the most fragrant basil in the world. The sauce is also popular along the French Riviera, where it is called *pistou*. The name comes from "pestle," as the cheese and basil were originally crushed with mortar and pestle.

3 cups uncooked rigatoni pasta (9 ounces)
1/4 cup Pesto (page 438) or prepared pesto
Shredded Parmesan cheese, if desired

1. Cook pasta as directed on package.

2. Drain pasta; return to saucepan. Add Pesto; toss until pasta is well coated. Sprinkle with cheese.

1 Serving (about 1 1/4 cups): Calories 400 (Calories from Fat 100); Fat 11g (Saturated 2g); Cholesterol 2mg; Sodium 60mg; Carbohydrate 66g (Dietary Fiber 3g); Protein 12g **% Daily Value:** Vitamin A 0%; Vitamin C 6%; Calcium 8%; Iron 20% **Diet Exchanges:** 4 Starch, 1 Vegetable, 1 Fat

GARDEN PASTA WITH PESTO: Add 1 large tomato, seeded and chopped (1 cup), and 1/4 cup sliced ripe olives with the Pesto.

Vermicelli with Fresh Herbs *Fast*

Prep: 10 min; Cook: 9 min ✱ *6 servings*

1 package (16 ounces) vermicelli
1 tablespoon capers
1/4 cup olive or vegetable oil
2 tablespoons chopped pine nuts
1 tablespoon chopped fresh parsley
2 teaspoons chopped fresh rosemary leaves
2 teaspoons chopped fresh sage leaves
1 teaspoon chopped fresh basil leaves
1 pint (2 cups) cherry tomatoes, cut into fourths
Freshly ground pepper, if desired

1. Cook vermicelli as directed on package.

2. While vermicelli is cooking, coarsely chop capers if they are large. Mix capers and remaining ingredients except tomatoes and pepper in medium bowl. Stir in tomatoes.

3. Drain vermicelli. Toss vermicelli and herb mixture in large bowl. Sprinkle with pepper.

1 Serving (about 1 1/2 cups): Calories 390 (Calories from Fat 110); Fat 12g (Saturated 2g); Cholesterol 0mg; Sodium 50mg; Carbohydrate 64g (Dietary Fiber 4g); Protein 11g **% Daily Value:** Vitamin A 4%; Vitamin C 10%; Calcium 2%; Iron 18% **Diet Exchanges:** 4 Starch, 1 Vegetable, 1 Fat

---

KEEPING PASTA DISHES HOT

Because the ingredients in this recipe are uncooked, they'll stay warmer if you toss them with the pasta in a prewarmed bowl. To warm your serving bowl, fill with hot water and let it stand while the pasta's cooking. Pour the water out just before you're ready to add the pasta.

Gorgonzola Linguine with Toasted Walnuts

Gorgonzola Linguine with Toasted Walnuts *Fast*

Prep: 10 min: Cook: 15 min ✳ 4 servings

How much is 8 ounces of linguine? All bundled up, 8 ounces of uncooked linguine is about 1 1/2 inches in diameter.

8 ounces uncooked linguine
1 tablespoon butter or stick margarine
1 clove garlic, finely chopped
1 1/2 cups whipping (heavy) cream
1/4 cup dry white wine or chicken broth
1/4 teaspoon salt
1/2 cup crumbled Gorgonzola cheese (about 2 ounces)
1/4 cup coarsely chopped walnuts, toasted (page 177)

1. Cook linguine as directed on package.

2. While linguine is cooking, melt butter in 10-inch skillet over low heat. Cook garlic in butter, stirring occasionally, until garlic is golden. Stir in whipping cream, wine and salt. Simmer about 6 minutes, stirring constantly, until slightly thickened; remove from heat. Stir in cheese until melted.

3. Drain linguine. Toss linguine and sauce. Sprinkle with walnuts.

1 Serving (about 1 1/2 cups): Calories 615 (Calories from Fat 370); Fat 41g (Saturated 23g); Cholesterol 120mg; Sodium 290mg; Carbohydrate 50g (Dietary Fiber 2g); Protein 14g **% Daily Value:** Vitamin A 26%; Vitamin C 0%; Calcium 16%; Iron 14% **Diet Exchanges:** 3 Starch, 7 Fat, 1/2 Skim Milk

> **Lighter Gorgonzola Linguine with Toasted Walnuts:** For 11 grams of fat and 360 calories per serving, substitute evaporated fat-free milk for the whipping cream; use 2 tablespoons finely chopped walnuts.

CHOPPING NUTS

Did you know that frozen nuts are easier to chop than room-temperature nuts? Put nuts in the freezer for at least an hour before chopping them.

Macaroni and Cheese

Prep: 25 min; Bake: 25 min ✳ *4 servings*

Mix up your cheeses! Try Vermont white Cheddar, or even a mixture of half sharp Cheddar and half Monterey Jack cheese with jalapeño peppers, in this great-tasting comfort food.

2 cups uncooked elbow macaroni (7 ounces)
1/4 cup butter or stick margarine
1/4 cup all-purpose flour
1/2 teaspoon salt
1/4 teaspoon pepper
1/4 teaspoon ground mustard
1/4 teaspoon Worcestershire sauce
2 cups milk
2 cups shredded sharp Cheddar cheese (8 ounces)

1. Heat oven to 350°.

2. Cook macaroni as directed on package.

3. While macaroni is cooking, melt butter in 3-quart saucepan over low heat. Stir in flour, salt, pepper, mustard and Worcestershire sauce. Cook over low heat, stirring constantly, until mixture is smooth and bubbly; remove from heat. Stir in milk. Heat to boiling, stirring constantly. Boil and stir 1 minute; remove from heat. Stir in cheese until melted.

4. Drain macaroni. Gently stir macaroni into cheese sauce. Pour into ungreased 2-quart casserole. Bake uncovered 20 to 25 minutes or until bubbly.

1 Serving (about 1 cup): Calories 605 (Calories from Fat 305); Fat 34g (Saturated 21g); Cholesterol 100mg; Sodium 790mg; Carbohydrate 51g (Dietary Fiber 2g); Protein 26g **% Daily Value:** Vitamin A 28%; Vitamin C 0%; Calcium 46%; Iron 14% **Diet Exchanges:** 2 1/2 Starch, 1 1/2 High-Fat Meat, 4 Fat, 1 Skim Milk

---

Lighter Macaroni and Cheese: For 10 grams of fat and 375 calories per serving, decrease butter to 2 tablespoons. Use fat-free (skim) milk and substitute 1 1/2 cups reduced-fat Cheddar cheese (6 ounces) for the 2 cups regular sharp Cheddar cheese.

Italian Sausage Lasagna

Prep: 1 hr 10 min; Bake: 45 min; Stand: 15 min ✳ *8 servings*

This is a great recipe to make ahead. Cover the unbaked lasagna with aluminum foil and refrigerate no longer than 24 hours or freeze no longer than 2 months. Bake covered 45 minutes; uncover and bake refrigerated lasagna 15 to 20 minutes longer or frozen lasagna 35 to 45 minutes longer until hot and bubbly.

1 pound bulk Italian sausage or lean ground beef
1 medium onion, chopped (1/2 cup)
1 clove garlic, finely chopped
3 tablespoons chopped fresh parsley
1 tablespoon chopped fresh or 1 teaspoon dried basil leaves
1 teaspoon sugar
1 can (14 1/2 ounces) whole tomatoes, undrained
1 can (15 ounces) tomato sauce
8 uncooked lasagna noodles (from 16 ounce box)
1 container (15 ounces) ricotta cheese or small curd creamed cottage cheese (2 cups)
1/2 cup grated Parmesan cheese
1 tablespoon chopped fresh or 1 1/2 teaspoons dried oregano leaves
2 cups shredded mozzarella cheese (8 ounces)

1. Cook sausage, onion and garlic in 10-inch skillet over medium heat, stirring occasionally, until sausage is no longer pink; drain.

2. Stir in 2 tablespoons of the parsley, the basil, sugar, tomatoes and tomato sauce, breaking up tomatoes with a fork or snipping with kitchen scissors. Heat to boiling, stirring occasionally; reduce heat. Simmer uncovered about 45 minutes or until slightly thickened.

3. Heat oven to 350°. Cook noodles as directed on package.

4. While noodles are cooking, mix ricotta cheese, 1/4 cup of the Parmesan cheese, the oregano and remaining 1 tablespoon parsley.

Italian Sausage Lasagna

5. Drain noodles. Spread 1/2 of the sausage mixture (about 2 cups) in ungreased rectangular baking dish, 13 × 9 × 2 inches. Top with 4 noodles. Spread one half of the cheese mixture (about 1 cup) over noodles. Sprinkle with one half of the mozzarella cheese. Repeat layers, ending with mozzarella and the remaining 1/4 cup Parmesan cheese.

6. Cover and bake 30 minutes. Uncover and bake about 15 minutes longer or until hot and bubbly. Let stand 15 minutes before cutting.

1 Serving: Calories 450 (Calories from Fat 200); Fat 22g (Saturated 11g); Cholesterol 70mg; Sodium 1,220mg; Carbohydrate 36g (Dietary Fiber 3g); Protein 30g **% Daily Value:** Vitamin A 20%; Vitamin C 14%; Calcium 48%; Iron 16% **Diet Exchanges:** 2 Starch, 3 Medium-Fat Meat, 1 Vegetable, 1 Fat

EASY ITALIAN SAUSAGE LASAGNA: Substitute 4 cups (from 48 ounce jar) spaghetti sauce with meat for the first 8 ingredients (do not use thick or extra-thick varieties).

CHOOSING SAUSAGE

Italian sausage comes in two styles: hot (flavored with hot red peppers) and mild. You can use either variety in this recipe, depending on whether you like a little hot bite to your food or not.

Creamy Seafood Lasagna

Prep: 20 min; Bake: 40 min; Stand: 15 min ✱ *8 servings*

When choosing your cheese for this lasagna, it's best to select regular or part-skim ricotta. Creamed cottage cheese, which is not as dry as ricotta, will thin the cheese sauce and make the lasagna a bit soupy.

12 uncooked lasagna noodles (12 ounces)
1/4 cup butter or stick margarine
2 cloves garlic, finely chopped
2/3 cup all-purpose flour
2 cups milk
1 1/2 cups chicken broth
1/4 cup dry sherry or chicken broth
2 cups shredded mozzarella cheese (8 ounces)
8 medium green onions, sliced (1/2 cup)
1 tablespoon chopped fresh or 1 teaspoon dried basil
    leaves
1/4 teaspoon pepper
1 package (8 ounces) frozen salad-style imitation crab-
    meat, thawed and chopped
1 package (4 ounces) frozen cooked salad shrimp,
    thawed
1 cup ricotta cheese
1/2 cup grated Parmesan cheese

1. Heat oven to 350°. Cook noodles as directed on package.

2. While noodles are cooking, melt butter in 3-quart saucepan over low heat. Stir in garlic and flour. Cook and stir 1 minute; remove from heat. Stir in milk, broth and sherry. Heat to boiling, stirring constantly. Boil and stir 1 minute.

3. Stir mozzarella cheese, onions, basil and pepper into sauce. Cook over low heat, stirring constantly, until cheese is melted.

4. Drain noodles. Spread 1 cup of the cheese sauce in ungreased rectangular baking dish, 13 × 9 × 2 inches. Top with 4 noodles. Spread half of the crabmeat and shrimp over noodles; spread with 1 cup of the cheese sauce. Top with 4 noodles. Spread ricotta cheese over noodles; spread with 1 cup of the cheese sauce. Top with 4 noodles. Spread with remaining crabmeat, shrimp and cheese sauce.

5. Bake uncovered 35 to 40 minutes or until hot in center. Sprinkle with Parmesan cheese. Let stand 15 minutes before cutting.

1 Serving: Calories 415 (Calories from Fat 155); Fat 17g (Saturated 10g); Cholesterol 75mg; Sodium 850mg; Carbohydrate 40g (Dietary Fiber 2g); Protein 28g **% Daily Value:** Vitamin A 16%; Vitamin C 2%; Calcium 46%; Iron 14% **Diet Exchanges:** 2 1/2 Starch, 3 Medium-Fat Meat

Spaghetti and Meatballs

Prep: 1 hr 10 min; Cook: 30 min ✱ *6 servings*

When you're crunched for time, substitute a 26-ounce jar of spaghetti sauce for the Italian Tomato Sauce and 1 1/2 pounds purchased cooked meatballs for the Meatballs.

Italian Tomato Sauce (page 436)
Meatballs (page 241)
4 cups hot cooked spaghetti
Grated Parmesan cheese, if desired

1. Make Italian Tomato Sauce.

2. Make Meatballs; drain.

3. Stir meatballs into sauce. Cover and simmer 30 minutes, stirring occasionally. Serve over spaghetti. Serve with cheese.

1 Serving (about 1 3/4 cups): Calories 380 (Calories from Fat 145); Fat 16g (Saturated 5g); Cholesterol 80mg; Sodium 490mg; Carbohydrate 40g (Dietary Fiber 3g); Protein 22g **% Daily Value:** Vitamin A 8%; Vitamin C 14%; Calcium 8%; Iron 20% **Diet Exchanges:** 2 Starch, 2 Medium-Fat Meat, 2 Vegetable, 1/2 Fat

SPAGHETTI AND BEEF SAUCE: Omit Meatballs. Cook 1 pound lean ground beef, 1 large onion, chopped (1 cup), and 2 cloves garlic, finely chopped, in 10-inch skillet over medium heat, stirring occasionally, until beef is brown; drain. Stir beef mixture into sauce. Simmer as directed in step 3.

EASY CASSEROLE CLEANUP

For quick casserole cleanup, line the casserole with heavy-duty aluminum foil, and grease or spray with cooking spray before filling and baking.

Manicotti

Prep: 40 min; Bake: 1 hr 30 min ✱ *7 servings*

Red Sauce (below)
2 packages (10 ounces each) frozen chopped spinach, thawed
2 cups small curd creamed cottage cheese
1/3 cup grated Parmesan cheese
1/4 teaspoon ground nutmeg
1/4 teaspoon pepper
14 uncooked manicotti shells
2 tablespoons grated Parmesan cheese

1. Make Red Sauce. Heat oven to 350°.

2. Squeeze spinach to drain; spread on paper towels and pat dry. Mix spinach, cottage cheese, 1/3 cup Parmesan cheese, the nutmeg and pepper.

3. Spread about one-third of the sauce in ungreased rectangular baking dish, 13 × 9 × 2 inches. Fill uncooked manicotti shells with spinach mixture. Place shells in sauce in dish. Pour remaining sauce evenly over shells, covering shells completely. Sprinkle with 2 tablespoons Parmesan cheese.

4. Cover and bake about 1 hour 30 minutes or until shells are tender.

Red Sauce

1 pound lean ground beef
1 large onion, chopped (1 cup)
2 large cloves garlic, finely chopped
1 can (28 ounces) whole tomatoes, undrained
1 can (8 ounces) mushroom pieces and stems, drained
1/4 cup chopped fresh parsley
1 tablespoon chopped fresh or 1 teaspoon dried basil leaves
1 teaspoon salt

Cook beef, onion and garlic in 10-inch skillet over medium heat 8 to 10 minutes, stirring occasionally, until beef is brown; drain. Stir in remaining ingredients, breaking up tomatoes with a fork or snipping with kitchen scissors. Heat to boiling; reduce heat. Cover and simmer 10 minutes.

1 Serving: Calories 380 (Calories from Fat 125); Fat 14g (Saturated 7g); Cholesterol 50mg; Sodium 720mg; Carbohydrate 39g (Dietary Fiber 5g); Protein 30g **% Daily Value:** Vitamin A 52%; Vitamin C 22%; Calcium 24%; Iron 24% **Diet Exchanges:** 2 Starch, 3 Lean Meat, 2 Vegetable

Stir-Fried Asian Beef and Noodles

Prep: 15 min; Marinate: 20 min; Cook: 8 min ✱ *6 servings*

1 pound beef boneless sirloin or round steak, cut into 2 × 1/4-inch strips
1 tablespoon vegetable oil
1 teaspoon cornstarch
1/2 teaspoon soy sauce
1 package (about 6 ounces) rice stick noodles
1 tablespoon vegetable oil
1 tablespoon finely chopped gingerroot
1 clove garlic, finely chopped
1 bag (16 ounces) frozen broccoli, carrots and cauliflower
1 tablespoon vegetable oil
3/4 cup beef broth
1/3 cup rice or cider vinegar
1/3 cup honey
3 tablespoons soy sauce
1 teaspoon sesame oil
1/4 teaspoon crushed red pepper
4 medium green onions, sliced (1/4 cup)

1. Toss beef, 1 tablespoon vegetable oil, the cornstarch and 1/2 teaspoon soy sauce in glass or plastic bowl. Cover and refrigerate 20 minutes. Soak noodles in cold water 5 minutes; drain.

2. Heat 12-inch skillet or wok over medium-high heat. Add 1 tablespoon vegetable oil; rotate skillet to coat with oil. Add gingerroot and garlic; stir-fry 30 seconds. Add vegetables; stir-fry until crisp-tender. Remove vegetables from skillet.

3. Add 1 tablespoon vegetable oil to skillet; rotate to coat. Add beef; stir-fry about 5 minutes or until brown. Remove beef from skillet.

4. Add broth, vinegar, honey, 3 tablespoons soy sauce, the sesame oil and red pepper to skillet. Stir in noodles; heat to boiling. Cook over medium heat about 2 minutes, stirring frequently, until noodles are tender. Stir in beef, vegetables and onions; cook and stir 1 minute.

1 Serving (about 1 cup): Calories 295 (Calories from Fat 90); Fat 10g (Saturated 2g); Cholesterol 35mg; Sodium 630mg; Carbohydrate 37g (Dietary Fiber 3g); Protein 17g **% Daily Value:** Vitamin A 24%; Vitamin C 20%; Calcium 4%; Iron 14% **Diet Exchanges:** 2 Starch, 1 Medium-Fat Meat, 2 Vegetable

Spaghetti Pie

Prep: 10 min; Cook: 16 min; Bake: 45 min; Stand: 5 min
✳ *6 servings*

If you hold your uncooked spaghetti together in a bundle, 4 ounces is about as big around as the size of a quarter.

4 ounces uncooked spaghetti
1/2 pound lean ground beef
1 small green bell pepper, chopped (1/2 cup)
1 small onion, chopped (1/4 cup)
1 jar (14 ounces) spaghetti sauce
1 teaspoon chili powder
1/2 teaspoon salt
1/4 teaspoon pepper
2 large eggs
1 cup small curd creamed cottage cheese
1/2 cup shredded mozzarella cheese (2 ounces)

1. Heat oven to 375°. Grease pie plate, 10 × 1 1/2 inches. Cook spaghetti as directed on package.

2. While spaghetti is cooking, cook beef, bell pepper and onion in 10-inch skillet over medium heat 8 to 10 minutes, stirring occasionally, until beef is brown; drain. Stir in spaghetti sauce, chili powder, salt and pepper. Cook 5 to 6 minutes, stirring occasionally, until sauce is thickened.

3. Drain spaghetti. Place spaghetti in pie plate; gently press on bottom and 1 inch up side of pie plate.

4. Mix eggs and cottage cheese; spread evenly over spaghetti. Spoon beef mixture over cottage cheese mixture. Sprinkle with mozzarella cheese.

5. Bake 35 to 45 minutes or until center is set. Let stand 5 minutes before cutting.

1 Serving: Calories 310 (Calories from Fat 115); Fat 13g (Saturated 5g); Cholesterol 100mg; Sodium 760mg; Carbohydrate 30 (Dietary Fiber 2g); Protein 20g **% Daily Value:** Vitamin A 12%; Vitamin C 18%; Calcium 12%; Iron 12% **Diet Exchanges:** 2 Starch, 2 Medium-Fat Meat

Easy Southwestern Stroganoff *Fast*

Prep: 5 min; Cook: 15 min **✳** *4 servings*

Top off this easy skillet supper with crushed corn chips or flavored tortilla chips and chopped fresh cilantro.

1 pound lean ground beef
1 cup water
1 jar (16 ounces) thick-and-chunky salsa
2 cups uncooked wagon wheel pasta (4 ounces)
1/2 teaspoon salt
1/2 cup sour cream

1. Cook beef in 10-inch skillet over medium heat 8 to 10 minutes, stirring occasionally, until brown; drain.

2. Stir water, salsa, uncooked pasta and salt into beef. Heat to boiling; reduce heat. Cover and simmer 10 to 15 minutes, stirring occasionally, until pasta is tender.

3. Stir in sour cream; cook just until hot.

1 Serving (about 1 cup): Calories 525 (Calories from Fat 205); Fat 23g (Saturated 10g); Cholesterol 85mg; Sodium 590mg; Carbohydrate 52g (Dietary Fiber 4g); Protein 31g **% Daily Value:** Vitamin A 12%; Vitamin C 18%; Calcium 10%; Iron 26% **Diet Exchanges:** 3 Starch, 3 Medium-Fat Meat, 1 Vegetable, 1 Fat

Lighter Easy Southwestern Stroganoff: For 8 grams of fat and 410 calories per serving, substitute ground turkey breast for the ground beef; use reduced-fat sour cream.

Straw and Hay Pasta

Straw and Hay Pasta

Prep: 15 min; Cook: 25 min ✳ *4 servings*

Serving fettuccine and spaghetti can sometimes be tricky without the help of kitchen tongs, pasta servers or a wooden pasta fork. These handy, inexpensive items let you easily grab the pasta and transfer it onto your plate without taking more than you want.

1 tablespoon butter or stick margarine
1 1/2 cups sliced mushrooms (4 ounces)
4 ounces fully cooked ham, cut into 1 x 1/4-inch strips
2 tablespoons chopped fresh parsley
2 tablespoons chopped onion
1/4 cup brandy or chicken broth
1 cup whipping (heavy) cream
1/4 teaspoon salt
1/4 teaspoon pepper
1 package (9 ounces) refrigerated plain fettuccine
1 package (9 ounces) refrigerated spinach fettuccine
1/2 cup shredded Parmesan cheese
Freshly ground pepper

1. Melt butter in 10-inch skillet over medium-high heat. Cook mushrooms, ham, parsley and onion in butter, stirring occasionally, until mushrooms are tender. Stir in brandy. Cook uncovered until liquid has evaporated.

2. Stir in whipping cream, salt and pepper. Heat to boiling; reduce heat. Simmer uncovered about 15 minutes, stirring frequently, until thickened.

3. Cook fettuccines as directed on package.

4. Drain fettuccines. Mix fettuccines and sauce. Sprinkle with cheese and pepper.

1 Serving (about 1 1/4 cups): Calories 730 (Calories from Fat 290); Fat 32g (Saturated 17g); Cholesterol 210mg; Sodium 680mg; Carbohydrate 87g (Dietary Fiber 4g); Protein 28g **% Daily Value:** Vitamin A 20%; Vitamin C 2%; Calcium 22%; Iron 34% **Diet Exchanges:** 5 Starch, 1 High-Fat Meat, 2 Vegetable, 4 Fat

Spaghetti Carbonara *Fast*

Prep: 10 min; Cook: 13 min ✱ 6 servings

We've substituted fat-free cholesterol-free egg product, which is pasteurized, for raw eggs, thereby eliminating the food safety issue of contracting salmonella from eating raw or undercooked eggs.

1 package (16 ounces) spaghetti
1 clove garlic, finely chopped
6 slices bacon, cut into 1-inch pieces
3/4 cup fat-free cholesterol-free egg product
1 tablespoon olive or vegetable oil
1/2 cup freshly grated Parmesan cheese
1/2 cup freshly grated Romano cheese
2 tablespoons chopped fresh parsley
1/4 teaspoon pepper
Freshly grated Parmesan cheese, if desired
Freshly ground pepper, if desired

1. Cook spaghetti in Dutch oven as directed on package.

2. While spaghetti is cooking, cook garlic and bacon in 10-inch skillet over medium heat, stirring occasionally, until bacon is crisp; drain.

3. Mix egg product, oil, 1/2 cup Parmesan cheese, the Romano cheese, parsley and 1/4 teaspoon pepper.

4. Drain spaghetti; return to Dutch oven. Add bacon mixture and egg product mixture. Cook over low heat, tossing mixture constantly, until egg product coats spaghetti. Remove from heat. Serve with Parmesan cheese and pepper.

1 Serving (about 1 1/2 cups): Calories 385 (Calories from Fat 80); Fat 9g (Saturated 3g); Cholesterol 10mg; Sodium 260mg; Carbohydrate 61g (Dietary Fiber 3g); Protein 18g **% Daily Value:** Vitamin A 4%; Vitamin C 0%; Calcium 12%; Iron 20% **Diet Exchanges:** 4 Starch, 1 Medium-Fat Meat

Chili Macaroni

Prep: 20 min; Cook: 25 min ✱ 8 servings

1 cup uncooked elbow macaroni (3 1/2 ounces)
1 pound lean ground beef
1 medium onion, chopped (1/2 cup)
2 cloves garlic, finely chopped
1 can (15 to 16 ounces) kidney beans, drained
1 can (14 1/2 ounces) diced tomatoes, undrained*
1 can (8 ounces) tomato sauce
1 can (6 ounces) tomato paste
1 tablespoon chili powder
1 teaspoon ground cumin
1 cup shredded Cheddar cheese (4 ounces)

1. Cook macaroni as directed on package.

2. While macaroni is cooking, cook beef, onion and garlic in 4-quart saucepan or Dutch oven over medium-high heat, stirring occasionally, until beef is brown; drain.

3. Drain macaroni. Stir macaroni and remaining ingredients except cheese into beef mixture. Heat to boiling, stirring occasionally; reduce heat. Simmer uncovered about 20 minutes, stirring occasionally, until hot. Sprinkle with cheese.

*1 can (14 1/2 ounces) whole tomatoes, undrained and tomatoes cut up, can be substituted for the diced tomatoes.

1 Serving (about 1 cup): Calories 335 (Calories from Fat 125); Fat 14g (Saturated 6g); Cholesterol 45mg; Sodium 730mg; Carbohydrate 35g (Dietary Fiber 6g); Protein 23g **% Daily Value:** Vitamin A 16%; Vitamin C 18%; Calcium 12%; Iron 24% **Diet Exchanges:** 2 Starch, 2 Lean Meat, 1 Vegetable, 1 Fat

Lighter Chili Macaroni: For 5 grams of fat and 255 calories per serving, substitute ground turkey breast for the ground beef and use reduced-fat cheese.

SOUTHWESTERN CHILI MACARONI: Substitute 4 ounces pasta of a similar size for the macaroni, 1 can (15 ounces) black beans, rinsed and drained, for the kidney beans and shredded Monterey Jack cheese for the Cheddar cheese. Add 1 can (4 ounces) chopped green chilies.

Chicken Tetrazzini

Prep: 20 min; Bake: 30 min ✳ *6 servings*

This rich casserole apparently was named for the opera singer Luisa Tetrazzini. Serve with Bacon-Spinach Salad (page 416) for a dinner that is *magnifique!*

1 package (7 ounces) spaghetti, broken into thirds
1/4 cup butter or stick margarine
1/4 cup all-purpose flour
1/2 teaspoon salt
1/4 teaspoon pepper
1 cup chicken broth
1 cup whipping (heavy) cream
2 tablespoons dry sherry or water
2 cups cubed cooked chicken or turkey
1 can (4 ounces) sliced mushrooms, drained
1/2 cup grated Parmesan cheese

1. Heat oven to 350°.

2. Cook spaghetti as directed on package.

3. While spaghetti is cooking, melt butter in 2-quart saucepan over low heat. Stir in flour, salt and pepper. Cook, stirring constantly, until mixture is smooth and bubbly; remove from heat. Stir in broth and whipping cream. Heat to boiling, stirring constantly. Boil and stir 1 minute.

4. Drain spaghetti. Stir spaghetti, sherry, chicken and mushrooms into sauce.

5. Pour spaghetti mixture into ungreased 2-quart casserole. Sprinkle with cheese. Bake uncovered about 30 minutes or until bubbly in center.

1 Serving (about 1 cup): Calories 480 (Calories from Fat 260); Fat 29g (Saturated 15g); Cholesterol 110mg; Sodium 680mg; Carbohydrate 34g (Dietary Fiber 2g); Protein 22g **% Daily Value:** Vitamin A 18%; Vitamin C 0%; Calcium 14%; Iron 14% **Diet Exchanges:** 2 Starch, 2 Medium-Fat Meat, 3 Fat, 1/2 Skim Milk

> **Lighter Chicken Tetrazzini:** For 12 grams of fat and 320 calories per serving, decrease butter to 2 tablespoons and Parmesan cheese to 1/4 cup; substitute fat-free (skim) milk for the whipping cream.

Asian Chicken and Noodles *Fast*

Prep: 15 min; Cook: 7 min ✳ *4 servings*

Made from sesame seed, sesame oil is available in light and dark varieties. The darker sesame oil is dark brown in color with a much stronger flavor. Teriyaki baste and glaze is a thick, brown-colored sauce; do not confuse it with teriyaki sauce or teriyaki marinade, which has a watery consistency. You can find teriyaki baste and glaze in the condiments or Asian foods section of your supermarket.

8 ounces uncooked soba (buckwheat) noodles*
1 tablespoon vegetable oil
1/2 pound boneless, skinless chicken breast halves, cut into thin slices
1 bag (16 ounces) fresh (refrigerated) stir-fry vegetables
1/4 cup chicken broth or water
1/2 cup teriyaki baste and glaze (from 12-ounce bottle)
1 teaspoon dark sesame oil
1/4 teaspoon crushed red pepper

1. Cook noodles as directed on package.

2. While noodles are cooking, heat vegetable oil in 10-inch skillet or wok over high heat. Add chicken; stir-fry 3 to 5 minutes or until no longer pink in center. Remove chicken from skillet.

3. Add vegetables and broth to skillet. Heat to boiling. Cover and boil about 2 minutes or until vegetables are crisp-tender.

4. Drain noodles. Mix teriyaki glaze, sesame oil and red pepper; stir into vegetables. Stir in chicken. Heat to boiling. Serve chicken mixture over noodles.

*Japanese udon noodles, whole wheat spaghetti, ramen noodles or angel hair pasta can be substituted for the soba noodles.

1 Serving (about 1 1/2 cups): Calories 315 (Calories from Fat 70); Fat 8g (Saturated 1g); Cholesterol 35mg; Sodium 2,160mg; Carbohydrate 48g (Dietary Fiber 4g); Protein 17g **% Daily Value:** Vitamin A 68%; Vitamin C 50%; Calcium 8%; Iron 10% **Diet Exchanges:** 3 Starch, 1 Lean Meat, 1 Vegetable

Cavatappi with Roasted Chicken and Vegetables

Prep: 25 min; Bake: 45 min ✻ *4 servings*

4 medium red potatoes, cut into 3/4-inch cubes
    (2 1/2 cups)
2 cups 1-inch cauliflowerets
1 large yellow or red bell pepper, cut into 1-inch pieces
4 medium roma (plum) tomatoes, cut into 1-inch pieces
    (1 1/2 cups)
1 medium onion, coarsely chopped (1/2 cup)
2 tablespoons olive or vegetable oil
1 pound boneless, skinless chicken breast halves
1 tablespoon chicken seasoning or seasoned salt
2 cups uncooked cavatappi or fusilli (corkscrew) pasta
    (6 ounces)
1/3 cup finely chopped fresh parsley
3 cloves garlic, finely chopped
2 tablespoons grated lemon or orange peel

1. Heat oven to 425°. Mix potatoes, cauliflowerets, bell pepper, tomatoes, onion and oil in 6-quart roasting pan. Top with chicken. Sprinkle with chicken seasoning.

2. Bake uncovered about 45 minutes, stirring vegetables occasionally, until vegetables are very tender and chicken is no longer pink when centers of thickest pieces are cut.

3. Cook and drain pasta as directed on package. Mix parsley, garlic and lemon peel; set aside.

4. Chop chicken. Toss chicken, vegetable mixture and pasta. Sprinkle with parsley mixture.

1 Serving: Calories 515 (Calories from Fat 110); Fat 12g (Saturated 2g); Cholesterol 70mg; Sodium 1120mg; Carbohydrate 74g (Dietary Fiber 8g); Protein 36g **% Daily Value:** Vitamin A 30%; Vitamin C 100%; Calcium 6%; Iron 28% **Diet Exchanges:** 4 Starch, 2 1/2 Lean Meat, 3 Vegetable

Ravioli with Pesto Cream *Fast*

Prep: 10 min; Cook: 8 min ✻ *4 servings*

Add wedges of melon, clusters of grapes and some garlic breadsticks to quickly round out this colorful meal.

2 teaspoons olive or vegetable oil
1/2 pound green beans, cut into 1 1/2-inch pieces
1/2 medium yellow bell pepper, cut into 1/2-inch
    pieces (1/2 cup)
3 roma (plum) tomatoes, cut into 1/2-inch pieces
    (1 cup)
1/2 teaspoon salt
16 ounces frozen sausage- or cheese-filled ravioli (from
    24-ounce package)
1/2 cup sour cream
3 tablespoons basil pesto
2 teaspoons grated lemon peel

1. Heat oil in 12-inch nonstick skillet over medium-high heat. Cook green beans and bell pepper in oil about 5 minutes, stirring frequently, until crisp-tender. Stir in tomatoes and salt. Cook 3 minutes.

2. While vegetables are cooking, cook and drain ravioli as directed on package. Mix sour cream, pesto and lemon peel in small bowl.

3. Toss hot cooked ravioli with vegetables and sour cream mixture.

1 Serving: Calories 360 (Calories from Fat 200); Fat 22g (Saturated 8g); Cholesterol 150mg; Sodium 1220mg; Carbohydrate 31g (Dietary Fiber 4g); Protein 14g **% Daily Value:** Vitamin A 28%; Vitamin C 32%; Calcium 18%; Iron 18% **Diet Exchanges:** 1 Starch, 1 High-Fat Meat, 3 Vegetable, 2 1/2 Fat

Italian Chicken and Couscous

Italian Chicken and Couscous

Prep: 15 min; Cook: 20 min; Stand: 5 min ✳ *4 servings*

Couscous, the most tiny of all pasta, is a staple of North African and some Middle Eastern cuisine. Since it is often used in place of rice, it is sometimes mistakenly thought of as a grain.

1 tablespoon olive or vegetable oil

2 cloves garlic, finely chopped

1 can (14 1/2 ounces) stewed tomatoes, drained and
   1/2 cup liquid reserved

1 pound boneless, skinless chicken breast halves, cut
   into 1/2-inch strips

1 medium onion, thinly sliced and separated into rings

1 1/2 teaspoons chopped fresh or 1/2 teaspoon dried
   oregano leaves

1/8 teaspoon pepper

1 1/2 cups chicken broth

1 medium zucchini, cut lengthwise in half, then cut
   crosswise into 1/4-inch slices

1/2 package (10-ounce size) couscous (3/4 cup)

1. Heat oil in 10-inch skillet over medium heat. Cook garlic in oil 1 minute, stirring frequently.

2. Stir in reserved tomato liquid, chicken, onion, oregano and pepper. Heat to boiling; reduce heat. Cover and simmer about 10 minutes, stirring occasionally, until chicken is no longer pink in center.

3. Stir in broth; heat to boiling. Stir in zucchini, couscous and tomatoes, breaking up tomatoes with a fork or snipping with kitchen scissors; remove from heat. Cover and let stand about 5 minutes or until couscous is tender and liquid is absorbed.

1 Serving (about 1 1/4 cups): Calories 330 (Calories from Fat 70); Fat 8g (Saturated 2g); Cholesterol 70mg; Sodium 520mg; Carbohydrate 37g (Dietary Fiber 4g); Protein 33g **% Daily Value:** Vitamin A 8%; Vitamin C 16%; Calcium 6%; Iron 12% **Diet Exchanges:** 2 Starch, 3 1/2 Very Lean Meat, 1 Vegetable, 1 Fat

Linguine with Red Clam Sauce

Prep: 40 min; Cook: 35 min; Stand: 30 min ✳ *6 servings*

6 cups hot cooked linguine or Homemade Pasta
(page 393)
Red Clam Sauce (below)
Chopped fresh parsley

1. Cook linguine as directed on package. If preparing Homemade Pasta, roll and cut into 1/8-inch strips for linguine.

2. Make Red Clam Sauce.

3. While clam sauce is cooking, heat 4 quarts water (salted if desired) to boiling in large pan. Add linguine. Boil uncovered 2 to 4 minutes, stirring occasionally, until firm but tender (*al dente*). Begin testing for doneness when linguine rise to surface of water.

4. Drain linguine. Toss linguine and sauce. Sprinkle with parsley.

Red Clam Sauce

1 pint shucked fresh small clams, drained and liquor
reserved*
1/4 cup olive or vegetable oil
3 cloves garlic, finely chopped
1 can (28 ounces) Italian-style pear-shaped tomatoes,
drained and chopped
1 small red chili, seeded and finely chopped
1 tablespoon chopped fresh parsley
1 teaspoon salt

Chop clams; set aside. Heat oil in 3-quart saucepan over medium-high heat. Cook garlic in oil, stirring frequently, until golden. Stir in tomatoes and chili. Cook 3 minutes, stirring frequently. Stir in clam liquor. Heat to boiling; reduce heat. Simmer uncovered 10 minutes. Stir in clams, parsley and salt. Cover and simmer about 15 minutes, stirring occasionally, until clams are tender.

*2 cans (6 1/2 ounces each) minced clams, undrained, can be substituted for the fresh clams. Decrease simmer time to 5 minutes.

1 Serving (about 1 1/2 cups): Calories 340 (Calories from Fat 100); Fat 11g (Saturated 1g); Cholesterol 15mg; Sodium 230mg; Carbohydrate 48g (Dietary Fiber 3g); Protein 15g **% Daily Value:** Vitamin A 20%; Vitamin C 34%; Calcium 8%; Iron 54% **Diet Exchanges:** 3 Starch, 1/2 Lean Meat, 1 Vegetable, 1 Fat

Spaghetti with White Clam Sauce *Fast*

Prep: 10 min; Cook: 15 min ✳ *4 servings*

1 package (7 ounces) spaghetti
1/4 cup butter or stick margarine
2 cloves garlic, finely chopped
2 tablespoons chopped fresh parsley
2 cans (6 1/2 ounces each) minced clams, undrained
Chopped fresh parsley
1/2 cup grated Parmesan cheese

1. Cook spaghetti as directed on package.

2. While spaghetti is cooking, melt butter in 1 1/2-quart saucepan over medium heat. Cook garlic in butter about 3 minutes, stirring occasionally, until light golden. Stir in 2 tablespoons parsley and the clams. Heat to boiling; reduce heat. Simmer uncovered 3 to 5 minutes.

3. Drain spaghetti. Pour sauce over spaghetti; toss. Sprinkle with parsley and cheese.

1 Serving (about 1 1/4 cups): Calories 395 (Calories from Fat 145); Fat 16g (Saturated 9g); Cholesterol 65mg; Sodium 310mg; Carbohydrate 43g (Dietary Fiber 2g); Protein 22g **% Daily Value:** Vitamin A 18%; Vitamin C 10%; Calcium 20%; Iron 76% **Diet Exchanges:** 3 Starch, 2 Medium-Fat Meat

CHAPTER 15
Salads & Salad Dressings

Salads & Salad Dressings

Low-Fat = *3g or less, except main dishes with 6g or less*　**Fast** = *Ready in 30 minutes or less*　■ = *Bread Machine directions*　● = *Slow Cooker directions*

Greek Salad (page 414)

Lighter = 1/3 fewer calories or 50% less fat

Salad Basics

The first salads were made of edible herbs and leaves sprinkled with salt. They've come a long way! Today, salads are still an array of greens, but they also include seafood, meat, cheese, pasta, fruit and veggies, all accented by dressings from tangy to sweet. Because of this versatility, salads are easy to enjoy in many different ways.

Appetizer salads are usually light and tangy to stimulate your appetite for the meal ahead. Tossed green salad and marinated vegetables are two typical varieties of appetizer salads.

Side-dish salads complement the main dish. They're usually heartier than appetizer salads, with dressings ranging from vinaigrette to creamy. Creamy Potato Salad (page 417) and Three-Bean Salad (page 421) are often enjoyed as side-dish salads.

Main-dish salads don't accompany the meal—they are the meal. They're usually larger and include more filling ingredients such as pasta, meat, poultry, seafood, eggs, cheese and beans. Taco Salad (page 429) and Cobb Salad (page 430) are hearty enough for a meal by themselves.

Dessert salads are a light, refreshing way to end a meal. They're usually a combo of fruits, nuts and/or cheese and are often held together with a sweet dressing of whipped cream or sour cream. Try 24-Hour Fruit Salad (page 421) for dessert sometime!

Storing and Handling Salad Greens

When you say "salad," people usually think about greens. Today there are so many varieties available, you can eat a week's worth and never have the same green twice. To ensure your greens are at their best, here are some great tips to follow.

- Store greens in their original wrap or in perforated vegetable or regular plastic bags in the crisper section of your refrigerator. Wait to wash them until you're ready to use them.

- When ready to use, wash greens in several changes of cold water, then shake off the excess moisture. Some greens such as spinach may be sandy; be sure to separate the leaves with your fingers to get all the grit out.

- You'll want your salad greens to be as dry as possible to allow the dressing to cling to the leaves. To dry greens, use a salad spinner, toss them in a cloth towel or blot with paper towels.

- Romaine and iceberg are longer-lasting lettuces; they'll stay fresh in the refrigerator up to one week. Most other greens will wilt after a few days.

- Iceberg lettuce should be cleaned before storing. Remove the core by striking the core end of the head against a flat surface, then twisting and lifting it out. Rinse by holding the head, cored end up, under cold running water to wash and refresh the leaves. Turn right side up and let the water run out. Store lettuce in plastic bag or airtight container in refrigerator for up to 2 weeks.

Selecting Salad Greens

The best salads start with the best ingredients, and that means fresh, fresh, fresh. No matter what kind of greens you choose, be sure they aren't wilted, bruised or discolored. Then pick the varieties that suit your salad best: large firm leaves to cup a main-dish salad or line a salad bowl, or tender, colorful greens to toss with your favorite dressing.

Know your greens! The Salad Greens Glossary on page 410 can help you make your selection, along with a stroll through your supermarket's produce section or a farmers' market where you may find even more exotic greens favored by other cultures. If you have the chance, try a taste, too.

Salad Greens Glossary

Arugula (or rocket): Has small, slender, dark green leaves similar to radish leaves and a slightly bitter, peppery mustard flavor. Choose smaller leaves for a less-distinctive flavor.

Belgian endive (or French): Has narrow, cupped, cream-colored leaves tinged with green and a slightly bitter flavor.

Bibb lettuce: Has tender, pliable leaves similar to Boston lettuce. Bibb is smaller than Boston but has the same delicate, mild flavor.

Boston lettuce (or butterhead): Has small rounded heads of soft, buttery leaves and a delicate flavor.

Cabbage: Comes in several varieties, each with its own distinct flavor. Green and red cabbage are the most familiar and readily available; look for compact heads of waxy, tightly wrapped leaves. Savoy cabbage has crinkled leaves, and Chinese (or napa) cabbage has long, crisp leaves.

Curly endive: Has frilly, narrow, somewhat prickly leaves with a slightly bitter taste.

Escarole: Another member of the endive family; has broad, wavy, medium green leaves and a slightly bitter flavor, although it's milder than Belgian or curly endive.

Frisée: A member of the chicory family; has slender, curly leaves ranging in color from yellow-white to yellow-green and a slightly bitter flavor.

Greens (beet, collard, chard, dandelion, mustard): All have a strong, biting flavor. Young greens are milder and more tender and can be tossed in salads; older greens are too bitter for salads and should be cooked for the best flavor.

Iceberg lettuce (or crisphead): Has a bland, mild flavor that makes it the most popular salad green. Look for solid, compact heads with tight leaves that range in color from medium green outer leaves to pale green inner ones.

Kale: Recognized by its sturdy but frilly leaves that usually are dark green and tinged with shades of blue and purple. A member of the cabbage family, it doesn't form a head, but it does have a mild cabbage taste. Choose young small leaves for the best flavor.

Leaf lettuce (red, green, oak leaf, salad bowl): Has tender but crisp leaves that don't form tight heads. These leafy bunches have a mild, bland flavor that's more full-bodied than iceberg lettuce.

Mesclun (field or wild greens): A mixture of young, delicate greens often including arugula, chervil, chickweed, dandelion, frisée, mizuma and oak leaf lettuce.

Mixed salad greens (prepackaged): Already cleaned and ready to use, you'll find these in the produce section of your supermarket. Choose from a variety of mixes, each with its own combination of colors, flavors and textures.

Radicchio: A type of endive, looks like a small, loose-leaf cabbage with smooth, tender leaves. The two most common radicchios in the U.S. are a ruby-red variety with broad, white veins and one with leaves speckled in shades of pink, red and green.

Romaine (or cos): Has narrow, elongated, dark green, crisp leaves sometimes tinged with red on the tips. The broad white center rib is especially crunchy. Romaine is the favored lettuce for Caesar Salad (page 413).

Sorrel (or sourgrass): Looks much like spinach, but the leaves are smaller. Sorrel has a sharp, lemony flavor.

Spinach: Has smooth, tapered, dark green leaves, sometimes with crumpling at the edges, and a slightly bitter flavor.

Watercress: Has small, crisp, dark green, coin-size leaves and a strong peppery flavor.

GREENS

Arugula

Boston or Bibb

Romaine

Curly Endive

Kale

Spinach

Iceberg

Mesclun Mix

Escarole

Radicchio

Watercress

Sorrel

Leaf Lettuce

Belgian Endive

Greens—Beet, Collard, Mustard

Tips for Tossed Salads

- Choose a variety of greens to create a medley of complementary textures, flavors and colors. For little dashes of flavor, add fresh herbs.

- Mix dark greens with light, crisp greens with tender, and straight greens with curly. Combine pale iceberg with dark green spinach, romaine with curly endive. For color accents, add red leaf lettuce, red cabbage or radicchio.

- Dressing clings much better to dry leaves, so use a salad spinner or paper towel to blot any leftover moisture that may be in the crevices.

- Greens go limp and the edges darken if you cut them with a knife; instead of cutting, tear them into bite-size pieces with your fingers. If you do use a knife, cut up the greens just before serving or use a serrated plastic salad knife (sold in the utensils/gadgets section in large department or discount stores).

- Serve salads family style from a large bowl or in small bowls or on plates for each person. If you're making individual servings, give your artistic flair the go-ahead and arrange the salad attractively on the plate. Try grouping the ingredients or layering them on a bed of greens.

- Tomatoes are watery, so wait until just before tossing to add slices or wedges to a salad so they won't dilute the dressing or cause the greens to go limp. Seeding the tomatoes first will also help.

- Pour dressing over greens just before serving, using only enough to lightly coat the leaves, then toss. Or serve the dressing on the side so each person can add as much or as little as desired. Salads that have been tossed with dressing don't make good leftovers because the salad will become soggy and limp.

- Put the finishing touch on your salad with onion or green bell pepper rings, a sprig of herbs, sliced green or ripe olives, halved cherry tomatoes or a sprinkling of nuts or cheese.

Mandarin Salad   *Fast*

Prep: 20 min ✱ 6 servings

1/4 cup sliced almonds
1 tablespoon plus 1 teaspoon sugar
Sweet-Sour Dressing (below)
1/2 small head lettuce, torn into bite-size pieces (3 cups)
1/2 bunch romaine, torn into bite-size pieces (3 cups)
2 medium stalks celery, chopped (1 cup)
2 medium green onions, thinly sliced (2 tablespoons)
1 can (11 ounces) mandarin orange segments, drained

1. Cook almonds and sugar in 1-quart saucepan over low heat, stirring constantly, until sugar is melted and almonds are coated; cool and break apart.

2. Make Sweet-Sour Dressing.

3. Toss almonds, dressing and remaining ingredients.

Sweet-Sour Dressing

1/4 cup vegetable oil
2 tablespoons sugar
2 tablespoons white or cider vinegar
1 tablespoon chopped fresh parsley
1/2 teaspoon salt
Dash of pepper
Dash of red pepper sauce

1. Shake all ingredients in tightly covered container.

2. Refrigerate until serving.

1 Serving (about 1 1/3 cups): Calories 180 (Calories from Fat 110); Fat 12g (Saturated 2g); Cholesterol 0mg; Sodium 220mg; Carbohydrate 18g (Dietary Fiber 2g); Protein 2g **% Daily Value:** Vitamin A 4%; Vitamin C 30%; Calcium 4%; Iron 4% **Diet Exchanges:** Vegetable, 1 Fruit, 2 Fat

Mandarin Salad

Caesar Salad *Fast*

Prep: 15 min ✳ 6 servings

1 clove garlic, cut in half
8 anchovy fillets, cut up*
1/3 cup olive or vegetable oil
3 tablespoons lemon juice
1 teaspoon Worcestershire sauce
1/4 teaspoon salt
1/4 teaspoon ground mustard
Freshly ground pepper
1 large or 2 small bunches romaine, torn into bite-size
   pieces (10 cups)
1 cup garlic-flavored croutons
1/3 cup grated Parmesan cheese

1. Rub large wooden salad bowl with cut clove of garlic. Allow a few small pieces of garlic to remain in bowl if desired.

2. Mix anchovies, oil, lemon juice, Worcestershire sauce, salt, mustard and pepper in salad bowl.

3. Add romaine; toss until coated. Sprinkle with croutons and cheese; toss.

*2 teaspoons anchovy paste can be substituted for the anchovy fillets.

1 Serving (about 1 3/4 cups): Calories 165 (Calories from Fat 125); Fat 14g (Saturated 3g); Cholesterol 10mg; Sodium 430mg; Carbohydrate 6g (Dietary Fiber 1g); Protein 5g **% Daily Value:** Vitamin A 14%; Vitamin C 24%; Calcium 10%; Iron 6% **Diet Exchanges:** 1 Vegetable, 3 Fat

CHICKEN CAESAR SALAD: Broil or grill 6 boneless, skinless chicken breast halves (page 277); slice diagonally and arrange on salads. Serve chicken warm or chilled.

SHRIMP CAESAR SALAD: Broil or grill 1 pound peeled deveined large shrimp (page 320); arrange on salads. Serve shrimp warm or chilled.

Greek Salad *Fast*

Prep: 20 min ✻ 8 servings

Tangy feta cheese is Greek in origin and is traditionally made from sheep or goat milk. It is sometimes referred to as "pickled" cheese because it's cured and stored in its own salty whey brine.

Lemon Dressing (below)
7 ounces spinach, torn into bite-size pieces (5 cups)
1 head Boston lettuce, torn into bite-size pieces
    (4 cups)
1/2 cup crumbled feta cheese (2 ounces)
4 medium green onions, sliced (1/4 cup)
24 pitted ripe olives
3 medium tomatoes, cut into wedges
1 medium cucumber, sliced

1. Make Lemon Dressing.

2. Toss dressing and remaining ingredients.

Lemon Dressing

1/4 cup vegetable oil
2 tablespoons lemon juice
1/2 teaspoon sugar
1 1/2 teaspoons Dijon mustard
1/4 teaspoon salt
1/8 teaspoon pepper

Shake all ingredients in tightly covered container.

1 Serving (about 1 3/4 cups): Calories 120 (Calories from Fat 90); Fat 10g (Saturated 3g); Cholesterol 10mg; Sodium 320mg; Carbohydrate 6g (Dietary Fiber 2g); Protein 3g **% Daily Value:** Vitamin A 22%; Vitamin C 30%; Calcium 8%; Iron 8% **Diet Exchanges:** 1 Vegetable, 2 Fat

Gorgonzola and Toasted Walnut Salad *Fast*

Prep: 20 min ✻ 6 servings

Toasted Walnut Dressing (below)
1 head radicchio, torn into bite-size pieces (4 cups)
1 head Bibb lettuce, torn into bite-size pieces (4 cups)
1/2 cup crumbled Gorgonzola or Roquefort cheese
    (2 ounces)
1/2 cup 1/2-inch pieces fresh chives
1/3 cup coarsely chopped walnuts, toasted (page 177)

1. Make Toasted Walnut Dressing.

2. Toss dressing and remaining ingredients.

Toasted Walnut Dressing

1/3 cup olive or vegetable oil
1/3 cup coarsely chopped walnuts, toasted
2 tablespoons lemon juice
1 clove garlic
1/8 teaspoon salt
Dash of pepper

Place all ingredients in blender or food processor. Cover and blend on high speed about 1 minute or until smooth.

1 Serving: Calories 250 (Calories from Fat 215); Fat 24g (Saturated 4g); Cholesterol 5mg; Sodium 210mg; Carbohydrate 5g (Dietary Fiber 2g); Protein 5g **% Daily Value:** Vitamin A 10%; Vitamin C 16%; Calcium 8%; Iron 4% **Diet Exchanges:** 1 Vegetable, 5 Fat

---

LEMON JUICE

One fresh lemon will give you about 2 to 3 tablespoons of juice. To get the most juice out of a lemon or lime, it should be at room temperature. Before squeezing, roll the lemon back and forth on the counter several times with firm pressure, which helps to burst the cells holding the juice. Or try zapping whole lemons in the microwave on High for about 20 seconds or so to warm them first, which also helps release the juice.

Roasted Beet Salad

Roasted Beet Salad

Prep: 15 min; Bake: 1 hr; Cool: 1 hr ✱ *4 servings*

4 medium beets (4 to 6 ounces each)
1/2 cup Fresh Herb Vinaigrette (page 433)
1/4 cup orange juice
4 cups bite-size pieces mixed salad greens
1 medium orange, peeled and sliced
1/2 cup walnut halves, toasted (page 177) and coarsely
    chopped
1/4 cup crumbled chèvre (goat) cheese

1. Heat oven to 400°. Remove greens from beets, leaving about 1/2 inch of stem. Wash beets well. Place in square pan, 8 × 8 × 2 inches. Add 1/2 cup water to pan. Cover tightly with aluminum foil. Bake about 1 hour or until tender.

2. Cool beets 1 hour. Remove skins from beets under running water. Cut beets into slices. Cut each slice in half.

3. Make Fresh Herb Vinaigrette as directed—except substitute orange juice for 1/4 cup of the vinegar.

4. Arrange salad greens on 4 salad plates. Top with beets, orange, walnuts and cheese. Drizzle with vinaigrette. Serve with remaining vinaigrette.

1 Serving: Calories 270 (Calories from Fat 205); Fat 23g (Saturated 4g); Cholesterol 8mg; Sodium 75mg; Carbohydrate 14g (Dietary Fiber 3g); Protein 5g **% Daily Value:** Vitamin A 8%; Vitamin C 22%; Calcium 8%; Iron 6% **Diet Exchanges:** 3 Vegetable, 4 Fat

Bacon-Spinach Salad

Fast & Low-Fat

Prep: 15 min; Cook: 10 min ✱ 4 servings

Don't forget to wash your spinach well, since it grows in sandy soil and you want to make sure it is free of any grit. You can also save time by using prewashed spinach found in the produce department.

4 slices bacon, diced
1/4 cup white or cider vinegar
8 ounces spinach or 2 bunches leaf lettuce, coarsely shredded (6 cups)
5 medium green onions, chopped (1/3 cup)
2 teaspoons sugar
1/4 teaspoon salt
1/8 teaspoon pepper

1. Cook bacon in 12-inch skillet over medium heat, stirring occasionally, until crisp. Stir in vinegar. Heat through; remove from heat.

2. Add spinach and onions to bacon mixture. Sprinkle with sugar, salt and pepper. Toss 1 to 2 minutes or until spinach is wilted.

To wash spinach, remove and discard spinach stems. Place leaves in a sink or bowl filled with cool water. Swish with your hands to rinse off the dirt. Lift the leaves up to drain off excess water. Repeat until no dirt remains, changing water if necessary.

1 Serving (about 1 1/2 cups): Calories 55 (Calories from Fat 25); Fat 3g (Saturated 1g); Cholesterol 5mg; Sodium 280mg; Carbohydrate 5g (Dietary Fiber 1g); Protein 3g **% Daily Value:** Vitamin A 34%; Vitamin C 22%; Calcium 4%; Iron 8% **Diet Exchanges:** 1 Vegetable, 1/2 Fat

Seven-Layer Salad

Prep: 25 min; Chill: 2 hr ✱ 6 servings

Many of the creamier dressings call for mayonnaise or salad dressing. What's the difference? Although very similar in flavor and appearance, salad dressing is usually a bit sweeter than mayonnaise.

6 cups bite-size pieces mixed salad greens
2 medium stalks celery, thinly sliced (1 cup)
1 cup thinly sliced radishes
8 medium green onions, sliced (1/2 cup)
12 slices bacon, crisply cooked and crumbled
1 package (10 ounces) frozen green peas, thawed and drained
1 1/2 cups mayonnaise or salad dressing
1/2 cup grated Parmesan cheese or shredded Cheddar cheese (2 ounces)

1. Place salad greens in large glass bowl. Layer celery, radishes, onions, bacon and peas on salad greens.

2. Spread mayonnaise over peas, covering top completely and sealing to edge of bowl. Sprinkle with cheese. Cover and refrigerate at least 2 hours to blend flavors but no longer than 12 hours. Toss before serving if desired. Store covered in refrigerator.

1 Serving (about 1 1/4 cups): Calories 540 (Calories from Fat 480); Fat 52g (Saturated 10g); Cholesterol 50mg; Sodium 700mg; Carbohydrate 10g (Dietary Fiber 4g); Protein 10g **% Daily Value:** Vitamin A 14%; Vitamin C 28%; Calcium 14%; Iron 10% **Diet Exchanges:** 1 High-Fat Meat, 2 Vegetable, 8 1/2 Fat

Lighter Seven-Layer Salad: For 11 grams of fat and 170 calories per serving, substitute 1/2 cup reduced-fat mayonnaise and 1 cup plain fat-free yogurt for the 1 1/2 cups mayonnaise. Decrease bacon to 6 slices and cheese to 1/4 cup.

Broccoli Sunshine Salad *Fast*

Prep: 15 min ✴ 6 servings

Stir the salad just before serving. If the dressing is too thick, thin it with a little vinegar.

1/2 cup mayonnaise or salad dressing
1 tablespoon sugar
2 tablespoons cider vinegar
3 cups broccoli flowerets (1/2 pound)
1/3 cup raisins
1/4 cup shredded Cheddar cheese (1 ounce)
4 slices bacon, crisply cooked and crumbled
2 tablespoons chopped red onion

1. Mix mayonnaise, sugar and vinegar in large bowl.

2. Add remaining ingredients; toss until evenly coated. Store covered in refrigerator.

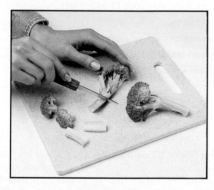

To make spears, cut lengthwise into 1/2-inch stalks. For pieces, cut the 1/2-inch stalks crosswise into 1-inch pieces (or size desired).

1 Serving (about 1/2 cup): Calories 220 (Calories from Fat 160); Fat 18g (Saturated 4g); Cholesterol 20mg; Sodium 210mg; Carbohydrate 12g (Dietary Fiber 2g); Protein 4g **% Daily Value:** Vitamin A 8%; Vitamin C 68%; Calcium 4%; Iron 4% **Diet Exchanges:** 2 Vegetable, 4 Fat

Lighter Broccoli Sunshine Salad: For 8 grams of fat and 130 calories per serving, use reduced-fat mayonnaise and cheese. Decrease bacon to 2 slices.

Creamy Potato Salad

Prep: 45 min; Chill: 4 hr ✴ 10 servings

6 medium round red or white potatoes (2 pounds), peeled
1 1/2 cups mayonnaise or salad dressing
1 tablespoon white or cider vinegar
1 tablespoon yellow mustard
1 teaspoon salt
1/4 teaspoon pepper
2 medium stalks celery, chopped (1 cup)
1 medium onion, chopped (1/2 cup)
4 Hard-Cooked Eggs (page 201), chopped
Paprika, if desired

1. Place potatoes in 3-quart saucepan; add enough water just to cover potatoes. Cover and heat to boiling; reduce heat to low. Cook covered 30 to 35 minutes or until potatoes are tender; drain. Let stand until cool enough to handle. Cut potatoes into cubes.

2. Mix mayonnaise, vinegar, mustard, salt and pepper in large glass or plastic bowl. Add potatoes, celery and onion; toss. Stir in eggs. Sprinkle with paprika. Cover and refrigerate at least 4 hours to blend flavors and chill. Store covered in refrigerator.

1 Serving (about 3/4 cup): Calories 345 (Calories from Fat 250); Fat 28g (Saturated 5g); Cholesterol 105mg; Sodium 480mg; Carbohydrate 21g (Dietary Fiber 2g); Protein 5g **% Daily Value:** Vitamin A 4%; Vitamin C 18%; Calcium 2%; Iron 8% **Diet Exchanges:** 1 Starch, 1 Vegetable, 5 Fat

Lighter Creamy Potato Salad: For 13 grams of fat and 210 calories per serving, use reduced-fat mayonnaise and 2 eggs.

Hot German Potato Salad

Prep: 25 min: Cook: 35 min ✱ *6 servings*

4 medium round red or white potatoes (1 1/3 pounds)

3 slices bacon, cut into 1-inch pieces

1 medium onion, chopped (1/2 cup)

1 tablespoon all-purpose flour

1 tablespoon sugar

1/2 teaspoon salt

1/4 teaspoon celery seed

Dash of pepper

1/2 cup water

1/4 cup white or cider vinegar

1. Place potatoes in 3-quart saucepan; add enough water just to cover potatoes. Cover and heat to boiling; reduce heat to low. Cook covered 30 to 35 minutes or until potatoes are tender; drain. Let stand until cool enough to handle. Cut potatoes into 1/4-inch slices.

2. Cook bacon in 10-inch skillet over medium heat until crisp. Remove bacon from skillet; drain on paper towels.

3. Cook onion in bacon fat in skillet over medium heat, stirring occasionally, until tender. Stir in flour, sugar, salt, celery seed and pepper. Cook over low heat, stirring constantly, until mixture is bubbly; remove from heat.

4. Stir water and vinegar into onion mixture. Heat to boiling, stirring constantly. Boil and stir 1 minute; remove from heat.

5. Stir in potatoes and bacon. Heat over medium heat, stirring gently to coat potato slices, until hot and bubbly.

1 Serving (about 2/3 cup): Calories 130 (Calories from Fat 20); Fat 2g (Saturated 1g); Cholesterol 5mg; Sodium 260mg; Carbohydrate 28g (Dietary Fiber 3g); Protein 3g **% Daily Value:** Vitamin A 0%; Vitamin C 10%; Calcium 0%; Iron 8% **Diet Exchanges:** 1 Starch, 2 Vegetable

Slow Cooker Directions: Increase flour to 2 tablespoons. Decrease water to 1/3 cup. Cut potatoes into 1/4-inch slices. Cook and drain bacon; refrigerate. Mix all ingredients except bacon in 3 1/2- to 6-quart slow cooker. Cover and cook on low heat setting 8 to 10 hours or until potatoes are tender. Stir in bacon.

Carrot-Raisin Salad *Fast*

Prep: 10 min ✱ *5 servings*

3 large carrots, shredded (2 1/2 cups)

1/2 cup raisins

1/2 cup mayonnaise or salad dressing

1 teaspoon lemon juice

Salad greens, if desired

1. Mix all ingredients except salad greens.

2. Serve on salad greens.

3. Store covered in refrigerator.

1 Serving (about 1/2 cup): Calories 225 (Calories from Fat 160); Fat 18g (Saturated 3g); Cholesterol 15mg; Sodium 140mg; Carbohydrate 17g (Dietary Fiber 2g); Protein 1g **% Daily Value:** Vitamin A 68%; Vitamin C 8%; Calcium 2%; Iron 4% **Diet Exchanges:** 2 Vegetable, 1/2 Fruit, 3 Fat

---

POTATO SALAD PASSION

Who would think that something as humble as the creamy type of potato salad could create so much passion and debate? But do a little digging into this creation, and you will find fierce loyalty for making it this way or that. It's generally agreed that round red potatoes, because of their waxy texture, stand up best to a cook's additions and mixing. But some folks will settle for it made only with baking potatoes. Do you add onion? Celery? Green bell pepper? Pickle relish? Barbecue sauce? And how many hard-cooked eggs do you use for each potato? Do you mash or smash some of the potatoes and leave the rest in chunks, or do you cut nice even pieces? Do you like throwing in a little yellow mustard, a lot of yellow mustard, some other type of mustard or no mustard at all? And how about vinegar—a little dash or a bit more? And a key decision—whether to use mayonnaise or salad dressing. Some like it made with cooked salad dressing. Maybe you add a little sour cream, too. Some add sugar; most add salt and pepper to taste. Do you make it a day ahead of time or insist on eating it the day it's made? Do you like to serve it ice cold or a tad warmer? As you can imagine, each cook puts her or his special spin on this very adaptable little recipe. Try our Creamy Potato Salad on page 417; it's a classic version we think you'll enjoy.

Cucumber Salad

Lighter Carrot-Raisin Salad: For 8 grams of fat and 140 calories per serving, use low-fat mayonnaise.

Cucumber Salad *Low-Fat*

Prep: 10 min; Chill: 3 hr ✳ *6 servings*

For a scalloped look, run fork tines down the length of each cucumber before slicing.

2 medium cucumbers, thinly sliced
1/3 cup cider or white vinegar
1/3 cup water
2 tablespoons sugar
1/2 teaspoon salt
1/8 teaspoon pepper
Chopped fresh dill weed or parsley, if desired

1. Place cucumbers in small glass or plastic bowl.

2. Shake remaining ingredients except dill weed in tightly covered container. Pour over cucumbers. Cover and refrigerate at least 3 hours to blend flavors.

3. Drain salad. Sprinkle with dill weed. Srore covered in refrigerator.

1 Serving (about 1/2 cup): Calories 25 (Calories from Fat 0); Fat 0g (Saturated 0g); Cholesterol 0mg; Sodium 200mg; Carbohydrate 7g (Dietary Fiber 1g); Protein 0g **% Daily Value:** Vitamin A 0%; Vitamin C 6%; Calcium 0%; Iron 0% **Diet Exchanges:** 1 Vegetable

CREAMY CUCUMBER SALAD: After draining salad, stir in 3/4 cup sour cream or plain yogurt. (If desired, omit vinegar and water; stir in sour cream.) Store covered in refrigerator.

Creamy Coleslaw

Prep: 15 min; Chill: 1 hr ✱ *8 servings*

1/2 cup mayonnaise or salad dressing
1/4 cup sour cream
1 tablespoon sugar
2 teaspoons lemon juice
2 teaspoons Dijon mustard
1/2 teaspoon celery seed
1/4 teaspoon salt
1/4 teaspoon pepper
1/2 medium head cabbage, finely shredded or chopped
    (4 cups)
1 small carrot, shredded (1/2 cup)
1 small onion, chopped (1/4 cup)

1. Mix all ingredients except cabbage, carrot and onion in large glass or plastic bowl. Add remaining ingredients; toss until evenly coated.

2. Cover and refrigerate at least 1 hour to blend flavors. Store covered in refrigerator.

To shred cabbage, place a flat side of 1/4 head of cabbage on a cutting board. Cut into thin slices with a large sharp knife. Cut slices several times to make smaller pieces.

1 Serving (about 2/3 cup): Calories 140 (Calories from Fat 115); Fat 13g (Saturated 3g); Cholesterol 15mg; Sodium 260mg; Carbohydrate 7g (Dietary Fiber 2g); Protein 1g **% Daily Value:** Vitamin A 12%; Vitamin C 32%; Calcium 4%; Iron 2% **Diet Exchanges:** 1 Vegetable, 2 1/2 Fat

> **Lighter Creamy Coleslaw:** For 6 grams of fat and 85 calories per serving, use reduced-fat mayonnaise and sour cream.

Sweet-and-Sour Coleslaw

Prep: 15 min; Chill: 3 hr ✱ *8 servings*

In a hurry? Use 6 1/2 cups packaged coleslaw mix, and omit the cabbage, carrot and bell pepper.

1/2 medium head cabbage, finely shredded (4 cups)
1 large carrot, finely shredded (1 cup)
1 medium green bell pepper, chopped (1 cup)
4 medium green onions, thinly sliced (1/4 cup)
1/2 cup sugar
1/2 cup white wine, white vinegar or cider vinegar
1/4 cup vegetable oil
1 teaspoon ground mustard
1/2 teaspoon celery seed
1/2 teaspoon salt

1. Place cabbage, carrot, bell pepper and onions in large glass or plastic bowl.

2. Shake remaining ingredients in tightly covered container. Pour over vegetables; stir. Cover and refrigerate at least 3 hours, stirring several times, until chilled. Serve with slotted spoon. Store covered in refrigerator.

1 Serving (about 3/4 cup): Calories 130 (Calories from Fat 65); Fat 7g (Saturated 1g); Cholesterol 0mg; Sodium 160mg; Carbohydrate 18g (Dietary Fiber 2g); Protein 1g **% Daily Value:** Vitamin A 16%; Vitamin C 58%; Calcium 2%; Iron 2% **Diet Exchanges:** 3 Vegetable, 1 Fat

Three-Bean Salad

Prep: 20 min; Chill: 3 hr ✱ *6 servings*

For a quickly made salad, use your favorite purchased Italian dressing instead of making the dressing from scratch.

1 cup Italian Dressing (page 431)
1 can (15 to 16 ounces) cut green beans, drained
1 can (15 to 16 ounces) wax beans, drained
1 can (15 to 16 ounces) kidney, black or garbanzo
    beans, rinsed and drained
4 medium green onions, chopped (1/4 cup)
1/4 cup chopped fresh parsley
1 tablespoon sugar
2 cloves garlic, finely chopped

1. Make Italian dressing.

2. Mix beans, onions and parsley in medium glass or plastic bowl.

3. Mix dressing, sugar and garlic. Pour over salad; toss. Cover and refrigerate at least 3 hours to blend flavors, stirring occasionally.

4. Just before serving, spoon bean mixture into bowl with slotted spoon.

1 Serving (about 3/4 cup): Calories 200 (Calories from Fat 90); Fat 10g (Saturated 2g); Cholesterol 0mg; Sodium 640mg; Carbohydrate 27g (Dietary Fiber 7g); Protein 8g **% Daily Value:** Vitamin A 4%; Vitamin C 20%; Calcium 6%; Iron 20% **Diet Exchanges:** 1 Starch, 2 Vegetable, 2 Fat

24-Hour Fruit Salad

Prep: 30 min; Chill: 12 hr ✱ *8 servings*

Whipped Cream Dressing (below)
1 can (16 1/2 ounces) pitted light or dark sweet
    cherries, drained
2 cans (20 ounces each) pineapple chunks in juice,
    drained and 2 tablespoons juice reserved for
    dressing
3 oranges, cut into small chunks*
1 cup miniature marshmallows

1. Make Whipped Cream Dressing.

2. Gently toss dressing and remaining ingredients in large glass or plastic bowl. Cover and refrigerate at least 12 hours to blend flavors but no longer than 24 hours. Store remaining salad covered in refrigerator.

2 cans (11 ounces each) mandarin orange segments, drained, can be substituted for the oranges.

Whipped Cream Dressing

2 large eggs, beaten
2 tablespoons sugar
2 tablespoons white vinegar or lemon juice
2 tablespoons reserved pineapple juice
1 tablespoon butter or stick margarine
Dash of salt
3/4 cup whipping (heavy) cream

1. Heat all ingredients except whipping cream just to boiling in 1-quart saucepan over medium heat, stirring constantly; cool.

2. Beat whipping cream in chilled medium bowl with electric mixer on high speed until stiff.

3. Fold in egg mixture.

1 Serving (about 1 cup): Calories 255 (Calories from Fat 90); Fat 10g (Saturated 6g); Cholesterol 80mg; Sodium 35mg; Carbohydrate 40g (Dietary Fiber 3g); Protein 4g **% Daily Value:** Vitamin A 10%; Vitamin C 32%; Calcium 6%; Iron 4% **Diet Exchanges:** 2 1/2 Fruit, 2 Fat

Lighter 24-Hour Salad: For 3 grams of fat and 180 calories per serving, omit Whipped Cream Dressing. For dressing, reserve 1/4 cup pineapple juice; fold juice into 2 cups frozen (thawed) reduced-fat whipped topping.

Waldorf Salad

Waldorf Salad   *Fast*

Prep: 10 min ✱ 4 servings

Instead of apples, why not try fresh pears instead?
Stirring in 2 tablespoons dried blueberries, cherries,
cranberries or raisins is perfect for adding a tasty flavor and pretty color.

1/2 cup mayonnaise or salad dressing
1 tablespoon lemon juice
1 tablespoon milk
2 medium unpeeled red eating apples, coarsely chopped
   (2 cups)
2 medium stalks celery, chopped (1 cup)
1/3 cup coarsely chopped nuts
Salad greens, if desired

1. Mix mayonnaise, lemon juice and milk in medium
bowl.

2. Stir in apples, celery and nuts. Serve on salad greens.
Store remaining salad covered in refrigerator.

1 Serving (about 3/4 cup): Calories 305 (Calories from Fat 250);
Fat 28g (Saturated 4g); Cholesterol 15mg; Sodium 180mg;
Carbohydrate 14g (Dietary Fiber 3g); Protein 2g **% Daily Value:**
Vitamin A 2%; Vitamin C 10%; Calcium 2%; Iron 2% **Diet
Exchanges:** 1 Fruit, 5 Fat

Lighter Waldorf Salad: For 13 grams of fat and
170 calories per serving, use reduced-fat mayonnaise; decrease nuts to 2 tablespoons.

Apples and Their Uses

The names sound just like autumn: Prairie Spy,
Winesap, Beacon, Fireside. Unfortunately, the names
don't give any hints on how to use the literally thousands of apple varieties. To clear up some of the confu-
sion and help you choose the best apple for eating or
cooking, we've drawn up this chart of some of the most
popular apple varieties, their characteristics and how
they can be used.

APPLE VARIETIES AND CHARACTERISTICS

Variety	Flavor	Texture	Baking	Eating and Salads	Pies	Sauce
Braeburn	Sweet-Tart	Crisp	●	●	●	●
Cortland	Slightly Tart	Slightly Crisp	●	●	●	●
Crispin/Mutsu	Sweet	Crisp	●	●	●	●
Criterion	Sweet	Crisp		●	●	●
Elstar	Sweet-Tart	Crisp	●	●		●
Empire	Sweet-Tart	Crisp	●	●	●	●
Fireside	Slightly Sweet	Slightly Crisp		●		
Fuji	Sweet	Crisp		●		
Gala	Sweet	Crisp		●		●
Ginger Gold	Sweet	Crisp		●		
Golden Delicious	Sweet	Crisp	●	●	●	●
Granny Smith	Tart	Crisp	●	●	●	●
Greening	Tart	Crisp	●		●	●
Haralson	Tart	Crisp	●	●	●	●
Honeycrisp	Sweet	Crisp	●	●		●
Honey Gold	Sweet	Slightly Crisp		●	●	
Ida Red	Slightly Tart	Slightly Crisp	●		●	●
Jonagold	Sweet-Tart	Crisp	●	●	●	●
Jonamac	Sweet-Tart	Tender		●		●
Jonathan	Slightly Tart	Tender		●	●	●
McIntosh	Sweet-Tart	Tender		●		●
Newtown Pippin	Slightly Tart	Crisp	●	●	●	●
Northern Spy	Slightly Tart	Crisp	●		●	●
Paula Red	Slightly Tart	Slightly Crisp		●	●	●
Prairie Spy	Slightly Sweet	Crisp	●	●	●	●
Red Delicious	Sweet	Crisp		●		
Regent	Sweet	Crisp		●	●	
Rome	Slightly Tart	Slightly Crisp	●		●	●
Spartan	Slightly Tart	Tender		●	●	●
Winesap	Slightly Tart	Crisp		●		
York Imperial	Slightly Tart	Slightly Crisp	●	●	●	●

Tips for Gelatin Salads

There are two types of gelatin: flavored and unflavored. You're probably most familiar with flavored gelatin that's premixed with sugar or artificial sweetener, coloring and flavors and that is easy to work with. Unflavored gelatin, because it's clear and plain, is used to gel or thicken mixtures of any flavor.

- For gelatin to gel or "set up," it must be dissolved completely in hot liquid. Here's how to handle the two types of gelatin:

  Flavored: Place the gelatin in a heatproof container, and add a boiling liquid such as fruit juice or water. Stir until dissolved.

  Unflavored: Sprinkle the gelatin on cold liquid, and let stand for 1 to 2 minutes to soften and swell. Then, stir in boiling liquid or heat over low heat until the gelatin is dissolved.

- You can add up to 1 1/2 cups of fruit or vegetable to a four-serving-size batch of gelatin. If you're making a gelatin mold, small pieces of fruit or veggies work best; larger chunks can tear the gelatin when you try to unmold it. If you're just making gelatin in a bowl, using larger chunks is okay.

- When adding fruit or vegetables, chill the gelatin mixture first, about 20 to 40 minutes, until it's the consistency of unbeaten egg whites. If the gelatin becomes thicker than that, place it over hot water or microwave on High for 5 to 10 seconds until it's the desired consistency.

- Before adding whipped or sour cream, chill the gelatin until it mounds when you drop a dollop from a spoon, about 30 to 40 minutes.

- Don't use *fresh or frozen* pineapple, pineapple juice, papaya or kiwifruit in a gelatin salad. They contain an enzyme that breaks down the gelatin so it won't set. However, you can use these fruits if they're canned.

- How long does gelatin take to "set up"? Chilling time depends on the amount of gelatin and the kind of container you're using; a metal container chills faster than a glass one. As a rule, a recipe for four servings takes about 3 hours; larger recipes need to be refrigerated 4 to 6 hours or overnight.

- Here's the secret for how to perfectly unmold a gelatin salad: Quickly dip—10 seconds—the mold into warm, not hot, water up to the line of the gelatin. Loosen an edge of the salad with the tip of a knife, then tip the mold slightly to allow air in and to break the vacuum. Rotate the mold so all sides are loose. Place a moistened serving plate on top of the mold. Holding both the mold and the plate firmly, turn the mold upside down and shake gently. Carefully lift the mold off the gelatin. If the gelatin doesn't come out, repeat the steps.

- Gelatin salads keep at least 24 hours; most keep up to 3 days. If the salad contains ingredients such as vinegar or lemon juice or if too much sugar was used, the gelatin will be softer and may leak liquid during storage.

Peach-Berry Fruit Mold *Low-Fat*

Prep: 15 min; Chill: 4 hr ✳ 8 servings

1 cup boiling water
1 package (4-serving size) peach-flavored gelatin
1 cup cold water
1 cup raspberries
1/2 cup blueberries
1 medium peach, peeled and coarsely chopped
Leaf lettuce, if desired

1. Pour boiling water on gelatin in medium bowl; stir until gelatin is dissolved. Stir in cold water. Refrigerate about 1 hour or until slightly thickened.

2. Spray 1-quart mold with cooking spray. Stir raspberries, blueberries and peach into gelatin. Spoon into mold. Cover and refrigerate at least 3 hours until firm.

3. Unmold gelatin onto lettuce leaves on serving plate (see Tips for Gelatin Salads, page 424).

1 Serving: Calories 50 (Calories from Fat 0); Fat 0g (Saturated 0g); Cholesterol 0mg; Sodium 30mg; Carbohydrate 14g (Dietary Fiber 2g); Protein 1g **% Daily Value:** Vitamin A 0%; Vitamin C 10%; Calcium 0%; Iron 0% **Diet Exchanges:** 1 Fruit

Piña Colada Mold *Low-Fat*

Prep: 10 min; Chill: 5 hr ✳ 8 servings

1 2/3 cups boiling water
1 package (4-serving size) pineapple-flavored gelatin
1 package (4-serving size) orange-flavored gelatin
1/2 cup frozen nonalcoholic piña colada concentrate
    (from 10-ounce can)
1 can (20 ounces) pineapple tidbits in juice, drained and
    juice reserved
1/2 cup flaked coconut

1. Pour boiling water on gelatins in medium bowl; stir until gelatins are dissolved. Stir in piña colada concentrate and reserved pineapple juice, using wire whisk, until concentrate is melted. Refrigerate 45 to 60 minutes or until slightly thickened.

2. Spray 2-quart mold with cooking spray. Stir pineapple and coconut into gelatin mixture. Spoon into mold. Cover and refrigerate at least 4 hours until firm.

3. Unmold gelatin onto serving plate (see Tips for Gelatin Salads, page 424).

1 Serving: Calories 180 (Calories from Fat 25); Fat 3g (Saturated 3g); Cholesterol 0mg; Sodium 70mg; Carbohydrate 37g (Dietary Fiber 1g); Protein 2g **% Daily Value:** Vitamin A 0%; Vitamin C 0%; Calcium 0%; Iron 2% **Diet Exchanges:** 2 1/2 Fruit, 1/2 Fat

Tabbouleh

Prep: 35 min; Chill: 1 hr ✱ 6 servings

3/4 cup uncooked bulgur
1 1/2 cups chopped fresh parsley
3 medium tomatoes, chopped (2 1/4 cups)
5 medium green onions, thinly sliced (1/3 cup)
2 tablespoons chopped fresh or 2 teaspoons crumbled
    dried mint leaves
1/4 cup olive or vegetable oil
1/4 cup lemon juice
3/4 teaspoon salt
1/4 teaspoon pepper
Whole ripe olives, if desired

1. Cover bulgur with cold water. Let stand 30 minutes; drain. Press out as much water as possible.

2. Place bulgur, parsley, tomatoes, onions and mint in medium glass or plastic bowl.

3. Shake remaining ingredients except olives in tightly covered container. Pour over bulgur mixture; toss. Cover and refrigerate at least 1 hour to blend flavors. Garnish with olives.

1 Serving (about 3/4 cup): Calories 160 (Calories from Fat 90); Fat 10g (Saturated 1g); Cholesterol 0mg; Sodium 320mg; Carbohydrate 19g (Dietary Fiber 5g); Protein 3g **% Daily Value:** Vitamin A 12%; Vitamin C 60%; Calcium 4%; Iron 10% **Diet Exchanges:** 1 Starch, 1 Vegetable, 1 Fat

Tuna-Macaroni Salad

Prep: 20 min; Chill: 1 hr ✱ 6 servings

1 package (7 ounces) elbow macaroni
1 cup mayonnaise or salad dressing
1 cup shredded Cheddar cheese (4 ounces), if desired
1/2 cup frozen green peas, thawed
1/4 cup sweet pickle relish, if desired
2 teaspoons lemon juice
3/4 teaspoon salt
1/4 teaspoon pepper
1 medium stalk celery, chopped (1/2 cup)
1 small onion, chopped (1/4 cup)
1 can (9 ounces) tuna, drained

1. Cook and drain macaroni and directed on package. Rinse with cold water; drain.

2. Mix macaroni and remaining ingredients. Cover and refrigerate at least 1 hour to blend flavors.

1 Serving (about 1 cup): Calories 520 (Calories from Fat 325); Fat 36g (Saturated 9g); Cholesterol 55mg; Sodium 780mg; Carbohydrate 30g (Dietary Fiber 2g); Protein 21g **% Daily Value:** Vitamin A 8%; Vitamin C 4%; Calcium 12%; Iron 14% **Diet Exchanges:** 2 Starch, 2 Medium-Fat Meat, 5 Fat

Crunchy Oriental Chicken Salad *Fast*

Prep: 10 min; Cook: 5 min ✱ *6 servings*

2 tablespoons butter or stick margarine
1 package (3 ounces) Oriental-flavor ramen noodle
    soup mix
2 tablespoons sesame seed
1/4 cup sugar
1/4 cup white vinegar
1 tablespoon sesame or vegetable oil
1/2 teaspoon pepper
2 cups cut-up cooked chicken
1/4 cup dry-roasted peanuts, if desired
4 medium green onions, sliced (1/4 cup)
1 bag (16 ounces) coleslaw mix
1 can (11 ounces) mandarin orange segments, drained

1. Melt butter in 10-inch skillet over medium heat. Stir in seasoning packet from soup mix. Break block of noodles into bite-size pieces over skillet; stir into butter mixture.

2. Cook 2 minutes, stirring occasionally. Stir in sesame seed. Cook about 2 minutes longer, stirring occasionally, until noodles are golden brown; remove from heat.

3. Mix sugar, vinegar, oil and pepper in large bowl. Add noodle mixture and remaining ingredients; toss.

1 Serving (about 1 1/4 cups): Calories 265 (Calories from Fat 110); Fat 12g (Saturated 4g); Cholesterol 50mg; Sodium 140mg; Carbohydrate 25g (Dietary Fiber 2g); Protein 16g **% Daily Value:** Vitamin A 4%; Vitamin C 26%; Calcium 6%; Iron 8% **Diet Exchanges:** 1 Starch, 1 Medium-Fat Meat, 2 Vegetable, 1 Fat

Salad Niçoise

Prep: 1 hr 20 min ✱ *4 servings*

1 package (10 ounces) frozen French-style green beans
3/4 cup Classic French Dressing (page 432)
1 head Bibb lettuce, torn into bite-size pieces (4 cups)
2 medium tomatoes, cut into sixths
2 Hard-Cooked Eggs (page 201), cut into fourths
1 can (6 ounces) tuna in water, drained and flaked
2 tablespoons sliced ripe olives
Chopped fresh parsley, if desired
6 anchovy fillets, if desired

1. Cook and drain green beans as directed on package. Refrigerate at least 1 hour until chilled.

2. Make Classic French Dressing.

3. Place lettuce in deep platter or salad bowl. Arrange green beans, tomatoes and eggs around edge of lettuce. Mound tuna in center; sprinkle with olives. Sprinkle parsley over salad. Garnish with anchovies. Serve with dressing. Store covered in refrigerator.

1 Serving (about 2 cups): Calories 165 (Calories from Fat 80); Fat 9g (Saturated 2g); Cholesterol 120mg; Sodium 270mg; Carbohydrate 8g (Dietary Fiber 3g); Protein 16g **% Daily Value:** Vitamin A 12%; Vitamin C 30%; Calcium 6%; Iron 12% **Diet Exchanges:** 2 Lean Meat, 2 Vegetable

Chicken Stuffed Tomatoes

Salmon-Stuffed Tomatoes *Fast*

Prep: 20 min ✻ 4 servings

1 cup uncooked rosamarina (orzo) pasta (6 ounces)*
4 large tomatoes
1 medium cucumber, peeled, seeded and chopped
   (1 cup)
1 can (14 3/4 ounces) salmon, drained and skin
   removed
1/2 cup ranch or creamy dill dressing

1. Cook and drain pasta as directed on package. Rinse with cold water; drain.

2. Cut stem ends from tomatoes. Remove pulp, leaving 1/2-inch wall. Chop tomato pulp; drain. Cut thin slice from bottom of each tomato to prevent tipping.

3. Mix pasta, chopped tomato and remaining ingredients. Spoon 1/2 cup pasta mixture into each tomato. Serve with remaining pasta mixture. Or cut tomato shells into halves or fourths; divide pasta mixture evenly among tomatoes.

*3 cups cold cooked rice can be substituted for the cooked pasta.

1 Serving: Calories 400 (Calories from Fat 180); Fat 20g (Saturated 3g); Cholesterol 45mg; Sodium 660mg; Carbohydrate 37g (Dietary Fiber 3g); Protein 21g **% Daily Value:** Vitamin A 14%; Vitamin C 60%; Calcium 24%; Iron 16% **Diet Exchanges:** 2 Starch, 2 Medium-Fat Meat, 1 Vegetable, 1 Fat

CHICKEN-STUFFED TOMATOES: Substitute 2 cups cut-up cooked chicken or turkey for the salmon.

SHRIMP-STUFFED TOMATOES: Substitute 2 packages (5 ounces each) frozen cooked salad shrimp, thawed

TUNA-STUFFED TOMATOES: Substitute 1 can (12 ounces) tuna, rinsed and drained, for the salmon.

Taco Salad

Prep: 1 hr 15 min ✱ *8 servings*

Tortilla Shells (right)
3/4 cup Thousand Island Dressing (page 432)
1 pound lean ground beef
2/3 cup water
1 tablespoon chili powder
1/2 teaspoon salt
1/4 teaspoon garlic powder
1/4 teaspoon ground red pepper (cayenne)
1 can (15 to 16 ounces) kidney beans, drained and
    can reserved
1 medium head lettuce, torn into bite-size pieces
    (10 cups)
1 cup shredded Cheddar cheese (4 ounces)
2/3 cup sliced ripe olives
2 medium tomatoes, coarsely chopped (1 1/2 cups)
1 medium onion, chopped (1/2 cup)
1 medium avocado, thinly sliced
Sour cream, if desired

1. Make Tortilla Shells and Thousand Island Dressing.

2. Cook beef in 10-inch skillet over medium heat 8 to 10 minutes, stirring occasionally, until brown; drain. Stir in water, chili powder, salt, garlic powder, red pepper and beans. Heat to boiling; reduce heat. Simmer uncovered 15 minutes, stirring occasionally. Cool 10 minutes.

3. Mix lettuce, cheese, olives, tomatoes and onion in large bowl. Toss with dressing. Add beef mixture and toss. Divide among Tortilla Shells. Garnish with avocado and sour cream. Serve immediately. Store covered in refrigerator.

Tortilla Shells

Reserved empty kidney bean can
Vegetable oil
8 flour tortillas (10 inches in diameter)

1. Remove label and both ends of kidney bean can. Wash can and dry thoroughly.

2. Heat oil (1 1/2 inches) in 3-quart saucepan to 375°. (Diameter of saucepan should be at least 9 inches.)

3. Place 1 tortilla on top of saucepan. Holding can with long-handled tongs, place can on center of tortilla. Push tortilla into oil by gently pushing can down.

4. Fry tortilla about 5 seconds or until set; remove can with tongs. Fry tortilla 1 to 2 minutes longer, turning tortilla in oil, until crisp and golden brown.

5. Carefully remove tortilla from oil, and drain excess oil from inside. Turn tortilla shell upside down on paper towels; cool.

6. Repeat with remaining tortillas.

1 Serving (about 2 cups): Calories 670 (Calories from Fat 360); Fat 40g (Saturated 7g); Cholesterol 70mg; Sodium 1,030mg; Carbohydrate 56g (Dietary Fiber 8g); Protein 29g **% Daily Value:** Vitamin A 8%; Vitamin C 18%; Calcium 30%; Iron 0% **Diet Exchanges:** 3 Starch, 2 High-Fat Meat, 2 Vegetable, 4 Fat

Lighter Taco Salads: For 9 grams of fat and 285 calories per serving, omit Tortilla Shells. Substitute ground turkey breast for the ground beef. Use reduced-fat Cheddar cheese, prepared Thousand Island dressing and sour cream. Omit avocado. Serve salad on about 12 baked tortilla chips.

Tossed Chef's Salad *Fast*

Prep: 25 min ✱ 5 servings

1/4 cup Classic French Dressing (page 432)*
1/2 cup julienne strips cooked meat (beef, pork or
    smoked ham)
1/2 cup julienne strips cooked chicken or turkey
1/2 cup julienne strips Swiss cheese
8 medium green onions, chopped (1/2 cup)
1 medium head lettuce, torn into bite-size pieces
    (10 cups)
1 small bunch romaine, torn into bite-size pieces
    (6 cups)
1 medium stalk celery, sliced (1/2 cup)
1/2 cup mayonnaise or salad dressing
2 Hard-Cooked Eggs (page 201), sliced
2 medium tomatoes, cut into wedges

1. Make Classic French Dressing.

2. Reserve a few strips of meat, chicken and cheese
for topping salad. Mix remaining meat, chicken
and cheese, the onions, lettuce, romaine and celery in
large bowl.

3. Mix mayonnaise and Classic French Dressing. Pour
over lettuce mixture; toss. Top with reserved meat,
chicken and cheese strips, the eggs and tomatoes. Store
remaining salad covered in refrigerator.

**1/4 cup prepared vinaigrette dressing can be substituted for
the Classic French Dressing.*

1 Serving (about 3 cups): Calories 380 (Calories from Fat 290);
Fat 32g (Saturated 6g); Cholesterol 130mg; Sodium 300mg;
Carbohydrate 9g (Dietary Fiber 4g); Protein 17g **% Daily Value:**
Vitamin A 32%; Vitamin C 58%; Calcium 18%; Iron 14% **Diet
Exchanges:** 2 High-Fat Meat, 2 Vegetable, 3 Fat

Cobb Salad

Prep: 1 hr 10 min ✱ 4 servings, about 3 cups each

This is a show-off salad! Instead of arranging salads
on individual serving plates, arrange it on a platter or
in a large, wide, shallow bowl.

Lemon Vinaigrette (below)
1 small head lettuce, finely shredded (6 cups)
2 cups cut-up cooked chicken
3 Hard-Cooked Eggs (page 201), chopped
2 medium tomatoes, chopped (1 1/2 cups)
1 ripe avocado, chopped
1/4 cup crumbled blue cheese (1 ounce)
4 slices bacon, crisply cooked and crumbled

1. Make Lemon Vinaigrette.

2. Divide lettuce among 4 salad plates or shallow bowls.
Arrange remaining ingredients in rows on lettuce.
Serve with vinaigrette.

Lemon Vinaigrette

1/2 cup vegetable oil
1/4 cup lemon juice
1 tablespoon red wine vinegar
2 teaspoons sugar
1/2 teaspoon salt
1/2 teaspoon ground mustard
1/2 teaspoon Worcestershire sauce
1/4 teaspoon pepper
1 clove garlic, finely chopped

Shake all ingredients in tightly covered container.
Refrigerate at least 1 hour to blend flavors.

1 Serving (about 3 cups): Calories 590 (Calories from Fat 440);
Fat 49g (Saturated 10g); Cholesterol 230mg; Sodium 640mg;
Carbohydrate 12g (Dietary Fiber 4g); Protein 30g **% Daily Value:**
Vitamin A 16%; Vitamin C 36%; Calcium 10%; Iron 14% **Diet
Exchanges:** 4 High-Fat Meat, 2 Vegetable, 3 Fat

HOMEMADE CROUTONS

Make your own croutons in one of
two ways:

- Spread one side of dry (not
  hard) bread with softened butter or margarine, and cut into
  1/2-inch cubes.

- Cut dry (not hard) bread into
  1/2-inch cubes, and toss with
  olive oil to lightly coat.

Then sprinkle either type of bread
cubes with grated Parmesan cheese
and Italian seasoning or your favorite
herbs and seasonings. Cook in
an ungreased heavy skillet over
medium heat 4 to 7 minutes, stirring
frequently, until golden brown.

Salad Dressing Basics

A salad needs as little as a squeeze of lemon juice or as much as a chunky blue cheese dressing. The choice is yours, and what a choice it is! Right now in your refrigerator, you probably have at least one kind of bottled dressing, and in your cupboard, the fixings for many, many more. While the selection of bottled, made-from-a-mix and homemade salad dressings grows by leaps and bounds, they all basically fall into three main categories:

Vinaigrette: Vinaigrette is the classic oil-and-vinegar combo with seasonings added. It's also called French dressing, but don't confuse it with the bottled red French dressing that contains tomato paste and other ingredients. Some of the seasonings you'll find added to vinaigrette dressing are Dijon mustard, sun-dried tomatoes, fruit and various herb-spice combinations.

Vinaigrette separates easily, so you'll need to give it a good shake before serving. Besides salad, you can drizzle vinaigrette onto meats, pasta, vegetables and fruit or use it as a marinade before grilling.

Mayonnaise: Mayonnaise is the base for many dressings. Because it's made with raw egg yolks or eggs, for food safety reasons we recommend buying commercial mayonnaise rather than making it at home.

Salad dressing:

Cooked: This salad dressing also contains eggs, but unlike mayonnaise, it's cooked. Use it for making meat, potato, pasta and vegetable salads.

Creamy: These salad dressings have a base of mayonnaise, sour cream, cream cheese, whipped cream, yogurt or buttermilk. Sweetened, they pair well with fruit; unsweetened, they're good with meat, pasta and potato and vegetable salads.

Italian Dressing *Fast*

Prep: 10 min ✳ About 1 1/4 cups

1 cup olive or vegetable oil
1/4 cup white or cider vinegar
2 tablespoons finely chopped onion
1 tablespoon chopped fresh or 1 teaspoon dried basil leaves
1 teaspoon sugar
1 teaspoon ground mustard
1/2 teaspoon salt
1/2 teaspoon dried oregano leaves
1/4 teaspoon pepper
2 cloves garlic, finely chopped

Shake all ingredients in tightly covered container. Shake before serving.

1 Tablespoon: Calories 105 (Calories from Fat 100); Fat 11g (Saturated 1g); Cholesterol mg; Sodium 60mg; Carbohydrate 1g (Dietary Fiber 0g); Protein 0g **% Daily Value:** Vitamin A 0%; Vitamin C 0%; Calcium 0%; Iron 0% **Diet Exchanges:** 2 Fat

Lighter Italian Dressing: For 5 grams of fat and 50 calories per serving, substitute 1/2 cup apple juice for 1/2 cup of the oil.

CREAMY ITALIAN DRESSING: Beat 1/2 cup Italian Dressing and 1/2 cup mayonnaise or salad dressing with hand beater or wire whisk until smooth. Store covered in refrigerator.

Classic French Dressing *Fast*

Prep: 5 min ✱ *About 1 1/2 cups*

1 cup olive or vegetable oil
1/4 cup white or cider vinegar
1/4 cup lemon juice
1/2 teaspoon salt
1/2 teaspoon ground mustard
1/2 teaspoon paprika

Shake all ingredients in tightly covered container. Shake before serving.

1 Tablespoon: Calories 80 (Calories from Fat 80); Fat 9g (Saturated 1g); Cholesterol 0mg; Sodium 50mg; Carbohydrate 0g (Dietary Fiber 0g); Protein 0g **% Daily Value:** Vitamin A 0%; Vitamin C 0%; Calcium 0%; Iron 0% **Diet Exchanges:** 2 Fat

CLASSIC RED FRENCH DRESSING: Mix 1/2 cup Classic French Dressing and 1/2 cup ketchup.

Thousand Island Dressing *Fast*

Prep: 15 min ✱ *About 1 cup*

1 cup mayonnaise or salad dressing
1 tablespoon chopped fresh parsley
2 tablespoons chopped pimiento-stuffed olives or sweet pickle relish
2 tablespoons chili sauce or ketchup
1 teaspoon finely chopped onion
1/2 teaspoon paprika
1 Hard-Cooked Egg (page 201), finely chopped

Mix all ingredients. Store covered in refrigerator.

1 Tablespoon: Calories 105 (Calories from Fat 100); Fat 11g (Saturated 2g); Cholesterol 20mg; Sodium 135mg; Carbohydrate 1g (Dietary Fiber 0g); Protein 1g **% Daily Value:** Vitamin A 2%; Vitamin C 0%; Calcium 0%; Iron 0% **Diet Exchanges:** 2 Fruit

> **Lighter Thousand Island Dressing:** For 5 grams of fat and 55 calories per serving, use reduced-fat mayonnaise; substitute 2 hard-cooked egg whites for the hard-cooked egg.

RUSSIAN DRESSING: Omit parsley, olives and egg. Increase chili sauce to 1/4 cup. Add 1 teaspoon prepared horseradish.

Honey-Dijon Dressing *Fast*

Prep: 5 min ✱ *About 1 cup*

1/2 cup vegetable oil
1/3 cup honey
1/4 cup lemon juice
1 tablespoon Dijon mustard

Shake all ingredients in tightly covered container. Shake before serving.

1 Tablespoon: Calories 85 (Calories from Fat 65); Fat 7g (Saturated 1g); Cholesterol 0mg; Sodium 15mg; Carbohydrate 6g (Dietary Fiber 0g); Protein 0g **% Daily Value:** Vitamin A 0%; Vitamin C 2%; Calcium 0%; Iron 0% **Diet Exchanges:** 1/2 Fruit, 1 Fat

HONEY–POPPY SEED DRESSING: Omit mustard. Add 1 tablespoon poppy seed.

Lime-Cilantro Dressing *Fast*

Prep: 10 min ✱ *About 1 cup*

1/2 cup olive or vegetable oil
1/3 cup lime juice or white vinegar
3 tablespoons chopped fresh cilantro
1 1/2 teaspoons ground cumin
1 teaspoon salt
1/8 teaspoon pepper
3 cloves garlic, finely chopped

Shake all ingredients in tightly covered container. Shake before serving.

1 Tablespoon: Calories 65 (Calories from Fat 65); Fat 7g (Saturated 1g); Cholesterol 0mg; Sodium 135mg; Carbohydrate 1g (Dietary Fiber 0g); Protein 0g **% Daily Value:** Vitamin A 0%; Vitamin C 2%; Calcium 0%; Iron 0% **Diet Exchanges:** 1 1/2 Fat

Fresh Herb Vinaigrette, Buttermilk (page 434) Dressing and Raspberry Vinaigrette

Fresh Herb Vinaigrette *Fast*

Prep: 10 min ✱ *About 1 cup*

1/2 cup olive or vegetable oil
1/2 cup white or cider vinegar
1 tablespoon chopped fresh herb leaves (basil, marjoram, oregano, rosemary, tarragon or thyme)
1 tablespoon chopped fresh parsley
1 medium green onion, finely chopped (1 tablespoon)

Shake all ingredients in tightly covered container. Shake before serving.

1 Tablespoon: Calories 65 (Calories from Fat 65); Fat 7g (Saturated 1g); Cholesterol 0mg; Sodium 0mg; Carbohydrate 0g (Dietary Fiber 0g); Protein 0g **% Daily Value:** Vitamin A 0%; Vitamin C 0%; Calcium 0%; Iron 0% **Diet Exchanges:** 1 1/2 Fat

Lighter Fresh Herb Vinaigrette: For 0 grams of fat and 5 calories per serving, substitute apple juice for the olive oil; decrease vinegar to 1/3 cup.

Raspberry Vinaigrette

Fast & Low-Fat

Prep: 10 min ✱ *1 cup*

1/3 cup seedless raspberry jam
1/2 cup red wine vinegar
1/4 cup olive or vegetable oil
1/4 teaspoon salt

Beat all ingredients with wire whisk until well blended. Store covered in refrigerator.

1 Tablespoon: Calories 45 (Calories from Fat 25); Fat 3g (Saturated 0g); Cholesterol 0mg; Sodium 40mg; Carbohydrate 5g (Dietary Fiber 0g); Protein 0g **% Daily Value:** Vitamin A 0%; Vitamin C 0%; Calcium 0%; Iron 0% **Diet Exchanges:** 1/2 Fruit, 1/2 Fat

Oriental Dressing *Fast & Low-Fat*

*Prep: 5 min * About 1 cup*

Toasting really brings out the flavor of sesame seed, so toast a whole 2-ounce package or jar of sesame seed (about 1/2 cup), then keep it in the freezer to use whenever you need some.

1/3 cup rice, white or cider vinegar
1/4 cup vegetable oil
3 tablespoons soy sauce
1 tablespoon sesame seed, toasted if desired (page 00)
2 tablespoons dry sherry or apple juice
1 teaspoon grated gingerroot or 1/4 teaspoon ground ginger
2 drops dark sesame oil, if desired

Shake all ingredients in tightly covered container. Shake before serving.

1 Tablespoon: Calories 40 (Calories from Fat 35); Fat 3g (Saturated 1g); Cholesterol 0mg; Sodium 170mg; Carbohydrate 1g (Dietary Fiber 0g); Protein 0g **% Daily Value:** Vitamin A 0%; Vitamin C 0%; Calcium 0%; Iron 0% **Diet Exchanges:** 1 Fat

Buttermilk Dressing

*Prep: 5 min; Chill: 2 hr * About 1 1/4 cups*

3/4 cup mayonnaise or salad dressing
1/2 cup buttermilk
1 teaspoon parsley flakes
1/2 teaspoon instant minced onion
1/2 teaspoon salt
Dash of freshly ground pepper
1 clove garlic, finely chopped

1. Mix all ingredients.

2. Cover and refrigerate at least 2 hours to blend flavors. Store covered in refrigerator.

1 Tablespoon: Calories 65 (Calories from Fat 65); Fat 7g (Saturated 1g); Cholesterol 5mg; Sodium 110mg; Carbohydrate 1g (Dietary Fiber 0g); Protein 0g **% Daily Value:** Vitamin A 0%; Vitamin C 0%; Calcium 0%; Iron 0% **Diet Exchanges:** 1 1/2 Fat

Lighter Buttermilk Dressing: For 3 grams of fat and 30 calories per serving, use reduced-fat mayonnaise and buttermilk.

BUTTERMILK-PARMESAN DRESSING: Add 1/3 cup grated Parmesan cheese and 1/2 teaspoon paprika.

Blue Cheese Dressing

*Prep: 10 min; Chill: 3 hr * About 1 2/3 cups*

3/4 cup crumbled blue cheese (3 ounces)
1 package (3 ounces) cream cheese, softened
1/2 cup mayonnaise or salad dressing
1/3 cup half-and-half

1. Reserve 1/3 cup of the blue cheese. Mix remaining blue cheese and the cream cheese in small bowl until well blended.

2. Stir in mayonnaise and half-and-half until creamy. Stir in reserved blue cheese. Cover and refrigerate at least 3 hours to blend flavors. Store covered in refrigerator.

1 Tablespoon: Calories 60 (Calories from Fat 55); Fat 6g (Saturated 2g); Cholesterol 10mg; Sodium 90mg; Carbohydrate 0g (Dietary Fiber 0g); Protein 1g **% Daily Value:** Vitamin A 2%; Vitamin C 0%; Calcium 2%; Iron 0% **Diet Exchanges:** 1 Fat

Lighter Blue Cheese Dressing: For 3 grams of fat and 35 calories per serving, decrease blue cheese to 1/2 cup. Substitute 1/2 package (8-ounce size) reduced-fat cream cheese (Neufchâtel) for the regular cream cheese and 1/4 cup fat-free (skim) milk for the half-and-half. Use reduced-fat mayonnaise.

CHAPTER 16

Sauces, Seasonings & Accompaniments

Sauces, Seasonings & Accompaniments

Low-Fat = 3g or less, except main dishes with 6g or less   *Fast* = Ready in 30 minutes or less   ■ = Bread Machine directions   ● = Slow Cooker directions

Savory Butters (page 458)

Lighter = 1/3 fewer calories or 50% less fat

Sauce Basics

Sauces, whether a simple butter sauce, savory barbecue sauce or an extra-special bordelaise sauce, often make a dish special. They make plain dishes sing and more complex dishes dance with flavor. Sauces shouldn't mask the other ingredients in a dish, but rather, they should enhance them. And sauces aren't just for savory dishes. Looking for a dessert sauce? See pages 195 to 197. Here are some super saucy ideas:

- **Mix with food:** Italian Tomato Sauce (page 436) layered in lasagna or White Sauce (page 440) as a creamy soup base.
- **Top food:** Hollandaise Sauce (page 440) spooned over steamed asparagus and Eggs Benedict (page 204) or Pan Gravy (page 442) over Garlic Mashed Potatoes (page 517).
- **Serve on the side:** Sweet-and-Sour Sauce (page 438) with chicken kabobs or Cranberry Sauce (page 439) with roast turkey.
- **Pool or drizzle on a plate** just like they do in restaurants, magazines and cookbooks: Fresh Tomato Sauce (page 436) under a slice of Meat Loaf (page 240) or Dill Sauce (page 441) under Broiled Fish Fillets (page 308).

Mixing Sauces

Lumps, be gone! To prevent lumping, use a wire whisk to mix sauces. Also, before you add flour to thicken a dish such as stew, mix it separately with a little bit of cold water first to keep the flour from clumping. The same goes for cornstarch.

A roux, a cooked mixture of fat (usually butter) and flour, is the most common way to thicken savory sauces. White Sauce (page 440), Velouté Sauce (page 442) and Brown Sauce (page 443) are some examples of roux-based sauces. When you're making a roux, stir the fat-and-flour mixture as it cooks, letting it bubble before adding the liquid. That bit of cooking does away with any raw flour taste, and the sauce will thicken the way it should.

Another way to thicken sauces is with cornstarch. As they cook, cornstarch-based sauces become clear, almost shiny, so they're perfect for sparkling fruit sauces.

You can also thicken sauces with egg yolks, but you must cook them thoroughly, to avoid bacterial contamination, and at low temperatures, to avoid overcooking them.

Sauces will thicken by reduction, too. Reductions boil the liquid until some of it evaporates, thereby concentrating and intensifying flavors as it thickens the sauce. You can speed up reduction by using a skillet with a large surface area instead of a saucepan.

Storing and Reheating Sauces

Put leftover sauces in covered containers and refrigerate immediately. Follow storage directions given in the recipe.

When reheating sauces, use a saucepan just large enough to hold the sauce to prevent too much evaporation, and stir the sauce frequently. If the sauce starts to stick to the pan, reduce the heat, stir more frequently and/or add a little liquid.

Not all sauces can be reheated the same way—some require different temperatures.

- *Unthickened sauces* (barbecue sauce): Reheat to boiling over medium heat.
- *Flour- or cornstarch-thickened sauces* (White Sauce, page 440): Use low or medium heat.
- *Egg-thickened sauces* (Hollandaise Sauce, page 440): Use low heat so they won't separate.

To reheat sauces in the microwave, a heatproof glass measuring cup works well. Choose a power setting similar to the one you'd use on the stovetop. Stir the sauce at least once during heating and again before serving.

Italian Tomato Sauce

Prep: 15 min; Cook: 50 min ✱ About 4 cups

This versatile sauce is perfect for meat loaf, meatballs or any variety of pasta.

2 tablespoons olive or vegetable oil
1 large onion, chopped (1 cup)
1 small green bell pepper, chopped (1/2 cup)
2 large cloves garlic, finely chopped
2 cans (14 1/2 ounces each) whole tomatoes, undrained
2 cans (8 ounces each) tomato sauce
2 tablespoons chopped fresh or 2 teaspoons dried basil leaves
1 tablespoon chopped fresh or 1 teaspoon dried oregano leaves
1/2 teaspoon salt
1/2 teaspoon fennel seed
1/4 teaspoon pepper

1. Heat oil in 3-quart saucepan over medium heat. Cook onion, bell pepper and garlic in oil 2 minutes, stirring occasionally.

2. Stir in remaining ingredients, breaking up tomatoes with a fork or snipping with kitchen scissors. Heat to boiling; reduce heat. Cover and simmer 45 minutes.

3. Use sauce immediately, or cover and refrigerate up to 2 weeks or freeze up to 1 year.

1/2 Cup: Calories 80 (Calories from Fat 35); Fat 4g (Saturated 1g); Cholesterol 0mg; Sodium 660mg; Carbohydrate 12g (Dietary Fiber 3g); Protein 2g **% Daily Value:** Vitamin A 14%; Vitamin C 32%; Calcium 4%; Iron 6% **Diet Exchanges:** 2 Vegetable, 1/2 Fat

Slow Cooker Directions: Use 1 medium onion. Substitute 1 can (28 ounces) diced tomatoes, undrained, for the 2 cans whole tomatoes. Use 1 can (8 ounces) tomato sauce. Mix all ingredients in 3 1/2- to 6-quart slow cooker. Cover and cook on low heat setting 8 to 10 hours.

Cucumbers and Tomatoes in Yogurt *Low-Fat*

Prep: 20 min; Chill: 30 min ✱ About 2 cups

This refreshing salsa or relish is served as a salad in northern India, where it is called *raita*. It is especially good with spicy foods, such as Tandoori Chicken and Chutney (page 294). You can also use it as a dip with pita or crackers.

1 medium cucumber
1 medium green onion, chopped (1 tablespoon)
1/2 teaspoon salt
1 medium tomato, chopped (3/4 cup)
1 tablespoon chopped fresh cilantro or parsley
1/4 teaspoon ground cumin
Dash of pepper
1/2 clove garlic, finely chopped
1/2 cup plain yogurt

1. Cut cucumber lengthwise in half; scoop out seeds. Chop cucumber (about 1 1/4 cups).

2. Mix cucumber, onion and salt; let stand 10 minutes. Stir in tomato.

3. Mix remaining ingredients except yogurt; toss with cucumber mixture. Cover and refrigerate at least 30 minutes to blend flavors.

4. Drain thoroughly. Just before serving, fold in yogurt. Store covered in refrigerator.

1/2 Cup: Calories 30 (Calories from Fat 10); Fat 1g (Saturated 1g); Cholesterol 5mg; Sodium 310mg; Carbohydrate 5g (Dietary Fiber 1g); Protein 2g **% Daily Value:** Vitamin A 4%; Vitamin C 16%; Calcium 4%; Iron 2% **Diet Exchanges:** 1 Vegetable

Fresh Tomato Sauce

Fresh Tomato Sauce

Fast & Low-Fat

Prep: 20 min ✱ About 4 cups

Make from garden-fresh tomatoes, and serve over freshly cooked pasta for a wonderful summer treat.

1 can (28 ounces) Italian-style pear-shaped tomatoes, drained
2 cloves garlic, finely chopped
1 tablespoon chopped fresh or 1 teaspoon dried basil leaves
1 teaspoon chopped fresh parsley or 1 teaspoon parsley flakes
1 teaspoon grated Parmesan cheese
1 teaspoon olive or vegetable oil
1/2 teaspoon salt
1/2 teaspoon pepper
6 medium tomatoes, diced (about 4 1/2 cups)
3/4 cup pitted Kalamata or ripe olives, cut in half
1 tablespoon capers, if desired

1. Place all ingredients except diced tomatoes, olives and capers in food processor or blender. Cover and process until smooth. Pour into bowl.

2. Stir in tomatoes, olives and capers.

3. Use sauce immediately, or cover and refrigerate up to 2 weeks or freeze up to 1 year.

1/2 Cup: Calories 60 (Calories from Fat 20); Fat 2g (Saturated 0g); Cholesterol 0mg; Sodium 420mg; Carbohydrate 10g (Dietary Fiber 2g); Protein 2g **% Daily Value:** Vitamin A 12%; Vitamin C 26%; Calcium 4%; Iron 8% **Diet Exchanges:** 2 Vegetable

Teriyaki Sauce *Fast*

Prep: 5 min ✻ About 2/3 cup

This mahogany-colored salty and slightly sweet sauce, gives a flavor burst to pork, chicken, shrimp, fish and vegetables.

1/4 cup vegetable oil
1/4 cup soy sauce
2 tablespoons ketchup
1 tablespoon white vinegar
1/4 teaspoon pepper
2 cloves garlic, finely chopped

1. Mix all ingredients.

2. Use sauce immediately, or cover and refrigerate up to 2 weeks or freeze up to 1 year.

1 Tablespoon: Calories 55 (Calories from Fat 45); Fat 5g (Saturated 1g); Cholesterol 0mg; Sodium 400mg; Carbohydrate 2g (Dietary Fiber 0g); Protein 0g **% Daily Value:** Vitamin A 0%; Vitamin C 0%; Calcium 0%; Iron 0% **Diet Exchanges:** 1 Fat

Sweet-and-Sour Sauce

Fast & Low-Fat

Prep: 10 min; Cook: 1 min ✻ About 1 1/2 cups

Douse this sauce on pork, poultry or seafood.

1/2 cup packed brown sugar
1 tablespoon cornstarch
1 can (8 ounces) crushed pineapple in juice, drained and juice reserved
1/3 cup white vinegar
1 tablespoon soy sauce
1/4 cup finely chopped green bell pepper

1. Mix brown sugar and cornstarch in 1-quart saucepan.

2. Add enough water to reserved pineapple juice to measure 1/2 cup; stir into sugar mixture. Stir in vinegar and soy sauce.

3. Heat to boiling over medium heat, stirring constantly. Boil and stir 1 minute. Stir in pineapple and bell pepper.

4. Use sauce immediately, or cover and refrigerate up to 2 weeks or freeze up to 1 year. Serving suggestions: pork, poultry, seafood.

1 Tablespoon: Calories 30 (Calories from Fat 0); Fat 0g (Saturated 0g); Cholesterol 0mg; Sodium 40mg; Carbohydrate 7g (Dietary Fiber 0g); Protein 0g **% Daily Value:** Vitamin A 0%; Vitamin C 2%; Calcium 0%; Iron 0% **Diet Exchanges:** 1 Fruit

Tartar Sauce

Prep: 5 min; Chill: 1 hr ✻ About 1 cup

Creamy tartar sauce is easy to make at home! Try using pickle relish versus the dill pickles for sweeter flavor.

1 cup mayonnaise or salad dressing
2 tablespoons finely chopped dill pickle or pickle relish
1 tablespoon chopped fresh parsley
2 teaspoons chopped pimiento
1 teaspoon grated onion

1. Mix all ingredients.

2. Cover and refrigerate about 1 hour or until chilled.

1 Tablespoon: Calories 100 (Calories from Fat 100); Fat 11g (Saturated 2g); Cholesterol 10mg; Sodium 90mg; Carbohydrate 0g (Dietary Fiber 0g); Protein 0g **% Daily Value:** Vitamin A 0%; Vitamin C 0%; Calcium 0%; Iron 0% **Diet Exchanges:** 2 Fat

Lighter Tartar Sauce: For 5 grams fat and 50 calories per serving, use reduced-fat mayonnaise.

Pesto *Fast*

Prep: 10 min ✻ About 1 1/4 cups

Try all the flavor variations of the traditional basil pesto (right)—all are equally as good! Keep pesto on hand to toss with pasta, spread on sandwiches, mix into salads or top hot meats or vegetables.

2 cups firmly packed fresh basil leaves
3/4 cup grated Parmesan cheese
1/4 cup pine nuts
1/2 cup olive or vegetable oil
3 cloves garlic

1. Place all ingredients in blender or food processor. Cover and blend on medium speed about 3 minutes, stopping occasionally to scrape sides, until smooth.

2. Use pesto immediately, or cover tightly and refrigerate up to 5 days or freeze up to 1 month (color of pesto will darken as it stands).

2 Tablespoons: Calories 150 (Calories from Fat 135); Fat 15g (Saturated 3g); Cholesterol 5mg; Sodium 115mg; Carbohydrate 2g (Dietary Fiber 1g); Protein 3g **% Daily Value:** Vitamin A 4%; Vitamin C 2%; Calcium 10%; Iron 2% **Diet Exchanges:** 1/2 Vegetable, 3 Fat

CILANTRO PESTO: Substitute 1 1/2 cups firmly packed fresh cilantro and 1/2 cup firmly packed fresh parsley for the fresh basil.

WINTER SPINACH PESTO: Substitute 2 cups firmly packed fresh spinach and 1/2 cup firmly packed fresh basil leaves or 1/4 cup dried basil leaves for the fresh basil.

SUN-DRIED TOMATO PESTO: Use food processor. Omit basil. Decrease oil to 1/3 cup; add 1/2 cup oil-packed sun-dried tomatoes (undrained).

Whipped Horseradish Sauce *Fast & Low-Fat*

Prep: 10 min ✱ *About 1 1/4 cups*

This sauce is sassy! The kick in this creamy sauce comes from the horseradish and vinegar. It's perfect with beef or other meats.

1/4 cup sour cream
3 tablespoons grated fresh horseradish or prepared horseradish
1 tablespoon white wine vinegar or white vinegar
1 teaspoon yellow mustard
1/4 teaspoon white pepper
1/2 cup whipping (heavy) cream

1. Mix all ingredients except whipping cream in small bowl.

2. Beat whipping cream in chilled small bowl with electric mixer on high speed until stiff; carefully fold into sour cream mixture.

3. Store covered in refrigerator.

1 Tablespoon: Calories 20 (Calories from Fat 20); Fat 2g (Saturated 2g); Cholesterol 0mg; Sodium 10mg; Carbohydrate 1g (Dietary Fiber 0g); Protein 0g **% Daily Value:** Vitamin A 2%; Vitamin C 0%; Calcium 0%; Iron 0% **Diet Exchanges:** 1 Serving is free

Cranberry Sauce *Low-Fat*

Prep: 15 min; Cook: 15 min; Chill: 3 hr ✱ *About 4 cups*

Be sure to cook the cranberries until they pop in order to release the natural pectin, which thickens the sauce. This sauce is a classic at Thanksgiving, but it's welcome any time, served with pork, turkey or chicken.

4 cups fresh or frozen cranberries (1 pound)
2 cups sugar
2 cups water
1 tablespoon grated orange peel, if desired

1. Wash cranberries; remove any stems or blemished berries.

2. Heat sugar and water to boiling in 3-quart saucepan over medium heat, stirring occasionally. Boil 5 minutes.

3. Stir in cranberries. Heat to boiling; boil about 5 minutes or until cranberries pop. Stir in orange peel. Cover and refrigerate about 3 hours or until chilled. Store covered in refrigerator.

1/4 Cup: Calories 110 (Calories from Fat 0); Fat 0g (Saturated 0g); Cholesterol 0mg; Sodium 0mg; Carbohydrate 29g (Dietary Fiber 1g); Protein 0g **% Daily Value:** Vitamin A 0%; Vitamin C 2%; Calcium 0%; Iron 0% **Diet Exchanges:** 2 Fruit

Herbed Butter Sauce *Fast*

Prep: 5 min; Cook: 5 min ✱ *About 1/2 cup*

Sometimes, simple is best, as with this easy butter sauce spiked with fresh herbs. It's sensational with fish, seafoood, poultry or vegetables.

1/2 cup stick butter*
2 tablespoons chopped fresh or 1 teaspoon dried herb leaves (basil, chives, oregano, savory, tarragon or thyme)
2 teaspoons lemon juice

1. Melt butter in heavy 1-quart saucepan or 8-inch skillet over medium heat.

2. Stir in herb leaves and lemon juice.

Do not use margarine or vegetable oil spreads.

1 Tablespoon: Calories 110 (Calories from Fat 110); Fat 12g (Saturated 7g); Cholesterol 30mg; Sodium 75mg; Carbohydrate 0g (Dietary Fiber 0g); Protein 0g **% Daily Value:** Vitamin A 8%; Vitamin C 0%; Calcium 0%; Iron 0% **Diet Exchanges:** 2 1/2 Fat

Hollandaise Sauce *Fast*

Prep: 10 min; Cook: 5 min ✳ About 3/4 cup

If this delicate sauce curdles (mixture begins to separate), add about 1 tablespoon boiling water and beat vigorously with wire whisk or hand beater until it's smooth. Serve it with cooked vegetables, eggs or grilled meats.

3 large egg yolks
1 tablespoon lemon juice
1/2 cup firm stick butter*

1. Stir egg yolks and lemon juice vigorously in 1 1/2-quart saucepan. Add 1/4 cup of the butter. Heat over *very low heat*, stirring constantly with wire whisk, until butter is melted.

2. Add remaining 1/4 cup butter. Continue stirring vigorously until butter is melted and sauce is thickened. (Be sure butter melts slowly so eggs have time to cook and thicken sauce without curdling.)

3. Store covered in refrigerator. To serve refrigerated sauce, stir in small amount of water when reheating over very low heat.

1 Tablespoon: Calories 85 (Calories from Fat 80); Fat 9g (Saturated 5g); Cholesterol 75mg; Sodium 55mg; Carbohydrate 0g (Dietary Fiber 0g); Protein 1g **% Daily Value:** Vitamin A 8%; Vitamin C 0%; Calcium 0%; Iron 0% **Diet Exchanges:** 2 Fat

*Do not use margarine or vegetable oil spreads.

BÉARNAISE SAUCE: Stir in 1 tablespoon dry white wine with the lemon juice. After sauce thickens, stir in 1 tablespoon finely chopped onion, 1 1/2 teaspoons chopped fresh or 1/2 teaspoon dried tarragon leaves and 1 1/2 teaspoons chopped fresh or 1/4 teaspoon dried chervil leaves. Serving suggestions: fish, meat.

White Sauce *Fast*

Prep: 5 min; Cook: 5 min ✳ About 1 cup

Also called Béchamel sauce, this is perfectly paired with vegetables, or use as a creamy sauce in casseroles. There are many flavored variations of this sauce as well (see right).

2 tablespoons butter or stick margarine
2 tablespoons all-purpose flour
1/4 teaspoon salt
1/8 teaspoon pepper
1 cup milk

1. Melt butter in 1 1/2-quart saucepan over low heat. Stir in flour, salt and pepper. Cook over medium heat, stirring constantly, until mixture is smooth and bubbly; remove from heat.

2. Gradually stir in milk. Heat to boiling, stirring constantly. Boil and stir 1 minute.

Stir flour, salt and pepper into melted butter. Cook, stirring constantly, until mixture is smooth and bubbly.

Heat sauce to boiling, stirring constantly. Boil and stir 1 minute.

Cheese Sauce (White Sauce variation)

1 Tablespoon: Calories 25 (Calories from Fat 20); Fat 2g (Saturated 1g); Cholesterol 5mg; Sodium 55mg; Carbohydrate 1g (Dietary Fiber 0g); Protein 1g **% Daily Value:** Vitamin A 2%; Vitamin C 0%; Calcium 2%; Iron 0% **Diet Exchanges:** 1 Serving is free

THICK WHITE SAUCE: Increase butter to 1/4 cup and flour to 1/4 cup.

THIN WHITE SAUCE: Decrease butter to 1 tablespoon and flour to 1 tablespoon.

CHEESE SAUCE: Stir in 1/4 teaspoon ground mustard with the flour. After boiling and stirring sauce 1 minute, stir in 1/2 cup shredded Cheddar cheese (2 ounces) until melted. Serve with eggs and vegetables or over toast for Welsh rabbit. About 1 1/3 cups sauce.

CURRY SAUCE: Stir in 1/2 teaspoon curry powder with the flour. Serve with chicken, lamb and shrimp.

DILL SAUCE: Stir in 1 teaspoon chopped fresh or 1/2 teaspoon dried dill weed and dash of ground nutmeg with the flour. Serve with fish.

MUSTARD SAUCE: Decrease butter to 1 tablespoon and flour to 1 tablespoon. After boiling and stirring sauce 1 minute, stir in 3 tablespoons yellow mustard and 1 tablespoon prepared horseradish. Serve with beef, veal, ham and vegetables.

Velouté Sauce *Fast & Low-Fat*

Prep: 5 min; Cook: 5 min ❋ About 1 cup

This classic sauce is a white sauce made with a light broth or stock base instead of milk. Offer it with chicken, fish, broccoli or carrots.

2 tablespoons butter or stick margarine
2 tablespoons all-purpose flour
1 cup chicken broth
1/4 teaspoon salt
1/8 teaspoon pepper
1/8 teaspoon ground nutmeg

1. Melt butter in 1 1/2-quart saucepan over low heat. Stir in flour. Cook over low heat, stirring constantly, until mixture is smooth and bubbly; remove from heat. (See photo page 440).

2. Gradually stir in broth. Heat to boiling, stirring constantly. Boil and stir 1 minute. Stir in salt, pepper and nutmeg.

1 Tablespoon: Calories 20 (Calories from Fat 20); Fat 2g (Saturated 1g); Cholesterol 5mg; Sodium 110mg; Carbohydrate 1g (Dietary Fiber 0g); Protein 0g **% Daily Value:** Vitamin A 0%; Vitamin C 0%; Calcium 0%; Iron 0% **Diet Exchanges:** 1 Serving is free

MORNAY SAUCE: Substitute 1/2 cup half-and-half for 1/2 cup of the chicken broth. Omit pepper and nutmeg. After boiling and stirring 1 minute, stir in 1/8 teaspoon ground red pepper (cayenne) and 1/2 cup grated Parmesan or shredded Swiss cheese with the salt; stir until cheese is melted. Serving suggestions: meat, fish, eggs, vegetables.

Pan Gravy *Fast & Low-Fat*

Prep: 5 min; Cook: 5 min ❋ About 1 cup

The secret to perfect gravy is using equal amounts of fat and flour, so measuring carefully is important. If you have plenty of pan drippings and like to use lots of gravy and are serving a crowd or like a little potato with your gravy, you can double or triple this recipe. Just place your cooked meat on warm platter; keep warm while preparing gravy. It's the perfect match for roasted meat, mashed potatoes and stuffing.

Drippings from cooked meat
2 tablespoons all-purpose flour
1 cup liquid* (meat juices, broth, water)
Browning sauce, if desired
Salt and pepper to taste

1. After removing meat from pan, pour drippings (meat juices and fat) into bowl or glass measuring cup, leaving brown particles in pan. Skim 2 tablespoons of fat from the top of the drippings and return fat to the pan. Discard any remaining fat; reserve remaining drippings.

2. Stir flour into fat in cooking pan. Cook over low heat, stirring constantly and scraping up brown particles, until mixture is smooth and bubbly; remove from heat.

3. Gradually stir in reserved drippings plus enough broth or water to equal 1 cup. Heat to boiling, stirring constantly. Boil and stir 1 minute. Stir in a few drops browning sauce if a darker color is desired. Stir in salt and pepper.

*Vegetable cooking water, consommé or tomato or vegetable juice can be substituted for part of the liquid.

1 Tablespoon: Calories 15 (Calories from Fat 10); Fat 1g (Saturated 0g); Cholesterol 0mg; Sodium 65mg; Carbohydrate 1g (Dietary Fiber 0g); Protein 1g **% Daily Value:** Vitamin A 0%; Vitamin C 0%; Calcium 0%; Iron 0% **Diet Exchanges:** 1 Serving is free

CREAMY GRAVY: Substitute milk for half of the liquid. Serve with turkey, chicken, pork and veal.

GIBLET GRAVY: Cook gizzard, heart and neck of fowl in 4 cups salted water 1 to 2 hours or until tender. Add liver the last 30 minutes. Remove meat from neck and finely chop with giblets. Substitute broth from giblets for the liquid. Stir giblets into gravy. Heat until hot.

THIN GRAVY: Decrease meat drippings to 1 tablespoon and flour to 1 tablespoon.

Brown Sauce *Fast & Low-Fat*

Prep: 5 min; Cook: 10 min ✱ *About 1 cup*

Known in France as *espagnole* sauce, this versatile creation can be a partner to beef, veal or pork.

2 tablespoons butter or stick margarine
1 thin slice onion
2 tablespoons all-purpose flour
1 cup beef broth
1/4 teaspoon salt
1/8 teaspoon pepper

1. Melt butter in 1 1/2-quart saucepan over low heat. Cook onion in butter, stirring occasionally, until onion is brown; discard onion.

2. Stir flour into butter. Cook over low heat, stirring constantly, until flour is deep brown; remove from heat.

3. Gradually stir in broth. Heat to boiling, stirring constantly. Boil and stir 1 minute. Stir in salt and pepper.

1 Tablespoon: Calories 15 (Calories from Fat 10); Fat 1g (Saturated 1g); Cholesterol 5mg; Sodium 110mg; Carbohydrate 1g (Dietary Fiber 0g); Protein 0g **% Daily Value:** Vitamin A 0%; Vitamin C 0%; Calcium 0%; Iron 0% **Diet Exchanges:** 1 Serving is free

BORDELAISE SAUCE: Decrease broth to 1/2 cup and add 1/2 cup dry red wine. Stir in 1/2 teaspoon chopped fresh parsley, 1/2 teaspoon finely chopped onion, 1 bay leaf and 3/4 teaspoon chopped fresh or 1/4 teaspoon dried thyme leaves with the broth. Remove bay leaf before serving. Serving suggestions: steaks, pork chops, hamburgers.

RAISIN OR DRIED CRANBERRY SAUCE: Substitute 1/2 cup apple cider for 1/2 cup of the broth. Stir in 1/4 cup raisins or dried cranberries with the broth. Serving suggestions: ham, pork, beef, poultry.

Peanut Sauce *Fast*

Prep: 5 min; Cook: 5 min ✱ *About 1 cup*

Peanut sauce tastes great with grilled poultry or meats.

1/2 cup creamy peanut butter
1 cup water
2 tablespoons lime juice
1/2 teaspoon ground coriander
1/2 teaspoon ground cumin
2 cloves garlic, finely chopped

1. Mix all ingredients in 1-quart saucepan with wire whisk. Heat over medium heat, stirring occasionally, until smooth and warm.

2. Use sauce immediately, or cover and refrigerate up to 3 days or freeze up to 2 months.

2 Tablespoons: Calories 100 (Calories from Fat 70); Fat 8g (Saturated 2g); Cholesterol 0mg; Sodium 75mg; Carbohydrate 4g (Dietary Fiber 1g); Protein 4g **% Daily Value:** Vitamin A 0%; Vitamin C 0%; Calcium 0%; Iron 2% **Diet Exchanges:** 1/2 High-Fat Meat, 1 Fat

Prune-Almond Sauce
Fast & Low-Fat

Prep: 30 min ✱ *About 2 cups sauce*

This sauce goes wonderfully with pork or ham and is equally delicious as a bread spread or pastry filling.

1 1/2 cups apple juice
1/2 package (16-ounce size) pitted prunes (2 cups)
2 tablespoons apple brandy, brandy or water
1 teaspoon grated lemon peel
1/2 cup slivered almonds

1. Heat apple juice and prunes to boiling in 2-quart saucepan; reduce heat. Cover and simmer about 20 minutes or until prunes are soft.

2. Drain prunes, reserving 1/2 cup liquid. Place prunes, reserved liquid, the brandy and lemon peel in blender or food processor. Cover and blend on high speed until smooth. Remove from blender. Stir in almonds. Store tightly covered in refrigerator up to 4 weeks.

1 Tablespoon: Calories 45 (Calories from Fat 10); Fat 1g (Saturated 0g); Cholesterol 0mg; Sodium 0mg; Carbohydrate 9g (Dietary Fiber 1g); Protein 1g **% Daily Value:** Vitamin A 2%; Vitamin C 0%; Calcium 0%; Iron 2**% Diet Exchanges:** 1/2 Fruit

PRUNE SAUCE: Omit apple brandy, lemon peel and almonds. Makes 1 1/2 cups sauce.

Creamy Herb-Mushroom Sauce

Creamy Herb-Mushroom Sauce *Fast*

*Prep: 5 min; Cook: 10 min * About 1 cup*

So rich, so creamy, so luscious—so good ladled over chicken, beef or pork.

1/4 cup butter or stick margarine

1 tablespoon finely chopped shallots

1 cup thinly sliced mushrooms (about 3 ounces)

1 tablespoon all-purpose flour

1 tablespoon chopped fresh or 1 teaspoon dried thyme leaves

1 tablespoon chopped fresh parsley or 1 teaspoon parsley flakes

1/2 cup half-and-half

1 tablespoon dry white wine, if desired

1. Melt butter in 2-quart saucepan over medium heat. Cook shallots and mushrooms in butter, stirring occasionally, until tender.

2. Stir in flour, thyme and parsley. Cook, stirring constantly, until slightly thickened.

3. Gradually stir in half-and-half and wine until smooth. Cook, stirring constantly, until thickened. Serve immediately.

2 Tablespoons: Calories 85 (Calories from Fat 70); Fat 8g (Saturated 5g); Cholesterol 20mg; Sodium 45mg; Carbohydrate 2g (Dietary Fiber 0g); Protein 1g **% Daily Value:** Vitamin A 6%; Vitamin C 0%; Calcium 2%; Iron 0% **Diet Exchanges:** 2 Fat

Seasonings Basics

For many cooks, how to season food to enhance its natural flavors or to add a new accent can be a big mystery. But with a little practice—and a little courage—you can unlock the mystery. Fresh herbs, ground spices, flavored oils and vinegars all lend themselves well to a variety of dishes. And with a little bit of practice, it will become second nature! And you're making the most of a wonderful world of new tastes and flavor combinations.

With ingredients you probably have on hand, you can blend your own seasoning mixes. Or the next time you're at the supermarket, choose a new seasoning, seasoning mix or marinade to experiment with.

The charts in this chapter will give you a general idea about herbs, spices, seeds and seasonings—their form, flavor and how they can be used. They're just a start, so explore and enjoy!

Storing Seasonings

To store most fresh herbs, wrap the stems in a damp paper towel, then put the herbs in a plastic bag and refrigerate.

Keep herbs such as parsley and cilantro fresh in a little "vase" in the refrigerator. Cut about 1/8 to 1/4 inch off the bottoms of stems so the water can be absorbed into the herb. Fill a jar with about two inches of water, place the stems in the water, then put a plastic bag over the herbs. Hold the bag in place with a rubber band around the neck of the jar. Most herbs will keep 1 to 2 weeks.

That spice rack hanging next to the stove may look homey, but being close to heat is tough on spices, dried herbs and seeds. Instead, store them in airtight containers away from heat, light and moisture but still within easy reach of where you'll be cooking. Dried herbs, spices and seasonings can be stored 1 to 2 years, although over time, the flavor may become weaker. Paprika, red pepper (cayenne) and chili powder should be refrigerated to retain color and guard against infestation. This is particularly important during the summer months and in hot climates.

After opening marinades, store them in the refrigerator.

Cooking with Herbs

A pinch of dried herbs or a snippet of fresh herbs adds oomph to just about any food, from iced tea to tomatoes. Some herbs grow wild and some are cultivated on herb farms, but you can easily grow kitchen favorites such as basil, parsley, oregano and chives in your garden or in windowsill pots. Keep your kitchen scissors handy to snip herbs for a simple but impressive garnish.

Herbs range in flavor from delicate and sweet to strong and savory. Sometimes just a little bit goes a long way, especially with the more bold herbs such as rosemary and oregano. If you're using an herb for the first time, start out with 1 teaspoon of fresh herb or 1/4 teaspoon of dried herb for every four servings. Taste, then add more—a little at a time—until the flavor's just right.

After measuring dried herbs, crumble them in your hand to release their flavor before adding to your recipe. Use a kitchen scissors or knife to cut fresh herbs. Because their flavor isn't as concentrated, you'll need three to four times more fresh herbs than dried.

Cooking with herbs is an adventure with exciting flavor combinations and uses for you to discover.

HERB CHART

Herb and Form	Flavor	Use
Basil (fresh and dried leaves, ground)	Sweet and spicy; a cross between cloves and black licorice; reminiscent of pesto	Eggs, meats, pesto, salads, soups, stews, tomato dishes
Bay leaves (dried leaves)	Earthy, grassy, slightly piney; reminiscent of beef stew	Meats, pickling, sauces, soups, stews, vegetables
Chervil (fresh and dried leaves)	Delicate, slightly peppery; tastes a bit like black licorice	Eggs, fish, salads, sauces, soups, stuffings
Chives (fresh, freeze-dried)	Tastes like mild green onions	Appetizers, cream soups, eggs, garnish, salads
Cilantro (fresh; also called Chinese parsley)	Slightly soapy; reminiscent of pico de gallo (salsa)	Chinese, Italian and Mexican dishes, garnish, pasta salads, pesto
Dill weed (fresh, dried)	Fresh, peppery and tangy; tastes like dill pickles	Breads, cheese, fish, salads, sauces, vegetables
Lemongrass (fresh)	Sour lemon flavor	Soups, tea, Thai dishes
Marjoram (fresh and dried leaves, ground)	Mild, slightly woodsy and flowery; reminiscent of spaghetti sauce	Cottage cheese, fish, lamb, poultry, sausages, soups, stews, stuffings, vegetables
Mint (fresh, dried)	Strong, cool, fresh, sweet; reminiscent of after-dinner mints	Beverages, desserts, fish, lamb, sauces, soups
Oregano (fresh and dried leaves, ground)	Stronger than marjoram, slightly bitter; reminiscent of pizza	Cheese, eggs, fish, Italian dishes, meats, sauces, soups, vegetables
Parsley (fresh curly leaf, fresh Italian flat leaf, flakes)	Slightly peppery; Italian parsley has a slightly stronger flavor	Garnish, herb mixtures, sauces, soups, stews
Rosemary (fresh and dried leaves)	Sweet, piney; reminiscent of pine needles	Casseroles, fish, lamb, salads, seafood, soups, vegetables
Sage (fresh and dried leaves, rubbed, ground)	Slightly musty, bitter; reminiscent of turkey stuffing	Fish, meats, poultry, salads, sausages, soups, stuffings
Savory (fresh, ground)	A cross between mint and thyme	Poultry, meats, salads, sauces, soups, stuffings, vegetables
Tarragon (fresh and dried leaves)	Astringent and aromatic; tastes like mild black licorice	Eggs, meats, pickling, poultry, salads, sauces, tomatoes
Thyme (fresh and dried leaves, ground)	Peppery, minty, light lemon flavor	Chowders, fish, meats, poultry, stews, stuffings, tomatoes

FRESH HERBS

Marjoram

Parsley—Curly

Parsley—Flat

Basil

Mint

Cilantro

Rosemary

Oregano

Sage

Chives

Thyme

Savory

Dill Weed

Lemongrass

Chervil

Tarragon

SPICE CHART

Spice and Form	Flavor	Use
Allspice (whole, ground; a spice, not a blend)	A cross between cloves and nutmeg; reminiscent of jerk chicken	Cakes, cookies, fruits, jerk seasoning, pickling, pies, poaching fish, spinach, stews
Cinnamon (stick, ground)	Sweet and woodsy; reminiscent of apple pie	Cakes, cappuccino, cookies, fruit desserts, hot chocolate, maple syrup, pies, pickling, puddings, winter hot drinks
Cloves (whole, ground)	Sweet, peppery; reminiscent of gingersnaps	Baked beans, desserts, fruits, gravies, ham, meats, pickling, pork, sausages, stews, syrups, tea, vegetables
Garlic (minced, powdered, dehydrated, flaked, fresh, paste, juice)	Slightly musty and reminiscent of garlic bread	Fish, meats, salads, oniony; sauces, sausages, soups, vegetables
Ginger (whole, cracked bits, ground, crystallized, fresh)	Spicy-hot and tangy; reminiscent of gingerbread	Baked goods, fish, fruits, meats, sauces, sausages, soups, tea, vegetables
Nutmeg (whole, ground; mace is the covering of the nutmeg seed and can be used the same way)	Sweet, spicy; reminiscent of eggnog	Apple or pear desserts, beverages, the cakes, cookies, parsnips, puddings, sauces, sweet potatoes, winter squash
Paprika (ground; made from dried sweet red peppers)	Ranges from sweet to hot, slightly bitter; reminiscent of Hungarian goulash	Casseroles, eggs, fish, garnish, meats, salads, soups, vegetables
Pepper, black, white and green (whole, ground, cracked; green sold packed in brine or dried)	Slightly hot with a hint of sweetness; black pepper is the strongest, green is the mildest	Meats, savory foods
Pepper, red (cayenne; ground)	Very hot and peppery	Barbecue and other sauces, chili, corn bread, eggs, fish, gravies, guacamole, meats, vegetables
Saffron (strands, powdered)	Distinctive flavor, softly bitter; reminiscent of paella	Spanish dishes
Turmeric (ground)	Fragrant, woodsy; reminiscent of curry	Curry powder, eggs, food color, pickling, poultry, rice, seafood

Cooking with Spices and Seeds

Centuries ago, spices were the treasures of kings, as much cherished and sought after as gold. Today, you don't have to sail the Seven Seas to find them—they're available at your supermarket. What are spices, exactly? Most consist of the seeds, shells, buds, fruit or flower parts, bark or roots of plants that grow in the tropical regions of the world.

If you want to crush or blend the seeds of spices, use a mortar and pestle, spice grinder or small electric grinder. Some cooks like to toast spices and seeds because toasting intensifies the flavor. Spices that are good for toasting include cumin, coriander, fennel seed, cardamom, cloves, cinnamon sticks and mustard seed. To toast, spread a thin layer of spice or seed in an ungreased skillet, and shake or stir over low heat. Watch so they don't burn! When the aroma really strengthens, take the skillet off the heat and pour out the spice or seed. Let it cool, then store in a container with a tight-fitting lid.

SPICES AND SEEDS

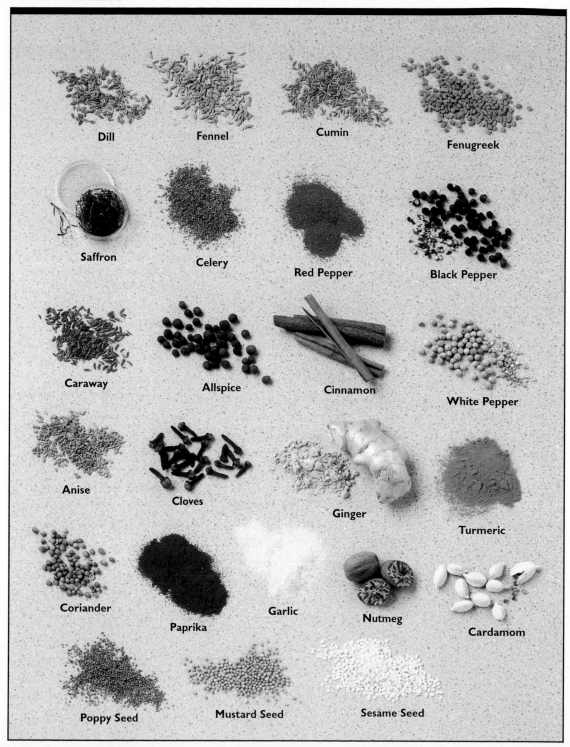

Dill

Fennel

Cumin

Fenugreek

Saffron

Celery

Red Pepper

Black Pepper

Caraway

Allspice

Cinnamon

White Pepper

Anise

Cloves

Ginger

Turmeric

Coriander

Paprika

Garlic

Nutmeg

Cardamom

Poppy Seed

Mustard Seed

Sesame Seed

SEED CHART

Seeds are little kernels of seasoning that you can sprinkle on top of dishes or mix into the food to give flavor, texture and eye appeal.

Seed and Form	Flavor	Use
Anise seed (whole)	Tastes like black licorice	Baked goods, candy, sweetened warm milk
Caraway seed (whole)	Tangy, strongly fragrant and a little smoky; reminiscent of caraway rye bread	Cabbage, cheese, dumplings, meats, pickling, rye bread, sauerkraut, soups, stews
Cardamom (whole pod, seeds, ground)	Strongly fragrant with a slight lemony-sweet flavor and a touch of pepper and ginger; reminiscent of Swedish cardamom bread	Coffee, curry, custard, fruits, Scandinavian breads, sausages
Celery seed (whole, ground)	Slightly bitter, like really strong celery	Meats, pickling, salads, sauces, soups, stuffings, tomato juice-based drinks
Coriander (whole, ground)	Mildly fragrant, a cross between lemon peel and caraway, like curry powder	Curry powder, marinades, Mexican and Spanish dishes, pastries, pickling, sausages, seafood
Cumin (whole, ground)	Strongly fragrant and slightly smoky, reminiscent of Mexican food	Cheese, chili, chili powder, curry powder, pickling, pork, sauerkraut
Dill seed (whole, ground)	Tangy; tastes like dill pickles	Fish, meats, pickling, processed meats, salads, sauces, soups
Fennel seed (whole, ground)	Sweet with a delicate black licorice flavor	Breads, eggs, fish, Italian dishes, sauces, sausages, soups, sweet pickles
Fenugreek seed (whole)	Pleasantly bitter and slightly sweet	Chutneys, curry powder
Mustard seed (whole, ground)	Hot, strongly fragrant with dusty aftertaste; reminiscent of yellow or Dijon mustard	Casseroles, Chinese dishes, meats, pickling, relishes, salads, vegetables
Poppy seed (whole)	Sweet and nutty, very crunchy; reminiscent of poppy seed muffins	Noodles, salad dressings, breads, cakes, cookies, cabbage, carrots
Sesame seed (whole)	Oily with a nutty, slightly sweet flavor; reminiscent of hummus, hamburger buns and breadsticks	Breads, dips, salad dressings, poultry, seafood

SEASONINGS

Crab Boil

Barbecue Spice

Fines Herbes

Herb Seasoning

Grill Seasoning

Five-Spice Powder

Apple Pie Spice

Curry Powder

Poultry Seasoning

Chili Powder

Pumpkin Pie Spice

Italian Seasoning

Tips for Seasoning Mixes

- Seasoning mixes and rubs are highly concentrated blends of dried herbs and spices that flavor the outside of the food as it cooks.

- Store seasoning mixes tightly covered in a cool, dry place for up to 6 months. After 6 months, they begin to lose their flavor or the flavor may actually change.

- Rubs, a dry or wet concentrated blend of spices, are a great way to give food more flavor than just sprinkling it with seasoning. Start by moistening poultry, meat or vegetables with a little vegetable or olive oil or even water. Then rub a seasoning or mix onto the food. Cook immediately, or for a more intense flavor, cover and refrigerate the food from 1 to 24 hours.

Rubs

A mixture of dry or wet seasonings rubbed completely over meat, using your fingers, before cooking. Rubs traditionally were used for barbecued meats cooked in dug-out earth pits, where the pitmasters had their own "secret rub." You can add a rub and immediately cook or grill the food or, for more flavor, cover and refrigerate about 1 hour.

Rubs may contain sugar or salt or even ground nuts. The "wet" seasonings get their name from added liquid, such as oil, mustard and reduced liquids such as wine, mixed with the dry seasonings and creating a paste.

You can easily mix together seasonings from your spice cabinet, or purchase ready-to-use rubs at the supermarket. Rubs also can be used to flavor a wide range of dishes such as condiments, soups and stews.

SEASONING CHART

Seasonings are nifty shortcuts for adding lots of flavor to food. They include blends of dry herbs, spices and salt as well as liquid blends such as red pepper sauce, Worcestershire sauce and marinades. Pick them up at the supermarket, or create your own seasoning collection at home.

Seasoning and Form	Flavor	Use
Apple pie spice (ground blend of cinnamon, cloves, nutmeg or mace, allspice and ginger)	Sweet and spicy; reminiscent of a spice rack	Chutneys, fruit pies, fruit sauces, pastries
Barbecue spice (ground blend of chili peppers, cumin, garlic, cloves, paprika, salt and sugar)	Savory and spicy; reminiscent of tomato with a bit of a smoky kick	Barbecue sauce, casseroles, cheese, eggs, meats
Chili powder (ground blend of chili peppers, cumin, coriander, garlic, onion powder, oregano, cloves, allspice or other spices)	Flavors from mild to hot, depending on the variety	Cocktail sauce, cottage cheese, eggs, Mexican dishes, soups, stews
Cinnamon-sugar (blend of ground cinnamon and granulated sugar)	Sweet and fragrant; reminiscent of cinnamon toast	Baked goods, fruit desserts, toast
Crab boil (blend of whole spices such as peppercorns, bay leaves, crushed red peppers, mustard seed, gingerroot)	Savory and fragrant; reminiscent of shrimp with cocktail sauce	Add to water when boiling seafood
Curry powder (ground blend of as many as twenty spices—ginger, turmeric, fenugreek seed, cloves, cinnamon, cumin seed, black pepper and red pepper are typical)	Strongly fragrant, ranges in "heat" from mild to hot; reminiscent of an Indian restaurant	Appetizers, chicken and shrimp salads, eggs, fish, fruit compotes, meats, sauces, split pea soup, vegetables
Fines herbes (blend of herbs such as parsley, chives and tarragon)	Delicate, yet tangy	Dips, eggs, fish, French dishes, poultry, salad dressings, salads, sauces, veal, vegetables
Five-spice powder (varied blend of five spices—star anise, cinnamon and cloves are usually used)	Slightly sweet and strongly fragrant; reminiscent of a Chinese restaurant	Chinese and other Asian dishes, marinades, meats, poultry, sauces
Grill seasoning (varied blends for different kinds of meat, poultry and fish)	Mild to spicy	Fish and seafood, meats, poultry, vegetables
Herb seasoning (varied blends of mild dried herb leaves such as marjoram, oregano, basil and chervil)	Mild and savory	Casseroles, meat loaves, salad dressings, salads, vegetables
Italian seasoning (blend of oregano, basil, red pepper, rosemary, garlic powder)	Savory and strongly fragrant; reminiscent of Italian dressing	Italian dishes, pasta, pizza
Poultry seasoning (ground blend of sage, thyme, marjoram, savory and sometimes rosemary and other spices)	Savory and musty; reminiscent of turkey stuffing	Meat loaves, poultry and other meat stuffings
Pumpkin pie spice (ground blend of cinnamon, nutmeg, cloves and ginger)	Sweet and aromatic; reminiscent of Thanksgiving	Cookies and bars, pumpkin pie, winter squash

Jamaican Jerk Seasoning

Fast & Low-Fat

Prep: 5 min ✳ *About 3 tablespoons*

The tradition of "jerking" meat is unique to Jamaica. Originally, the spicy seasonings were applied to wild boar to make it more edible. Today, most foods that are jerked are beef, pork and chicken.

1 tablespoon instant minced onion
2 teaspoons dried thyme leaves
1 teaspoon ground allspice
1 teaspoon ground pepper
1/2 teaspoon salt
1/2 teaspoon ground cinnamon
1/4 teaspoon ground red pepper (cayenne)

1. Mix all ingredients in storage container with tight-fitting lid.

2. Store in cool, dry place up to 6 months. Stir before each use.

TO USE AS A RUB: Brush 1 tablespoon vegetable oil over 3- to 3 1/2-pound cut-up broiler-fryer chicken or 1 1/2 pounds boneless meat (chicken, pork, beef). Rub with seasoning.

TO USE AS A MARINADE: Mix seasoning, 1/2 cup dry red wine or chicken broth, 1 tablespoon olive or vegetable oil and 1 clove garlic, finely chopped. Use to marinate chicken, pork or beef.

1 Teaspoon Dry Dressing: Calories 5 (Calories from Fat 0); Fat 0g (Saturated 0g); Cholesterol 0mg; Sodium 130mg; Carbohydrate 0g (Dietary Fiber 0g); Protein 0g **% Daily Value:** Vitamin A 0%; Vitamin C 0%; Calcium 0%; Iron 0% **Diet Exchanges:** 1 Serving is free

Southwestern Rub *Low-Fat*

Prep: 10 min: Marinate: 30 min ✳ *About 3 tablespoons*

Because this rub has oil in it, it's known as a "wet rub" rather than the more typical "dry rub."

1 tablespoon chili powder
1 tablespoon vegetable oil
1 teaspoon ground cumin
1/4 teaspoon salt
1/4 teaspoon ground red pepper (cayenne)
1 large clove garlic, finely chopped

1. Mix all ingredients.

2. Spread rub evenly on 1 pound boneless meat (chicken, pork, beef) or 2 1/2 pounds 1/2-inch-thick pork chops (about 8). Cover and refrigerate at least 30 minutes or up to 24 hours. Cook meat as desired.

1 Teaspoon: Calories 20 (Calories from Fat 20); Fat 2g (Saturated 0g); Cholesterol 0mg; Sodium 75mg; Carbohydrate 1g (Dietary Fiber 0g); Protein 0g **% Daily Value:** Vitamin A 2%; Vitamin C 0%; Calcium 0%; Iron 2% **Diet Exchanges:** 1 Serving is free

Tips for Marinades and Marinating

By soaking food in a marinade, or seasoned liquid, you'll add flavor to foods or tenderize less-tender cuts of meat such as round steak. Marinating is especially tasty for grilled or broiled meats and vegetables. And it's easy to do, with little fuss and with great results.

- For mixing and marinating, use glass or plastic containers or heavy plastic food-storage bags. Glass and plastic won't react with the acid, such as vinegar, wine or lemon juice, in the marinade. It's best not to use earthenware containers because they're porous and the marinade may seep into the pottery.

- Use about 1/4 to 1/2 cup marinade for each 1 to 2 pounds of meat, poultry, fish or vegetables.

- Marinate food, covered, in the refrigerator—not at room temperature—and turn the food occasionally.

- The marinade will soak about 1/4 inch into the food. For more flavor, you can marinate from 15 minutes to 2 hours or longer. If you're tenderizing meat, marinate it for up to 24 hours. If marinated longer than 24 hours, the texture of the meat may become mushy.

- To avoid bacterial contamination, *never* serve cooked meat on the same unwashed platter used to carry raw marinated meat to the oven or grill.

- If you want to use the same marinade that raw meat, poultry or fish has been marinating in as a sauce, you need to cook it first. To avoid bacterial contamination, you *must* heat it to a rolling boil and boil 1 minute, stirring constantly, before serving.

Garlic Marinade

Prep: 10 min; Cook: 5 min; Marinate: 8 hr
✳ *About 3/4 cup*

1/4 cup vegetable oil
4 cloves garlic, finely chopped
1 tablespoon chopped fresh or 1 teaspoon dried
    rosemary leaves, crumbled
1/2 teaspoon ground mustard
2 teaspoons soy sauce
1/4 cup red or white wine vinegar
1/4 cup dry sherry or apple juice

1. Heat oil in 10-inch skillet over medium-high heat. Cook garlic in oil, stirring frequently, until golden. Stir in rosemary, mustard and soy sauce; remove from heat. Stir in vinegar and sherry; cool.

2. Place 1 to 1 1/2 pounds boneless or 3 to 4 pounds bone-in beef, pork or lamb in shallow glass or plastic dish or resealable plastic food-storage bag. Pour marinade over meat. Cover dish or seal bag and refrigerate, turning meat occasionally, at least 8 hours but no longer than 24 hours.

3. Remove meat from marinade; reserve marinade. Cook meat as desired, brushing occasionally with marinade.

4. Remaining marinade must be boiled to be served as a sauce (if not boiled, discard marinade). Heat marinade to boiling, stirring constantly; boil and stir 1 minute.

1 Tablespoon: Calories 50 (Calories from Fat 45); Fat 5g (Saturated 1g); Cholesterol 0mg; Sodium 50mg; Carbohydrate 1g (Dietary Fiber 0g); Protein 0g **% Daily Value:** Vitamin A 0%; Vitamin C 0%; Calcium 0%; Iron 0% **Diet Exchanges:** 1 Fat

Lemon-Herb Marinade

Prep: 10 min; Marinate: 4 hr ✳ *About 2/3 cup*

1/3 cup vegetable oil
2/3 teaspoon grated lemon peel
2 tablespoons lemon juice
1 tablespoon dry vermouth, dry white wine or beef
    broth
1 teaspoon chopped fresh or 1/4 teaspoon crumbled
    dried sage leaves
1 teaspoon chopped fresh or 1/4 teaspoon dried
    oregano leaves
1/2 teaspoon salt
1/4 teaspoon coarsely ground pepper

1. Mix all ingredients in shallow glass or plastic dish or resealable plastic food-storage bag.

2. Add up to 2 pounds boneless beef, pork, chicken or turkey, turning to coat with marinade. Cover dish or seal bag and refrigerate, turning meat occasionally, at least 4 hours but no longer than 24 hours.

3. Remove meat from marinade; reserve marinade. Cook meat as desired, brushing occasionally with marinade.

4. Remaining marinade must be boiled to be served as a sauce (if not boiled, discard marinade). Heat marinade to boiling, stirring constantly; boil and stir 1 minute.

1 Tablespoon: Calories 65 (Calories from Fat 65); Fat 7g (Saturated 1g); Cholesterol 0mg; Sodium 110mg; Carbohydrate 0g (Dietary Fiber 0g); Protein 0g **% Daily Value:** Vitamin A 0%; Vitamin C 0%; Calcium 0%; Iron 0% **Diet Exchanges:** 1 1/2 Fat

Fajita Marinade

Prep: 5 min; Marinate: 4 hr ✱ About 1/2 cup

Don't limit yourself to using this tasty marinade for only Fajitas (page 234). Meats marinated in this mixture and then cooked also make great salads or sandwiches.

1/4 cup vegetable oil
1/4 cup red wine vinegar
1 teaspoon sugar
1 teaspoon dried oregano leaves
1 teaspoon chili powder
1/2 teaspoon garlic powder
1/2 teaspoon salt
1/4 teaspoon pepper

1. Mix all ingredients in shallow glass or plastic dish or resealable plastic food-storage bag.

2. Add about 1 pound boneless or 2 to 3 pounds bone-in beef, pork or chicken, turning to coat with marinade. Cover dish or seal bag and refrigerate, turning meat occasionally, at least 4 hours but no longer than 24 hours.

3. Remove meat from marinade; reserve marinade. Cook meat as desired, brushing occasionally with marinade.

4. Remaining marinade must be boiled to be served as a sauce (if not boiled, discard marinade). Heat marinade to boiling, stirring constantly; boil and stir 1 minute.

1 Tablespoon: Calories 65 (Calories from Fat 65); Fat 7g (Saturated 1g); Cholesterol 0mg; Sodium 155mg; Carbohydrate 1g (Dietary Fiber 0g); Protein 0g **% Daily Value:** Vitamin A 2%; Vitamin C 0%; Calcium 0%; Iron 0% **Diet Exchanges:** 1 1/2 Fat

Teriyaki Marinade *Low-Fat*

Prep: 5 min; Marinate: 1 hr ✱ About 1/2 cup

1/4 cup water
1 tablespoon packed brown sugar
3 tablespoons soy sauce
1 tablespoon lemon juice
1 tablespoon vegetable oil
1/8 teaspoon coarsely ground pepper
1 clove garlic, finely chopped

1. Mix all ingredients in shallow glass or plastic dish or resealable plastic food-storage bag.

2. Add about 1 pound boneless or 2 to 3 pounds bone-in beef, pork or chicken, turning to coat with marinade. Cover dish or seal bag and refrigerate, turning meat occasionally, at least 1 hour but no longer than 24 hours.

3. Remove meat from marinade; reserve marinade. Cook meat as desired, brushing occasionally with marinade.

4. Remaining marinade must be boiled to be served as a sauce. Heat marinade to boiling, stirring constantly; boil and stir 1 minute.

1 Tablespoon: Calories 25 (Calories from Fat 20); Fat 2g (Saturated 0g); Cholesterol 0mg; Sodium 340mg; Carbohydrate 2g (Dietary Fiber 0g); Protein 0g **% Daily Value:** Vitamin A 0%; Vitamin C 0%; Calcium 0%; Iron 0% **Diet Exchanges:** 1 Serving is free

Meat can be marinated in a resealable plastic food-storage bag. Using the bag makes it easy to turn the meat to coat all sides.

Condiment Basics

Everyone is familiar with the Big Three—ketchup, mustard and salsa—but the condiment family is much larger. Other members include relishes, steak sauce, chutneys, jams, jellies and spreads as delicious serve-yourself accompaniments that add zest to everyday foods. Some of the most popular condiments are:

- **Salsa:** In Mexico, the word means "sauce," and salsa has taken cooking by storm. It isn't just for tortilla chips anymore. Fruit salsas, made from pineapple, peaches, apricots, raspberries and more, are fabulous paired with grilled and roasted meat and poultry. Look for cooked as well as fresh versions in this cookbook, such as Tomato Salsa (below).

- **Chutney:** Like salsa, chutney hails from a different culture, in this case India. This chunky, spicy, cooked condiment usually contains fruit, vinegar, sugar and spices. Serve chutneys, such as Golden Fruit Chutney (page 457), with curried dishes and grilled meats, as a spread for bread and as a partner to cheese.

- **Relish:** Relishes are undergoing a renaissance! Fresh or cooked, relishes are made up of small pieces of fruits or vegetables. They're also colorful complements to meats, poultry, fish and sandwiches.

Make condiments head of time, then serve them right from the refrigerator or at room temperature, depending on the ingredients. Your supermarket is a mecca for a fabulous array of already-prepared condiments. Look for them in the condiment and international food sections as well as in the refrigerator and freezer cases.

Tomato Salsa *Low-Fat*

Prep: 20 min; Chill: 1 hr ✳ *About 3 1/2 cups*

Chilies contain oils that will irritate your skin if you rub your face or eyes after touching chilies. Wearing plastic gloves, or putting your hands in plastic bags, prevents the oils from transferring onto your skin. After chopping chilies, wash hands, especially under your nails, and utensils in soapy water.

Serve with tortilla chips, crackers, vegetables, fish, chicken or eggs.

3 large tomatoes, seeded and chopped (3 cups)
1 small green bell pepper, chopped (1/2 cup)
8 medium green onions, sliced (1/2 cup)
3 cloves garlic, finely chopped
2 tablespoons chopped fresh cilantro
1 tablespoon finely chopped seeded jalapeño chilies
2 to 3 tablespoons lime juice
1/2 teaspoon salt

Mix all ingredients in glass or plastic bowl. Cover and refrigerate at least 1 hour to blend flavors but no longer than 1 week.

2 Tablespoons: Calories 10 (Calories from Fat 0); Fat 0g (Saturated 0g); Cholesterol 0mg; Sodium 5mg; Carbohydrate 2g (Dietary Fiber 0g); Protein 0g **% Daily Value:** Vitamin A 2%; Vitamin C 14%; Calcium 0%; Iron 0% **Diet Exchanges:** 1 Serving is free

BLACK BEAN–TOMATO SALSA: Stir in 1 can (15 ounces) black beans, rinsed and drained. About 5 cups salsa.

Corn Relish *Low-Fat*

Prep: 10 min; Cook: 5 min; Chill: 4 hr ✳ *About 2 cups*

Brats, hot dogs and hamburgers are favorites with this relish.

2 cups frozen corn, thawed, or 1 can (15 1/4 ounces) whole kernel corn, drained
2 tablespoons chopped green bell pepper
1 tablespoon finely chopped onion
1 jar (2 ounces) diced pimientos, drained
1/2 cup sugar
1/2 cup cider vinegar or white vinegar
1/2 teaspoon celery seed
1/4 teaspoon salt
1/4 teaspoon mustard seed
1/4 teaspoon red pepper sauce

1. Mix corn, bell pepper, onion and pimientos in medium heatproof glass or plastic bowl.

2. Heat remaining ingredients to boiling in 1-quart saucepan, stirring occasionally. Boil 2 minutes. Pour over corn mixture; stir.

3. Cover and refrigerate at least 4 hours to blend flavors but no longer than 5 days.

Golden Fruit Chutney

2 Tablespoons: Calories 45 (Calories from Fat 0); Fat 0g (Saturated 0g); Cholesterol 0mg; Sodium 40mg; Carbohydrate 11g (Dietary Fiber 1g); Protein 1g **% Daily Value:** Vitamin A 0%; Vitamin C 4%; Calcium 0%; Iron 0% **Diet Exchanges:** 2 Vegetable

Golden Fruit Chutney *Low-Fat*

Prep: 20 min; Cook: 45 min; Cool: 2 hr
✱ *About 4 1/2 cups*

Chutney is both a little sweet and a little sour. Try adding a spoonful onto turkey, grilled pork chops, ham or steak.

1 cup golden raisins

1/2 cup packed brown sugar

3/4 cup pineapple or apple juice

1/2 cup cider vinegar

1 1/2 teaspoons ground ginger

1 teaspoon ground mustard

1/8 teaspoon ground red pepper (cayenne)

1 can (20 ounces) pineapple chunks in juice or syrup, undrained

2 packages (6 ounces each) dried apricots, coarsely chopped (2 cups)

1. Heat all ingredients to boiling in 3-quart saucepan or 4-quart Dutch oven, stirring occasionally; reduce heat. Cover and simmer 30 minutes.

2. Uncover and simmer about 15 minutes, stirring occasionally, until mixture is very thick. Cool about 2 hours. Cover and refrigerate up to 2 weeks, or freeze up to 2 months.

1 Tablespoon: Calories 30 (Calories from Fat 0); Fat 0g (Saturated 0g); Cholesterol 0mg; Sodium 0mg; Carbohydrate 8g (Dietary Fiber 1g); Protein 0g **% Daily Value:** Vitamin A 2%; Vitamin C 0%; Calcium 0%; Iron 2% **Diet Exchanges:** 1/2 Fruit

Slow Cooker Directions: Drain pineapple. Mix all ingredients in 3 1/2- to 6-quart slow cooker. Cover and cook on low heat setting 6 to 7 hours or until very thick.

Cranberry-Orange Relish *Low-Fat*

Prep: 20 min; Chill: 24 hr ✳ *About 2 1/2 cups*

A food processor can be used to chop the cranberries and oranges. Using a fine blade will give a velvety texture, and a coarse blade will give a rougher texture. This relish is a natural with pork, ham or poultry.

1 cup sugar
1 tablespoon finely chopped crystallized ginger, if
    desired
1 package (12 ounces) fresh or frozen cranberries
    (3 cups)
1 unpeeled orange

1. Place sugar and ginger in medium bowl.

2. Wash and dry cranberries; remove any stems or blemished berries.

3. Wash and dry orange; cut into 1-inch pieces (with peel) and remove seeds.

4. Place half of the cranberries and orange pieces in food processor. Cover and process, using short on-and-off motions, about 15 seconds or until evenly chopped. Transfer cranberry mixture into sugar mixture. Repeat with remaining cranberries and orange pieces.

5. Cover and refrigerate at least 24 hours to blend flavors but no longer than 1 week.

2 Tablespoons: Calories 50 (Calories from Fat 0); Fat 0g (Saturated 0g); Cholesterol 0mg; Sodium 0mg; Carbohydrate 13g (Dietary Fiber 1g); Protein 0g **% Daily Value:** Vitamin A 0%; Vitamin C 10%; Calcium 0%; Iron 0% **Diet Exchanges:** 1 Fruit

Savory Butters *Fast*

Prep: 5 min ✳ *About 1/2 cup*

Top grilled or broiled beef or fish steaks, pork chops or chicken breasts with these easy butters, or toss with hot pasta, rice or vegetables. And of course, they are also great as a spread for bread.

Beat ingredients for one of the flavor variations, below. If desired, chill about 1 hour to blend flavors.

*Do not use vegetable oil spreads (page 91).

1 Teaspoon: Calories 35 (Calories from Fat 35); Fat 4g (Saturated 2g); Cholesterol 10mg; Sodium 25mg; Carbohydrate 0g (Dietary Fiber 0g); Protein 0g **% Daily Value:** Vitamin A 2%; Vitamin C 0%; Calcium 0%; Iron 0% **Diet Exchanges:** 1 Fat

GARLIC BUTTER: 1/2 cup softened butter, 1 to 2 cloves garlic, finely chopped, or 1/4 to 1/2 teaspoon garlic powder.

HERB BUTTER: 1/2 cup softened butter, 2 tablespoons to 1/4 cup chopped fresh or 1 to 2 teaspoons dried herb leaves (basil, chives, oregano, savory, tarragon or thyme), 2 teaspoons lemon juice and 1/2 teaspoon salt.

ITALIAN PARMESAN BUTTER: 1/2 cup softened butter, 2 tablespoons grated Parmesan cheese and 1/2 teaspoon Italian seasoning.

LEMON-PEPPER BUTTER: 1/2 cup softened butter, 2 tablespoons finely shredded lemon peel, 1 teaspoon lemon juice and and 1/8 to 1/4 teaspoon pepper.

SESAME BUTTER: 1/2 cup softened butter, 2 tablespoons toasted sesame seed (page 00), 2 teaspoons Worcestershire sauce and 1 teaspoon garlic salt.

Sweet Butters *Fast*

Prep: 5 min ✳ About 1/2 cup butter

You'll especially enjoy the aroma of these butters when they're served on warm breads, rolls and biscuits.

Beat ingredients for one of the flavor variations, below. If desired, chill about 1 hour to blend flavors.

*Do not use vegetable oil spreads (see page 91).

1 Teaspoon: Calories 45 (Calories from Fat 35); Fat 4g (Saturated 2g); Cholesterol 10mg; Sodium 25mg; Carbohydrate 2g (Dietary Fiber 0g); Protein 0g **% Daily Value:** Vitamin A 2%; Vitamin C 0%; Calcium 0%; Iron 0% **Diet Exchanges:** 1 Fat

ALMOND BUTTER: 1/2 cup softened butter, 1 tablespoon finely chopped almonds and 1/2 teaspoon almond extract.

HONEY BUTTER: 1/2 cup softened butter, 1/2 cup honey.

LEMON POPPY SEED BUTTER: 1/2 cup softened butter, 1 tablespoon finely shredded lemon peel and 1 teaspoon poppy seed.

ORANGE BUTTER: 1/2 cup softened butter, 1 teaspoon grated orange peel and 1 tablespoon orange juice.

PECAN BUTTER: 1/2 cup softened butter, 1/4 cup chopped pecans and 2 tablespoons packed brown sugar.

RASPBERRY BUTTER: 1/2 cup softened butter, 1/2 cup raspberries, crushed, and 1 tablespoon sugar; or 1/4 cup raspberry jam.

Cream Cheese Spreads *Fast*

Prep: 5 min ✳ About 2/3 to 1 cup

These spreads are great with your favorite bagels and breads.

Mix cream cheese and milk until blended. Stir in ingredients for one of the flavor variations, below.

1 Tablespoon: Calories 45 (Calories from Fat 35); Fat 4g (Saturated 2g); Cholesterol 10mg; Sodium 35mg; Carbohydrate 0g (Dietary Fiber 0g); Protein 2g **% Daily Value:** Vitamin A 2%; Vitamin C 0%; Calcium 4%; Iron 0% **Diet Exchanges:** 1 Fat

CHILI CHEDDAR SPREAD: 1 package (3 ounces) cream cheese, softened, 1/3 cup shredded Cheddar cheese, 1/4 cup whole kernel corn, 3/4 teaspoon chili powder and a sliced green onion.

CHIVE-SWISS-CREAM CHEESE SPREAD: 1 package (3 ounces) cream cheese, softened, 2 tablespoons milk, 1/2 cup finely shredded Swiss cheese and 1 tablespoon chopped fresh chives.

NUTTY OLIVE CREAM CHEESE SPREAD: 1 package (3 ounces) cream cheese, softened, 2 tablespoons milk, 1/2 cup finely chopped walnuts and 1/4 cup finely chopped pimiento-stuffed olives.

PEANUT BUTTER–HONEY CREAM CHEESE SPREAD: 1 package (3 ounces) cream cheese, softened, 2 tablespoons milk, 1/4 cup crunchy peanut butter and 1 tablespoon honey.

Strawberry Freezer Jam and Blueberry Freezer Jam

Strawberry Freezer Jam *Low-Fat*

Prep: 15 min; Cook: 5 min; Stand: 24 hr
✱ *About 5 half-pints*

1 quart (4 cups) strawberries, cut in half
4 cups sugar
3/4 cup water
1 package (1 3/4 ounces) powdered fruit pectin

1. Mash strawberries with potato masher or in food processor until slightly chunky (not pureed) to make 2 cups crushed strawberries. Mix strawberries and sugar in large bowl. Let stand at room temperature 10 minutes, stirring occasionally.

2. Mix water and pectin in 1-quart saucepan. Heat to boiling, stirring constantly. Boil and stir 1 minute. Pour hot pectin mixture over strawberry mixture; stir constantly 3 minutes.

3. Immediately spoon mixture into freezer containers, leaving 1/2-inch headspace. Wipe rims of containers; seal. Let stand at room temperature about 24 hours or until set.

4. Store in freezer up to 6 months or in refrigerator up to 3 weeks. Thaw frozen jam and stir before serving.

1 Tablespoon: Calories 45 (Calories from Fat 0); Fat 0g (Saturated 0g); Cholesterol 0mg; Sodium 0mg; Carbohydrate 11g (Dietary Fiber 0g); Protein 0g **% Daily Value:** Vitamin A 0%; Vitamin C 6%; Calcium 0%; Iron 0% **Diet Exchanges:** 1 Fruit

RASPBERRY FREEZER JAM: Substitute 3 pints (6 cups) raspberries (3 cups crushed) for the strawberries. Increase sugar to 5 1/4 cups.

Blueberry Freezer Jam *Low-Fat*

Prep: 30 min; Stand: 24 hr ✱ *About 5 half-pints*

2 pints (4 cups) blueberries, crushed (2 1/2 cups)
3 cups sugar
1 teaspoon grated orange peel, if desired
1/2 cup water
1 package (1 3/4 ounces) powdered fruit pectin

1. Mix blueberries, sugar and orange peel in large bowl. Let stand 20 minutes, stirring occasionally, until sugar is dissolved.

2. Mix water and pectin in 1-quart saucepan. Heat to boiling, stirring constantly. Boil and stir 1 minute. Pour hot pectin mixture over blueberry mixture; stir constantly 3 minutes.

3. Immediately spoon mixture into freezer containers, leaving 1/2-inch headspace. Wipe rims of containers; seal. Let stand at room temperature about 24 hours or until set.

4. Store in freezer up to 6 months or in refrigerator up to 3 weeks. Thaw frozen jam and stir before serving.

1 Tablespoon: Calories 35 (Calories from Fat 0); Fat 0g (Saturated 0g); Cholesterol 0mg; Sodium 0mg; Carbohydrate 9g (Dietary Fiber 1g); Protein 0g **% Daily Value:** Vitamin A 0%; Vitamin C 2%; Calcium 0%; Iron 0% **Diet Exchanges:** 1/2 Fruit

Apple Butter *Low-Fat*

Prep: 30 min; Cook: 2 hr; Cool: 2 hr ✱ About 4 cups

Use as a spread for toast, bagels, biscuits and other breads.

12 medium Granny Smith or other cooking apples,
    peeled and cut into fourths (4 pounds)
1 1/2 cups packed brown sugar
1 1/4 cups apple juice
1 tablespoon ground cinnamon
1 tablespoon lemon juice
1 teaspoon ground allspice
1 teaspoon ground nutmeg
1/2 teaspoon ground cloves

1. Heat all ingredients to boiling in 4-quart Dutch oven, stirring occasionally; reduce heat. Cover and simmer 1 hour.

2. Mash apples with potato masher or large fork.

3. Simmer uncovered about 1 hour, stirring occasionally, until mixture is very thick. Cool about 2 hours.

4. Spoon apple butter into container. Store covered in refrigerator up to 3 weeks.

1 Tablespoon: Calories 30 (Calories from Fat 0); Fat 0g (Saturated 0g); Cholesterol 0mg; Sodium 0mg; Carbohydrate 9g (Dietary Fiber 1g); Protein 0g **% Daily Value:** Vitamin A 0%; Vitamin C 0%; Calcium 0%; Iron 0% **Diet Exchanges:** 1/2 Fruit

Slow Cooker Directions: Decrease apple juice to 1/2 cup. Mix all ingredients in 5- to 6-quart slow cooker. Cover and cook on low heat setting 8 to 10 hours or until apples are very tender. Mash apples with potato masher or large fork. Cook uncovered on low heat setting 1 to 2 hours, stirring occasionally, until very thick.

Lemon Curd *Low-Fat*

Prep: 15 min; Cook: 10 min ✱ About 2 cups

This is a tart, refreshing custard. It makes a tasty spread for Scones (page 56) or a filling for Silver White Cake (page 96).

1 cup sugar
1 tablespoon finely shredded lemon peel
1 cup lemon juice (5 large lemons)
3 tablespoons firm butter or stick margarine,* cut up
3 large eggs, slightly beaten

1. Mix sugar, lemon peel and lemon juice in heavy 1 1/2-quart saucepan with wire whisk.

2. Stir in butter and eggs. Cook over medium heat about 8 minutes, stirring constantly, until mixture thickens and coats back of spoon (do not boil). Immediately pour into one 1-pint container or two 1-cup containers.

3. Store covered in refrigerator up to 2 months.

Do not use vegetable oil spreads (page 91).

1 Tablespoon: Calories 50 (Calories from Fat 20); Fat 2g (Saturated 1g); Cholesterol 25mg; Sodium 15mg; Carbohydrate 7g (Dietary Fiber 0g); Protein 1g **% Daily Value:** Vitamin A 2%; Vitamin C 0%; Calcium 0%; Iron 0% **Diet Exchanges:** 1/2 Fruit, 1/2 Fat

KEY LIME CURD: Substitute lime peel for the lemon peel and Key lime juice for the lemon juice.

PEELING APPLES

To peel apples, use a swivel-bladed vegetable peeler. It peels more quickly than a knife and will remove the peel without taking much of the apple flesh. Or use a crank-type apple peeler to save time. Once the apples are peeled, cut them into fourths, and cut out the core.

Herb Vinegar *Low-Fat*

Prep: 10 min; Stand: 10 days ✱ About 2 cups

Flavored vinegars can add a more distinctive taste to your favorite recipes. And making them yourself not only gives satisfaction, but it's also usually less costly than buying them.

2 cups white wine vinegar or white vinegar
1/2 cup firmly packed fresh herb leaves (basil, chives,
    dill weed, mint, oregano, rosemary or tarragon)

1. Shake vinegar and herb leaves in tightly covered glass jar or bottle. Let stand in cool, dry place 10 days.

2. Strain vinegar; discard herb. Place 1 sprig of fresh herb in jar to identify if desired. Store covered at room temperature up to 6 months.

1 Tablespoon: Calories 5 (Calories from Fat 0); Fat 0g (Saturated 0g); Cholesterol 0mg; Sodium 0mg; Carbohydrate 0g (Dietary Fiber 0g); Protein 0g **% Daily Value:** Vitamin A 0%; Vitamin C 0%; Calcium 0%; Iron 0% **Diet Exchanges:** 1 Serving is free

BERRY VINEGAR: Substitute 2 cups berries, crushed, for the herb.

GARLIC VINEGAR: Substitute 6 cloves garlic, cut in half, for the herb.

GINGER VINEGAR: Substitute 1/2 cup chopped peeled gingerroot for the herb.

LEMON VINEGAR: Substitute peel from 2 lemons for the herb.

Herbed Oil

Prep: 5 min; Stand: 3 days ✱ About 3/4 cup

1 jar (0.37 ounce) dried basil, thyme or oregano leaves
    (about 1/2 cup)*
1/4 cup water
1 cup vegetable oil

1. Mix basil and water in container with wide mouth and tight-fitting lid. Add oil; cover and shake. Let stand undisturbed in cool, dry place 3 days.

2. Strain oil; discard basil. Carefully pour clear oil into clean container with tight-fitting lid, being careful not to pour any brown liquid into container. Store tightly covered at room temperature in dark place. Use to brush on poultry, cook vegetables in, toss with cooked pasta or in salad dressings.

*Do not use fresh herbs. Fresh herbs cannot be stored in oil, not even in the refrigerator due to the possibility of botulism food poisoning.

2 Teaspoons: Calories 110 (Calories from Fat 110); Fat 12g (Saturated 2g); Cholesterol 0mg; Sodium 0mg; Carbohydrate 0g (Dietary Fiber 0g); Protein 0g **% Daily Value:** Vitamin A 0%; Vitamin C 0%; Calcium 0%; Iron 0% **Diet Exchanges:** 2 1/2 Fat

---

USING HERBED OIL

Flavored, or infused, oils add their unique flavor to other foods. Because oil absorbs flavors easily, it carries whatever additional flavor is added to it. Stir herbed oils into freshly cooked pasta or potatoes, sprinkle over salads or drizzle over cooked vegetables. Or pour a small amount on a butter plate, and dip crusty breads into it. Shake a plain or flavored vinegar and herbed oil together for a quick salad dressing.

CHAPTER 17
Stews, Soups & Sandwiches

Low-Fat = 3g or less, except main dishes with 6g or less   *Fast* = Ready in 30 minutes or less   ■ = Bread Machine directions   ● = Slow Cooker directions

Easy Cioppino (page 470)

Lighter = 1/3 fewer calories or 50% less fat

Stews and Soups Basics

Stews and soups are soul-satisfying dishes that can be main-course hearty or a light beginning to a meal. Stews tend to be chunky concoctions of meat, poultry, fish and vegetables or a medley of vegetables alone. Made on top of the stove or in the oven, stews are stick-to-your-ribs meals. Soups, on the other hand, can be clear or creamy, hot or cold, quickly cooked or slowly simmered, a perfect beginning or a hearty main course. One thing stews and soups have in common: Both are savored in just about every culture and cuisine around the world.

Tips for Stews and Soups

- Be sure to use the size of pan specified in the recipe. A too-small pan can lead to spillovers or let the mixture heat so slowly that some vegetables and meats overcook.

- Timesaving tip: Buy fresh or frozen cut-up or chopped vegetables from the produce or frozen food section or the deli of your supermarket.

- Use a sharp chef's knife or food processor to chop raw vegetables.

- Using a food processor or blender makes quick work of blending and pureeing cream soups.

- Don't skimp on cooking time. All that simmering over low heat allows the full flavor from the ingredients to develop.

- When thickening stews and soups with a flour mixture, keep lumps from forming by mixing the flour thoroughly in a little cold water with a wire whisk before adding it to the liquid you want to thicken.

- To avoid a starchy undercooked taste and uneven consistency, heat the thickened liquid to boiling, and boil for the time specified in the recipe.

- Heat soups made with dairy products *slowly*. If you let creamy or cheesy soups come to a boil, the ingredients may separate and curdle, but it won't effect the taste.

- To remove fat easily from stews, soups or broths, chill it for several hours or overnight in the refrigerator. Any fat will rise to the surface and solidify. Skim off the fat and toss.

- You don't have to thicken only with flour. Here are some great ways to make a thicker, creamier soup.

  - In a blender or food processor, puree one or more of the cooked vegetables from the recipe with a little of the stew or soup liquid. Stir the thick puree back into to the stew or soup.

  - Stir unseasoned, dry mashed potato mix into the stew or soup to thicken it.

Tips for Slow Cookers

- For easy cleanup, spray the inside of the slow cooker with cooking spray before adding the food. Let your slow cooker cool before washing; otherwise the liner could crack.

- Fill your slow cooker one-half to three-fourths full of food to ensure that the liquid doesn't simmer away during the long hours of cooking and to keep the food moist and tender.

- Vegetables such as carrots and potatoes often take longer than meat to cook. So cut them into bite-size pieces, and put them in the bottom of the cooker (which gets hotter) with the meat on top. Add tender vegetables such as fresh mushrooms, tomatoes and zucchini during the last 30 to 45 minutes to prevent overcooking.

- Don't put a frozen block of veggies in your slow cooker—it will take too long to thaw. Thaw them first, or run them under warm water to separate the pieces.

- Slow cooking makes economical sense because you can use less-expensive cuts of meat. The moist heat and slow cooking is perfect for tenderizing the meat as it cooks.

- Use dried leaf herbs rather than ground because they keep their flavor better over the long cooking time. Or stir in fresh herbs during the last hour of cooking.

- Allow enough cooking time. Remember, most soups, stews and one-dish meals take 8 to 10 hours to cook on the low heat setting.

- A slow cooker that's opened doesn't cook, so don't peek! Removing the cover adds 15 to 20 minutes to the cooking time.

- Milk, sour cream and cheese may break down during the long cooking time. Wait to add these ingredients until the last 30 minutes of cooking unless a recipe states otherwise.

- Fish and seafood can fall apart or get tough if they're slow cooked too long. Add these ingredients in the last hour of cooking.

- Pasta and rice will be at their best if you cook them according to package directions first, and then add them to the slow cooker just before serving.

- Be a safe slow cooker. The long cooking times at low temperatures can be a boon for harmful bacteria unless you:

  - Remove leftovers from the slow cooker and transfer them to the refrigerator or freezer as soon as you've finished eating. Do not let cooked food stand at room temperature longer than 1 hour.

  - Cook and drain ground meats to destroy harmful bacteria before adding them to the slow cooker.

  - Add only thawed foods to your slow cooker—no frozen meats or vegetables.

  - Do not cook whole poultry, such as a whole chicken or Rock Cornish hens, in a slow cooker because safe cooking temperatures cannot be reached quickly enough near the bone.

Storing and Reheating Stews and Soups

In most cases, the flavors in stews and soups mellow and meld with age. So make them ahead of time, cover and refrigerate for up to 3 days. (But store those made with fish or shellfish no longer than 1 day.)

Stews thickened with flour or cornstarch may separate after freezing. If you plan to freeze one of these stews, save the thickening step until you reheat it.

Soups freeze very well, so it's easy to double the recipe and freeze half of it so you'll always have a meal on hand when you need it. Just pour the soup into freezer containers, leaving 1/4- to 1/2-inch headspace (it expands as it freezes). Freeze broth in freezer containers or in ice-cube trays. Once the broth is frozen, transfer the "broth cubes" to a heavy plastic freezer bag. Soups and broths can be kept frozen for 2 to 3 months.

Freezing may affect the flavor and texture of some soups:

- The flavor of green bell pepper intensifies, and onion gradually loses its flavor. So you may need to adjust the seasoning to taste during reheating.

- Freezing makes potatoes soft and grainy. So wait to add the cooked potatoes until it's time to reheat.

- Thick soups tend to become thicker during storage. Add a little broth, milk or half-and-half while reheating, until the soup reaches the desired consistency.

Thaw soups in the refrigerator; once they've thawed, use them right away. Heat broth-based soups over medium heat, stirring occasionally, until hot. You can also reheat these soups in the microwave. Reheat thick purees or soups containing milk, cream, eggs or cheese over low heat, stirring frequently. Don't let them boil, or the ingredients may separate.

Beef Stew *Low-Fat*

Prep: 15 min; Cook: 3 hr 30 min ✳ *8 servings*

1 pound beef stew meat, cut into 1/2-inch pieces
1 medium onion, cut into eighths
1 package (8 ounces) baby-cut carrots (about 30)
1 can (14 1/2 ounces) diced tomatoes, undrained
1 can (10 1/2 ounces) condensed beef broth
1 can (8 ounces) tomato sauce
1/3 cup all-purpose flour
1 tablespoon Worcestershire sauce
1 teaspoon salt
1 teaspoon sugar
1 teaspoon dried marjoram leaves
1/4 teaspoon pepper
12 new potatoes (1 1/2 pounds), cut into fourths
2 cups sliced mushrooms (about 5 ounces) or 1 package (3.4 ounces) fresh shiitake mushrooms, sliced

1. Heat oven to 325°.

2. Mix all ingredients except potatoes and mushrooms in ovenproof 4-quart Dutch oven. Cover and bake 2 hours, stirring once.

3. Stir in potatoes and mushrooms. Cover and bake 1 hour to 1 hour 30 minutes or until beef and vegetables are tender.

1 Serving (about 1 1/4 cups): Calories 220 (Calories from Fat 55); Fat 6g (Saturated 2g); Cholesterol 30mg; Sodium 770mg; Carbohydrate 31g (Dietary Fiber 4g); Protein 14g **% Daily Value:** Vitamin A 50%; Vitamin C 20%; Calcium 4%; Iron 18% **Diet Exchanges:** 1 Starch, 1 Medium-Fat Meat, 3 Vegetable

Slow Cooker Directions: Chop onion (1/2 cup). Omit tomato sauce. Increase flour to 1/2 cup. Mix all ingredients except beef in 3 1/2- to 6-quart slow cooker. Add beef (do not stir). Cover and cook on low heat setting 8 to 9 hours or until vegetables are tender. Stir well.

Burgundy Beef Stew

Prep: 15 min; Cook: 1 hr 50 min ✳ *8 servings*

6 slices bacon, cut into 1-inch pieces
2 pounds beef stew meat, cut into 1-inch pieces
1/2 cup all-purpose flour
1 1/2 cups dry red wine or beef broth
1 1/2 teaspoons chopped fresh or 1/2 teaspoon dried thyme leaves
1 1/4 teaspoons salt
1 teaspoon beef bouillon granules
1/4 teaspoon pepper
1 clove garlic, finely chopped
1 dried bay leaf
2 tablespoons butter or stick margarine
3 cups sliced mushrooms (1/2 pound)
4 medium onions, sliced
Chopped fresh parsley, if desired

1. Cook bacon in 4-quart Dutch oven over low heat, stirring occasionally, until crisp; remove bacon with slotted spoon. Refrigerate bacon.

2. Coat beef with flour. Cook beef in bacon drippings over medium-high heat, stirring frequently, until brown. Drain excess fat from Dutch oven.

3. Add wine and just enough water to cover beef in Dutch oven. Stir in thyme, salt, bouillon granules, pepper, garlic and bay leaf. Heat to boiling; reduce heat. Cover and simmer about 1 hour 30 minutes or until beef is tender.

4. Melt butter in 12-inch skillet over medium heat. Cook mushrooms and onions in butter, stirring frequently, until onions are tender. Stir mushroom mixture and bacon into stew. Cover and simmer 10 minutes. Remove bay leaf. Garnish stew with parsley.

1 Serving (about 1 1/4 cup): Calories 285 (Calories from Fat 145); Fat 16g (Saturated 7g); Cholesterol 70mg; Sodium 750mg; Carbohydrate 13g (Dietary Fiber 2g); Protein 24g **% Daily Value:** Vitamin A 2%; Vitamin C 4%; Calcium 2%; Iron 18% **Diet Exchanges:** 3 Medium-Fat Meat, 3 Vegetable

Cincinnati-Style Chili (variation of Chili)

Chili

Prep: 25 min; Cook: 1 hr 10 min ✱ *4 servings*

This recipe is sometimes called *chili con carne*, Spanish for "chili with meat." Everyone has a favorite chili; if you like yours hotter, either increase the chili powder, add 1/2 teaspoon red pepper sauce or add a jalapeño chili, seeded and chopped.

1 pound lean ground beef
1 medium onion, chopped (1/2 cup)
1 clove garlic, finely chopped
1 can (14 1/2 ounces) diced tomatoes, undrained
1 can (8 ounces) tomato sauce
1 tablespoon chili powder
3/4 teaspoon ground cumin
1/4 teaspoon salt
1/4 teaspoon pepper
1 can (15 or 16 ounces) kidney or pinto beans, rinsed
    and drained, if desired

1. Cook beef, onion and garlic in 3-quart saucepan over medium heat 8 to 10 minutes, stirring occasionally, until beef is brown; drain.

2. Stir in remaining ingredients except beans. Heat to boiling; reduce heat. Cover and simmer 1 hour, stirring occasionally.

3. Stir in beans. Heat to boiling; reduce heat. Simmer uncovered about 10 minutes, stirring occasionally, until desired thickness.

1 Serving (about 1 1/4 cups): Calories 395 (Calories from Fat 155); Fat 17g (Saturated 7g); Cholesterol 65mg; Sodium 970mg; Carbohydrate 37g (Dietary Fiber 10g); Protein 33g **% Daily Value:** Vitamin A 18%; Vitamin C 22%; Calcium 8%; Iron 36% **Diet Exchanges:** 2 Starch, 3 Lean Meat, 1 Vegetable, 1 Fat

CINCINNATI-STYLE CHILI: For each serving, spoon about 3/4 cup beef mixture over 1 cup hot cooked spaghetti (page 390). Sprinkle each serving with 1/4 cup shredded Cheddar cheese and 2 tablespoons chopped onion. Top with sour cream if desired.

White Chili

White Chili *Low-Fat*

Prep: 30 min; Cook: 25 min ✳ 6 servings

"Accessorizing" your chili is half the fun. Serve several bowls of toppings—shredded cheese, crushed tortilla chips, chopped green onions, diced tomatoes, chopped fresh cilantro, sliced avocado, sour cream—for sprinkling over the chili.

1 tablespoon vegetable oil

2 medium onions, chopped (1 cup)

2 cloves garlic, finely chopped

3 cups chicken broth

2 tablespoons chopped fresh cilantro or 1/2 teaspoon ground coriander

2 tablespoons lime juice

1 teaspoon ground cumin

1/2 teaspoon dried oregano leaves

1/4 teaspoon red pepper sauce

1/4 teaspoon salt

1 can (11 ounces) white shoepeg or whole kernel corn, drained

1 can (15 to 16 ounces) great northern beans, drained

1 can (15 to 16 ounces) butter beans, drained

2 cups chopped cooked chicken breast

1. Heat oil in 4-quart Dutch oven over medium heat. Cook onions and garlic in oil, stirring occasionally, until onions are tender.

2. Stir in remaining ingredients except chicken. Heat to boiling; reduce heat. Simmer uncovered 20 minutes. Stir in chicken; simmer until hot.

1 Serving (about 1 1/3 cups): Calories 320 (Calories from Fat 55); Fat 6g (Saturated 1g); Cholesterol 40mg; Sodium 940mg; Carbohydrate 46g (Dietary Fiber 11g); Protein 31g **% Daily Value:** Vitamin A 0%; Vitamin C 6%; Calcium 10%; Iron 32% **Diet Exchanges:** 2 Starch, 2 Lean Meat, 3 Vegetable

Hungarian Goulash

Prep: 30 min; Cook: 1 hr 40 min ✹ 6 servings

Paprika, a popular Hungarian flavoring, enhances the color and flavor of this stew. You can use either the mild or hot variety of paprika in this stew, depending on how much you like the flavor of heat.

1 tablespoon vegetable oil or bacon fat
1 1/2 pounds beef boneless chuck, tip or round roast
    or pork boneless shoulder, cut into 3/4-inch cubes
1/2 cup beef broth
3 tablespoons paprika
1 1/2 teaspoons salt
1/2 teaspoon caraway seed
1/4 teaspoon pepper
3 large onions, chopped (3 cups)
2 cloves garlic, finely chopped
1 can (14 1/2 ounces) whole tomatoes, undrained
1/4 cup cold water
2 tablespoons all-purpose flour
6 cups hot cooked noodles (page 390)

1. Heat oil in 4-quart Dutch oven or 12-inch skillet over medium heat. Cook beef in oil about 15 minutes, stirring occasionally, until beef is brown; drain.

2. Stir in remaining ingredients except water, flour and noodles, breaking up tomatoes with a fork or snipping with kitchen scissors. Heat to boiling; reduce heat. Cover and simmer about 1 hour 15 minutes, stirring occasionally, until beef is tender.

3. Shake water and flour in tightly covered container; gradually stir into beef mixture. Heat to boiling, stirring constantly. Boil and stir 1 minute. Serve over noodles.

1 Serving (about 1 cup): Calories 495 (Calories from Fat 160); Fat 18g (Saturated 6g); Cholesterol 120mg; Sodium 810mg; Carbohydrate 54g (Dietary Fiber 5g); Protein 34g **% Daily Value:** Vitamin A 26%; Vitamin C 14%; Calcium 6%; Iron 36% **Diet Exchanges:** 3 Starch, 3 Medium-Fat Meat, 2 Vegetable

Lighter Hungarian Goulash: For 7 grams of fat and 335 calories per serving, omit vegetable oil; spray Dutch oven with cooking spray before heating. Reduce beef to 1 pound. Use noodles made without egg yolks.

Everyday Cassoulet

Prep: 20 min; Bake: 1 hr 10 min ✹ 8 servings

Traditionally, the French cassoulet requires long, slow cooking. This stew, however, has been streamlined so that it will be on the table more quickly.

1 pound Polish or smoked sausage, cut diagonally into
    1-inch pieces
1 can (15 to 16 ounces) great northern beans, rinsed
    and drained
1 can (15 to 16 ounces) kidney beans, rinsed and
    drained
1 can (15 ounces) black beans, rinsed and drained
1 can (15 ounces) tomato sauce
3 medium carrots, thinly sliced (1 1/2 cups)
2 small onions, thinly sliced and separated into rings
2 cloves garlic, finely chopped
1/2 cup dry red wine or beef broth
2 tablespoons packed brown sugar
2 tablespoons chopped fresh or 1 1/2 teaspoons dried
    thyme leaves

1. Heat oven to 375°.

2. Mix all ingredients in ungreased 3-quart casserole. Cover and bake 1 hour to 1 hour 10 minutes or until mixture is hot and bubbly and carrots are tender.

1 Serving (about 1 cup): Calories 400 (Calories from Fat 155); Fat 17g (Saturated 6g); Cholesterol 30mg; Sodium 1,010mg; Carbohydrate 51g (Dietary Fiber 12g); Protein 23g **% Daily Value:** Vitamin A 38%; Vitamin C 10%; Calcium 14%; Iron 34% **Diet Exchanges:** 3 Starch, 2 Medium-Fat Meat, 1 Vegetable

Lighter Everyday Cassoulet: For 7 grams of fat and 295 calories per serving, use low-fat smoked sausage.

Shrimp Gumbo

Prep: 20 min; Cook: 1 hr 10 min ✳ *6 servings*

1/4 cup butter or stick margarine
2 medium onions, sliced
1 medium green bell pepper, cut into thin strips
2 cloves garlic, finely chopped
2 tablespoons all-purpose flour
3 cups beef broth
1/2 teaspoon red pepper sauce
1/4 teaspoon salt
1/4 teaspoon pepper
1 bay leaf
1 package (10 ounces) frozen cut okra, thawed
1 can (14 1/2 ounces) whole tomatoes, undrained
1 can (6 ounces) tomato paste
1 1/2 pounds uncooked fresh or frozen medium
    shrimp in shells*
3 cups hot cooked rice (page 348)
1/4 cup chopped fresh parsley

1. Melt butter in 4-quart Dutch oven over medium heat. Cook onions, bell pepper and garlic in butter 5 minutes, stirring occasionally. Stir in flour. Cook over medium heat, stirring constantly, until bubbly; remove from heat.

2. Stir in remaining ingredients except shrimp, rice and parsley, breaking up tomatoes with a fork or snipping with kitchen scissors. Heat to boiling; reduce heat. Simmer uncovered 45 minutes, stirring occasionally.

3. Peel shrimp. (If shrimp are frozen, do not thaw; peel in cold water.) Make a shallow cut lengthwise down back of each shrimp; wash out vein (see How to Devein Shrimp, page 320).

4. Stir shrimp into gumbo. Cover and simmer about 5 minutes or until shrimp are pink and firm. Remove bay leaf. Serve soup in bowls over rice. Sprinkle with parsley.

*1 pound frozen uncooked peeled deveined medium shrimp, thawed, can be substituted for the 1 1/2 pounds shrimp in shells.

1 Serving (about 1 1/2 cups): Calories 295 (Calories from Fat 80); Fat 9g (Saturated 5g); Cholesterol 125mg; Sodium 1,130mg; Carbohydrate 40g (Dietary Fiber 5g); Protein 19g **% Daily Value:** Vitamin A 24%; Vitamin C 46%; Calcium 12%; Iron 24% **Diet Exchanges:** 2 Starch, 1 Lean Meat, 2 Vegetable, 1 Fat

Quick Jambalaya *Fast*

Prep: 15 min; Cook: 15 min ✳ *4 servings*

1 package (8 ounces) brown-and-serve sausage links
1 1/2 cups uncooked instant rice
1 1/2 cups chicken broth
1 teaspoon chopped fresh or 1/4 teaspoon dried
    thyme leaves
1/4 teaspoon chili powder
1/8 teaspoon ground red pepper (cayenne)
1 small green bell pepper, chopped (1/2 cup)
1 small onion, chopped (1/4 cup)
1 can (14 1/2 ounces) stewed tomatoes, undrained
1 package (10 ounces) frozen quick-cooking cleaned
    shrimp

1. Cut sausages diagonally into 1-inch slices. Cook as directed on package, using deep 10-inch skillet; drain.

2. Stir in remaining ingredients. Heat to boiling, stirring occasionally; reduce heat. Simmer uncovered 10 minutes, stirring occasionally.

1 Serving (about 1 1/2 cups): Calories 460 (Calories from Fat 200); Fat 22g (Saturated 8g); Cholesterol 140mg; Sodium 1,120mg; Carbohydrate 43g (Dietary Fiber 2g); Protein 24g **% Daily Value:** Vitamin A 10%; Vitamin C 26%; Calcium 8%; Iron 26% **Diet Exchanges:** 2 Starch, 2 Medium-Fat Meat, 3 Vegetable, 2 Fat

Lighter Quick Jambalaya: For 1 gram of fat and 240 calories per serving, omit sausage links.

Oyster Stew *Fast*

Prep: 10 min; Cook: 10 min ✳ 4 servings

1/4 cup butter or stick margarine
1 pint shucked oysters, undrained
2 cups milk
1/2 cup half-and-half
1/2 teaspoon salt
Dash of pepper

1. Melt butter in 1 1/2-quart saucepan over low heat. Stir in oysters. Cook, stirring occasionally, just until edges curl.

2. Heat milk and half-and-half in 2-quart saucepan over medium-low heat until hot. Stir in salt, pepper and oyster mixture; heat until hot.

1 Serving (about 1 cup): Calories 285 (Calories from Fat 180); Fat 20g (Saturated 12g); Cholesterol 115mg; Sodium 710mg; Carbohydrate 12g (Dietary Fiber 0g); Protein 14g **% Daily Value:** Vitamin A 22%; Vitamin C 4%; Calcium 24%; Iron 46% **Diet Exchanges:** 1 Medium-Fat Meat, 3 Fat, 1 Skim Milk

Easy Cioppino *Low-Fat*

Prep: 25 min; Cook: 45 min ✳ 6 servings

Cioppino is a San Francisco fish stew made with tomatoes and a variety of fish and shellfish.

2 tablespoons butter or stick margarine
1 medium onion, chopped (1/2 cup)
1 medium green bell pepper, chopped (1 cup)
2 cloves garlic, finely chopped
1 can (14 1/2 ounces) Italian-style stewed tomatoes, undrained
1 cup dry red wine, nonalcoholic red wine or beef broth
1 cup spicy eight-vegetable juice
1 bottle (8 ounces) clam juice
1 teaspoon salt
1 pound halibut or haddock steaks, cut into bite-size pieces
12 clams or mussels, cleaned (page 324)
1 pound uncooked peeled deveined medium shrimp with tails on, thawed if frozen

1. Melt butter in 4-quart Dutch oven over medium-high heat. Cook onion, bell pepper and garlic in butter about 5 minutes, stirring occasionally, until tender.

2. Stir in tomatoes, wine, vegetable juice, clam juice and salt. Heat to boiling; reduce heat. Cover and simmer 15 minutes.

3. Stir in fish and clams. Heat to boiling; reduce heat. Cover and simmer 5 minutes.

4. Stir in shrimp. Heat to boiling; reduce heat. Cover and simmer about 5 minutes or until fish flakes easily with fork and shrimp are pink and firm. Discard any unopened clams.

1 Serving (about 1 1/3 cups): Calories 175 (Calories from Fat 45); Fat 5g (Saturated 3g); Cholesterol 125mg; Sodium 970mg; Carbohydrate 9g (Dietary Fiber 2g); Protein 25g **% Daily Value:** Vitamin A 18%; Vitamin C 36%; Calcium 8%; Iron 34% **Diet Exchanges:** 3 Very Lean Meat, 2 Vegetable

Tips for Broths

• Wash vegetables, then cut into large pieces. There's no need to peel or trim them first.

• *You* control the amount of salt and spices in homemade broths. Follow the recipe, then adjust seasonings to your taste. Remember, as broths evaporate, their flavor becomes more concentrated or intense.

• Short on time? Toss leftover cooked vegetables, meat and/or pasta or rice into broth, and you've got soup!

• Freeze leftover sauces and strongly flavored vegetable cooking liquid. Use them to replace some of the water in recipes that call for broth.

• If you don't have time to make your own broth, try one of these quick alternatives:

Ready-to-serve broth: 1 can (14 1/2 ounces) chicken, beef or vegetable broth equals about 1 3/4 cups broth.

Condensed broth: 1 can (10 1/2 ounces) condensed chicken or beef broth diluted with 1 soup can water equals 2 2/3 cups broth.

Bouillon: 1 chicken, beef or vegetable bouillon cube or 1 teaspoon bouillon granules mixed with 1 cup water equals 1 cup broth.

Broth or Stock Base: Follow directions on container; each brand is different.

Fish Broth *Low-Fat*

Prep: 20 min; Cook: 40 min ✱ About 6 cups

1 1/2 pounds fish bones and trimmings
4 cups cold water
2 cups dry white wine or clam juice
1 tablespoon lemon juice
1 teaspoon salt
1/2 teaspoon dried thyme leaves
1 large celery stalk with leaves, chopped
1 small onion, sliced
3 medium mushrooms, chopped
3 sprigs parsley
1 bay leaf

1. Rinse fish bones and trimmings with cold water; drain. Mix bones, trimmings, 4 cups cold water and remaining ingredients in 4-quart Dutch oven or stockpot; heat to boiling. Skim foam from broth; reduce heat. Cover and simmer 30 minutes.

2. Cool about 10 minutes. Strain broth through cheesecloth-lined sieve; discard skin, bones, vegetables and seasonings. Use broth immediately, or cover and refrigerate up to 24 hours or freeze up to 6 months.

1 Cup: Calories 40 (Calories from Fat 10); Fat 1g (Saturated 0g); Cholesterol 0mg; Sodium 360mg; Carbohydrate 1g (Dietary Fiber 0g); Protein 3g **% Daily Value:** Vitamin A 0%; Vitamin C 0%; Calcium 0%; Iron 0% **Diet Exchanges:** 1 Serving is free

Vegetable Broth *Low-Fat*

Prep: 20 min; Cook: 1 hr 10 min ✱ About 8 cups

6 cups coarsely chopped mild vegetables (bell peppers, carrots, celery, leeks, mushroom stems, potatoes, spinach, zucchini)
1 medium onion, coarsely chopped (1/2 cup)
1/2 cup parsley sprigs
8 cups cold water
2 tablespoons chopped fresh or 2 teaspoons dried basil leaves
2 tablespoons chopped fresh or 2 teaspoons dried thyme leaves
1 teaspoon salt
1/4 teaspoon cracked black pepper
4 cloves garlic, finely chopped
2 bay leaves

1. Heat all ingredients to boiling in 4-quart Dutch oven or stockpot; reduce heat. Cover and simmer 1 hour, stirring occasionally.

2. Cool about 10 minutes. Strain broth through cheesecloth-lined sieve; discard vegetables and seasonings. Use broth immediately, or cover and refrigerate up to 24 hours or freeze for up to 6 months. Stir before measuring.

1 Cup: Calories 5 (Calories from Fat 0); Fat 0g (Saturated 0g); Cholesterol 0mg; Sodium 270mg; Carbohydrate 2g (Dietary Fiber 0g); Protein 0g **% Daily Value:** Vitamin A 0%; Vitamin C 0%; Calcium 0%; Iron 0% **Diet Exchanges:** 1 Serving is free

---

QUICK HOMEMADE SOUP

Keep broths on hand to make quick homemade soups anytime. Stir bite-size pieces of fresh or frozen vegetables and uncooked pasta or rice into simmering broth. Cook 12 to 15 minutes or until the vegetables and pasta or rice are tender. If you'd like, add small chunks of cooked beef, poultry or fish, and heat through.

Chicken and Broth *Low-Fat*

Prep: 25 min; Cook: 1 hr ✱ *About 4 cups broth and*
2 1/2 to 3 cups cooked chicken

3- to 3 1/2-pound cut-up broiler-fryer chicken*
4 1/2 cups cold water
1 teaspoon salt
1/2 teaspoon pepper
1 medium stalk celery with leaves, cut up
1 medium carrot, cut up
1 small onion, cut up
1 sprig parsley

1. Remove any excess fat from chicken. Place chicken, giblets (except liver) and neck in 4-quart Dutch oven or stockpot. Add remaining ingredients; heat to boiling. Skim foam from broth; reduce heat. Cover and simmer about 45 minutes or until juice of chicken is no longer pink when centers of thickest pieces are cut.

2. Remove chicken from broth. Cool chicken about 10 minutes or just until cool enough to handle. Strain broth through cheesecloth-lined sieve; discard vegetables.

3. Remove skin and bones from chicken. Cut chicken into 1/2-inch pieces. Skim fat from broth. Use broth and chicken immediately, or cover and refrigerate broth and chicken in separate containers up to 24 hours or freeze for up to 6 months.

*3 to 3 1/2 pounds chicken necks, backs and giblets (except liver) can be used to make broth.

1 Cup: Calories 155 (Calories from Fat 55); Fat 6g (Saturated 2g); Cholesterol 65mg; Sodium 700mg; Carbohydrate 1g (Dietary Fiber 0g); Protein 24g **% Daily Value:** Vitamin A 0%; Vitamin C 0%; Calcium 2%; Iron 6% **Diet Exchanges:** 3 Very Lean Meat, 1 Fat

Slow Cooker Directions: Decrease water to 3 cups. Increase salt to 1 1/4 teaspoons. Mix all ingredients in 3 1/2- to 6-quart slow cooker. Cover and cook on low heat setting 8 to 10 hours or until juice of chicken is no longer pink when centers of thickest pieces are cut. Continue as directed in step 2.

Beef and Broth *Low-Fat*

Prep: 30 min; Cook: 3 hr 15 min
✱ *About 6 cups broth and 1 cup cooked beef*

2 pounds beef shank cross-cuts or soup bones
6 cups cold water
1 teaspoon salt
1/4 teaspoon dried thyme leaves
1 medium carrot, cut up
1 medium stalk celery with leaves, cut up
1 small onion, cut up
5 peppercorns
3 whole cloves
3 sprigs parsley
1 bay leaf

1. Remove marrow from centers of bones. Melt marrow in 4-quart Dutch oven over low heat, or heat 2 tablespoons vegetable oil until hot. Cook beef shanks in marrow over medium heat until brown on both sides.

2. Add water; heat to boiling. Skim foam from broth. Stir in remaining ingredients; heat to boiling. Skim foam from broth; reduce heat. Cover and simmer 3 hours.

3. Remove beef from broth. Cool beef about 10 minutes or just until cool enough to handle. Strain broth through cheesecloth-lined sieve; discard vegetables and seasonings.

4. Remove beef from bones. Cut beef into 1/2-inch pieces. Skim fat from broth. Use broth and beef immediately, or cover and refrigerate broth and beef in separate containers up to 24 hours or freeze up to 6 months.

1 Cup: Calories 130 (Calories from Fat 45); Fat 5g (Saturated 1g); Cholesterol 40mg; Sodium 580mg; Carbohydrate 2g (Dietary Fiber 0g); Protein 21g **% Daily Value:** Vitamin A 0%; Vitamin C 0%; Calcium 0%; Iron 10% **Diet Exchanges:** 3 Very Lean Meat, 1/2 Fat

Slow Cooker Directions: Decrease water to 5 cups. Increase salt to 1 1/4 teaspoons. Heat 2 tablespoons vegetable oil in 10-inch skillet over medium heat. Cook beef in oil until brown on both sides. Mix remaining ingredients in 3 1/2- to 6-quart slow cooker; add beef. Cover and cook on low heat setting 8 to 10 hours. Continue as directed in step 3.

Vegetable-Beef Soup

Prep: 50 min; Cook: 4 hr ✱ *7 servings*

Beef and Broth (page 472)
1 ear corn or 1/2 cup frozen whole kernel corn
2 medium potatoes, cubed (2 cups)
2 medium tomatoes, chopped (1 1/2 cups)
1 medium carrot, thinly sliced (1/2 cup)
1 medium stalk celery, sliced (1/2 cup)
1 medium onion, chopped (1/2 cup)
1 cup 1-inch pieces green beans
1 cup shelled green peas or 1 cup frozen green peas
1/4 teaspoon pepper

1. Make Beef and Broth. If necessary add enough water to broth to measure 5 cups. Return strained beef and broth to 4-quart Dutch oven.

2. Cut kernels from corn cob. Stir corn and remaining ingredients into broth. Heat to boiling; reduce heat. Cover and simmer about 30 minutes or until vegetables are tender.

1 Serving (about 1 1/2 cups): Calories 235 (Calories from Fat 90); Fat 10g (Saturated 4g); Cholesterol 50mg; Sodium 410mg; Carbohydrate 20g (Dietary Fiber 4g); Protein 20g **% Daily Value:** Vitamin A 18%; Vitamin C 14%; Calcium 2%; Iron 16% **Diet Exchanges:** 1 Starch, 2 Lean Meat, 1 Vegetable, 1/2 Fat

BARLEY-VEGETABLE-BEEF SOUP: Omit potatoes. Stir 2/3 cup uncooked barley and 1/2 teaspoon salt into Beef and Broth in step 1. Heat to boiling; reduce heat. Cover and simmer 30 minutes. Stir in remaining ingredients. Cover and simmer about 30 minutes or until barley and vegetables are tender.

Chicken Noodle Soup ***Low-Fat***

Prep: 1 hr 25 min; Cook: 30 min ✱ *6 servings*

Chicken and Broth (page 472)
2 medium carrots, sliced (1 cup)
2 medium stalks celery, sliced (1 cup)
1 small onion, chopped (1/4 cup)
1 tablespoon chicken bouillon granules
1 cup uncooked medium noodles (2 ounces)
Chopped fresh parsley, if desired

1. Make Chicken and Broth. Refrigerate cut-up chicken. Add enough water to broth to measure 5 cups.

2. Heat broth, carrots, celery, onion and bouillon granules to boiling in 4-quart Dutch oven; reduce heat. Cover and simmer about 15 minutes or until carrots are tender.

3. Stir in noodles and chicken. Heat to boiling; reduce heat. Simmer uncovered 7 to 10 minutes or until noodles are tender. Sprinkle with parsley.

1 Serving (about 1 cup): Calories 110 (Calories from Fat 25); Fat 3g (Saturated 1g); Cholesterol 30mg; Sodium 1,000mg; Carbohydrate 9g (Dietary Fiber 1g); Protein 13g **% Daily Value:** Vitamin A 32%; Vitamin C 2%; Calcium 2%; Iron 6% **Diet Exchanges:** 1/2 Starch, 1 1/2 Very Lean Meat

CHICKEN RICE SOUP: Substitute 1/2 cup uncooked regular long-grain rice for the uncooked noodles. Stir in rice with the vegetables. Cover and simmer about 15 minutes or until rice is tender. Stir in chicken; heat until chicken is hot.

QUICK CHICKEN SOUP: Make as directed—except substitute 3 cans (14 1/2 ounces each) ready-to-serve chicken broth and 2 cups cut-up cooked chicken or turkey for the Chicken and Broth. Omit chicken bouillon granules.

Gazpacho *Low-Fat*

Prep: 20 min; Chill: 1 hr ✳ 8 servings

1 can (28 ounces) whole tomatoes, undrained
1 medium green bell pepper, finely chopped (1 cup)
1 cup finely chopped cucumber
1 cup croutons
1 medium onion, chopped (1/2 cup)
2 tablespoons dry white wine or chicken broth
2 tablespoons olive or vegetable oil
1 tablespoon ground cumin
1 tablespoon white vinegar
1/2 teaspoon salt
1/4 teaspoon pepper

1. Place tomatoes, 1/2 cup of the bell pepper, 1/2 cup of the cucumbers, 1/2 cup of the croutons, 1/4 cup of the onion and the remaining ingredients in blender or food processor. Cover and blend on medium speed until smooth.

2. Cover and refrigerate at least 1 hour. Serve remaining vegetables and croutons as accompaniments.

1 Serving (about 1/2 cup): Calories 75 (Calories from Fat 35); Fat 4g (Saturated 1g); Cholesterol 0mg; Sodium 320mg; Carbohydrate 10g (Dietary Fiber 2g); Protein 2g **% Daily Value:** Vitamin A 6%; Vitamin C 48%; Calcium 4%; Iron 8% **Diet Exchanges:** 2 Vegetable, 1/2 Fat

Cream of Broccoli Soup

Prep: 35 min; Cook: 10 min ✳ 8 servings

1 1/2 pounds broccoli
2 cups water
1 large stalk celery, chopped (3/4 cup)
1 medium onion, chopped (1/2 cup)
2 tablespoons butter or stick margarine
2 tablespoons all-purpose flour
2 1/2 cups chicken broth
1/2 teaspoon salt
1/8 teaspoon pepper
Dash of ground nutmeg
1/2 cup whipping (heavy) cream
Shredded cheese, if desired

1. Remove flowerets from broccoli; set aside. Cut stalks into 1-inch pieces, discarding any leaves.

2. Heat water to boiling in 3-quart saucepan. Add broccoli flowerets and stalk pieces, celery and onion. Cover and heat to boiling; reduce heat. Simmer about 10 minutes or until broccoli is tender (do not drain).

3. Carefully place broccoli mixture in blender. Cover and blend on medium speed until smooth.

4. Melt butter in 3-quart saucepan over medium heat. Stir in flour. Cook, stirring constantly, until mixture is smooth and bubbly; remove from heat. Stir in broth. Heat to boiling, stirring constantly. Boil and stir 1 minute.

5. Stir in broccoli mixture, salt, pepper and nutmeg. Heat just to boiling. Stir in whipping cream. Heat just until hot (do not boil or soup may curdle). Serve with cheese.

1 Serving (about 1 cup): Calories 110 (Calories from Fat 70); Fat 8g (Saturated 5g); Cholesterol 25mg; Sodium 520mg; Carbohydrate 7g (Dietary Fiber 2g); Protein 4g **% Daily Value:** Vitamin A 12%; Vitamin C 42%; Calcium 4%; Iron 4% **Diet Exchanges:** 2 Vegetable, 1 Fat

CREAM OF CAULIFLOWER SOUP: Substitute 1 head cauliflower (about 2 pounds), separated into flowerets, for the broccoli. Add 1 tablespoon lemon juice with the onion in step 2.

Borscht

Prep: 25 min; Cook: 3 hr 40 min ✳ 6 servings

3/4 pound beef boneless chuck, tip or round, cut into 1/2-inch cubes
1 smoked pork hock
4 cups water
1 can (10 1/2 ounces) condensed beef broth
1 teaspoon salt
1/4 teaspoon pepper
4 medium beets, cooked (page 498), or 1 can (15 ounces) sliced beets, drained
1 large onion, sliced
2 cloves garlic, finely chopped
2 medium potatoes, cubed (2 cups)
3 cups shredded cabbage
2 teaspoons dill seed or 1 sprig dill weed
1 tablespoon pickling spice
1/4 cup red wine vinegar
3/4 cup sour cream
Chopped fresh dill weed, if desired

1. Heat beef, pork, water, broth, salt and pepper to boiling in 4-quart Dutch oven; reduce heat. Cover and simmer 1 hour to 1 hour 30 minutes or until beef is tender.

2. Shred beets, or cut into 1/4-inch strips. Remove pork from soup; let stand until cool enough to handle. Remove pork from bone; cut pork into bite-size pieces.

3. Stir pork, beets, onion, garlic, potatoes and cabbage into soup. Tie dill seed and pickling spice in cheesecloth bag or place in tea ball; add to soup. Cover and simmer 2 hours.

4. Stir in vinegar. Simmer uncovered 10 minutes. Remove spice bag. Serve sour cream with soup. Sprinkle with chopped dill weed.

1 Serving (about 1 1/4 cups): Calories 275 (Calories from Fat 115); Fat 13g (Saturated 6g); Cholesterol 60mg; Sodium 750mg; Carbohydrate 22g (Dietary Fiber 3g); Protein 20g **% Daily Value:** Vitamin A 4%; Vitamin C 20%; Calcium 6%; Iron 16% **Diet Exchanges:** 2 Medium-Fat Meat, 4 Vegetable, 1/2 Fat

Slow Cooker Directions: Decrease water to 3 cups. Mix all ingredients except vinegar, sour cream and chopped dill weed in 4- to 6-quart slow cooker. Cover and cook on low heat setting 8 to 10 hours or until beef is tender. Remove pork hock; let stand until cool enough to handle. Remove pork from bone; cut into bite-size pieces. Stir pork and vinegar into soup. Cover and cook on low heat setting 10 minutes. Serve sour cream with soup. Sprinkle with chopped dill weed. 8 servings.

Beer-Cheese Soup *Fast*

Prep: 15 min: Cook: 10 min ✳ 4 servings

2 tablespoons butter or stick margarine
1 small onion, chopped (1/4 cup)
1 medium stalk celery, thinly sliced (1/2 cup)
2 tablespoons all-purpose flour
1/4 teaspoon pepper
1/4 teaspoon ground mustard
1 can or bottle (12 ounces) beer or nonalcoholic beer
1 cup milk
2 cups shredded Cheddar cheese (8 ounces)
Popped popcorn, if desired

1. Melt butter in 2-quart saucepan over medium heat. Cook onion and celery in butter about 2 minutes, stirring occasionally, until tender.

2. Stir in flour, pepper and mustard. Stir in beer and milk. Heat to boiling over medium heat, stirring constantly. Boil and stir 1 minute; reduce heat to low.

3. Gradually stir in cheese. Heat over low heat, stirring constantly, just until cheese is melted. Sprinkle each serving with popcorn.

1 Serving (about 1 cup): Calories 345 (Calories from Fat 235); Fat 26g (Saturated 16g); Cholesterol 80mg; Sodium 430mg; Carbohydrate 12g (Dietary Fiber 1g); Protein 17g **% Daily Value:** Vitamin A 20%; Vitamin C 2%; Calcium 38%; Iron 4% **Diet Exchanges:** 1 Starch, 2 Medium-Fat Meat, 2 1/2 Fat

CHEESE SOUP: Substitute 1 can (10 1/2 ounces) condensed chicken broth for the beer. Serve topped with paprika if desired.

Cream of Mushroom Soup *Fast*

Prep: 15 min: Cook: 15 min ✳ 4 servings

1 pound mushrooms
1/4 cup butter or stick margarine
3 tablespoons all-purpose flour
1/2 teaspoon salt
1 cup whipping (heavy) cream
1 can (14 1/2 ounces) ready-to-serve chicken broth
1 tablespoon dry sherry, if desired
Freshly ground pepper

1. Slice enough mushrooms to measure 1 cup. Chop remaining mushrooms.

2. Melt butter in 3-quart saucepan over medium heat. Cook sliced and chopped mushrooms in butter about 10 minutes, stirring occasionally, until mushrooms are golden brown. Sprinkle with flour and salt. Cook, stirring constantly, until thickened.

3. Gradually stir in whipping cream and broth; heat until hot. Stir in sherry. Sprinkle with pepper.

1 Serving (about 1 cup): Calories 350 (Calories from Fat 280); Fat 31g (Saturated 19g); Cholesterol 95mg; Sodium 870mg; Carbohydrate 12g (Dietary Fiber 1g); Protein 7g **% Daily Value:** Vitamin A 22%; Vitamin C 2%; Calcium 6%; Iron 10% **Diet Exchanges:** 3 Vegetable, 6 Fat

Lighter Cream of Mushroom Soup: For 7 grams of fat and 145 calories per serving, decrease butter to 2 tablespoons and substitute 1 cup evaporated fat-free milk for the whipping cream.

French Onion Soup

French Onion Soup

Prep: 20 min; Cook: 50 min ✱ *4 servings*

The long, slow cooking of the onions gives this soup its rich flavor and color.

2 tablespoons butter or stick margarine
4 medium onions, sliced
2 cans (10 1/2 ounces each) condensed beef broth
1 1/2 cups water
1/8 teaspoon pepper
1/8 teaspoon dried thyme leaves
1 bay leaf
4 slices French bread, 3/4 to 1 inch thick, toasted
1 cup shredded Swiss or mozzarella cheese (4 ounces)
1/4 cup grated Parmesan cheese

1. Melt butter in 4-quart nonstick Dutch oven over medium-high heat. (If desired, cook onions in 12-inch nonstick skillet; after cooking, transfer onions to Dutch oven to complete the soup.) Stir in onions to coat with butter. Cook uncovered 10 minutes, stirring every 3 to 4 minutes.

2. Reduce heat to medium-low. Cook 35 to 40 minutes longer, stirring well every 5 minutes, until onions are light golden brown (onions will shrink during cooking).

3. Stir in broth, water, pepper, thyme and bay leaf. Heat to boiling; reduce heat. Cover and simmer 15 minutes. Remove bay leaf.

4. Set oven control to broil. Place bread in 4 ovenproof bowls or individual casseroles. Add onion soup. Top with Swiss cheese. Sprinkle with Parmesan cheese. Place bowls on cookie sheet or in pan with shallow sides.

5. Broil with cheese about 5 inches from heat 1 to 2 minutes or just until cheese is melted and golden brown. Watch carefully so cheese does not burn. Serve with additional French bread if desired.

1 Serving (about 1 1/4 cups): Calories 310 (Calories from Fat 145); Fat 16g (Saturated 10g); Cholesterol 45mg; Sodium 1,130mg; Carbohydrate 25g (Dietary Fiber 3g); Protein 20g **% Daily Value:** Vitamin A 10%; Vitamin C 6%; Calcium 38%; Iron 10% **Diet Exchanges:** 1 Starch, 2 High-Fat Meat, 2 Vegetable

GOLDEN ONION SOUP: Omit French bread and Swiss and Parmesan cheeses; do not broil.

Wild Rice Soup

Prep: 20 min; Cook: 25 min ✱ *5 servings*

The next time you serve wild rice as a side dish, cook more than you need and freeze the leftover to have on hand for making this soup.

2 tablespoons butter or stick margarine
2 medium stalks celery, sliced (1 cup)
1 medium carrot, coarsely shredded (1 cup)
1 medium onion, chopped (1/2 cup)
1 small green bell pepper, chopped (1/2 cup)
3 tablespoons all-purpose flour
1/4 teaspoon pepper
1 1/2 cups cooked wild rice (page 348)
1 cup water
1 can (10 1/2 ounces) condensed chicken broth
1 cup half-and-half
1/3 cup slivered almonds, toasted (page 177), if desired
1/4 cup chopped fresh parsley

1. Melt butter in 3-quart saucepan over medium-high heat. Cook celery, carrot, onion and bell pepper in butter about 4 minutes, stirring occasionally, until tender.

2. Stir in flour and pepper. Stir in wild rice, water and broth. Heat to boiling; reduce heat. Cover and simmer 15 minutes, stirring occasionally.

3. Stir in half-and-half, almonds and parsley. Heat just until hot (do not boil or soup may curdle).

1 Serving (about 1 cup): Calories 205 (Calories from Fat 100); Fat 11g (Saturated 6g); Cholesterol 30mg; Sodium 390mg; Carbohydrate 23g (Dietary Fiber 3g); Protein 7g **% Daily Value:** Vitamin A 44%; Vitamin C 18%; Calcium 8%; Iron 6% **Diet Exchanges:** 1 Starch, 2 Vegetable, 2 Fat

> **Lighter Wild Rice Soup:** For 1 gram of fat and 150 calories per serving, spray saucepan with cooking spray before heating. Omit butter. Substitute 1 cup evaporated fat-free milk for the half-and-half.

CHICKEN–WILD RICE SOUP: Stir in 2 cups cubed cooked chicken or turkey with the half-and-half.

Hearty Tomato Soup *Fast*

Prep: 15 min; Cook: 10 min ✱ *8 servings*

2 tablespoons butter or stick margarine
1 medium onion, finely chopped (1/2 cup)
1 clove garlic, finely chopped
1/2 teaspoon paprika
1 1/2 teaspoons chopped fresh or 1/2 teaspoon dried basil leaves
2 packages (3 ounces each) cream cheese, softened
1 1/4 cups milk
2 cans (10 3/4 ounces each) condensed tomato soup
2 cans (14 1/2 ounces each) whole tomatoes, undrained

1. Melt butter in 3-quart saucepan over medium heat. Cook onion and garlic in butter about 2 minutes, stirring occasionally, until onion is tender; remove from heat.

2. Stir in paprika, basil and cream cheese. Gradually stir in milk and soup. Beat with hand beater or wire whisk until cheese is melted and soup is smooth.

3. Stir in tomatoes, breaking up tomatoes with a fork or snipping with kitchen scissors. Heat over medium heat, stirring frequently, until hot.

1 Serving (about 1 cup): Calories 195 (Calories from Fat 110); Fat 12g (Saturated 7g); Cholesterol 35mg; Sodium 710mg; Carbohydrate 19g (Dietary Fiber 2g); Protein 5g **% Daily Value:** Vitamin A 20%; Vitamin C 22%; Calcium 10%; Iron 8% **Diet Exchanges:** 4 Vegetable, 2 Fat

New England Clam Chowder

New England Clam Chowder *Low-Fat*

Prep: 10 min; Cook: 25 min ✽ 4 servings

This classic chowder from colonial days is a white chowder made with milk or cream.

1/4 cup cut-up bacon or lean salt pork
1 medium onion, chopped (1/2 cup)
2 cans (6 1/2 ounces each) minced or whole clams*
1 medium potato, diced (1 cup)
1/2 teaspoon salt
Dash of pepper
2 cups milk

1. Cook bacon and onion in 2-quart saucepan over medium heat, stirring occasionally, until bacon is crisp and onion is tender; drain off fat.

2. Drain clams, reserving liquor. Add enough water, if necessary, to clam liquor to measure 1 cup.

3. Stir clams, clam liquor, potato, salt and pepper into bacon and onion. Heat to boiling; reduce heat. Cover and simmer about 15 minutes or until potato is tender.

4. Stir in milk. Heat, stirring occasionally, just until hot (do not boil or soup may curdle).

*1 pint shucked fresh clams with their liquor can be substituted for the canned clams. Chop clams and stir in with the potato in step 3.

1 Serving (about 1 cup): Calories 190 (Calories from Fat 55); Fat 6g (Saturated 2g); Cholesterol 40mg; Sodium 480mg; Carbohydrate 18g (Dietary Fiber 1g); Protein 17g **% Daily Value:** Vitamin A 12%; Vitamin C 12%; Calcium 20%; Iron 68% **Diet Exchanges:** 1 Lean Meat, 2 Vegetable, 1/2 Skim Milk, 1/2 Fat

Manhattan Clam Chowder *Low-Fat*

Prep: 15 min; Cook: 20 min ✱ *4 servings*

In this chowder, tomatoes replace the milk or cream used in New England Clam Chowder.

1/4 cup finely chopped bacon or salt pork
1 small onion, finely chopped (1/4 cup)
2 cans (6 1/2 ounces each) minced or whole clams*
2 medium potatoes, diced (2 cups)
1/3 cup chopped celery
1 cup water
2 teaspoons chopped fresh parsley
1 teaspoon chopped fresh or 1/4 teaspoon dried
    thyme leaves
1/2 teaspoon salt
1/8 teaspoon pepper
1 can (14 1/2 ounces) whole tomatoes, undrained

1. Cook bacon and onion in Dutch oven over medium heat, stirring occasionally, until bacon is crisp and onion is tender; drain off fat.

2. Stir in clams and clam liquor, potatoes, celery and water. Heat to boiling; reduce heat. Cover and simmer about 10 minutes or until potatoes are tender.

3. Stir in remaining ingredients, breaking up tomatoes with a fork or snipping with kitchen scissors. Heat to boiling, stirring occasionally.

1 pint shucked fresh clams with their liquor can be substituted for the canned clams. Chop clams and stir in with the potatoes in step 2.

1 Serving (about 1 1/2 cups): Calories 155 (Calories from Fat 20); Fat 2g (Saturated 0g); Cholesterol 30mg; Sodium 550mg; Carbohydrate 23g (Dietary Fiber 3g); Protein 14g **% Daily Value:** Vitamin A 12%; Vitamin C 28%; Calcium 8%; Iron 72% **Diet Exchanges:** 1 Starch, 1 Very Lean Meat, 2 Vegetable

Corn Chowder

Prep: 15 min; Cook: 20 min ✱ *6 servings*

1/2 pound bacon, cut up
1 medium onion, chopped (1/2 cup)
2 medium stalks celery, chopped (1 cup)
2 tablespoons all-purpose flour
4 cups milk
1/8 teaspoon pepper
1 can (14 3/4 ounces) cream-style corn
1 can (16 ounces) tiny whole potatoes, drained and
    diced
Chopped fresh parsley, if desired
Paprika, if desired

1. Cook bacon in 3-quart saucepan over medium heat until crisp. Drain fat, reserving 3 tablespoons in saucepan. Drain bacon on paper towels; set aside.

2. Cook onion and celery in bacon fat over medium heat about 2 minutes, stirring, until tender. Stir in flour. Cook over medium heat, stirring constantly, until mixture is bubbly; remove from heat.

3. Gradually stir in milk. Heat to boiling, stirring constantly. Boil and stir 1 minute.

4. Stir in pepper, corn and potatoes. Heat until hot. Stir in bacon. Sprinkle each serving with parsley and paprika.

1 Serving (about 1 cup): Calories 255 (Calories from Fat 80); Fat 9g (Saturated 4g); Cholesterol 20mg; Sodium 570mg; Carbohydrate 35g (Dietary Fiber 4g); Protein 12g **% Daily Value:** Vitamin A 10%; Vitamin C 10%; Calcium 20%; Iron 12% **Diet Exchanges:** 1 Starch, 1 Vegetable, 1 Skim Milk, 1 Fat

CHOWDER CHAT

Red or white? And we aren't talking about wine. In the world of clam chowder, there are two wonderful versions to choose from—New England Clam Chowder, a rich, hearty cream-based variety, or Manhattan Clam Chowder, a lighter tomato and vegetable-based chowder. The word, chowder, comes from the French word *chaudiere*, a large cauldron that the seamen used to make their hearty stews in. Which do you prefer? We've given you both recipes to do some taste-testing of your own.

Senate Bean Soup

Prep: 20 min; Stand: 1 hr; Cook: 3 hr 15 min
✻ *8 servings*

2 cups dried navy beans (1 pound)
12 cups water
1 ham bone, 2 pounds ham shanks or 2 pounds smoked
    pork hocks
2 1/2 cups mashed cooked potatoes
2 teaspoons salt
1/4 teaspoon pepper
1 large onion, chopped (1 cup)
2 medium stalks celery, chopped (1 cup)
1 clove garlic, finely chopped

1. Heat beans and water to boiling in 4-quart Dutch oven. Boil uncovered 2 minutes; remove from heat. Cover and let stand 1 hour.

2. Add ham bone. Heat to boiling; reduce heat. Cover and simmer about 2 hours or until beans are tender.

3. Stir in remaining ingredients. Cover and simmer 1 hour.

4. Remove ham bone; let stand until cool enough to handle. Remove ham from bone. Remove excess fat from ham; cut ham into 1/2-inch pieces. Stir ham into soup.

1 Serving (about 1 1/2 cups): Calories 285 (Calories from Fat 80); Fat 9g (Saturated 3g); Cholesterol 15mg; Sodium 930mg; Carbohydrate 45g (Dietary Fiber 9g); Protein 15g **% Daily Value:** Vitamin A 4%; Vitamin C 6%; Calcium 10%; Iron 18% **Diet Exchanges:** 3 Starch, 1 Very Lean Meat

Slow Cooker Directions: Decrease water to 8 cups and salt to 1 1/2 teaspoons. Mix all ingredients except mashed potatoes in 4- to 6-quart slow cooker. Cover and cook on high heat setting 8 to 9 hours or until beans are tender. Remove ham bone; let stand until cool enough to handle. Remove excess fat from ham; cut ham into 1/2-inch pieces. Stir ham and mashed potatoes into soup. Cover and cook on high heat setting 15 minutes. **11 servings.**

SOUTHWESTERN BEAN SOUP: Add 1 can (4 ounces) chopped green chilies, 1 tablespoon chili powder and 1 teaspoon ground cumin with remaining ingredients in step 3. Top with salsa if desired.

Cuban Black Bean Soup *Low-Fat*

Prep: 20 min; Cook: 2 hr 15 min **✻** *8 servings*

2 tablespoons vegetable oil
1 large onion, chopped (1 cup)
3 cloves garlic, finely chopped
2 2/3 cups dried black beans (1 pound)
1 cup finely chopped fully cooked ham
3 cups beef broth
3 cups water
1/4 cup dark rum or apple cider
1 1/2 teaspoons ground cumin
1 1/2 teaspoons dried oregano leaves
1 medium green bell pepper, chopped (1 cup)
1 large tomato, chopped (1 cup)
Chopped Hard-Cooked Eggs (page 201), if desired
Chopped onions, if desired

1. Heat oil in 4-quart Dutch oven over medium heat. Cook 1 cup onion and the garlic in oil, stirring occasionally, until onion is tender.

2. Stir in remaining ingredients except eggs and additional chopped onions; heat to boiling. Boil 2 minutes; reduce heat. Cover and simmer about 2 hours or until beans are tender.

3. Serve soup with eggs and onions.

1 Serving (about 1 1/2 cups): Calories 240 (Calories from Fat 55); Fat 6g (Saturated 1g); Cholesterol 10mg; Sodium 640mg; Carbohydrate 40g (Dietary Fiber 10g); Protein 17g **% Daily Value:** Vitamin A 2%; Vitamin C 16%; Calcium 10%; Iron 22% **Diet Exchanges:** 2 Starch, 1 Very Lean Meat, 2 Vegetable

Slow Cooker Directions: Decrease water to 1 3/4 cups. Mix all ingredients except hard-cooked eggs and additional chopped onions in 3 1/2- to 6-quart slow cooker. Cover and cook on high heat setting 6 to 8 hours or until beans are tender. Serve soup with eggs and onions.

Split Pea Soup *Low-Fat*

Prep: 20 min; Cook: 2 hr 30 min ✳ 8 servings

Split peas are a variety of pea grown specifically for drying. They are found with dried beans and lentils in the supermarket.

2 1/4 cups dried split peas (1 pound), sorted and rinsed
8 cups water
1/4 teaspoon pepper
1 large onion, chopped (1 cup)
2 medium stalks celery, finely chopped (1 cup)
1 ham bone, 2 pounds ham shanks or 2 pounds smoked pork hocks
3 medium carrots, cut into 1/4-inch slices (1 1/2 cups)

1. Heat all ingredients except carrots to boiling in 4-quart Dutch oven, stirring occasionally; reduce heat. Cover and simmer 1 hour to 1 hour 30 minutes.

2. Remove ham bone; let stand until cool enough to handle. Remove ham from bone. Remove excess fat from ham; cut ham into 1/2-inch pieces.

3. Stir ham and carrots into soup. Heat to boiling; reduce heat. Cover and simmer about 30 minutes or until carrots are tender and soup is desired consistency.

1 Serving (about 1 1/2 cups): Calories 195 (Calories from Fat 45); Fat 5g (Saturated 2g); Cholesterol 15mg; Sodium 220mg; Carbohydrate 34g (Dietary Fiber 12g); Protein 16g **% Daily Value:** Vitamin A 36%; Vitamin C 4%; Calcium 4%; Iron 12% **Diet Exchanges:** 2 Starch, 1 Very Lean Meat, 1 Vegetable

Slow Cooker Directions: Decrease water to 7 cups. Mix all ingredients in 4- to 6-quart slow cooker. Cover and cook on high heat setting 3 to 4 hours or until peas are tender. Remove ham bone; let stand until cool enough to handle. Remove excess fat from ham; cut ham into 1/2-inch pieces. Stir ham into soup.

Chicken, Artichoke and Red Onion Pizza *Fast*

Prep: 5 min; Bake: 10 min ✳ 4 servings

Artichoke hearts add a distinctive flavor to this easy pizza. Serve the pizza for a light supper, or cut into small squares for a great appetizer. If roasted red bell peppers aren't available, use canned pimientos.

2 teaspoons butter or stick margarine
1 large red onion, sliced (2 cups)
1 package (16 ounces) Italian bread shell or ready-to-serve pizza crust (12 to 14 inches in diameter)
1 cup cubed cooked chicken or turkey
1 jar (6 to 7 ounces) marinated artichoke hearts, drained and sliced
3 tablespoons sliced drained roasted red bell peppers (from 7-ounce jar)
1 cup shredded sharp Cheddar cheese (4 ounces)

1. Heat oven to 400°. Melt butter in 8-inch skillet over medium heat. Cook onion in butter 3 to 5 minutes, stirring occasionally, until crisp-tender.

2. Spread onion over bread shell. Top with chicken, artichoke hearts, bell peppers and cheese.

3. Bake 8 to 10 minutes or until cheese is melted.

1 Serving: Calories 440 (Calories from Fat 170); Fat 19g (Saturated 10g); Cholesterol 65mg; Sodium 670mg; Carbohydrate 43g (Dietary Fiber 4g); Protein 28g **% Daily Value:** Vitamin A 10%; Vitamin C 16%; Calcium 38%; Iron 14% **Diet Exchanges:** 2 Starch, 2 High-Fat Meat, 3 Vegetable

---

PREPARING SPLIT PEAS

Before tossing the peas into the soup pot, you'll need to sort through them to remove any foreign objects. Spread the peas out in a shallow pan, and inspect them for any small rock pebbles or stones, grit, discolored peas, or dried and shriveled peas which should be discarded. Then place the peas in a bowl, and cover them with water. After a minute or two, remove any skins or split peas that float to the top. Finally, rinse the split peas in a colander.

Pizza

Pizza

Prep: 45 min: Rest: 30 min: Bake: 20 min

✱ *2 pizzas, 8 slices each*

This recipe includes several options for some of the ingredients. Choose your favorite ones, or add a few of your own, to create your own pizza.

Pizza Crust (right) or 2 ready-to-serve pizza crusts
   (12 inches in diameter)
1 pound lean ground beef, pork, lamb or turkey
1 large onion or 1 medium green bell pepper, chopped
   (1 cup)
1 teaspoon Italian seasoning
2 cloves garlic, finely chopped
1 can (8 ounces) pizza sauce
1 can (4 ounces) sliced mushrooms or chopped green
   chilies, drained
2 cups shredded mozzarella, Cheddar, Monterey Jack or
   brick cheese (8 ounces)
1/4 cup grated Parmesan or Romano cheese

1. Make dough for Pizza Crust; let rest 30 minutes. Partially bake as directed for thin crusts or thick crusts.

2. While crusts are baking, cook beef, onion, Italian seasoning and garlic in 10-inch skillet over medium heat 8 to 10 minutes, stirring occasionally, until beef is brown and onion is tender; drain.

3. Spread pizza sauce over partially baked crusts. Top with beef mixture, mushrooms and cheeses.

4. Bake thin-crust pizzas at 425° for 8 to 10 minutes, thick-crust pizzas at 375° about 20 minutes, or until cheese is melted.

Pizza Crust

2 1/2 to 3 cups all-purpose* or bread flour
1 tablespoon sugar
1 teaspoon salt
1 package regular or quick active dry yeast
   (2 1/4 teaspoons)
3 tablespoons olive or vegetable oil
1 cup very warm water (120° to 130°)

Mix 1 cup of the flour, the sugar, salt and yeast in large bowl. Add 3 tablespoons oil and the warm water. Beat with electric mixer on medium speed 3 minutes, scraping bowl frequently. Stir in enough remaining flour until dough is soft and leaves sides of bowl. Place dough on lightly floured surface. Knead 5 to 8 minutes or until dough is smooth and springy. Cover loosely with plastic wrap and let rest 30 minutes. Continue as directed below for thin crusts or thick crusts.

FOR THIN CRUSTS: Heat oven to 425°. Grease 2 cookie sheets or 12-inch pizza pans with oil. Divide dough in half. Pat each half into 12-inch circle on cookie sheets. Partially bake 7 to 8 minutes or until crust just begins to brown. Add toppings and bake as directed in step 4.

FOR THICK CRUSTS: Grease 2 square pans, 8 × 8 × 2 inches, or 2 round pans, 9 × 1 1/2 inches, with oil. Sprinkle with cornmeal. Divide dough in half. Pat each half in bottom of pan. Cover loosely with plastic wrap and let rise in warm place 30 to 45 minutes or until almost double. Move oven rack to lowest position. Heat oven to 375°. Partially bake 20 to 22 minutes or until crust just begins to brown. Add toppings and bake as directed in step 4.

*Do not use self-rising flour.

1 Slice: Calories 195 (Calories from Fat 80); Fat 9g (Saturated 4g); Cholesterol 25mg; Sodium 340mg; Carbohydrate 18g (Dietary Fiber 1g); Protein 12g **% Daily Value:** Vitamin A 2%; Vitamin C 4%; Calcium 12%; Iron 10% **Diet Exchanges:** 1 Starch, 1 High-Fat Meat, 1 Vegetable

CHEESE PIZZA: Omit beef, onion, Italian seasoning and garlic. Increase shredded cheese to 3 cups.

Calzone

Prep: 45 min; Rest: 30 min; Bake: 25 min ✱ 6 servings

A calzone is a stuffed pizza that looks like a big turnover.

Pizza Crust (page 482)
2 cups shredded mozzarella cheese (8 ounces)
1/4 pound salami, cut into thin strips
1/2 cup ricotta cheese
1/4 cup chopped fresh basil leaves
2 roma (plum) tomatoes, chopped
Freshly ground pepper
1 large egg, slightly beaten

1. Make dough for Pizza Crust; let rest 30 minutes.

2. Heat oven to 375°. Grease 2 cookie sheets.

3. Divide dough into 6 equal parts. Roll each part into 7-inch circle on lightly floured surface with floured rolling pin.

4. Top half of each dough circle with mozzarella cheese, salami, ricotta cheese, basil and tomatoes to within 1 inch of edge. Sprinkle with pepper. Carefully fold dough over filling; pinch edges or press with fork to seal securely.

5. Place calzones on cookie sheets. Brush with egg. Bake about 25 minutes or until golden brown.

Top half of each dough circle with filling ingredients. Carefully fold dough over filling; pinch edges or press with fork to seal securely.

1 Serving: Calories 460 (Calories from Fat 200); Fat 22g (Saturated 9g); Cholesterol 80mg; Sodium 970mg; Carbohydrate 44g (Dietary Fiber 2g); Protein 24g **% Daily Value:** Vitamin A 10%; Vitamin C 2%; Calcium 34%; Iron 18% **Diet Exchanges:** 3 Starch, 2 High-Fat Meat, 1/2 Fat

Lighter Calzone: For 8 grams of fat and 350 calories per serving, use reduced-fat mozzarella cheese and fat-free ricotta cheese; substitute cooked chicken for the salami.

Sandwich Basics

The beauty of the versatile sandwich is that can be served cold or hot; grilled, baked or fried; layered, stacked, rolled or wrapped; open-face with knife and fork; cut in half or quartered. Almost every cuisine has its own version of a sandwich: filled Mexican tortillas, Middle Eastern pitas, Italian calzones, Chinese pork buns and the list goes on. Serve a hearty sandwich such as the Submarine Sandwich (page 490), and it's a full-size meal.

Tips for Sandwiches

- Firm-textured breads work best for sandwiches because they're sturdy enough to hold the filling without collapsing. Look beyond the usual when choosing sandwich bread: try nut breads, buns, tortillas, hard rolls.

- Just say no to soggy sandwiches! Seal the sides of the bread that touch the filling by spreading them to the edges with spreads such as butter or cream cheese. If the filling is saucy, such as for Sloppy Joes (right), toast the bread before assembling the sandwich. Toasting helps seal the bread, too.

- Some like 'em thick, some like 'em thin, so fill sandwiches according to individual likes and dislikes.

- Hold together mixed fillings—chopped eggs, cut-up pieces of meat, vegetables—with mayonnaise, salad dressing, cream cheese, barbecue sauce or other sandwich spreads. Season with a little mustard, herbs, salt or pepper, if you like.

- When freezing sandwiches, keep the following in mind:
  - Sandwiches can be frozen for up to 1 month.
  - Mayonnaise, sour cream, hard-cooked eggs, tomatoes and lettuce don't freeze well, so wait to add them until just before serving.
  - Wrap sandwiches individually in moisture- and vaporproof wrap.
  - Sandwiches take about 3 hours to thaw at room temperature. Pack frozen sandwiches for school or work, and they'll be ready to eat by lunchtime. If it's going to be longer than 3 hours before sandwiches are eaten, put them in the refrigerator or on ice to keep them safe to eat.

Sloppy Joes *Fast*

Prep: 10 min; Cook: 20 min ✳ *6 sandwiches*

Lightly toasting the hamburger buns under the broiler will add flavor and a little crunch to this favorite sandwich.

1 pound lean ground beef
1 medium onion, chopped (1/2 cup)
1/4 cup chopped celery
1 cup ketchup
1 tablespoon Worcestershire sauce
1 teaspoon ground mustard
1/8 teaspoon pepper
6 hamburger buns, split

1. Cook beef, onion, and celery in 10-inch skillet over medium heat 8 to 10 minutes, stirring occasionally, until beef is brown; drain.

2. Stir in remaining ingredients except buns. Heat to boiling; reduce heat. Simmer uncovered 10 to 15 minutes, stirring occasionally, until vegetables are tender.

3. Fill buns with beef mixture.

1 Sandwich: Calories 325 (Calories from Fat 115); Fat 13g (Saturated 5g); Cholesterol 45mg; Sodium 780mg; Carbohydrate 35g (Dietary Fiber 2g); Protein 19g **% Daily Value:** Vitamin A 4%; Vitamin C 6%; Calcium 8%; Iron 16% **Diet Exchanges:** 2 Starch, 1 1/2 High-Fat Meat, 1 Vegetable

Lighter Sloppy Joes: For 3 grams of fat and 235 calories per serving, substitute ground turkey breast for the ground beef; spray skillet with cooking spray before heating.

Barbecued Roast Beef Sandwiches

Barbecued Roast Beef Sandwiches *Fast & Low-Fat*

Prep: 25 min; Cook: 5 min ✳ *6 sandwiches*

You can make these family-pleasing sandwiches even more quickly by using 1 cup prepared barbecue sauce for the Zesty Barbecue Sauce and packaged meats for the beef. Heat the barbecue sauce just to boiling, and stir in 3 packages (2 1/2 ounces each) sliced cooked chicken, ham, turkey, beef or pastrami, cut into 1-inch strips.

Zesty Barbecue Sauce (right)
1 pound thinly sliced cooked roast beef, cut into 1-inch strips (3 cups)
6 hamburger buns, split

1. Make Zesty Barbecue Sauce.

2. Stir beef into sauce. Cover and simmer about 5 minutes or until beef is hot.

3. Fill buns with beef mixture.

Zesty Barbecue Sauce
1/2 cup ketchup
3 tablespoons white vinegar
2 tablespoons chopped onion
1 tablespoon Worcestershire sauce
2 teaspoons packed brown sugar
1/4 teaspoon ground mustard
1 clove garlic, finely chopped

Heat all ingredients to boiling in 1-quart saucepan over medium heat, stirring constantly; reduce heat. Simmer uncovered 10 minutes, stirring occasionally.

1 Sandwich: Calories 270 (Calories from Fat 55); Fat 6g (Saturated 2g); Cholesterol 55mg; Sodium 540mg; Carbohydrate 30g (Dietary Fiber 1g); Protein 25g **% Daily Value:** Vitamin A 2%; Vitamin C 2%; Calcium 6%; Iron 20% **Diet Exchanges:** 2 Starch, 3 Very Lean Meat

Gyros

Prep: 25 min; Cook: 15 min ✽ 4 sandwiches

This Greek sandwich features lamb-filled pita breads.

4 pita breads (6 inches in diameter)
1/2 cup plain yogurt
1 tablespoon chopped fresh or 1 teaspoon dried mint
    leaves
1 teaspoon sugar
1 small cucumber, seeded and chopped (3/4 cup)
1 pound ground lamb or beef
2 tablespoons water
1 tablespoon lemon juice
1/2 teaspoon salt
1/2 teaspoon ground cumin
1/2 teaspoon dried oregano leaves
1/4 teaspoon pepper
2 cloves garlic, finely chopped
1 small onion, chopped (1/4 cup)
2 tablespoons vegetable oil
2 cups shredded lettuce
1 medium tomato, chopped (3/4 cup)

1. Split each pita bread halfway around edge with knife; separate to form pocket.

2. Mix yogurt, mint and sugar in small bowl. Stir in cucumber.

3. Mix lamb, water, lemon juice, salt, cumin, oregano, pepper, garlic and onion. Shape mixture into 4 thin patties.

4. Heat oil in 10-inch skillet over medium heat. Cook patties in oil 10 to 12 minutes, turning frequently, until no longer pink in center. Place cooked patty in each pita pocket. Top with yogurt mixture, lettuce and tomato.

1 Sandwich: Calories 450 (Calories from Fat 215); Fat 24g (Saturated 8g); Cholesterol 75mg; Sodium 640mg; Carbohydrate 36g (Dietary Fiber 2g); Protein 24g **% Daily Value:** Vitamin A 4%; Vitamin C 20%; Calcium 12%; Iron 18% **Diet Exchanges:** 2 Starch, 2 High-Fat Meat, 1 Vegetable, 1 1/2 Fat

Reuben Sandwiches

Prep: 20 min; Cook: 20 min ✽ 6 sandwiches

Although the traditional Reuben sandwich is served grilled, it also is delicious served cold without grilling. If you decide to skip the grilling, omit the 1/4 cup butter or stick margarine in step 2.

1/3 cup mayonnaise or salad dressing
1 tablespoon chili sauce
12 slices rye bread
6 slices (1 ounce each) Swiss cheese
3/4 pound thinly sliced cooked corned beef
1 can (16 ounces) sauerkraut, drained
1/4 cup butter or stick margarine, softened*

1. Mix mayonnaise and chili sauce. Spread over 6 slices bread. Place cheese, corned beef and sauerkraut on mayonnaise mixture. Top with remaining bread slices. Spread 1 teaspoon butter over each top slice of bread.

2. Place sandwiches, butter sides down, in skillet. Spread remaining butter over top slices of bread. Cook uncovered over low heat about 10 minutes or until bottoms are golden brown. Turn and cook about 8 minutes longer or until bottoms are golden brown and cheese is melted.

*Spreads with at least 65% vegetable oil can be used (page 91).

1 Serving: Calories 410 (Calories from Fat 250); Fat 28g (Saturated 12g); Cholesterol 55mg; Sodium 1,110mg; Carbohydrate 30g (Dietary Fiber 5g); Protein 14g **% Daily Value:** Vitamin A 12%; Vitamin C 8%; Calcium 34%; Iron 16% **Diet Exchanges:** 2 Starch, 1 Medium-Fat Meat, 4 Fat

Lighter Reuben Sandwiches: For 11 grams of fat and 310 calories per serving, use fat-free mayonnaise; substitute thinly sliced turkey or chicken for the corned beef. Omit butter; spray skillet with cooking spray before heating.

American Grilled Cheese *Fast*

Prep: 10 min; Cook: 15 min ✻ 4 sandwiches

Dunk these sandwiches into bowls of steaming tomato soup.

12 slices process American cheese (about 8 ounces)
8 slices white or whole wheat bread
1/3 cup butter or stick margarine, softened*

1. Place 3 slices cheese on each of 4 slices bread. Top with remaining bread slices. Spread 1 teaspoon butter over each top slice of bread.

2. Place sandwiches, butter sides down, in skillet. Spread remaining butter over top slices of bread. Cook uncovered over medium heat about 5 minutes or until bottoms are golden brown. Turn and cook 2 to 3 minutes longer or until bottoms are golden brown and cheese is melted.

Spreads with at least 65% vegetable oil can be used (page 91).

1 Serving: Calories 470 (Calories from Fat 295); Fat 33g (Saturated 21g); Cholesterol 90mg; Sodium 1,260mg; Carbohydrate 26g (Dietary Fiber 1g); Protein 18g **% Daily Value:** Vitamin A 26%; Vitamin C 0%; Calcium 38%; Iron 10% **Diet Exchanges:** 10 Iron, 2 Starch, 2 High-Fat Meat, 2 1/2 Fat

PESTO-PARMESAN GRILLED CHEESE: Spread pesto lightly over each bread slice before adding cheese in step 1. Sprinkle butter-topped slices with Parmesan cheese before grilling.

Beef Burritos *Fast*

Prep: 30 min ✻ 8 servings

2 cups shredded cooked beef
1 cup prepared refried beans
8 flour tortillas (10 inches in diameter)
2 cups shredded lettuce
2 medium tomatoes, chopped (1 1/2 cups)
1 cup shredded Cheddar cheese (4 ounces)

1. Heat beef and refried beans separately. Warm tortillas as directed on package.

2. Place about 1/4 cup of the beef on center of each tortilla. Spoon about 2 tablespoons beans onto beef. Top with 1/4 cup of the lettuce, 3 tablespoons tomatoes and 2 tablespoons cheese.

3. Fold one end of tortilla up about 1 inch over filling; fold right and left sides over folded end, overlapping. Fold remaining end down.

1 Serving: Calories 280 (Calories from Fat 90); Fat 10g (Saturated 4g); Cholesterol 45mg; Sodium 410mg; Carbohydrate 31g (Dietary Fiber 4g); Protein 20g **% Daily Value:** Vitamin A 4%; Vitamin C 6%; Calcium 14%; Iron 18% **Diet Exchanges:** 2 Starch, 2 Lean Meat

Chicken Tacos *Fast*

Prep: 15 min; Cook: 10 min ✻ 5 servings

Perfectly ripe avocados are silky smooth and have the best flavor. Avocados are ripe and ready to use when they yield to gentle pressure but still feel slightly firm.

1 small avocado
Lemon juice
2 tablespoons vegetable oil
2 cups chopped cooked chicken
1 can (4 ounces) chopped green chilies, drained
1 small onion, sliced
10 taco shells
2 cups shredded Monterey Jack cheese (8 ounces)
1/3 cup sliced pimiento-stuffed olives
1 cup shredded lettuce
Taco sauce, if desired
Sour cream, if desired

1. Cut avocado in half; remove pit and avocado peel (see page 23). Cut halves into slices. Sprinkle with lemon juice to keep avocado from turning brown.

2. Heat oil in 10-inch skillet over medium heat. Cook chicken, chilies and onion in oil, stirring occasionally, until chicken is hot. Heat taco shells as directed on package.

3. Spoon about 1/4 cup chicken mixture into each shell. Top with cheese, olives, lettuce and avocado. Serve with taco sauce and sour cream.

1 Serving: Calories 535 (Calories from Fat 350); Fat 39g (Saturated 13g); Cholesterol 90mg; Sodium 710mg; Carbohydrate 22g (Dietary Fiber 5g); Protein 29g **% Daily Value:** Vitamin A 22%; Vitamin C 16%; Calcium 38%; Iron 12% **Diet Exchanges:** 1 Starch, 3 High-Fat Meat, 1 Vegetable, 3 Fat

Garden Vegetable Wraps

Garden Vegetable Wraps *Fast*

Prep: 15 min ✳ *4 servings*

These fun, portable sandwiches have endless possibilities. Try different flavors of cream cheese, chopped fresh broccoli, sliced green onions or shredded zucchini. Or add your favorite cheeses and deli meats. Anything goes!

1/2 cup cream cheese (about 4 ounces)
4 flour tortillas (8 to 10 inches in diameter)
1 cup lightly packed spinach leaves
1 large tomato, thinly sliced
3/4 cup shredded carrot
8 slices (1 ounce each) Muenster or Monterey Jack cheese
1 small yellow bell pepper, chopped (1/2 cup)

1. Spread 2 tablespoons of the cream cheese over each tortilla. Top with spinach and tomato to within 1 inch of edge. Sprinkle with carrot. Top with cheese slices. Sprinkle with bell pepper.

2. Roll up tortillas tightly. Serve immediately, or wrap securely with plastic wrap and refrigerate no longer than 24 hours.

Top tortilla with filling ingredients to within 1 inch of edge. Roll up tortilla tightly.

1 Serving: Calories 460 (Calories from Fat 270); Fat 30g (Saturated 18g); Cholesterol 35mg; Sodium 660mg; Carbohydrate 31g (Dietary Fiber 3g); Protein 20g **% Daily Value:** Vitamin A 68%; Vitamin C 38%; Calcium 50%; Iron 14% **Diet Exchanges:** 2 Starch, 2 High-Fat Meat, 2 Fat

Chicken Salad Sandwiches *Fast*

Prep: 15 min ✳ *4 sandwiches*

Choose hearty breads, buns or croissants for these ever-popular sandwiches.

1 1/2 cups chopped cooked chicken or turkey
1/2 cup mayonnaise or salad dressing
1/4 teaspoon salt
1/4 teaspoon pepper
1 medium stalk celery, chopped (1/2 cup)
1 small onion, chopped (1/4 cup)
8 slices bread

1. Mix all ingredients except bread.

2. Spread chicken mixture on each of 4 slices bread. Top with remaining bread.

1 Serving: Calories 450 (Calories from Fat 280); Fat 31g (Saturated 6g); Cholesterol 60mg; Sodium 630mg; Carbohydrate 27g (Dietary Fiber 2g); Protein 18g **% Daily Value:** Vitamin A 4%; Vitamin C 2%; Calcium 6%; Iron 12% **Diet Exchanges:** 2 Starch, 2 Medium-Fat Meat, 3 Fat

> **Lighter Chicken Salad Sandwiches:** For 9 grams of fat and 270 calories per serving, use fat-free mayonnaise.

EGG SALAD SANDWICHES: Substitute 6 Hard-Cooked Eggs (page 201), chopped, for the chicken.

HAM SALAD SANDWICHES: Substitute 1 1/2 cups chopped fully cooked ham for the chicken. Omit salt and pepper. Stir in 1 teaspoon yellow mustard.

TUNA SALAD SANDWICHES: Substitute 2 cans (6 ounces each) tuna in water, drained, for the chicken. Stir in 1 teaspoon lemon juice.

Montana Panini *Fast*

Prep: 8 min; Cook: 5 min ✳ *6 sandwiches*

Avocado Ranch Dressing (below)
3/4 pound thinly sliced cooked deli turkey or chicken
12 slices bacon, crisply cooked and broken in half
1 large tomato, sliced
6 slices (1 ounce each) Colby–Monterey Jack cheese
12 slices sourdough bread, 1/2 inch thick
3 tablespoons butter or stick margarine, softened*

1. Make Avocado Ranch Dressing.

2. Layer turkey, bacon, tomato, cheese and dressing on 6 slices bread. Top with remaining bread slices. Spread butter on top slices of bread.

3. Place sandwiches, butter sides down, in 12-inch skillet. Spread butter over top slices of bread. Cover and cook over medium heat 4 to 5 minutes, turning once, until bread is crisp and cheese is melted.

*Spreads with at least 65% vegetable oil can be used (page 91).

Avocado Ranch Dressing

1/4 cup ranch dressing
1 small avocado, mashed (see page 00)

Mix ingredients.

1 Sandwich: Calories 515 (Calories from Fat 300); Fat 33g (Saturated 10g); Cholesterol 75mg; Sodium 1,680mg; Carbohydrate 31g (Dietary Fiber 3g); Protein 27g **% Daily Value:** Vitamin A 20%; Vitamin C 14%; Calcium 22%; Iron 14% **Diet Exchanges:** 2 Starch, 3 Lean Meat, 4 Fat

Submarine Sandwich

Submarine Sandwich   *Fast*

Prep: 15 min ✱ 6 servings

Create a submarine sandwich to your taste by using your favorite cheeses, meats and vegetables. Try flavored cream cheese or mayonnaise instead of butter.

1 loaf (1 pound) French bread

1/4 cup butter or stick margarine, softened

4 ounces Swiss cheese, sliced

1/2 pound salami, sliced

2 cups shredded lettuce

2 medium tomatoes, thinly sliced

1 medium onion, thinly sliced

1/2 pound fully cooked ham, thinly sliced

1 medium green bell pepper, thinly sliced

1/4 cup Creamy Italian Dressing (page 431) or bottled
    dressing

6 long wooden picks or small skewers

1. Cut bread horizontally in half. Spread butter over bottom half.

2. Layer cheese, salami, lettuce, tomatoes, onion, ham and bell pepper on bread.

3. Drizzle with dressing. Top with remaining bread half. Secure loaf with picks. Cut into 6 serving pieces.

1 Serving: Calories 605 (Calories from Fat 315); Fat 35g (Saturated 15g); Cholesterol 90mg; Sodium 1,780mg; Carbohydrate 46g (Dietary Fiber 3g); Protein 30g **% Daily Value:** Vitamin A 14%; Vitamin C 46%; Calcium 26%; Iron 20% **Diet Exchanges:** 3 Starch, 3 High-Fat Meat, 1 1/2 Fat

Low-Fat = *3g or less, except main dishes with 6g or less*　　**Fast** = *Ready in 30 minutes or less*　　■ = *Bread Machine directions*　　● = *Slow Cooker directions*

Mashed Potatoes (page 517)　　*Lighter* = *1/3 fewer calories or 50% less fat*

Vegetable Basics

A fabulous bounty of vegetables is just waiting to be picked at your local grocery store, supermarket and farmers' market. It's a year-round cornucopia of familiar favorites and exotic newcomers, from carrots to jicama, green beans to broccoli rabe. Available fresh, frozen, canned and dried, there's a vegetable to fit every need. Vegetables bring color, texture and flavor to our plates, but they also bring something more—a wealth of healthy nutrients.

New and Specialty Vegetables Glossary

Baby Vegetables: A few vegetables, including broccoli, carrots, corn, eggplant and potatoes are available in some markets as "small," "tiny," "new" or "baby." They look like miniature versions of the larger ones, but their skin may be thinner and their flesh more delicate.

Broccoli Rabe (Broccoletta, Broccoli Raab, Brocoletti di Rape, Rapini): Although this vegetable is related to the cabbage and turnip families, it has none of those characteristics. It has long, slender, dark green stalks with small clusters of broccoli-like buds and lots of leafy greens. The entire vegetable is edible and has a pungent, bitter flavor. Refrigerate unwashed and wrapped in a plastic bag up to 5 days. Available year-round.

Celeriac (Celeri-Rave, Celery Knob, Celery Root, Turnip-Rooted Celery): This vegetable is grown especially for its large, knobby root that ranges in size from that of an apple to a small cantaloupe. The stems and leaves are inedible and are often removed before it reaches stores. Peel the heavy brown skin from the root; the interior is creamy white. The mild flavor tastes like a combination of celery and parsley. It can be cooked or served raw, grated or chopped in salads. Refrigerate unwashed in a plastic bag up to 1 week. Available October through April.

Daikon: A large black or white radish of Asian origin. It ranges from six to fifteen inches in length and has a diameter of two to three inches and sometimes more. Its flesh is crisp, juicy and white with a sweet, fresh flavor. It can be served raw in salads or as a garnish or cooked in a stir-fry. Refrigerate wrapped in plastic up to 1 week. Scrub with a brush under running water before using. Available year-round.

Elephant Garlic: A large, white-skinned member of the leek family with bulbs the size of a small grapefruit and very large cloves that average one ounce each. It has a milder flavor than common garlic and doesn't leave a strong aftertaste or odor. Store in a cool, dry place. Available year-round.

Jicama (Ahipa, Mexican Potato, Yam Bean): A crunchy, juicy root vegetable with a sweet, nutty flavor, especially popular in Mexico. Under the thick brown skin, which should be peeled before using, is ivory flesh that does not discolor and can be served raw in salads or on a vegetable platter with a dip. When cooked, it retains its crisp, water chestnut–like texture and flavor. Refrigerate up to 2 weeks. Available year-round.

Longbean (Asparagus Bean, Chinese Longbean, Yard-Long Bean): Although this looks like a long version of the common green bean, it is actually from the same plant family as the black-eyed pea. The flavor is similar to green beans but is milder and not as sweet. They are normally harvested when about a foot long but sometimes can grow to three feet. Usually they are cut in half or into smaller pieces and sautéed or stir-fried. If overcooked, they become mushy. Refrigerate unwashed in a plastic bag up to 5 days. Available year-round.

Mushrooms: Specialty mushrooms may be available fresh but are often sold in dried form. If purchased dried, they must be rehydrated as directed on the package. Generally, one ounce of dried mushrooms equals about four ounces of fresh mushrooms after being rehydrated. There are literally thousands of varieties of mushrooms; the following are some of the most popular.

- **Chanterelle:** A trumpet-shaped wild mushroom often sold dried. It has a delicate, nutty flavor and a chewy texture. It can be cooked as a separate side dish or added to soups, sauces and stir-fries; it should never be eaten raw. Available in dried form year-round.

- **Cremini (Brown):** A dark brown, slightly firmer version of the cultivated white mushroom but with a slightly stronger flavor. When allowed to grow to its full size, it is known as a portobello mushroom. Available year-round.

- **Enoki:** Grown in clumps from a single base, this fresh mushroom has a long, thin stem and tiny, snow-white cap. They are prized for their delicate size and fresh, grapelike flavor. Cut them away from the base and trim one or two inches from the stems before using. They may be eaten raw or added to cooked dishes at the last minute to prevent over cooking. Usually available year-round.

- **Morel:** A ruffled, cone-shaped wild mushroom belonging to the truffle family. It may be two to four inches long and range in color from tan to dark brown. The smoky, earthy, nutty flavor, prized by food lovers, can be enjoyed by simply sautéing them in butter. Fresh wild morels are usually available April through June, and cultivated morels may be available at other times during the year. Dried are available year-round.

- **Oyster:** A fan-shaped mushroom that grows both wild and cultivated on rotting tree trunks—the mushrooms are perfectly edible. The robust, earthy flavor complements pork and game dishes as well as sauces and stir-fries. Fresh and dried oyster mushrooms are normally available year-round.

- **Padi Straw (Straw):** Especially popular in Asian cooking, this mushroom is so named because it is grown on straw that has been used in a rice paddy. Shaped like tiny 1- to 1 1/2-inch coolie hats, they are smooth and mild in flavor; never eat them raw. Most often available dried and found year-round.

- **Porcini:** This mushroom has an earthy flavor popular in French and Italian cooking. Fresh, they range from one to ten inches in diameter. The firm texture complements beef, veal and fish. Most often available dried and found year-round.

- **Portobello:** A very large, dark brown mushroom, often up to six inches in diameter, that has a dense, meaty texture. It can be grilled and used in a sandwich or sliced for a salad or main dish. The crimini mushroom is a younger version of the portobello. Available year-round.

- **Shiitake (Golden Oak):** Originally from Japan and Korea, this mushroom is now grown in the U.S. The average shiitake mushroom is three to six inches in diameter and has a full-bodied, almost steaklike flavor. Available fresh in the spring and fall; dried are available year-round.

- **Wood Ear:** The slightly chewy texture of this mushroom makes it an excellent substitute for meat in stir-fry dishes. It is mild in flavor and absorbs the flavor of the ingredients cooked with it. Dried are available year-round.

Onions:
- **Boiler Onion:** A small onion, one inch in diameter, available in white, gold, red or purple. Boilers have a mild onion flavor and are often used as a side dish or roasted with meat or poultry. They can also be added to stews. Store in a cool, dry place up to 1 month. Available year-round.

- **Cipolline:** A sweet, delicately flavored onion originally grown in Italy. It can be baked, broiled, stuffed or used in the same way as other onions. Store in a cool, dry place up to 2 weeks. Peak season is September through February.

- **Maui:** A sweet, juicy, mild onion from the Hawaiian island of Maui. When grown outside Hawaii, it is more like the common yellow onion. Good for making caramelized onions and adding to sandwiches and salads or using in the same way as other onions. Store in a cool, dark place, or refrigerate in plastic wrap up to 2 weeks. Available year-round.

Parsley Root (Hamburg Parsley, Rooted Parsley, Turnip-Rooted Parsley): Originally popular only in Europe, it is now grown in the United States. Although the leaves can be used like regular parsley, it is grown mostly for its root. It is often used in soups and stews and tastes like a combination of carrot and celery. Refrigerate in a plastic bag up to 1 week. Available year-round.

Potatoes:
- **Purple:** Minerals in the soil cause this potato to have its vibrant color. It is a small potato with a dense texture that is good for boiling. The purple color fades during cooking.

- **Yellow (Yellow Finnish, Yukon Gold):** The skin and flesh of this potato ranges from buttery yellow to golden. It has a mild butterlike flavor, is good for boiling and makes excellent mashed potatoes. The yellow color fades just slightly during cooking.

VEGETABLES

Salsify

Parsley Root

Daikon

Celeriac

Baby Peppers

Longbean

Jicama

Baby Carrots

Yuca Root

Baby Bok Choy

Baby Patty Pan

Taro Root

Water Chestnuts

Broccoli Rabe

Jerusalem Artichoke

Baby Broccoli

Baby Zucchini

Radicchio: A leafy salad vegetable from the chicory family. Its small loose head has tender leaves with a bittersweet flavor. Most commonly available in burgundy red, it is attractive in mixed salads. Refrigerate in a plastic bag up to 1 week. Available year-round; peak season is midwinter to early spring.

Salsify (Oyster Plant): A long, narrow root with the texture of a carrot and a subtle oyster flavor. The white interior can be eaten raw in salads, added to soups and meats and sautéed as a side dish. Refrigerate in a plastic bag up to 2 weeks. Available June through February.

Squash: The following specialty squash are considered winter squash, which means they have hard, thick skins and seeds. Many varieties are available all year, but the peak season is normally late summer, fall and sometimes into the winter.

- **Carnival:** A small, pumpkin-shaped squash with cream, orange and green coloring. The delicate yellow flesh can be baked or steamed and tastes a bit like sweet potatoes or butternut squash.

- **Delicata (Sweet Potato Squash):** This oblong squash ranges from five to nine inches long and is about two to three inches in diameter. It has pale yellow skin with green stripes. The seed cavity is small, so the squash yields a lot of edible flesh. It can be baked or steamed and has a sweet, buttered corn flavor.

- **Golden Nugget:** A round squash about the size of a softball with a bright orange shell that has ridges. The orange flesh is moist and sweet but slightly bland. It can be baked or steamed.

- **Kabocha (Delica, Edisu, Haka):** Forest green skin with light striations characterizes this squash that ranges from nine to twelve inches in diameter. The moist, golden flesh is almost fiberless and has a rich, sweet flavor similar to a sweet potato or pumpkin. It is usually baked or steamed.

- **Sugar Loaf (Orange Delicata):** A shorter, more squat squash than the Delicata with orange or tan skin and green stripes. Its flesh is moist and creamy and has a sweet, buttered-corn flavor, as does the Delicata.

- **Sweet Dumpling:** This small, softball-size squash has green and white stripes. It is naturally sweet and is good stuffed with rice or stuffing.

Taro Root (Dasheen): This starchy potato-like root has a nutty flavor when cooked. It ranges in length from five inches to over twelve inches. The flesh is usually creamy white or pale pink and sometimes becomes tinged with purple when cooked. It is used like a potato and can be boiled, fried or baked; the edible leaves can be steamed and served like spinach. In Hawaii, it is used to make poi. Refrigerate up to 4 days. Available year-round.

Water Chestnut: A common Asian ingredient that is now cultivated in the U.S. It is the underwater tuber of an aquatic plant that grows in shallow waters. Under the brownish black skin is white, crunchy flesh that is bland with a hint of sweetness. It can be served raw or cooked. Although available fresh, it is most often sold in cans. Refrigerate fresh water chestnuts tightly wrapped in a plastic bag up to 1 week. Available year-round.

Yuca Root (Cassava, Manioc): A tuber native to South America that is also grown in Asia and Africa. There are two types of yucca—bitter and sweet. Yuca has tough, brown skin and flesh that is hard, dense and white. The bitter variety must be cooked before eating. It is usually prepared like potatoes and has a starchy, slightly sweet flavor. Store in a cool, dry place up to 3 days. Available year-round.

Selecting and Cooking

Fresh Vegetables

Look up the specific vegetable in the Fresh Vegetable Cooking Chart (page 497) to find guidelines on selection, prep and cooking. Ripeness, age, size, moisture content and storage method can affect cooking times.

When cooking, use about 1 cup of water per pound of vegetables.

Salting the cooking water is optional. If you decide to salt the water, use 1/4 teaspoon salt per cup of water.

Baby (or miniature) vegetables, such as beans, beets, broccoli, carrots, corn, eggplant, potatoes and squash, are either harvested early in their growing stages or genetically bred to be true miniatures and tend to be more expensive than their full-size counterparts. They're tender and delicately flavored; eat them raw or cooked. Baby veggies often are cooked in a small amount of butter or margarine to enhance their flavor. Because of their size, they may cook faster than their full-size relatives, so check for doneness several minutes before the minimum cooking time.

Frozen Vegetables

You'll find frozen vegetables available not only individually but also in creative combinations, with or without sauce or with additions such as pasta or rice. Many offer suggestions for adding cooked meat or poultry to make a main dish.

When buying frozen vegetables, choose packages that aren't opened or damaged or where the contents aren't in a solid block, which means they may have been thawed and refrozen (except boxed vegetables such as spinach, which are frozen in a block).

Cook frozen vegetables according to package directions. The blanching and freezing process that the manufacturer has done tenderizes them somewhat, so they'll cook in less time than fresh vegetables.

Store-Bought Canned Vegetables

Choose cans without dents or other damage.

Heat the vegetables, undrained, until hot; drain before serving.

Home-Canned Vegetables

Don't cook or eat home-canned vegetables if the jar isn't completely and tightly sealed.

As a safety precaution, boil all low-acid home-canned foods (tomatoes, green beans, corn, carrots and beets are the most commonly canned vegetables) for at least 10 minutes before serving.

Vegetable Doneness

Knowing when vegetables are done just right can mean the difference between an inviting dish and an overdone or underdone disappointment.

Check doneness at the minimum cooking time; cook longer if necessary.

Because vegetables continue to cook even after you've taken them out of the microwave, cook veggies in the microwave until *almost* tender or crisp-tender.

Cook vegetables such as potatoes, eggplants, peas and greens until tender. Cook other vegetables, such as asparagus, broccoli, beans, carrots, mushrooms and bell peppers, just until crisp-tender to preserve their bright color and vitamin and mineral content.

Storing Vegetables

Different vegetables have different needs, so properly storing vegetables makes a difference in their shelf life. It's best to buy veggies in quantities you can use quickly to minimize storage time. Storage times and techniques for optimum freshness are given below.

Refrigerator crisper or in a plastic bag in refrigerator: If your refrigerator crisper isn't two-thirds full, put veggies in perforated vegetable or regular plastic bags before putting them in the crisper.

- *1 to 2 days:* asparagus, beet greens, chard, collard greens, green peas, green onions, fresh lima beans, mushrooms, mustard greens, spinach, turnip greens.

- *3 to 5 days:* bell peppers, broccoli, Brussels sprouts, cauliflower, celery, cucumber, green beans, okra, summer squash.

- *1 or 2 weeks:* beets, cabbage, carrots, parsnips, radishes, turnips.

Refrigerate uncovered, 1 or 2 days: Sweet corn in husks, fully ripe tomatoes. Let *unripe* tomatoes ripen at room temperature but away from direct sunlight, which will make them mushy and pulpy.

Cool (between 45° and 60°), dark, dry, well-ventilated place 2 weeks: garlic, onions, potatoes, uncut winter squash with hard rinds. To reduce spoiling, store onions and potatoes separately. Potatoes stored at warmer temperatures will begin to sprout and shrivel, so use them within 1 week. A greenish tinge on potatoes is caused by long exposure to light; cut or scrape it off before cooking. Refrigerating can cause potatoes to become sweeter and turn dark when cooked.

Cooking Fresh Vegetables

Questions about cooking veggies? Look no further than this comprehensive guide for buying, prepping and cooking vegetables. For each vegetable, we've provided one or more cooking options. Before you consult the chart, you may want take a refresher course on these cooking methods in the section below.

Conventional Directions

Baking:

1. Preheat the oven.
2. Place vegetables in baking pan (place vegetables in skin, such as potatoes, directly on oven rack).
3. Bake for amount of time in chart. Directions will state whether to bake covered or uncovered.

Boiling:

1. Heat 1 inch water (salted, if desired) to boiling in saucepan, unless directed otherwise. Add vegetables.
2. Heat to boiling; reduce heat to low.
3. Boil gently (simmer) for amount of time in chart. Directions will state whether to cook covered or uncovered.
4. Drain.

Sautéing:

1. Heat butter, margarine, vegetable oil or olive oil in 10-inch skillet over medium-high heat. Add vegetables.
2. Cook uncovered, stirring frequently, for amount of time in chart.

Steaming:

1. Place steamer basket in 1/2 inch water in saucepan or skillet (water should not touch bottom of basket). Place vegetables in steamer basket.
2. Cover tightly and heat to boiling; reduce heat to low.
3. Steam for amount of time in chart.

Microwave Directions

1. Use microwavable casserole (1, 1 1/2 or 2 quart, or other size if given), unless directed otherwise.
2. Add amount of water (salted, if desired) if given. Add vegetables. You'll note that for some vegetables, we direct you to cook them with just the water that clings to them from being rinsed; no additional water is necessary.
3. Cover with lid, or cover with plastic wrap, folding plastic back 1/4 inch along one edge or corner to vent steam (we refer to this as "vented plastic wrap" in chart).
4. Microwave on High, unless directed otherwise, for amount of time in chart. Stir, rearrange or turn over vegetables once or twice during cooking if directed to in chart.
5. Vegetables continue to cook a short time after being microwaved. Many vegetables call for a stand time after cooking, which completes the cooking and equalizes the temperature throughout the food. Once you've microwaved vegetables a couple of times, determining how long to cook the vegetable before the stand time will become easier.
6. Drain.

FRESH VEGETABLE COOKING CHART

Vegetable with Amounts for 4 Servings	To Prepare	Conventional Directions*	Microwave Directions**
Artichokes, Globe (4 medium; 1 pound) Choose plump compact globes that are heavy in relation to their size, with fresh, green inner leaves.	Remove discolored leaves; trim stem even with base. Cut 1 inch off top and discard. Snip off points of the remaining leaves with scissors. Rinse with cold water. To prevent discoloration, dip into cold water mixed with small amount of lemon juice (1 tablespoon lemon juice per 1 quart water). To fill and bake, remove center leaves and the choke before cooking. (Choke is the fuzzy growth covering artichoke heart.)	**Boil:** Use 6 quarts water and 2 tablespoons lemon juice. Boil uncovered 20 to 30 minutes, rotating occasionally, until leaves pull out easily and bottom is tender when pierced with knife. **Steam:** Covered 20 to 25 minutes or until bottom is tender when pierced with knife.	*1 medium:* Place in 4-cup glass measuring cup; add 1/4 cup water. Cover with vented plastic wrap. Microwave 5 to 7 minutes or until leaves pull out easily. *2 medium:* Place in 8 × 4-inch loaf pan; add 1/4 cup water. Cover with vented plastic wrap. Microwave 9 to 11 minutes or until leaves pull out easily.
Artichokes, Jerusalem (4 medium; 1 pound) Choose smooth, firm, light-colored tubers with the fewest "knobs." Tubers should be free of blotches, green-tinged areas and sprouts.	Scrub artichokes; peel thinly if desired. Leave whole, or cut into 1/4-inch slices or 1/2-inch cubes. To prevent discoloration, toss with cold water mixed with small amount of lemon juice (1 tablespoon lemon juice per 1 quart water).	**Boil:** *Whole*—covered 20 to 25 minutes. *Slices or cubes*—covered 7 to 9 minutes or until crisp-tender. **Steam:** covered 15 to 20 minutes or until crisp-tender. **Note:** Can also be fried; see Fried Potatoes (page 515) for directions.	*Slices or cubes*—Place in 1-quart casserole; add 2 tablespoons water. Cover. Microwave 5 to 7 minutes, stirring once, until crisp-tender. Let stand 2 minutes.
Asparagus (1 1/2 pounds) Choose smooth, round, tender, medium-size green spears with closed tips.	Break off tough ends as far down as stalks snap easily. Wash asparagus; remove scales if sandy or tough. (If necessary, remove sand particles with a vegetable brush.) For spears, tie whole stalks in bundles with string, or hold together with band of aluminum foil. Or cut stalks into 1-inch pieces.	**Boil:** *Spears*—Place stalks upright in deep, narrow pan. Boil uncovered 6 to 8 minutes or until crisp-tender. *Pieces*—Boil uncovered 4 to 6 minutes or until crisp-tender **Steam:** Covered 6 to 8 minutes or until crisp-tender.	Place spears in 8 × 4-inch loaf pan or pieces in 1-quart casserole; add 2 tablespoons water. Cover with vented plastic wrap. Microwave 4 to 6 minutes or until crisp-tender. Let stand 2 minutes.
Beans, Green, Purple Wax and Yellow Wax (1 pound) Choose bright, smooth, crisp pods. Will feel pliable and velvety. When cooked, purple wax beans will turn dark green.	Wash beans; remove ends. Leave beans whole, or cut into 1-inch pieces.	**Boil:** Boil uncovered 6 to 8 minutes or until crisp-tender. **Steam:** Covered 10 to 12 minutes or until crisp-tender.	Place pieces in 1-quart casserole; add 1 cup water. Cover. Microwave 10 to 12 minutes or until crisp-tender. Let stand 5 minutes; drain.

continues

FRESH VEGETABLE COOKING CHART (cont.)

Vegetable with Amounts for 4 Servings	To Prepare	Conventional Directions*	Microwave Directions**
Beans, Lima (3 pounds unshelled; 3 cups shelled) Choose broad, thick, shiny pods that are plump with large seeds.	Wash beans. Shell just before cooking. To shell beans, remove thin outer edge of pod with sharp knife or scissors. Slip out beans.	**Boil:** Boil uncovered 5 minutes. Cover and boil 15 to 20 minutes longer or until tender.	Place in 1-quart casserole; add 1 cup water. Cover. Microwave on High 4 to 5 minutes or until boiling. Microwave on Medium-Low (30%) 20 to 25 minutes or until tender. Let stand 5 minutes; drain.
Beets (5 medium; 1 1/4 pounds) Choose firm, round, smooth, deep red beets with fresh, unwilted tops.	Cut off all but 1 inch of beet tops. Wash beets; leave whole with root ends attached.	**Boil:** Use 6 cups water, 1 tablespoon white vinegar (to preserve color) and salt if desired. Boil covered 40 to 50 minutes or until tender. **Steam:** Covered 45 to 50 minutes or until tender. Add boiling water during steaming if necessary.	Place in 1 1/2-quart casserole; add 2 cups water. Cover. Microwave 18 to 20 minutes, rearranging once, until tender. Let stand 5 minutes; drain.
Broccoli (1 1/2 pounds) Choose firm, compact, dark green clusters; avoid thick, tough stems.	Trim off large leaves; remove tough ends of lower stems. Wash broccoli; peel if desired. *For spears,* cut lengthwise into 1/2-inch-wide stalks. *For pieces,* cut lengthwise into 1/2-inch-wide stalks, then cut stalks crosswise into 1-inch pieces. If desired, cut flowerets into bite-size pieces.	**Boil:** *Spears*—uncovered 5 to 7 minutes or until stems are crisp-tender. *Flowerets*—uncovered 3 to 5 minutes or until crisp-tender. **Steam:** Covered 10 to 11 minutes or until stems are crisp-tender.	*Spears*—Place with just the water that clings to spears in 8-inch square dish in spoke pattern with flowerets in the center. Cover with vented plastic wrap. Microwave 6 to 8 minutes or until stems are crisp-tender. Let stand 2 minutes. *Pieces*—Place with just the water that clings to pieces in 2-quart casserole. Cover. Microwave 5 to 7 minutes or until crisp-tender. Let stand 2 minutes.
Brussels Sprouts (1 pound) Choose unblemished, bright green sprouts with compact leaves.	Remove any discolored leaves; cut off stem ends. Wash sprouts; cut large sprouts in half.	**Boil:** Uncovered 8 to 12 minutes or until tender. **Steam:** Covered 8 to 12 minutes or until tender.	Place in 1-quart casserole add 2 tablespoons water. Cover. Microwave 5 to 6 minutes or until tender. Let stand 2 minutes; drain.
Carrots (1 pound; 6 to 7 medium) Choose firm, nicely shaped carrots with good color.	Peel carrots thinly; cut off ends. Leave baby-cut carrots whole, or cut carrots lengthwise into julienne strips, cut crosswise into 1/4-inch slices or shred.	**Boil:** *Baby-cut whole*—covered 7 to 10 minutes. *Julienne strips*—covered 6 to 10 minutes. *Slices*—covered 6 to 10 minutes. *Shredded*—covered 5 minutes or until tender. **Steam:** *Baby-cut whole*—covered 8 to 10 minutes. *Slices*—covered 6 to 9 minutes or until tender.	*Baby-cut whole or Julienne strips* Place in 1-quart casserole; add 2 tablespoons water. Cover. Microwave 5 to 7 minutes, stirring once, until crisp-tender. (Baby-cut carrots may take 2 to 3 minutes longer to cook.) Let stand 5 minutes; drain.

FRESH VEGETABLE COOKING CHART (cont.)

Vegetable with Amounts for 4 Servings	To Prepare	Conventional Directions*	Microwave Directions**
Cauliflower (2 pounds; 1 medium head) Choose clean, non-spreading flower clusters (the white portion) and green leaves.	Remove outer leaves and stalk; cut off any discoloration. Wash cauliflower. Leave whole, cutting cone-shaped center to remove core, or separate into flowerets.	**Boil:** *Whole*—uncovered 10 to 12 minutes. *Flowerets*—uncovered 5 to 7 minutes or until tender. **Steam:** *Whole*—covered 18 to 22 minutes. *Flowerets*—covered 6 to 8 minutes or until tender.	Place flowerets in 2-quart casserole; add 2 tablespoons water. Cover. Microwave 8 to 10 minutes or until tender. Let stand 2 minutes; drain.
Corn (4 ears) Choose bright green, tight-fitting husks, fresh-looking silk, plump but not too large kernels.	Refrigerate unhusked corn until ready to use. (Corn is best when eaten as soon after picking as possible.) Husk ears and remove silk just before cooking.	**Boil:** Place ears in enough unsalted cold water to cover (salt toughens corn). Add 1 tablespoon sugar and 1 tablespoon lemon juice to each gallon of water if desired. Heat to boiling. Cover and boil 6 to 8 minutes. **Steam:** Covered 5 to 7 minutes or until tender.	Wrap ears in microwavable plastic wrap, or place in 8-inch square dish and add 1 tablespoon water. Cover with plastic wrap. *1 ear:* Microwave 2 to 3 minutes, turning once. Let stand 2 minutes. *2 ears:* Microwave 3 to 4 minutes, turning once. Let stand 2 minutes. *4 ears:* Microwave 6 to 8 minutes, turning once. Let stand 2 minutes.
Eggplant (1 1/2 pounds; 1 medium) Choose smooth, glossy, taut-skinned eggplant that is free from blemishes and rust spots. Caps and stems should be intact and free of mold.	Just before cooking, wash eggplant; peel if desired. Cut into 1/2-inch cubes or 1/4-inch slices.	**Boil:** Covered 5 to 8 minutes or until tender. **Sauté:** Melt 3 to 4 tablespoons butter or margarine in 10-inch skillet over medium-high heat. Cook eggplant in butter uncovered 5 to 10 minutes, stirring frequently, until tender. **Steam:** Covered 5 to 7 minutes or until tender.	*Cubes*—Place in 1 1/2-quart casserole; add 2 tablespoons water. Cover. Microwave 7 to 9 minutes, stirring twice, until tender. Let stand 5 minutes. *Slices*—Arrange slices, overlapping, in a circle around edge of 9-inch pie plate; add 2 tablespoons water. Cover with vented plastic wrap. Microwave 5 to 7 minutes or until tender. Let stand 5 minutes.
Fennel (1 pound; 3 to 4 medium) Choose compact, unblemished, smooth, whitish-green bulbs without cracks. Tops should be fresh and feathery.	Remove feathery tops (slice to use as a seasoning) and tough or discolored outer ribs; trim base. Cut bulbs lengthwise into fourths	**Boil:** Covered 8 to 11 minutes or until tender. **Steam:** Covered 12 to 15 minutes or until tender.	Place in 1-quart casserole; add 2 tablespoons water. Cover. Microwave 4 1/2 to 5 1/2 minutes or until crisp-tender. Let stand 2 minutes.

continues

FRESH VEGETABLE COOKING CHART (cont.)

Vegetable with Amounts for 4 Servings	To Prepare	Conventional Directions*	Microwave Directions**
Greens: Beet, Chicory, Collards, Escarole, Kale, Mustard, Spinach, Swiss Chard, Turnip (1 pound) Choose tender, young, unblemished leaves with bright green color.	Remove root ends and imperfect leaves. Wash several times in water, lifting out each time; drain.	**Cook:** *For greens except spinach,* cover and cook with just the water that clings to leaves over medium-high heat 8 to 10 minutes or until tender. *For spinach,* cover and cook with just the water that clings to the leaves over medium-high heat 3 to 5 minutes or until tender.	*For beet tops, chicory or escarole,* place in 2-quart casserole; add 2 tablespoons water. Cover. Microwave 8 to 10 minutes, stirring once, until tender. *For collards, kale, mustard, spinach, Swiss chard or turni*p, place in 2-quart casserole; add 2 tablespoons water. Cover. Microwave 4 to 6 minutes, stirring once, until tender.
Kohlrabi (1 pound; 4 medium) Choose firm, purple-tinged white bulbs with no soft spots or yellowing leaf tips. Those under 3 inches in diameter are most tender.	Cut off root ends and tops. Wash; peel thinly. Cut into 1/2-inch pieces or cubes.	**Boil:** Covered 15 to 20 minutes or until tender **Steam:** Covered 8 to 12 minutes or until tender.	Place in 1-quart casserole; add 2 tablespoons water. Cover. Microwave 3 1/2 to 5 minutes, stirring once, until tender. Let stand 2 minutes
Leeks (2 pounds; 6 medium) Choose white bulbs with pliable, crisp, green tops. Bulbs less than 1 1/2 inches in diameter are the most tender.	Remove green tops to within 2 inches of white part (reserve greens for soup or stew). Peel outside layer of bulbs. Wash leeks several times in cold water; drain. Cut large leeks lengthwise into fourths.	**Boil:** Covered 10 to 12 minutes or until tender. **Steam:** Covered 10 to 12 minutes or until tender.	Place in 1-quart casserole; add 2 tablespoons water. Cover. Microwave 4 to 5 minutes, stirring once, until tender. Let stand 2 minutes.
Mushrooms (1 pound) Choose creamy white to light brown caps, closed around the stems; if slightly open, gills should be light pink or tan.	Rinse mushrooms; trim off stem ends. Do not peel. Leave whole, or cut into 1/4-inch slices.	**Sauté:** *Whole or slices*—Melt 1/4 cup butter or margarine in 10-inch skillet over medium-high heat. Cook mushrooms in butter uncovered 4 to 5 minutes, stirring frequently, until tender. **Steam:** Covered 4 to 5 minutes or until tender.	*Whole or slices*—Place in 1-quart casserole; add 1 tablespoon butter, margarine or vegetable oil. Cover with paper towel. Microwave 3 to 4 minutes or until tender.
Okra (1 pound) Choose tender, unblemished, bright green pods, less than 4 inches long.	Wash okra; remove ends. Leave whole, or cut into 1/2-inch slices.	**Boil:** Uncovered about 10 minutes or until tender. **Steam:** Covered 6 to 8 minutes or until tender.	*Whole*—Place in 1-quart casserole; add 1/4 cup water. Cover. Microwave 5 to 6 minutes, stirring once until tender. Let stand 2 minutes.

FRESH VEGETABLE COOKING CHART (cont.)

Vegetable with Amounts for 4 Servings	To Prepare	Conventional Directions*	Microwave Directions**
Onions, White, Yellow or Red (1 1/2 pounds; 8 to 10 small) Choose firm, well-shaped onions with unblemished, papery skins and no sign of sprouting.	Peel onions in cold water to prevent eyes from watering. See cooking directions for piece size.	**Bake:** Place large onions in ungreased baking dish. Pour water into dish until 1/4 inch deep. Cover and bake in 350° over 40 to 50 minutes or until tender. **Boil:** *Small*—covered 15 to 20 minutes. *Large*—covered 30 to 35 minutes or until tender. **Sauté:** Cut onions into 1/4-inch slices. Melt 3 to 4 tablespoons butter, margarine or olive or vegetable oil in 10-inch skillet over medium-high heat. Cook onions in butter uncovered 6 to 9 minutes, stirring frequently, until tender. **Steam:** *Small*—covered 15 to 20 minutes. *Large*—covered 30 to 35 minutes or until tender.	*Whole*-Place in 1 1/2-quart casserole; add 1/4 cup water. Cover. Microwave 7 to 9 minutes or until tender. Let stand 2 minutes.
Parsnips (1 1/2 pounds; 6 to 8 medium) Choose firm, nicely shaped, unblemished parsnips that are not too wide.	Scrape or peel. Leave whole, or cut into halves or fourths or 1/4-inch slices or strips.	**Boil:** *Whole or halves*—covered 10 to 15 minutes. *Slices* or *strips*—covered 7 to 9 minutes or until tender. **Steam:** *Whole or halves*—covered 15 to 20 minutes. *Slices or strips*—covered 8 to 10 minutes or until tender.	*Slices or strips*—Place in 1-quart casserole; add 2 tablespoons water. Cover. Microwave 5 to 6 minutes, stirring once, until tender. Let stand 2 minutes.
Pea Pods, Snow (Chinese) (1 pound) Choose flat, crisp and evenly green pods with a velvety feel.	Wash pods; remove tips and strings.	**Boil:** Boil uncovered 2 to 3 minutes, stirring occasionally, until crisp-tender **Steam:** Covered 3 to 5 minutes or until crisp-tender.	Place in 1-quart casserole with just the water that clings to the pea pods. Cover. Microwave 6 to 7 minutes, stirring once, until crisp-tender. Let stand 2 minutes.
Peas, Green (2 pounds) Choose plump, tender, bright green pods.	Wash and shell peas just before cooking.	**Boil:** Boil uncovered 5 to 10 minutes or until tender. **Steam:** Covered 8 to 10 minutes or until tender.	Place peas with just the water that clings to them in 1-quart casserole. Cover. Microwave 4 to 6 minutes, stirring once, until tender. Let stand 2 minutes.

continues

FRESH VEGETABLE COOKING CHART (cont.)

Vegetable with Amounts for 4 Servings	To Prepare	Conventional Directions*	Microwave Directions**
Peas, Sugar Snap (1 pound) Choose smooth bright-green pods that are filled with peas.	Snip off stem ends and remove strings if present.	**Boil:** Boil uncovered 4 to 5 minutes, stirring occasion-ally, until crisp-tender. **Steam:** Covered 6 to 7 minutes or until crisp-tender.	**Microwave:** Place in 1-quart casserole with just the water that clings to the pea pods. Cover. Microwave 6 to 7 minutes, stirring once, until crisp-tender.
Peppers, Bell (2 medium; 1/2 pound) Choose well-shaped, shiny, bright-colored, unblemished peppers with firm sides.	Wash peppers; remove stems, seeds and membranes. Leave whole to stuff and bake, or cut into thin slices or rings.	**Sauté:** *Slices or rings*—Melt 1 to 2 tablespoons butter or margarine in 10-inch skillet over medium-high heat. Cook peppers in butter uncovered 3 to 5 minutes, stirring frequently, until crisp-tender. **Steam:** *Slices or rings*-covered 4 to 6 minutes or until crisp-tender.	Place peppers with just the water that clings to them in 1-quart casserole. Cover. Microwave 3 to 4 minutes, stirring once, until crisp-tender. Let stand 2 minutes.
Potatoes, New (1 1/2 pounds new potatoes; 10 to 12) Choose nicely shaped, smooth, firm potatoes with unblemished skins (some are very delicate). Choose potatoes of similar size, about 1 1/2 inches in diameter.	Scrub potatoes.	**Boil:** Place potatoes in 2-quart saucepan. Add water just to cover. Heat to boiling; reduce heat to low. Boil gently (simmer) covered 15 to 20 minutes or until tender. **Steam:** Covered 18 to 22 minutes or until tender.	Place in 1 1/2-quart casse-role; add 1/4 cup water. Cover. Microwave 9 to 11 minutes, stirring once, until tender. Let stand 5 minutes.
Potatoes, Sweet, and Yams (4 medium; 1 1/2 pounds) Choose nicely once, shaped, smooth, firm potatoes with even-colored skins. (See varieties of potatoes, page 512.) Choose potatoes of similar size.	Scrub potatoes, but do not peel. *To bake*—Pierce potatoes to allow steam to escape. *To boil or steam*—Leave whole, or cut into large pieces.	**Bake:** Bake uncovered in 375° oven about 45 minutes, in 350° oven about 1 hour, in 325° oven about 1 hour 15 minutes or until tender. **Boil:** Place potatoes in 2-quart saucepan. Add water just to cover. Heat to boiling; reduce heat to low. Boil gently (simmer) covered: *Whole*—20 to 25 minutes or until tender. *Pieces*—10 to 15 minutes or until tender. **Steam:** *Whole*—covered 15 to 20 minutes or until tender.	*Whole:* Pierce potatoes to allow steam to escape. Arrange on paper towel in spoke pattern with narrow ends in center. Microwave 9 to 11 minutes, turning until tender. Cover and let stand 5 minutes.

FRESH VEGETABLE COOKING CHART (cont.)

Vegetable with Amounts for 4 Servings	To Prepare	Conventional Directions*	Microwave Directions**
Potatoes, White and Red (6 medium; 2 pounds) Choose nicely shaped, smooth, firm potatoes with unblemished skins, free from discoloration.	*To bake*—Choose potatoes of similar size. Scrub potatoes, but do not peel; if desired, rub with shortening for softer skins. Pierce potatoes to allow steam to escape.*To boil or steam*—Scrub potatoes. Leave skins on whenever possible, or peel thinly and remove eyes. Leave whole, or cut into large pieces.	**Bake:** Bake uncovered in 375° oven 1 hour to 1 hour 15 minutes, in 350° oven 1 hour 15 minutes to 1 hour 30 minutes, in 325° oven about 1 hour 30 minutes or until tender. **Boil:** Place potatoes in 2-quart saucepan. Add water just to cover. Heat to boiling; reduce heat to low. Boil gently(simmer) covered: *Whole or pieces*—20 to 30 minutes or until tender. **Steam:** Covered 30 to 35 minutes or until tender.	*Whole*—Pierce potatoes to allow steam to escape. Place on paper towels. *1 potato:* Microwave 4 to 5 minutes, turning once, until tender. Cover, let stand 5 minutes. *2 potatoes:* Microwave 6 to 8 minutes, turning once, until tender. Cover; let stand 5 minutes. *3 potatoes:* Arrange in spoke pattern with narrow ends in center Microwave 8 to 10 minutes, turning once, until tender. Cover; let stand 5 minutes. *4 potatoes:* Arrange in spoke pattern with narrow ends in center Microwave 12 to 14 minutes, turning once, until tender. Cover; let stand 5 minutes.
Rutabagas (1 1/2 pounds; 2 medium) Choose rutabagas that are heavy, well shaped (round or elongated) and smooth.	Wash rutabagas; peel thinly. Cut into 1/2-inch cubes or 2-inch pieces.	**Boil:** Covered 20 to 25 minutes or until tender. **Steam:** Covered 20 to 25 minutes or until tender.	Place in 2-quart casserole; add 1/4 cup water. Cover. Microwave 13 to 15 minutes, stirring twice, until tender. Let stand 5 minutes.
Squash, Summer (Chayote, Crookneck, Green Zucchini, Pattypan, Straightneck, Yellow Zucchini) (1 1/2 pounds) Choose squash that are heavy in relation to size, with smooth and glossy skin. Small squash are more tender.	Wash squash; remove stem and blossom ends, but do not peel. Cut small squash in half. Cut large squash into 1/2-inch slices or cubes.	**Boil:** *Slices*—uncovered 5 to 10 minutes. *Cubes*—uncovered 3 to 6 minutes or until tender. **Steam:** Covered 5 to 7 minutes or until tender.	Place in 1 1/2-quart casserole; add 1 tablespoon water. Cover. Microwave 4 to 6 minutes, stirring once, until almost tender. Let stand 2 minutes.

continues

FRESH VEGETABLE COOKING CHART (cont.)

Vegetable with Amounts for 4 Servings	To Prepare	Conventional Directions*	Microwave Directions**
Squash, Winter (Acorn, Buttercup, Butternut, Spaghetti) and Pumpkin (2 pounds) Choose squash that are heavy in relation to size, with good yellow-orange color and hard, tough rinds with no soft spots.	Wash squash. *To bake—* Cut each squash lengthwise in half; remove seeds and fibers. *To boil—*Peel squash if desired. Cut into 1-inch slices or cubes.	**Bake:** Place squash halves, cut sides up, in ungreased 13 × 9-inch baking dish. Sprinkle cut sides with salt and pepper. Dot with butter or margarine. Pour water into dish until 1/4 inch deep. Cover and bake in 400° oven 30 to 40 minutes, in 350° oven about 40 minutes, in 325°oven about 45 minutes or until tender. **Boil:** *Slices or cubes—*covered 10 to 15 minutes or until tender. **Steam:** *Slices—*covered 12 to 15 minutes. *Cubes—*covered 7 to 10 minutes or until tender.	*For whole squash except spaghetti—*Pierce with knife in several places to allow steam to escape. Place on paper towel. Microwave uncovered 5 minutes or until squash feels warm to the touch. Cut in half; remove seeds. Arrange halves, cut sides down, in shallow dish. Microwave 5 to 8 minutes, or until tender. Let stand 5 minutes. *For whole spaghetti—*Pierce with knife in several places to allow steam to escape. Place on paper towel. Micro-wave uncovered 18 to 23 minutes, turning once, until tender. Let stand 10 min-utes. Cut in half; remove seeds and fibers.
Turnips (1 pound; 4 medium) Choose turnips that are smooth, round and firm, with fresh tops.	Cut off tops. Wash turnips peel thinly. Leave whole, or cut into 1/2-inch pieces.	**Boil:** *Whole—*covered 25 to 30 minutes. *Pieces—* covered 15 to 20 minutes or until tender. **Steam:** *Pieces—*covered 15 to 20 minutes or until tender.	*Pieces—*Place in 1-quart casserole; add 2 tablespoons water. Cover. Microwave 6 to 8 minutes, stirring once, until tender. Let stand 2 minutes.

*See also page 496.
**See also page 496.

Grilling Fresh Vegetables

Grilling takes vegetables beyond the ordinary. They pick up that wonderful smoky flavor of grilled foods, their sugars caramelize and their colors deepen and brighten. For perfect grilled veggies every time, follow these simple steps:

1. Make your selection, then prep the veggies by following the directions in the Fresh Vegetable Cooking Chart, page 497.

2. Grill the vegetables four to five inches from medium heat.

3. To prevent them from drying out, brush the veggies occasionally with melted butter, margarine, olive oil, vegetable oil or your favorite bottled or homemade dressing.

4. Use the chart at right as a guide for *approximate* grilling times. The kind of grill you have and the weather can affect grilling time.

TIMETABLE FOR GRILLING VEGETABLES

Vegetable	Time
Asparagus spears, whole	20 minutes
Bell peppers, cut into 1-inch strips	15 minutes
Broccoli spears, cut lengthwise in half	20 minutes
Carrots, small whole, partially cooked*	10 minutes
Cauliflowerets, cut lengthwise in half	20 minutes
Cherry tomatoes, whole	10 minutes
Corn on the cob, husked and wrapped in aluminum foil	20 minutes
Eggplant, cut into 1/4-inch slices	15 minutes
Green beans, whole	15 minutes
Mushrooms, whole	10 minutes
Onions, cut into 1/2-inch slices	10 minutes
Pattypan squash, whole	15 minutes
Potatoes, cut into 1-inch wedges, partially cooked*	10 minutes
Zucchini, cut into 3/4-inch pieces	15 minutes

Before grilling, cook in boiling water 5 to 10 minutes or just until crisp-tender.

Hazelnut-Parmesan Asparagus

Fast

Prep: 15 min; Cook: 10 min ✳ 8 servings

2 cups water
2 pounds asparagus spears
2 tablespoons butter or stick margarine
1 package (8 ounces) sliced mushrooms (3 cups)
1 1/2 teaspoons chopped fresh or 1/2 teaspoon dried basil leaves
1/4 teaspoon salt
1/4 teaspoon coarsely ground pepper
1/4 cup shredded Parmesan cheese
1/4 cup chopped hazelnuts (filberts)

1. Heat water to boiling in 12-inch skillet. Add asparagus. Heat to boiling; reduce heat to medium. Cover and cook 4 to 6 minutes or until crisp tender. Drain; set aside.

2. Melt butter in skillet over medium-high heat. Stir in mushrooms. Cook 2 to 3 minutes, stirring frequently, until mushrooms are light brown.

3. Stir asparagus, basil, salt and pepper into mushrooms until vegetables are coated with seasonings and asparagus is heated through. Sprinkle with cheese and hazelnuts.

1 Serving: Calories 85 (Calories from Fat 55); Fat 6g (Saturated 1g); Cholesterol 2mg; Sodium 160mg; Carbohydrate 5g (Dietary Fiber 1g); Protein 4g **% Daily Value:** Vitamin A 8%; Vitamin C 12%; Calcium 6%; Iron 4% **Diet Exchanges:** 1 Vegetable, 1 Fat

Favorite Green Bean Casserole

Prep: 20 min; Bake: 40 min ✳ 6 servings

1 can (10 3/4 ounces) condensed cream of mushroom, cream of celery or cream of chicken soup
1/2 cup milk
1/8 teaspoon pepper
2 cans (15 ounces each) French-style green beans, drained*
1 can (2.8 ounces) French-fried onions

1. Heat oven to 350°.

2. Mix soup, milk and pepper in 2-quart casserole or square baking dish, 8 × 8 × 2 inches. Stir in beans. Sprinkle with onions.

3. Bake uncovered 30 to 40 minutes or until hot in center.

2 bags (16 ounces each) frozen cut green beans can be substituted for the canned beans. Cook as directed on package for minimum time; drain.

1 Serving (about 3/4 cup): Calories 160 (Calories from Fat 90); Fat 10g (Saturated 2g); Cholesterol 5mg; Sodium 850mg; Carbohydrate 17g (Dietary Fiber 3g); Protein 4g **% Daily Value:** Vitamin A 6%; Vitamin C 6%; Calcium 8%; Iron 10% **Diet Exchanges:** 1/2 Starch, 2 Vegetable, 1 1/2 Fat

Green Beans Olé

Prep: 10 min; Cook: 30 min ✱ 4 servings

1 pound green beans, cut into 1-inch pieces
4 slices bacon, cut up
1 medium onion, chopped (1/2 cup)
1 medium tomato, chopped (3/4 cup)
1 clove garlic, finely chopped
1 teaspoon chopped fresh or 1/2 teaspoon dried
    oregano leaves
1/2 teaspoon salt
Dash of pepper
2 tablespoons lemon or lime juice

1. Place beans in 1 inch water in 2-quart saucepan. Heat to boiling; reduce heat. Simmer uncovered 10 to 15 minutes or until crisp-tender; drain. Immediately rinse with cold water; drain.

2. Cook bacon in 10-inch skillet over medium-high heat, stirring occasionally, until crisp. Remove bacon from skillet, reserving 1 tablespoon fat in skillet. Drain bacon on paper towels.

3. Cook onion in bacon fat over medium heat, stirring occasionally, until tender. Stir in tomato, garlic, oregano, salt and pepper. Simmer uncovered 5 minutes. Stir in beans; heat through. Drizzle with lemon juice. Garnish with bacon.

1 Serving: Calories 70 (Calories from Fat 25); Fat 3g (Saturated 1g); Cholesterol 5mg; Sodium 410mg; Carbohydrate 11g (Dietary Fiber 4g); Protein 4g **% Daily Value:** Vitamin A 6%; Vitamin C 10%; Calcium 6%; Iron 6% **Diet Exchanges**: 2 Vegetable, 1/2 Fat

Broccoli with Pine Nuts *Fast*

Prep: 5 min; Cook: 15 min ✱ 4 servings

1 cup water
1 1/2 pounds broccoli, cut into spears
1/4 cup butter or stick margarine
1/2 cup pine nuts, almonds or pecans

1. Heat water to boiling in 2-quart saucepan. Add broccoli. Cook uncovered 5 to 7 minutes or until stems are crisp-tender; drain.

2. Melt butter in 8-inch skillet over medium heat. Cook pine nuts in butter about 5 minutes, stirring frequently, until golden brown. Stir pine nuts into broccoli.

1 Serving: Calories 235 (Calories from Fat 200); Fat 22g (Saturated 9g); Cholesterol 30mg; Sodium 110mg; Carbohydrate 9g (Dietary Fiber 5g); Protein 5g **% Daily Value:** Vitamin A 28%; Vitamin C 34%; Calcium 6%; Iron 6% **Diet Exchanges:** 2 Vegetable, 4 Fat

Herbed Broccoli

Herbed Broccoli *Fast*

Prep: 15 min; Cook: 10 min ✱ *4 servings*

1 pound broccoli, cut into flowerets and stems into
 1 × 1/2-inch pieces (4 cups)*
2 tablespoons olive or vegetable oil
1 teaspoon chopped fresh or 1/4 teaspoon dried basil
 leaves
1 teaspoon chopped fresh or 1/4 teaspoon dried
 oregano leaves
1/2 teaspoon salt
1 clove garlic, finely chopped
2 roma (plum) tomatoes, seeded and chopped

1. Heat 1 inch water to boiling in 10-inch skillet. Add broccoli. Heat to boiling. Boil 5 to 7 minutes or until crisp-tender; drain and set aside. Wipe out and dry skillet with paper towel.

2. Heat oil in same skillet over medium heat. Stir in remaining ingredients. Heat about 1 minute, stirring frequently, until hot. Add broccoli; toss gently.

*2 packages (10 ounces each) frozen chopped broccoli, cooked and drained, can be substituted for the fresh broccoli. Omit step 1; cook broccoli as directed on package.

1 Serving: Calories 65 (Calories from Fat 45); Fat 5g (Saturated 1g); Cholesterol 0mg; Sodium 320mg; Carbohydrate 5g (Dietary Fiber 2g); Protein 2g **% Daily Value:** Vitamin A 10%; Vitamin C 58%; Calcium 4%; Iron 4% **Diet Exchanges:** 1 Vegetable, 1 Fat

Sweet-Sour Red Cabbage *Fast & Low-Fat*

Prep: 20 min; Cook: 10 min ✱ 6 servings

Cabbage can be shredded by thinly slicing with a knife or using the largest holes of a shredder or the shredding blade with your food processor. Cut the cabbage through the core into fourths. Cut away core and discard; shred remaining cabbage. Or, substitute 1 bag (16 ounces) coleslaw mix for the red cabbage.

1 medium head red cabbage (1 1/2 pounds), shredded
4 slices bacon, diced
1/4 cup packed brown sugar
2 tablespoons all-purpose flour
1/2 cup water
1/4 cup white vinegar
1/4 teaspoon salt
1/8 teaspoon pepper
1 small onion, sliced

1. Heat 1 inch water to boiling in 10-inch skillet. Add cabbage. Heat to boiling. Boil 4 to 6 minutes or until crisp-tender. Drain and reserve. Wipe out and dry skillet with paper towel.

2. Cook bacon in same skillet over medium heat, stirring occasionally, until crisp. Remove bacon with slotted spoon; drain on paper towels. Drain fat, reserving 1 tablespoon in skillet.

3. Stir brown sugar and flour into bacon fat in skillet. Stir in water, vinegar, salt, pepper and onion. Cook over medium heat about 5 minutes, stirring frequently, until mixture thickens.

4. Stir in cabbage. Cook until hot.

1 Serving (about 2/3 cup): Calories 110 (Calories from Fat 25); Fat 3g (Saturated 1g); Cholesterol 5mg; Sodium 190mg; Carbohydrate 20g (Dietary Fiber 3g); Protein 4g **% Daily Value:** Vitamin A 2%; Vitamin C 38%; Calcium 8%; Iron 6% **Diet Exchanges:** 4 Vegetable

Slow Cooker Directions: Cook bacon as directed in step 2, reserving 1 tablespoon fat. Refrigerate bacon. Decrease water to 1/3 cup and vinegar to 3 tablespoons. Mix fat, brown sugar, flour, water, vinegar, salt and pepper in 3 1/2- to 6-quart slow cooker. Stir in cabbage and onion. Cover and cook on low heat setting 6 to 7 hours or until tender. Crumble bacon; stir into cabbage.

Glazed Carrots

Prep: 30 min; Cook: 10 min ✱ 6 servings

1 1/2 pounds carrots, cut into julienne strips*
    (page 8)
1/3 cup packed brown sugar
2 tablespoons butter or stick margarine
1/2 teaspoon salt
1/2 teaspoon grated orange peel

1. Heat 1 inch water to boiling in 2-quart saucepan. Add carrots. Heat to boiling; reduce heat. Simmer uncovered 6 to 9 minutes or until crisp-tender. Drain and reserve.

2. Cook remaining ingredients in 12-inch skillet over medium heat, stirring constantly, until bubbly.

3. Stir in carrots. Cook over low heat about 5 minutes, stirring occasionally, until carrots are glazed and hot.

*1 1/2 bags (16-ounce size) frozen sliced carrots, cooked as directed on package, or fresh baby-cut carrots can be substituted for the 1 1/2 pounds julienne carrots.

1 Serving (about 1/2 cup): Calories 120 (Calories from Fat 35); Fat 4g (Saturated 2g); Cholesterol 10mg; Sodium 260mg; Carbohydrate 23g (Dietary Fiber 3g); Protein 1g **% Daily Value:** Vitamin A 100%; Vitamin C 8%; Calcium 4%; Iron 4% **Diet Exchanges:** 2 Vegetable, 1 Fruit

Glazed Carrots (page 508)

Scalloped Corn

Prep: 10 min; Cook: 8 min; Bake: 35 min ✱ *8 servings*

2 tablespoons butter or stick margarine

1 medium onion, finely chopped (1/4 cup)

1/4 cup finely chopped green bell pepper

2 tablespoons all-purpose flour

1/2 teaspoon salt

1/2 teaspoon paprika

1/4 teaspoon ground mustard

Dash of pepper

3/4 cup milk

1 can (15 1/4 ounces) whole kernel corn, drained

1 egg, slightly beaten

1 cup cornflakes cereal

1 tablespoon butter or stick margarine, melted

1. Heat oven to 350°.

2. Melt 2 tablespoons butter in 10-inch skillet over medium heat. Cook onion and bell pepper in butter, stirring occasionally, until crisp-tender. Stir in flour, salt, paprika, mustard and pepper. Cook, stirring constantly, until smooth and bubbly; remove from heat

3. Stir in milk. Heat to boiling, stirring constantly. Boil and stir 1 minute; remove from heat. Stir in corn and egg. Pour into ungreased 1-quart casserole.

4. Mix cornflakes and 1 tablespoon butter; sprinkle over corn mixture. Bake uncovered 30 to 35 minutes or until center is set.

1 Serving: Calories 135 (Calories from Fat 55); Fat 6g (Saturated 3g); Cholesterol 40mg; Sodium 350mg; Carbohydrate 17g (Dietary Fiber 1g); Protein 4g **% Daily Value:** Vitamin A 10%; Vitamin C 8%; Calcium 4%; Iron 10% **Diet Exchanges:** 1 Starch, 1 Fat

MUSHROOMS

Portobello

Maitake

Oyster

White

Shitake

Cremini (Brown)

Enoki

Morel

Sautéed Mushrooms *Fast*

Prep: 15 min; Cook: 5 min ✳ *4 servings*

An easy way to slice fresh mushrooms is to use a hard-cooked egg slicer, available at grocery stores, specialty cookware stores and in the cookware sections at chain stores.

2 tablespoons butter or stick margarine
2 tablespoons olive or vegetable oil
2 cloves garlic, finely chopped
1/2 teaspoon salt
1/4 teaspoon pepper
1 pound mushrooms, sliced (6 cups)
Chopped fresh parsley, if desired

1. Heat all ingredients except mushrooms and parsley in 12-inch skillet over medium-high heat until butter is melted. Stir in mushrooms.

2. Cook 4 to 6 minutes, stirring frequently, until mushrooms are light brown. Sprinkle with parsley.

1 Serving: Calories 140 (Calories from Fat 115); Fat 13g (Saturated 5g); Cholesterol 15mg; Sodium 340mg; Carbohydrate 5g (Dietary Fiber 1g); Protein 2g **% Daily Value:** Vitamin A 4%; Vitamin C 2%; Calcium 0%; Iron 8% **Diet Exchanges:** 1 Vegetable, 2 1/2 Fat

Lighter Sautéed Mushrooms: For 3 grams of fat and 55 calories per serving, omit oil and decrease butter to 1 tablespoon; use nonstick skillet.

Caramelized Onions

Prep: 5 min; Cook: 50 min ✳ *About 1 3/4 cups*

Sweet varieties of onions contain more sugar than other varieties and it is the sugar that caramelizes, resulting in a deep golden brown color and rich flavor. If you can't find any of the onions we suggest, regular yellow onions can be used—just sprinkle about 1 tablespoon of brown sugar over the onions and cook as directed.

ONIONS

Yellow

Green

Boiler

Red

Pearl

Cipolline

Shallots

Vidalia

Walla Walla

Maui

2 tablespoons butter*
3 large sweet onions (Vidalia, Walla Walla or Spanish),
      sliced (8 cups)
1/4 teaspoon salt

1. Melt butter in 12-inch nonstick skillet over medium-high heat. Stir in onions to coat with butter. Cook uncovered 10 minutes, stirring every 3 to 4 minutes.

2. Reduce heat to medium-low. Sprinkle salt over onions. Cook 35 to 40 minutes longer, stirring well every 5 minutes, until onions are light golden brown (onions will shrink during cooking).

*Do not use margarine or vegetable oil spreads.

1 Serving: Calories 80 (Calories from Fat 45); Fat 5g (Saturated 3g); Cholesterol 10mg; Sodium 180mg; Carbohydrate 10g (Dietary Fiber 2g); Protein 1g **% Daily Value:** Vitamin A 2%; Vitamin C 6%; Calcium 2%; Iron 0% **Diet Exchanges:** 2 Vegetable, 1/2 Fat

Desired color for caramelized onions

POTATOES

Purple | Sweet | Yam | Russet/Idaho

New Red | Round Red | Round White | Fingerling | Yellow/Yukon Gold

Peas and Almonds *Fast*

Prep: 5 min; Cook: 7 min ✳ 6 servings

2 tablespoons butter or stick margarine
1/4 cup slivered almonds
1 bag (16 ounces) frozen green peas, thawed and
   drained
1/2 teaspoon salt

1. Melt butter in 10-inch skillet over medium heat. Cook almonds in butter 2 to 3 minutes, stirring occasionally, until light brown.

2. Stir in peas and salt. Cook 3 to 5 minutes, stirring frequently, until peas are tender.

1 Serving: Calories 85 (Calories from Fat 45); Fat 5g (Saturated 2g); Cholesterol 5mg; Sodium 270mg; Carbohydrate 10g (Dietary Fiber 4g); Protein 4g **% Daily Value:** Vitamin A 6%; Vitamin C 4%; Calcium 2%; Iron 6% **Diet Exchanges:** 2 Vegetable, 1 Fat

Twice-Baked Potatoes

Prep: 1 hr 35 min; Bake: 20 min ✳ 8 servings

These potatoes can be put in the fridge or freezer (wrapped up tightly) before being baked again. Bake refrigerated potatoes 30 minutes; frozen potatoes about 40 minutes.

4 large baking potatoes (8 to 10 ounces each)
1/4 to 1/2 cup milk
1/4 cup butter or stick margarine, softened
1/4 teaspoon salt
Dash of pepper
1 cup shredded Cheddar cheese (4 ounces)
1 tablespoon chopped fresh chives

1. Heat oven to 375°. Gently scrub potatoes, but do not peel. Pierce potatoes several times with fork to allow steam to escape while potatoes bake.

2. Bake 1 hour to 1 hour 15 minutes or until potatoes feel tender when pierced in center with fork.

3. When potatoes are cool enough to handle, cut lengthwise in half; scoop out inside, leaving a thin shell. Mash potatoes in medium bowl with potato masher or electric mixer on low speed until no lumps remain. Add milk in small amounts, beating after each addition with potato masher or electric mixer on low speed (amount of milk needed to make potatoes smooth and fluffy depends on kind of potatoes used).

4. Add butter, salt and pepper; beat vigorously until potatoes are light and fluffy. Stir in cheese and chives. Fill potato shells with mashed potato mixture. Place on ungreased cookie sheet.

5. Increase oven temperature to 400°. Bake about 20 minutes or until hot.

Scoop out potatoes from shells using a soup spoon. Carefully scoop out the inside of each potato half, leaving about a 1/4-inch shell.

1 Serving: Calories 180 (Calories from Fat 100); Fat 11g (Saturated 7g); Cholesterol 30mg; Sodium 210mg; Carbohydrate 16g (Dietary Fiber 1g); Protein 5g **% Daily Value:** Vitamin A 8%; Vitamin C 8%; Calcium 8%; Iron 2% **Diet Exchanges:** 1 Starch, 2 Fat

Scalloped Potatoes

Prep: 20 min; Bake: 1 hr 40 min; Stand: 5 min
* *6 servings*

3 tablespoons butter or stick margarine
1 small onion, finely chopped (1/4 cup)
3 tablespoons all-purpose flour
1 teaspoon salt
1/4 teaspoon pepper
2 1/2 cups milk
6 medium peeled or unpeeled potatoes, thinly sliced (6 cups)
1 tablespoon butter or stick margarine

1. Heat oven to 350°. Grease bottom and side of 2-quart casserole with shortening.

2. Melt 3 tablespoons butter in 2-quart saucepan over medium heat. Cook onion in butter about 2 minutes, stirring occasionally, until tender. Stir in flour, salt and pepper. Cook, stirring constantly, until smooth and bubbly; remove from heat.

3. Stir in milk. Heat to boiling, stirring constantly. Boil and stir 1 minute.

4. Spread potatoes in casserole. Pour sauce over potatoes. Cut 1 tablespoon butter into small pieces; sprinkle over potatoes. Cover and bake 30 minutes. Uncover and bake 1 hour to 1 hour 10 minutes longer or until potatoes are tender. Let stand 5 to 10 minutes before serving (sauce thickens as it stands).

1 Serving: Calories 225 (Calories from Fat 90); Fat 10g (Saturated 6g); Cholesterol 30mg; Sodium 500mg; Carbohydrate 30g (Dietary Fiber 2g); Protein 6g **% Daily Value:** Vitamin A 12%; Vitamin C 12%; Calcium 12%; Iron 2% **Diet Exchanges:** 1 Starch, 1 Vegetable, 1/2 Skim Milk, 2 Fat

HAM AND SCALLOPED POTATOES: Stir 1 1/2 cups cubed fully cooked ham into potatoes before pouring sauce over potatoes in step 4.

Roasted Rosemary-Onion Potatoes

Au Gratin Potatoes

Prep: 25 min; Bake: 1 hr 20 min ✳ *6 servings*

2 tablespoons butter or stick margarine

1 small onion, chopped (1/4 cup)

1 tablespoon all-purpose flour

1/2 teaspoon salt

1/4 teaspoon pepper

2 cups milk

2 cups shredded natural sharp Cheddar cheese
   (8 ounces)

6 medium potatoes, peeled and thinly sliced (6 cups)

1/4 cup dry bread crumbs

Paprika, if desired

1. Heat oven to 375°.

2. Melt butter in 2-quart saucepan over medium heat. Cook onion in butter about 2 minutes, stirring occasionally, until tender. Stir in flour, salt and pepper. Cook, stirring constantly, until bubbly; remove from heat.

3. Stir in milk. Heat to boiling, stirring constantly. Boil and stir 1 minute; remove from heat. Stir in 1 1/2 cups of the cheese until melted.

4. Spread potatoes in ungreased 1 1/2-quart casserole. Pour cheese sauce over potatoes. Bake uncovered 1 hour.

5. Mix remaining 1/2 cup cheese and the bread crumbs; sprinkle over potatoes. Sprinkle with paprika. Bake uncovered 15 to 20 minutes or until top is brown and bubbly and potatoes are tender.

1 Serving: Calories 340 (Calories from Fat 160); Fat 18g (Saturated 11g); Cholesterol 55mg; Sodium 540mg; Carbohydrate 31g (Dietary Fiber 2g); Protein 15g **% Daily Value:** Vitamin A 14%; Vitamin C 10%; Calcium 30%; Iron 6% **Diet Exchanges:** 1 Starch, 1 Skim Milk, 4 Fat

Roasted Rosemary-Onion Potatoes

Prep: 15 min; Bake: 25 min ✳ 4 servings

4 medium potatoes (1 1/3 pounds)
1 small onion, finely chopped (1/4 cup)
2 tablespoons olive or vegetable oil
2 tablespoons chopped fresh or 2 teaspoons dried
    rosemary leaves
1 teaspoon chopped fresh or 1/4 teaspoon dried
    thyme leaves
1/4 teaspoon salt
1/8 teaspoon pepper

1. Heat oven to 450°. Grease bottom and sides of jelly roll pan, 15 1/2 × 10 1/2 × 1 inch, with shortening.

2. Cut potatoes into 1-inch chunks. Mix remaining ingredients in large bowl. Add potatoes; toss to coat. Spread potatoes in single layer in pan.

3. Bake uncovered 20 to 25 minutes, turning occasionally, until potatoes are light brown and tender when pierced with fork.

1 Serving: Calories 190 (Calories from Fat 65); Fat 7g (Saturated 1g); Cholesterol 0mg; Sodium 160mg; Carbohydrate 33g (Dietary 4Fiber g); 3Protein g **% Daily Value:** Vitamin A 0%; Vitamin C 14%; Calcium 2%; Iron 10% **Diet Exchanges:** 2 Starch, 1 Fat

Fried Potatoes *Fast*

Prep: 10 min; Cook: 20 min ✳ 4 servings

The potatoes can be sliced ahead of time, but be sure to put them in a bowl of cold water so they don't turn brown or black. Drain and pat dry with paper towels before cooking, so water won't make the hot fat spatter.

2 tablespoons vegetable oil
4 medium peeled or unpeeled potatoes, thinly sliced
    (4 cups)
1 medium onion, thinly sliced, if desired
1 1/2 teaspoons salt
1/4 teaspoon pepper

1. Heat oil in 10-inch nonstick skillet over medium heat. Place potatoes and onion in skillet; sprinkle with salt and pepper.

2. Cover and cook over medium heat 10 minutes, stirring occasionally. Uncover and cook 10 minutes, stirring occasionally, until potatoes are brown and tender.

1 Serving: Calories 220 (Calories from Fat 90); Fat 10g (Saturated 3g); Cholesterol 10mg; Sodium 920mg; Carbohydrate 32g (Dietary Fiber 2g); Protein 3g **% Daily Value:** Vitamin A 2%; Vitamin C 14%; Calcium 0%; Iron 2% **Diet Exchanges:** 2 Starch, 1 1/2 Fat

---

NEED TO BREATHE

Store onions, garlic, potatoes and other root vegetables in baskets or on wire racks that allow air to circulate around them. Ideally, you should store them in a dry, cool, dark place.

Oven-Fried Potato Wedges   *Low-Fat*

Prep: 10 min; Bake: 30 min ✱ *4 servings*

If you love seasoned french fries but not the fat, then you'll love this recipe for making them from scratch—and they're so easy! The wedges of potato are sprayed with cooking spray, sprinkled with seasonings and baked in the oven instead of being deep-fried.

3/4 teaspoon salt
1/2 teaspoon sugar
1/2 teaspoon paprika
1/4 teaspoon ground mustard
1/4 teaspoon garlic powder
3 medium baking potatoes (8 to 10 ounces each)
Cooking spray

1. Heat oven to 425°. Mix salt, sugar, paprika, mustard and garlic powder.

2. Gently scrub potatoes, but do not peel. Cut each potato lengthwise in half; cut each half lengthwise into 4 wedges. Place potato wedges, skin sides down, in ungreased rectangular pan, 13 × 9 × 2 inches.

3. Spray potatoes with cooking spray until lightly coated. Sprinkle with salt mixture.

4. Bake uncovered 25 to 30 minutes or until potatoes are tender when pierced with fork. (Baking time will vary depending on the size and type of the potato used.)

To cut potatoes into wedges, cut each potato lengthwise in half. Turn potatoes cut sides down, and cut each half lengthwise into 4 wedges.

1 Serving: Calories 105 (Calories from Fat 0); Fat 0g (Saturated 0g); Cholesterol 0mg; Sodium 450mg; Carbohydrate 24g (Dietary Fiber 2g); Protein 2g **% Daily Value:** Vitamin A 2%; Vitamin C 10%; Calcium 0%; Iron 6% **Diet Exchanges:** 1 1/2 Starch

Hash Brown Potatoes

Prep: 15 min; Cook: 30 min ✱ *4 servings*

4 medium peeled or unpeeled boiling potatoes
    (1 1/2 pounds)
2 tablespoons finely chopped onion
1/2 teaspoon salt
1/8 teaspoon pepper
2 tablespoons vegetable oil

1. Shred enough potatoes to measure 4 cups. Rinse well; drain and pat dry.

2. Mix potatoes, onion, salt and pepper. Heat 1 tablespoon of the oil in 10-inch nonstick skillet over medium heat. Pack potato mixture firmly in skillet, leaving 1/2-inch space around edge.

3. Cook over medium-low heat about 15 minutes or until bottom is brown. Drizzle oil evenly over potatoes. Cut potato mixture into fourths; turn over.* Cook about 12 minutes longer or until bottom is brown.

*Potato mixture can be kept in one piece if desired. Place large plate over skillet; turn skillet upside down to invert potatoes onto plate. Slide potatoes back into skillet.

1 Serving: Calories 180 (Calories from Fat 80); Fat 9g (Saturated 1g); Cholesterol 0mg; Sodium 150mg; Carbohydrate 25g (Dietary Fiber 2g); Protein 2g **% Daily Value:** Vitamin A 0%; Vitamin C 8%; Calcium 0%; Iron 2% **Diet Exchanges:** 1 Starch, 2 Vegetable, 1 Fat

Potato Pancakes *Low-Fat*

Prep: 15 min; Cook: 20 min ✱ *16 pancakes*

Serve with sour cream, sliced green onions, applesauce or maple syrup.

4 medium baking potatoes (1 1/2 pounds), peeled
4 large eggs, beaten
1 small onion, finely chopped (1/4 cup), if desired
1/4 cup all-purpose flour
1 teaspoon salt
1/4 cup vegetable oil

1. Shred enough potatoes to measure 4 cups. Rinse well; drain and pat dry.

2. Mix potatoes, eggs, onion, flour and salt. Heat 2 tablespoons of the oil in 12-inch skillet over medium heat. For each pancake, pour about 1/4 cup batter into skillet. Flatten each with spatula into pancake about 4 inches in diameter.

3. Cook pancakes about 2 minutes on each side or until golden brown. Cover to keep warm while cooking remaining pancakes. Repeat with remaining batter; as batter stands, liquid and potatoes will separate, so stir to mix as necessary. Add remaining oil as needed to prevent sticking.

1 Serving: Calories 65 (Calories from Fat 25); Fat 3g (Saturated 1g); Cholesterol 55mg; Sodium 160mg; Carbohydrate 8g (Dietary Fiber 1g); Protein 2g **% Daily Value:** Vitamin A 2%; Vitamin C 4%; Calcium 0%; Iron 2% **Diet Exchanges:** 1/2 Starch, 1/2 Fat

Mashed Potatoes

Prep: 10 min; Cook: 25 min ✱ *4 to 6 servings*

6 medium round red or white potatoes (2 pounds)
1/3 to 1/2 cup milk
1/4 cup butter or stick margarine, softened
1/2 teaspoon salt
Dash of pepper

1. Place potatoes in 2-quart saucepan; add enough water just to cover potatoes. Heat to boiling; reduce heat. Cover and simmer 20 to 30 minutes or until potatoes are tender; drain. Shake pan with potatoes over low heat to dry (this will help mashed potatoes be fluffier).

2. Mash potatoes in pan until no lumps remain.* Add milk in small amounts, mashing after each addition (amount of milk needed to make potatoes smooth and fluffy depends on kind of potatoes used).

3. Add butter, salt and pepper. Mash vigorously until potatoes are light and fluffy. If desired, sprinkle with small pieces of butter or sprinkle with paprika, chopped fresh parsley or chives.

*To mash potatoes with an electric mixer, follow these guidelines:

- *For unlined, stainless steel or glass saucepans, beat potatoes in saucepan with electric mixer on low speed as directed above.*

- *For nonstick or for saucepans that are not shiny inside (such as saucepans made of anodized steel, which are dark gray in color), transfer potatoes to medium bowl after step 1. Beat potatoes with electric mixer on low speed as directed above.*

1 Serving: Calories 290 (Calories from Fat 110); Fat 12g (Saturated 7g); Cholesterol 30mg; Sodium 400mg; Carbohydrate 44g (Dietary Fiber 4g); Protein 5g **% Daily Value:** Vitamin A 10%; Vitamin C 18%; Calcium 4%; Iron 12% **Diet Exchanges:** 2 Starch, 3 Vegetable, 1 Fat

Lighter Mashed Potatoes: For 6 grams of fat and 235 calories per serving, use fat-free (skim) milk and decrease butter to 2 tablespoons.

BUTTERMILK MASHED POTATOES: Substitute buttermilk for the milk.

GARLIC MASHED POTATOES: Cook 6 cloves garlic, peeled, with the potatoes.

HORSERADISH MASHED POTATOES: Add 2 tablespoons prepared mild or hot horseradish with the butter, salt and pepper in step 3.

Potato Casserole Supreme

Potato Casserole Supreme

Prep: 15 min; Bake: 50 min ✳ 8 servings

1 can (10 3/4 ounces) condensed cream of mushroom
    soup
1 can (10 3/4 ounces) condensed cream of chicken
    soup
1 container (8 ounces) sour cream
1/2 cup milk
1/4 teaspoon pepper
1 package (30 ounces) frozen shredded hash brown
    potatoes
8 medium green onions, sliced (1/2 cup)
1 cup shredded Cheddar cheese (4 ounces)

1. Heat oven to 350°. Grease rectangular baking dish,
13 × 9 × 2 inches.

2. Mix soups, sour cream, milk and pepper in very
large bowl. Stir in potatoes and onions. Spoon into
baking dish.

3. Bake uncovered 30 minutes. Sprinkle with cheese.
Bake uncovered 15 to 20 minutes or until golden brown
on top and bubbly around edges.

1 Serving: Calories 325 (Calories from Fat 135); Fat 15g (Saturated
8g); Cholesterol 40mg; Sodium 1,060mg; Carbohydrate 39g
(Dietary Fiber 3g); Protein 9g **% Daily Value:** Vitamin A 10%;
Vitamin C 10%; Calcium 16%; Iron 6% **Diet Exchanges:** 2 Starch, 2
Vegetable, 3 Fat

Candied Sweet Potatoes

Prep: 45 min; Cook: 5 min ✳ 6 servings

6 medium sweet potatoes or yams (2 pounds)*
1/3 cup packed brown sugar
3 tablespoons butter or stick margarine
3 tablespoons water
1/2 teaspoon salt

1. Place sweet potatoes in 2-quart saucepan; add
enough water just to cover potatoes. Heat to boiling;
reduce heat. Cover and simmer 20 to 25 minutes or
until tender; drain. When potatoes are cool enough to
handle, slip off skins; cut potatoes into 1/2-inch slices.

2. Heat remaining ingredients in 10-inch skillet over medium heat, stirring constantly, until smooth and bubbly. Add potatoes. Gently stir until glazed and hot.

*1 can (23 ounces) sweet potatoes, drained and cut into 1/2-inch slices, can be substituted for the fresh sweet potatoes; omit step 1.

1 Serving: Calories 210 (Calories from Fat 55); Fat 6g (Saturated 4g); Cholesterol 15mg; Sodium 250mg; Carbohydrate 40g (Dietary Fiber 3g); Protein 2g **% Daily Value:** Vitamin A 100%; Vitamin C 22%; Calcium 4%; Iron 4% **Diet Exchanges:** 2 Starch, 1 Fruit, 1 Fat

Lighter Candied Sweet Potatoes: For 2 grams of fat and 175 calories per serving, decrease butter to 1 tablespoon; use nonstick skillet.

MASHED SWEET POTATOES: Cook potatoes as directed in step 1, except do not cut into slices. Omit 1/3 cup brown sugar, 3 tablespoons butter, 3 tablespoons water and 1/2 teaspoon salt. Add 2 tablespoons butter or stick margarine and 1/2 teaspoon salt to cooked, skinned potatoes. Mash potatoes in pan until no lumps remain.

ORANGE SWEET POTATOES: Substitute orange juice for the water. Add 1 tablespoon grated orange peel with the brown sugar.

PINEAPPLE SWEET POTATOES: Omit water. Add 1 can (8 ounces) crushed pineapple in syrup, undrained, with the brown sugar.

Spinach Soufflé

Prep: 25 min; Bake: 35 min ✱ 4 to 6 servings

Soufflés stay fluffy and are easiest to serve when two forks or a fork and spoon are used to divide the servings.

1 package (9 ounces) frozen chopped spinach, thawed
3 tablespoons all-purpose flour
1/2 teaspoon dried dill weed
1/4 teaspoon salt
1/4 teaspoon pepper
1 cup milk
1 cup shredded Cheddar cheese (4 ounces)
5 large eggs

1. Heat oven to 350°. Grease bottom and side of 2-quart casserole with shortening.

2. Squeeze spinach to drain; spread on paper towels and pat dry. Mix flour, dill weed, salt, pepper and milk in 2-quart saucepan. Cook over medium-high heat, stirring constantly, until thickened; remove from heat. Stir in cheese and spinach.

3. Separate eggs; set egg whites aside. Beat egg yolks in large bowl with wire whisk. Gradually stir in spinach mixture. Beat egg whites in large bowl with electric mixer on high speed until stiff. Gently fold egg whites into egg yolk mixture.

4. Spoon spinach mixture into casserole. Bake uncovered 30 to 35 minutes or until golden brown and puffed.

1 Serving: Calories 270 (Calories from Fat 155); Fat 17g (Saturated 9g); Cholesterol 300mg; Sodium 470mg; Carbohydrate 11g (Dietary Fiber 1g); Protein 19g **% Daily Value:** Vitamin A 50%; Vitamin C 43%; Calcium 32%; Iron 10% **Diet Exchanges:** 1 1/2 High-Fat Meat, 1 Vegetable, 1 Skim Milk, 1 Fat

CORN SOUFFLÉ: Omit dill weed. Substitute 1 1/2 cups frozen whole kernel corn, thawed, for the spinach.

Wilted Spinach *Fast*

Prep: 20 min; Cook: 10 min ✱ 4 servings

2 tablespoons olive or vegetable oil
1 medium onion, chopped (1/2 cup)
1 slice bacon, cut up
1 clove garlic, finely chopped
1/2 teaspoon salt
1/4 teaspoon pepper
1/4 teaspoon ground nutmeg
1 pound spinach leaves
2 tablespoons lime juice

1. Heat oil in 4-quart Dutch oven over medium heat. Cook onion, bacon and garlic in oil, stirring occasionally, until bacon is crisp; reduce heat to low.

2. Stir in salt, pepper and nutmeg. Gradually add spinach. Toss just until spinach is wilted. Drizzle with lime juice.

1 Serving (about 1/2 cup): Calories 95 (Calories from Fat 70); Fat 8g (Saturated 1g); Cholesterol 0mg; Sodium 390mg; Carbohydrate 6g (Dietary Fiber 3g); Protein 3g **% Daily Value:** Vitamin A 68%; Vitamin C 22%; Calcium 8%; Iron 12% **Diet Exchanges:** 1 Vegetable, 1 1/2 Fat

SQUASH

Banana

Turban

P[...]

Kabucha

Delicata

Carnival

Yellow Summer Squash

Acorn

Green Zucchini

Spaghetti

Butternut

Golden Nugget

Chayote

Sweet Dumpling

Pattypan

Jack Be Little

Glazed Acorn Squash

Prep: 10 min; Bake: 1 hr ✱ *4 servings*

2 acorn squash (1 to 1 1/2 pounds each)
4 tablespoons maple-flavored syrup
4 tablespoons whipping (heavy) cream, butter or stick margarine

1. Heat oven to 350°.

2. Cut each squash lengthwise in half; remove seeds and fibers. Place squash, cut sides up, in ungreased rectangular pan, 13 × 9 × 2 inches. Spoon 1 tablespoon maple syrup and 1 tablespoon whipping cream into each half.

3. Bake uncovered about 1 hour or until tender.

1 Serving: Calories 210 (Calories from Fat 45); Fat 5g (Saturated 3g); Cholesterol 15mg; Sodium 35mg; Carbohydrate 47g (Dietary Fiber 9g); Protein 3g **% Daily Value:** Vitamin A 12%; Vitamin C 18%; Calcium 10%; Iron 10% **Diet Exchanges:** 2 Starch, 1 Fruit, 1 Fat

Slow Cooker Directions: Use squash that are 3/4 to 1 pound each. Cut squash crosswise in half; remove seeds and fibers. Pour 1/4 cup water into 5- to 6-quart slow cooker. Place squash halves, cut sides up, in cooker. (Stacking squash halves in cooker may be necessary.) Spoon 1 tablespoon maple syrup and 1 tablespoon whipping cream into each half. Cover and cook on high heat setting 3 to 4 hours or until tender.

APPLE-STUFFED ACORN SQUASH: Omit maple syrup and whipping cream. Bake squash halves 30 minutes. Mix 1 large tart red apple, diced, 2 tablespoons chopped nuts, 2 tablespoons packed brown sugar and 1 tablespoon butter or stick margarine, melted. Spoon apple mixture into squash halves. Bake about 30 minutes longer or until tender.

Mixed Roasted Vegetables

Prep: 25 min; Bake: 45 min ✱ *8 servings*

1 medium unpeeled eggplant (1 1/2 pounds), cut into 2-inch chunks
1 medium green bell pepper, cut into 1-inch pieces
1 medium red bell pepper, cut into 1-inch pieces
1 medium onion, cut into 8 wedges and separated
2 medium zucchini, cut into 1-inch pieces
1/2 pound whole mushrooms

1/3 cup chopped fresh or 2 tablespoons dried basil leaves
3 tablespoons olive or vegetable oil
2 tablespoons red wine vinegar
1 teaspoon dried oregano leaves
1/2 teaspoon salt
1/4 teaspoon pepper
1 medium tomato, seeded and cut into 2-inch pieces
Grated Parmesan cheese, if desired

1. Heat oven to 350°.

2. Place eggplant, bell peppers, onion, zucchini and mushrooms in 3-quart casserole. Sprinkle evenly with basil.

3. Mix oil, vinegar, oregano, salt and pepper. Drizzle evenly over vegetables.

4. Bake uncovered 30 minutes. Add tomatoes; toss to coat. Bake uncovered about 15 minutes or until vegetables are tender. Serve with cheese.

1 Serving (about 1 cup): Calories 90 (Calories from Fat 55); Fat 6g (Saturated 1g); Cholesterol 0mg; Sodium 150mg; Carbohydrate 11g (Dietary Fiber 4g); Protein 2g **% Daily Value:** Vitamin A 12%; Vitamin C 42%; Calcium 2%; Iron 6% **Diet Exchanges:** 2 Vegetable, 1 Fat

Ratatouille

Prep: 20 min; Cook: 15 min ✱ *6 servings*

1 medium unpeeled eggplant (1 1/2 pounds), cut into 1/2-inch cubes
2 small zucchini (1/2 pound), cut into 1/2-inch slices
1 medium green bell pepper, chopped (1 cup)
1 medium onion, finely chopped (1/2 cup)
2 medium tomatoes, cut into fourths
1/4 cup olive or vegetable oil
1 1/2 teaspoons salt
1/4 teaspoon pepper
2 cloves garlic, finely chopped

Cook all ingredients in 12-inch skillet over medium heat 10 to 15 minutes, stirring occasionally, until zucchini is tender.

1 Serving (about 1 cup): Calories 120 (Calories from Fat 80); Fat 9g (Saturated 1g); Cholesterol 0mg; Sodium 600mg; Carbohydrate 12g (Dietary Fiber 4g); Protein 2g **% Daily Value:** Vitamin A 6%; Vitamin C 26%; Calcium 2%; Iron 4% **Diet Exchanges:** 2 Vegetable, 1 1/2 Fat

FRUITS

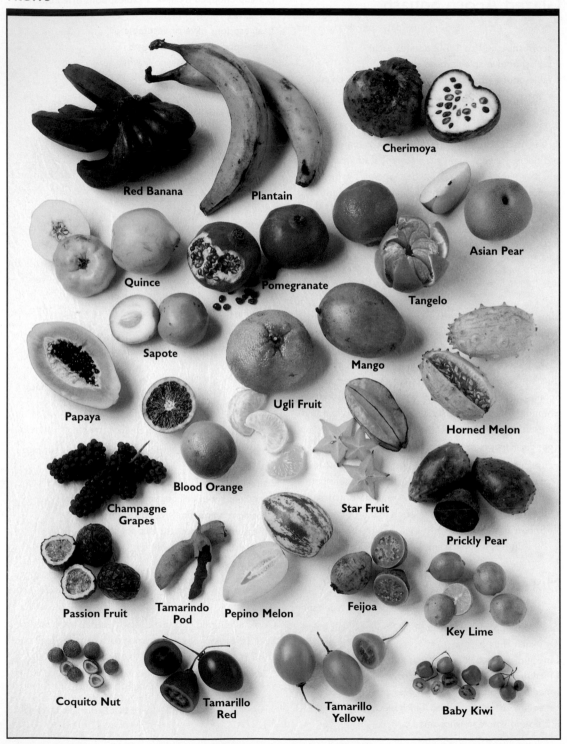

Red Banana

Plantain

Cherimoya

Quince

Pomegranate

Asian Pear

Tangelo

Sapote

Mango

Papaya

Ugli Fruit

Horned Melon

Blood Orange

Champagne
Grapes

Star Fruit

Prickly Pear

Passion Fruit

Tamarindo
Pod

Pepino Melon

Feijoa

Key Lime

Coquito Nut

Tamarillo
Red

Tamarillo
Yellow

Baby Kiwi

Fruit Basics

Tips for Fruit

The array of fresh fruit available year-round is truly amazing—from familiar apple varieties to exotic ugli fruit. But you'll find most fruits at the best price and flavor when they're in season.

- Look for fruit that doesn't have bumps or bruises. Unfortunately, there isn't one rule for determining if fruit is ripe—it varies from fruit to fruit. A pear is ripe if it gives slightly when pressed near the stem. Some fruit, such as blackberries, cherries, grapes, pineapples and watermelon, don't ripen any more after they've been picked. Other fruit, including peaches, cantaloupe and blueberries, ripen in color, texture and juiciness after picking, and kiwifruit, pears and papayas ripen in flavor, too.

- Whole or cut up, fruit by itself makes a simple dessert, especially when paired with a selection of cheeses. Of course, fruit also can be used in toppings and baked into a delicious variety of desserts.

- If a fresh fruit isn't available or in season, canned or frozen fruits can be substituted in many recipes.

- To learn more about the apple varieties that work well in desserts, check out Apples and Their Uses on page 422.

Tropical and Specialty Fruits Glossary

Apples:

- **Crab Apple:** This small red apple, about 1 1/2 to 2 inches in diameter, has a sweet-sour taste. Peak season is November to December. Select fruit that has a pleasant aroma and no bruises. Crab apples are served cooked, not raw.

- **Lady Apple:** An apple the size of a table-tennis ball that is red to yellow in color. Fruit has a smooth, firm surface and a sweet-tart taste. Peak season is November to December. Select fruit without bruises; serve raw or cooked.

Asian Pear: Over 100 varieties exist of this crunchy, sweet and very juicy fruit that has the texture of a pear and the crispness of an apple. Ranges from large and golden brown to tiny and yellow-green. Peak season is late summer through early fall. Fruit is sold ripe; store in the refrigerator up to 3 months.

Babáco: Resembling a star when cut crosswise, this extremely juicy five-sided fruit is related to the papaya, often being called "mountain papaya." Peak season is usually October through November. When mature, the fruit is soft with golden yellow skin and has the aroma of strawberries, pineapples and papayas. Use within 1 or 2 days.

Baby Kiwi: Bite-size berries are the size of grapes with smooth green skin and no fuzz. Flesh is sweet, soft and creamy and contains edible tiny black seeds. Limited season from early to mid autumn. Fruit is delicate; refrigerate up to 3 days.

Bananas/Plantains:

- **Burro Banana:** Squat and square in shape, this banana has a tangy lemon-banana flavor. Available year-round. When ripe, the peel is yellow with black spots and the flesh is creamy.

- **Ice Cream Banana (Blue Java):** This banana resembles a burro banana but has a very creamy taste and texture that is said to melt in your mouth like ice cream. Peak season is during the summer months. When unripe, the skins have a bluish cast to them. When ripe, the skin turns yellow and the fruit yields to gentle pressure.

- **Manzano:** Short and chubby in shape, this banana has a mild flavor combination of apples and strawberries. Available year-round. When peel is fully black, manzanos are at their peak flavor.

- **Niño:** Another short, chubby banana, this one has a rich, sweet flavor and a soft, creamy texture. Available year-round. Ripe niños are yellow with some black spots.

- **Plantain:** Large and long with thick skin and pointed ends, this fruit is most often served as a vegetable because of its lower sugar content. Available year-round. Cooked when the skin is green, the fruit is starchy with no banana taste; cooked when the skin is yellow or brown and the fruit is ripe, it has a sweet banana taste and a slightly chewy texture.

- **Red Banana:** Heavier and chunkier than yellow bananas, the flavor is sweeter with a hint of raspberry. Available year-round. When ripe, the skin is purplish and the flesh is creamy with a touch of pink or orange.

Cape Gooseberry: Also known as golden berry, these sweet-tart berries are 1 1/2 to 2 inches long and light green to orange-red with a papery orange-yellow skin. They have small, soft edible seeds. Peak season is February to July. When ripe, they smell a bit like pineapple. Keep at room temperature a few days or in the refrigerator up to 1 month.

Champagne Grapes: A black corinth varietal, these tiny, reddish-purple, seedless grapes are crunchy, sweet and juicy. Peak season is July through October. Select fragrant, unblemished fruit with fresh stems. Store in a plastic bag in the refrigerator.

Cherimoya (Custard Apple): Heart-shaped fruit with thin green skin that resembles a closed pine cone. Pulp is creamy white with large black almond-shaped seeds and a sweet custard taste. Fruit is available year-round. Select firm fruit; ripen at room temperature until fruit yields to gentle pressure, then refrigerate.

Citrus:

- **Blood Orange:** Deep-red flesh that is sweet and juicy is characteristic of this orange. The peel is smooth or pitted with a red blush. Peak season is December through May. Select fruit that has a sweet fragrance, no blemishes and is firm and heavy for its size. Store at cool room temperature up to 1 week or in the refrigerator up to 2 weeks.

- **Clementine Orange:** Similar to a tangerine, this fruit is flatter in shape. The orange skin is loose and easy to peel. Flesh is orange, sweet and usually seedless. Peak season is January through March. Select fruit that is heavy for its size. Store in refrigerator.

- **Honey Tangerine:** Very sweet and juicy, this fruit is a cross between a tangerine and an orange. The flesh is orange with a touch of green, and the peel

is easy to remove. Peak season is January through mid-March. Select fruit that is firm with some give and heavy for its size. Store in refrigerator.

- **Key Lime:** The Florida Keys are the primary growing area for this yellowish lime that is smaller and rounder than a green Persian lime. The flesh is yellow, less acidic and full of seeds. Available year-round. Select fruit that is heavy for its size. Store in a closed bag in the refrigerator up to 1 week.

- **Kumquat:** Resembling a miniature orange football, this one- to two-inch fruit is entirely edible. The skin is sweet, and the orange pulp is tart. Peak season is December through May. Select firm fruit with a fresh scent that has no soft spots. Store in refrigerator up to 2 weeks.

- **Lavender Gem (Wekiwa):** Crossing a grapefruit with a Sampson tangelo produced this hybrid fruit. It resembles a miniature grapefruit with bright yellow peel. The flesh is pinkish with small seeds and has a delicate, sweet grapefruit taste. Peak season is December through February. Select fruit that is heavy for its size. Store in the refrigerator.

- **Meyer Lemon:** Favored for its mild, juicy flesh, this lemon has smooth, bright yellow peel. Peak season is November through May. Select fruit that is heavy for its size. Refrigerate in a plastic bag up to 10 days.

- **Oro Blanco:** Crossing a pummelo with a grapefruit created this fruit with a thick, yellow peel. The name means "white gold" in Spanish. The flesh is sweet and juicy with a grapefruit flavor and no bitterness or acidity. The peak season is November through February. Select fruit that is heavy for its size. Store in the refrigerator.

- **Pummelo:** The largest of all citrus, this fruit ranges in size from a small cantaloupe to a basketball. The thick peel is green to yellow, and the sweet-tart flesh ranges from white to pink or rose red. Fruit is sweeter, firmer and less juicy than a grapefruit. Peak season is November to March. Select fruit that yields to gentle pressure. Refrigerate 1 to 2 weeks.

- **Tangelo:** Tangelos are a cross between a pummelo (an ancestor of the grapefruit) and a tangerine.

Tangelos can range in size from that of a tiny orange to a small grapefruit. The skin can be rough to smooth and range in color from yellow-orange to deep orange. They are juicy, sweet-tart and contain few seeds. The most common variety is the Minneola. Peak season is November through March.

- **Ugli Fruit:** An exotic tangelo from Jamaica that combines the characteristics of tangerines, grapefruits and Seville oranges. The fruit is large like a grapefruit and easy to peel like a tangerine. The flesh is sweet and very juicy. Peak season occurs winter to spring with limited availability. Select fruit that yields to gentle pressure and has a fragrant aroma.

Coconut: The fruit of the coconut palm has a thick, fibrous, brown, oval husk surrounding a thin, hard shell that encloses white flesh. The center is hollow and filled with coconut milk. Available year-round. Select coconuts that are heavy for their size and sound full of liquid. Store at room temperature up to 6 months. When opened, store meat in refrigerator up to 4 days or freeze up to 6 months.

Coquito Nut: Nuts are the size and shape of marbles and resemble miniature smooth, brown coconuts. They have a hollow center with white flesh that is hard, crunchy and sweet like coconut. The nuts come from a Chilean palm that takes up to 50 years to produce and remains productive for hundreds of years. Available year-round. Store in an airtight container in the refrigerator up to 2 weeks.

Donut Peach: A peach that has rounded sides that pull into the center, creating the look of a doughnut. The sweet, juicy fruit has light yellow skin with a red blush and a white to pale orange flesh. Peak season is mid-August. Select fruit free of brown spots. Store at room temperature until soft to the touch, then refrigerate.

Feijoa: This small, egg-shaped fruit has a thin, slightly bumpy, lime green to olive green skin. Flesh has a granular texture with a creamy color. Taste is a unique blend of pineapple, quince and lemon. New Zealand fruit is available from spring to early summer, and California fruit from fall to early winter. Ripen fruit at room temperature. It is ready to eat when it yields slightly to gentle pressure and has a sweet smell. Store in the refrigerator up to 5 days, and peel bitter skin before eating.

Fig: Over six hundred varieties of this teardrop-shaped fruit exist. The peel can be purple, green or red, and the very sweet flesh ranges from creamy to purplish in color. Peak season is July to August. Select firm fruit, and ripen at room temperature until flesh is soft.

Horned Melon (Kiwano): The name is derived from the spikes that cover this yellow to orange melon. The bright lime green pulp is jellylike in texture with edible seeds that resemble those in a cucumber. The flavor is a blend of cucumber and lime. Available year-round. The melon is at its peak ripeness when it is golden orange. Refrigeration is not necessary.

Kiwifruit: Egg-shaped fruit that has thin, fuzzy, brown skin. Flesh is emerald green and fine textured, has tiny edible black seeds and a flavor that resembles strawberries and melons. Available year-round. Ripen at room temperature or in the refrigerator until flesh yields to gentle pressure.

Loquat: Originating in China, this pear-shaped fruit was introduced into the United States as a Japanese plum. The fruit is the size of an apricot with yellowish orange skin. The creamy flesh is orange, juicy and tender with one or more inedible seeds. It has a sweet and slightly acid flavor with a hint of cherries, plums and grapes. Peak season occurs sporadically during the spring months. Ripen at room temperature until flesh yields to gentle pressure.

Lychee: Chinese evergreen trees produce this small fruit the size of a large grape that has a tough, reddish brown, bumpy peel. Flesh has a grapelike texture with a single black seed and a flavor resembling a melon. Fruit comes from trees up to forty feet tall that take up to 15 years to mature. Peak season is June and July. Store in refrigerator.

Mango: Yellowish red, oblong fruit that has a thick rind. The golden flesh is juicy and tangy-sweet with a single large seed. Mangoes are the most consumed fruit in the world and have been cultivated for over 6,000 years. Available year-round. Store at room temperature until flesh yields to gentle pressure, then refrigerate up to 3 days.

Papaya: Large, oblong, yellowish green fruit that contains black seeds. The flesh of Hawaiian fruit is bright yellow to orange, and the flesh of Mexican fruit is bright orange to salmon red. Available year-round. Store at room temperature until fruit yields to gentle pressure, then refrigerate up to 3 days.

- **Maradol Papaya:** The average weight of this long, round papaya with yellow to green peel is 3 to 5 pounds. The sweet and juicy flesh is salmon red and contains black seeds that need to be removed before eating. Available year-round. Select fruit that is soft to the touch. Refrigerate up to 3 days.

- **Sunrise Papaya:** This yellow papaya with a red blush is heavier, meatier and sweeter than the more common variety. Peak season is January through June. Ripen at room temperature until flesh gives to gentle pressure, then refrigerate.

Passion Fruit: Egg-shaped fruit of the passionflower family that is purplish in color with leathery skin. The flesh is golden and jellylike with a tart lemony flavor and small, black, edible seeds. New Zealand fruit is available March through June, and California fruit from July through May. Select fruit that is large and heavy. Ripen at room temperature until the skin is almost black and very wrinkled, then refrigerate.

Pepino Melon: Tear-drop-shaped melon has smooth, green skin and flesh that is golden yellow and fragrant. The flavor is slightly sweet with a taste of cantaloupe and cucumber. Fruit is available from late fall to mid-spring. Select melons that are heavy for their size. As the fruit ripens, the skin will turn yellow and develop purple stripes. Store in the refrigerator, and use in 3 to 4 days.

Persimmon:

- **Fuyu:** Persimmon shaped like a flattened ball that has skin ranging in color from pale orange to brilliant red-orange. The flesh is coreless with few seeds and has a sweet flavor. Peak season is September through mid-December. Store in a cool place. Fruit can be eaten when firm or soft.

- **Hachiya:** Heart-shaped persimmon has smooth, brilliant reddish orange skin and flesh. The taste is extremely astringent when immature, and sweet and spicy when ripe. Peak season is September through mid-December. Ripen at room temperature, and eat fruit when very soft.

Pomegranate: Leathery red rind covers this round fruit that is filled with tiny seeds encased in red juicy pulp. The seeds have a sweet and tangy taste and are sectioned between shiny, tough, white membranes. Although available September through December, peak season is October. Refrigerate up to 3 months.

Prickly (Cactus) Pear: The pear-shaped fruit of cactus plants has medium green to dark magenta skin. The flesh ranges from pale green to ruby red and contains small edible seeds. The peak season is from September through April. Store at room temperature until fruit yields to slight pressure, then refrigerate up to 5 days.

Quince: One of the earliest known fruits is apple shaped and ranges from apple to grapefruit size. The golden skin usually has a woolly surface, and the white flesh is firm and somewhat dry with an acidic pine-apple taste. In ancient times, this fruit was called "golden apple" and was considered an emblem of love and happiness. Peak season is September through December. Select large, smooth fruit, and store in the refrigerator for several weeks.

Rainier Cherries: Shiny yellow cherries have a red blush and a very sweet, delicate flavor. The flesh is white, firm and finely textured with colorless juice. Peak season is April through June. Cherries are shipped ripe; store in the refrigerator.

Rambutan: Growing in clusters on ornamental-type trees, this fruit has soft hairy spines protruding from reddish brown, leathery skin. Its name comes from the Malay word *rambut*, meaning "hair." When peeled, pale flesh with a single seed is revealed. The fruit is sweet with a texture similar to grapes. A small crop is available in June and July and a large crop November through January. Store in refrigerator up to 1 week.

Red Currants: This tart, juicy berry is about the size of a pea and usually used in jellies, sauces, juice, pies, cakes or as a beautiful garnish for food platters. Peak season is mid-June through July.

Sapote: Coreless, juicy fruit the size and shape of an apple has delicate, thin green skin that bruises easily. The flesh is yellowish, and the mild flavor is a combination of peaches, lemons and mangoes. Peak season is August through November. Select fruit that is hard, and ripen at room temperature about 3 days. Refrigerate ripe fruit.

Starfruit (Carambola): When sliced crosswise, this fruit resembles a star, thus its name. The skin and flesh are yellow, and the taste is sweet with a lemon tartness. Available year-round. Store at room temperature until a few brown spots appear on the ridges, then refrigerate.

Tamarillo: This egg-shaped fruit with a stem is related to the tomato and potato. The smooth, glossy skin is scarlet to golden yellow, and the flesh is golden apricot in color with tiny edible seeds. It has a slightly bitter tomato taste. Peak season is May through August. Ripen at room temperature until flesh yields to slight pressure and becomes fragrant. Refrigerate up to 1 week.

Tamarind: Brownish, barklike pods about five inches long are filled with a tart apricot-lemon-flavored pulp that is very sticky. Pulp is often used to make a flavorful drink in Mexico. Available year-round. Store pods in refrigerator up to 1 month, or remove pulp and freeze.

Yellow Seedless Watermelon: An oval-shaped melon that has smooth green skin. The sweet, crisp and juicy flesh is bright yellow with a few white seeds. Melons are available sporadically year-round depending on the variety and are most available August through September. Store at room temperature until cut, then refrigerate.

Applesauce *Fast & Low-Fat*

Prep: 5 min; Cook: 20 min ✳ *6 servings*

Zap it! To microwave, decrease the water to 1/4 cup, and put all the ingredients in 2-quart microwavable casserole. Cover tightly and microwave on High for 10 to 12 minutes, stirring and breaking up apples every 3 minutes, until apples are tender. With a scoop of vanilla ice cream, and sprinkle of cinnamon-sugar, it makes a great dessert.

4 medium cooking apples (1 1/3 pounds), peeled and cut into fourths
1/2 cup water
1/4 cup packed brown sugar or 3 to 4 tablespoons granulated sugar
1/4 teaspoon ground cinnamon
1/8 teaspoon ground nutmeg

1. Heat apples and water to boiling in 2-quart saucepan over medium heat, stirring occasionally; reduce heat. Simmer uncovered 5 to 10 minutes, stirring occasionally to break up apples, until tender.

2. Stir in remaining ingredients. Heat to boiling. Boil and stir 1 minute.

1 Serving (about 1/2 cup): Calories 90 (Calories from Fat 0); Fat 0g (Saturated 0g); Cholesterol 0mg; Sodium 5mg; Carbohydrate 22g (Dietary Fiber 2g); Protein 0g **% Daily Value:** Vitamin A 0%; Vitamin C 2%; Calcium 0%; Iron 2% **Diet Exchanges:** 1 1/2 Fruit

Slow Cooker Directions: Decrease water to 1/4 cup. Mix all ingredients in 3 1/2- to 6-quart slow cooker. Cover and cook on high heat setting 1 hour 30 minutes to 2 hours or until apples are tender; stir.

Frozen Pineapple on a Stick

Prep: 20 min; Freeze: 2 hr; Stand: 10 min ✳ *8 servings*

To prepare fresh pineapple, twist the top off and cut the pineapple lengthwise into eighths. Cut the fruit from the rind, and cut off the pineapple core. Cut the wedges lengthwise in half to form spears. You can make and freeze this recipe up to 1 week ahead of time.

8 pieces fresh pineapple, about 3 × 1 inch
1/4 cup pineapple or orange juice
3/4 cup shredded coconut, toasted (page 177)

1. Line cookie sheet with waxed paper. Insert wooden skewer into narrow end of each piece of pineapple.

2. Dip pineapple into juice, then roll in coconut, coating completely. Place on cookie sheet.

3. Cover and freeze 1 to 2 hours or until firm. Let stand 10 minutes before serving.

1 Serving: Calories 90 (Calories from Fat 25); Fat 3g (Saturated 3g); Cholesterol 0mg; Sodium 25mg; Carbohydrate 16g (Dietary Fiber 1g); Protein 1g **% Daily Value:** Vitamin A 0%; Vitamin C 22%; Calcium 0%; Iron 2% **Diet Exchanges:** 1 Fruit, 1/2 Fat

Rhubarb Sauce, Apple Sauce (page 527) and Strawberry-Rhubarb Sauce (variation of Rhubarb sauce)

Rhubarb Sauce   *Fast & Low-Fat*

Prep: 10 min; Cook: 15 min ✱ 6 servings

Rhubarb varies in sweetness, so add sugar to taste. Besides making a great accompaniment to savory food such as pork, this sauce also can be served for dessert, either by itself or over pound cake or ice cream.

1/2 to 3/4 cup sugar
1/2 cup water
1 pound rhubarb, cut into 1-inch pieces (4 cups)
Ground cinnamon, if desired

1. Heat sugar and water to boiling in 2-quart saucepan, stirring occasionally. Stir in rhubarb; reduce heat. Simmer uncovered about 10 minutes, stirring occasionally, until rhubarb is tender and slightly transparent.

2. Stir in cinnamon. Serve sauce warm or chilled.

1 Serving (about 1/2 cup): Calories 75 (Calories from Fat 0); Fat 0g (Saturated 0g); Cholesterol 0mg; Sodium 0mg; Carbohydrate 18g (Dietary Fiber 1g); Protein 1g **% Daily Value:** Vitamin A 0%; Vitamin C 2%; Calcium 14%; Iron 0% **Diet Exchanges:** 1 Fruit

STRAWBERRY-RHUBARB SAUCE: Substitute 1 cup strawberries, cut in half, for 1 cup of the rhubarb. After simmering rhubarb, stir in strawberries; heat just to boiling.

Fruit Kabobs with Yogurt

Fast & Low-Fat

Prep: 20 min ✱ 8 servings

4 cups bite-size pieces assorted fresh fruit (pineapple, cantaloupe, strawberries, kiwifruit)
3 cups strawberry low-fat yogurt

1. Thread 4 to 6 pieces fruit on each of eight 8-inch bamboo skewers.

2. Serve fruit kabobs with yogurt.

1 Kabob: Calories 125 (Calories from Fat 10); Fat 1g (Saturated 1g); Cholesterol 5mg; Sodium 25mg; Carbohydrate 26g (Dietary Fiber 2g); Protein 5g **% Daily Value:** Vitamin A 6%; Vitamin C 74%; Calcium 14%; Iron 2% **Diet Exchanges:** 1 Fruit, 1 Skim Milk

Low-Fat = *3g or less, except main dishes with 6g or less*   **Fast** = *Ready in 30 minutes or less*   ■ = *Bread Machine directions*   ● = *Slow Cooker directions*

Lighter = 1/3 fewer calories or 50% less fat

Menu Planning Basics

America is a melting pot of cultures, experiences and lifestyles. Nowhere is that more evident than in the kitchen, in what we eat. The variety of foods and flavors and fresh ingredients available make cooking and eating an everyday adventure for the entire household.

The way we approach everyday entertaining has changed, too. Most social gatherings have gone from traditional, formal occasions, to more casual get-togethers, potlucks and hassle-free gatherings.

These changes make meal planning and entertaining fun! The perks of planning menus, whether they are for everyday dinners or entertaining purposes, is that it makes cooking easier because you are sure you will have everything you need on hand. The following tips can take some of the guesswork out of planning menus.

- **Choose from the hundreds of recipes in this book** to create menus to fit any occasion. Or combine a recipe with convenience foods from your supermarket deli or carryout to make a meal.
- **Make a list.** Some people carry a mental meal-planning checklist in their heads; others prefer to write everything down. Whatever your technique, a list will help make grocery shopping faster and more economical, and it will cut down on those last-minute dashes to pick up missing items. Don't forget to do a quick check of what you already have on hand, and work those ingredients into your plan.
- **Keep your eating patterns and preferences in mind**. Does your family eat two main meals plus snacks rather than the more traditional three meals a day or eat a heavier meal at noon instead of in the evening? Or how about a special family night that features a meatless, ethnic or other type of dinner with a theme?
- **Plan the main course first.** Then plan the other foods, such as vegetables and breads, to complement your main course.
- **Make sure flavors go together instead of competing with each other**. A strongly flavored main

dish needs a milder-flavored side dish for balance; a subtle main dish works well with a boldly flavored side dish. If the meal has been on the heavier side, choose a lighter dessert; if the meal was a bit lighter try something indulgent and rich.

- **Involve all your senses—sight, taste, smell, touch.** Keep flavors, textures, colors, shapes and temperatures in mind. For example, serve spicy with mild; creamy with crisp; white or brown with red, yellow or green; tiny pieces with big chunks; and hot dishes with cold.
- **Use seasonings, sauces, condiments, salsas, relishes and marinades** to jazz up easy-to-make plainer foods, such as broiled fish, cooked pasta or steamed vegetables. See Chapter 16 for more information.
- **Use the Food Guide Pyramid** (page 531). It provides the recommended number of servings from each food group in order to maintain a balanced and healthful diet. The guide will help you plan an entire day of meals that include at least the minimum recommended number of servings from each food group.
- **Aim for moderation and variety.** Try planning meals with less than 30 percent of their total calories from fat, and include plenty of complex carbohydrates and fiber. Emphasize grain-based foods as well as lots of different vegetables and fruits. Eat moderate amounts of low-fat dairy foods and lean meats and only a few fats and sweets each day.
- **Watch that fat.** To control fat, saturated fat and cholesterol, choose more plant-based foods, such as cereals, rice, pasta and beans. Use meat, poultry and fish in smaller amounts rather than as the main feature. Try the lighter variations for recipes in this book, and use fats and oils sparingly in all your cooking. Look for the Low-Fat symbol on recipes throughout this cookbook to help you choose the right ones for your menu.

Nutrition Glossary

Complex carbohydrates. Saturated fat. Unsaturated fat. The terms used by nutritionists and health experts and on package labels can be confusing. Here's a basic explanation of some of the most commonly used terms:

Carbohydrate: A key source for our energy needs. Sugars are simple carbohydrates; starches are complex carbohydrates.

Cholesterol: Fatlike substance found in animal-based foods. Our bodies also make cholesterol because we need it for our hormones to function properly.

Dietary fiber: Technically a complex carbohydrate. Fiber is the part of plant-based foods that isn't broken down or used by our bodies.

Fat: A powerful energy source. Fat provides more than twice the amount of energy supplied by carbohydrates or proteins. It's also a source of essential nutrients and insulates and protects body organs.

- **Saturated:** Found primarily in animal-based foods. This fat is solid at room temperature. Diets high in saturated fats have been linked to higher levels of blood cholesterol.
- **Unsaturated:** Found mostly in plant-based foods. This fat is usually liquid at room temperature. Unsaturated fats may be monounsaturated or polyunsaturated.

Food Guide Pyramid: A nutrition education guide from the U.S. Department of Health and Human Services and U.S. Department of Agriculture. It groups foods according to their primary nutrient content and outlines the recommended number of servings from each food group needed to maintain a balanced and healthful diet. See diagram on page 531.

Minerals: Elements other than carbon, hydrogen, oxygen and nitrogen that are nutritionally essential in very small amounts. Minerals are inorganic elements, such as calcium and iron, and are found in foods and water.

Nutrients: Substances that build, repair and maintain body cells. Nutrients include protein, carbohydrate, fat, water, vitamins and minerals.

Protein: Provides energy and structural support of body cells. Protein, made from building blocks of amino acids, is important for growth.

Vitamins: Essential for controlling body processes. Vitamins are found in small amounts in many foods. Unlike minerals, vitamins are organic compounds that contain carbon. Some common vitamins include vitamins A, B vitamins (such as thiamin, niacin, riboflavin) and vitamin C, among others. Folic acid has gained a lot of attention in recent years and is being added to more and more food products. This vitamin is necessary for all cells to function. It may protect against heart disease and nerve damage.

How Much Is a Serving from the Food Pyramid?

Breads, Cereal, Rice and Pasta Group: 1 slice bread; a small roll or muffin; 1/2 bun, bagel or English muffin; 1/2 to 1 1/2 cups ready-to-eat cereal (depends on density of individual cereals); 1/2 cup cooked cereal, rice or pasta; 3 or 4 small or 2 large crackers; 2 breadsticks (4 × 1/2 inch); 3 cups popcorn; 2 medium cookies.

Fruit Group: 1 medium fresh fruit or 1/2 grapefruit; 1 medium wedge melon; 3/4 cup fruit juice; 1/2 cup berries; 1/2 cup cooked or canned fruit; 1/4 cup dried fruit.

Vegetable Group: 1/2 cup chopped raw, cooked or canned vegetables; 3/4 cup vegetable juice; 1 cup raw leafy vegetables; 1 medium potato.

Meat, Poultry, Fish, Dry Beans, Eggs and Nuts Group: 2 to 3 ounces cooked lean meat, poultry or fish (3 ounces is about the size of deck of cards); 4 ounces tofu. Count the following as 1 ounce of meat: 1 egg; 3 egg whites; 2 tablespoons peanut butter or whole nuts or seeds; 1/2 cup cooked dried beans.

Milk, Yogurt and Cheese Group: 2 cups cottage cheese; 1 cup milk, yogurt or pudding; 1 1/2 ounces cheese; 1 1/2 cups ice cream, ice milk or frozen yogurt.

Fats, Oils and Sweets: Use sparingly.

FOOD GUIDE PYRAMID

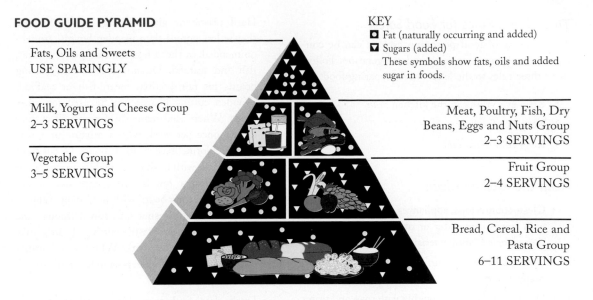

Fats, Oils and Sweets
USE SPARINGLY

Milk, Yogurt and Cheese Group
2–3 SERVINGS

Vegetable Group
3–5 SERVINGS

KEY
◻ Fat (naturally occurring and added)
▽ Sugars (added)
These symbols show fats, oils and added
sugar in foods.

Meat, Poultry, Fish, Dry
Beans, Eggs and Nuts Group
2–3 SERVINGS

Fruit Group
2–4 SERVINGS

Bread, Cereal, Rice and
Pasta Group
6–11 SERVINGS

Source: U.S. Department of Agriculture, U.S. Department of Health and Human Services

Food Safety Basics

America's food supply is one of the safest in the world. Farmers and ranchers, food processors, supermarkets and restaurants must follow strict rules and regulations while getting food to you. These requirements end, however, when the food goes into your shopping cart, leaves the store and goes to your kitchen.

So why should we worry about food safety? Because most of the illnesses reported from "bad food" are caused by bacterial contamination. Nearly all these cases can be linked to improper food handling, in our homes, supermarkets and restaurants, which means they could have been prevented.

Microorganisms are with us always. They're on us and on animals, in the air and water and on raw food. Some bacteria are useful, such as those that cause cheese and beer to ferment. But other bacteria cause foods to spoil, and even others cause food poisoning.

Beware the "Danger Zone"

The main difference between food-spoiling and food-poisoning bacteria is the temperatures at which they survive and grow. Bacteria that cause food to spoil can grow at refrigerator temperatures (below 40°). They usually make the food look or smell bad, which is an obvious clue to throw it out.

Most bacteria that cause food poisoning *don't* grow at refrigerator temperatures. The best temperature for these microorganisms to reproduce is around 100°. But the actual temperature varies with the organism and may range from 40° to 140°, or the "danger zone." These are pathogens, the type of bacteria that if eaten may lead to illness, disease or even death.

To prevent these bacteria from becoming harmful, they must be stopped from multiplying. Pathogenic bacteria are among the most important organisms to control because of the illness they cause in humans. The majority of them are invisible attackers; they can't be seen, smelled or tasted.

If contaminated food is eaten, people most often get sick within 4 to 48 hours, and it's not always easy to tell if the problem is the flu or food poisoning. Use your judgment to determine if and when medical care is needed. Call a doctor or go to a hospital immediately if symptoms are severe, such as vomiting, diarrhea, fever or cramps, or if the victim is very young, elderly, pregnant, has a weakened immune system or is already ill.

Three Basic Rules for Food Safety

The majority of food-poisoning bacteria can be controlled by cleaning, cooking and refrigeration. Follow these three rules to the letter when preparing food:

1. Keep everything in the kitchen *clean*.
2. Keep hot foods *hot*.
3. Keep cold foods *cold*.

Keep the Kitchen Clean

- Clean countertops, appliances, utensils and dishes with hot, soapy water or other cleaners, such as those labeled "antibacterial."
- Clean refrigerator surfaces regularly with hot, soapy water.
- Wash your hands thoroughly with soap and water for at least 20 seconds before handling food. Twenty seconds is about how long it takes to recite or sing the alphabet. If you stop handling food to do something else, wash your hands again—especially after blowing your nose, using the bathroom, changing diapers or touching pets.
- If you sneeze or cough while preparing food, turn your face away and cover your mouth and nose with a tissue; wash your hands afterward.
- Wash your hands and all utensils and surfaces with hot, soapy water after contact with raw poultry, meat, fish or seafood.
- If you have any kind of skin cut or infection on your hands, cover it with a bandage or wear protective plastic or rubber gloves.

- Hard plastic or glass cutting boards, because they're less porous than wooden boards, are recommended as the safest for raw poultry, meat, fish and seafood. Do not use wooden cutting boards for raw poultry, meat, fish or seafood. Wooden cutting boards can be used for other foods. When used regularly, sanitize all cutting boards once per week with a mixture of 1 teaspoon chlorine bleach to 1 quart (4 cups) of water. Rinse with fresh water and let air dry or pat dry with paper towels. After each use, always wash your cutting board with hot, soapy water; if the board is dishwasher safe, run it through the dishwasher (some plastic cutting boards may warp in the dishwasher). When your cutting board is battered with deep scratches and cuts, it's time to get a new one.
- Don't chop fresh vegetables, salad ingredients, fruit or any food that won't be fully cooked on a cutting board that was used for raw poultry, meat, fish or seafood without cleaning it as directed above. Wash any knives or utensils that were used hot, soapy water, too.
- Don't transfer bacteria from raw meat to cooked meat. For example, don't carry raw hamburgers to the grill on a platter, then put the cooked burgers back on the same unwashed platter.
- Wash the meat keeper and crisper drawers of your refrigerator often, and keep containers for storing food in the refrigerator very clean. Make it a habit to go through your refrigerator once a week to throw out perishable foods that are past their prime.

FOR MORE FOOD SAFETY INFORMATION

For information about safe food handling and foodborne illness, contact:

- Your local health department
- Extension home economists, listed in the phone book
- USDA's Meat and Poultry Hotline, 800-535-4555, or

TTY 800-256-7072 (weekdays, 10 A.M. to 4 P.M. eastern standard time). Or, check out the USDA's Web site at www.fsis.usda.gov.

- Food Safety Education, USDA-FSIS, Room 2942-S, 14000 Independence Avenue SW, Washington, DC 20250

- Consumer Information Center, 719-948-4000. Pueblo, CO 81009
- www.fightbac.org for up-to-the-minute food safety and food handling information

- Use paper towels when working with, or cleaning up after, raw foods, such as poultry and meats.
- Keep pets out of the kitchen. After playing with pets, be sure to your wash hands before handling food. Teach kids to do this, too.
- Wash kitchen linen often because bacteria "hang out" in towels, sponges and cloths used over and over. Throw out dirty or mildewed dish sponges.

Keep Hot Food Hot

- Bacteria thrive at room temperature or in luke-warm food. So don't allow hot foods to stand at room temperature for more than 2 hours, including prep time. Keeping hot foods hot means keeping them at 140° or higher.
- Don't partially cook or heat perishable foods, then set them aside or refrigerate to finish cooking later. During cooking, the food may not reach a temperature high enough to destroy bacteria.
- Don't worry about the safety of your slow cooker. With the direct heat from the pot, the lengthy cooking times and the steam created within the container, your slow cooker destroys harmful bacteria.
- Roast meat or poultry at 325° or above. Lower temperatures can encourage bacterial growth before cooking is complete.
- Cook meat and poultry completely, following the "doneness" times and temperatures recommended throughout this book. A meat thermometer comes in handy for making sure meat is done.
- Keep cooked food hot, or refrigerate it until ready to serve. This includes carryout foods and meals-to-go, too.
- Reheat leftovers, stirring often, until "steaming" hot (165°). Using a cover while reheating retains moisture and helps the leftovers heat through to the center. Heat soups, sauces and gravies to a rolling boil for 1 minute, stirring constantly, before serving (some cream-based recipes may curdle, but will taste the same). Do not taste leftover food that looks or smells strange to see if it's okay. When in doubt, throw it out!

Keep Cold Food Cold

- Bacteria thrive at room temperature, so don't allow cold foods to stand at room temperature for more than 2 hours, including prep time. Keeping cold foods cold means keeping them at 40° or lower.
- The most perishable foods are eggs, milk, seafood, fish, meat and poultry or the dishes that contain them, such as cream pies or seafood salad. When you shop, make your meat, poultry, fish and seafood selections last. Place them in plastic bags to prevent juices from dripping on other foods in your cart.
- Take perishable foods straight home, and refrigerate them immediately. If the time from the store to home is longer than 30 minutes, bring a cooler with freezer packs or filled with ice and put perishable groceries inside. Short stops during hot weather can cause perishable groceries in a hot car to reach unsafe temperatures very quickly.
- Buy "keep refrigerated" foods only if they are in a refrigerated case and are cold to the touch. Follow the "keep refrigerated," "safe handling" and "use by" labels on these products; this includes carryout foods and meals to go, as well.
- Frozen foods should be frozen solid without lots of ice crystals, which indicate the food may have thawed and refrozen.
- Foods chill faster if you allow space between them when stocking your refrigerator and freezer and if you divide large amounts into smaller ones and store foods in shallow containers.
- Buy a refrigerator thermometer to make sure your refrigerator is cooling at 35° to 40°. Use a freezer thermometer to check that your freezer is maintaining 0° or colder. If your power goes out, keep the refrigerator and freezer doors closed to protect food up to 2 days.
- When cleaning your refrigerator or freezer, pack perishables in a cooler with freezer packs or filled with ice.
- Never thaw foods at room temperature—thaw only in the refrigerator or microwave. If you thaw foods in the microwave, finish cooking them immediately.

More Tips for Keeping Food Safe to Eat

Canned Foods: Don't buy or use food in leaking, bulging or dented cans or in jars with cracks or loose or bulging lids. If you are in doubt about a can of food, don't taste it! Return it to your grocer, and report it to your local health authority.

Eggs: Store uncooked "do-ahead" recipes containing raw eggs in the refrigerator only for up to 24 hours before cooking. Even though it's tempting, don't eat unbaked cookie dough or cake batter containing raw eggs.

Foods made with cooked eggs—cheesecakes, cream fillings, custards, quiches and potato salads—must be served hot or cold, depending on the recipe. Refrigerate leftovers immediately after serving. Also see Handling and Storing Eggs Safely (page 199) and Cooking Eggs (page 200).

Raw eggs give some dishes, such as frosting, mousse and traditional Caesar salad dressing, a unique texture. When making these recipes, don't use raw eggs in the shell; use only pasteurized egg products or substitutes found in the dairy or freezer case. It's also okay to use reconstituted dried eggs or egg whites. Some processors are beginning to market eggs that are pasteurized in the shell, but they're not available nationwide yet.

Fruits and Vegetables: Wash with cold running water, using a scrub brush if necessary.

Ground Meat: Don't eat or taste raw ground meat—it's not safe! The process of grinding meat exposes more of the meat surface to bacteria so be sure to cook ground meat thoroughly. Make sure ground beef dishes such as burgers and meat loaf are completely cooked to 160° in the center of the thickest portion.

Ham: Most hams are fully cooked, but others need cooking. With so many varieties of hams, it can be confusing, so check the label. If you have any doubts, cook it so its internal temperature reaches 160°.

Luncheon Meats, Hot Dogs: Keep refrigerated, and use within 2 weeks. If the liquid that forms around hot dogs is cloudy, throw them out. Although hot dogs are fully cooked, you should reheat them until they're steaming hot all the way through.

Marinades: Marinate foods in a heavy plastic food-storage bag or nonmetal dish in the refrigerator, not at room temperature. Either discard leftover marinades or sauces that have had contact with raw meat or heat them to a rolling boil and boil 1 minute, stirring constantly, before serving.

Milk: Keep fresh milk products refrigerated. You can store unopened evaporated milk and nonfat dry milk in the cupboard up to several months. Refrigerate whole dry milk because it contains fat, and use it within a few weeks. Do not drink unpasteurized milk or milk products.

Poultry: Cook all poultry products according to the directions. Ground poultry, like ground beef, is susceptible to bacterial contamination and should be cooked to at least 165°. Stuff poultry just before you're ready to cook it to keep any bacteria in the raw poultry from tainting the stuffing. So that the stuffing will cook all the way through, stuff poultry loosely—about 3/4 cup of stuffing per pound of poultry, since it will expand while it cooks. The center of the stuffing should reach 165°. Within 2 hours of serving, refrigerate poultry, stuffing and giblets in separate containers. Use the leftovers within 4 days, or freeze them.

Keep Buffet Food Safe

- Serve food at buffets in small dishes. Rather than adding fresh food to a dish that already has had food on it, wash the dish or use a different one.

- Keep foods hot (at least 140°) with a slow cooker, fondue pot, chafing dish or warming tray. Warming units heated by canned cooking fuel are safe to use, but don't depend on units heated with candles because they don't get hot enough to keep foods safe from bacteria.

- Refrigerate salads made with seafood, poultry or meat. Chill both the food and the dish before serving.

- Place containers of cold foods in crushed ice to keep them below 40°.

- Hot or cold foods should not stand at room temperature for more than 2 hours. If in doubt, toss it.

- Store leftovers in the refrigerator for the amount of time recommended in our Cold Food Storage Chart on pages 540 to 541.

Keep Away-from-Home Food Safe

- Pack lunches in insulated lunch bags or in a small cooler with a freeze-pack, frozen juice box or small plastic bottle of frozen water to keep food cold. Keep the bag or cooler out of the sun. Put perishable foods carried in an uninsulated lunch bag in the refrigerator.

- Wash thermoses and rinse with boiling water after each use. Be sure hot foods are boiling when poured into thermoses. Wash fruits and vegetables before packing.

- Chill picnic food *before* packing in an ice-filled cooler. Because beverage coolers will be opened more frequently, use one cooler for beverages and one for perishable foods.

- Tightly wrap raw meat, poultry, fish and seafood or pack them in a separate cooler to keep them from dripping onto other foods. Bring along a bottle of instant hand sanitizer, antibacterial moistened towelettes or a bottle filled with soapy water for washing hands and surfaces after handling raw poultry, meat, fish or seafood.

- At restaurants or potlucks, salad bars and buffets should look clean. Make sure cold foods are cold and hot foods are steaming.

Table Settings and Entertaining

Setting the Table

Was setting the table one of your responsibilities when you were a kid? If those early lessons are a bit hazy or if you're teaching a youngster the basics, here are some guidelines for setting the table.

Sample Table Setting

- Allow plenty of room for each place at the table. It's hard to enjoy a meal when you're squashed.

- Whether you're serving a weekday dinner or springtime luncheon, create a welcoming table with colorful place mats, a bowl of fruit for a simple centerpiece or your cherished china and silver.

- Place the knives, forks and spoons one inch from the edge of the table. Place the flatware used first farthest from the dinner plate; the simple rule is to work from the outside in. The forks are typically placed to the left of the plate. The knife (with the blade toward the plate) and then the spoons are placed to the right of the plate. Place a seafood fork to the right of the spoons.

- If you're using a butter plate, place it above the fork. Place the butter knife horizontally or vertically on the rim or edge of the butter plate.

- If you're serving a salad *with* the main course, place the salad plate to the left of the forks and the salad fork at either side of the dinner fork.

- Arrange glasses above the knife. The water glass is usually at the tip of the knife, with beverage and/or wine glasses to the right of the water glass.

- If you're serving coffee or tea at the table, place the cup slightly above and to the right of the spoons.

- Place the napkin either in the center of the dinner plate, to the left of the forks or in another creative spot at each place setting. There are lots of nifty ways to fold napkins; check your local library or bookstore for ideas.

- Place dessert flatware horizontally above the top of the dinner plate, or bring it to the table with the dessert.

- Before dessert, clear the table of serving dishes, plates, glasses, salt and pepper shakers and flatware that won't be used for dessert. Bring coffee or tea cups, saucers, spoons and cream and sugar to the table if you plan to serve it with dessert.

Setting a Buffet Table

Letting guests serve themselves is easy and convenient for small or large groups, casual or formal occasions. There are basically three types of buffets:

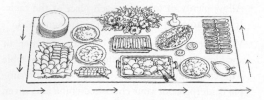

Sample Buffet

True Buffet: Guests pick up their food, beverage and flatware from the buffet table, then find a place to sit—although seating may be limited to a picnic blanket or lawn chairs. Keep in mind your guests might be balancing plates on their laps, so be sure to use real plates or very sturdy paper or plastic plates. Also, try to serve foods that don't need to be cut with a knife to make eating easier for your guests. Butter the rolls or breads ahead of time, and make sure there are places where guests can set their beverages.

Seated Buffet: Guests serve themselves from the buffet table, then sit at a table set with glasses, flatware and napkins. With this type of buffet, you're not limited to "fork-only" food.

Semi-Buffet: Guests serve themselves from the buffet table, then sit at a set table. The host may serve accompaniments, such as sauce or gravy, at the table. Or the host may fill plates from the buffet table, then serve them to the seated guests. This style of buffet often is used at holidays when turkey and roasts are carved at the table.

Buffet Tips

- Set up the buffet where it will be most convenient for serving, clearing and traffic: the dining room table, a sideboard, a picnic table, two card tables placed together, a kitchen center island or counter or desk.

- Make sure the traffic can flow easily around the serving area.

- If possible, place the buffet in the center of the room so guests can help themselves from all sides of the table. For a large group, set up identical serving lines on two sides of the table. To save space, place the table against a wall and leave three sides open for serving.

- Be sure guests know where the line starts. Place the food in order, so they can serve themselves without backtracking. Arrange the plates first, then the main course and vegetables, followed by salad, condiments and bread. If it's a true buffet, put the flatware and napkins last so your guests' hands will be free while serving themselves.

- While guests finish the main course, clear the buffet table and arrange the dessert, dessert plates and flatware on the buffet table or on a side table.

Entertaining Tips

What's the secret to successful parties? Good company, good food—and planning and preparing as much ahead of time so you can enjoy your party. Here are a few tips for making your next party a success.

- As you draw up your guest list, keep in mind the number of guests you want (Don't forget your budget!). Consider combinations of personalities—really interesting parties often include people with varied backgrounds.

- Encourage mingling! Spend time introducing your guests. For a large group, try providing name tags with "teaser" information about each guest, such as an unusual hobby or best vacation.

- Invite your guests plenty of time ahead—10 days to 2 weeks for casual events, 2 or more weeks for more formal events. Send written invitations for a formal event, but it's okay to call or e-mail your guests for casual get-togethers.

- Be specific in your invitation about time, food and dress. For example, "Come for a dress-up dessert party on New Year's Eve at 11 P.M." or "Come to a football party and pig roast on Saturday the 14th at 2 P.M. It'll be outside, so dress for the weather."

- Have enough food and beverages so you won't run out. Be sure to have nonalcoholic beverages on hand.

- Plan a varied menu, but don't wear yourself out! Choose foods you're comfortable preparing, including some you can make ahead of time; pick up the rest from the deli, or ask guests to bring something. See Menu Planning Basics, page 529.

- Plan foods suitable to the weather, seasonal availability, guests' preferences or diet needs and the serving style you plan to use.
- Make it easy. Consider hiring a college student, next-door neighbor's kid or your own children to help with serving and cleanup.

Food for a Crowd

The following charts will help you figure out how much food you'll need. Also consider the time of day, weather and number of dishes being served. Plan on one drink per hour per guest; if it's very warm, plan on two.

AMOUNTS OF FOOD FOR A CROWD

Food Item	Per Serving	12 Servings	24 Servings	48 Servings
Meat, Poultry and Shellfish (bone-in, unshelled)	3/4 pound	9 pounds	18 pounds	36 pounds
Meat, Poultry and Fish (boneless)	1/4 pound	3 pounds	6 pounds	12 pounds
Chicken Salad, Side Dish	1/2 cup	1 1/2 quarts	3 quarts	1 1/2 gallons
Main Dish	1 cup	3 quarts	1 1/2 gallons	3 gallons
Potato Salad, Baked Beans or Coleslaw	1/2 cup	1 1/2 quarts	3 quarts	1 1/2 gallons
Meat Cold Cuts	2 1/2 ounces	2 pounds	4 pounds	8 pounds
Cheese Slices	1 ounce	1 pound	2 pounds	4 pounds
Rolls	1 1/2 rolls	2 dozen	3 dozen	6 dozen
Crackers	4 crackers	8 ounces	1 pound	2 pounds
Tossed Salad	1 1/2 cups	4 1/2 quarts	9 quarts	4 1/2 gallons
Salad Dressing	2 tablespoons	1 1/2 cups	3 cups	1 1/2 quarts
Dip	2 tablespoons	1 1/2 cups	3 cups	1 1/2 quarts
Chips	1 ounce	12 ounces	1 1/2 pounds	3 pounds
Fruit or Vegetable Dippers	4 pieces	4 dozen	8 dozen	16 dozen
Cakes, 13 × 9″, 12-cup Ring or 9″ Layer	1/16 cake	1 cake	2 cakes	3 cakes
Cookies	2	2 dozen	4 dozen	8 dozen
Ice Cream	1/2 cup	2 quarts	1 gallon	2 gallons
Coffee, Brewed	3/4 cup	9 cups water	18 cups water	36 cups water
Ground Coffee		1 1/2 cups	3 cups	5 cups
Tea, Brewed	3/4 cup	9 cups water	18 cups water	36 cups water
Loose Tea		1/4 cup	1/2 cup	1 cup
Tea Bags		12 bags	24 bags	48 bags
Iced Tea	1 cup	3 quarts	1 1/2 gallons	3 gallons
Punch	1/2 cup	1 1/2 quarts	3 quarts	1 1/2 gallons
Mineral Water	8 ounces	3 quarts	6 quarts	12 quarts
Ice	4 ounces	3 pounds	6 pounds	12 pounds

FRUIT AND VEGETABLE YIELDS

Fruits	Approximate Yield
Cantaloupe, 4-pound	36 chunks
Grapes, 1 pound seedless	12 to 15 clusters
Honeydew, 2-pound	36 chunks
Pineapple, 3- to 4-pound	40 chunks
Strawberries, 1-pound large	20 to 25 berries

Vegetables	Approximate Yield
Asparagus, 1 pound	30 to 45 spears
Bell pepper, 1 large	24 strips, 3 1/2 × 1/2
Broccoli or cauliflower, 2 pounds	32 flowerets, 1 1/4"
Carrots, 1 pound	65 sticks, 3 × 1/2"
Celery, 4 medium stalks	33 sticks, 4 × 1/2"
Cucumbers, 2 large	45 sticks, 4 × 3/4"
Mushrooms, 1 pound	20 medium
Pea pods, 4 ounces	30 pea pods
Zucchini, 3 medium	35 slices, 1/2"

Salad Greens	Bite-Size Pieces
Boston lettuce, 1/2-pound head	6 cups
Iceberg lettuce, 1 1/2-pound head	12 cups
Leaf lettuce, 1-pound bunch	8 cups
Romaine, 1 1/2-pound bunch	12 cups
Spinach, 3/4-pound bunch	8 cups

Storing Food in the Refrigerator and Freezer

There's more to storing food in the refrigerator and freezer than opening the door, putting the food away and closing the door! Following are tips and a time chart for keeping refrigerated and frozen foods safe.

Refrigerator

- Keep your refrigerator at 40° or slightly lower. Adjust the temperature to a colder setting after you've added large amounts of room-temperature or warm foods. Readjust the temperature to the normal setting after about 8 hours.

- For extra security, we recommend buying a refrigerator/freezer thermometer. Check it often to make sure your appliances are maintaining proper temperatures.

- Before putting food in the refrigerator, cover it or close the original containers tightly to prevent the food from drying out or transferring odors from one food to another. Store produce and strong-flavored foods in tightly covered containers or plastic bags.

- Keep foods in the refrigerator until just before you're ready to use them.

Freezer

- The proper temperature for your freezer is 0° or lower.

- Wrap food in moistureproof, vaporproof containers and wraps.

- Label and date all packages and containers.

- To prevent freezer burn (a loss of moisture which can effect the flavor and texture of food), remove as much air from packages as possible.

- Store purchased frozen foods in their original packages.

- Use foods that have been in the freezer the longest before using other foods.

- Always thaw frozen meats, poultry and seafood in the refrigerator—never at room temperature. Thawing takes about 5 hours per pound of frozen food. Or thaw food in your microwave following the manufacturer's directions, then cook immediately.

- To maintain the best flavor and texture of frozen food, follow the times given in the Cold Foods Storage Chart (page 540). If you keep frozen foods slightly longer, they still will be safe to eat.

More Tips for Freezing and Thawing Foods

Baked Products: Cool them completely, then wrap in airtight packaging for freezing. Allow frostings to set at room temperature, or freeze frosted baked goods uncovered *before* packaging to set them, then wrap and freeze.

Breads: Refrigerate bread only during hot, humid weather. To thaw frozen bread, loosen the wrap and let it stand at room temperature for 2 to 3 hours.

Cakes:

- **Filled:** Cakes filled and frosted with plain sweetened whipped cream can be frozen. Refrigerate cakes with custard filling; do not freeze because the filling can separate.
- **Frosted:** To thaw frozen frosted cakes, loosen the wrap and place overnight in the refrigerator.
- **Unfrosted:** To thaw frozen unfrosted cakes, loosen the wrap and let stand at room temperature for 2 to 3 hours.

Cheesecakes: Thaw frozen cheesecakes in their wrapping in the refrigerator for 4 to 6 hours.

Cookies: See Storing Cookies and Bars (page 141).

Dairy Products: Check packages for the use-by or sell-by date, and refrigerate in their original containers. The refrigeration time in the chart is for *opened* products.

- **Cream Cheese and Hard Cheese:** If hard cheese is moldy, trim 1/2 inch from the affected area and rewrap cheese tightly. Thaw frozen cheeses, wrapped, in the refrigerator. Because the texture changes, use cheese that has been frozen only in baked goods such as casseroles, egg dishes, lasagna and pizza.

- **Ice Cream, Sorbet, Frozen Yogurt:** Keep frozen in the original containers. To reduce ice crystals, place aluminum foil or plastic wrap directly on the surface and re-cover with lids. For best quality, do not thaw and refreeze these foods.
- **Whipped Cream:** Contrary to popular belief, you can freeze both unsweetened and sweetened whipped cream. Drop small mounds of whipped cream onto waxed paper; freeze, then place in an airtight container. To thaw, let stand about 15 minutes at room temperature.

Eggs: See Handling and Storing Eggs Safely, page 199.

Meat Products: Check packages for the use-by or sell-by date. If meat is wrapped in white butcher paper, unwrap it and repackage tightly in moisture- and vapor-resistant materials such as plastic wrap, aluminum foil or plastic freezer bags.

Rewrapping meat packaged in clear plastic wrap isn't necessary, but you may want to put it a plastic bag in case the original packaging leaks. To freeze, wrap packages with heavy-duty aluminum foil or freezer wrap or place in freezer bags.

Pies: To freeze pies, see Pie Yields and Storage (page 116). Do not freeze custard, cream and unbaked pumpkin pies.

- **Frozen unbaked fruit pies:** Unwrap and carefully cut slits in the top crust. Bake at 425° for 15 minutes. Reduce oven temperature to 375° and bake 30 to 45 minutes longer or until the crust is golden brown and juice begins to bubble through the slits.
- **Frozen baked fruit and pecan pies:** Unwrap and thaw at room temperature until completely thawed. Or unwrap and thaw at room temperature 1 hour, then heat in oven at 375° for 35 to 40 minutes or until warm.
- **Frozen baked pumpkin pies:** Unwrap and thaw in the refrigerator.

COLD FOOD STORAGE CHART

Foods	Refrigerator (34° to 40°)	Freezer (0° or below)
Baked Products		
Breads—coffee cakes, muffins, quick breads and yeast breads	5 to 7 days	2 to 3 months
Cakes—unfrosted and frosted	3 to 5 days	Unfrosted—3 to 4 months Frosted—2 to 3 months
Cheesecakes—baked	3 to 5 days	4 to 5 months
Cookies—baked	Only if stated in recipe	Unfrosted—no longer than 12 months Frosted—no longer than 3 months
Pies—unbaked or baked fruit pies, baked pecan and baked pumpkin pies	Baked pumpkin pies, 3 to 5 days. Store fresh fruit or baked fruit pies and baked pecan pies loosely covered at room temperature no longer than 3 days.	Unbaked fruit pies—2 to 3 months Baked fruit pies—3 to 4 months
Pie Shells—unbaked or baked	Store in freezer	Unbaked shells—no longer than 2 months Baked shells—no longer than 4 months
Dairy Products		
Cheese		
Cottage and ricotta	1 to 10 days	Not recommended
Cream	No longer than 2 weeks	No longer than 2 months
Hard	3 to 4 weeks	6 to 8 weeks
Ice Cream, Sorbet and Frozen Yogurt	Freeze only	2 to 4 months
Milk Products		
Buttermilk	No longer than 1 week	Not recommended
Cream, half-and-half and whipping	No longer than 5 days	Not recommended
Cream, whipped	1 or 2 days	No longer than 3 months
Regular milk—whole, 2%, 1% and fat-free (skim)	No longer than 5 days	No longer than 1 month
Sour Cream	No longer than 1 week	Not recommended
Yogurt	No longer than 3 weeks	No longer than 1 month
Eggs		
Raw		
Whole in shell	3 weeks	Not recommended
Yolks, whites	2 to 4 days. Cover yolks with cold water.	See Handling and Storing Eggs Safely, page 199.
Cooked		
Whole in shell	1 week	Not recommended
Yolks, whites	1 week	Not recommended

Foods	Refrigerator (34° to 40°)	Freezer (0° or below)
Fats and Oils		
Butter	No longer than 2 weeks	No longer than 2 months
Margarine and Spread	No longer than 1 month	No longer than 2 months
Mayonnaise and Salad Dressing	No longer than 6 months	Not recommended
Meats		
Uncooked		
Chops	3 to 5 days	4 to 6 months
Ground	1 to 2 days	3 to 4 months
Roasts and Steaks	3 to 5 days	6 to 12 months
Cooked	3 to 4 days	2 to 3 months
Processed		
Cold cuts	Opened—3 to 5 days Unopened—2 weeks	Not recommended Not recommended
Cured bacon	5 to 7 days	No longer than 1 month
Hot dogs	Opened—1 week Unopened—2 weeks	1 to 2 months 1 to 2 months
Ham		
• Canned, unopened	6 to 9 months	Not recommended
• Whole or half, fully cooked	5 to 7 days	1 to 2 months
• Slices, fully cooked	3 to 4 days	1 to 2 months
Poultry		
Uncooked		
Whole (including game birds, ducks and geese)	1 to 2 days	No longer than 12 months
Cut up	1 to 2 days	No longer than 9 months
Giblets	1 to 2 days	No longer than 3 months
Cooked	3 to 4 days	4 months
Seafood		
Fin Fish		
Uncooked full-flavor fish (mackerel, salmon, trout, tuna, etc.)	1 to 2 days	2 to 3 months
Uncooked mild-flavor fish (cod, flounder, grouper, halibut, orange roughy, snapper, etc.)	1 to 2 days	4 to 6 months
Cooked and breaded fish	Store in freezer	2 to 3 months
Shellfish		
Uncooked	1 to 2 days	3 to 4 months
Cooked	3 to 4 days	1 to 2 months

Cooking at Higher Altitudes

If you live at elevations of 3,500 feet or higher, you have some unique cooking challenges. Air pressure is lower, so water has a lower boiling point and liquids evaporate faster. That means recipes for both conventional and microwave cooking need to be adjusted so they'll turn out right. Unfortunately, no set of rules applies to all recipes; sometimes the only way to make improvements is through trial and error. Here are some guidelines to help you conquer your high-altitude cooking challenges:

- Boiling foods such as pasta, rice, vegetables and cooked eggs will take longer.

- When you microwave, you may need to add more water and cook foods longer. However, this guideline may be affected by the type and amount of food, the water content of the food and the elevation.

- Cooking meat in boiling liquid or steam takes longer, sometimes as much as 50 percent to 100 percent. Cooking large meat cuts, such as roasts and turkeys, in the oven also takes longer. You can create your personal guidelines by using a meat thermometer and writing down how long meats take to cook.

- You can improve most baked goods made with baking powder or baking soda—not yeast—with one or more of the following changes:
  - Increase the oven temperature by 25°.
  - Increase the liquid.
  - Decrease the baking powder or baking soda.
  - Decrease the sugar and/or use a larger pan.

- Very rich recipes, such as pound cakes, will turn out better if you decrease the fat. Quick breads and cookies usually don't need as many adjustments.

- Yeast bread dough rises faster at high altitudes and can easily overrise. Let dough rise for a shorter time (just until double). Flour dries out more quickly at high altitudes, too, so use the minimum amount in the recipe, or decrease the amount by 1/4 to 1/2 cup.

- If you're using a mix, look for specific directions right on the package.

- Because water evaporates faster at higher altitudes, boiled candy, cooked frostings and other sugar mixtures concentrate faster. Watch the recipe closely during cooking so it doesn't scorch. You also may want to reduce the recipe temperature by 2° for every 1,000 feet of elevation. Or use the cold water test for candy (page 163).

- Deep-fried foods can be too brown on the outside but undercooked on the inside. So that both the outside and inside of food are done at the same time, reduce the temperature of the oil by 3° for every 1,000 feet of elevation and increase frying time, if necessary.

Microwave Basics

What would we do without our microwaves? Not only do they save on cooking time, they save on cleanup time because there are fewer dishes to wash. Be sure to follow the manufacturer's operating instructions for your microwave and information on microwavable utensils. Plus, here are some basics to keep in mind.

MORE HIGH-ALTITUDE TIPS

If you're new to high-altitude cooking, call your local U.S. Department of Agriculture (USDA) Extension Service office, listed in the phone book under "county government," for answers to your questions. Recipes are also available from the Food Science and Human Nutrition Cooperative Extension Service at Colorado State University, 200 Gifford Building, Colorado State University, Fort Collins, CO 80523-1571. Phone 970-491-7334 for brochures. Check your library and local bookstores for high-altitude cookbooks.

Starting Food Temperature: The colder the food, the longer the cooking time. Foods tested for this book were taken from their normal storage areas—freezer, refrigerator or cupboard shelf.

Food Volume: Increase the cooking time if you increase the amount of food.

Food Density: Porous foods, such as breads and cakes, cook quickly. Dense foods, such as roasts and potatoes, need longer cooking.

Sizes: Because small pieces of food cook faster than large ones, keep pieces about the same size so they'll cook more evenly.

Shapes: Round or doughnut-shaped foods or foods in round or ring-shaped containers cook most evenly. Watch foods with uneven shapes more closely during cooking.

Moisture, Sugar, Fat: Foods containing these ingredients cook or heat quickly.

Standing Time: Allows foods to finish cooking or distribute heat more evenly.

Microwave Techniques

Try these techniques to speed up heating, cook food evenly and make some foods look better when microwaved.

Add color to uncooked food by coating with crumbs or brushing with a sauce or glaze before microwaving.

For even cooking, arrange food in a circle with thickest parts to the outside.

Cover food with a lid or plastic wrap. Turn back a corner or two-inch edge of wrap to vent steam for faster cooking. Use waxed paper or microwavable paper towels to prevent spattering.

If the food is very moist (such as batters), put it on an *upside-down dish* so the bottom center will cook better.

Check food at the minimum time to avoid overcooking. Cook longer if necessary.

Stir food from the outer edge to the center for faster and more even cooking.

If food can't be stirred and your microwave doesn't have a turntable, *rotate the dish* one-half or one-quarter turn several times during cooking cycle to help the food cook more evenly.

Turn some foods over after part of the cooking time for more even cooking.

Microwave Testing for This Book

We used countertop microwaves with 700 to 800 watts for testing the microwave directions in this book. If your microwave has a rating of less than 700 watts, lengthen the cooking time; more than 800 watts, shorten the cooking time.

Microwave Cooking and Heating

These quick, practical tips will help you prepare food in your microwave. We've referred to many of them in recipes throughout this book. **Remember: Use only microwavable utensils!**

MICROWAVE COOKING AND HEATING CHART

Food, Utensil and Tips	Power Level	Amount	Time
Bacon, thinly sliced (cook) Place on plate or bacon rack lined with paper towels. Place paper towels between layers; cover with paper towel. Microwave until crisp.	High (100%)	1 slice 2 slices 4 slices 6 slices 8 slices	30 seconds to 1 1/2 minutes 1 to 2 minutes 2 to 3 minutes 3 to 5 minutes 4 to 6 minutes
Brown Sugar, hard (soften) Place in glass bowl; cover with damp paper towel, then plastic wrap. Repeat heating once or twice	High (100%)	1 to 3 cups	1 minute; let stand 2 minutes until softened.
Caramels (melt) 4-cup glass measuring cup, uncovered.	High (100%)	1 bag (14 ounces) unwrapped caramels mixed with 2 to 4 tablespoons milk or water	2 to 3 minutes, stirring once or twice
Chocolate, Baking (unsweetened or semisweet) (melt) Place unwrapped squares in glass dish or measuring cup, uncovered.	Medium (50%)	1 to 3 ounces	1 1/2 to 2 1/2 minutes
Chocolate Chips (melt) Place in glass bowl or glass measuring cup, uncovered. Chips will not change shape.	Medium (50%)	1/2 to 1 cup	2 to 3 minutes
Coconut (toast) Place in 2-cup glass measuring cup or pie plate, uncovered. Stir every 30 seconds.	High (100%)	1/4 to 1/2 cup 1 cup	1 1/2 to 2 minutes 2 to 3 minutes
Cream Cheese (soften) Remove foil wrapper or cover. Place in glass bowl or leave in plastic tub, uncovered.	Medium (50%)	3-ounce package 8-ounce package 8-ounce tub	45 to 60 seconds 1 to 1 1/2 minutes 45 to 60 seconds
Dried Fruit (soften) Place in 2-cup glass measuring cup; add 1/2 teaspoon water for each 1/2 cup fruit. Cover with plastic wrap, turning back a corner or 1/4-inch edge to vent steam.	High (100%)	1/4 to 1/2 cup 1/2 to 1 cup	30 to 45 seconds 45 to 60 seconds; let stand 2 minutes
Fruit, Frozen (thaw) Leave in plastic bag or pouch or transfer to glass bowl; thaw until most of ice is gone, stirring or rearranging twice.	Medium (50%)	16-ounce bag	3 to 5 minutes

Food, Utensil and Tips	Power Level	Amount	Time
Fruit, Refrigerated (warm) Place on floor of microwave.	High (100%)	1 medium	15 seconds
		2 medium	20 to 30 seconds; let stand 2 minutes
Honey (dissolve crystals) In jar with lid removed, uncovered. Stir every 20 to 30 seconds or until crystals dissolve.	High (100%)	1/2 to 1 cup	45 seconds to 1 1/2 minutes
Ice Cream (soften) In original container; remove any foil. Let stand 2 to 3 minutes.	Low (10%)	1/2 gallon	2 to 3 minutes
Margarine or Butter (melt) Remove foil wrapper. Place in glass bowl or measuring cup. Cover with paper towel.	High (100%)	1 to 8 tablespoons 1/2 to 1 cup	30 to 50 seconds 60 to 75 seconds
Margarine or Butter (soften) Remove foil wrapper. Place in glass bowl or measuring cup; uncovered.	High (100%)	1 to 8 tablespoons 1/2 to 1 cup	10 to 20 seconds 15 to 30 seconds
Muffins or Rolls (small to medium) (heat) Place on plate, napkin or napkin-lined basket; uncovered.	High (100%)	1 2 3 4	5 to 10 seconds 10 to 15 seconds 12 to 20 seconds 20 to 30 seconds
Muffins (large to jumbo) (heat) Place on plate or napkin, uncovered. Let stand 1 minute.	High (100%)	1 2 3 4	10 to 20 seconds 20 to 30 seconds 30 to 40 seconds 40 to 50 seconds
Nuts, Chopped (toast) Place in glass measuring cup, uncovered; add 1/4 teaspoon vegetable oil for each 1/4 cup nuts. Stir every 30 seconds until light brown.	High (100%)	1/4 to 1/2 cup 1/2 to 1 cup	2 1/2 to 3 1/2 minutes 3 to 4 minutes
Snacks (crisp popcorn, pretzels, corn chips or potato chips) Place in paper-towel-lined basket, uncovered.	High (100%)	2 cups 4 cups	20 to 40 seconds 40 to 60 seconds
Syrup (heat) Place in glass measuring cup or pitcher, uncovered. Stir every 30 seconds.	High (100%)	1/2 cup 1 cup	30 to 45 seconds 45 to 60 seconds
Water (boil) In glass measuring cup.	High (100%)	1 cup	2 to 3 minutes

Home Canning

There's something deeply satisfying about looking at a row of jewel-toned jellies, scarlet tomatoes or golden peaches that you've just "put up" or canned yourself with produce from your garden or local farmers' market. Home canning isn't hard, but you have to be careful to ensure that the food you preserve is safe from bacterial contamination.

To destroy spoilage organisms such as molds, yeast and bacteria, you need to process food for a long enough time at high enough temperatures. But one organism, *clostridium botulinum*, can be destroyed only if you process food correctly in a pressure canner. If *clostridium botulinum* survives and grows in a sealed jar of food, it can produce a poisonous toxin, which if eaten—even in small amounts—may be fatal.

The acidity of the food will determine which canning method you use:

- The pressure canner method is recommended by the U.S. Department of Agriculture (USDA) for nonacid foods, such as meat, poultry, seafood and vegetables.
- The water canner method is recommended for all acid foods, such as fruits, tomatoes with added acid, jams, jellies and pickled vegetables.
- *The open kettle method*, a process where boiling-water or pressure-canning is not used, *is not recommended, ever.*
- If you are unsure about the safety of certain home-canned foods, boiling the food for 10 minutes at altitudes below 1,000 feet will destroy these toxins. Boil 1 additional minute per 1,000 feet of additional elevation.

MORE HOME-CANNING HELP

Contact your local USDA Extension Service office listed in the phone book under "county government," or check out the USDA's Web site, www.usda.gov. Or, call the Ball and Kerr Home Canning Hot Line at 1-800-240-3340.

Helpful Nutrition and Cooking Information

Nutrition Guidelines

We provide nutrition information for each recipe that includes calories, fat, cholesterol, sodium, carbohydrate, fiber and protein. Individual food choices can be based on this information.

Recommended Intake for a Daily Diet of 2,000 Calories As Set by the Food and Drug Administration

Total Fat	Less than 65g
Saturated Fat	Less than 20g
Cholesterol	Less than 300mg
Sodium	Less than 2,400mg
Total Carbohydrate	300g
Dietary Fiber	25g

Criteria Used for Calculating Nutrition

■ The first ingredient was used wherever a choice is given (such as 1/3 cup sour cream or plain yogurt).

■ The first ingredient amount was used wherever a range is given (such as 3 to 3 1/2 pound cut-up broiler-fryer chicken).

■ The first serving number was used wherever a range is given (such as 4 to 6 servings).

■ "If desired" ingredients (such as sprinkle with brown sugar if desired) and recipe variations were not included.

■ Only the amount of a marinade or frying oil that is estimated to be absorbed by the food during preparation or cooking was calculated.

Ingredients Used in Recipe Testing and Nutrition Calculations

■ Ingredients used for testing represent those that the majority of consumers use in their homes: large eggs, 2% milk, 80% lean ground beef, canned ready-to-use chicken broth, and vegetable oil spread containing not less than 65% fat.

■ Fat-free, low-fat or low-sodium products are not used, unless otherwise indicated.

■ Solid vegetable shortening (not butter, margarine, nonstick cooking sprays or vegetable oil spread as they can cause sticking problems) is used to grease pans, unless otherwise indicated.

Equipment Used in Recipe Testing

We use equipment for testing that the majority of consumers use in their homes. If a specific piece of equipment (such as a wire whisk) is necessary for recipe success, it will be listed in the recipe.

■ Cookware and bakeware without nonstick coatings were used, unless otherwise indicated.

■ No dark-colored, black or insulated bakeware was used.

■ When a baking pan is specified in a recipe, a metal pan was used; a baking dish or pie plate means oven-proof glass was used.

■ An electric hand mixer was used for mixing only when mixer speeds are specified in the recipe directions. When a mixer speed is not given, a spoon or fork was used.

Equivalent Measures

3 teaspoons = 1 tablespoon
4 tablespoons = 1/4 cup
5 tablespoons + 1 teaspoon = 1/3 cup
8 tablespoons = 1/2 cup
12 tablespoons = 3/4 cup
16 tablespoons = 1 cup (8 ounces)
2 cups = 1 pint (16 ounces)
4 cups (2 pints) = 1 quart (32 ounces)
8 cups (4 pints) = 1/2 gallon (64 ounces)
4 quarts = 1 gallon (128 ounces)

Common Abbreviations

degree	° (or dg)	package	pkg
dozen	doz	pint	pt
gallon	gal	pound	lb (or #)
hour	hr	quart	qt
inch	" (or in.)	second	sec
minute	min	tablespoon	Tbsp (or T)
ounce	oz	teaspoon	tsp (or t)

Metric Conversion Guide

Volume

U.S. Units	Canadian Metric	Australian Metric
1/4 teaspoon	1 mL	1 ml
1/2 teaspoon	2 mL	2 ml
1 teaspoon	5 mL	5 ml
1 tablespoon	15 mL	20 ml
1/4 cup	50 mL	60 ml
1/3 cup	75 mL	80 ml
1/2 cup	125 mL	125 ml
2/3 cup	150 mL	170 ml
3/4 cup	175 mL	190 ml
1 cup	250 mL	250 ml
1 quart	1 liter	1 liter
1 1/2 quarts	1.5 liters	1.5 liters
2 quarts	2 liters	2 liters
2 1/2 quarts	2.5 liters	2.5 liters
3 quarts	3 liters	3 liters
4 quarts	4 liters	4 liters

Weight

U.S. Units	Canadian Metric	Australian Metric
1 ounce	30 grams	30 grams
2 ounces	55 grams	60 grams
3 ounces	85 grams	90 grams
4 ounces (1/4 pound)	115 grams	125 grams
8 ounces (1/2 pound)	225 grams	225 grams
16 ounces (1 pound)	455 grams	500 grams
1 pound	455 grams	1/2 kilogram

Note: The recipes in this cookbook have not been developed or tested using metric measures. When converting recipes to metric, some variations in quality may be noted.

Measurements

Inches	Centimeters
1	2.5
2	5.0
3	7.5
4	10.0
5	12.5
6	15.0
7	17.5
8	20.5
9	23.0
10	25.5
11	28.0
12	30.5
13	33.0

Temperatures

Fahrenheit	Celsius
32°	0°
212°	100°
250°	120°
275°	140°
300°	150°
325°	160°
350°	180°
375°	190°
400°	200°
425°	220°
450°	230°
475°	240°
500°	260°

Index